THE MIND OF THE BIBLE-BELIEVER

THE MIND OF THE BIBLE-BELIEVER

EDMUND D. COHEN

PROMETHEUS BOOKS
700 East Amherst St., Buffalo, NY 14215

92 91 90 89 88   4 3 2 1

Original edition published in 1986 by Prometheus Books

Library of Congress Cataloging-in-Publication Data

Cohen, Edmund D.
The mind of the Bible-believer.

Includes index.
1. Bible—Psychology. 2. Christianity—Psychology. 3. Protestant churches—United States. 4. Evangelicalism—United States. 5. United States—Church history. I.Title.
BS645.C63 1986   230′044   86-42574
ISBN: 0-87975-495-8

Contents

Now, therefore, I, Ronald Reagan, President of the United States of America, in recognition of the contributions and influence of the Bible on our Republic and our people, do hereby proclaim 1983 the year of the Bible in the United States. I encourage all citizens, each in his or her own way, to reexamine and rediscover its priceless and timeless message. —Ronald Reagan[1]

The search for trustworthy authority and the resurgence of interest in biblical archaeology points to a high involvement of laity and clergy in Bible study groups in the 80s. Already we have seen interest widening in the Catholic community, and the appearance of new translations throughout the Christian community worldwide indicates that the decade to come will be Bible-centered, indeed. —George Gallup, Jr.[2]

If anyone comes to you and does not bring this teaching, do not receive him into *your* house, and do not give him a greeting; for the one who gives him a greeting participates in his evil deeds. —2 John, 10-11[3]

Introduction: An Illusion Revisited

To what did it point that 1983 was proclaimed "year of the Bible" by President Ronald Reagan? Or that the second-generation, public-opinion surveyor turned Evangelical enthusiast, George Gallup, Jr., said, "the decade to come will be Bible-centered, indeed"? Can supernaturalistic religion really play a major rôle in the lives of contemporary enlightened Americans? To what extent are the politicized Evangelicals, the television preachers, and the other sensational features of the Evangelical subculture that are made conspicuous by the mass media, representative of conservative Christianity in America? Who buys all those Bibles in modern, accessible translation that fill shelves in every bookstore and sell literally by the ton, year after year?[4] And what do the people who buy them do with them? Is there really a resurgence of conservative Christianity in

1. *Federal Register,* vol. 48, no. 26 (Feb. 7, 1983), pp. 5527-28.
2. George Gallup, Jr., and David Poling, *The Search for America's Faith* (Nashville: Abingdon Press, 1980), p. 142.
3. *New American Standard Bible.* Italics indicate a word implied but not present in the underlying Greek texts.
4. Richard N. Ostling, "Rivals to the King James Throne," *Time,* Apr. 20, 1981, p. 62.

America? Could it be that the politicized Evangelicals and television preachers are but a side effect of a larger psychic sea-change quietly occurring? Is that why churches in such large numbers and bewildering variety continue to be built up, maintained, and faithfully attended across the American landscape?

I have been though a strange, personal odyssey with the Christians, one that has left me with just the right combination of background and experience to understand and unravel the causes of what, I assure the reader, is a conservative Christian resurgence of immense proportions. Growing up nominally Jewish, raised in a way that never made the traditional or theological side of Judaism attractive or compelling to me, I lacked the usual formative experiences of attachment to one religion or another, which congeal thought about religion in most people. As a young adult, I became a psychologist, earning a Ph.D. in that field at the age of twenty-five. The lack of scientific justification for any of the techniques psychologists earn their living administering, and the rise of public relations, lobbying, and the endless ad hominem attacks on dissenters rather than substance for response to problems within psychologists' circles all alienated me profoundly from my chosen field. As a new assistant professor in a state college, I developed an interest in the work of the Swiss psychiatrist, C. G. Jung, taking me still farther from the mainstream of my field. I studied with Jung's disciples in Zürich, Switzerland, and realized that, despite the intellectual merit of the underlying ideas, here was another kind of psychotherapy so obviously lacking in benefit to anyone that I did not even need controlled, statistical research to know it. I worked out some of my ambivalence by writing a book about Jung.[5] But that exercise brought me to what I experienced as an intellectual dead end. Perhaps having such an enterprise as psychology had been just another of those aspirations of our century that did not pan out. I went back to school, became a lawyer, and spent several fascinating years involved in the panoply of human drama that surrounds the general-practice attorney.

A crucial feature of Jungian thought that I had never worked out was the premise of personal religious quest as the ultimate human motive. Considering myself a spiritual, somehow religious person took on inflated importance after I had ripped apart and discarded everything that the modern, secular competitors of the religious practitioners had to offer. Some very humane and cultured clergy had been my close friends, and I had seen at close range the characteristic difficulties attending the enlightened, liberal practitioner of religion. Nevertheless, the impresion that there was sublime wisdom to the Bible after all, and that something psychologically very salutary was at work in people steeped in it, had been powerfully engraved on my mind. I got involved in an attractive, large liberal church in Washington, D.C., which also attracted an impressive assortment of Capitol Hill luminaries.

There is an ironic reason why what subsequently happened could happen. Anyone but me, when encountering unexpected manifestations around religious

5. Edmund D. Cohen, *C. G. Jung and the Scientific Attitude* (New York: Philosophical Library, 1975). Paperback ed., Totowa, N.J.: Littlefield Adams & Co., 1976.

people, could shrug them off, reassuring himself that some expert he might ask, or list of books he might read, would explain away what supposedly only seemed so remarkable to the untrained senses. But I knew intimately about all that could possibly answer to that description. So when I came among more intense, genuinely Bible-steeped believers than those in that liberal church, I knew that I—and anyone else in the pertinent academic fields—really knew from nothing about the indubitably psychologically powerful and seemingly salutary effects to be observed in these people. I got involved, and, bereft of any intellectual resource that I thought validly refuted it, became a believer myself. The experience, in retrospect, resembled nothing so much as a bout of substance abuse. For me, breaking out of that sticky process and gaining the insight for this book were the same event. Perhaps the experience is so little known because those who get really enmeshed in it seldom come out, or articulate their experience if they finally do find their way out.

To understand what really goes on within the Bible-believer, and consequently to understand how an unpopular spin-off of Judaism happened to take over the entire Western world, penetrating language and ethnic barriers with apparent ease, we must first take into account that we are part of late developments in a history viewed out of proportion. We all want very much to view the several religions, each with persons we care for attached to it, as imparting the same benign message—which they do not. And we want to think that the humane, sensible things that Christian leaders have been saying for about two and a half of the nineteen centuries since the New Testament as we know it emerged are what Christianity and other religions intrinsically stand for. We want to think that the enlightened, liberal practitioners of the several religions, whom we all know and appreciate, are the ones authentically in touch with the Bible's true meaning, and that the conservative Evangelical upstarts, with their startlingly retrograde social views, are the ones who have distorted that meaning. The terrible truth is that, when one really gets to know the Bible, the social views implicit in it are by far more retrograde than those of any contemporary politicized Evangelical. The liberal Christians, understandably believing their own respective establishments' propaganda, never realize that they are heirs to a laudable tradition of rebellion *against* the Bible's true import, and that all their modern theology was actually designed, in its time, to contain and obfuscate that import, not make it plainer. Each successive phase of theology in the Christian era has, in effect, amounted to an effort to rationalize whatever philosophical wisdom was current in any given period as implicit in the Bible as well, so that scholars could entertain it in good conscience, and not appear to inveigh against religious authority. But when we scrutinize the Bible so as to separate it from subsequent, overlying traditions—as the Bible-believers do with fast-increasing intellectual facility—we will be astonished to realize how little didactic content is intrinsically there. For readers coming from a liberal religious background, this will, therefore, be a phenomenally painful book. What I have to tell them is that maintenance of their illusions cannot coexist with an effective response to the retrograde social views and inconspicuous personal misery being spread far and wide by the new conservative Evangelicals.

The major thesis of this work is that the Bible—for our purposes, consisting of the New Testament, the Jewish Scriptures slightly rearranged to form the Old Testament, and excluding the Apocrypha—is a psychological document. The claimed didactic content, so long and so bitterly debated, is incidental to the document's psychological purpose. To become bogged down in its supposed didactic content is to cooperate with the psychological strategems operating on the believer. Debating the merits of the Bible along familiar, epistemological lines only ensures that the debate will remain safely clear of the truly sensitive issues and vulnerabilities in the Bible-believer's experience of his religion.

Proponents of New Testament Christianity are not wrong to say that theirs is unlike any other religion, that it exhibits a palpably different quality from any other. We shall show that this qualitative difference is not, as they suppose, an indication of New Testament Christianity's singular, divine origin, and all others' lesser pedigree, but, instead, the fingerprints of the brilliant men who contrived it. The New Testament came into existence in a profoundly unusual and intense historical situation. After a long, grinding period of unrest, the Roman Empire leveled its military might at Israel, devastating it and destroying the Second Temple in A.D. 70. That left a situation wherein every kind of constructive, this-worldly activity for Jews in Israel was made completely futile. Hence, the enormous emphasis on life after death in Christianity, sharply contrasting with the scant Old Testament mention of the topic and elaborating wildly upon the competing theological views in Israel in Jesus' day. I contend that the New Testament grew out of a profound sense of spoliation of the Jewish identity, when events turned so powerfully against the historic Jewish expectation of God's special favor. More importantly, it grew out of its authors' practical need to have a tightly knit, supportive and informal network of people around them, when the formal institutions were all tightly under the control of foreign oppressors and many prominent Jews behaved basely and disloyally.

The New Testament is nothing other than a psychological manipulation—a depth-psychotechnology—designed so to knit its people together. The psychological acumen and artfulness with which it was done is unsurpassed. We shall have much excitement in sorting out what it has to teach modern psychology. It worked much too well, and continues to work absurdly long after the historical situation that called it into being has been forgotten. For reasons we shall examine, it worked best on people without Jewish ethnic roots. Whereas other religions, as well as variations of Christianity subsequent to the New Testament, probably do spontaneously reflect the cultures and times that have given rise to them (this question is not focally examined herein), I contend that New Testament Christianity was, instead, deliberately contrived and field-tested over a few eventful decades. This depth-psychotechnology concealed in the New Testament—whereof the new, conservative, upstart pastors are unwittingly the restorers and new practitioners—I call the *Evangelical mind-control system.* Its spread today is driven by a strong grass-roots movement toward authentically New Testament religion; that movement cannot rightly be called a return, because it occurs in quarters where, if there ever was authentic biblicism before, it was too long ago to retain much effect. The movement's character is much different from what appears in the mass media, and it is not nearly as overtly political as the typical media coverage makes it appear. In the most ascendant of the new conservative churches in any North American locality, the visitor will hear content straight out of the Bible. Not political speeches à la Jerry Falwell or Pat Robertson, and not even playing to lower-middle-class prejudices, as Jimmy Swaggart does. One would not think that anything all that socially significant was taking place. But it is, as we shall see. The resurgence of New Testament religion I call the new *mini-Reformation* (within a classification scheme to which we shall come presently).

How is it that such a development has escaped scholarly notice? The meandering path of scholarly study of religion reveals some of the answer. Evidently, the negative psychological effects of real New Testament religion were well known during the Enlightenment. These effects, then as now in the mini-Reformation, took their worst toll on pastors, who partook of secular education and were happy to encase the New Testament in an ever-thicker gloss of secular learning. We shall see that the Enlightenment had fought New Testament religion almost to a standstill by the time of the American Revolution. The next wave of conservative Christianity was besmirched by defense of slavery, and by moral as well as military defeat in the Civil War, dealing conservative Christianity a blow from which it never recovered until the 1970s. The intellectual discussion of matters pertaining to conservative Christianity west of the Atlantic Ocean focused on the seeming conflict of Darwinism and the Bible. I submit that the underlying significance of the ensuing discussion had little to do with the intellectual merit of the contending views but rather with pastors tacitly glad to gain room to reshape their religion into something more agreeable, and to refrain from making so strong a defense as lay in their power. In the first half of the present century, the overwhelming majority of clergy were happy to modernize their theology. By 1960, there were not enough articulate or reputable spokesmen for conservative Christianity to form a decent-sized choir.

In Europe, in the mid-nineteenth century, leading up to the formation of the new theology that American clergy would receive so gladly, the pivotal figure was a philosopher who is no longer well known: Ludwig Andreas Feuerbach (1804–1872). For now, it will suffice for us to sketch his main, seminal idea. He explained the God-concept as having arisen from indoctrinating people not to attribute their more positive qualities to themselves but rather to project them and believe that those qualities belong to a divine Other, all occurring under the clergy's constant assault on men's and women's natural self-esteem. Feuerbach was a precursor of modern ideological humanism; his writing is permeated by bitterness against the use of religion to cool out opposition to exploitation by authoritarian political leadership. His influence on subsequent thinkers—theological, sociological, and psychological—was enormous. But those who came after him failed to pick up on his correct intimation that the relevant questions about religion are psychological; Feuerbach's successors all went for the epistemological decoy issues.

The only other provider of any appreciable psychological insight into conservative Christianity was Sigmund Freud. In *The Future of an Illusion,* published in 1927, he said:

> It has been repeatedly pointed out . . . in how great detail the analogy between religion and obsessional neurosis can be followed out, and how many of the peculiarities and vicissitudes in the formation of religion can be understood in that light. And it tallies well with this that devout believers are safeguarded in a high degree against the risk of certain neurotic illnesses; their acceptance of the universal neurosis spares them the task of constructing a personal one.[6]

After Freud, there was no further incisive or reductive study of the psychology of religion. We shall have much to say about the causes of that strange silence. Gordon W. Allport dropped a hint that will hold us until we return to the question:

> During the past fifty years [i.e., to 1949] religion and sex seem to have reversed their positions. Writing in the Victorian age William James could bring himself to devote barely two pages to the role of sex in human life which he labeled euphemistically the "instinct of love." Yet no taboos held him back from directing the torrent of his genius into the *Varieties of Religious Experience.* On religion he spoke freely and with unexcelled brilliance. Today, by contrast, psychologists write with the frankness of Freud or Kinsey on the sexual passions of mankind, but blush and grow silent when the religious passions come into view. Scarcely any modern textbook writers in psychology devote as much as two shamefaced pages to the subject—even though religion, like sex, is an almost universal interest of the human race [footnote omitted].[7]

Allport's fleeting observation that a taboo still operates unrecognized, inhibiting the uncovering of the true, psychological inner workings of Christianity, was as close as he ever got to a useful insight. Like every other behavioral-science writer on religion since Freud, Allport was willing to see nothing else but benign, kindly, modernist theology at the core of Christianity. He was entirely unsuspecting that a depth-psychological manipulation reflecting psychological acumen far beyond his own or that of any of his contemporaries is there instead. Unwittingly, the end result of the modernists has been to make the public, including those informed by scholarly writing, unsuspecting of the real causes common to both the original rise of New Testament Christianity and its present resurgence, which is taking place contrary to every preceding expert prediction. The modern goes unwarned about the psychological harm that can be done to him. Hence, this is the book I wish had been available to me before I became a "believer."

---

6. Trans. James Strachey (New York: W. W. Norton, 1961), pp. 43–44.
7. *The Individual and His Religion* (New York: Macmillan, 1950), pp. 1–2.

In the following chapters, the conceptual tools of the behavioral sciences are substantially reworked, to make them serviceable for the task of showing how the Bible manipulation works. For me, it turns out that mastering the intellectual content of psychology, largely while teaching advanced courses in social psychology, theories of personality, and the history of psychology, and then putting all that aside for ten years and occupying my mind with completely different things, was fortunate. Discussion in these areas has grown stagnant, partly through too specialized and microscopic an approach. The combination of a fertile problem to work on and a fortunate string of personal experiences unlike any a psychologist or professor would normally have has made for a situation where questions that were unyielding to a piecemeal approach finally yielded. Despite the concentration of emphasis on the Bible in what follows, this is essentially a psychology book. My contention is that the Bible is history's most successful psychological manipulation, achieving with uncanny facility what motivational researchers and psychological warfare experts of our own day have only dreamed of. We will backtrack through the Bible, sorting out the unsurpassed psychological understanding that went into its making. The Bible is a masterpiece of the highest magnitude in that sense, and we shall come out with even more appreciation for the brilliance of its conception and the superb craftsmanship of its execution than the devout student ever could have.

A few details about the mechanics of what follows must be mentioned. For me, a footnote is a way to include matter that would break the train of thought of the text but which is important for understanding nevertheless. Some of this work's most important nuggets of substance are in the notes. For the many Bible quotations, I have mainly used the King James version because it is familiar, has been the transmitting medium of the phenomenon we shall explore more than any other translation, and is in the public domain. Most often, the details wherein the King James uses a quaint word, or suffers from some other translation difficulty, are stumbling blocks for the modern translator as well. In those situations, it most often seemed best to me to use the King James and put some explanatory matter in brackets at the place where the hard-to-translate detail occurs. Where it worked better, I have occasionally quoted from one of the recent translations widely used and recommended by the more studious, contemporary conservative Christians. The reader accustomed to scholarly writing about the Bible should judge this work by taking into account that the effect of the translated text on the Bible-believer who is exposed to it year in and year out is the matter of paramount relevance in this work. When I go into the underlying ancient language, it is to get at what the original authors had in mind and hopefully to infer how the text affected its "hearers" initially. I am well aware that many things that an expert in Semitics would know cast various Bible details in a different light and bring out implications the modern believer would find strange; these are not relevant to the text's effect on more ordinary, unknowing people, and this work's neglect of the matter is, accordingly, deliberate. Italics in Bible quotations denote words the translators have added, to make the translation less elliptical than the underlying ancient-language text. In other quotations herein, whatever italics are present are carried over from the text quoted unless otherwise indicated.

What I have really aimed to do in this work is to be my century's Feuerbach. I have done what he set out to do but could not really do because the psychological knowledge needed for it was unavailable to him. We are living in a time when a very significant and rapidly growing portion of our population is coming under Evangelical mind-control. These people have been set up for some very miserable personal experiences thereby—ones that have escaped our notice much as the widespread spouse and child abuse going on close to home did until our consciousness was raised—and they have been made listeners to radical-right political rhetoric they would otherwise reject. The new biblicism has become a substantial social problem for commentators to learn about and whose worst results mental-health professionals must treat. Our time sorely needs another Feuerbach. My application for the job is herewith cheerfully submitted.

Philadelphia, Pennsylvania
February 1986

No one knows . . . whether at the end of this tremendous development entirely new prophets will arise, or there will be a great rebirth of old ideas and ideals, or, if neither, mechanized petrification, embellished with a sort of convulsive self-importance. —Max Weber, *The Protestant Ethic and the Spirit of Capitalism*[1]

. . . [A] propensity to religious extremism does not require explanation since it is entirely consistent with basic religious tenets and authentic religious orientations. It is religious moderation or religious liberalism, the willingness of religious adherents to accommodate themselves to their environment, to adapt their behavioral and belief patterns to prevailing cultural norms, to make peace with the world, that requires explanation. —A professor of political studies at Bar-Ilan University, Israel[2]

Chapter 1

The "Old-Time Religion" and the New "Mini-Reformation"

In February 1982, I attended the convention of the National Religious Broadcasters at the Sheraton Washington (D.C.) Hotel. The leaders in bringing the conservative Christian message on radio and television, including some faces familiar from television, were nearly all present or represented. In the Grand Ballroom, from the same podium that President Reagan addressed the convention and from which Jerry Falwell had given a press conference explaining why he thinks the viewership ratings underestimate his influence and following, I heard the orthodox theologian Francis A. Schaeffer (1912–1984) give his gala dinner address. His remarks included the following:

> It is a post-Christian world in that the countries that used to have a Christian mentality, a Christian consensus, now function largely on a contrary, absolutely opposite consensus, that . . . the final reality is not a personal, infinite God who is the creator of all else, but rather that the final reality is only material or energy that has existed forever, and exists in its present form only on the basis of sheer chance. And which . . . is therefore totally neutral and silent in regard to any value of human life and silent concerning any moral value and silent concerning any basis for law. If we fail to recognize this change in our country and in society

1. Trans. Talcott Parsons (New York: Charles Scribner's Sons, 1958), p. 182.
2. Charles S. Liebman, "Extremism as a Religious Norm," *Journal for the Scientific Study of Religion* 22 (1983): 75, 79.

from functioning on a Judeo-Christian basis which was the foundation of this country, at least, in the form of a memory, up to almost the immediate past, if we fail to really notice and understand this change . . . to the new consensus . . . we have failed in our loyalty to Jesus Christ . . . . if there is not a confrontation concerning these things, our children and our grandchildren will not call us blessed . . . . it indeed is . . . the natural and inevitable change . . . when there is a shift from the Christian foundation, a Christian consensus . . . to a humanistic one. . . .

We have shifted in our view of law in this country from the concept that there is a law-giver . . . someone who indeed is the base therefore . . . to law becoming only that which a few people decide is for the good of society, quite arbitrarily, according to their own limited views at the given moment. Now, this is the real reason for the break-down in morals, values, and the reason law is now only this arbitrary series of decisions. . . .

It should be noticed that this view, which is dominant now in our culture . . . is is the very opposite of that upon which the founding fathers . . . built this country . . . . they founded this country on the base that there is a God who is the Creator, who gave the inalienable rights . . . . The freedoms we have could never have been brought forth by this other world view, and, believe me, as it increasingly takes over, in the northern European countries, in the western world, and specifically in the United States . . . these freedoms are going to be lost. . . .

Eighty years ago, this country still was functioning on a totally Christian consensus—far from perfect—not a golden age—but was functioning on a Christian consensus or at least the memory of it. . . .

And today, we who are Christians, and others who love liberty, and human life, should be acting today as they [the founding fathers of the United States and of the Reformation] acted in their day. If we do not act now, to use every means to get rid of such tyranny, and the hidden censorship which we face on every side, if we don't act now I do not think we are going to get another opportunity. . . .

[A] conservative humanism is no better than a liberal humanism. . . .

And we must absolutely use every means at our disposal, every legal means . . . to roll back the awful and inevitable results brought forth by this other world view . . . . This is true spirituality because true spirituality is Christ being the Lord of all of life, and not just that which is usually called religion. Christ is the Lord of all of life, or He's not Lord, really, of any part of life. . . .

We should make plain that we are not calling for a theocracy in name or in fact . . . we must not wrap our Christianity in our flag . . . what we want to do is to return to a real freedom . . . for everyone . . . and that means all religions, but that nevertheless, that those who hold the historic view that brought forth this country have a right in the political processes to bring the Christian viewpoints into the courts of law and into . . . our government. . . .

When a government . . . negates the law of God, it abrogates its authority. . . . At a certain point it is not only the privilege, but it is the duty of the Christian to disobey the government.

For many years, Schaeffer had operated a renowned retreat center for conservative Evangelical elite in L'Abri, Switzerland, and written prolifically. His are the only recent Evangelical books that consistently appeal to well-educated, nonclergy, conservative Christians. Only in the last few years of his life, when he knew he was dying of cancer, did Schaeffer go off on the militant tangent these comments reflect. What did he mean that government must embody his theology, or else Christians ought to flout it, but far be it from him to advocate theocracy, and the rights of those who do not share his theology are somehow to be protected by whatever it is he is advocating? Was our country founded on, or did it ever have, a "Christian consensus"? Do our values of individual freedom and protection of dissenting points of view have a specifically Christian pedigree? I, who knew enough of the Bible that I ought to have figured out that so accomplished a Bible expositor could never come by such conclusions honestly, had no problem with the speech except for a minor, pedantic one, as to the characterization of all humanistic thought as reductionism, as antithetical to any ordering principle other than "pure chance." I excused the oversimplification as Schaeffer's concession to time constraints. For the duration of that long, lost weekend I spent under Evangelical mind-control, my normal critical faculties were kaput. I went away in a high state of exhilaration.

The key heretical feature of Schaeffer's remarks—the part about Christians having the privilege and duty of disobeying government they find insufficiently biblical—later turned out to be the tonesetter of his ultimate influence. The idea became current in Evangelical circles.[3] A few young Evangelical fanatics took it as a mandate to burn or bomb abortion clinics, and probably half a year too late for Schaeffer to know of it, the American television public got to see some of them, unrepentant, with those distinctive, sappy-sweet expressions on their faces, being led off to prison. The impression that there could be a fascistic, kamikaze danger from these new, conservative Evangelicals was indelibly made, and many people were permanently sensitized to spot Evangelical Trojan horses in the future.

A Historical View

We shall proceed to sketch, with broad brush, the influence of Protestant Christianity in the United States. In colonial America, the only serious efforts to order society or governmental institutions along religious lines occurred in New England in the seventeenth century. *The Scarlet Letter,* by Nathaniel Hawthorne, accurately conveys the flavor of local theocracy in that period. The Salem witch trials were tightly contained in time and geography. At the beginning of the eighteenth century, the religious fervor of the Puritans in Massachusetts and the Baptists in Rhode Island was in decline. In Virginia, the

3. Schaeffer made similar remarks on the major conservative Christian television programs that season. In *A Christian Manifesto* (Westchester, Ill.: Crossway Books, 1981), p. 120, probably the most widely distributed of his books, he said, "State officials must know that we are serious about stopping abortion . . . . This may include doing such things as sit-ins in legislatures and courts, including the Supreme Court, when other constitutional means fail . . . . *the bottom line* is that at a certain point there is not only the right, but the duty, to disobey the state."

established Church of England had never had much fervor to lose: the aristocrats were not greatly influenced by it and the common people were alienated from it.

The most important American religious figure of the period leading up to independence, who touched or was touched by every trend that need concern us, was Jonathan Edwards (1703–1758). The son and grandson of New England Puritan clergy, Edwards was educated at Yale. His horizons were profoundly expanded by the works of John Locke. Even though he vigorously rejected those parts of Locke that conflicted with his Calvinist theology, especially the concept of free will, the influence of Locke led Edwards to a new psychological formulation of salvation.

We shall return to that psychological formulation when we cover the later developments arising from it. In order to understand Edwards' immediate time, his style concerns us more than his intellectual substance. Edwards was the first notable dramatic, theatrical preacher to reach outside the relatively closed church congregation, to motivate people by stirring up fear of hellfire and damnation, and to focus on the recruitment and development of new converts. In 1740, George Whitefield came to America and held the series of evangelistic meetings known as the Great Awakening. These conspicuous meetings, partaking of the quality of media events in our own time, were on a much larger scale than the ones Edwards had conducted.

In Edwards' own congregation in Northampton, Massachusetts, the suicide of a prominent church member awakened the people from their fascination with hellfire and damnation preaching. Edwards attempted to carry on the Puritan fathers' tradition of rebuke from the pulpit. The congregation rebelled and dismissed Edwards in 1750. For six years, Edwards was a missionary to the Indians at Stockbridge outpost, Massachusetts. There, he devoted his time to scholarly writing, which helped pave the way for him to be offered the presidency of the forerunner of Princeton University. He died shortly after assuming that post.

Unlike later American expressions of religious fervor, the Great Awakening was thoroughly Calvinist in content. What did that entail? In Western Europe, the Reformation, the rise of Protestant Christianity in the sixteenth century, had as its main feature reliance on the authority of the Bible as the antidote for the authority of the Roman Catholic church. The royalty of northwestern Europe bridled at having to share with Rome their funds and their political control. In religious scholars such as Erasmus of Rotterdam and Martin Luther, the potential was found to make the princes' desire for independence from Rome into a positive religious project. Translation of the Bible, first into Latin and then into the spoken languages, broke the monopoly of the clergy in information about religion. Erasmus, the Latin translator of the Bible and very much a part of the Renaissance, was subtle and cautious in his scholarly books on the Bible. His criticisms of Rome were implicit and understated.

Catholic theologians of the period said of the Reformation, "Erasmus laid the egg, and Luther hatched it!"[4] Luther, who had been a particularly timorous Catholic monk, found relief from his besetting salvation doubts and his inability to make his life free enough from sin according to the teaching of Ephesians 2:8, namely, that salvation is entirely by God's grace and a person's works have no effect upon it. This emphasis had great social importance, since it contradicted the Catholic church's claim of the right to dispense forgiveness of sin, and indulgences from particular sins, in exchange for money paid to the church. Luther had no interest in the Renaissance or in harmonizing the Bible with humanist learning. He translated the Bible with immense artistry into German, and he sought to make practice and doctrine conform to the Bible.

On the whole, the Reformation chose not humanity but rigor in its approach to the Bible. Luther carried that rigor far, but not to its fullest extent. He did not provide a rendition of the Bible's teaching so convincingly authoritative as to standardize Protestantism. Such a rendition was provided by John Calvin.

John (or Jean) Calvin (1509–1564) was born in France, trained as a lawyer, had contacts with humanist scholarship quite similar to those of the young Erasmus, and experienced a sudden, dramatic Christian conversion. A persecuted Protestant in France, he went to Basel, Switzerland. His ability to settle disputes by demonstrating, through careful scholarship, what the Bible taught enabled him to make himself indispensable in bringing order in the fluid, anarchic situation that religious conflict had left in its wake in Geneva. Although he held no formal position except pastor of the church there, the civil leaders in Geneva were dependent on him, and he dictated what the laws would be and how they were enforced. His laws involved constant intrusion of police into private homes to check that the furnishings were not too lavish and the women's underclothes not too luxurious. As in the Catholic Inquisition, heresy was a capital crime, and Calvin instigated many capital heresy prosecutions, including the celebrated case of Michael Servetus, which awakened public opinion and brought prosecution for heresy to an end within a very few years.[5] At the height

---

4. Stefan Zweig, *Erasmus of Rotterdam*, trans. Eden and Cedar Paul (New York: Viking Press, 1934), p. 157.

5. Servetus was an eccentric, generalist scholar, whose discovery of pulmonary blood circulation would probably have earned him his place in history without Calvin. Servetus' theological interest was in opposing the doctrine of the Trinity; however, his theology was so orthodox in all other respects that he cannot be claimed as a forerunner of modern Unitarianism. Of him, a pro-Calvin commentator, Hunter A. Mitchell, in *The Teachings of Calvin*, 2nd ed. (London: James Clarke & Co., 1950), p. 241, said, "He might well have passed for orthodox, had he not proceeded to explanation and definition."

For years, Servetus had sent Calvin his writings, to the point of making a nuisance of himself. Calvin clandestinely provided the writings that Servetus had sent him to the Catholic Inquisition authorities in Vienne, France, where Servetus practiced medicine. Servetus was convicted of heresy and sentenced to death. He escaped, but still obsessed by the desire to confront Calvin, went to Geneva. Calvin, through intermediaries, instigated a heresy prosecution against Servetus and participated in his long, spectacular, and, from Calvin's point of view, successful trial.

Undoubtedly, Servetus, seeking to imitate in a bizarre way the ministry and death of Jesus, found, in Calvin, someone with an equally bizarre proclivity to imitate Caiaphas.

of the Calvin theocracy in Geneva, the heresy prisoners were kept handcuffed in their cells to prevent them from committing suicide to avoid the torture chambers.[6]

Calvin's theology, set out in successive editions of his *Institutes of the Christian Religion,* had no strong rival as the authoritative elucidation of Protestantism until late in the eighteenth century. The five points of Calvinism summarize Calvin's theology; they have long been used to teach its fundamentals. (1) The nature of man, owing to Adam's fall, is totally depraved, so that nothing good can come from him without God's gracious intervention. (2) God decided before creating the world which people would receive salvation; that number might be a very small portion of humanity, God's elect. (3) Christ's sacrifice on the cross redeemed the elect only. (4) God's grace is irresistible by the elect, so that a decision or voluntary action by the recipient is not involved in salvation. (5) Those who are saved cannot lose their salvation.

These five points came to be formulated in response to the five points with opposite meanings propounded by Jacobus Arminius, the founder of a sect in Holland attempting to humanize Christianity; the sect was persecuted after Calvinism prevailed there. It will serve our purposes to view Arminianism as open and democratic in its implication and Calvinism as closed, authoritarian, and aristocratic. We shall return to the relationship of these points to the Bible's contents.

All this will, hopefully, aid us in putting ourselves into the minds and milieu of the Puritans and other religiously minded American colonials. We begin to see how preoccupation with the question of whether one is included or left out of the circle of the elect could become quite morbid. Consider a sermon passage that is probably the best known of Edwards' writings:

> The God that holds you over the pit of hell, much as one holds a spider, or some loathsome insect over the fire, abhors you, and is dreadfully provoked, his wrath towards you burns like fire; he looks upon you as worthy of nothing else, but to be cast into the fire; he is of purer eyes than to bear to have you in his sight; you are ten thousand times more abominable in his eyes than the most hateful venomous serpent is in ours. You have offended him infinitely more than ever a stubborn rebel did his prince; and yet it is nothing but his hand that holds you from falling into the fire every moment. It is to be ascribed to nothing else, that you did not go to hell the last night, that you was [sic] suffered to awake again in this world, after you closed your eyes to sleep.[7]

Instead of a cross, Servetus was put on a pyre, his books inserted in between his chains and his body, and instead of a crown of thorns, he wore a crown of sulfur-soaked laurel leaves. Calvin stayed home and was not in the crowd of Christians who came out to see Servetus slowly burned to death. These events are described in detail by Stefan Zweig in *The Right to Heresy,* trans. Eden and Cedar Paul (New York: Viking Press, 1936).

6. Ibid., p. 63.

7. "Sinners in the Hands of an Angry God," preached July 8, 1741. In Ola Elizabeth Winslow, ed., *Jonathan Edwards: Basic Writings* (New York: New American Library, 1966), p. 159. Includes a useful foreword and bibliography.

Clearly, what made the Great Awakening work was fear. For a while, there would be a frenzy of interest in doing something to prepare for the afterlife, followed by a lull, a return to normal routine, and perhaps an avoidance of thinking about the nagging fear beneath the surface. In Edwards' church, there were such lulls, and from 1744 to 1748, there was not one new candidate for membership. The unattractiveness of Calvinst religion has turned out, in the fullness of time, to be geographically discernible, and in North America and in Europe the localities and the universities where there was fervent Calvinism are today the ones with the least interest in conservative Christianity. Protestant Christianity needed to change—and did change—to continue to play a strong rôle in the expanding United States of the next century. We can notice three trends that began in this pre-Revolutionary time, and remained:

1. *The voluntary church.* The presence in close proximity of churches with different old-country origins, with no one of them in a position to gain (or regain) governmental establishment, led to cooperation and competition. Even Edwards himself first preached in a Presbyterian church, although his background and the church where he preached most of his adult life were Congregationalist. One of the vicissitudes of the Great Awakening, and the ferment and controversy it generated within local churches, was loss of members from Congregationalist to Baptist churches. Those communities, and the ones to come, in the south and west became marketplaces of religious views, and individual conscience and preference became the criteria for choosing within the market. This was a far cry from the conflicts over governmental establishment of church denominations and legal disputes over the manner of existence of nonestablished denominations east of the Atlantic.

2. *The para-church ministry.* A biographer of Edwards writes:

> Whitefield was . . . responsible for connecting in the popular mind the idea of a revival with the coming of a strange preacher. Previous to his visit, parishes had been content to listen to the village minister for life. If revivals came, he reaped his own harvest . . . . By the summer of 1741, a ministerial migration was in progress, and pulpit as well as pew was enjoying the novelty of new faces . . . . their congregations had . . . opportunity to make comparisons; they had also heard some startling criticisms of their own pastor by visiting ministers who assumed Whitefield's prerogatives in denunciation and abuse. . . .[8]

For the first time, dispensers of religious teaching were not mutually exclusive, and one could remain in a church and still be availed of teaching from outside. This trend was to develop into a diverse network of organizations and activities and was a means of cross-fertilization.

3. *The infusion of secular learning in religious views.* We have mentioned, and will later dwell on, Edwards' psychological formulation of salvation. This small and seemingly innocuous adjustment was to open the way for the modal

8. Ola Elizabeth Winslow, *Jonathan Edwards: A Biography* (New York: Macmillan, 1941), pp. 195–96.

American theology to change from Calvinism to Arminianism. We shall see several other important instances where one period's avant garde, ivory-tower idea became a staple of the thinking of the next group of younger men being educated for the ministry.

Moving on to the American Revolution, we confront the question of the religious bases, if any, of our governmental institutions. Nearly all of us will have had a distorted first introduction to this topic: those who are older, or who have been in religious schools, will have first heard a rendition not unlike Schaeffer's, and those who are younger, and who have been in public schools since important Supreme Court decisions on prayer and other exposure to religion in such schools, will have received the early impression that the founding fathers were all deists and admirers of the French Revolution. Indeed, the third man to be elected president of the United States, Thomas Jefferson, was a deist, openly denying the divinity of Christ, as was Benjamin Franklin. Max Weber gave some additional fame to Franklin, depicting him from his own writings as an extreme example of the Protestant ethic continuing to govern values and behavior after the supernaturalistic religion has died away or been rejected.[9] Most of the Revolutionary founding fathers were churchgoers, after the customs of their home communities, but none was a representative of religious fervor in public life, as for example, Roger Williams and William Penn had been in earlier generations.

In combing the social-science literature on religion, I found "Civil Religion in America," an article by Robert N. Bellah,[10] to be the publication, of authors still living, second most frequently referred to. This shows how those conflicting childhood impressions as to our country's religious origins carry over to the grownup American social scientist. Bellah combed the inaugural and farewell addresses of the presidents and other salient historical papers and found:

> The words and acts of the founding fathers, especially the first few presidents, shaped the form and tone of the civil religion as it has been maintained ever since. Though much is selectively derived from Christianity, this religion is clearly not itself Christianity. For one thing, neither Washington nor Adams nor Jefferson mentions Christ in his inaugural address; nor do any of the subsequent presidents, although not one of them fails to mention God. The God of the civil religion is not only rather "unitarian," he is also on the austere side, much more related to order, law, and right than to salvation and love. Even though he is somewhat deist in cast, he is by no means simply a watchmaker God. He is actively interested and involved in history, with a special concern for America. . . .
>
> At a time when the society was overwhelmingly Christian, it seems unlikely that this lack of Christian reference was meant to spare the feelings of the tiny non-Christian minority. Rather the civil religion expressed what those who set the precedents felt was appropriate under the circumstances. It reflected their private

9. Weber, *Protestant Ethic,* pp. 48–51.
10. *Daedalus* 96 (Winter 1967): 1–21.

as well as public views.[11]

This special form of religion, distinct from churchly or private religion, has remained remarkably consistent up to the present day. It remains quite consistent, even when the individual religious backgrounds of the public officials expressing it differ: from the president least inclined toward organized religion (probably Jefferson) to the one most so inclined (probably Lincoln) to the most recent presidents in a time alleged to be "secularized," the sort of religiously toned view one is apt to hear expressed by an incumbent of public office has not changed since the United States was founded.

The course of Protestant Christianity after the Revolution has been closely studied by historian Richard Hofstadter:

> If one compares American society at the close of the Revolution, still largely hemmed in east of the Alleghenies, with the much vaster American society of 1850, when the denominational pattern was basically fixed, one is impressed by the gains of the groups committed to evangelicalism. At the end of the Revolution the three largest and strongest denominations were the Anglicans, the Presbyterians, the Congregationalists. Two of these had once been established in one place or another, and the third had a strong heritage in America. By 1850, the change was striking. The largest single denomination was then the Roman Catholic. Among Protestant groups the first two were now the Methodists and the Baptists, once only dissenting sects. . . .
>
> In the mid-eighteenth century, America had a smaller proportion of church members than any other nation in Christendom . . . it has been estimated that in 1800 about one of every fifteen Americans was a church member; by 1850 it was one of seven. In 1855 slightly more than four million persons were church members in a population of over twenty-seven million . . . . There were many more church-goers than church members—at least if we are to judge by the twenty-six million church seating accommodation reported in 1860 for a population of thirty-one million. The . . . Methodists and Baptists . . . together had almost seventy percent of all Protestant communicants.[12]

The ascendance of Methodist and Baptist churches coincides with the change of the modal theology from Calvinist to Arminian, which we have mentioned. The Baptist movement was always decentralized, often fragmented, and the range of theological views within it tended to mirror, perhaps lagging behind, the views in contention in other Protestant groups. For understanding the popular, Evangelical Christianity of nineteenth-century America, one personality, John Wesley (1703–1791), the cofounder of Methodism, towers above

---

11. Ibid., pp. 7–8. The notion of a "civil religion," a form of religion reduced to the lowest common denominator, belief in an omnipotent and good God, an afterlife with rewards and punishments, and proscription of intolerance, to facilitate the smooth working of society, with all more specific religious views left to individual conscience, had been advocated by Jean Jacques Rousseau, whose writings the founding fathers knew well.

12. *Anti-Intellectualism in American Life* (New York: Random House, 1963,), pp. 87, 89–90.

all others. Just how ripe America was for a movement such as Methodism is shown by the smallness of its start. The Methodist movement had been identified with Tory sentiment earlier and had practically no following in the newly independent United States. I think John Wesley to be as important a shaper of American society as any of the founding fathers.

The Methodist movement began in the 1730s at Oxford, where Wesley, his brother, Charles, and Whitefield had been educated as an "elite gathering of . . . scholars, who practiced a systematic and rigorous discipline of study, prayer, philanthropy, sacramental observance, and personal piety."[13] In his younger years, Wesley was troubled, sickly, but academically promising. In 1735, having trouble finding direction, Wesley accepted the offer of James Oglethorpe to go to Georgia and minister to the English settlers and Indians there. A present-day Methodist spokesman candidly describes Wesley's sojourn:

> His missionary service in Georgia had been a dismal failure. Rigid emphasis upon rules, rules, rules angered and repulsed most colonists. They hated or ignored the conscientious priest who insisted on reading morning and evening prayers, who arbitrarily excluded people from the Lord's Supper, and who baptized babies by immersion.[14]

After his return to England, the personality of the sickly, priggish, nearly middle-aged cleric was transformed, and his health improved, so that he became a vigorous traveler and worker, remaining so well into his eighties. He and his brother, Charles, began to preach at every opportunity. Wesley became adamantly Arminian, precipitating a break with Whitefield. This meant emphasis on good works, and hence, social action. For the first time, preaching to the effect that meeting human needs was a Christian teaching caught on. A widely respected college history text describes the effect:

> Although the beliefs of the Methodists diverged entirely from those of the enlightened rationalists, both groups worked in their different ways to improve the condition of society. Where the *philosophes* advised public reform, the Methodists favored private charity and where the *philosophes* attacked the *causes* of social evils, the Methodists accepted these evils as part of God's plan and sought to mitigate their *symptoms* . . . . They began agitation against drunkenness, the trade in slaves, and the barbarous treatment of prisoners, the insane, and the sick. John Wesley established schools for coalminers' children and opened dispensaries for the poor in London and Bristol.[15]

The English Methodist movement provided the model for the Evangelicalism of expanding America in the nineteenth century, with its itinerant evange-

---

13. Donald F. Durnbaugh, *The Believers' Church: The History and Character of Radical Protestantism* (New York: Macmillan, 1968), p. 132.
14. Charles W. Keysor, *Our Methodist Heritage* (Elgin, Ill.: David C. Cook, 1973), p. 17.
15. Crane Brinton, John B. Christopher, and Robert Lee Wolff, *A History of Civilization,* vol. 2, 2nd ed. (Englewood Cliffs, N.J.: Prentice-Hall, 1960), p. 87.

lists, rescue missions, missionary organizations, Salvation Army, and generally upbeat, civic-minded tone. The Baptist denominations, with their emphasis on a knowing and deliberate entry into the Christian life by adult baptism, easily absorbed the Arminian theology of the Methodists: that anyone could decide to be a Christian and receive its blessings if his attitude were right and he performed such good works as he was able, as a necessary but not sufficient condition of those blessings. Believing that anybody could be saved militated toward emphasis on the recruitment of new converts and to charitable outreach to the unsaved, coupled with recruitment.

Both in America and in Great Britain, the private charity prompted by Wesleyanism helped greatly to ease the anomie and harshness of newly forming industrial centers, which were attracting people from the shelter of country life and into America from other countries. One hears that Wesley and his followers may have it to their credit that England did not suffer a proletarian/intellectual ideological revolution, as France did. This may well be so. More certainly, it saved Protestantism from petrifying, declining, and giving way to "secularization" in the early nineteenth century.

The Arminian, Evangelical, socially conscious Christianity emanating from Wesley is what I mean by the term *old-time religion.* Our sketch of it will suffice until we take up twentieth-century developments. Now, we shall look at the theological and psychological interior of the old-time religion and see what made it such a profound departure from what had gone before.

We have pointed out that Protestantism's most basic premise is the authority of the Bible, in contradistinction to other Christ-centered religions, which have additional writings claimed to be canonical or which give credit to revelations claimed to be received directly by church leaders from time to time. We have emphasized that the modal American theology before the advent of our old-time religion was Calvinism. We are preparing, all the while, to analyze the implications of a renewed biblicism in present-day conservative Christianity. Hence, we must sort out what the Bible actually contains, pertaining to each theological issue, to understand those who follow or claim to follow its teaching.

To assess Calvinism, I carefully read the New Testament to see which verses would support only a Calvinist interpretation and which would support only an Arminian interpretation. I found one hundred thirty-three verses clearly militating in favor of Calvinism,[16] and only twenty-three clearly militating in favor of Arminianism.[17] No biblical story, parable, or larger development has an Arminian dénouement. Calvinism is the clear winner, in accurate rendition of

---

16. The verses consistent only with Calvinism are: Matt. 2:6; 7:16-20; 9:37-38; 10:5-6; 11:25, 27; 13:24-30; 37-43; 15:13, 24; 20:23, 28; 22:2-14; 24:22; 25:32-34; Mark 4:11-12, 15-20; Luke 1:77; 3:17; 6:43-45; 8:5-15; 10:22; 13:23-30; 14:23; 16:31; 18:7; John 1:12-13; 3:6; 6:44, 65; 10:14, 16, 26; 15:16; 17:2; Acts 2:39; Rom. 8:29-30, 33; 9:15-16, 21-24; 10:20; 11:5; 2 Cor. 10:7, 18; Gal. 1:15; Eph. 1:4-5; 2:8; 2 Thess. 2:11-12; 2 Tim. 2:10, 19-20; 1 Pet. 2:8; Jude 4; Rev. 7:3-15; 13:8; and 22:11.

17. The verses consistent only with Arminianism are: Matt. 11:28; Luke 2:10; 11:9-10; 13:34; 20:38; Acts 2:17; Rom. 10:9, 13; Gal. 5:13; Eph. 4:6; Phil. 2:10-11; Col. 1:28; 1 Tim. 2:4, 6; 2 Tim. 2:21; Titus 2:11; 2 Pet. 3:9; and Rev. 22:17-19, 21.

the Bible's contents. Of course, one can much more easily and plausibly find ways to strain the language of twenty-three verses to reconcile them with one hundred thirty-three than the reverse.[18]

It does not matter whether or not one engages in semantic gymnastics to reconcile the verses. The contradiction of these verses, so much more obvious if one looks at them grouped together than if they remain buried in the rest of the text, is essential to the psychological effect.

If salvation is not available to all, is salvation doubt a necessary consequence of deep Bible knowledge, such as Edwards and Wesley possessed? What does the Bible have to say about indicators of salvation? It cannot be emphasized too strongly that the Bible gives only this, for a working definition, as a criterion observable or distinguishable by the believer: ". . . he that shall endure unto the end, the same shall be saved."[19] The point that a true saint of the church can be known only when the entire span of his life is known is made numerous times in the New Testament.[20] Apparently, one cannot measure a saint until he is dead. Examples in the early church of individuals who wanted to be Christians, but turned out in the long run to lack the right stuff, include Judas, Ananias, Sapphira, and Simon the Sorcerer; in the later church period, whole ostensible churches, or even the majority of them, outwardly professed the faith but were condemned.[21]

Besides endurance or perseverance to the end, only ambiguous, even teasing allusions are given. In one place, the believers are told: "Examine yourselves, whether ye be in the faith; prove your own selves. Know ye not your own selves, how that Jesus Christ is in you, except ye be reprobates?"[22] In another place: "Let us therefore come boldly unto the throne of grace, that we may obtain mercy, and find grace to help in time of need."[23] But, ". . . work out your own

---

18. For instance, a present-day Calvinist would be likely to explain away Matt. 11:28 by saying that an unsaved person is not "heavy-laden" in the way contemplated, because the Holy Spirit has not convicted him, or Rom. 10:13, saying that one of the nonelect cannot have the desire to call upon the name of the Lord. Calvin, faced with 1 Tim. 2:4 ("[God] will have all men to be saved, and to come unto the knowledge of the truth"), perhaps the clearest of these verses, simply announced that God had meant to say, "all orders of men," or "nationalities." *Institutes of the Christian Religion,* Book 3, chap. 24, para. 16.

19. Matt. 24:13. Another definition, not really adding anything, is 1 John 2:3, "And hereby we do know that we know him, if we keep his commandments." Until all that is to happen in the individual's life has happened, his keeping of the commandments cannot be measured. (The Calvinists describe good behavior as "evidences of salvation," thereby bringing this verse into seeming harmony with others teaching that God's grace, and not the keeping of the law, effect salvation, namely, Gal. 5:3-4 and Eph. 2:8.)

20. Matt. 10:22; 24:12-51; 25:1-13; Mark 13:13, 35-37; Luke 12:35-40, 42-48; 21:19; Rom. 2:7; 8:25; 1 Thess. 5:2-8; 1 Tim. 4:16; 2 Tim. 2:12; 4:7; Heb. 3:12, 14; James 1:12; 5:11; Rev. 2:17; 3:3-13; 13:10, and 16:15.

21. Matt. 7:21-23; 8:11-12; Luke 22:3 ff. (Judas); Acts 5:1-11 (Ananias and Sapphira); 8:9-24 (Simon the Sorcerer); 2 Cor. 11:13-15, 26; Phil. 1:15, 17-18; 1 John 2:19; and Rev., chaps. 2 and 3, generally.

22. 2 Cor. 13:5.

23. Heb. 4:16.

salvation with fear and trembling."[24] Also, "Do ye look on things after the outward appearance? If any man trust to himself that he is Christ's, let him of himself think this again, that as he *is* Christ's, even so *are* we Christ's."[25]

Weber, who had no occasion to be interested in the Bible-authenticity of Calvinism, supposing capitalism to be an aftereffect of Calvinism, after the erosion of its supernaturalistic underpinnings, paused to describe the psychological consequences of not being able to know whether oneself or one's fellow was saved:

> [T]he Calvinist's intercourse with his God was carried on in deep spiritual isolation. To see the specific results of this peculiar atmosphere, it is only necessary to read Bunyan's *Pilgrim's Progress* . . . . In the description of Christian's attitude after he had realized that he was living in the City of Destruction and he had received the call to take up his pilgrimage to the celestial city, wife and children cling to him, but stopping his ears with his fingers and crying, "life, eternal life," he staggers forth across the fields. No refinement could surpass the naive feeling of the tinker who, writing in his prison cell, earned the applause of a believing world, in expressing the emotions of the faithful Puritan, thinking only of his own salvation. It is expressed in the unctuous conversations which he holds with fellow-seekers on the way . . . . Only when he himself is safe does it occur to him that it would be nice to have his family with him.[26]

In understanding what intense psychological pressure the Protestant believer was under in the time of Edwards and Wesley, we can interrelate the seemingly unconnected trends of hyperreligious revival, "normal" periods characterized by slight or absent overt awareness of religious concerns, and civic life with a sort of amorphous, quasi-religious spirit to it, but dissociated from formal religion. When the Calvinistic early indoctrination of those who set the precedents was not showing on the surface, was it truly absent? Consider the following anecdote Hofstadter tells about Franklin:

> One thinks . . . of Benjamin Franklin listening to Whitefield's preaching in Philadelphia, emptying his pockets for the support of one of the Awakener's favored charities, and, after the regular clergy had refused their pulpits to Whitefield, contributing to the erection of a meeting house that would be available to any preacher. This rapprochement between pietism and rationalism reached a peak at the time of Jefferson's presidency, when the dissenting groups, notably the Baptists, gladly threw their support behind a man who, rationalist or not, stood so firmly for religious freedom.[27]

This portrait of the least reverent of our founding fathers, feeling emotionally moved to contribute at a revival meeting, does not bespeak a mind free

---

24. Phil. 2:12.
25. 2 Cor. 10:7.
26. Weber, *Protestant Ethic,* pp. 106–7. Footnotes omitted.
27. Hofstadter, *Anti-Intellectualism in American Life,* pp. 119–20.

from underlying religious fear. If Franklin's behavior could be manipulated by Whitefield's pitch, then who in that milieu was immune from such manipulation? For anyone who was thoughtful, the problem of religious fear must have been at least a latent problem, needing resolution in some manner.

The resolution of the problem of religious fear, required by the Zeitgeist, was the psychological reformulation of salvation, contemporaneously and independently put into theory by Edwards and into practice by Wesley. Perhaps the most condensed of Edwards' statements of it is found in "A Treatise Concerning Religious Affections," first published in 1746 and quite influential on those who came after:

> True religion is evermore a powerful thing; and the power of it appears, in the first place, in its exercises in the heart, its principal and original seat. Hence true religion is called the *power of godliness,* in distinction from external appearances, which are *the form* of it, 2 Tim. iii. 5. *Having a form of godliness, but denying the power of it.* The spirit of God, in those who have sound and solid religion, is a spirit of powerful, holy affection; and, therefore, God is said *to have given them the Spirit of power, and of love, and of a sound mind* (2 Tim. i. 7). And such, when they receive the spirit of God, in his sanctifying and saving influences, are said to be *baptized with the Holy Ghost, and with fire;* by reason of the power and fervour of those exercises which the Spirit of God excites in them, and whereby *their hearts,* when grace is in exercise, may be said to *burn within them.* (Luke xxiv. 32.)[28]

Besides setting down almost a blueprint for the Pentecostalism of nearly a century and a half later, and the "second blessing" theology underlying it, Edwards makes the individual's emotions integral to his religious life. To counterbalance fear, he prescribes an experience of hope and love. Although Edwards, staying within the Calvinistic constraints, never goes so far as to say that one can know by the emotional experience that one is saved—and remove or reduce the uncertainty—we can see it intimated in personal reminiscences that he wrote in his mid-thirties, about his conversion experience in his late teens:

> Indeed, I was at times very uneasy, especially towards the latter part of my time at college; when it pleased God, to seize me with a pleurisy; in which he brought me nigh to the grave, and shook me over the pit of hell. . . . I had great and violent inward struggles, till, after many conflicts with wicked inclinations, repeated resolutions, and . . . vows to God, I was brought wholly to break off all former wicked ways, and all ways of known outward sin. . . . My concern continued and prevailed, with many exercising thoughts and inward struggles; but yet it never seemed to be proper, to express that concern by the name of terror. . . .
>
> It used to appear like a horrible doctrine to me. But I remember the time very well, when I seemed to be convinced, and fully satisfied, as to this sovereignty of God, and his justice in thus eternally disposing of men according to his sovereign pleasure. . . . And there has been a wonderful alteration in my

28. Winslow, ed., *Jonathan Edwards,* p. 191.

> mind . . . from that day to this. . . . The doctrine has very often appeared exceedingly pleasant, bright, and sweet. . . .
>
> An inward, sweet sense of these things, at times, came into my heart; and my soul was led away in pleasant views and contemplations of them.[29]

Tenuously, and by blunting the emotions appropriate to the biblical doctrine, Edwards attained some peace of mind. We can be tempted all too easily to compare him with Winston Smith, when he has at last learned to love Big Brother. But for almost any other believer, lacking Edwards' grasp of the theological issues and his intellectual integrity in facing them, dispelling the fear and doubt by cultivating a set of thoughts and emotions consistent with the believer's notion of a saved person's mental life, went far toward reducing the tension. If he could convince himself that the thoughts and emotions were of supernatural origin, so much the better. Edwards could not, and did not, stretch the matter that far.

Wesley, whom we saw at a juncture chosen to emphasize his rigidity and dissonance of personality before his creative phase began, stretched the matter that far and farther. On the ship to America, in 1736, Wesley had spent time with a group of Moravians, and through them had become acquainted with Peter Böhler. In his Journal entry for May 24, 1738, Wesley wrote:

> In my return to England, January, 1738, being in imminent danger of death, and very uneasy on that account, I was strongly convinced that the cause of that uneasiness was unbelief. . . . Böhler . . . affirmed of true faith in Christ . . . that it had those two fruits inseparably attending it, 'dominion over sin and constant peace from a sense of forgiveness'. . . .
>
> When I met Peter Böhler again, he consented to put the dispute upon the issue . . . Scripture and experience. . . . [considering] the words of God . . . I found they all made against me, and was forced to retreat to my last hold, 'that experience would never agree with the *literal interpretation* of those scriptures. Nor could I therefore allow it to be true, till I found some living witness of it.' He replied, he could show me such at any time. . . . the next day he came again with three others, all of whom testified, of their own personal experience, that a true living faith in Christ is inseparable from a sense of pardon for all past and freedom from all present sins.

In the same Journal entry, he described the famous experience he had at Aldersgate, during Whitsuntide, when he had a sudden but gentle conversion experience, and felt his "heart strangely warmed." Böhler had taught him that sudden conversion experiences were normal.[30]

Whereas Edwards wanted a subjective experience of hope and love to counteract or at least counterbalance the fear, Wesley, very deftly and subtly, made

---

29. Ibid., pp. 82-84.

30. Clifford W. Towlson, *Moravian and Methodist: Relationships and Influences in the Eighteenth Century* (London: Epworth Press, 1957). The historical passage of the sudden-conversion idea from the Moravians, through the Methodists, and into the mainstream of American Protestantism is shown in detail, and the important passages from the journals, etc. of the key figures are digested.

individual judgment and conscience a counterbalance, or check upon, the literal authority of Scripture. He went boldly ahead, preaching from those parts of the Scripture that agreed with the Arminian theology and social concern that made Methodism so responsive to the needs of the time. He cut the Gordian knot of precise Bible scholarship. All the while, he conspicuously claimed to be the arch-exponent of biblicism. In his Journal, on June 5, 1766, he wrote, "My ground is the Bible. Yea, I am a Bible-bigot. I follow it in all things, both great and small." But what he followed was not the letter of it, but its spirit as he, Wesley, in his sole discretion, saw it. Those who minded, commiserated with one another about it in churches that were being eclipsed by the new approach.

Because the overwhelming majority of Wesley's writings affirmatively, brightly, and attractively present his position, and because very little in them criticizes others, it is easy for the Wesleyan to miss the point that the authority of Scripture is made subordinate to common sense in Wesleyanism, and the groundwork is laid for greater departures in theology later. The following passage, from Wesley's sermon "Free Grace," preached in Bristol in 1740, a polemic against Calvinism, clearly illustrates the elevation of common sense to the position of superior or governing priciple in interpreting Scripture:

> . . . let it be observed that this doctrine [Calvinism] represents our blessed Lord, "Jesus Christ the righteous," . . . as a hypocrite, a deceiver of the people, a man void of common sincerity. For it cannot be denied, that he every where speaks as if he was willing that all men should be saved. Therefore, to say he was not willing that all men should be saved, is to represent him as a mere hypocrite and dissembler. It cannot be denied that the gracious words which came out of his mouth, are full of invitations to all sinners. To say then, he did not intend to save all sinners, is to represent him as a gross deceiver of the people. You cannot deny that he says, "Come unto me, all ye that are weary and heavy laden." [Matt. 11:28] If, then, you say he calls those who cannot come; those whom he knows to be unable to come; those whom he can make able to come, but will not; how is it possible to describe greater insincerity! You represent him as mocking his helpless creatures, by offering what he never intends to give. You describe him as saying one thing and meaning another; as pretending the love which he had not. Him, in "whose mouth was no guile," [1 Pet. 2:22] you made full of deceit, void of common sincerity;—then, especially, when drawing nigh the city, he went over it and said, "Oh Jerusalem, Jerusalem, thou that killest the prophets and stonest them that are sent unto thee, how often *would I* have gathered thy children together,—and *ye would not;"* . . . . [Luke 13:34] Now if you say, *they would,* but *he would not,* you represent him (which who could hear?) as weeping crocodile's tears; weeping over the prey which himself had doomed to destruction!
>
> Such blasphemy this, as one would think might make the ears of a Christian to tingle! But there is yet more behind; for just as it honours the Son, so doth this doctrine honour the Father. It destroys all his attributes at once; it overturns both his justice, mercy, and truth: yea, it represents the most holy God as worse than the devil, as both more false, more cruel, and more unjust. More *false;* because the devil, liar as he is, hath never said, "He willeth all men to be saved:" [1 Tim. 2:4] more *unjust;* because the devil cannot, if he would be guilty of

such injustice as you ascribe to God, when you say, that God condemned millions of souls to everlasting fire, prepared for the devil and his angels, for continuing in sin, which, for want of that grace *he will not* give them, they cannot avoid: and more *cruel;* because that unhappy spirit "seeketh rest and findeth none;" [Matt. 12:43] so that his own restless misery is a kind of temptation to him to tempt others. But God resteth in his high and holy place; so that to suppose him, of his own mere motion, of his pure will and pleasure, happy as he is, to doom his creatures, whether they will or no, to endless misery, is to impute such cruelty to him, as we cannot impute even to the great enemy of God and man. It is to represent the Most High God (he that hath ears to hear, let him hear!) [Matt. 11:15] as more cruel, false, and unjust than the devil! [paragraph numbers and Greek repetitions of Bible phrases omitted][31]

What should be noted is that our "old-time religion," Evangelicalism during its halcyon days in America, was biblical only in a very superficial sense. In its deeper substance, it evaded the Bible's teaching, especially the negative implications of that teaching. The outer forms and traditions were retained, but in every psychologically significant instance a modern, functional idea was substituted for the biblical one and clothed in biblical language. The indoctrination of a new generation with ideas contradicting those that best bring out the unity, continuity, and direction of the Bible, achieved *containment* of the Bible's teaching. When the Bible is approached with Arminian or Wesleyan assumptions, it is rendered remote, confusing, and impenetrable, and Bible knowledge becomes a matter of concrete facts and events. No new translation of the Bible had displaced the King James version, and English had changed enough since its time so as to impede understanding even further. Methodist and Baptist clergy in the United States tended to have modest formal education, and they were not academically oriented. These were no sticklers for precise Bible scholarship. Clergy and lay study of the Bible became more or less harmless.

This obscuring of the Bible's teaching led to an intellectual doctrine of sorts, *dispensationalism.* The dispensationalist separates the Bible into as many as seven epochs, each with different theological rules. Such a view excuses the Bible student from looking for unity, continuity, and consistency in the entire Bible, as Calvinism had done. The permeation of what passed for theological scholarship in the United States with dispensationalism also gave rise to the various forms of *millennialism,* the study of scenaria of end-time events.[32]

---

31. John Emory, ed., *The Works of the Reverend John Wesley, A.M.,* 7 vols.; vol. 5 (New York: J. Emory and B. Waugh, 1831), p. 488.

32. The seminal thinker in dispensationalism was John Nelson Darby (1800-1882). He is also known for his vocal criticism of the worldliness of visible churches, and his exhortations against too close identification with them. Thus, "Darbyism" has come to be a term of opprobrium among denomination-oriented clergy, used for para-church ministries. There is very little secondary-source material on Darby, and the major encyclopedias do not carry articles on him. A goodly application of library effort turned up little to add to Durnbaugh, *Believers' Church,* pp. 164-70. The lack of scholarly writing about such a figure is symptomatic of Evangelicals' lack of appreciation of their own history.

The main nineteenth-century trend, then, was substitution of something more practical and useful for the religion of fear and loneliness within the four corners of the Bible. This functionalization of Protestantism brought it closer to the civil religion and also gave rise to an even more psychological conception of salvation than that of Edwards and Wesley, wherein salvation became a matter of mind-cure.

An image of the further progress of the civil religion in America that has affected every academic since is from Alexis de Tocqueville, in his chronicle of his travels in the United States in the 1840s, *Democracy in America.* This is the first of many social scientists' views we will cover, and always we will look at the partisan viewpoint of the social scientist. (Everyone comes to the topic of religion with a partisan viewpoint of some kind.)

De Tocqueville was a Frenchman, a republican, and at least nominally, a Roman Catholic. He was careful to stress that he found American Roman Catholics similar in outlook to the Protestants, particularly in holding the view that separation of church and state was best for the prosperity of both. De Tocqueville was not particularly knowledgeable theologically, and thought the main psychological purpose of religion to be provision for life after death, as an antidote for the discouragement of physical death being the end. He saw only the civically beneficial implications of religious fear: the motivation of honesty in business dealings and truthfulness of statements given under oath. The following imparts his most basic impression about American religion:

> The Americans combine notions of Christianity and of liberty so intimately in their minds that it is impossible to make them conceive of the one without the other; and with them this conviction does not spring from that barren, traditionary faith which seems to vegetate rather than to live in the soul.
>
> I have known of societies formed by Americans to send out ministers of the Gospel into the new Western states, to found schools and churches there, lest religion should be allowed to die away in those remote settlements, and the rising states be less fitted to enjoy free institutions than the people from whom they came. I met with wealthy New Englanders who abandoned the country in which they were born in order to lay the foundations of Christianity and of freedom on the banks of the Missouri or in the prairies of Illinois. Thus religious zeal is perpetually warmed in the United States by the fires of patriotism. These men do not act exclusively from a consideration of a future life; eternity is only one motive of their devotion to the cause. If you converse with these missionaries of Christian civilization, you will be surprised to hear them speak so often of the goods of this world, and to meet a politician where you expected to find a priest.[33]

Cast free from its former biblical moorings, *Christianity* came to denote anything good or wholesome in American life. The term ceased to have any more specific meaning than that and was easily amended to *Judeo-Christian*

33. Alexis de Tocqueville, *Democracy in America,* ed. Phillips Bradley, vol. 1 (New York: Random House, 1945), p. 317.

later, when a non-Christian minority became significant in American life. So long as Christianity was seen as having a salutary and unifying effect on society, it received gentle treatment from social scientists.

A different image, important as a chronicle of the mind-cure aspect of Evangelicalism preceding it and perhaps more important for the influence that it wielded on subsequent developments, is found in William James' *The Varieties of Religious Experience.* James (1842–1910) was one of the pioneers of scientific psychology and was far ahead of his time in moving that field away from trying to study mental elements in isolation and the "chemistry" of their behavior to *functionalism,* the study of mental activity in relation to adaptation to the environment, the ultimate purpose of mental activity. Philosophically, James was a pragmatist, but in a better and more durable sense than others we associate with that term. James was passionate about being democratic in his conduct toward other people and fair in dealing with contending points of view. With James, pragmatism did not boil down to reductionistic materialism, or to ends justifying means. He was absolutely earnest in being for fair discussion of all points of view and permanently tentative about all conclusions, lest new discovery require that a conclusion be abandoned or a point of view changed. Consistently, he favored productive involvement with what is outside, and disliked withdrawal, detachment, imagination not tempered by realism and practicality.

We will return to the technical psychological content of *Varieties* in the next chapter, dealing now only with James' stand as a proponent of Evangelicalism as a form of mind-cure. The religion James saw around him during the last quarter of the nineteenth century, that he thought salutary and wanted to encourage, he characterized as "healthy-minded." "Repentance according to such healthy-minded Christians means *getting away from* the sin, not groaning and writhing over its commission."[34] In contrast is the melancholy, withdrawn "sick soul":

> [N]either Bunyan nor Tolstoy could become what we have called healthy-minded. They had drunk too deeply of the cup of bitterness ever to forget its taste, and their redemption is into a universe two stories deep. Each of them realized a good which broke the effective edge of his sadness; yet the sadness was preserved as a minor ingredient in the heart of the faith by which it was overcome.[35]

James goes on to describe religious conversion:

> To be converted, to be regenerated, to receive grace, to experience religion, to gain an assurance, are so many phrases which denote the process, gradual or sudden, by which a self hitherto divided, and consciously wrong, inferior and unhappy, becomes unified and consciously right, superior and happy, in consequence of its firmer hold upon religious realities. This at least is what conversion

34. William James, *The Varieties of Religious Experience* (New York: New American Library, 1958), p. 113.
35. Ibid., p. 155.

> signifies in general terms, whether or not we believe that a direct divine operation is needed to bring such a moral change about. . . .[36]

> To say that a man is 'converted' means, in these terms, that religious ideas, previously peripheral in his consciousness, now take a central place, and that religious aims form the habitual centre of his energy.[37]

Then he states three characteristics of religious conversions: (1) "The central one is the loss of all worry, the sense that all is ultimately well with one. . . ." (2) "[T]he sense of perceiving truths not known before." (3) "[T]he objective change which the world often appears to undergo . . . . the precise opposite of . . . that dreadful unreality and strangeness . . . experienced by melancholy patients. . . . "[38]

Despite James' rejection of the idea of biblical authority out of hand,[39] *Varieties* was received as it was offered, as a strong testimonial in favor of Evangelicalism. Those clergy educated enough to be reading a book by James had already rejected Bible authority at least tacitly and were primarily concerned with what they could do to conserve their position. From Europe, they were receiving the works of such theologians as Schleiermacher, Ritschl, Barth, Bultmann, and Tillich. All of these were responses to the perceived and admitted need to find something new for Christianity to stand for, when the old supernaturalism was assumed to be untenable and indefensible. The rise of the theory of evolution was to mark the occasion for practically all effort by academics to defend biblical Christianity to cease.

Because the matter of a cosmology in which the earth is not the center was much more acute from the standpoint of Roman Catholic doctrine than from a biblical point of view, no great conflict between Protestantism and the natural sciences took place until after the publication (in 1859) and popularity of *Origin of the Species* by Charles Darwin. And much more in the United States than in Europe the issue of the tenability of the Bible seemed to hinge on this one issue.

Although a lively political controversy still rages over the question of equal time in the schools for so-called scientific creationism, the evolution question is not and has never been dispositive in determining whether or not biblical authority is intellectually defensible. In the intervening time, fundamentalists have noticed that the Bible says sufficiently little as to leave room for the dinosaurs to have existed before the flood of Noah's day; for the "days" before the creation

---

36. Ibid., p. 157.
37. Ibid., p. 162.
38. Ibid., pp. 198–99.
39. Ibid., p. 23. "[I]f our theory of revelation-value were to affirm that any book, to possess it, must have been composed automatically or not by the free caprice of the writer, or that it must exhibit no scientific and historic errors and express no local or personal passions, the Bible would probably fare ill at our hands. But if . . . our theory should allow that a book may well be a revelation . . . if only it be a true record of the inner experiences of great-souled persons wrestling with the crises of their fate, then the verdict would be much more favorable."

of the sun and the moon as timekeepers, on the third day of creation, to have had more than twenty-four hours, indeed, to have continued for whole geological epochs; and for God to have been perfectly able to create the isotopes partly decayed, so that carbon dating would give spurious results. Fundamentalists have also noticed that the further discoveries, relied upon by evolutionists of an earlier day, that indicate how man descended from the higher primates and how one species evolved from another have not been made. Instead, later developments have detracted from the credibility of the random-mutation-natural-selection-by-reproductive-advantage-of-the-fittest rendition of evolution.[40] That rendition was harder to assail before modern physics exploded the neat, time-space-causality environment of nineteenth-century science. When the fundamentalists criticize Carl Sagan, or the local high-school biology teacher, for representing as science that which is really a mix of science, science fiction, and ideologically toned speculation, their criticism is not without validity.

These days, a few believing Christians can be found in each of the pertinent scientific disciplines who thoughtfully find ways to reconcile what is known in their respective disciplines with the biblical account of creation.[41] Accommodations between Christianity and those sciences can readily be formed, and room found for the biblical account not to be false. For the purposes of this work, the reader is asked to do what courts of law are often asked to do in preliminary proceedings: to view the question of discrepancy between the Bible and the current state of any of the natural sciences in the light most favorable to the Bible, assuming if possible, for purposes of discussion, that any such discrepancy is only apparent. If the encroachment of the natural sciences were the real issue, then all those clergy and theologians of our grandparents' day would not have backed down so readily.

The Twentieth Century

At the beginning of the twentieth century, the great majority of Protestants were to be found in the "mainline" denominations we have encountered,[42] church participation having become part of expected, conventional, "respectable" behavior. Having *some* recognizable church affiliation mattered much more than which one it was, and it was not considered polite to discuss religion with someone from a different denomination. Clergy entering the twentieth cen-

40. Arthur Koestler, *The Ghost in the Machine* (New York: Macmillan, 1967), pp. 127-50.

41. For examples of the sort of discussion that takes place, see David L. Bender and Bruno Leone, eds., *Science and Religion: Opposing Viewpoints* (St. Paul: Greenhaven Press, 1981), a supplementary text designed to stimulate discussion of these issues in high-school classes.

42. Martin E. Marty, *A Nation of Behavers* (Chicago: University of Chicago Press, 1976). Marty saw six zones of activity in American religion: Mainline, Evangelicalism-Fundamentalism, Pentecostal-Charismatic, New Religions (i.e., Eastern and cult religions), Ethnic, and Civil.

tury mirrored, more than anything, the society around them. They were pragmatic, progressive, and interested in business as usual. No leader or spokesperson led them to transform the religion, which Wesley had made amendable, into the eclectic mix of civic religion, and whatever was salient in the surrounding culture, that it became.

Very few religious leaders desired to have Protestantism be anything other than a beneficent, uncontroversial institution that could change with the times. There was, in fact, only one conspicuous, academically respectable dissenter up to the last quarter of the century, J. Gresham Machen. He described the mainline church scene of the twenties:

> The period of apparent harmony in which the Church in America found itself . . . was, I believe, a period of the deadliest peril; loyalty to Church organizations was being substituted for loyalty to Christ; Church leaders who never even mentioned the centre of the gospel in their preaching were in undisputed charge of the resources of the Church; at board meetings or in the councils of the Church, it was considered bad form even to mention, at least in any definite and intelligible way, the Cross of Christ. A polite paganism, in other words, with reliance upon human resources, was being quietly . . . substituted for the heroism of devotion to the gospel.[43]

Machen's efforts brought him extreme difficulties and a task he did not want: leadership of a faction. In 1923, Machen's denomination, the Presbyterian Church in the U.S.A., not the most liberal of the strong, mainline denominations, took action implementing the operative parts of the Auburn Affirmation, replacing scriptural "inerrancy" or "infallibility" (terms used to avoid the word *literal* when it is the hortatory rather than the factual content of the Bible that the conservative Christian is most concerned to uphold) with a statement resembling nothing so much as academic freedom in higher education. Each individual was to answer only to his own conscience (and to God) for what he advocated. This result was a comeuppance to conservatives, who had started the bickering in attempting to get Harry Emerson Fosdick ousted from his pulpit.

The same dissension between liberals and conservatives soon caused a rupture within the faculty of Princeton Theological Seminary, where Machen was a faculty member. Machen became the founder and president of Westminster Theological Seminary in Philadelphia in 1929, taking with him the losing minority of conservative Princeton faculty. The focus of controversy within the denomination became the doctrinal purity of funded missionaries and Machen's criticisms of Pearl Buck, who was one of those missionaries and whose best-selling books disagreed with the church's doctrine. Finally, in another coup by the liberals, in 1934, Machen was defrocked and put out of the ministry. This received national newspaper coverage, comparable to that accompanying the decredentialing of Hans Küng by the pope, much more recently. In turn, Machen became involved in founding two splinter conservative Presbyterian

43. *What Is Faith?* (Grand Rapids, Mich.: Wm. B. Eerdmans, 1925), pp. 40-41.

denominations.

What interests us about Machen and the developments surrounding him is the extreme rarity, up to the last quarter of the twentieth century, of thoughtful, intellectually responsive defense of biblical Christianity. Machen himself was more than a rarity; he was an anomaly. Westminster was the only real stronghold of such defense, at least through the sixties, and even the most celebrated of its faculty, John Murray and Cornelius Van Til,[44] have had little influence outside the circle of those they had personally taught. The most conspicuous protégé of Machen has turned out to be Carl McIntire, the famous reactionary radio preacher of the fifties. McIntire formed the nucleus of further schism in Machen's own new denomination. On New Year's Day, 1937, after exhausting himself on a speaking tour in North Dakota, trying to heal rifts caused by McIntire, Machen died at the age of fifty-six.[45]

The mainline clergy knew that a loose approach to the Bible promoted happiness of the individual church participant and constructive involvement of the church in the surrounding world better than a rigorous approach did. They collectively declared the theological issues that had caused salvation-doubt suffering, such as Edwards and Wesley experienced, obsolete and spared themselves similar suffering. Liberal clergy would enjoy some halcyon years, when events

---

44. Van Til (1895-1987), reacting to the logical positivism of his day, and its tendency to confuse the results of empirical investigation with the assumptions from which such investigation proceeded, developed what he called a *presuppositional apologetics:* only that which agrees with the Bible can be truly intelligible and enlightening, and the Christian need not be interested in the "natural" man's chaotic and meaningless methodology. On closer study, one realizes that, yes, he is saying that all secular philosophy and all natural science, including medicine, not done in a spirit of obedience to God is meaningless and unintelligible. No secular intellectual endeavor can have a good or successful outcome! Also, this "apologetics" takes apologetics, as a discipline, completely out of the business of trying to convince or to evangelize unbelievers.

In writing about other theologians, Van Til demonstrated great skill and care. But in writing about secular philosophers, he was true to his view that there was nothing of value to look for in them and engaged in ham-handed oversimplification. In devising a closed system, where the methods and the conclusions were laid out in advance, and what did not fit the system became, by definition, a nonproblem, Van Til unwittingly imitated the positivists and radical behaviorists whom he so disliked.

Francis Schaeffer, who came out of the same sort of Reformed tradition as Van Til, used similar ideas but toned them down for more worldly Christian enthusiasts. There is an unacknowledged intellectual debt owed to Van Til by Schaeffer, similar to the one I have elsewhere described as owed to C. G. Jung by Erich Fromm. Cohen, *C. G. Jung and The Scientific Attitude,* pp. 124-25. Also, there is an extreme fringe group called *reconstructionists* or *post-millennialists,* who advocate implementing a reactionary political program to prepare the world for Christ's second coming; they claimed to be followers of Van Til during years when he was still alive but no longer mentally able to follow their progress and repudiate them, as he undoubtedly would have done.

45. An account of these events, rich in detail and color but neglecting the rôle of McIntire and his followers, is Ned B. Stonehouse, *J. Gresham Machen: A Biographical Memoir* (Philadelphia: Westminster Theological Seminary, 1977). For more on the activities of McIntire, see Gary K. Clabaugh, *Thunder on the Right* (Chicago: Nelson-Hall Co., 1974), pp. 69 ff.

would provide works needing to be done, in civil-rights advocacy, in bringing help to the disadvantaged, and in protesting the Vietnam war. A clergyman who was an adoptee, through his postgraduate education experiences, into the ranks of liberal, mainline clergy, Martin Luther King, Jr., was arguably the greatest man of his time. But in periods not presenting good causes to champion, mainline churches and their clergy would suffer identity confusion and lose followers. The generosity of financial support of the following they kept would diminish.

Modernist Theology

Although liberal church does not spring from any particular seminal thinker, there is one theologian whose views thoroughly permeate the later liberal church phenomenon. Also, there is no social scientist of religion, writing after the theologian came on the scene, whose thinking was not so much influenced by him that misunderstanding is certain, if the implications of the theologian's views are not appreciated. The influence of all other modernist theologians (with the possible exception of Dietrich Bonhoeffer) was so limited to seminary circles that we may safely neglect them in this work. That key provider of a new wineskin for the new wine was Paul Tillich (1886–1965).

To understand Tillich, we must digress and sketch some of the essential features of the milieu from which he came. We cannot overemphasize how much our Anglo-American culture is the poorer for its failure to assimilate more than it has of the intellectual and artistic richness of Germany before Hitler, and the gap or partial vacuum in all our cultural lives, from the failure, so far, of that culture to come back to life since World War II. In Germany then, the focus of the religious debate was not on creation and evolution but on the philosophical implications of theology. Discussion progressed toward insight into the phenomenon of Christianity, toward seeing what makes it concern and motivate humans, in sharp contrast to the Anglo-American habit of focusing only on religion-related issues one can discuss without being inwardly touched, without having the sensitive roots of one's own deeply held views exposed.

A philosopher relatively unfamiliar to the present-day social scientist, Ludwig Andreas Feuerbach ruined his academic career with his angry analysis of conventional religions. But he crucially influenced others better known, including Nietzsche, Marx, Engels, and Freud, and received thoughtful and respectful treatment from subsequent theologians, particularly the modernists, for whom he, more than the evolutionists, was the presenter of the challenge they had to answer.

Prefiguring the depth psychologists,[46] Feuerbach understood religions

46. The concept of the unconscious was not "discovered" by Freud, Breuer, and Janet, as American psychology students are taught, but was in circulation among intellectuals by the end of the eighteenth century. In the mid-nineteenth century, the writings of Eduard von Hartmann and C. G. Carus about the unconscious were widely known. It is the medical application, not the

generally, and Christianity specifically, as arising from the *projection* and *hypostatization* of human qualities and aspirations into the deity or deities.

> Man—this is the mystery of religion—projects his being into objectivity, and then again makes himself an object to this projected image of himself thus converted into a subject; he thinks of himself, is an object to himself, but as the object of an object, of another being than himself.[47]

> Man denies as to himself only what he attributes to God . . . man in relation to God, denies his own knowledge, his own thoughts, that he may place them in God. Man gives up his pesonality; but in return, God, the Almighty, infinite, unlimited being, is a person; he denies human dignity, the human *ego;* but in return God is to him a selfish, egoistical being, who in all things seeks only himself, his own honour, his own ends . . . [48]

> Religion is the disuniting of man from himself; he sets God before him as the antithesis of himself. God is not what man is—man is not what God is . . . God and man are extremes: God is the absolutely positive, the sum of all realities; man the absolutely negative, comprehending all negations.[49]

Feuerbach advocated, in place of conventional religions, self-fulfillment and harmony with nature.

> [My] purpose . . . is to transform theologians into anthropologists, lovers of God into lovers of man, candidates for the next world into students of this world, religious and political flunkeys of heavenly and earthly monarchs and lords into free, self-reliant citizens of the earth . . . I negate the fantastic hypocrisy of theology and religion only in order to affirm the true nature of man.[50]

The life-denying implication of Christianity became the "slave morality" of Nietzsche. Freud saw, as he did in practically everything, the Oedipal problem being projected in a stern, threatening, powerful God the Father. Marx heard "the sigh of the oppressed creature," and felt "the feelings of a heartless world . . . the spirit of unspiritual conditions . . . the opium of the people." The

---

discovery, of the unconscious that the early psychoanalysts have to their credit. Such precursors of the psychological learning theorists as Hermann Ebbinghaus and Hermann von Helmholtz were well aware of unconscious mental contents and inferences and can be described as having tried to answer the question, "Where are our thoughts when we are not thinking them?" See Lancelot Law Whyte, *The Unconscious Before Freud* (London: Tavistock Publications, 1959).

47. Ludwig Feuerbach, *The Essence of Christianity,* trans. George Eliot [Mary Ann Evans] (New York: Harper & Row, 1957), pp. 29-30.

48. Ibid., p. 27.

49. Ibid., p. 33.

50. Feuerbach, *Lectures on the Essence of Religion,* trans. Ralph Manheim (New York: Harper & Row, 1967), p. 23.

"I and thou" relationship, of one part with another, of the fragmented individual personality[51] became the groundwork for the thought of Martin Buber. Tillich would find a way to accept Feuerbach's entire analysis, and not only justify the continued existence of traditional religion but also provide an affirmative program for it.

Because of our historic place and time, we must pause to look at the nonreductionistic and nonrelativistic (i.e., allowing for there to be absolutes in the structure of our experience) philosophical heritage of the European thinkers. This is important for two purposes besides introducing Tillich. Firstly, we need to show those readers who have been surrounded by Evangelicalism that the criticism directed by educated Evangelicals toward all secular thought—alleging that it is "atomistic" or presupposes that order came from chaos with no cause—does not apply to all secular thought.[52] There is plenty of pertinent secular thinking recognizing that wholes have properties that their component parts lack, that neither nature nor our apparatus for coping with the natural environment around us is limitlessly plastic, and that one does not need to hold to a particular conventional religion to hold that a teleological process does operate in nature. Secondly, we need to keep in mind that nonreductionistic and nonrelativistic views are the kind most lacking in our Anglo-American social sciences. In the next chapter, we will see something of the malaise and intellectual stagnation in the psychology field, due in large measure to the failure to follow leads furnished by European nonreductionistic thinkers.

Immanuel Kant (1724–1804) read the writings of the empiricist philosophers John Locke and David Hume early in life, and experienced what he termed an awakening from his dogmatic slumber. He was not content, as we should not be, with the idea that human knowledge comes totally or even primarily from without and makes its impression on our tabula rasa mind.

> There are two ultimate sources from which knowledge comes to us: either we receive ideas in the form of impressions, or, by our spontaneous faculty of conception, we know an object by means of those ideas [i.e., spontaneous conceptions]. In the former case, the object is *given* to us; in the latter case it is *thought* in relation to the impressions that arise in our consciousness. Perception and conception, therefore, are the two elements that enter into all our knowledge. To every conception some form of perception corresponds, and no perception yields knowledge without conception. Both may be either pure or empirical; *empirical,* if sensation, which occurs only in the actual presence of an object is implied; *pure,* if there is no intermixture of sensation. . . . Pure perceptions or pure conceptions alone are possible *a priori,* while empirical perceptions or empirical

51. Feuerbach, *Essence of Christianity,* p. 158.
52. Cornelius Van Til, in *Apologetics* (Phillipsburg, N.J.: Presbyterian and Reformed Pub. Co., 1976), p. 75, says, "Over against this Christian theistic position, any non-Christian philosophy virtually denies the unity of truth. It may speak much of it and even seem to contend for it, as idealistic philosophers do, but in the last analysis non-Christian philosophy is atomistic." This is a truly outrageous statement.

conceptions are possible only *a posteriori*.[53]

Understanding takes place through the dialectically counterposed processes of *analysis* and *synthesis*. Synthesis depends on prestructuring, and the forms or rules that prestructuring follows Kant calls *categories*. The ability of humans to have in common and communicate their conceptions, which may to a high degree be intuitively apprised, depends on the universality of the categories, their sameness from individual to individual. Underlying the *phenomena,* the objects of experience, are the *noumena,* the categorical source of that which enables mere sensory or imaginative impressions to be understood.

> A conception which cannot be known in any way to have objective reality may be called problematic, if it is not self-contradictory, and if it is bound up with the knowledge gained through certain conceptions the range of which it serves to limit. Now the conception of a *noumenon,* that is, of a thing that cannot be an object of sense, but is thought, by pure understanding alone, as a thing in itself, is certainly not self-contradictory; for we cannot know with certainty that sensibility is the only possible mode of perception. Moreover, the conception of a noumenon is necessary to prevent sensuous perception from claiming to extend to things in themselves, and to set a limit to the objective validity of sensuous knowledge. In the end, however, we are unable to understand how such noumena are possible at all, and the realm beyond the sphere of phenomena is for us empty.[54]

The chief difficulty or source of illusion in human knowledge is our inability to see where the object of knowledge ends and our prestructured category for apperceiving it begins. Space, time, and causality are prominent among the properties that Kant believed to be subjective conditions, and are not inherent in the phenomena within them. More than a century later, relativity physics (not a "relativistic" enterprise in the sense we have been contemplating), by mathematical inferences, knowing indirectly what the time, space, and causality-bound human mind cannot know directly, has demonstrated time to be a function of velocity, so that there are no such things as simultaneity and instantaneous space, indicated matter and energy to be a function of each other, and cast doubt (through the Heisenberg irregularity principle) on the very idea of causality. By the use of the most "pure," intuitively apprised means of knowledge, a kind of knowledge about alien, mind-boggling, but indubitably real (and dangerous) things has been gained.[55]

In the practical realm, Kant sought to develop ethical categoricals, i.e.,

---

53. John Watson, trans. and ed, *The Philosophy of Kant as Contained in Extracts from His Own Writings* (Glasgow: James Maclehose & Sons, 1901), p. 40

54. Ibid., p. 132.

55. The presence in man of unsolicited mental gifts, so that the intrinsic ability to split the atom, to create works of art, and do other creative things for the first time, must have been present long before it was ever consciously dreamed of, and cannot be accounted for by a random-mutation-natural-selection view of evolution. This is the most serious deficiency of any nonteleological evolutionary theory.

categorical imperatives, and he progressed from the biblical Golden Rule:[56]

> In all cases I must act in such a way *that I can at the same time will that my maxim should become a universal law.*[57]
>
> *Act so as to use humanity, whether in your own person or in the person of another, always as an end, never as merely a means.*[58]

From his categorical imperatives, Kant inferred that God must exist, and in describing the attributes of God as his philosophy implied him, only incidental similarities to the God of the Bible emerged. The conventional saints of Kant's day took offense, and after the publication of his *Religion Within the Limits of Reason Alone,* in 1793, he came under a Prussian government injunction to publish no more writings on religion.

The modernist theologians, including Tillich, emulated Kant.[59] They were focally aware that there was more that was real than the Newtonian/Euclidean apparent world of the senses. Tillich, coming after the revolution in physics, was aware that the human unconscious, being discussed by the depth-psychologists, partook of a reality outside time and space. He, the depth-psychologist C. G. Jung, and the philosopher Ernst Cassierer developed a viewpoint that was to have a substantial impact on psychological and philosophical thought and would thoroughly permeate religious thought for a generation. In a period in which closed schools of thought, each with its fervent adherents, such as logical positivism, behaviorism, Freudianism, social Darwinism, communism, and fascism, flourished, Cassierer, Jung, and Tillich sought a unified solution to the problem of meaning in them all.

The *symbol* is the key concept in the aspired-to unified view. Human understanding is seen as arranging itself along a continuum of explicit to implicit. A notation, character, or image that is totally explicit is a *sign.* A sign stands arbitrarily, by convention, for its referent and is interchangeable with other possible signs of the same referent. An eight-sided red shield requiring us to bring our motor vehicle to a full stop before proceeding would be an example of a sign in this sense, and mathematical notations, as part of the most explicitly and exhaustively defined field of knowledge, are also a sign system, or nearly so.

---

56. Matt. 7:12; Luke 6:31. The Golden Rule was formulated long before Jesus, in the sixth century B.C., by Confucius, "What you do not want done to yourself, do not do to others," and by Lao-tse, with the added feature of returning good for evil, "Recompense injury with kindness. There are three things which I grasp as precious: the first is Compassion, the second Moderation, and the third is Modesty or Humility." Gerald L. Berry, *Religions of the World* (New York: Barnes & Noble, 1947), pp. 52, 50.

57. Watson, ed., *Philosophy of Kant,* p. 230.

58. Ibid., p. 246.

59. To the claim that the modernist theologians, such as Schleiermacher, Ritschl, Barth, and Bultmann, served to make Christianity relevant to the intellectual concerns of their times, the answer can be made that they only clothed the philosophers' ideas in biblical terms, repackaged them for seminary audiences, and reinforced the idea that the indefensibility of biblical Christianity was a foregone conclusion.

The symbol, in contradistinction to the sign, participates in context with its referent, possesses properties that make it rather than others the fitting representation of the referent, and is not interchangeable. The symbol stands for that which those using it cannot make totally explicit, for that which is partially unconscious, for that which is involved in a creative process of coming to consciousness, a process proceeding from unknowing toward knowledge.

Because we are concerned with Tillich, we will stay close to his rendition of the properties of symbols. He enumerated six such properties: (1) Pointing beyond itself and (2) participation in that to which it points, we have already indicated. (3) The symbol "opens up levels of reality which otherwise are closed for us." (4) It "unlocks dimensions and elements of our soul which correspond to the dimensions and elements of reality." (5) "Symbols cannot be produced intentionally." They are spontaneous, and occur to us rather than being invented by us. (6) They grow to meet the needs of their users, and when the creative process of the referent coming to consciousness is finished, when it has become explicit or nearly so, the symbol dies. Symbol systems are dynamic and ever-changing.[60]

A larger symbol system is commonly referred to as a *myth,* and that something is a myth or has "mythic" quality means it prompts a response or resonance in those for whom it has meaning. *Mythic* is a complimentary term, indicating spiritual or psychological truth, not an opprobrious term, for literal untruth, error, or ignorance. At the apex of all myths is *ultimate reality,* which is infinite, perfect, and complete and which we can grasp only in bits and pieces through provisional, fluctuating symbols and myths because we are finite, imperfect, and incomplete. The inaccessibility of ultimate reality can discourage us from according it its proper place of importance in our lives, according to Tillich. The harmonious, "healthy" personality is one with a symbolic life, shared in a religious community, inclined toward the ultimate, and avoiding too one-sided or obsessive concern with this-worldly, "idolatrous" concerns. "Existential disappointment" is the result of nonultimate concerns becoming paramount for the individual.

> The more idolatrous a faith the less it is able to overcome the cleavage between subject and object . . . the act of faith leads to a loss of center and to a disruption of the personality.[61]

> God is the basic symbol of faith, but not the only one. All the qualities we attribute to him, power, love, justice, are taken from finite experiences and applied

60. Paul Tillich, *The Dynamics of Faith* (New York: Harper & Row, 1957), pp. 42–43. The idea that Christianity could change, withdrawing its projections, for example, by separating inward moral purity from outward ritual purity, when for the Jewish religion they had seemed identical, was already noted by Feuerbach, in *The Essence of Christianity,* p. 32: "In relation to the Israelite, the Christian is an *esprit fort,* a free-thinker. Thus do things change. What yesterday was still religion is no longer such to-day; and what to-day is atheism, tomorrow will be religion."

61. Tillich, *Dynamics of Faith,* p. 12.

> symbolically to that which is beyond finitude and infinity. If faith calls God "almighty" it uses the human experience of power in order to symbolize the content of its infinite concern, but it does not describe a highest being who can do as he pleases. So it is with all the other qualities and with all the actions, past, present and future, which men attribute to God. They are symbols taken from our daily experience, and not information about what God did once upon a time or will do sometime in the future. Faith is not the belief in such stories, but it is the acceptance of symbols that express our ultimate concern in terms of divine actions.[62]

> For only in the community of spiritual beings is language alive. Without language there is no act of faith, no religious experience! This refers to language generally and to the special language in every function of man's spiritual life. The religious language, the language of symbol and myth, is created in the community of believers and cannot be fully understood outside this community. But within it, the religious language enables the act of faith to have a concrete content . . .[63]

Tillich's views filled acute needs of the generation of mainline church clergy succeeding the one that had won its freedom by innovations like the Auburn Affirmation. Where clergy and laity who rejected even the truncated version of the Bible's salvation plan that remained after the Wesleyan revolution found themselves together with others who still accepted it, and these desired to continue to get along, one could simply say that one group was responding to a different level of the symbolism in the ritual and teaching from the other.[64] The outward appearances could remain conservatively supernaturalistic, to be taken at face value by those who wanted to do so, but they could be taken as symbolizing some sublime, ineffable inner experience by the more sophisticated. No longer would anything doctrinal need be a sticking point. Because *ultimate concern* necessarily involves poignant things the person having the faith experience cannot put into words, the lack of clear explanations or resolutions of differences in beliefs would no longer be bothersome, or indicative of hypocrisy. Any good work and prosecution of any good cause could be a reflection of ultimate concern.

Tillich wrote little to guide Christians toward a new, ultimately concerned

---

62. Ibid., pp. 47–48
63. Ibid., p. 24.
64. Empirical evidence of departure from older, supernaturalistic religious ideas, and greatly differing ideas existing together within the same religious groups, was gathered in California church populations in Rodney Stark, Bruce D. Foster, Charles Y. Glock, and Harold E. Quinley, *Wayward Shepherds: Prejudice and the Protestant Clergy* (New York: Harper & Row, 1971). In the more liberal mainline denominations (i.e., United Church of Christ, United Methodist, Episcopal, and United Presbyterian), approximately half of the clergy reported personally important doubts about the existence of God, and only about one-third firmly believed in the divinity of Jesus. About 80 percent believed in life after death, but only half as many believed in a fiery fate for some, beyond the grave. For each sort of church, parishioners were somewhat, but not greatly, more supernaturally inclined in answering each question.

idea-content or scriptural interpretation for a new generation of Christians. He himself seemed to be weary of the Gospel story and rarely mentioned it in those last years of his life when he was so influential. This void was largely filled by C. G. Jung's rich investigations into mythic and religious symbolism. Jung saw in the death-to-life transformation of the Gospel story an image of the individual's innate, teleological, "authentic" destiny unfolding. The demands for submission and obedience to the Bible were reinterpreted as openness to one's own unconscious destiny unfolding, and living out that innate destiny rather than being stultified, disunited with oneself, living by artificial prescriptions imposed from without.[65] The emphasis became intensely individualistic, and the idea of obligation imposed from without drops out of the new Christianity for the follower of Tillich or Jung. Goodness toward others and social concern were expected to arise as byproducts of the development and unfolding of the true Self.

The period following Tillich—from approximately 1965, and coinciding with political turmoil in American society—saw no birth of new symbols to take the place of those thought to be worn out and dead. Rather, the indications from liberal theologians were ones of acute distress. For a time, theologians loudly bewailing the spiritual bankruptcy of Christianity held the limelight. The cover of the April 8, 1966, *Time* magazine consisted of a black background, with the question, "Is God Dead?" in red letters as large as the space allowed. The sophisticated publications in theology thereafter involved such topics as the synthesis of Christianity with Marxism and the gender-neutering of the Bible.

Sociologist Peter L. Berger, who possesses truly formidable and rare knowledge of the theology and social science that pertains, attracted considerable attention with his notion of *secularization,* "the process by which sectors of society and culture are removed from the domination of religious institutions and symbols."[66] He saw the longer, historical process, leading up to our own time, as consisting of the narrowing and fragmenting of church-supplied definitions of reality. In a religiously pluralistic society, where religion is determined primarily within the family, conflicting definitions of reality encountered outside the home undercut the "plausibility" of the reality definition supplied by the church, and the lack of a governmental mandate for it deprives that definition of its "legitimacy."[67]

---

65. Cohen, *C. G. Jung and the Scientific Attitude,* pp. 65–69.

66. *The Sacred Canopy* (Garden City, N.Y.: Doubleday & Co., 1967), p. 107.

67. In interviews reported later in this work with persons answering to the label "religiously disillusioned," I was struck by frequent reports of first encounters with a different doctrine puncturing the childhood religious indoctrination. When a child first learns that significant others hold supernaturalistic views, some of which must be false for others to be true, the awkwardness or unlikelihood of the whole proposition comes into focus. Very often, this starts with more than one denomination being represented within the same nuclear family. The "plausibility" often gets cut off even closer to the ground than Berger anticipated. Even in people who report the generalized, free-form, wish-fulfilling sort of religious belief that, as we shall see, is normal in present-day America, I sense deep resistance to specificity in religious doctrines or beliefs. Beliefs lacking sharp features do not lead to contradictions.

> At the risk of some simplification, it can be said that Protestantism divested itself as much as possible from the three most ancient and most powerful concomitants of the sacred—mystery, miracle, and magic. This process has been aptly caught in the phrase [of Weber's] "disenchantment of the world" [*Entzauberung der Welt*]. The Protestant believer no longer lives in a world ongoingly penetrated by sacred beings and forces. Reality is polarized between a radically transcendent divinity and a radically "fallen" humanity that, *ipso facto,* is devoid of sacred qualities. Between them lies an altogether "natural" universe, God's creation to be sure, but in itself bereft of numinosity [a term for magicalness or holiness originated by Rudolf Otto, and frequently used by Jung]. In other words, the radical transcendence of God confronts a universe of radical immanence, of "closedness" to the sacred. Religiously speaking, the world becomes very lonely indeed.[68]

Berger's analysis, the only well-articulated, intellectually intensive one since Tillich, implicitly follows those earlier social-science authors, such as Freud and Durkheim, who saw all religions as serving to explain the origins of the cosmos and the group's relation to that cosmos. When the natural sciences came along, challenged the religious cosmology, and substituted for it a more competent one, religions would necessarily be obsolete and would decline. Without the hoped-for renovation of the religious symbols, the best sociological opinion included predictions of gloom and doom for organized religions.

If a social scientist of religion is religiously affiliated, the affiliation tends to be mainline. The tacit assumption, arising both from social-science training and from inside the mainline churches has been that the redefined religion of personal growth is the only kind of religion still having a mainstream rôle to play. Having the preponderance of corporate church history behind those churches where that view prevails aids in that misperception. Intensely supernaturalistic religion has been assumed to remain significant only in "sects" or "cults" on the fringes of society, involving only disadvantaged, ignorant, or hypersuggestible people, largely rural or nonwhite. Social scientists have difficulty thinking of religion apart from the denominations, since their categories for differentiating one mode of religion from another, as well as their sources of statistical data on a regional or national scale, have come from the denominations. The proportion of effort in the social sciences applied to religion has been tiny, and the topic has generally been regarded as unimportant, uninteresting, or pertaining to history rather than current events.

In 1972, a book was published that hit the liberal-church and social-science-of-religion establishments like a bomb. This was *Why Conservative Churches Are Growing,* by Dean M. Kelley,[69] a National Council of Churches executive on sabbatical. In contemporary writing on religion, Kelley's is the only publication I found discussed more often than Bellah's "Civil Religion in America"—and that, despite the conspicuous absence of reference to Kelley's work in the more serious academic sociology publications to which it is relevant. Ostensibly,

68. Berger, *Sacred Canopy,* pp. 111–12.
69. (New York: Harper & Row, 1972).

the academic sociologists resented an empirical study by one not a member of their guild. But the findings Kelley reported must have come as a traumatic surprise, a shock, to those steeped in what has passed for scholarly writing on this topic.

Using his experience in the church world and statistics that denominations routinely gather, Kelley traced the progress of the larger church denominations. For the major historical denominations—Episcopalians, United Presbyterians, United Methodists, and United Church of Christ (which had resulted from the merger of several Congregationalist denominations)—Kelley found that membership had steadily increased from the beginnings of the United States until the mid-1960s. Then, the membership leveled off and began to decline, just at the time when the discussion about "death of God" theology was most in vogue. (The membership decline in these denominations has accelerated in the years following Kelley's book.)[70] In the same years when the membership decline was beginning, there was a precipitous decline, a falling out of the bottom, in church-school enrollment; this apparently indicated that the character of participation in the churches was becoming more superficial. Indicators of economic activity in the denominations, such as budgets, building, and publications, closely followed the downward trend of the membership statistics. This, in itself, did not surprise church professionals, but it did disappoint their hopes that by good public relations, by making themselves useful in meeting human needs, and by being tolerant, nondogmatic and nonjudgmental the church could hold its own.

But conservative church denominations, principally the Southern Baptists and certain denominations composed of seceding dissenters, from situations paralleling the events in Presbyterianism involving Machen, experienced no falling off of growth or vitality.[71] Contrary to the conventional wisdom of mainline church professionals, those churches that were least "reasonable," "tolerant," and "relevant" were (and are) the ones not declining. Those churches that continued to emphasize the primacy of the Bible, and to take for real the supernatural salvation plan set out in it, continued to add to their numbers each year.

Beyond that, Kelley's book is not useful to us for its analysis but only for pointing out the blind spots that all of us looking at conservative Christianity

70. See Frank S. Mead, *Handbook of Denominations in the United States,* 7th ed. (Nashville: Abingdon Press, 1980). These trends occur in the context of low birth and death rates and increased life span, leading to increase in the average age, the "graying" of Americans. This would tend to mute the effect on membership statistics of younger people not following the church memberships of their parents, and church-membership decline in that circumstance is all the more significant. Preliminary data for 1983 indicate a leveling off of losses in mainline denomination membership and continuing growth in conservative denominations. *New York Times,* June 19, 1985, p. A20.

71. To compare liberal- with conservative-denomination membership trends, Kelley compared United Presbyterian Church in the U.S.A. with Presbyterian Church in the U.S. (Southern), United Methodist Church with Wesleyan Church, Lutheran Church in America with Lutheran Church—Missouri Synod, Reformed Church in America with Christian Reformed Church, and American Baptist Convention with Southern Baptist Convention.

from outside have shared with him. His views on the nature of religion and his own personal religiosity are so permeated with Tillich that it never occurs to him to examine the possibility that all those people are in conservative churches because they take the supernatural salvation plan at face value. His sources of theory are Berger and expressly Tillichian social scientists, including Bellah, Milton Yinger, Rodney Stark, and Charles Y. Glock. To him, all conservative denominations are alike, and it does not occur to him to distinguish one from another.

Kelley classed the conservative Protestant denominations together with the fast-growing *special-doctrine, Christ-centered religions,* the Seventh-Day Adventists, Christian Scientists, Jehovah's Witnesses, and Mormons. He perceived no interesting differences in implication between the growth of denominations with conspicuous, dearly held doctrines detracting from the authority of the Bible (and consequently rejecting and not cooperating with other religious organizations) and the growth of denominations that proceed from the premise of paramount biblical authority, which can respect and cooperate with other church organizations that they think sincerely devoted, if mistaken, in their efforts to follow the Bible. He shared with the academic sociologists a blind spot as to Pentecostal or "charismatic" denominations, and he made only slight mention of the most conspicuous success story in conservative Protestant denominations, the Assemblies of God, even while stressing the smaller and much less significant Christian Reformed Church.[72] He showed no inkling at all that a network of independent or loosely affiliated churches and para-church organizations might supersede the denomination as the pattern for conservative churchly affiliates to follow. He saw only the impressive presence in nondeclining churches of commitment, discipline, and missionary zeal, and the contrasting lack of those qualities in the declining, mellow mainline churches.

For recommendations for "conserving strength in an adverse era," [73] Kelley could only plead for more imparting of ultimate meaning (which he did not seem to know how to explain, but seemed to equate with work for positive

---

72. The Christian Reformed Church is similar in form but not in history to traditional Presbyterianism. Its membership consists primarily of descendants of Dutch Calvinist immigrants, and its principal success has been in retaining the loyalty of its young people.

In contrast, the Assemblies of God is the product of coalescence, in 1914, of various rural white churches that had emulated black churches in their emphasis on emotionalism and manifestations purporting to be the 1 Corinthians 12 gifts of the Spirit—glossolalia and prophecy. While this denomination reports only about one-half million members in the United States, it does not attach as much significance to membership as other denominations do, and its church-school enrollment of approximately 1.3 million and its more than 9,000 churches indicate such strength of participation as typically would coincide with membership of from 2 to 2.5 million. This denomination proceeds from the premise of paramount biblical authority, and its charismatic practices do not cause the kind of sharp estrangement from other conservative Protestants that exists for the special-doctrine, Christ-centered religions. Its success has been in the building of a respectable, socially heterogeneous body from what had been despised, "henhouse" sects. See William W. Menzies, *Anointed to Serve* (Springfield, Mo.: Gospel Publishing House, 1971).

73. Kelley, *Why Conservative Churches Are Growing,* p. 176.

social change), for enthusiasm rather than lukewarmth, and for more demands made on prospective church members before they are admitted to membership—in other words, getting more members by making the hurdles to membership higher. The church professional reading Kelley's book must have gotten an icy chill from its lack of hope or of recommendations they were in a position to follow.

As it has become evident that organized religion as a whole is not dying out as a result of "secularization" and that the liberal churches have not made good their aspiration to renovate and redefine the Christian symbolism along lines other than those of the supernatural salvation plan, the social science of religion has made very little further progress. If one peruses the journals that carry articles on it, such as *Sociological Analysis* and *Journal for the Scientific Study of Religion* (representing the disciplines of sociology and psychology, respectively), one finds that the need to study conservative religion is mentioned from time to time, and a few articles on microscopic aspects of it do appear. While some good empirical survey work is being done, theory and explanation are in disarray.

Some recent surveys, looking at religious questions in samples of the general population rather than in specific denominations, exist; they interest us primarily because we are developing the premise that independent churches and para-church organizations that do not show up in any routinely compiled demographic sources are superseding the denomination as the corporate vehicles for conservative Protestantism. George Gallup, Jr., son and heir of the famous pollster and an Evangelical enthusiast with moderately liberal theological views, has been active in this field. He reports that consistently the overwhelming majority (percentages in the high nineties) of people in the United States believe in God. He reports that the percentage believing in the divinity of Jesus was 81 percent in 1952, dipped to 71 percent in 1965, and rose again to 80 percent in 1978. While 59 percent of the American people belonged to some church organization in 1978, a large majority believe that one can be a good Christian and be unchurched, and a very large minority are dubious or critical of organized religion. On questions pertaining to basic doctrine, the unchurched generally lag behind the churched about 20 percent in proreligious or orthodox answers. For example, 98 percent of the churched and 76 percent of the unchurched say that they pray to God, and faith in the resurrection is professed by 93 percent of the churched and 68 percent of the unchurched. Only 20 percent of the unchurched respond in the negative to the question of whether the Bible is supernaturally inspired.[74] Gallup recognizes that there is an obvious discrep-

74. George Gallup, Jr., and David Poling, *The Search for America's Faith* (Nashville: Abingdon Press, 1980), p. 90. At the orthodox end, this particular survey was flawed, because the response that the Bible "is to be taken literally, word for word," forces the knowledgeable orthodox believer, who has in mind that the Bible contains much parable and hyperbole, to respond. "The Bible is the inspired word of God but not everything in it should be taken literally." This would deflate the orthodox category, and inflate the liberal, middle category. (The unbelief response, to which the statistic pertains, characterizes the

ancy between the behavior and reported religiosity of his unchurched respondents and comments:

> The unchurched stance is difficult to sort out; it may be that inactive Christians are parroting orthodox views because those are the creeds and philosophies they were taught early in life and presently are resisting. Is it possible that men and women who are currently inactive and defined as unchurched propose the "proper" answer in a poll or punch the orthodox response because that was the last one they heard just before they dropped out and decided they had no place to go theologically?[75]

To put the question more pointedly, is the religious belief being expressed entirely of an optimistic, wish-fulfilling sort, or is there some discomfort, fear, and loneliness associated with it, which the respondents would rather not think about or face? Does the low level of action arising from religious belief stem from belief that their religion is so undemanding that no action is wanted, or does it reflect ambivalence? Are the proreligion views so popularly expressed anything more than an approved, grown-up equivalent of Santa Claus or the tooth fairy? Are the religious beliefs anything more than a last resort of comforting escape into fantasy, reserved for those times when all practical action has failed, or is some substantial aid or comfort derived from them? Merely by showing us that these questions are still pertinent, and perhaps poignant, Gallup has achieved a great deal. I suspect that most Americans are so out of touch with their true inner attitudes on these matters that they could not easily articulate those attitudes to a good interviewer, much less have the structured public-opinion survey tap them.

Until October 1983, there was no intensive sociological survey work available to take us beyond the foregoing. When the plan for the present work was first laid, it appeared that I would have no opportunity to test my impressionistic observations of conservative Protestantism against sociological work that was free of my pronounced biases. Fortunately, a major work, obviously the most important in years, appeared: *All Faithful People: Change and Continuity in Middletown's Religion,* by Theodore Caplow, Howard M. Bahr, and Bruce A. Chadwick.[76] *Middletown* is a pseudonym for Muncie, Indiana, the community chosen by Robert S. and Helen Merrell Lynd for their classic, cross-sectional studies because it was demographically representative, i.e. con-

---

Bible as "an ancient book of fables, legends, history, and moral perceptions recorded by men." Three percent of the churched respondents in the same poll chose this response.) On page 136 the authors report another study, where the orthodox response was, "The Bible is the word of God and is *not* mistaken in its statements and teachings." That response was chosen by 42 percent of the general public (churched and unchurched) and by 100 percent of a conservative church sample.

75. Ibid., p. 135.

76. (Minneapolis: University of Minnesota Press, 1983).

stituted a stratified sample, of the United States population as a whole.[77] Building on the Lynds' work, Caplow and his colleagues have the benefit of good longitudinal data from as far back as 1924, as well as the Lynds' efforts to reconstruct what was then still living memory, which went as far back as 1890. Longitudinal data is very rare in the social science of religion.

Caplow and his colleagues characterized the Lynds' work as follows:

> They found that the role of the minister was to reinforce the property-centered values of an industrial society and to put his imprimatur on the Magic Middletown creed [a variety of what we have called civil religion]. The Lynds concluded that ministers were overworked and lacked the time to read and to study in order to overcome deficiencies in their intellectual training. The churches, according to the Lynds, served to reinforce class boundaries in the community and to rationalize the social system. . . . Finally, the Lynds concluded that industrialization was leading to increased secularization, that each generation was less religious than the previous one, and that the business class was more secularized than the working class.[78]

> Robert Lynd was trained to be a Presbyterian minister but had already turned away from organized religion when he began to observe Middletown's churches . . . according to one of his principal informants who was still living in Middletown when we arrived there. The two Middletown books were read, correctly or incorrectly, as exposés of grass-roots Protestantism. By contrast, most of the investigators involved in the Middletown III project are active in the church. . . . With a bias that differs so fundamentally from that of the Lynds, we run a considerable risk of misreading the comparison between their data and our own.[79]

Although Caplow and his colleagues never say in what kinds of churches they are active, it is fairly evident that they are theologically liberal and that they began their work with the tacit expectation that churches generally were declining, like the ones in their own experience. The researchers had predicted decline, in comparison with the Lynds' data, of the number of churches per capita of the population, the proportion of the population attending church services, the proportion of "rites of passage" (marriages, burials, etc.) held under religious auspices, the proportion of marriages with both parties from the same religious group, and the proportion of individual income contributed to churches. Instead, their data show that all of those measures *increased!* The only things they expected to decline that *had* declined were the degree of attention to secular topics in sermons and political activity in organized religious

77. *Middletown: A Study in American Culture* (New York: Harcourt and Brace, 1929) and *Middletown in Transition: A Study in Cultural Conflicts* (New York: Harcourt and Brace, 1937).
78. Caplow, et al., *All Faithful People,* p. 40.
79. Ibid., p. 33.

groups.[80] The occurrence of religious issues in the governmental and civic life of Middletown neither increased nor decreased, from earlier measures by the Lynds.

The leading tendency in churches in Middletown in the seventies and beyond is clearly conservative. Although Caplow and his colleagues make no mention of Kelley, their findings are entirely consistent with his in this respect. Middletown had been a traditional Methodist stronghold. While the Methodists remained the strongest single denomination there, theirs was the one that had diminished most. Earlier, there had been a strong tendency for working-class people to be marginal, nonmember participants of mainline churches dominated by the more affluent. In the seventies, conservative churches with Southern, or "henhouse"-sect roots, were the conspicuous successes, the mean socioeconomic level of the members rising as their numbers increased. The most rapidly growing church in Middletown in the seventies was one "which advertises itself as independent, fundamental, and evangelistic," having grown from an average attendance of 85 in 1967, to 1,200 in 1977.[81] That church was strongly identified with the personality of its pastor, who had built it up so successfully.

A particularly interesting detail is what the researchers call the "common creed." We have encountered civil religion, separate and apart from private or organized religion, throughout America's national existence, and, through Gallup, gained some indication of a common core of popular religious views—if not commonplaces or clichés—that individuals perceive to be their religious beliefs. This "popular religion" savors strongly of civil religion, but it belongs to the private, family, and church spheres of life. Our earlier observation, that our old-time religion was only superficially biblical, pertains. Caplow and his colleagues were surprised to find a high degree of homogeneity of response across denominations, social classes, ages, and sexes:

> The religious experiences reported by members of all of Middletown's Protestant denominations—and some non-Protestants, too—in response to questions . . . run in opposition to the religious dogmas that are the raisons d'être of Middletown's separate denominations, neither affirming nor contradicting them. The themes most often repeated are the following. (1) Prayer is internally efficacious; it strengthens the sufferer to endure or to surmount his or her suffering. (2) Prayer is externally efficacious; it can avert danger and cure the sick. (3) Bible reading is internally efficacious in the same manner as prayer. (4) The Bible guarantees the eventual safety of those who read and believe it. (5) Jesus takes care of those who have made a commitment to him. (6) Morality of any kind is predicated on the existence of God. (7) God provides all of life's meaning and

80. It is my view that the influence of polticized conservative Protestantism, and the related phenomenon of conservative television ministries, is much overrated by the mass media, and seeing fragments of the religious programs themselves, while changing channels, enhances the general public's mistaken impression. Political and television religion are marginal activities, only superficially involving their clientèle, and are not representative of the widespread, deep involvement in Bible-centered churches, which we are scrutinizing.

81. Caplow, et al., *All Faithful People*, p. 67.

hope. (8) The presence of God, when directly experienced, is not challengeable by argument. (9) Personal immortality is promised by God and therefore is certain although not clearly visualizable. These nine themes (it might be more accurate to call them attitudes) seem to provide the basic pattern for Middletown's dominant religion as described by its believers in 1924 and again in 1978.[82]

To be sure, the context of these core beliefs did change with the times. The researchers present attitude-survey data, which they summarize by saying, "Middletown's Christians have become much less chauvinstic, less punitive, and less antiscientific."[83] The proportion of high-school-age youth giving orthodox answers to questions about religious belief was much less in 1978 than in 1924, and in the later data, about half of those young people who were churched and held orthodox religious attitudes also believed that non-Christian religions could provide access to God and disclaimed zeal for the conversion of non-Christians.

> Religious fervor no longer goes hand in hand with missionary zeal, and the reason may be that Middletown people are not aware of having a common creed and holding it strongly. Their division into numerous denominations conceals from them the extent to which they agree, and their stereotyped misreading of social change persuades them that religion is weaker than it is. Devout Christians in Middletown, like happily married couples there, regard themselves as exceptional; surrounded by people just like themselves, they think they stand quite alone. This almost universal illusion explains, at least in part, why Middletown people are so reluctant to lay down the law or to expound the prophets for the benefit of their neighbors. In this sense, there is less community in Middletown today than there was in 1924 or in 1890, when it was customary for respectable people to perceive themselves as participating in a moral consensus. It is possible to regard the loss of this moral unanimity as a kind of decadence, but it is equally plausible to argue that the manners and morals of Middletown have been improved by it.[84]

Summing up, we find that beneath those surface appearances that Schaeffer took for the loss of a preexisting Christian consensus and Berger took for "secularization,"[85] a deep, abiding loyalty to Christianity remains and an intensely active church life goes on. The Bible is greatly venerated—consistently, the researchers found that larger percentages of groups surveyed believed the Bible to be divinely inspired than affirmed the divinity of Jesus or had no doubts about the existence of God—even if nearly all knowledge about its contents is second-hand. If the impressions that led to salvation-doubt suffering

---

82. Ibid., p. 91.
83. Ibid., pp. 94–95.
84. Ibid., pp. 98–99.
85. Caplow and his colleagues, whose characteristic mode of expression is moderate and unpolemic, ask: "If Berger, trained both as a sociologist and a theologian, could be so badly mistaken about the facts of religion in the observable contemporary world, is it not possible that he and less critical colleagues are equally mistaken about the facts of religion in those vanished eras from which secularization started?" Ibid., p. 34.

in an earlier day have registered at all in people like those who go to church in Middletown, those impressions are buried more deeply than in the days of the Great Awakening. As to the presence of such impressions in the lower recesses of the contemporary American psyche, we shall be breaking difficult, new ground!

Before I became familiar with the foregoing statistical sources, my impressionistic observations in conservative churches paralleled them. I have visited, heard the local radio programs of, and heard second-hand descriptions of quite a few of them, particularly in the suburbs of Washington, D.C., and Philadelphia.[86] At every hand in such conservative churches, the operative premise is making thought and conduct ever more biblical, peeling and stripping away those "mere human traditions" that do not pass the biblical test. Where I hear of a church that has grown large quickly, I always find a particular pastor's preaching at the center of it. Often, the pastor turns out to be surprisingly unimpressive outwardly, lacking polish and smoothness in his delivery. *The quality that distinguishes the pastor of the fast-growing, conservative church is his own process of "growth," in delving into the Bible, relating one passage to another—as the young Calvin did—to find consistency, unity, and continuity in it, and getting rid of those preconceptions about what is biblical for which biblical justification cannot be found.* Proceeding from the premise that the Bible is so uniquely good and beneficial, imparting the wisdom of the greatest intelligence in the universe, of course it is exciting to discover things in it one did not anticipate were there. Those who come to sit in the pews, who have been inculcated with that same premise at every hand, appreciate being involved in such excitement.

To the new biblicists, human traditions are potential pitfalls, and the Bible is the means to avoid pitfalls. Of course, looking at the Bible to find out what is in it, without the hidden or open agenda of forcing it to fit conceptions of right or good exterior to it, takes one over the same ground Calvin trod. While there is very little veneration of Calvin in independent conservative churches, what occurs is, in effect, the reinvention of Calvinism, as fast as the pastor's intellectual capabilities and the ability of the congregation to follow him will permit. Complete trust in and submission to the Bible's teachings are the goals. When the pastor fearlessly advocates obedience to a strange or distasteful conclusion from the Bible's teaching, that only goes to prove how far above the sin-cursed, wicked little minds of humans the Bible's teachings are, and how much integrity the pastor possesses, to persevere even when his own clouded common sense is offended by what he is preaching. This is done in genuine ignorance of history. Secular history, to the new biblicist, is bunk. Many have been confused by sanitized, misleading renditions of religious history and are glad to be encouraged to ignore history other than the Bible.

---

86. For additional pertinent, impressionistic observations, see R. Stephen Warner, "Research Note: Visits to a Growing Evangelical and a Declining Liberal Church in 1978," *Sociological Analysis* 44 (1983):243-54.

This emergence of intensely biblicist churches and supporting para-church activities, as the cutting edge of conservative Protestantism, is what I refer to as the *new "mini-Reformation."* Its corporate vehicles are churches and a network of unaccredited seminaries, teaching-materials sources, retreat centers, and opinion leaders, such as Schaeffer, Jay Adams, Harold Camping, Donald G. Bloesch, and Charles Ryrie. It transcends denominations, constituting a trend in some conservative denominations and being present in some atypical churches within the liberal denominations.[87] It transcends older theological labels and can have its psychological effect just as readily in surroundings where a fine intellectual effort is made to reconcile the various teachings of the Bible as it can in a more rustic setting, where the pew-sitters tend not to react outwardly or consciously to Bible teachings in tension with one another. (Indeed, Pentecostal and charismatic churches, where the manifest content contains much to offend the Bible purist, tend to be the most Bible-authentic in their appraoch to worship and devotions, a feature that will have significance for us.) The dividing line between old-time religion and the new mini-Reformation can be very subtle in conservative churches not on the cutting edge. Most conservative churches are in what I believe to be an early phase in the *transition* toward mini-Reformationism.

I find it useful to think of conservative churches on a continuum, with pure old-time religion at one pole and pure mini-Reformationism at the other. The most consistent features of old-time-religion churches are stress on personal decision as the prelude to salvation, a salvation experience occurring at a definite and memorable time, and a toning down of the Bible's fear message. These churches assure the believer that by cultivating the right attitudes and performing good works one may preserve one's candidacy for Heaven, and much gracious latitude is given for stumbling and straying along the way. The key to salvation is in one's own pocket at all times.

Spiritual-gift and faith-healing theatrics, if they are present, are found at the old-time religion end of the spectrum, but are neither necessary nor particularly material.[88] Religion on television is usually old-time religion. At this end

---

87. One finds within the United Presbyterian Church some churches that would be more at home in one of the Machen denominations; within the United Methodist Church, churches that resemble nothing so much as Assemblies of God churches. Within Episcopalianism, one finds churches with a very sacramental approach, mimicking pre–Vatican II Roman Catholicism, and others with a charismatic-Pentecostal flavor. The liberal denominations have, for an incentive to tolerate these churches, their revenue, since they tend to be the economically stronger ones within the denomination. The atypical churches have, for incentive to stay and keep peace with the liberal denomination, its claim to their land and buildings. Seceding churches are usually the losers in court cases over church property.

For evaluating statistical research, we should keep in mind that atypical churches reduce the homogeneity of the denomination of any religious-content variable we may desire to measure. Accordingly, mean differences in variables across denominations will be deflated by the presence of atypical churches.

88. In the Bible itself, all references to signs, wonders, and gaudy purported prophets, in what from the standpoint of the apostolic age is the future, are negative. See Matt. 24:3–31; Mark 8:11–12; 13:4–23; Luke 17:20–21; Acts 20:29–30; 2 Cor. 11:13–15; 1 Tim. 4:1–3; 2 Tim. 4:3–4; and Rev. 13:13–14; 19:20–21. Thus, the new mini-Reformationist believer, even if he does not accept the old Re-

of the spectrum, per capita contribution is lower than in mini-Reformationism, in keeping with relative shallowness of involvement; the most extreme cases of small contributions from many are the television ministries. These expressions, conspicuous to the outside observer and apt to attract the attention of the behavioral scientist looking for externalities to observe "objectively," are not the ones that involve people most deeply or persistently.

At the mini-Reformationist end of the spectrum, the emphasis is on the Bible itself and on the ordering of life to conform to it. No visually observable thing or behavior will reliably distinguish the mini-Reformationist church from a liberal, mainline church, although the former's physical plant is likely to be newer and more plain. One feature I have found to be a very reliable quick test indicating a mini-Reformationist or advanced transitional church is the presence of a Sunday-evening service; with the exceptions that a mini-Reformationist church with only a handful of people will sometimes lack a Sunday-evening service, and a church of some other sort may very rarely be so large as to have a whole shift coming on Sunday evening who did not come in the morning, this test works fairly well.[89] One must listen to the preaching and teaching to identify a mini-Reformationist church positively. If pressed for easy criteria, whereby one might reliably distinguish a small sample of mini-Reformationist preaching or teaching from other kinds, I would recommend looking for the following: (1) themes of separation and alienation of the believers from the surrounding world, (2) the characterization of the believer as chosen by God in his sovereignty, (3) emphasis away from reward or benefit for the believer in this life, and (4) negative characterization of the individual person, apart from his condition as a believer. Sunday school and other classes in the transitional church often will have content more strictly biblical than that of the Sunday sermon.

We briefly encountered some other clues to the biblicist Zeitgeist: the presidential Year-of-the-Bible proclamation, the opinion of Gallup—not particularly a biblicist himself—that the eighties would be "Bible-centered, indeed," and the flooding of Evangelical circles with new translations of the Bible which, I can say from personal experience, represent a quantum leap in accessibility of the Bible—and impetus to study it—particularly to younger Evangelicals. Some other indicators, which had no parallels in the preceding decades, are:

---

formed view that Heb. 1:1–2 and Rev. 22:18–19 foreclose the possibility of supernatural manifestations that are of God, or messages from him, will come to recognize them as spiritually dangerous ground, that one does best to avoid, to preserve one's candidacy for Heaven. In Assemblies of God churches, which have a historical, Pentecostal tradition to preserve, but which are, to a high degree transitional churches, I have noticed the development of a remarkably fine feeling for keeping the glossolalia, etc., contained and toned down but still vestigially present, as a sign of the group's historical identity.

89. Here, I have to complain of a liberal blind spot and faulty work by Caplow and his colleagues. They give the impression that the rise of Sunday entertainment (car trips, sporting events, etc.) has taken over the post-noon part of Sunday, even for the most orthodox. *All Faithful People,* pp. 72–73. In the March 1976 Yellow Pages for Muncie, Indiana, I found twenty churches, including all the prominent conservative ones that Caplow and his colleagues specially mentioned, with paid ads listing Sunday-evening services.

1. For the first time in this century, there is a widely accepted textbook of Evangelical theology, *Essentials of Evangelical Theology,* by Professor Donald G. Bloesch, of Dubuque Theological Seminary.[90] Bloesch writes, "For authentic evangelicalism the test of a sound theology is not whether it is successfully correlated with general wisdom, but whether it is in conformity with its object, the revealed Word of God,"[91] and proceeds to discuss many of the same theological issues we have touched on. Bloesch speaks of the issues represented by the five points of Calvinism and strains in the direction of the closed-salvation plan, comparing and contrasting older and modernist theologians. Through this work, the discussion of those issues is revived, taking on a mien of currency and contemporaneity.

Bloesch was one of the leaders in the "Chicago Call," a convocation of Evangelical leaders, mostly the more biblicist minority faculty of mainline theological seminaries, and representatives of religious publishers, in May 1977.[92] The coalescence of religious academics calling for renewal in historic and biblical Christianity, discussing theological issues, and presenting both sides on the major issues of biblical teachings in tension aids the mini-Reformation, plowing the ground ahead of it for it to be sown, but it lacks the crucial feature that enabled Christianity to elicit intense personal involvement and drastic behavior from people in earlier times, particularly the first century A.D., and during the Reformation. Containment of the negative aspects of the Bible's teaching, particularly the fear message, tacitly remains in their agenda. Their discussion remains on the plane of the abstract, and they hesitate to take the crucial step, rendition of the Bible into concise doctrine and prescripts for human conduct. They keep one foot on the gas, and the other on the brake. They continue to look for immense ideas underlying the biblical obscurities, not seeing that the true significance of those obscurities is psychological, and the obscurities are interspersed with prescripts that are not obscure at all. The Calvinists among conservative Protestants were not participants in the Chicago Call, and there remains a rift between the Calvinist academics and the larger group of Evangelical academics, who do not see that the actual doing of what the call exhorts implies the reinvention of Calvinism, more or less.

2. The key development in the mini-Reformation is the biblical or "nouthetic" counseling movement founded by Jay E. Adams (1929-). In the late sixties, Adams was a professor of "practical theology" at Westminster Theological Seminary, long after the death of Machen and when Van Til was passing into retirement. Adams, a Calvinist equipped with clearly articulated doctrine, became interested in the mental-health professions. He correctly sized up their shortcomings and identified the conflicts between theory and practice in those professions on the one hand, and correct biblical doctrine on the other. He then developed a series of applications of biblical doctrines to the various

90. 2 vols. (San Francisco: Harper & Row, 1978).
91. Ibid., vol. 1, p. 15.
92. See Robert E. Webber and Donald G. Bloesch, eds., *The Orthodox Evangelicals: Who They Are and What They Are Saying* (Nashville: Thomas Nelson, 1978.)

diagnoses that are typically referred to a mental-health professional, for pastors and the church community to aid the individual, supposedly to meet the problem. These applications follow from the Scriptures themselves and seem perfectly reasonable, proceeding from the premise of paramount biblical authority. Because those who do the counseling are themselves under what we shall call mind-control, they consistently misperceive the results of the attitudes and practices they guide the counselee in applying. If there are untoward results too clear to be misperceived, then the counselor can reassure himself that it was God's will, since God's rules were followed. The biblical attitudes and practices can produce satisfyingly dramatic subjective changes, at least in the short run, and they do help to contain some kinds of problem, especially substance abuse. But they cause deterioration in the personalities of some others and lead to drastic disruptions in the lives of still others. What such counseling amounts to, despite the uniform well-meaning of those who counsel, is exploitation of the problems and vulnerabilities of the counselees to bring them under mind-control.

The first of Jay Adams' prolific books on counseling, *Competent to Counsel,*[93] has sold over 250,000 copies. That number enormously understates the breadth of its influence. The book is on such a level that its readership must consist of pastors and fairly sophisticated church leaders. The great mass of people in transitional churches, moving gradually toward the closed-salvation plan, cannot take Adams' unrelieved, Calvinist presentation "cold turkey," so one encounters widespread, watered-down renditions of it.[94] What makes biblical counseling so important is the restoration of the mind-set of finding *prescripts for action* in the Bible, in people who are innocent of knowledge of past times when that was done. Bible study becomes very serious business.

3. A very unusual phenomenon, important more for reaching mini-Reformationist pastors and church leaders than pew-sitters, is Harold Camping (1921-). Camping was trained as a civil engineer and grew rich in the building business in the San Francisco Bay area. Raised in the Christian Reformed Church, much of his private life was given over to activity as a churchman. In the late fifties, he became involved on the business side of a religious radio station, and, having enough means to be a full-time volunteer, he proceeded to build what is now the Family Radio network, with proliferating, satellite-fed stations and translators in strategic U.S. population areas, affiliate stations elsewhere, and a shortwave network in various languages, including Mandarin Chinese. Family Radio is a very sincere and cost-effective operation, in sharp contrast to the vulgarity and this-worldly preoccupation that is the norm of religious broadcasting.

---

93. (Phillipsburg, N.J.: Presbyterian and Reformed Pub. Co., 1970).

94. Application of large portions of the biblical-counseling project can be seen on Charles E. Stanley's "In Touch Ministries" television program. The techniques have proven powerful enough to enable Stanley to take over the Southern Baptist Convention, the largest U.S. Protestant denomination. He displaced proponents of Chicago Call-style theology, whose numbers include Billy Graham, and Bailey Smith (the maker of the famous gaffe about God not hearing the prayers of Jews).

In the process, Camping has become a self-taught Bible scholar—in my opinion, the equal if not the better of any credentialed academic in conservative Protestant circles. He stands astride his radio world empire, and it broadcasts a half-hour teaching program of him several times each day and a one-and-a-half-hour telephone call-in program, where he answers questions about the Bible. He also writes books, which Family Radio sends out free of charge.[95]

Although there is no immediate connection of Camping with the biblical-counseling movement, much of what occurs on the call-in program amounts to biblical counseling, and we will scrutinize some examples from it. The callers ask the same questions over and over, showing that, for the most part, they are not attentive listeners. Apparently, rank-and-file listeners to the other programming are unable to follow him. However, it is clear that the preaching in many mini-Reformationist churches I have visited has been influenced by him as much as I, myself, have been. My analyses of Bible issues in this work all owe him a debt, and I have to say that without him, my progress through and out of orthodox Christianity would have taken much longer than it did, and would have been far more destructive to me personally than it was.

Although these opinion leaders are a more interesting and effective lot than any who have appeared on the secular intellectual scene for quite some time, that is not what makes them significant. At every hand in church circles, Bible authenticity is lauded, even if it be only lip service. As one studies the Bible for oneself, one finds out which leaders are being true to it and which ones invoke it for the sake of values exterior to it. In the horizontally mobile church marketplace, increasing numbers of people look for Bible authenticity and go where they think they find it. That they choose the sternness and demandingness of mini-Reformationism over the pleasantness and easy encouragement of old-time religion or the liberal church will have significance for us.

What the Bible Really Teaches on Social Issues

What social implications of biblicism can we clarify before we begin our deep, subterranean journey into its psychology? There are some social issues where biblicism and recent progress in our society agree, and the developing believer can construe the social progress as evidence of the salutariness of biblicism. Living in the eighties, when, in the United States, the crucial battles over civil rights for nonwhites are behind us and the prevailing ethos deprecates racism, the believer finds that all along the Bible made no racial distinctions. All of the group antagonisms told of in the Bible are along tribal or political lines. The existence of races per se is never discussed. The premise of the common ancestry of all humanity is laid down early, and when the fact of dark skin color arises, it is in contexts clearly inconsistent with racism.[96] My own experience in con-

95. Program information and Camping's books can be obtained from Family Stations, Inc., 290 Hegenberger Road, Oakland, California 94621.
96. See Song of Sol. 1:5; Acts 8:25-39.

servative churches has convinced me that the antiracist reconstruction goes deep and will prove to be permanent. The antiracist civic project of the rest of society enables the fundamentalists to assimilate an aspect of the Bible's teaching that they glossed over or contained before. There is relief from a certain underlying dissonance or tension in that.[97]

A similar salutary situation exists, in relations between conservative Christians and Jews. Without any significant exceptions, my experience was that conservative Christians are well aware that there is no biblical basis for the folkloric notions about Jewish people that arose as a side effect of *shtetl* and ghetto existence in Europe or that used to be part of the doctrine of the Roman Catholic church. More practically, I was vigilant for, but did not find any appreciable tendency for conservative Christians to identify their hated "secular humanism" as Jewish. It may be useful to remember that anti-Jewish persecutions based on racist rhetoric are a nineteenth- and twentieth-century proclivity, and even in Reformation times, persecutions were based on professed beliefs rather than heredity. The individual could escape if he would make the desired doctrinal declaration. Even as there is no biblical reason for the Christian believer to treat the individual, unconverted Jew differently from the Gentile unbeliever, the currently fashionable Evangelical enchantment with contemporary Israel has no strong biblical basis. We will take up the possible future attitude of conservative Christians toward Israel in Chapter 5.

The decline of negative attitudes toward nonwhites and Jews removed some of the inducement that had existed to gloss over major features of the Bible's contents. That is one reason why a mini-Reformation could get started in the last quarter of the century, and not earlier. This insight enables us to reconstruct some history and to understand what must have led the mainline clergy of our grandparents' day to become adroit at passing over the Bible lightly enough to avoid finding what they did not want to find. Those clergy had to be resourceful, indeed, to avoid the effects of the Bible's teaching on slavery, which deals a major shock in the life of the Evangelical enthusiast.

> Slaves, obey your earthly masters in everything; and do it, not only when their eye is on you and to win their favor, but with sincerity of heart and reverence for the Lord. Whatever you do, work at it with all your heart, as working for the Lord, not for men, since you know that you will receive an inheritance from the

97. Up to the sixties, whenever one encountered a fundamentalist private primary or secondary school, one could justly assume that it was a segregation academy. In the intervening time, such bad things happened in public schools that the welfare of one's children became a legitimate reason for the existence of Christian schools, and for the biblicist, this blends with the motif of separateness and estrangement from the surrounding world. It has been credibly estimated that there are 10,000 such schools operating in the United States. MacNeil/Lehrer News Hour, Jan. 5, 1984.

One of my interviews with "religiously disillusioned" persons was with a highly qualified and motivated science teacher in a public middle school, who had become alienated from fundamentalism in a rough and tumble, industrial neighborhood, and he was an active lay teacher in a liberal, mainline church. When I asked him about the rôle of fear in his life, he answered that being maimed or killed by a pupil, so that he would be unable to care for his wife and child, was his most immediate fear.

> Lord as a reward. It is the Lord Christ you are serving. Anyone who does wrong will be repaid for his wrong, and there is no favoritism. Masters, provide your slaves with what is right and fair, because you know that you also have a Master in heaven.[98]

Consistently, the Bible presupposes the institution of slavery.[99] That the Christian, receiving the biblical exhortation, can continue to be a slaveowner is clearly contemplated and approved.[100] The explicit mandates and the figurative language agree; the motif of man existing only as a slave of Satan or else as a bondservant of the Lord constantly recurs.[101]

In the antebellum South, the freethinking that earlier had been present in the cities and among the aristocracy died out as the nineteenth century progressed. Then as now, the South was a stronghold of fundamentalism. While clergy were prominent in the abolition movement, conservative clergy were even more prominent among the Southern apologists for and defenders of slavery.[102] A respected historian has written:

> The growing need of defending the institution of slavery . . . tended to produce religious uniformity in the South. . . . By pointing to the undeniable words of the Holy Scriptures, religious leaders . . . presented a plausible defense of slavery and fostered a reactionary movement in the Southern church.
>
> The Northern abolitionists, on the other hand, since the letter of the Bible was against them, appealed to "the spirit of Christianity." Prominent abolitionists . . . proclaimed radical ideas in regard to religious dogma, denying miracles, attacking such revered beliefs as the holiness of the Sabbath and the literal interpretation of the Bible. . . . Thus the abolitionists tended to discredit religious liberalism in the eyes of Southern people.[103]

The typical Christian abolitionist centered his argument on the Golden Rule. The contemporary biblicist will see that "as ye would that men should do to you," in context, has to mean whatever helps preserve salvation candidacy, not what makes earthly life more pleasant. Since there is little prospect of the contemporary conservative Christian being called upon to defend actual slavery, it does not seem relevant; he will simply praise God for having solved that problem in another time and say, ". . . ye thought evil against me; *but* God meant it unto good . . . to save such people alive."[104]

---

98. Col. 3:22-4:1. *New International Version. Doulos,* euphemistically translated *servant* in the King James, and its cognates clearly intend forced servitude for indefinite term in the New Testament. The appropriate modern English translation is *slave* or its cognate. Hire or employment, the few times it is mentioned, is denoted by *misthos* or its cognate.
99. Luke 17:8-10; John 13:16; 1 Cor. 7:21-22; Eph. 6:5-8; 1 Tim. 6:1; Titus 2:9; 1 Pet. 2:18.
100. Eph. 6:9; Col. 4:1 and Philemon.
101. See pp. 106-27.
102. Much of what we have called old-time religion was the religious liberalism of its day. For example, Charles Grandison Finney (1792-1875), a major evangelist and stylesetter in loose construction of the Bible, so that there could be old-time-religion and clerical antagonists of slavery, was president of Oberlin College during the Civil War years. Originally a lawyer and untrammeled by seminary training, he had been tutored by a Presbyterian minister, who, although he certified Finney for the ministry, had found him a bad theology pupil and asked him not to reveal publicly who his tutor had been.
103. Clement Eaton, *Freedom of Thought in the Old South* (Durham, N.C.: Duke University Press, 1940), pp. 292-93.
104. Gen. 50:20.

Now, in venturing to say what a Bible teaching "in context, has to mean" I make some tacit assumptions needing explanation. In liberal Christianity, Bible teachings such as the foregoing one on slavery and others relating to social issues, including, for example, the place of women, marriage, the obligation of the church to meet the physical needs of unbelievers, and the relation of the believer to secular, civil authority, that are neither progressive nor democratic, are taken simply as reflecting the prejudices of the times and localities in which the Bible authors found themselves, and, by Holy Spirit–given discernment, to be severed from the inspired part.[105] It is easy to see that, in practice, this gives the pastor, if not everyone in the church, the right to discard whatever he wants of the Bible's teaching and to keep whatever he wants of what is left. By picking and choosing, one can make the rules into whatever one wishes. If followed to the ultimate extreme, the Bible can be emptied of its content altogether in this manner.

The passage where the Scripture refers most clearly to itself, and the one the mini-Reformationist is most likely to have memorized, is 2 Timothy 3:16 and 17:

> All scripture *is* given by inspiration of God, and *is* profitable for doctrine, for reproof, for correction, for instruction in righteousness: That the man of God may be perfect, thoroughly furnished unto all good works.

Just before this, verse 15 speaks of "the holy scriptures, which are able to make thee wise unto salvation. . . ." Keeping in mind that, in the Gospels, Jesus, the great majority of the time, and always when speaking in public, spoke in parables, in stories not claimed to be literally true but told in order to teach by illustration and allegory, we see that the Bible contemplates that every bit of itself will be taken as authoritative, but explicitly provides that far from all of it is to be taken *literally*.[106] As to whether conflicting spiritual interpretations ought to coexist, or in the extreme case, whether the Scriptures will permit themselves to be regarded as a sort of verbal Rorschach blot, to which the Holy Spirit will inspire a different projection in one believer than in another, the Scriptures say, "no prophecy of the scripture is of any private interpretation."[107]

The Scriptures make understanding of themselves a communal rather than an individualistic affair, and place such a premium on good doctrine that all mention of gradations of punishment in Hell hinge upon scriptural knowledge.

---

105. Often quoted as a purported example of Scripture not meant to be taken as inspired or mandatory is 1 Cor. 7:10-12. "And unto the married I command, *yet* not I, but the Lord, Let not the wife depart from *her* husband: But and if she depart, let her remain unmarried, or be reconciled to *her* husband: and let not the husband put away *his* wife. But to the rest speak I, not the Lord: If any brother hath a wife that believeth not, and she be pleased to dwell with him, let him not put her away."

What should be noted here is that in the first instance, Paul refers to a topic on which the Lord—i.e., Jesus—has spoken, and Paul is repeating what he said. Then, he gives a new revelation on a topic Jesus did not broach, i.e., what to do about an unbelieving spouse. If the comments on unbelieving spouses are taken as some parenthetical material inserted by Paul, the context is wrecked, and one cannot make sense out of the passage.

106. Mark 4:11, 34.

107. 2 Pet. 1:20.

Not murder or blasphemy but failing to be a doer of the Word when one knows better and being a false teacher are the things declared to bring more severe eternal punishment than other transgressions.[108] The understanding of Scripture is clearly declared to transcend reason, and the believer is put on notice that if his views on the Scriptures are too clear and pat, or are not mystifying enough, he runs the risk of being a false teacher.

> Now we have received, not the spirit of the world, but the spirit which is of God; that we might know the things that are freely given to us of God. Which things also we speak, not in the words which man's wisdom teacheth, but which the Holy Ghost teacheth; comparing spiritual things with spiritual. But the natural man receiveth not the things of the Spirit of God: for they are foolishiness unto him: neither can he know *them,* because they are spiritually discerned.[109]

> For we know in part, and we prophesy in part. But when that which is perfect is come, then that which is in part shall be done away. . . . For now we see through a glass, darkly; but then face to face. . . .[110]

As understanding the Scriptures is claimed to be impossible by mere intellect and to require divine intervention, God takes full responsibility for the inability of the nonelect to understand them. "God will send upon them a deluding influence so that they might believe what is false."[111] Considering that the Scriptures put in the category of sin everything that is not part of the religious program ("whatsoever *is* not of faith is sin"),[112] we can fairly say that the Scriptures, as a whole, assume an antiintellectual posture as to their own interpretation.

The operative principles, then, are that the Bible is to be taken in its entirety, not à la carte, and to the exclusion of other sources. "The Bible, the whole Bible, and nothing but the Bible." It is to be taken on a figurative, allegorical level as well as a literal or factual one, the most abstract levels tending to be the most instructive where it really counts. Often, the historicity of the events is neither here nor there, in relation to the figurative instruction to be derived

---

108. Luke 12:46-48 (not doing God's will despite knowing better); Matt. 18:6; Mark 9:42; Luke 17:2; and James 3:1 (false teachers).

109. 1 Cor. 2:12-14.

110. 1 Cor. 13:9-10, 12.

111. 2 Thess. 2:11. *New American Standard Bible.*

112. Rom. 14:23. Other Scriptures, adding up to a prescribed content for the consciousness of the believer to the exclusion of all else, are discussed in Chapter 4.

This antiintellectual trend manifested itself in the thought of Finney (see note 102), the great Civil War-era abolitionist, old-time religionist, and president of Oberlin College. Hofstadter said of Finney and others like him: "The minds of these men had been toughened by constant gnawing on Calvinist and neo-Calvinist theology and disciplined by the necessity of carving out their own theological framework. But their culture was exceptionally narrow; their view of learning was extremely instrumental; and instead of enlarging their intellectual inheritance, they steadily contracted it. . . . As to literature [Finney said]: 'I cannot believe that a person who has ever known the love of God can relish a secular novel'. . . . Looking upon piety and intellect as being in open enmity, Finney found young ministers coming 'out of college with hearts as hard as college walls'. . . . However prosperous the state of intellect was among fledgling ministers, he was against it." *Anti-Intellectualism in American Life,* pp.91-95.

from them. The antiintellectualism of the mini-Reformationist resides in deprecation of whatever is exterior to the Bible, not in simplism, concreteness of approach, or intolerance of ambiguity.

The issue of figurative as opposed to literal understanding of Bible teachings quickly becomes important, even to the unintelligent or thoughtless believer, because of the many promises included in the Bible. If the believer takes literally such promises as "If thou canst believe, all things *are* possible to him that believeth,"[113] given by Jesus to the father of a spirit-possessed, mute boy pertinent to healing him, or "And these signs shall follow them that believe; In my name shall they cast out devils . . . . They shall take up serpents; and if they drink any deadly thing, it shall not hurt them; they shall lay hands on the sick and they shall recover,"[114] then events in his immediate surroundings will quickly prove them false, and invalidate the entire religious scheme. To be sure, those, Mark 11:23-24 and John 14:12, are the only promises that can be demonstrated to be literally false, as others turn out to have qualifications to their operation, such as applicability only to apostles,[115] or operation only if done in God's name, which might mean in his will. By the outcome, the believer learns whether his object was in God's will or not.[116] The mini-Reformationist knows well that healing and casting out devils are consistent biblical figures of salvation, and poison and serpent bites are figures for the efforts of Satan to divert or mislead the elect. What should be noted is that those conspicuous manifestations of Christianity—believing literal things that fly in the face of reality—are not a major tendency in the resurgence of conservative Protestantism we are scrutinizing. The thoughtful, nonunintelligent believer has no trouble getting around the promises by spiritualizing them.

A negative implication of the mini-Reformation is that closer scrutiny of the passages that have commonly been thought to confer on the believer a duty of charitable works, even though they benefit unbelievers, leads to reinterpreting the passages as having only evangelization or indoctrination in view. Whereas transitional, old-time-religion churches still do worthwhile charitable works on quite a large scale, deeply involving their people with inner-city and third-world people needing the help (and liberal churches advocate the same, but are less and less successful at marshalling the resources and participation to do it), true mini-Reformationist enterprises tend to limit their attention to spreading the Gospel and inducting converts.

Let us consider those passages, treading the same ground that the fearless, Bible-authentic, mini-Reformationist pastor we have described will cover, pertaining to charitable works. In Matthew 25:31-46, the last judgment and the separation of the elect sheep from the nonelect goats are described. Those who met Jesus unawares in the guise of the least of their fellow man, and gave him food to eat and water to drink, clothed him, visited him in prison, and extended

---

113. Mark 9:23.
114. Mark 16:17-18.
115. Matt. 16:19; 17:20; 18:19; 21:21-22; Luke 17:6; John 14:13.
116. John 14:13-14; 15:16; 16:23-24, 26.

him hospitality will go to the right to Paradise, and those who did not, to the left into eternal punishment. In all the events in the New Testament that purport to be historical, from the activities being urged, only extension of hospitality is actually engaged in, by Jesus or anyone following him. Never do the early Christians visit anyone in prison or clothe anyone inadequately clothed. They are usually the recipients, rather than the givers of hospitality, and their hospitality is for each other, not the unbelieving surrounding world. Even when Jesus multiplies the loaves and the fishes, it is for people who are not depicted as hungry or in need, and a more abstract teaching is implied.

If we look at the urged activities as symbols and look for the same symbols in other contexts, harmony and continuity begin to appear. Even before taking his first disciples, Jesus began his ministry by reading from Isaiah 61:2 in the synagogue at Nazareth: "The Spirit of the Lord *is* upon me, because he hath anointed me to preach the gospel to the poor; he hath sent me to heal the broken-hearted, to preach deliverance to the captives, and recovering of sight to the blind, to set at liberty them that are bruised, To preach the acceptable year of the Lord. And he closed the book, and he gave *it* again to the minister, and sat down. And the eyes of all them that were in the synagogue were fastened on him. And he began to say unto them, This day is this scripture fulfilled in your ears." (Luke 4:18-21)

Activities similar to the ones seemingly urged on believers are described as "fulfilled" by the beginning of Jesus' ministry, in contradistinction from other pivotal events in it, such as the incarnation, atonement, or resurrection. The images of food and water are absent, and Jesus expressly says that he has come to preach to the poor, as opposed to meeting their physical needs. The notions of release from captivity or prison, gaining of sight, and clothing of nakedness all converge as kinds of relief from the sin affliction.[117] For someone looking to get more in touch with the Bible, that harmonizing insight will satisfy far better than understanding the verses to be prescripts for charitable works.[118]

Another insight, far more unfamiliar than that of understanding good-work related symbols as figures of salvation, emerges when we notice toward whom the urged activities are to be directed. Consider Luke 10:25-37:

> And, behold, a certain lawyer stood up, and tempted him, saying, Master, what shall I do to inherit eternal life? He said unto him, What is written in the law? how readest thou? And he answering said, Thou shalt love the Lord thy God with all thy heart, and with all thy soul, and with all thy strength, and with all thy mind; and thy neighbour as thyself. And he said unto him, Thou hast answered

---

117. Prior to exploring the content and implications of the concept of sin in Chapter 4, it will suffice to note that sin is seen as a form of power or hold over the person, that the higher supernatural power releases. Accordingly, note the way our charitable-work symbols occur elsewhere in the Bible: Gen. 3:7, 21; 9:21-27; Isa. 4:1; 64:6; Matt. 22:11-12; and James 5:2 (garments and nakedness); John 4:7-38; 6:33-35; and 1 Cor. 11:24-29 (food and drink); Ps. 142:7 and Gal. 5:1 (release from prison); Mark 4:12 and Rev. 3:17-18 (sight).

118. Cf. Matt. 5:42; 10:42; 19:21; Mark 14:7; Luke 14:13-15; John 13:29; Rom. 12:20; Gal. 6:10; James 1:27; and Rev. 3:17-18.

> right: this do, and thou shalt live. But he, willing to justify himself, said unto Jesus, And who is my neighbour? And Jesus answering said, a certain *man* went down from Jerusalem to Jericho, and fell among thieves, which stripped him of his raiment, and wounded *him,* and departed, leaving *him* half dead. And by chance there came down a certain priest that way: and when he saw him, he passed by on the other side. And likewise a Levite. . . . But a certain Samaritan, as he journeyed, came where he was: and when he saw him, he had compassion *on him,* And went to *him,* and bound up his wounds, pouring in oil and wine, and set him on his own beast, and brought him to an inn, and took care of him. And on the morrow when he departed, he took out two pence, and gave *them* to the host, and said unto him, Take care of him; and whatsoever thou spendest more, when I come again I will repay thee. Which now of these three, thinkest thou, was neighbour unto him that fell among the thieves? And he said, He that shewed mercy on him. Then said Jesus unto him, Go and do thou likewise.

As the lowly Samaritan is the one doing the ministering, the passage does not inform us what categories of persons should be the recipients of ministry. Here, the wounded man in the road is not described: we may infer that he is an observant Jew, since he is coming down from Jerusalem, but this is not certain. That he is "half dead," when salvation is consistently symbolized by bringing to life one who is fully dead, may well indicate the robbery victim to be one of the elect. The Samaritan goes into debt, for the ministry to the robbery victim to be carried on to completion in his absence, intimating the redemptive atonement, and identifying Jesus with the Samaritan. Otherwise, we are left to infer that going into debt for charitable purposes is morally better than paying cash for them, that philanthropies are more godly if put on the American Express card.

The lawyer's question, "And who is my neighbor?" never gets a straight answer from Jesus. A politician or used-car salesman should envy the adroitness of his evasion. By asking the rhetorical question as to who was neighbor to the victim, he deflected attention from the aspect of the parable relevant to the lawyer's question, the matter of who was neighbor to the Samaritan. The qualities of neighborliness exemplified by thc Samaritan are the qualities of Jesus himself rescuing and redeeming a half-alive one of God's elect. Demonstrating love for such a neighbor, one's savior, turns out to be a redundant declaration of love for God himself, who is incarnated in the Savior. The emphasis is all on love of the deity in his various aspects, and the question of right attitude towards "neighbors" in the more familiar sense gets lost in the shuffle. A relationship with God, eclipsing relationships with other humans, is intimated. Although the believers are constantly exhorted to be humble, and deem themselves capable of nothing without Jesus, here they are exhorted to exercise the office of surrogate savior to the elect as they go. When Jesus taught love of "enemies," as in Matthew 5:44 and Luke 6:27, 35, ministry to the needy was not in view. From Paul's telling the believers to give food and drink to their "enemy," in Romans 12:20, we infer that literal food and drink cannot have been meant if their purpose, to "heap coals of fire on his head," is to be reconciled with the more benign motives believers are otherwise exhorted to have. The point is also made by Jesus rebuking his disciples for having the temerity to say that the money value of the precious ointment used to anoint him should have been given to the poor instead, in Matthew 26:6-13 and Mark 14:3-9.

Taken together, the passages parabolically depicting good works can only be interpreted as contemplating a ministry that is predominantly spiritual and meant to be of ultimate benefit only to the elect. Otherwise, they are unintelligible. Speaking from personal experience, intense Bible study does tend to wean believers away from concern with charitable works. When the new mini-Reformationist pastor involves himself and his flock in the oriental mind-game of sorting out the passages, interest in the traditional old-time-religion philanthropies recedes into the background.

Implications far more dreadful than loss of interest in traditional philanthropies lie in the Bible's teachings on the duties of the believers toward secular civil authority. To understand the unrelievedly severe and authoritarian posture of the Bible on this topic, we must look at the historical situation of the early Christians, particularly remembering that neither participatory democracy nor Christians in leadership positions were contemplated or even dreamed of by the New Testament authors. The biblical claim of sempiternal comprehensiveness, "[t]hat the man of God may be perfect, thoroughly furnished unto all good works," is quickly punctured, and the absence of biblical answers to the insistent problems of our own time becomes apparent.

In Jesus' time, messianic expectations coincided with nationalistic aspirations. Israel was a Roman colony. The Jewish people were divided into contending parties, ranging from collaborationism to nationalistic zealotry. As Israel had once been a militarily strong nation, enforcement of antisedition laws was a high priority to the Romans. The classical scholar Hugh J. Schonfield described Jesus' situation:

> All this had long been known to Jesus, though most Christians even today have never given serious thought to the situation he faced. . . . But Jesus was well aware of them and proceeded circumspectly. . . . When Jesus travelled round the country preaching on the highly political as well as spiritual theme of the Kingdom of God he spoke in parables, so that the spies and informers who made it their business to be present wherever crowds gathered round a public speaker would be unable to detect anything subversive or inflammatory in what he said. He conveyed that he was speaking cryptically in his parables by adding, 'He who hath an ear to hear, let him hear,' in other words, 'He who can catch my meaning, let him do so.'
>
> Jesus was not interfered with at this time because so far as the State was concerned he gave the impression of being a harmless religious enthusiast. Some of his sayings, indeed, would meet with the full approval of the authorities. His instructions were excellent for these stubborn rebellious Galileans, and might help to keep them in order. 'Resist not evil,' the preacher declared, 'and whosoever shall smite thee on the right cheek, turn to him the other also. And whosoever

> shall force thee to go a mile, go with him two.' This was with reference to the *angaria*, military requisitioning of labour and transport. 'Love your enemies, bless them that curse you, do good to them that hate you, and pray for them which despitefully use you, and persecute you.'
>
> But Jesus was not acting as an unpaid Government agent, though he was intentionally warning the people against taking the law into their own hands and retaliating. If they resorted to violence, if they even nourished hatred in their hearts, not only would they be playing into the hands of their enemies to their own undoing, they would be abandoning the path God had marked out for them as a 'kingdom of priests and a holy nation' to win the heathen to God.[119]

In view of the overwhelming military superiority of Rome, Jesus' counsel may well have been the wisest and most far-sighted in circulation. It did not prevail, and the college history text by Brinton, et al., describes the result:

> The exception [to the rule that by measured modifications of, and concessions to local traditions, Rome, in the first and second centuries, A.D., was successful in governing its conquered provinces peacefully] was Palestine, where Roman efforts to maintain a satellite kingdom met stubborn opposition from the Jews. The more the Romans intervened in Jewish life, the more the Jews rebelled, and the more blood was shed on both sides. Finally, in 70 A.D., after a Roman siege of Jerusalem lasting four years, the remnant of the old Jewish state was destroyed. The results were the persecution of Judaism as a religion and the gradual dispersion of the Jews abroad.[120]

After having come back from conquest and exile so many times before, this time the Jewish nation did not come back—until 1948! The Temple was destroyed, not to be rebuilt, and the unconscious but not irrelevant notion that the rituals and sacrifices it stood for lost their validity casts its shadow over the place still.[121]

With Roman provincial government, retaining local officials and traditions, went Roman law. That law had a high degree of consistency, integrity and predictability about it. As Schonfield pointed out, by holding to the letter of

---

119. *The Passover Plot* (New York: Bernard Geis Associates, 1965), pp. 81-82. The Bible quotations are Matt. 11:15; 5:39, 41, 43-44; and Exod. 19:6. Schonfield, who was a biblical-languages scholar in university settings and published his own New Testament translation, departs from the familiar renditions.

This work, the best known of many Schonfield wrote on the origins of Christianity, attracted much notoriety, seemingly promising to prove that Jesus had staged his crucifixion, so that by the use of a drug, he might survive it and carry on his program. The presence of gaps, in the available substantial facts, so large that such a sensational scenario could fit them, and the difficulty, if not impossibility, of establishing any particular scenario from them, are what emerge. One felt misled by the advance publicity, and the fine quality of the scholarly work could all too easily go unappreciated. In retrospect, Schonfield's books are a very helpful complement to others by scholars reverently defending an orthodox point of view. One must take into account that Schonfield wrote as a Jew looking askance at what he regarded as a contamination of his religion. He regarded Christianity as a composite of Judaism and more mundane religious and philosophical elements, as the cluttering of his beloved, pure, elegant monotheism with so much pagan kitsch.

120. *History of Civilization*, vol. 1, p. 117.

121. See Matt. 27:51.

Roman laws against sedition, Jesus was able to go about his ministry, violating their spirit flagrantly, and enjoying Roman protection against those of his fellow Jews who took offence. When he came before Pilate, we see that if not out of integrity, then out of habit, Pilate tries to give the law its right application and find Jesus innocent. Only when the Pharisees put their full political weight behind it, does the tide of events turn toward an unjust verdict. Finally, we see Paul using his Roman citizenship, gained from his birth as a well-connected Pharisee, to manipulate the system, and retain considerable freedom of movement. At all times, the mighty inescapability of Roman authority had to be intellectually reconciled with the omnipotence and immanence of God. Like Abraham with little Isaac on Mount Moriah, or Job, the Christian was to see obedience as the auspicious path, regardless how events in the short run seemed to confute it.

The main passage on civil authority is Romans 13:1-7:

> Let every person be subject to the governing authorities. For there is no authority except from God, and those that exist have been instituted by God. Therefore he who resists the authorities resists what God has appointed, and those who resist will incur judgment. For rulers are not a terror to good conduct, but to bad. Would you have no fear of him who is in authority? Then do what is good, and you will receive his approval, for he is God's servant for your good. But if you do wrong, be afraid, for he does not bear the sword in vain; he is the servant of God to execute his wrath on the wrongdoer. Therefore one must be subject, not only to avoid God's wrath but also for the sake of conscience. For the same reason you also pay taxes, for the authorities are ministers of God, attending to this very thing. Pay all of them their dues, taxes to whom taxes are due . . . respect to whom respect is due, honor to whom honor is due.[122]

Less complete articulations of the same teaching are found elsewhere in the Bible.[123] The newer translations confront the contemporary believer with its force much more plainly than the King James translation did, as the expressions "higher powers" and "powers that be" have an inappropriately quaint, muted connotation for the modern reader.[124] Several times, members of the Roman military become followers of Christ. Jesus has nothing but praise for their obedience to hierarchical authority, and there is no indication that they are to refrain from any gruesome soldierly duties.[125] Even in the Revelation of John, we find that all the wrath is for individual sinners and apostate churches, not for wicked civil authorities.

The only activities connected with biblically approved disobedience to authority are evangelization and preaching. In all instances, it was the Jewish religious authorities, having some civil powers derived from and subordinate to

122. *Revised Standard Version.*

123. Prov. 8:15; Matt. 22:21; Luke 3:13-14; 20:25; Titus 3:1; 1 Pet. 2:13-15; 2 Pet. 2:10; and Rev. 1:5.

124. See p. 7 regarding use of Bible quotations in this work.

125. Matt. 8:5-10; Luke 7:2-10; Acts 10; 22:25-30; 27:43; Eph. 6:10-18; Phil. 2:25; 2 Tim. 2:4.

Roman authority, never Roman dignitaries themselves, whom the apostles disobeyed or showed disrespect. There is no indication that disobedience is justified where mere human life or liberty is at stake. All the believer is really given are the examples of Peter and John, continuing to preach after the Jewish authorities had forbidden them to do so, saying, "We ought to obey God rather than men,"[126] and Paul using his oratorical wiles to create a diversion, setting the Pharisees and Sadducees against each other, and disrupting their efforts to cooperate to silence him.[127] Besides these narrow exceptions, pertaining to preparation of others for the next life only, there is no relief within the Bible from the prescript of absolute obedience to the state.

Accordingly, the great moral leaders martyred in the name of Christianity in recent times, Martin Luther King, Jr., and Dietrich Bonhoeffer,[128] do not receive a good report from the Bible purist. While a weak biblical arugment might be made for the Christian soldier to disobey his superior when he knows the superior's order to be in disobedience to a higher superior's order, or a state policy,[129] none can be made for distinguishing active from passive civil disobedience, or combatants from noncombatants in war. The Bible gives the believer abundant rôle models for facing one's own or dear ones' martyrdom confidently and nobly, but none for lifting a finger to rescue another from martyrdom, or from this-worldly injustice. The Bible's thinly scattered mentionings of "conscience," which we shall scrutinize in the next chapter, do not provide a biblically approved source for filling in gaps in the Bible's teaching. If no extrabiblical standard of morality is applied to augment the Bible's limitations, one is forced to conclude that Bonhoeffer and King were "unprofitable servants," and that one might faithfully perform duties like those of an Eichmann or a Heydrich, and still be a child of God.

Our historical broad-brush sketch of old-time religion and the new mini-Reformation now complete, we can ask this work's central question: Why should orthodox, biblical Christianity have survived so long, and why should it be enjoying a resurgence in enlightened, democratic, twentieth-century North America? What draws contemporary people to it, if it is as irrelevant, unattractive, and retrograde as all that?

The short answer is that its "spiritual" content—the cleansing, rebirth, peace, prayer, perfect guidance and so on—taken by the conservative religious people as true at face value, by the skeptics of an earlier time for hollow chimera, and by the liberal religionists as the symbolic expression of something ineffable and sublime, is none of those things. These three have been the basic

126. Acts 5:29. See generally Acts 4 and 5.

127. Acts 23:1-10. The commentators usually see verse 5 as Paul apologizing to Ananias.

128. The notion of *costly grace,* discipleship and sacrifice in Christian life, as opposed to *cheap grace,* lip service and superficiality, is probably the best known of Bonhoeffer's contributions to theology, and he lived out their implicaiton by remaining and being killed as a dissident in Nazi Germany. It will be noted, however, that theologically he was rather a bull in the china shop, discarding the emphasis on grace, the most central insight of the old Reformation.

129. Luke 3:13-14 may have this implication.

approaches to the study of Christianity, and they do not suffice. Instead, we will take a fourth way, looking at those contents for their *psychological effect* rather than their intellectual content, to succeed, where all others have failed, in understanding what takes place. To do this, I must first lay a foundation of psychological ideas and terms that I will employ.

The initial word does not lie within the province of the theologian, but of the historian and the psychologist.—Hugh J. Schonfield, *The Passover Plot*[1]

Chapter 2

Psychological Premises and Concerns

A classic experiment in social psychology shows that our minds tend not to distinguish views communicated to us by reputable sources from views communicated by disreputable ones, over time. When groups of college students heard the same presentation in favor of leniency towards juvenile delinquents, with the communicator represented in one instance as an experienced and highly educated juvenile-court judge, in another instance with the communicator represented as a layperson with no particular relation to the topic, and in the third instance with the communicator represented as an ex-juvenile delinquent and adult career criminal, the immediate changes in attitude corresponded to the credibility of the source. In the first instance, the immediate result was a large shift in views toward leniency, in the second a lesser shift in the same direction, and in the third instance no shift, or a negative shift, toward more strictness. But when the groups' attitudes were remeasured after several weeks, all three groups showed similar attitudes. The students who thought they had heard the judge had receded part way toward their initial levels, the ones who thought they had heard the layperson remained about the same as immediately after hearing the presentation, and those who thought they had heard a criminal ex-delinquent make a presentation in favor of leniency toward those like himself showed influence toward his views after the passage of time, in contrast to their views expressed immediately after hearing him. The persuasive presentation of the low-credibility source had had a "sleeper effect."

The insight from this and related studies, among the few from the fertile years of the group-dynamics movement that have not been narrowed beyond practical application or clouded by subsequent studies, is that we tend to remember the message after we have forgotten the source.[2] We are at risk in our

1. (New York: Bernard Geis Associates, 1965), p. 51.
2. Carl I. Hovland, "Effects of the Mass Media of Communication," in Gardner Lindzey, ed., *Handbook of Social Psychology* (Cambridge, Mass.: Addison-Wesley Co., 1954), pp. 1062-1103, 1071-75.

views when we have been exposed to irresponsible presenters of opinions and supposititious facts. Also, we are reminded that we are neither as objective nor as independent thinking as we think we are. I will have much more to say about half-forgotten things a person unthinkingly believes, influencing other related attitudes.

Psychology is at its best when it enables a person to correct the distortion of view that comes of being the phenomenon studied. Although a truism, that bears repeating. I believe Arthur Koestler said it best: "The self which directs the searchlight of my attention can never be caught in its [own] focal beam."[3]

Because the reader may have been exposed to some learning about religious psychology and harbor some tacit notions that this work goes against, I will touch on every major development that has been current in the field. Fortunately, there are not many of them. I will show where some psychological propositions with wide currency have been plain wrong; even the best have mistaken collateral issues for central ones. We will see how some of the best insights of modern psychology were known, at least intuitively, to the biblical authors. Those insights are incorporated in the biblical program, more deftly than they ever have been since, even on Madison Avenue. This chapter is meant to furnish the technical background for, and explanation of the terminology to be used in, the next chapters, on the mind-control system.

Since the topic of individual susceptibility to group pressures or suggestions pertains both to our topic and our own process of being informed about it, we need to dwell on it. The leading thinkers of the group-dynamics movement of the forties and fifties, who gave us what has become the standard material for college courses in social psychology, were great optimists about the nature of man and his perfectability through education. After a series of experiments had shown individual judgment to be very susceptible to group influence, in judgments in an ambiguous situation,[4] the psychologist Solomon E. Asch set out to create an experimental situation in which the individual's initial correct judgment in an unambiguous situation would conflict with the judgments expressed by other members of a group, so that the individual forced to be a minority of one could be studied. The individual would find himself one of a group asked to judge which of three lines of assorted lengths was nearest to being as long as a fourth line. All four lines were on a poster displayed on an easel in front of the group. Unbeknown to the subject, the other members of the group had been organized to agree on an obviously wrong answer. The great majority of subjects would yield to the group, and a lesser majority of them would quickly come to *believe* the group, over the obvious evidence of their

3. *The Ghost in the Machine* (New York: Macmillan, 1967), p. 212.

4. Muzafer Sherif, *The Psychology of Social Norms* (New York: Harper & Brothers, 1936). The ambiguous situation was created by having small groups of subjects view a point of light in a darkened room. That produces the "autokinetic effect," the illusion that the point of light oscillates from side to side. The apparent movement, caused by internal physiological factors, had no objective distance of travel, so all estimates of travel by subjects were necessarily subjective. Individual tendencies to estimate a particular distance of travel soon gave way to a group "norm."

own eyesight.[5] The experiment and later variants of it stand as a monument to people's illusions about the independence of judgment they exercise and their true dependence on the collective judgments of others, on what "they say."

The laboratory experiments in susceptibility to group pressure, which reached the peak of their currency during the McCarthy era, never effectively studied judgments on controversial matters. A situation that repeated itself several times in the years when I taught psychology at George Mason University may serve us in lieu of such an experiment. In the second semester of a senior-level undergraduate course in abnormal psychology, I used various materials, including films, to promote class discussion. One such film, "Transorbital Lobotomy: Part II" by Walter Freeman, showed a young man diagnosed as "catatonic schizophrenic," who had no known previous psychiatric history but who had suddenly become intensely detached, withdrawn, and unresponsive and was hospitalized. Within a few days of that first admission to the hospital, Dr. Freeman performed his famous (now no longer performed) transorbital lobotomy, where a surgical instrument is inserted through each eye socket and neural connections between the frontal lobes and the midbrain are severed. This was done with such speed and lack of postoperative discomfort as to make it seem trivial. After such an operation, the patient was relaxed, passive, compliant, muted in affect, and often the most acute symptoms subsided. The patient became easy to manage, and often capable of some outward semblance of normal life, although with initiative and spontaneity greatly impaired and the depth of his personality greatly reduced.

The film next showed the patient "demonstrated" in his postoperative state, talking and putting on a short musical performance, in a wooden, affectless, hollow way. Dr. Freeman made it clear he thought such compliance and manageability so desirable that this patient might even be an improvement on nature. Because the patient, fortuitously, died of causes unrelated to his psychiatric problems shortly thereafter, the film was able to end with Dr. Freeman dissecting his brain and congratulating himself that the lesions were just where they were supposed to be. (An aspect of the film that the students generally did not recognize was the dead-ringer resemblance of Dr. Freeman, in appearance, voice, and speech, to his contemporary, Senator Joseph McCarthy. Having a lookalike of Senator Joe advocating the surgical alteration of people into passive conformists made the film more poignant than any existentialist-absurdist fiction could ever be. Or so it seemed to me.)

---

5. "Effects of Group Pressure upon the Modification and Distortion of Judgments," in Eleanor E. Maccoby, Theodore M. Newcomb and Eugene L. Hartley, eds., *Readings in Social Psychology*, 3rd ed. (New York: Holt, Rinehart and Winston, 1958), pp. 174–83.

Tendency not to yield in a group-pressure situation such as this has been shown to be correlated with personality factors, such as "field independence," going by internal, gravitational clues rather than visual ones in adjusting a vertical rod perpendicular to the ground, ability to find the embedded figure in a picture puzzle with many distracting contours, and low hypnotic suggestibility. Resistance to group pressure is more characteristic of males than females. See Edmund D. Cohen, *Some Related Variables in the Interpersonal Risk (IR) Theory* (Ann Arbor, Mich.: University Microfilms, 1969).

The undergraduates seeing the film purported to have the humane values and disrespect for authority of the then waning Vietnam era. In the course, we had already covered research findings showing spontaneous recovery by most first-admission mental patients within the first sixty days, regardless of whether they receive psychotherapy or not. My hope was that the students would pick up on Freeman's resort to such a drastic measure so soon after the patient's first admission, without trying less drastic treatment first or seeing if the patient would recover spontaneously.

Repeatedly, the undergraduates were unperturbed by what they had seen, despite anything I might say, and they accepted the film at face value. If anything, they would look askance at me, just as they did whenever I had the temerity to tell them that something with the dignity of being printed in a textbook was wrong. After all, here I was, only a psychologist, contradicting something a psychiatrist said. I may have previously lost some of my credibility with them by expressing skepticism as to the massive use of mood-altering drugs in psychiatry being a true treatment, as opposed to a mere short-sighted expedient in the management of patients. The students shared neither my sentiment that one's thoughts and emotions are something sacrosanct nor my horror at having someone tinker experimentally with another person, surgically or chemically.

Both of the insights from the group-pressure experiments apply. When the undergraduates saw that what was presented in the film was "official," that the source was "credible," and did not sense horror in their fellow students, they took what they had seen in stride. There were no minorities of one among my students on this topic. Do people get their cues from their peers, as to what will alarm or offend them and what will not, rather than from their individual appraisal of a potential cause for alarm or offense? Judging from the way groups of people get worked up, seemingly over nothing at some times, and blandly shrug off alarming signs fairly bellowing at them at other times—perhaps they do. Are people normally so other-directed that the actions of others take precedence over their own inner-directed thoughts and standards? Perhaps Gallup's repeated registering of fairly orthodox religious opinions in the absence of action reflecting that the opinions are truly meant can be explained in this way. Perhaps his respondents live as they see others live, and answer survey questions as they think they are expected to answer survey questions. Do people innately abhor intrusion in their person by those seen to have authority? Perhaps not so much as one would like to think.

A provocative variation on the theme of man's overdeveloped tendency to conform is found in Arthur Koestler's work on the origins of intelligence. He saw tension between the "self-assertive," individualistic tendency, and the "self-transcending," integrative, conforming tendency as the major theme in human psychological evolution. Drawing on that theme, from his intensive later research in the life sciences and his earlier experiences as a journalist and novelist writing about the great secular mass movements of the thirties and forties, he wrote:

> For the last three or four thousand years, Hebrew prophets, Greek philosophers, Indian mystics, Chinese sages . . . American pragmatists, have discussed the perils of violence, and appealed to man's better nature, without much noticeable effect. There must be a reason for this failure.
>
> The reason . . . lies in a series of fundamental misconceptions . . . which prevented him from learning the lessons of the past, and . . . now put his survival in question. The first of these . . . is putting the blame for man's predicament on his selfishness, greed, etc.; in a word, on the aggressive, self-assertive tendencies of the individual. . . . I would like to suggest that the *integrative tendencies of the individual are incomparably more dangerous than his self-assertive tendencies.* The sermons of the reformers were bound to fall on deaf ears because they put the blame where it did not belong.[6]

Koestler goes on to show how sporadic and minor the history of violence and inhumanity attributable to individual aggressiveness is, compared with the violence wrought by well-disciplined groups. Mass movements and organizations carry out violence with a persistency and consistency not found in violent individuals. Like his contemporary Eric Hoffer,[7] he saw the inadequate, inwardly spoliated individual attempting to lose himself in the group ideology to be the most dangerous form of human life.

What we should note most about group pressure and the tendency to conform is that they work more powerfully than the person subjected to them realizes. Separating people from competing influence, or discrediting or defining as illegitimate potential competing influencers, will be sufficient to control the attitudes of a goodly proportion of the population. This is the simplest and least subtle of the psychological insights embodied in the Evangelical mind-control system.

To know that susceptibility to group pressure is pervasive does not help us to understand those who resist. It will be noted that our two strands of communicator credibility, and perceived popularity of the doctrine being inculcated, correspond to Berger's "legitimacy" and "plausibility." Reasoning that religious indoctrination would subside as those two factors subsided, Berger came dramatically to the wrong conclusion. More is needed than to replace liberal optimism, which was disappointed in those who discovered how susceptible to badness man is, with its simple opposite.

Brainwashing

Discussion of the conformist streak in man calls to mind the topics of cults, brainwashing, deprogramming, "snapping," and related phenomena that have been important social issues in recent years. For the purpose of the present work, it is necessary to touch on these topics in order to dispel potentially misleading impressions the reader may have received, either directly or through

6. *Ghost in the Machine,* p. 233.
7. *The True Believer* (New York: Harper & Brothers, 1951).

others uncritically accepting them. The topic is one that genuine scholars have been reticent to take up, so it has been particularly troubled by sensationalists masquerading as scholars, claiming to have uncovered some arcane secret of inducing rapid or instantaneous personality change.

Following World War II, the extreme situations individuals had been and were being placed in by totalitarian regimes provided much for behavioral scientists to write about. Among these was brainwashing, the use of pressure techniques, often having more to do with incarceration, physical abuse, dietary and sleep deprivation and the like than with psychological sublety. While I will draw on some of the insights of that literature, its application to situations where the paramount question is why the individual in a position to choose, chooses as he does is limited.

Our observation about the "sleeper effect" of persuasion efforts by low-credibility communicators applies to books. Something like Gresham's law operates, where irresponsible books, which are ignored or generally condemned after they first appear, keep cropping up. Such a book is *Battle for the Mind: A Physiology of Conversion and Brain-Washing,* by William Sargant.[8] Sargant was a member of the same aberrational minority of psychiatrists as Freeman—the lobotomists. He espoused a peculiar combination of views, including Pavlovian classical conditioning and liberal Methodist Christianity, and he expressed in an unusually dissonant way his inability to come to some resolution of his ambivalence toward viewing man as nothing but a response mechanism.

Sargant delved into Pavlovian theory on the counterposition, at a physiological level, of excitation and inhibition in response to stimuli, and built his thesis on it. The thesis is that sudden pervasive changes in ideology, including religious experiences that form a bridge from doubt to faith, experiences accompanied by subjective certainty as to the newfound religious convictions, come after a barrage of excitatory stimuli so strong as to elicit a wave of response inhibition, causing higher mental activity to subside and the individual to be rendered open and vulnerable to suggestion for a short time. It took me more than one reading to be sure that, yes, Sargant was really equating the physical brutality and cruelty of the Chinese prison camp with hearing a ringing, emotional sermon delivered by John Wesley! The other major problem with the analysis is its presumption that sudden conversions are what they appear to be: the possibilities that a conversion, if truly sudden and without a long-term history, might be transitory, or, if it is lasting might have a historical development underlying it, received no consideration from Sargant. The McCarthy-era undertone of preoccupation with the fear of subversion, and overeagerness to eliminate freedom in the name of freedom, is all too apparent in Sargant's presentation.

With the rise of religious cults, perhaps filling a void left by the decline of the Aquarian counterculture with its search for alternative life-styles in the sixties, has come renewed interest in the psychology of religious indoctrination.

8. (New York: Doubleday & Co., 1957.)

Forcible deindoctrination, or deprogramming, of persons who joined eccentric, sequestered religious groups was in vogue for a time and then subsided.[9]

The only widely known recent publication purporting to offer a social-science explanation of sudden ideological conversions is *Snapping,* by Flo Conway and Jim Siegelman.[10] Much of it consists of a pseudoscholarly smokescreen about information theory, cybernetics, and mathematical modeling of physical fields where sudden changes take place, such as earthquakes and avalanches. The authors do not succeed in relating those imposing topics to ideological conversion, and the real substance of their work is warmed-over Sargant. While every-

---

9. Deprogramming consisted of forcibly carrying off the cult member, usually a young person whose parents sponsored the deprogrammer, and administering arguments against the cult; this was accompanied by sleep deprivation, bullying, and declarations of love for the person being so bullied. The best-known practitioner of deprogramming was Ted Patrick, who finally was imprisoned for the criminal abductions that some of his efforts had constituted. Patrick was raised in a poor, black neighborhood in Chattanooga, Tennessee, surrounded by the church-going and variety of religion-oriented exploitations and frauds endemic to such a place. As a child, he had a speech impediment that isolated him from other children, and he went through a phase of absorption in Bible reading. ". . . I began to emerge from my Bible obsession and to see that book in a larger context. Once I began to lead a more normal life [after overcoming the speech impediment], I could judge, looking back, how abnormal and even morbid I'd been in my religious thinking." Ted Patrick with Tom Dulack, *Let Our Children Go!* (New York: Ballantine Books, 1977), p. 215. Before developing deprogramming, Patrick was an official in the Reagan gubernatorial administration in California, espousing the sort of *ad libitum* Christianity often observed in Reagan's inner circle.

Legally, it appears that deprogramming will not be an option in the United States in the coming years. The leading case on the use of guardianship laws, existing in every jurisdiction to enable a court to appoint a guardian (other terms, such as *custodian* or *committee,* may be used) over the person or property of one unable to make decisions for himself, usually a person who is demented, senile, or comatose, is *Katz* v. *Superior Court,* 73 Cal. App. 3d 952, 141 Cal. Rptr. 234 (1977). In it, the California guardianship law, insofar as it made the criterion for suspending a person's civil rights and appointing a guardian over him, "[inability] properly to care for himself," was held unconstitutionally vague and therefore void. The California legislature enacted a new law, narrowing the criterion to inability to care for personal (i.e., physical) needs, and requiring that consistent inability to care for them, over and above isolated instances, be shown. On the legislative front, special enabling laws for deprogramming have been proposed but not carried, in the legislatures of Connecticut, Minnesota, Ohio, Oregon, and Texas. In New York, where the Jewish community is particularly concerned about loss of young people to cults and conservative churches, a deprogramming enabling act passed in the legislature in 1980 and 1981, but it was vetoed by Governor Hugh Carey. In my opinion, that was wise, since such a law would have had a troubled course, culminating in its being ruled unconstitutional by the courts.

Evangelicals, who often see the mote in someone else's eye more easily than the beam in their own, have been active in decrying the cults. In the late seventies, all of the major Evangelical publishers had anticult books on their lists. Walter Martin's *The New Cults* (Santa Ana, Calif.: Vision House Publishers, 1980) and other titles by him stand out as the best of these, giving journalistically professional and useful factual background about the various eccentric religious groups alleged to be cults. In December 1982, two young women who had become members of Assemblies of God were forcibly subjected to deprogramming by their mother and stepfather, who were subsequently prosecuted, along with eight others, for kidnapping. After that, public anticult activity, and support for deprogramming enabling legislation on the part of Evangelicals, abruptly stopped. Evangelicals were brought dangerously close to the insight that it is only cosmetic social acceptability, and not any distinction of kind, that demarcates them from the cults. Ted Patrick has since denounced Jerry Falwell saying, "Falwell leads the biggest cult in the nation." Randy Frame, "And Now—Deprogramming of Christians Is Taking Place," *Christianity Today,* Apr. 22, 1983, p. 31.

10. (New York: Dell Publishing Co., 1978).

thing they present is geared to systems that change suddenly, pervasively, and irreversibly when underlying stresses exceed a threshold level, they do recognize that their interview data on ideological conversions admit to many instances that were reversible or not sudden. They speak repeatedly of this or that observation "confirming" the "thesis" of snapping. If one brings together the elements of that "thesis" in a concise statement, it comes out: "Ideological conversion is sudden unless it is not sudden, and irreversible unless it is reversible." No conceivable set of facts fails to "confirm" that thesis. It fits all and discriminates none. Like the doctrine of any good religion, it is not disprovable.

What Conway and Siegelman with all their enthusiasm, superficiality, and credulity toward the claims and conclusions of their sources attempted, the serious scholars, by and large, do not attempt. What good is social science if it does not tackle the hard and relevant questions? If there are no real scholars to inhabit the edifice that the likes of Weber, James, and Jung built up, should we be surprised if we find intellectual barbarians crouching in its ruins?

There is a more telling similarity in the approach of Conway and Siegelman to the religious hucksters they criticize than the use of the rhetorical device of the nondisprovable hypothesis. That is their credulity as to the genuineness of apparently sudden and ahistorical ideological change. It seems they, like those who are converted under old-time religion revivalism, are fascinated by the prospect of there being some turning point where the hurts and habits from one's past are erased, preternaturally exploded by some magic bullet. We will see how the new mini-Reformationism tones down emphasis on sudden, salutary personality change, so that it does not fly in the face of daily experience but does retain it. The false promise of radical renewal is endemic to Christianity. It will be our approach to maintain a posture of skepticism toward sudden deliverances from the influence of the personal past, and to keep in mind the familiar depth-psychology insight that troublesome past influences, seemingly gone, remain with us at a subconscious level and find unruly ways to manifest themselves if we do not stay in touch with them, if we lack a sensible, conscious standpoint toward them.

Other Psychological Approaches

In Chapter 1, I made reference to social-science approaches to the study of religion which were themselves reflections of, and participants in, the liberal theological process that has dominated the learned books and the historic mainline denominations. We covered content enlightening our earlier, more macroscopic, historical and sociological discussion. We now need to cover, with a more microscopic, individual, psychological focus, more of that work, and distinguish the plainly unsuccessful approaches from those that shed light but mistook peripheral issues for core ones. Occasionally, I will have to speculate about their true concerns when it seems that the original authors have not made them plain—keeping the fact in mind when we entertain such speculations.

William James' views on religious conversions, and on the dichotomy of "healthy-minded" versus "sick-soul" religion, have already served us, as a reflection of the benefits claimed for the believer in nineteenth-century, old-time revivalist religion.[11] Having studied just enough of him to know that he was the proponent of a better, more refined sudden-conversion idea than those we have just covered, as well as to be surprised that one of the major founding fathers of that most secular of disciplines, psychology, had such encouraging things to say about the Evangelical churches of his day, we can anticipate that no concise treatment of James will do him justice.[12] But we do want to know how far his friendliness to Evangelicalism extended, when biblically authentic Protestantism will necessarily be "sick-soul" religion, because preoccupation with sin is endemic to it, and that the "right, superior and happy" converted person, in James' view, is inherently unlike the pilgrim in desperate suspense about whether he can persevere to the end or not. I shall restrict the focus to the background of a few of his ideas that influenced later key contributors.

Just as James was sincere in deeming it crucial to treat with fairness contending points of view, so was he sincere in including his own philosophizing within the principles that all human knowledge is subject to human psychological limitations, that human choices are necessarily implicated in human knowledge, that truly objective knowledge based on absolute truth is not in prospect for all practical purposes. In his lecture, "The Will to Believe," delivered in 1896, he said:

> Our passional nature not only lawfully may, but must, decide an option between propositions, whenever it is a genuine option that cannot by its nature be decided on intellectual grounds; for to say, under such circumstances, "Do not decide, but leave the question open," is itself a passional decision,—just like deciding yes or no,—and is attended with the same risk of losing the truth.

Accordingly, James thought it perfectly proper to look ahead to the human consequence of any given idea, in deciding whether to be its proponent or not. Without absolute human knowledge, belief in a supreme being was legitimate, if it did good things like bringing the believer inner peace or enabled him to find it gratifying to engage in philanthropy. Without absolute truth, good outcomes make the difference in what we, here on the ground, deem to be true. This is utterly different from the behavioral scientists and mental-health professionals we have all known, who had a kindly, genial façade good for "establishing rapport," but whose intellectual substance, if not so relativistic as to defy specification, turned out to sustain nothing better than the view that man is a physico-chemical automaton. They made us shudder to think what would hap-

---

11. See pp. 27-28.
12. Indeed, psychology has fared best when it tried to maintain Jamesian breadth, and it has suffered when others made a more narrow, technical field of it. For a good, recent survey of James' thought, see Patrick Kiaran Dooley, *Pragmatism as Humanism: The Philosophy of William James* (Chicago: Nelson-Hall, 1974).

pen if they were ever in a position to put into practice the implications of their views. James disliked views that encouraged inhumane action, or discouraged humane action by making it seem futile. A determinist position could not be intrinsically right, because its psychological implication is fatalism. He had high tolerance for ambiguity, but low tolerance for absurdity. To be a humanist in this sense—be it secular humanism or unbiblically religious humanism—is something much different from being a mere materialist. If a label for James is appropriate, it is *meliorist.*

There were some social concerns of the turn-of-the-century period that, although James barely mentioned them, he must surely have had in mind, in assessing the implications, were others to try to translate his philosophizing into action. These were so pervasively insistent in that day that we are safe in inferring their influence on James. First, the mental-health and social-service professions did not exist then. Psychiatrists, or alienists as they were known, were simply the custodians of warehouses for seriously disturbed and organically impaired patients; their specialty had little content and less prestige in those days. Applied psychology did not exist. There was a huge, highly publicized prevalence of alcoholism and a temperance movement that eventually led to the enactment of the Twenty-first Amendment to the U.S. Constitution. Rowland H's famed encounter with C. G. Jung, leading up to the founding of Alcoholics Anonymous, was still far in the future. There were few resources in any American community, other than old-time-religion philanthropic ones, for ministering to any of these problems.[13]

The existence of social problems and suffering people being attended to only under religious auspices was a powerful reason for the researcher into religion and conspicuous shaper of informed opinion of James' day to be very gentle, and to try to encourage what was good. The controversial nature of the topic, and the repercussions if one said the wrong thing, had to be considered. If that is not what was behind James' rhapsodic treatment of religious emotionalism, what are we to think? Are we to believe that the descendant of a dour bunch of Calvinist Presbyterians did not have the slightest hint that the biblical teaching might have contributed to making the "sick soul" sick? Are we to believe that he took the sugary accounts of the religious converts entirely at face value? Are we to believe that he was no more critical than Conway and Siegelman? This troubled me, since reading *Varieties* at an impressionable time in my life (I was a college student) added much to my wrong expectations and selective credulity, which in turn led to my own religious phase.

Some details yield a possible solution. Scrutinizing James' quotations from "sick-soul" authors, particularly Jonathan Edwards, one finds that James has skirted the doctrinal issues and conveyed far less than he must have understood

13. In *Varieties of Religious Experience,* James refers in passing to release from alcoholism in the case histories, and makes one direct reference to alcohol as an inferior substitute for religious mystical experience (New York: New American Library, 1958), p. 297. Interestingly, there is no reference to Freud and Breuer's newly published *Studies on Hysteria,* probably indicating that James had not yet read it.

about the causes of their melancholy. We note that hardly anything about religion is to be found in his main work, *The Principles of Psychology.* After finishing *Varieties* he said, "I've had enough of the squashy popular-lecture style."[14] How was he to know that so little on the topic would be written after *Varieties* and that this group of summer lectures would be taken so much more seriously than he had meant it to be?

What of the "healthy-minded" versus "sick-soul" dichotomy? Underlying it is the "tough-minded" versus "tender-minded" dichotomy, the most memorable of James' contributions to personality theory. The tough-minded personality is described as "emipricist, i.e., going by facts, sensationalistic, materialistic, pluralistic, irreligious, fatalistic, skeptical"; the tender-minded, as "rationalist, i.e., going by principles, intellectualistic, idealistic, monistic, religious, free willistic, dogmatical."[15] A consistent streak of invidiousness runs through James' treatment of these personality types: he preferred the cheerful, practical, outgoing type to the melancholic, inadequate, contemplative type. The types lend themselves to caricature as praise of the Yankee progressive over the European decadent. In the same vein, James' terms for explicit versus tacit or intuitive understanding are, respectively, "front-door" versus "back-door" experiences. With slight modifications, James' seminal idea would become Jung's still useful and current psychological types.

The healthy-minded and tough-minded types largely overlap, and we see that there is some difficulty about the healthy-minded convert, "that religious ideas, previously peripheral in his consciousness, now take a central place, and that religious aims form the habitual centre of his energy."[16] Healthy-mindedness and religiosity, in the larger context of James' work, turn out to be a contradiction in terms. The healthy-minded Evangelical is unmasked as one who adapts to the norms and forms of churchliness but is inwardly untouched (or no longer touched) by their content or implications. To the new mini-Reformationist, such a person would be a goat among the sheep! As a practical matter, the dimension of healthy-minded versus sick-soul has not worked out in my observations. That seeming inner unification really consists of making the gap of inner dividedness so wide that one loses consciousness of what is on the other side. I shall return to this later.

The next significant representative of academic psychology to take up the religion problem was Gordon W. Allport, a generation removed from James at Harvard and very much a reflector of his influence. In private life, Allport was a liberal churchman, and was among those who presumed it was settled that the liberal redefinition of Christianity *was* Christianity. His approach to religion grew out of his emphasis on the uniqueness of the individual; academic and practicing psychologists spoke well of Allport but incorporated little of his later thinking into their own.

Allport's contribution that lends itself best to concise treatment, that fairly

14. Dooley, *Pragmatism as Humanism,* p. 4.
15. Ibid., p. 119.
16. See p. 28.

conveys the flavor—and which other social scientists did pick up on—is the dichotomy of *intrinsic* versus *extrinsic* religion.[17] Intrinsic religion is seeking to put into practice the principles, sensitivities, and decencies that the inner meaning of the religion implies. I perceive no distinction between intrinsic religion and Tillich's ultimate concern. Extrinsic religion is concentration on the norms, forms, and selfish advantages that can be derived from churchliness. The purported negative side-effects of religion, such as self-righteousness and ethnic prejudice, are seen as belonging to extrinsic religion. Allport expected that differentiating extrinsic from intrinsic motives for church participation would show two rather distinct types of people, with different motives, participating in the same churches. Empirical research has generally failed to confirm this.

The most widely known empirical social scientists specializing in the study of religion (and, unlike Allport and Berger, not well known for anything else) were Rodney Stark and Charles Y. Glock. Although they were trained and affiliated as sociologists rather than psychologists, their essential work and thought parallels Allport's. They came to prominence with a major statistical study of anti-Semitism in Protestantism, funded by and the copyright property of B'nai B'rith.[18] The study showed substantial prevalence of negative sentiment toward Jews among Protestants and a strong tendency for that sentiment to color memories and interpretations of Bible content. Glock and Stark, in that early work, showed colossal ignorance of the underlying religious issues.[19] In their day, one heard much in the behavioral sciences about how ignorance of a topic was helpful in studying it objectively or operationally, avoiding prejudices affecting one's observations and letting one's impressions be genuinely fresh.

---

17. "Personal Religious Orientation and Prejudice," in *The Person in Psychology: Selected Essays* (Boston: Beacon Press, 1968), pp. 237-68.

18. *Christian Beliefs and Anti-Semitism* (New York: Harper & Row, 1966).

19. Glock and Stark apparently had no inkling what source other than Roman Catholic doctrine could possibly be authoritative for Protestants. A key construct was "particularism," the belief that one's own was the only true faith, all others being outside God's grace. To measure particularism, the respondents were asked whether they disagreed (0), agreed (1) or strongly agreed (2) with the propositions of the necessity of prayer, baptism, and regular participation in the sacraments as necessary for salvation; thus, a respondent could score from 0 to 6. Among Protestants, only a very traditionally oriented Episcopalian would think baptism or regular communion (the only other sacrament that can be in view for a Protestant) were indispensable. The usual biblicist view points out that one of the thieves crucified with Jesus (Luke 23:39-43) was saved and died on the cross, without ever having a chance to be baptized or receive communion. The idea that baptism or communion is a necessary work that man must perform to be saved flies in the face of the central insight of the Reformation: that salvation is by unilateral divine grace. Luther, Calvin, Bloesch, or Jay Adams, doubtless, would score no higher than 2 on particularism. Glock and Stark found no significant correlations of "particularism" with other variables.

The researchers also tried to make a projective text of Bible knowledge. They asked whether Peter, Paul, and the rest of the apostles were Jewish, whether Pontius Pilate had wanted to spare Jesus from the cross, and the like, looking for indications of attitude toward modern Jews in the answers. The questions have clear biblical right answers, and only ignorance could produce the "non-anti-Semitic" response that Pilate wanted to crucify Jesus all along, or the "anti-Semitic" one, that Peter and Paul were *goyim*. The uncontrolled variable of Bible knowledge spoiling the result is obvious.

In a later study, they and others investigated anti-Semitism in Protestant clergy.[20] This time, their work avoided any obvious display of ignorance about Protestantism. The researchers correctly identified the tension found in the more conservative of the pastors surveyed between lack of personal animosity toward Jews and the theological conviction that Jews who do not want Jesus for their messiah are outside God's grace. Apparently feeling constrained not to show enmity or intolerance themselves towards others' religious views, the researchers came to no conclusion, and made no prediction, based on that insight. What is most interesting about the study is its information on "orthodoxy," i.e., freedom from important doubts about the existence of God, the divinity of Christ, and rewards and punishments in the afterlife. In liberal-church clergy, the prevalence of such doubts is strikingly higher than in the general population surveyed by Gallup.[21] It is fascinating to compare the two books, and see that mainline church pastors are actually *less* biblical in their beliefs than the general public.

Stark and Glock's *American Piety: The Nature of Religious Commitment*[22] is the most representative larger work of the social psychology of religion of the sixties. Statistical data from a cross-section of religions and denominations were studied. This was just at the time when the membership, church school, and financial activity of the mainline denominations was leveling off and getting ready to decline, as would be evident to Dean M. Kelley, using updated data from the same sources four or five years later. The researchers stretched the data, to hold onto the premise that liberal churches were still growing and that conservative ones represented a declining *derrière garde.*[23] The main idea is that "religious commitment," meaning persistence of church participation, is motivated partly by the old religious ideas, in which Stark and Glock saw no point and tacitly equated with extrinsic religion, and partly by the new liberal theology, intrinsic religion. They looked for the redefined Christian message somehow to have caused church participants to know specific buzz words they had never been taught. The researchers were disappointed to find "ethicalism," social concern, etc. not particularly evident in the persistently churchly.

Besides these, there are some valuable academic behavioral-science studies on detailed topics, and we will benefit from a few of the mental-health related ones presented in Chapter 5. However, except for depth psychology, what we

---

20. Rodney Stark, Bruce D. Foster, Charles Y. Glock, and Harold E. Quinley, *Wayward Shepherds: Prejudice and the Protestant Clergy* (New York: Harper & Row, 1971).

21. George Gallup, Jr., and David Poling, *The Search for America's Faith* (Nashville: Abingdon Press, 1980).

22. (Berkeley: University of California Press, 1968).

23. Stark and Glock noticed that National Council of Churches data then showed conservative churches growing faster than moderate or liberal ones. This was in contrast to National Opinion Research Center data, intensively gathered in California, showing the reverse. They rationalized this, saying that the weaker churches would have the higher proportion of deadwood (i.e., former participants still on the rolls), and since the conservative churches were the weaker ones, they must have the more inflated apparent membership. In other words, by proceeding from the premise that the conservative churches were weaker, they came to the conclusion that the conservative churches were indeed weaker, regardless of the data.

have covered is representative. Never has a behavioral-science investigator into religion *predicted* anything of interest. Stark and Glock never foresaw that within a very few years Evangelicals would uniformly forget about being antipathetic toward the Jews (that antipathy having had more to do with perception of a connection between Jews and communism, that subsequent events made untenable, than with any religious issue), and become supporters of Israel, even becoming customers on a large scale for Israel tourism. Neither did those researchers foresee the events that an outsider to the behavioral sciences, Kelley, would bring to light only four years after *American Piety.* Of all the explanatory work we have covered so far, it appears that Weber is the only investigator whose work we might still profitably read for its insight; the rest is for the dustbin.

Sigmund Freud

The most famous figure in depth psychology,[24] the only still well-known behavioral-science student of religion who had no part in the attempted liberal redefinition of Christianity, and my precursor in the seminal insight (but not the methods) of the present work, is Sigmund Freud (1856–1939). The first member of a well-to-do Jewish family from Moravia to be permitted to pursue higher education, Freud grew up with a strong sense of alienation from the Christianity-permeated, Viennese belles-lettres culture surrounding him as he received that education. He was not so well-versed in the humanities and ethnological scholarship that flowered among the German speakers in his time as his reputation would seem to indicate. Rather, he became a radical—we would say, naïve—materialist, under some of the same influences that shaped Marx. He focused on a few things that appealed to him and made them into a doctrine with authoritarian and cultic overtones. As one notes the books about depth psychology published these days, one is struck by how few improve the ideas and their application and how many rehash who-did-what-to-whom in Freud's early circle. To be sure, some of the things he emphasized have very wide application and shed great light. He was an able author, to whom English translations have never done justice. But the virtue of clarity never completely overcomes its cognate vice, oversimplification.

What follows assumes familiarity with the standard, later Freudian concepts: ego, superego, id, repression, resistance, libido, Oedipus complex, and the five stages of psychosexual development. The reader may wish to review them in a psychology textbook or dictionary. Later, our approach will deliberately and self-consciously avoid the restrictions of Freudianism and be more "generally psychodynamic," using Jungian terms since they happen to work well for

24. I use the term *depth psychology* to include those psychologies that have an unconscious or subconscious portion of the mind as a key concept. I avoid the term *psychoanalysis,* because, among professionals, some understand it to mean a distinctively Freudian kind of psychology and others use it more generally and distinguish Freudianism as "orthodox psychoanalysis."

the purpose. The reasons for this will become clear as we examine some general implications of Freud's thought and show what his seminal insights into religion were and why they could not advance beyond rudimentariness and yet stay authentically Freudian.

First, we have mentioned that Freud was a radical materialist. All through his career, he proclaimed himself the proponent of a scientific Weltanschauung, with the empirical scientific method as its centerpiece.[25] He regarded his work as bridging the boundary between psychology and biology.[26] Although he lived when the weight of scientific opinion held the Darwinian random-mutation-natural-selection idea, operating according to the Mendelian arithmetic ratios, to be the ultimate intellectual breakthrough in genetics, Freud had a predilection for Lamarckianism, the view that adaptations and even ideas acquired by a particular individual during its lifetime could be hereditarily transmitted. Even his faithful disciple and biographer, Ernest Jones, found this peculiar.[27] The debate that persisted in Freudian circles over whether one had to be a member of the medical profession to reach the highest level of initiate status reflects the materialistic view that the ultimate objects of psychological study are body processes.

Secondly, the Freudian concepts are highly specific and exclusive. From that primitive, insensate part of the personality, the id, are said to emanate two drives: the erotic drive, with its specific aim being sexual possession of the parent of the opposite sex, and the self-destructive drive, with its aim being the reduction of all tension and return of the organism to its inorganic state. Since the attainment of either of these aims would have consequences that are antisocial, to say the least, only displacements, substitute gratifications that are not fully satisfying and that leave some tension undischarged, are possible. The ego develops through the five psychosexual stages to mediate and cope with the outside world, where there are objects in which the psychological energy, or libido, that the erotic drive consists of, can be invested. The superego, the internalization of those prohibitions that are inculcated in the child, is a related development. Because the potentialities of the drives are so terrible, it arouses anxiety—psychic pain—for them and their true nature to become conscious. Hence, they are repressed by the "censor," the superego. The individual's true nature remains hidden from him, and his socially acceptable illusions about himself remain intact.

Thus, all socially acceptable human strivings require redirection of these energies to objects other than their true aims. Sublimation and restraining and delaying what gratification is realistically possible are necessary.

Freud laid great stress on the recurring patterns of males having guilt complexes for having desired to commit jealous acts of aggression toward the father

25. Sigmund Freud, *New Introductory Lectures on Psychoanalysis,* trans. James Strachey (New York: W. W. Norton & Co., 1965), p. 139.
26. Ernest Jones, *The Life and Work of Sigmund Freud,* vol. 3 (New York: Basic Books, 1957), p. 302.
27. Ibid., pp. 309-14.

(which he thought to have been frequently committed in primitive societies), and fearing the retaliation from him—i.e., castration—such acts would deserve. That is the Oedipus complex. In females, Freud thought desire for seduction by the father,[28] guilt about that desire, and preoccupation with penis envy were the recurrent patterns.

Thirdly, the Freudian concepts have inherent in them a means of explaining away every conceivable contrary observation as a disguised derivative of the recurrent patterns; persons who say otherwise are discredited. The symbolism of dreams, slips of the tongue, and neurotic symptoms—as well as art and religion—all exist for the purpose of disguising the recurrent patterns so that some savor of them can get past the "censor" and come to consciousness. Freudian psychoanalysis consists of bringing up painfully repressed material, one sublethal dose at a time, so that little by little it can be made conscious and its potential for producing disturbances in the form of neurotic symptoms can be lessened. Such analysis is an interminable and rather distasteful ritualized process, and expectations for improvement are kept modest.

Those who say that any theory other than the sexual one is worthy of consideration are diagnosed as having such great unanalyzed resistance to its operation in their own lives that the truth remains hidden from them. The less relevant the theory seems to a critic, the more the Freudian becomes convinced that the critic must have horribly intense, and therefore intensely repressed, sexual complexes. If someone doubts the sexual theory, that also proves that he should not be allowed into the high secular priesthood of psychotherapists, since his insight into his own unconscious motives is so deficient. When Freud's prized early disciples, Jung and Alfred Adler, finally rejected the sexual theory, they were also accused of currying the favor of outsiders to the movement, who found the sexual theory scandalous or distasteful.

These artifices should have a familiar ring to readers with an Evangelical background. To the same ends, the dissenter from Christianity is told that he hasn't given himself freely enough, or that he values his sin-cursed, fleshly mind too much, or that God (or Satan) has given him a spirit of blindness because he is not one of the elect, or that, like Simon the Sorcerer, his heart is not right, etc., ad nauseam. The Scriptures equip the believer with the ready-made oriental opprobrium, "The dog *is* turned to his own vomit again; and the sow that was washed to her wallowing in the mire."[29] In Freudianism as in Christianity, considering the content on its merits is declared contrary to the rules of the game. In both, *argumentum ad hominem* is considered proper and is taught to

---

28. Early in his psychotherapy experience, Freud thought that actual early seductions by their fathers were the cause of neurotic symptoms in his female patients. He was horrified by the idea that these might be prevalent, or even usual. Later, he concluded that female patients' desire for such seduction and guilt about the desire—both unconscious—explained his observations. This began a tradition among psychotherapists to discount the possibility of father-daughter incest, except in terribly deprived social backgrounds, and retarded recognition of sexual abuse of children as a social problem. See Jeffrey M. Masson, *The Assault on Truth* (New York: Penguin Books, 1985).
29. 2 Pet. 2:22.

new initiates by example.

The restriction of Freudianism most material to our topic is its understanding of repression. Psychological contents are said to be kept out of conscious awareness by the censoring superego only because they violate taboos that parents in the first instance—and thereafter the rest of society—have inculcated. Those psychological contents all pertain to the erotic and self-destructive drives, or impulses as they are called. The Freudian is open to no other accounting for the difficulty or inability of the individual to get in touch with what is taking place in the inner recesses of his own mind. This means that the mechanism of dissociation, which will loom large in what we are to develop herein, is thought to be only incomplete, or somehow unperfected, repression. Relevant subconscious developments in the analysand that fail to follow the prescribed pattern are ridiculed as "resistance" or ignored. In the Freudian himself, unconscious motivation not fitting the pattern is apt to go unanalyzed and be acted out.[30]

From this black-and-white perspective, Freud, in *Totem and Taboo,* extrapolated to the view that human civilization grew up from primitive bands, in which submitting to social order came from guilt over acts of patricide. The paradox of the individual's drives needing to be repressed so that there can be a civilized society to provide, in turn, for individuals' needs is fundamental to Freudian thinking. Like others of his time, Freud attempted to develop a general view of the social purposes served by religion that all religions would fit.[31]

In Freud's own background, his air of superiority over those who give credence to religious supernaturalism is most noticeable. He came from a secularized, cultivated home, with few and unobtrusive vestiges of Jewish ritual only on special occasions and Passover Eve.[32] He did not think in terms of mystical or supernaturalistic belief being possible for Jews in modern times.[33] As a small child, he had a Catholic nanny, who took him with her to mass. A poignant

30. Before leaving Vienna as a refugee in 1939, Freud released his manuscript *Moses and Monotheism* for publication. By the same means that he claimed proved the Judeo-Christian conception of God to be a disguised way of ventilating the primordial urge to patricide (with its emphasis on guilt, or "sin," and atoning sacrifice), Freud claimed to have proved that Moses was an Egyptian and that the monotheistic religion was an idea that came into being in expression of that nation's political hegemony under Pharaoh Amenhotep IV; another place and people for its followers, including Moses, was needed to transplant it, after a coup against that Pharaoh succeeded. No Freudian analyzes the unconscious motives that go toward the release of such a manuscript by a Jew when the Jewish people are undergoing unprecedented persecution. Rather, many Freudians took the opportunity for a collateral attack on Jung's ideas, by falsely accusing Jung of anti-Semitism, when, in fact, he maintained a low profile in order to conserve the deteriorating position of medical psychology in countries under Nazi control, and he also quietly aided Jewish victims of persecution. See Edmund D. Cohen, *C. G. Jung and the Scientific Attitude* (New York: Philosophical Library, 1975), pp. 99-109.

31. Famous proponents, in this vein, of speculative theories of the origins of religion not materially different from Freud's include Emile Durkheim, Wilhelm Wundt (in his *Völkerpsychologie),* and J. H. Leuba. See Jan de Vries, *Perspectives in the History of Religions,* trans. Kees W. Bolle (Berkeley: University of California Press, 1967), pp. 142-61.

32. Jones, *Sigmund Freud,* p. 350.

33. Cohen, *C. G. Jung,* pp. 13-14.

image in the history of these ideas is little Sigmund, age two and a half, acting out for his parents the Catholic ritual he had seen.[34]

Bringing together Freud's two main statements on the rôle of religion,[35] we can distinguish three religious functions. First, the *explanatory* function, seen as losing its significance irretrievably with the rise of the natural sciences, responds to the need for an articulate explanation of man's origins and purposes. As well as providing purported cosmological facts, religion purports to provide "the humanization of nature . . . . the gods . . . . exorcize the terrors of nature . . . reconcile men to the cruelty of Fate, particularly as it is shown in death, and . . . compensate them for the sufferings and privations which a civilized life in common has imposed on them."[36]

Secondly, the *wish-fulfilling* function has two parts. Staying close to his view that Oedipal ambivalence is all-pervasive, Freud said, "the terrifying impression of helplessness in childhood aroused the need for protection . . . through love—which was provided by the father; and the recognition that this helplessness lasts throughout life made it necessary to cling to the existence of a father, but this time a more powerful one."[37] Also, in a way that detracts somewhat from his teaching about the self-destructive urge, Freud indicated that denial of death, along with denial that blind, banal, ultimately material principles rule our lives, are part of the wish-fulfilling function. The wish for "a benevolent Providence"[38] to watch over us—for our lives to be part of a purposeful context resolving itself in a life after this life—is described as fundamental, although how this can arise from the two drives is not explained. (For a brief moment, Freud wrote like Victor Frankl.) Of fear of punishment in the afterlife, he made practically no mention. It does not appear that he had read Max Weber or knew of the life experiences of the major protagonists of the Reformation.

Thirdly, by the *social regulatory* function, according to Freud, religion serves to extend parental controls against antisocial impulse gratification into adult life. All the emphasis is on guilt as the means for internalization of those controls. Shame, fear of sanctions, and affirmative integrity or desire for good are deemphasized, and they are unclear in their relation to the core ideas.

Summing up his position, Freud wrote:

> The final judgment of science on the religious *Weltanschauung,* then, runs as follows. While the different religions wrangle with one another about which of

34. Jones, *Sigmund Freud,* p. 349.
35. In *The Future of an Illusion,* trans. James Strachey (New York: W. W. Norton, 1961) and *New Introductory Lectures on Psychoanalysis,* Lecture 35, "The Question of a *Weltanschauung.*" In the latter Freud concisely restated his views for a series of lectures delivered in 1933.
36. *Future of an Illusion,* pp. 16–18. The notion that an impersonal universe is intolerable for man, conflicting with a perceived human need for the universe to be rational and to have the property of personality, is a very popular one with modern conservative Christian apologists. It is prominent in the thinking of J. Gresham Machen, Cornelius Van Til, and Carl Henry.
37. Ibid., p. 30.
38. Ibid., p. 19.

them is in possession of the truth, in our view the truth of religion may be altogether disregarded. Religion is an attempt to get control over the sensory world, in which we are placed, by means of the wish-world, which we have developed within as a result of biological and psychological necessities. But it cannot achieve its end. Its doctrines carry with them the stamp of the times in which they originated, the ignorant childhood days of the human race. Its consolations deserve no trust. Experience teaches us that the world is not a nursery. The ethical commands, to which religion seeks to lend its weight, require some other foundation instead, since human society cannot do without them, and it is dangerous to link up obedience to them with religious belief. If one attempts to assign to religion its place in man's evolution, it seems not so much to be a lasting acquisition as a parallel to the neurosis which the civilized individual must pass through on his way from childhood to maturity.[39]

Freud stands quite alone among behavioral scientists as a destructive critic of religion—at least, in print. Even so, he makes some concessions to religious people likely to be offended, carefully pointing out he has not disproved any nondisprovable religious propositions[40] and assuasively distinguishing religious illusions from pathological delusions.[41] His critique retains enough currency that when Hans Küng was invited to give the Terry Lecture at Yale, in 1978, he chose it as his topic and conferred on Freud this fair accolade:

Is one-sidedness the price of genius? Some apparently exaggerated views of Freud, which he links with his psychoanalytical theory, may be of a personal character and are perhaps founded in his own psychological development. But even if in practice he is often very dogmatic and unwilling to make formal corrections and even if he neglects or depreciates what is opposed to his teaching, *he is right in his positive claims* [my italics].[42]

We see the highest level to which Freud's making of positive claims rises in the following:

It may . . . be asked why religion does not put an end to this dispute which is so

---

39. Jones, *Sigmund Freud,* pp. 359–60. (Jones' translation of a passage from "The Question of a *Weltanschauung.*")

40. *Future of an Illusion,* p. 53.

41. Ibid., p. 31. Here, he backpedals briskly, saying that illusions are distinguished from delusions by their relative simplicity, their wish-fulfilling character, and their lack of demonstrable contrariness to reality, i.e., disprovability. But clinical experience, as well as Freud's usages generally, show religious views neither more simple than clinical delusions nor less wish-fulfilling, and delusions lend themselves to rationalizations rendering them nondisprovable just as readily as religious doctrines in the hands of apologists do.

42. *Freud and the Problem of God* (New Haven, Conn.: Yale University Press, 1979), p. 102. The lecture was taken from Küng's larger work, *Does God Exist?,* trans. Edward Quinn (New York: Vintage Books, 1981), p. 312. That work covers the history of proof and disproof of the existence of God as a philosophical problem, and covers depth psychology at considerable length. Küng's mastery of Jung's work (pp. 290 ff.) inclines me generally to trust his scholarship. See also Küng's excellent essay on Feuerbach (pp. 191 ff.).

> hopeless for it by frankly declaring: 'It is a fact that I cannot give you what is commonly called "truth"; if you want that, you must keep to science. But what I have to offer you is something incomparably more beautiful, more consoling and more uplifting than anything you could get from science. And because of that, I say to you that it is true in another, higher sense.' It is easy to find the answer to this. *Religion cannot make this admission because it would involve its forfeiting all its influence on the mass of mankind* [my italics].[43]

Had someone in Freud's time seriously applied that insight to the phenomenon of mainline-church liberalization, the important events that behavioral scientists such as Berger, Glock, and Stark failed to foresee even shortly before they occurred could have been predicted. For once, the behavioral sciences could have called one correctly. From Freud's having had such an insight and from his failure and the failure of his emulators to follow it through, we can anticipate what direction we should go.

What did Freud do right? First, we see that there is an element of truth to the claim that it helps to stand apart from, and avoid giving preferential treatment to, the phenomenon studied. By refusing to apply a double standard, by not applying more lenient intellectual standards to religious truth claims than to others, Freud did a thing for us to emulate. In the case of religion, we learn from others' experience that trying to study the religious phenomenon and defend a kind of religious truth claim at the same time leads in the end to failure at both tasks. Being worried about saying the wrong thing from a position of high visibility, as James and Jung among others must surely have been, does not make for analyses of lasting value.

Secondly, we see that looking beneath surface impressions—not for something great and profound but for something simple and schematic—is productive. We are looking for something *less* than meets the eye. We are looking for things from which all that stuff theologians study serves to divert our attention. Even the Freudian basic, the Oedipal conflict, turns out to be a more clever, elegant answer than the true one. Unlike a person, or even a work of art, the essential aspect of a religion is not its *genius,* defying explication. To be sure, a religion has such an aspect, but its symbolism or synthetic content (in the Kantian sense) turns out to be peripheral to its true purpose, as well as pretentious. When we strip religion of its pretenses, we will find a programmatic and explicit answer to the question of Christianity's hold on people. Many things, if studied analytically or reductively, are oversimplified, distorted, defiled, deprived of some essential dignity that ought to be left intact. But the Evangelical mind-control system is not one of them.

Thirdly, we learn that the religious problem, if present, is not to be severed from the larger context of motives and conflicts of the person. By pointing out that religion, as a ready-made, obsessive-compulsive neurosis, may substitute for other symptomatology of a neurosis and provide for the management and palliation of it, Freud makes a good start. But he did not examine religious

43. "The Question of a *Weltanschauung,*" p. 151.

indoctrination as a possible cause of any problems a psychotherapist is called upon to treat, and he would probably think a psychotherapist considering such a hypothesis was subtly resisting the true, terrible Oedipal core of the problem. Practicing psychotherapists know that extreme religious indoctrinations do cause some of their patients' problems, but they seldom explore the theoretical implications of that insight. It will be part of our task to consider seriously that religious indoctrination might be an important factor in many troubled people seen by psychotherapists, and that the inability of the latter to identify religious problems, or get their patients to open up about them, is a major shortcoming that needs remediation. This shortcoming is, of course, of the same substance as the belief lately held in the behavioral sciences that orthodox religion was disappearing, with no likelihood of a resurgence in view.

What is there in Freud's approach that we should take note to avoid? Above all, its rigidity is to be avoided. When we hear mental-health professionals using Freudian terms but evidently having in mind dynamics other than Freud's Oedipal conflict and erotic and death impulses, it is not that they are unworthily resisting the truth; it is simply that they are using common sense. Hence, we must build up terminology that does not imply something more specific than we really mean to say.

Equally important, the misuse of history is to be avoided. Rigidity and misuse of history are related, in that it is one's rigid theoretical presuppositions that one serves, by tailoring history to fit them.

An instance of the faulty use of history concerning us is Freud's third function, his general statement that the maintenance of social order is always a key issue. Even the most superficial review of the early history of Christianity reveals a situation in which there were abundant external controls imposed by the Roman Empire. Early Christianity advocated maintenance of the status quo regarding those controls, and could occupy itself with other issues precisely because it had neither the need to address that issue nor the opportunity to do so effectively. History puts us on notice that the genius of biblical Christianity is something far removed from protecting society against spontaneous acting out of impulses. To be sure, the transformation of early Christianity into Roman Catholicism brought the church enterprise into the business of upholding social controls. But that transformation got rid of much of the psychological subtlety that had enabled Christianity to increase its following with neither prestige nor social power on its side; this enables it to reassert itself today in contemporary American society despite appearances and common-sense expectations to the contrary.

C. G. Jung

The other major depth psychologist who addressed the religion question was Carl Gustav Jung (1875–1961; pronounced "yoong"). Jung is widely honored, not so widely read, and usually misunderstood when he is read. We will take up some aspects of his thought piecemeal.[44] Although I have long ago ceased to be a follower of his, I still think his work to be the intellectual high-water mark in the psychology world. Yet, among his followers, stagnation and a lack of any real contribution to human welfare has been the rule. Also, he was a key figure in the attempted liberal redefinition of religion, indeed hinging everything on it. The practical failure of that redefinition, with which history now confronts us, and the failure of Jung's psychology to take more firm root are related, and they surely have important issues concealed in them that need to be articulated and studied in the future. We will limit ourselves to Jung's views on religion and then to those of his positive, general-psychology contributions that will be major tools in this work. In contrast to Freud, who had essentially the right specific insight about religion but conceptual tools that do not accommodate the subtleties we need to emphasize, Jung had the wrong insight about religion but the right conceptual tools.

A Protestant and a Swiss with a deep sense of local roots, Jung had a much different background from that of other members of Freud's early circle. Jung was named for his grandfather, who had been an eminent scholar holding the position of rector of the University of Basel. Jung's father possessed a Ph.D. in philology and linguistics and had succumbed to the fate of many an intellectual with no salable profession in the nineteenth century: he had become an overeducated country parson, with doubts and inner conflicts over his religious vocation that he had to keep hidden. Very many of those American mainline pastors who welcomed liberalization, and whose actions reflected that they wanted no part of Bible authenticity, must have had similar stories. But such pastors did not chronicle their inner struggles, and there were no behavioral scientists to interview and study them. Early in his own university-student years, Jung made these sensitive observations about his father:

> It was clear to me that something quite specific was tormenting him, and I suspected that it had to do with his faith. From a number of hints he let fall I was convinced that he suffered from religious doubts. . . . From my attempts at discussion I learned in fact that something of the sort was amiss, for all my questions were met with the same old lifeless theological answers, or with a resigned shrug which aroused the spirit of contradiction in me. . . . He had to quarrel with somebody, so he did it with his family and himself. Why didn't he do it with God, the dark author of all created things, who alone was responsible for all the sufferings of the world?[45]

---

44. Jung has fared particularly poorly at the hands of the academic psychology-textbook writers, who generally leave their readers with the impression that the concept of the collective unconscious is a Lamarckian notion, or else one with racist implications (that the different races have correspondingly different unconscious minds or some such thing). Neither impression is correct. The various books with Calvin S. Hall as author or coauthor are worth noting as exceptions to this trend. Besides my earlier book, *C. G. Jung and the Scientific Attitude,* a good place to start to become familiar with Jung is *Analytical Psychology: Its Theory and Practice* (New York: Vintage Books, 1970), a series of lectures Jung gave in English in 1934.

45. *Memories, Dreams, Reflections,* recorded and edited by Aniela Jaffé, trans. Richard and Clara Winston (New York: Vintage Books, 1965), p. 92.

Although the relationship between father and son was basically a good one and from an early age Jung understood and appreciated that his father's irritability and surliness were accompanied by tolerance and, within his limitations, helpfulness, there were never open or candid conversations between father and son about the father's problems. Jung had read everything in his father's library and was able to reconstruct the effect of the theological learning of the day on his father, from its effect on himself. After spending much time in Biedermann's *Christliche Dogmatik,* then a standard work on Protestant doctrine, and trying to harmonize the various definitions set out in it, the fifteen-year-old Jung concluded it was "nothing but fancy drivel . . . whose sole aim was to obscure the truth. . . . I was . . . once more seized with pity for my father, who had fallen victim to this mumbo-jumbo."[46] "He could not even defend himself against the ridiculous materialism of the psychiatrists. This, too, was something one had to believe, just like theology, only in the opposite sense. I felt more certain than ever that both of them [i.e., materialism and theology] lacked epistemological criticism as well as experience."[47]

At a very early age, Jung began to have the experiences that would shape his views on religion and guide him away from acceptance of conventional religious formulations. When he was three or four years old, Jung dreamed that he walked down a stair from a meadow into an underground cavern containing a magnificently decorated throne room. Sitting on the throne, in regal splendor, was a phallus as big as a tree trunk, pointing upward. For our purposes, it will have to suffice to say that this was a primitive religious symbol that would, in the first instance, lend some additional ring of truth to Freud's sexual theory when Jung would first encounter it, and also force Jung to look beyond conventional Christianity's sharp distinction between spiritual, sacred things on the one hand, and earthly, profane things on the other. Neither with his father nor with Freud, who would become something of a father figure to him, would Jung be able to share such a dream as this.[48]

For a time, when he was about sixteen years old, Jung was preoccupied with thoughts of God sitting on his throne and a beautiful cathedral. When these thoughts would come to mind, Jung would become filled with terror, at the intimation of another thought following from these, so terrible that thinking it might be blasphemy against the Holy Ghost, for which there can be no forgiveness.[49] He was in a state of agitation about this for a number of days, lost sleep over it, and would awaken, resisting the coming to consciousness of the offending forbidden thought. Then, thinking that a good God would not allow such a strong temptation to think something without wanting it thought, Jung confronted it:

> I gathered all my courage, as though I were about to leap forthwith into hell-fire,

---

46. Ibid., p. 59.
47. Ibid., p. 94.
48. Ibid., p. 11–13.
49. Matt. 12:22–32; Mark 3:28–30; and Luke 12:10.

> and let the thought come. I saw before me the cathedral, the blue sky. God sits on His golden throne, high above the world—and from under the throne an enormous turd falls upon the sparkling new roof, shatters it, and breaks the walls of the cathedral asunder.[50]

As Jung matured, this and many related impressions meant that a radical distinction had to be made between the mystery of God and poor, human conventional religions. Like Kant, about whose influence on Jung we shall have more to say, Jung came to conceive of God in such ways as his own intellectual growth, including his extensive research in comparative religion, indicated God's nature to be. As with Kant, that conception had no more than incidental similarity to the God of the Bible. The reader will remember that Tillich's conception of symbols and the never-ending transformation of God as the symbol of ultimate reality are derived from Jung, who also took seeking after God to be a symbol for the unfolding of one's own personality, including that part that partakes of the infinite. Jung accepted only so much of Feuerbach's formulation as called for the attributes of God also to be the projected attributes of man, but saw the existence of God as necessary in order for man to have such attributes to project. This is to say that through the noumenal realm, in the Kantian sense, man has a relation to the reality beyond the time-space-causality apparent world of his senses, has a relation to all other human beings who have part of their personality unconsciously extending down into the noumenal realm also, and has a relation to the mystery of God.

Jung saw the personal religious quest of the mature individual during the second half of life (from about age thirty-five on) as life's true main issue. The religious symbols that one finds meaningful, or that one creates himself, and the rituals and expressive activities that enable one to get in touch with something deep within are thought, in Jungian circles, to be the things a truly mature, "individuated" person will make his main objects of concern. Although Jung's writings on the individual religious quest depict the "individuated" seeker after inner truth as someone who has successfully coped with the economic and family demands of the external surroundings,[51] Jungians turn out to be escapists and to regard their fellow humans and civic questions with aesthetically superior disdain.[52]

---

50. *Memories, Dreams, Reflections,* p. 39.

51. Jung's idea that the relationship of the religious quest to life's more mundane strivings was hierarchical, with the individual's energies turning to the higher striving after the lower has been accomplished (or never having the opportunity to seek the higher level because there has been failure or blocking in the lower), was translated by Abraham Maslow into the doctrine of self-actualization, or seeking after "peak experiences." This doctrine did not correspond to the empirical data available to Maslow, and empirical work following him generally failed to verify his key premise that creature needs, when they had once been satisfied, fell away and gave rise to interest in stimuli not implicated in the satisfaction of creature needs, stimuli in and for themselves. Maslow was derelict in failing to acknowledge his intellectual debt to Jung. See Cohen, *C. G. Jung,* pp. 122-24.

52. I studied at the Jung Institute in Zürich, Switzerland in the winter of 1970-71 and described the experience in my book. Ibid., pp. 138-53. Of the people I met there, I wrote, "Analysis was a matter of connoisseurship rather than utility with them. Instead of being a means to a more effective life, analysis *was* life for them. They did not read newspapers, or follow anything that went on in the outside world. They prided themselves on putative superior individuation, and dis-

In Jung's view, the ultimately religious journey from immaturity to maturity and from inner confusion and chaos to inner differentiation and character comes about through the synthesis of opposites. A psychic state or condition at a particular time, expressible in symbols, will finally combine with another, from the unconscious, that is in some way its opposite, and a higher synthesis will emerge. Shortly, we will develop some technical terms for describing that process. Right now, we are concerned with the rôle of Christianity in Jung's thinking, keeping in mind that Jung's God had as much disdain for human churchly conventions as Jung's followers did, for people who live in the here-and-now. The following is the quotation I think most representative of Jung's views on Christianity:

> All opposites are of God, therefore man must bend to this burden; and in so doing he finds that God in his "oppositeness" has taken possession of him, incarnated himself in him. He becomes a vessel filled with divine conflict. We rightly associate the idea of suffering with a state in which the opposites violently collide with one another, and we hesitate to describe such a painful experience as being "redeemed." Yet it cannot be denied that the great symbol of the Christian faith, the Cross, upon which hangs the suffering figure of the Redeemer, has been emphatically held up before the eyes of Christians for nearly two thousand years. This picture is completed by the two thieves, one of whom goes down to hell, the other into paradise. One could hardly imagine a better representation of the "oppositeness" of the central Christian symbol. Why this inevitable product of Christian psychology should signify redemption is difficult to see, except that the conscious recognition of the opposites, painful though it may be at the moment, does bring with it a definite feeling of deliverance. It is on the one hand a deliverance from the distressing state of dull and helpless unconsciousness, and on the other hand a growing awareness of God's oppositeness, in which man can participate if he does not shrink from being wounded by the dividing sword which is Christ. Only through the most extreme and most menacing conflict does the Christian experience deliverance into divinity, always provided that he does not break, but accepts the burden of being marked out by God.[53]

The theme of pain and tension attending psychological growth or "individuation" is very characteristic of Jung, and his extensive writing on the ancient literary theme of alchemy gave him the opportunity to express himself at great length on it. What should be noted here is that Jung made no concession at all to the Bible's own declarations about its meaning and import. The whole Christian symbolism becomes a way of expressing a process of personal growth that is unashamedly individualistic, applying all its emphasis and pertinence to life this side of the grave. The questions of the reality of God, apart from the humans who construct him through projection, and of another life beyond the

---

dained those less withdrawn than themselves as benighted and unconscious. To me, they seemed like refugees from reality, people for whom life's sorrows must have been overwhelming for them to withdraw so completely. . . . It was a bad imitation of Thomas Mann's *The Magic Mountain,* or Solzhenitsyn's *Cancer Ward."* Pp. 146–47.

53. *Answer to Job* in *Psychology and Religion: West and East,* trans. R. F. C. Hull, 2nd ed. (Princeton University Press, 1969), pp. 416-17, par. 65.

grave become almost immaterial. The religious quest for personal growth takes the foreground as the most exciting thing we can have in view, regardless of which way those questions are answered.

The process of individuation meant, for Jung, moving toward the divine nature, a process that can never be perfected, always leaving some still finer nuance to be experienced. In the person undergoing individuation, the divine or godly nature becomes relatively less unconscious, hence the characteristic Christian feature of God needing to take on a human nature as man moves toward a godly nature. In the climactic passage from *Answer to Job,* Jung's most significant work on Judeo-Christian religion, the rôles of God and man almost become reversed:

> Besides his love of mankind a certain irascibility is noticeable in Christ's character, and, as is often the case with people of emotional temperament, a manifest lack of self-reflection. There is no evidence that Christ ever wondered about himself, or that he ever confronted himself. To this rule there is only one significant exception—the despairing cry from the Cross: "My God, my God, why hast thou forsaken me?"[54] Here his human nature attains divinity; at that moment God experiences what it means to be mortal man and drinks to the dregs what he made his faithful servant Job suffer. Here is given the answer to Job, and, clearly, this supreme moment is as divine as it is human, as "eschatological" as it is "psychological."[55]

From the foregoing, a few highlights from a large, intricate, detailed body of work in the same vein published by Jung, we can see that liberal religious intellectuals like Tillich had good reason to think that a radical redefinition of the Christian symbols for modern man could take place—if it were not already *in* place in the form of Jung's books—awaiting a new crop of seminarians well enough prepared in psychology to sort it out. From our vantage point two decades or so later, we see that almost nobody sorted out Jung's religious views, and we appreciate a bit more deeply the disappointment that came with the deterioration of the institutions that had these futuristic high hopes. I, personally, was one of the tiny handful who became adept at Jungian lore. After failing to observe in myself, in the Jungians with whom I became acquainted, or in the case histories and other data presented what I could be satisfied to call "individuation," I ended up in orthodox Christianity. Now, with such a past, I come with a disrespectfully reductionistic psychology-of-religion theory. What happened?

In the first place, instead of being seen by the liberal clergy as one alternative approach among others, each with its different respective implications, Jung's views caused, or at least worsened, conceptual confusion as to what historic Christianity is. In the spiritual transformation of the individual through the synthesis of opposites within the psyche, we can see a refined variation of the American Evangelical notion of mind-cure, chronicled by James, of the

54. Can Jung mean here that the distress expressed by Jesus in the Garden of Gethsemane was not significant?
55. Ibid., p. 408, par. 647.

conversion experience liberating a new creature lacking the negative features of the old creature. In hindsight, we can see that the opportunity probably existed—and may exist still in liberal or early transitional religious circles—to formulate a workable religious doctrine of curative personal transformation with some purported biblical justification, parallel to Wesley's doctrine of philanthropy to the poor and afflicted. But instead, liberal clergy were all too eager to think of Jung as one of their own, not as an outsider the emulation of whom would require difficult changes.

Jung himself would encourage the liberal clergy, answering, when asked, that he considered himself a professing Christian. He meant by that, in large part, Christian in the sense of Gnosticism, one of the variations in understanding the teachings of Jesus that existed in the first century. The choice of the particular writings we know as the Bible placed Gnosticism outside the Christian establishment and made it a heresy, regarded as subversive, persecuted, and suppressed. We shall have more to say about Gnosticism in the next chapter, letting it suffice for now to point out that interpreting Jesus' statements about the next life as contemplating something other than tangible future menace was what the early church found so subversive in Gnosticism. Jung would praise Gnosticism when the opportunity occurred, and he wore a Gnostic signet ring, visible in many photos and a couple of oil paintings of him. To the Bible purist, profession of Christianity and praise of Gnosticism together are an offensive combination. Placing Jung in perspective, Hans Küng described him as "in principle friendly toward" Christianity and asked the rhetorical question, "But how far does this friendliness extend?"[56]

From Jung's violently negative early reaction to orthodox Christianity, we receive the clue that he would make of religion something psychologically so different from orthodox Christianity that the two could not coexist. The mental habits going with the one would conflict with those of the other, so that to do the one, a person would have to unlearn the habits of the other. The leading psychological feature of the personal religious quest, as seen by Jung, is an attitude of inward-directed openness, a kind of letting go that permits whatever is stirring in the inner recesses of the mind to have its own way enough so that the conscious mind can get in touch with it. What rises up from within is not to be permitted to be drowned out by what comes in from outside. Jungian religiosity is contemplative and meditative.

As we develop our catalogue of the mental habits and attitudes that make up orthodox Christianity, we shall see that there is enmity between it and genuine openness to the unconscious. Against the reasonable expectation of the latter-day liberal Christian, namely, that our modern state of psychological understanding could allow such an approach to succeed despite the failure of Gnosticism in ancient times, we must set over our recent data indicating the breathtaking superiority of orthodox Christianity over liberal religion and secular substitutes for religion at gaining adherents and holding onto them. In the relative sociological vitality of orthodox Christianity, we witness first-century

56. *Does God Exist?*, p. 293.

history repeating itself! Underlying the similar outward forms and symbols of liberal and orthodox Christianity, there must be very different respective psychological processes. And one important unfortunate characteristic they both have in common—the tendency to withdraw from philanthropy and service to others as religious projects—has different causes in each.

Jung elevated the playing of his particular kind of Gnostic mind-game to the position of paramount human endeavor, superior to any other. To the Jungian, a person whose most abiding, long-range interest in life is in some other art or science is inferior, his concern "idolatrous," in Tillichian terms. The failure in practice of Jung's sort of religious quest to be relevant or productive in any significant number of lives, the lack of rôle-models from it that one would want to emulate, prove Jung wrong in this respect.

Does Jung's overvaluing of the religious proclivity in human nature vitiate his contribution as a whole? I contend that it does not. There is nothing necessary or essential to Jung's general psychodynamic contribution in his religious theory. If anything, the distaste in mental-health circles for what was seen as tiresome fixation on a passé topic, on a problem thought to be on its way to self-resolution through the disappearance of supernaturalistic religion in civilized society as the twentieth century waned, had a dampening effect on interest in Jung's psychology overall. Because I now see that Jung's religious theory is not integral to his work as a whole but rather is an idiosyncrasy of his and of those personally attracted to him, *I propose to sever the religious theory from the rest of Jung's psychology.* It has been with this end in view that I have gotten the religious theory "out of the way" before setting out the Jungian terms and didactic models I will employ. I deliberately seek to instill in the reader (and in myself) the habit of thinking of them separately.

The best way to unfold Jung's substantive psychodynamic ideas is chronologically. His ideas grew out of earlier contributions, more familiar than his own to today's Anglo-American reader, and of course the former makes more sense in context. It is important to remember that Jung's psychology is very much a product of the cultural and intellectual life of the German-speaking world that died and has not truly come back to life since the Hitler-era poisoning of the soil where it grew. Creatively, Jung's career lends itself to division into three phases. The first extended from his earliest psychiatric work before the turn of the century to his break with Freud in the days leading up to World War I; it centered on the concept of the psychological complex. Jung briefly called his own school "complex psychology," before settling on the rubric "analytical psychology." After the break with Freud, Jung experienced a period of unproductivity and relative inactivity known to his followers as his "fallow period." Credible rumors have it that Jung was psychotic during this time. The second phase began with the publication of *Psychological Types,* in 1920, and overlapped with the succeeding phase, lasting until approximately 1948; it consisted of development and refinement of the structure of the psyche and the psychological types. The third phase had a very long prelude and could be seen taking shape in the book *Symbols of Transformation,* later extensively revised, but first published in 1912, providing the Freudians with something tangible to ridicule. Studying symbolic content—the archetypes—as opposed to personality dynamics characterized the last phase of Jung's work; this fostered his reputation as an apostle of withdrawn hypereccentricity.

At the turn of the century, after doing his Doctor of Medicine dissertation on the case of a young girl who was ostensibly a psychic medium through whom spirits of the dead spoke, Jung worked with seriously disturbed mental patients at Burghölzli Hospital in Zürich, under the kindly and moderate leadership of Eugen Bleuler, who authored, in succeeding editions, the leading textbook in pre-World War I psychiatry. In those days, there was extensive psychiatric activity in France, where hypnotism was used to relieve symptoms caused by unconscious memories of catastrophic past experiences not consciously remembered by the individual exhibiting the symptoms. In the winter of 1902-03, Jung took a leave of absence to study under the leading French depth psychiatrist, Pierre Janet (1859-1947)[57] in Paris.

A concept of Janet's that proves to be indispensable is psychic energy, derived from Henri Bergson's *élan vital.* Because of Freud, the habit of thinking of psychic energy, or libido, as sexual in character, is strong. Within the medical profession, "level of libido" remains a euphemism in speaking of the sexual drive, or absence of it.[58] It is absolutely crucial for our purposes to think of libido as having the widest conceivable range of possible expressions and characters. To make the concept more clear and exclusive is to falsify the underlying reality. Janet thought of consciousness as tension in a field composed of psychic energy and of neurosis as a lowering of the level of that tension, as *abaissement de niveau mental.* For Jung, as for us, this French expression is handy for describing a situation where a human adaptation attempt is less than thoughtful or rational, and yet does not exhibit a definite neurotic pattern or mechanism we can identify.

Psychic energy in the Jungian sense does not behave like physical energy, and is only indirectly related to the metabolism or physical energetics of the human body. Where the laws predicting the resultant of physical forces are mechanical, mathematical, and causal, psychic energy is immanent, purposive,

57. Janet's work contained a wealth of seminal ideas that have surfaced repeatedly in the subsequent history of psychology. Janet called the represssed content giving rise to the neurotic symptom the "unconscious fixed idea." The seminal idea that became Adler's concept of compensation for (or overcoming of) feelings of inferiority, Janet had called *sentiments d'incomplétude.* The faculty of adaptation to surroundings through attention, Janet called *fonction du réel.* Janet's work lacked the crispness and clarity of Freud's, and the French depth psychologists never clearly turned away from hypnotism toward the talking or "insight" treatment, as the Jewish German-speakers did. Such things make all the difference in determining what body of work posterity will favor. Late in life Janet was bitter toward Freud, accusing him of usurping recognition rightfully belonging to Janet.

58. There is still considerable prevalence of the *idée fixe* in the mental-health professions that lack of strong or persistent sexual drive or interest necessarily indicates neurotic conflict needing remedy. But both human experience and observation of the restricted and chemically predetermined rôle of sexuality in nonhuman species point to no more fundamentality of sexuality in the human makeup than many another trait. The importance of sexuality in the human makeup admits to wide individual differences.

and teleological in its behavior. Its quantity is not fixed, and it is not conserved; nor are the ratios of the products of its conversion predictable. The most obvious consequence of psychic energy is application of the person's capabilities to the environment. When a person is motivated, has drive, concentrates his thought and feeling persistently, and accomplishes something, we witness what Jung called the progression of psychic energy. Adaptation to the environment is the concomitant of the progressive phase of the flow of psychic energy. The Freudian notions that psychic energy is invested in objects (animate and inanimate) in the surroundings and that grief, sense of loss, feeling drained in a very real way of one's psychic energy are the concomitants of loss or destruction of an object in which psychic energy has been invested (i.e., to which libido has been cathected, in Freudian terms) remain useful and valid in my view.

Psychic energy cannot always progress. The regressive phase of the flow of libido concerns us, since it is necessary for conditions to be created allowing libido to flow progressively in its turn, and the regressive phase is implicated in those psychopathological conditions that interfere with progressive flow. Regression occurs for some ultimately adaptive reasons. The field of psychic energy becomes differentiated through the formation of symbols, as we have covered in our discussion of Tillich. We take in fact-data from the senses, as well as our subjective and affective responses to them, by symbolization. It is in the regressive, internalizing phase that all these "inputs" are digested into a form that is "meaningful" for us, that structures our relation to our situation so that progressive flow toward it can take place. The regressive phase allows rest and regeneration to take place: sleep and dreaming are regressive-phase activities.[59] The regeneration of libido after the loss of an object in which quantities of it have been invested will naturally tip the balance toward the regressive phase, drying up the resources needed for progress for a time.

Regression also occurs when progression is blocked. One condition that blocks progression is failure or inadequacy of the person's adaptive mechanisms—the psychological functions we shall come to presently—to cope with the external situation presented. We find that division of psychic energy, apportionment of it to purposes that do not complement each other, is what all pathological conditions intrerfering with progressive flow of libido have in common. This is where the mechanism of dissociation and the apportionment of psychic energy into complexes come into play.

When Jung was working toward his understanding of complexes, he had returned from France and had been most impressed by the early writings of Freud, whom he would not meet for some years. During this time, around 1905, Jung worked in and was a pioneer contributor to some techniques familiar

59. In an interesting recent theoretical thrust, directed to the well-known empirical findings that rapid-eye-movement (REM) sleep corresponds to dreaming activity, biologists Francis Crick and Graeme Mitchison, in "The Function of Dream Sleep," *Nature* 304 (July 1983), pp. 111–14, speculate that dreaming is implicated in discarding superfluous mental content, or "tuning up" the memory residue from sensations coming in. Such an idea agrees with the generally unfavorable experience with psychotherapeutic approaches turning attention too focally toward dreams.

to the present-day American mental-health professional. The first of these was the word-association test, where a list of words is read and the subject is asked to respond spontaneously to each one with another word. Previous investigators had used such a test, concentrating on the content of the responses. Jung noticed that the reaction times revealed more than the responses themselves, and he learned to look for correspondences among those words that produced hesitation or blocking before a response was given. Often, this would provide a clue to what the subject was unconsciously in conflict about, and more than occasionally it brought to light some transgression about which the subject had a bad conscience. From this, Jung moved to measuring rate of respiration, heart rate, and galvanic skin response (GSR) and found that questioning the subject on topics of bad conscience produced disturbances in these. So, in this early experimental phase, Jung became one of the fathers of the present-day lie detector; that device has changed little since Jung lost interest in it.

These experimental researches, and certain experiences with individual cases, such as the supposititious medium about whom Jung had written his dissertation, pointed to organized centers of activity within a personality, not consciously known to the ego-personality and working at cross-purposes to it. Such an unconscious energetic center within the personality becomes so distinctly separated or dissociated from the ego-personality because it has meaning or represents an attitude incompatible with the conscious attitude.

> A complex, then, is a grouping of energy-laden psychic contents which are compatible and belong together. It has a coherent set of values and objectives (e.g., its feeling tone). If it is prominent enough to include a sizable share of the personality's energy, it takes on a personality of its own, and possibly even its own consciousness. Thus the ego-personality is itself a complex, and the most important one. When a person is particularly complex-ridden, the energy available to the ego-personality is reduced. A neurotic person's symptoms can be better understood as the manifestations of complexes (splinter personalities) competing with the ego-personality for control.[60]

The relationship of the complexes within the individual psyche lends itself to the analogy of a parliament. In a normal person, there is a majority party (the ego-personality) governing and a relatively docile, loyal opposition (the complexes). The opposition creates minor disturbances from time to time and gains some concessions. In a neurotic person, there is also a majority party, but the opposition is disruptive and combative, largely because the majority party has been too narrow and intransigent, not allowed the minority a hearing, and made too few concessions. In the schizophrenic,[61] no party is able to form a

---

60. Cohen, *C. G. Jung,* pp. 8–9. Footnote omitted. Definitions of terms, glossed over here for the sake of brevity, can be found in that work.

61. The term *schizophrenic* typically has a meaning for the general reader that is quite wrong from the standpoint of the mental-health professions. Schizophrenia is a condition where the personality is more aptly described as shattered or fragmented than "split," and distorted ideation immediately identifiable by one familiar with it when it is encountered is present. A personality with two or more stable and well-defined disparate aspects, and lacking "schizy" ideation, would be described as hysterical rather than schizophrenic.

government and confusion reigns. This is to say, there must be cooperation between the ego-personality and the rest of the personality for progressive flow to occur.

It will be noted that in this model there is no equivalent to the reified agent of the superego or "censor" of the Freudian model. Because the complexes, although dissociated from conscious awareness, are part of a field of energy where every part is interrelated with every other part, it makes little difference whether we think in terms of the ego-personality expelling psychic contents it finds incompatible, the psychic contents withdrawing of themselves, or the complexes attracting them away. The features of psychic contents making them incompatible with one another are as varied as the meanings that symbols can convey, and it is not only transgression against taboos instilled from without that triggers psychic contents to become dissociated. That which is dissociated is always in some way a matter of bad conscience to the person, but conscience includes a variety of processes, ranging from a transcendental appreciation of right and wrong that is universal and innate to conventions that have been instilled from without that have no moral or taboo connotations at all and that lose their dissociation-triggering (or alternatively, anxiety-arousing) power after ever so little lucid reflection about them.

Looking at the psyche in terms of complexes, dissociation becomes the root ego-defense mechanism, and voluntary suppression of mental contents, repression of those contents that are taboo to the conscious attitude, and convenient forgetting of what does not agree with the conscious attitude are variations of it. The two purposes of banishment of mental contents from consciousness that the general-psychology lore of ego-defense mechanisms boils down to—(1) avoiding negative emotions that accompany the mental contents if they are in consciousness, and (2) avoiding confronting incongruity or conflict in attitudes[62]—turn out to be equal in importance; the tacit mental habit of rating the first more fundamental than the second is an important one for us to break. Subtle strategies for managing dissociation are among the most important features of the Evangelical mind-control system. (This point is crucial for understanding the following chapters.)

Having brought his own work this far, Jung could accommodate his views to those of Freud, for the relatively brief period of his life when he was Freud's disciple. After the break with Freud, and the "fallow period" which may, in

62. To the psychology-oriented reader, the management of incongruity of attitudes will call to mind Leon Festinger's cognitive-dissonance hypotheses, where the human tentency to make attitudes consistent will cause one attitude to be distorted to accommodate another. A typical demonstration is the comparison of one group of subjects paid well for performing an onerous task with another group paid badly for performing the same task. The badly paid subjects come to misperceive the task as interesting and enjoyable, ostensibly to make their continuing to perform it seem reasonable to themselves, while those who can justify their perseverance in the task by high pay correctly perceive it as boring. What should be noted is that the reduction of cognitive dissonance by distorting an attitude or perception is an alternative self-deceiving, ego-defensive strategy to dissociation, which may be understood as banishment of the *relation* between the dissonant attitudes from consciousness; those two strategies are to be distinguished from the more difficult activity of radically reordering attitudes and actions, to make sense.

part, be understood as a time of regeneration of the psychic energy invested in the Freudian circle and cut off, Jung developed his ideas on the structure of the psyche. We have mentioned how consciousness is necessarily a process that separates mental contents; it must put many things aside while it is focusing, concentrating, and working upon a few mental contents. Mental contents that are totally interrelated and interdependent at subconscious levels need, for the sake of adaptation to surroundings, to be perceived and handled as separate. Naïve consciousness exaggerates separateness and underrates interrelatedness. It is easy for us to see causal relation, but requires more sophistication for us to see organic interrelation and interdependence. Historically, the German-speakers were better than others at devising psychologies accounting for the organic interrelation of psychological processes, and our underlying theme that the Nazi-era catastrophe has had a crucial indirect effect, impoverishing our Anglo-American psychology in this regard, should be kept in mind.

The entire second phase of Jung's work was devoted to studying the interrelatedness of seemingly separate phenomena in the psyche. Unlike the emphasis on dissociation, the specifics of Jung's relational concepts are not crucial to understanding the Evangelical mind-control system, and the coming chapters could, substantially, stand without them.

The most important complex, and the only one we have specifically treated so far, is the *ego-personality*. That hyphenated term was used because the complex to which it refers does not coincide with the "ego" or "self" in some other psychologies. The ego-personality is the person's awareness of himself, including his memories and knowledge, at a particular time. It is an entity that changes, grows, and becomes more differentiated with maturity. The ego-personality is not to be confused with the *persona,* the image or mask presented to the outside world. How much the ego-personality is identified with the persona differs from individual to individual; we shall shortly cover some personality attributes affecting that identification. These complexes are essentially conscious.

As we move into the unconscious reaches, it is important to note that the relationship of unconscious elements to conscious ones is primarily *compensatory*. Compensation is as important within the psyche as causality is in the apparent world of the senses exterior to us. Unconscious elements tend to embody psychological opposites to the conscious attitude. The whole point of paying attention to dreams and spontaneous manifestations from the unconscious is that these are compensatory to the conscious attitude, containing what the conscious attitude is deficient in, or has been neglecting. The ebb and flow of psychic energy will enrich the ego-personality and make it more complete as the individual matures.

The unconscious complex of that which, from the standpoint of the conscious attitude, is related to bad conscience—treacherous, inferior and sinister—is the *shadow*. In dreams and fantasy, the shadow is personified as an inferior or sinister figure of the same sex as the person producing it. Unreasonable dislike of others and out-group prejudice result from projection of the shadow, and insight into our own inferior side, so that such projections may be recognized for what they are and withdrawn, is important in relieving such prejudice.[63] A more deeply unconscious complex, thought to occur more in the advanced stages of Jungian analysis, is the *anima* (in a male) or *animus* (in a female). Occurring in dreams and fantasy as an opposite-sex figure with mysterious, exotic, magnetic qualities, this complex represents those qualities that are missing from the conscious attitude, and is implicated in the growth and development of the ego-personality. Since it represents psychological opposites to the qualities strongly present and differentiated in the conscious attitude, it is personified as a figure of the opposite sex to the person to whom it belongs.[64] Projection of the animus or anima accounts for romantic infatuation, and such projections have to be understood for what they are and withdrawn, to avoid having them get in the way of a truly loving relation to a mate. Still deeper is the *Self.* (This term is used in a much different way than other psychologies and symbolic-interactionist sociology use it, and I have found it convenient to capitalize it when writing about it.) The Self represents the final complete quintessence toward which the person is growing, and it is often represented by a child or some abstract personification in dreams and fantasy. There is an affinity between the Self and the God-idea, and the personal religious quest and actualization of the Self (i.e., individuation) are substantially the same thing to a Jungian.

The relations of the qualities embodied in the complexes are brought out by the psychological types. Before Jung, many philosophers had been interested in opposites dichotomies in the human personality. Among these were tough-mindedness versus tender-mindedness and healthy-minded versus sick-soul religion, studied by James. (One can see much influence of James on Jung, both in dichotomies and in ideas on the nature and purpose of consciousness. The influence of Anglo-American and continental thinkers on each other was a two-way street.) Keeping in mind that logical or philosophical opposites are not necessarily the same as psychological opposites, Jung sought to make prominent those pairs of opposites he thought had been most useful in thinking about, comparing, and contrasting the cases in his clinical experience.

Jung's best known dichotomy is *introversion* versus *extraversion.* These terms have become a part of the language, and since the way they are popularly

---

63. The closest thing to an original didactic insight in the Bible is psychological, not philosophical or moral. Jesus comes tantalizingly close to the seminal concept of projection as it is known to modern depth psychology: "And why beholdest thou the mote that is in thy brother's eye, but considerest not the beam that is in thine own eye? Or how wilt thou say to thy brother, Let me pull out the mote out of thine eye; and, behold, a beam *is* in thine own eye? Thou hypocrite, first cast out the beam out of thine own eye; and then shalt thou see clearly to cast out the mote out of thy brother's eye." Matt. 7:3–5. Luke 6:41–42 is a parallel account.

64. Note that a Jungian explanation of homosexuality would be overidentification of the ego-personality with the anima or animus, so that the persona rather than it is romantically projected. This would agree with the wittiness and creative access to their own unconscious that is the style of some homosexuals. For such a person, the homosexuality would be fundamental to his personality makeup, and the effect of a "treatment" regime aimed at instilling heterosexuality would be detrimental. It is possible that such a pattern and homosexuality that is merely reactive or due to impeded maturation are fundamentally different types, and the latter would experience transition to heterosexuality as a concomitant of psychological growth.

used is correct, our treatment of them can be brief. The extravert typically feels understimulated by his surroundings and moves toward what is exterior to him, to increase the amount of stimulation he derives from it. His style involves the outward flow of psychic energy, and is empathic. The introvert typically feels overstimulated by his surroundings, and withdraws from them to reduce the stimulation received from them. His style emphasizes abstraction rather than empathy, and he is apt to crave to exercise control over his surroundings as the extravert does not.

The other important dichotomies are the four functions, which can be diagrammed thus:

Thinking

Sensation + Intuition

Feeling

By *thinking,* Jung meant mental activity involving an objective viewpoint, dealing with matters exterior, separate, and apart from individual intents and purposes. It includes logical deduction, ratiocination, induction, judgment, and comparison. *Feeling,* the psychological opposite of thinking, means subjective mental activity, dealing with matters exterior according to the individual's intents and purposes, i.e., valuing them according to their goodness or badness, preciousness or worthlessness, pleasantness or unpleasantness. Feeling and emotion are different matters, and Jung did not study emotions apart from the specific situations in which they occur. Thinking and feeling are called the *rational* functions because they both are kinds of *reflection.*

To say that a person is a thinking type indicates that his most conscious, best-differentiated mode of dealing with what is exterior is by thinking; such a person is least differentiated in the area of feeling, and is given to extremes and sudden lurches in his loves and hates. It would be characteristic of a thinking-type man to become intensely infatuated with a woman who evokes the projection of primitive contents in his subconscious, like the professor who is ruined by his love for the cabaret girl in the film *The Blue Angel.* If he becomes neurotic, the symptoms of the thinking type are characteristically in the area of feeling, such as confusion about how to relate to persons and objects. Existential neurosis is exclusively the province of the thinking type.

The unpremeditated, feeling-type contemplation of other persons and objects is subjective, and in a differentiated way, full of finer nuances, developing without sudden lurches. One thinks of a housewife or someone who is very devoted to some group or cause as feeling types. Obsessive thoughts, thoughts out of control would be characteristic neurotic symptoms of a feeling type. Jung thought of the French people, with their exceptional refinement of manners, food, wine, and expression of emotion, as having a feeling-type national character.

Sensation and intuition are called the *irrational* functions because they are both kinds of *perception.* The explicit data of perception, those of which one is focally aware,[65] are received through the sensation function. A sensation-type person is one well adapted to the reality of things around him, who deals in facts and prefers stable, orderly surroundings. The tacit, subliminal data of perception are received through the intuition function. An intuition-type person distinguishes himself when there are insufficient facts. He responds adaptively, as if he could see around corners, despite the ambiguity of a situation. If he has artistic proclivities (the intuition type does not necessarily have them), it will be the sensual expression that fascinates him because that expression partakes of sensation, which for him is underdifferentiated and problematical. The executive who is able to make important decisions despite the absence of satisfactory criteria and the drifter who easily copes with—and needs—a constant change of surroundings are examples of intuition types.

Each individual (in addition to his location on the introversion-extraversion dimension) has one of the four functions most developed and most characteristically used as the channel for progressive flow, the *main* function. The opposite or reciprocal function is his *inferior* function, manifesting itself in contrast or as an undercurrent, the function closest to the unconscious and the one implicated in the assimilation of unconscious contents to consciousness. The sense wherein the inferior function is inferior is its poor response to voluntary or conscious control; there can be prodigiously effective action on the surroundings through the inferior function, but only spontaneously, intermittently, and unpredictably. The one function cannot long be observed without the inextricable supporting context of the other.

At every hand, in Jung's psychology, we encounter a field of psychic energy becoming differentiated in some manner, yielding contents, symbols, complexes, all intimately interrelated and developing toward a final state of completeness immanent in the entire field, or being blocked in some way in that development. Are there characteristic, consistent regularities in these patterns in the flux? That is what the third phase of Jung's work was about.

In his work with patients, Jung was fascinated by symbolic content that the patients produced, relevant to their problems so that insight into it could help them practically, that matched in minute detail the symbolic content produced by others and in obscure books and art works. A few times, Jung reported very detailed patient productions that exactly matched obscure, unpublished ancient documents to which Jung could be positive his patients had had no exposure.[66] Similar human experiences produce similar symbols, across time and across cultures. Symbols are universal, and much of our response to them is innate. That there are universal symbols that arise in the same way because the human psyche retains the same structure across races, nations, cultures, and time is, in

65. Sensation and intuition correspond respectively to focal awareness and peripheral or tacit awareness as described by Michael Polanyi, *Personal Knowledge* (New York: Harper Torchbooks, 1964), pp. 55–65.
66. Cohen, *C. G. Jung,* pp. 29–33.

brief, the hypothesis of the *collective unconscious.* The collective unconscious is sharply different from the *personal unconscious,* which is the repository of forgotten personal memories. What should be noted is that the process whereby a human experience interacts with the prestructuring of the psyche to produce a universal symbol, capable of communicating the experience to other humans with similarly prestructured psyches, is much different from the process whereby an experience or memory is registered but not positioned so that the ego-personality can recall it.

The notion of a prestructured psyche goes to the very heart of the difference between psychology done by German-speakers and Anglo-American psychology. Shortly, we shall have much more to say about the German-speakers' psychology and why we need to have some of its tools at hand—or else we will be unable to handle our topic. Against a great weight of misteaching, we must keep in mind that inheritance of the personal memories of ancestors (a variation of the Lamarckian notion of genetic transmission of acquired characteristics) is *not* part of these ideas, and was never a part of Jung's thinking.

The structures or universal symbols Jung called *archetypes.* They are the psychological equivalent of Kant's categories. Archetypes are pure form. An archetype "might be compared to the crystal lattice which is preformed in the crystalline solution. It should not be confused with the variously structured axial system of the individual crystal."[67] The archetype represents the operation, on a different level, of the same process that gives rise to a *Gestalt* (literally, form, shape, or configuration) in Gestalt psychology. More on this presently.

While biological prestructuring is of the essence in understanding what archetypes are, their complete, full essence does not repose in the biological organism, existing in the apparent sense-world of time, space, and causality. Jung's psychology and that other production of German-speakers just before the catastrophe, Gestalt psychology, are the only kinds of psychology taking into account relativity physics. All others—all those entrenched in American universities today—go blithely on, as if the Newtonian view were as comprehensive as it seemed to be to the most accomplished natural scientist circa 1890. The crucial idea—that our consciousness, with its inherent limitation to time and space and its necessary proclivity to ignore interrelatedness so that it can focus on details segregated from the flux—is one-sided, and we must thoughtfully adjust, correct, and allow for that one-sidedness in making inferences in psychology.

Albert Einstein held a university position in Zürich in the early twenties, was sometimes a dinner guest in Jung's home, and held forth on relativity, the space-time continuum, the problem of causality, and so forth, to Jung, Bleuler, and other psychiatrists. That contact impressed Jung with the philosophical implications of relativity physics more quicky and thoroughly than print-media accounts for nontechnical readers could have. It must surely have helped to

---

67. C. G. Jung, "The Psychological Foundations of Belief in Spirits," in *The Structure and Dynamics of the Psyche,* trans. R. F. C. Hull, 2nd ed. (Princeton, N.J.: Princeton University Press, 1969), p. 311, par. 589 n.

fortify him against the disguisedly antiintellectual blight of logical positivism and operationism that was soon to get started in Anglo-American behavioral-science quarters.

The major implication of relativity physics for depth psychology is that the unconscious part of the psyche exists outside space and time. It touches the inanimate universe, other psyches, and perhaps even a creator supreme being in ways that we are, by nature, unable to observe directly, and can reach—if at all—only by inferences from indirect observations. On the existence of a supreme being, Jung, like Koestler after him, knew that the capabilities of humanity for knowledge and for adaptation had been built up neither gradually nor specifically in response to selective pressures in the environment, giving the possessors of some discrete trait propagatory advantage over its nonpossessors. Jung expressed this in comments in favor of teleological thinking, rather than against Darwin or other evolutionists. He expressed it in a delightfully disarming way, in an interview with an American historian of psychology, Richard I. Evans, in 1957. Evans asked Jung about the sexual instinct, relevant to his time as a disciple of Freud, and Jung answered:

> Nobody knows where instincts come from. They are there and you find them. It is a story that was played millions of years ago. Their sexuality was invented, and I don't know how this happened; I wasn't there! Feeding was invented very much longer ago than even sex, and how and why it was invented, I don't know. So we don't know where the instinct comes from. It is quite ridiculous, you know, to speculate about such an impossibility. So the question is only—where do those cases come from where instinct does not function. That is something within our reach. . . .[68]

That statement must have startled Evans, when practically any other mental-health professional or behavioral scientist would have answered such a question with pompous, scientifically unsupported speculations about what selective pressures had been encountered in evolution and what instincts were present in our supposititious infrahuman ancestors. The way the environment, the collective unconscious, and the human experience fit together[69] led Jung to be inclined toward the idea of a creator supreme being. Not the God of the Bible, but the one of whom Einstein wrote, "I cannot believe that God plays dice with the world."[70]

---

68. Richard I. Evans, *Conversations with Carl Jung* (New York: Van Nostrand Reinhold Co., 1964), p. 40. The interview was given in English, and the quotation reflects Jung speaking extemporaneously in that language.

69. The idea of intimate fitting together of events—or destiny—intrudes itself whenever there are meaningful correspondences of events without discoverable causes and against the statistical weight of probability. Jung experienced many such correspondences, and like many natural scientists, particularly physicists, Jung was persuaded to modify his early strong stand against the possibility of such things. Jung and the renowned physicist Wolfgang Pauli collaborated on parapsychological phenomena in *Synchronicity: An Acausal Connecting Principle* in *The Structure and Dynamics of the Psyche,* pars. 816-997.

70. Lincoln Barnett, *The Universe and Dr. Einstein* (New York: Mentor Books, 1952), p. 36.

We can put together several of the foregoing concepts, and see how Jung thought the process of human knowledge, taking in ethical, aesthetic, as well as intellectual understanding, takes place. Jung saw far too active, energy-consuming, and intricate a process at work in giving order to, and making sense of, the stimuli of the exterior world of the senses, to have any use for the Cartesian idea of impressions passively being made on a tabula rasa mind, or a modern psychological idea of associations or stimulus-response connections. Rather, there needed to be an archetype to make a whole out of the profusion of sensory or mental parts. The application of the archetypes to stimuli, Jung saw as occurring through *projection.* This makes projection something far more than mistaken attribution of one's own ulterior motives to another; indeed, it becomes the process of all right perceptions as well as subjectively distorted misperceptions. Progressive flow of libido partakes of the projection of archetypes on the things they fit. The withdrawal of projections that do not fit—and consequently result in the blocking of progressive flow, reformulation of them, and projecting them again, in a constant ebb and flow—correspond to progressive and regressive flow.

Understanding the practically inexhaustible output of fantasy in the dreams and spontaneous waking reverie of each of us as having its source in the collective unconscious is some help in understanding psychologically those products, while general psychology scarcely takes us beyond common knowledge. Indeed, in the days before hallucinogenic drugs became an influence in our culture, mention of the archetypes of the collective unconscious among American mental-health professionals consistently met with cocksure rejection of the idea out of hand, and ridicule; afterwards, the same mention has typically been met with respectful silence, even meekness. The complexity of the process whereby inner prestructuring and experiences from without and within are made intelligible, and how little we understand that process, is brought home to us. We begin to realize that the process might be fragile. When we encounter someone whose notion of who or what he is, is distorted by his failure to withdraw an unfitting archetypal projection (which Jung called inflation) or someone who has autochthonous ideas or emotions rushing in on him and carrying him away (which Jung called invasion), we see that the ability to distinguish fantasy from nonfantasy—because of the onesidedness of consciousness, we hesitate to call it "reality"—is precious. We shall see just how fundamental an assault it is, on a person whose relation to his own outer and inner life is not totally conventional or "other-directed," to receive social encouragement for failing to distinguish fantasy from nonfantasy. Fortunately for those of us who live in Western, developed countries, religions and certain disreputable pop-psychotherapies are the only activities where we receive consistent social encouragement for failure to make that distinction.

In evaluating Jung, what should be noted is the long agenda of unfinished business left behind. Jung took Kant's categories and insight about human thought and extended them to cover man's creative and emotional life. Jung understood that we cannot really reach the absolutes themselves, that we deceive ourselves if we think we have any understanding about ourselves without its compensatory opposite with some aspect of truth needing yet to be integrated. To avoid mistaking our provisional, one-sided formulation for the absolute of which it is at best a caricature, we have to employ Jamesian pragmatism as a working modus operandum. If we learn anything from Jung, it is that we can do no better than take James' advice about fairness to contending points of view and having decent regard for other human beings temper what we regard as "true."

If Jung did anything wrong, it is that he let himself be overwhelmed by his newfound appreciation of how much there was to be known, beyond the one-sidedness of our consciousness. He and his followers let introverted attention to that vastness turn into obsession. They wallowed in their dream accounts, ancient mythologies, and personal religious quests. In view of the experience of Jung and his followers, Kant's comment, "In the end, however, we are unable to understand how . . . noumena are possible at all, and the realm beyond the sphere of phenomena is for us, empty," should ring in our ears as an admonition. The extraverted side of living—having intellectual understanding help us in coming to terms with the world, trying to find ways to make it a better and less dangerous place to be—is the most we can do in this finite, one-sided condition of ours.

The Bible View of Human Nature

There remains yet one more psychological concern for us to take up to be ready to break new ground. That is the general one of "nature-of-man" issues in psychology. These issues are important to us for several reasons. First, we find that the Bible implicitly takes stands on them. Sometimes, it expresses or intimates a stand that much later became an enlightening one in psychology. Sometimes, it takes a stand on such an issue that is grossly outside what modern psychological knowledge (and the common sense of its own day) could allow, and we find that a mind-control purpose is served by so doing. Secondly, we find that the conventional wisdom of the contemporary mental-health professions can be traced back to reaction to chafing religious conventions of an earlier time. The furious retreat of the mainline pastors early in the present century must surely have been intended to avoid—and evidently it did avoid—the criticisms that otherwise would have come from the newly emerging mental-health professionals. Doing things in whatever way was opposite to what the old way was perceived to have been did not make for intelligent conventional wisdom in liberal clergy and the new mental-health professionals. Thirdly, the psychology field is, itself, divided on these issues, and any kind of applied psychology will necessarily rest on a potentially controversial assumption involving one or more of those issues. To make the reader play the additional game of figuring out what the underlying assumption is does not aid understanding.

A pervasive theme in the interaction of the old religious conventions and the new mental-health doctrines is the meaning of judgmentalness. When I was a graduate student in psychology in the middle sixties, the client-centered psychotherapy of Carl Rogers was much in vogue, and since Rogers was an ex-pastor, we students were to conclude that his ideas were biblical or Christian. The idea was that moral responsibility for one's actions is no big deal, that making too much of that issue had been one of the major mistakes of the past; the new enlightened mental-health professionals would correct all of this. One was only to repeat back in different words to the "client" what he had said, in order to avoid imposing one's own suggestions or in any way derogating from the client's right to make his own decisions. This way therapists bore no responsibility and needed no more skill or knowledge than they could pick up in fifteen minutes of classroom time.[71] While more common sense and moderation than the rhetoric implied was usually to be found in actual practice, the talk was pure mellowness and permissiveness. When the topic of criminals and criminal behavior came up, the silliest platitudes would be recited. When one of the proponents of radical nonjudgmentalness personally became the victim of a crime, a dramatic conversion to law-and-order harshness and mean-spiritedness would often ensue.

Since my own upbringing had been nominally Jewish, I did not realize that the theme of radical nonjudgmentalness was a liberal takeoff from Jesus' actions concerning the woman taken in adultery,[72] and "Judge not, that ye be not judged."[73] Against the old way, perceived as having involved instilling guilt and an individual sense of wrongness and inferiority—"when in doubt, condemn!"—the liberal way was always to approve and instill self-esteem, regardless whether or not the facts of the situation warranted it.

As will often prove to be the case, the perceived old-fashioned way of doing things—frequently a result of mistaking Roman Catholic doctrine for the Bible—turns out to have little to do with what the Bible actually teaches. The notions that the liberal church person or unreligious collegiate person holds about the Bible do little to help that person understand what someone who becomes steeped in the Bible goes through. In this case, we shall see that the Bible has a very precise but dual standard on judging others. In the case of non-Christians, the believer is to be just as nonjudgmental as the most extreme liberal. The believer is to be a good witness and leave up to God the judging of the unbeliever.[74] Regarding a fellow believer, the believer is to be just as judg-

71. During the same period, the other popular cause in the mental-health professions was Skinner's operant conditioning, the ultimate outworking of operationism. I studied under professors who were proponents of Skinnerism and would seriously say, "I don't know what people mean when they talk about consciousness because I cannot know anything that is not operationally defined." The psychodynamically oriented clinical students would correctly diagnose the hysterical condition that underlies such a statement. As a teacher, I found that I could exhaust the conceptual content of Skinnerism in about seventy-five minutes of classroom time, and the unit would become redundant and repetitious if I tried to make it longer. The tendency for mental-health professionals to want only what is intellectually undemanding, coming with the dramatic increase in the numbers of personnel following World War II, has been ruinous.
72. John 8:1–11.
73. Matt. 7:1.
74. Matt. 5:44; Luke 6:27–37; John 12:47; 1 Cor. 5:12–13; and 1 Pet. 3:1–2.

mental as he can be without hypocrisy, i.e., he should refrain from judging the brother (or sister) in an area where the judge is also derelict.[75] Believers are urged constantly to correct, admonish, and reprove one another. They are to keep one another under constant doctrinal surveillance.

The basic nature-of-man issues in psychology present themselves as dichotomies: free will and determinism, heredity and environment, mind and body, and good (gentle, benign) and evil (aggressive, predatory). If the progress of the issues behind these opposites in the history of psychology is any indication, they are unresolvable, and if the opposites represent faulty conceptualizations of the issues, we lack better ones. Each of these issues is integral to a biblical issue we need to be aware of.

The basic question underlying the free will/determinism dichotomy is whether any particular set of events can occur in more than one way. In theoretical physics, Heisenberg, with his irregularity principle, profoundly upset the habit of nineteenth-century science of thinking in terms of mechanistic causality and of events being the mathematically calculable resultants of forces in a field. On the cutting edge of the natural sciences, the question remains unresolved. On the level of experience, we do not know if we are really free, or if it is only our lack of knowledge of the forces shaping the outcome that lets us think we are free. The Jamesian objection to determinism, that a view leading to discouragement and fatalism is not a fit one for humans to regard as true, retains its currency.

This issue has manifested itself popularly as a controversy between the older, religious, conventional view that stresses free will and moral responsibility and an "enlightened" mental-health view that says human behavior is only the sum of the causal factors bearing upon it; the only way to change behavior, if so, is to change the causal factors. When the psychology field got started in its own right, essentially materialistic solutions to all intellectual problems were expected, and the field has never come to terms with the abandonment of that position by the hard sciences. When I was a graduate student, no presentation about psychotherapy or planned personality change was complete without the refrain, "We all know that moral suasion doesn't work!" That refrain would usually prompt some signs of animation from a professional or graduate-student audience, not unlike the shouts of "Amen!" at a Salvation Army meeting.

One can best see the present state of this issue in the relations between the mental-health professions and the legal system. Efforts to supersede the premise of moral responsibility for actions with some other premise have been attempted, but always with a notorious lack of success and a return to older legal conceptions for want of anything else that will work tolerably in practice.[76]

---

75. Luke 17:3; 1 Cor. 5:9–13; Gal. 6:1; 2 Thess. 3:14; 1 Tim. 5:20; and Heb. 3:13 (judging other believers). Matt. 7:2; Luke 6:37; Rom. 2:1 and James 4:11 (judging only in matters where oneself is not derelict).

76. Two important cases stand out in my memory as illustrating the problem in context, and they make better reading than the large amount of unenlightening secondary-source material about it. In *United States* v. *Brawner,* 471 F.2d 969 (D.C. Cir. 1972), the Federal Appeals Court for the busy District of Columbia jurisdiction put a modified form of the mid-nineteenth century M'Naughten rule of insanity defense in criminal cases back into effect. Eighteen years earlier, the

The distinctively modern concern with free will versus determinism has brought mass confusion to the field of theology. The doctrinaire materialism and mechanist determinism of the last century pushed the American old-time religionists—not that erudite a lot—into the position of defending free will as a prerequisite for regarding persons as morally responsible for their acts. The liberal mainline pastors of the next generation ran from the seeming inescapability of the doctrine of determinism, just as they did from the seeming unimpeachability of evolution and natural selection. When mental-health professionals came along with their public-relations campaigns to spread the belief that emotional and behavior problems were symptoms of disease that mental-health professionals' services should be purchased to treat, the pastors ran to get on the bandwagon. In hindsight, we can see that the pastors collectively were quite wise to take in stride subtle undermining of their authority by the mental-health professionals in order to deflect what could have been devastating attacks on themselves, apparently justified by the scientific understanding of the day. The pastors did, after all, substantially eliminate the things they had done before, that mental-health professionals would have wanted to criticize.

Within theological circles also, the notion grew that "free-willism" was a view with Arminian affinities, and determinism, one with Calvinst affinities. To some degree, this developed into a straw-man argument, whereby old-time-religion proponents could make their more orthodox competitors seem to take a position against popular ideology. (Note that James had made his "tender-minded" person "free-willistic" but did not expressly make his "tough-minded" person deterministic. As almost a lone voice in favor of free will in psychology in his time, he saw the determinist doctrine as one to be reckoned with.) The supposedly orthodox idea was that predestination, foreknowledge, and election meant that God had made his world determinist.[77]

What should be noted about determinism in the Bible parallels observations we will be making repeatedly: The biblical authors were just as brilliant and

---

same court, responding to the Zeitgeist, had ruled that instead of the traditional tests of ability to distinguish right from wrong and ability to make one's behavior conform to the requirements of the law, defendants were to be acquitted by reason of insanity if their criminal acts were the product of mental disease or defect. It had been intended to let mental-health professionals testify from their technical knowledge without encumbrance by legal definitions that clashed with their technical ones. Instead, despite vigorous attempts to refine and develop guidelines for the new standard, the experience had been that the experts would state their conclusions without the attorney questioners having success in making the reasoning behind the conclusions (if any) intelligible to the judges and juries, and the results tended toward the extremes of blind acceptance of the mental-health expert's testimony, the decision-making power meant for the judge and jury going to the mental-health professionals de facto, or else blind, cynical rejection of the mental-health testimony by judges and juries.

In *Baxtrom* v. *Herold,* 383 U.S. 107 (1966), the U.S. Supreme Court overturned a procedure of New York state for detaining prisoners judged by mental-health professionals to be dangerous to society, after the prisoners' sentences had expired. As the validity of the predictions of dangerousness was unsupported by scientific evidence, using such predictions as a criterion for deprivation of liberty deprived the prisoners of their right to due process of law.

77. Most salient among the verses lending themselves to a determinist reading are: Matt. 25:34; Acts: 2:23; 17:26; Rom. 8:29–30; Heb. 4:3; 1 Pet. 1:2; and Rev. 17:8.

perspicacious in their observations as the great men of letters who came later, and their handling of the matter of whether humans could control events or not fares far better with us in the late twentieth century than with people not long ago, who thought themselves intellectually bound to a deterministic premise. Looking more closely, we find that the Bible does indeed plainly tell us that whoever is to be saved (i.e., whoever is predestined to election) is so, "from the foundation of the world." As to whether less momentous things are predetermined or not, the Bible is silent. From the myriad exhortations to do or refrain from doing, we infer that there is some choice. But despite implication of the notion of free choice by the exhortations, we find that explicit references to humans choosing, deciding, or selecting something occur only occasionally in the Old Testament[78] and are conspicuously absent from the New Testament.[79] The New Testament constantly exhorts the reader to do or to think, but never at any point does it commit itself to the idea that following the exhortations lies within the power of human decision, or that everybody can follow them. Throughout the Bible, a fatalist interpretation fits the major events well. For the proposition that man, before the fall of Adam, was created in God's image to have any meaning within the context of the rest of the Bible, there is probably no defensible alternative to a doctrine of free will in the minor, morally insignificant events of life. But where it really counts—in the doing of what is righteous and preserves candidacy for Heaven—we are taught that we cannot choose to do those things because that does not lie within our fallen character,[80] and in that crucial respect a determinism is at work in us, from which, to be "free," we need salvation.[81]

The issue of free will and determinism as it interests the philosopher or the psychologist, then, is not particularly relevant so far as the Bible is concerned. We find, however, a great deal of good psychological insight in the Bible's treatment of the human experience of freedom or the lack of it: the Bible's appreciation of the universal human experience of some sort of inertia within, interfering with good intentions, is not so far removed from our discussion of the complexes. Relative freedom of choice, and an indefinite and illusive threshold of overcoming of that freedom by impinging forces, is what both our common sense and the Bible tacitly presuppose.

The biblical issue integral to the secular issue of free will and determinism is moral responsibility. The contending schools of thought all agree that the Bible teaches the moral responsibility of humans for their actions, as must be so if the

---

78. Josh. 24:15 and Prov. 1:29 are Old Testament references to human choice that have been popular with old-time-religion Christians.
79. The only explicit reference to human choice, decision, or selection in the New Testament is Phil. 1:22, where Paul describes the inner conflict to which he is subjected by his conflicting desires: to die so he can be with Christ or to live to continue the evangelistic tasks appointed to him. He speaks of choosing between the two, but in a context indicating that he has no real choice. The closest I have been able to find to a New Testament passage indicating someone had a free choice about a moral matter is Luke 7:30.
80. Matt. 15:19; Rom. 3:10–23; and Gal. 5:17–21.
81. John 8:34–36; Rom. 6:17–19 and 2 Pet. 2:19–20.

wicked are to be capable of deserving to go to Hell. Since the Bible clearly teaches that fallen man lacks the ability within himself ("in his own strength," as the Evangelicals say) to avoid wickedness, we are faced with a contradiction between unfreedom in the significant moral areas of life and responsibility for the consequences of that unfreedom, so eloquently portrayed by John Wesley.[82] That contradiction is real: it is no paradox pointing beyond itself to a greater truth, and no pair of compensatory opposites in counterposition.[83] Drumming it into the believer that there is *responsibility* where there is no *ability* will turn out to be a key feature of the mind-control system.

That the issue of nativism and empiricism manifests itself as a dichotomy of heredity versus environment in Anglo-American psychology and popular thought reflects the one-sidedness of the culture, which we have referred to several times. Anglo-American psychology has largely been the psychology of individual differences. So huge is the portion of psychologists' effort that has gone toward measuring and rating individuals along various trait continua, that the term *heredity* calls to mind the question whether a genetic prediction of some test score or measurement is possible, and the conclusion that the score or measurement is environmentally determined if such a genetic prediction is not possible. That emphasis has crowded out that other kind of psychology for which I have said that German-speakers have shown more aptitude than English-speakers: the study of the relationship of innate prestructuring and experience in the psychological functioning of an individual.

Psychologies stressing innate prestructuring, "nativistic" psychologies have generally failed to take root in the English-speaking world. This has been true for the originators of Gestalt psychology, most of whom were Jewish and who relocated in the United States during the rise of Hitler, as well as Jung's psychology. Those originators did receive considerable respect and recognition, the most lasting effect of which has been the theft of some of their key terms, particularly *Gestalt* and *holism,* by American hucksters with pop-psychology commodities to sell, lacking any of the meaty intellectual content of Gestalt psychology.[84] Whereas the Anglo-American mind wants to understand a phe-

---

82. See pp. 24–25.

83. Max Weber also saw the contradiction: "It is unnecessary . . . to analyse the various inconsistent attempts to combine with the predestination and providence of God the responsibility and free will of the individual. They began as early as . . . Augustine. . . . " *The Protestant Ethic and the Spirit of Capitalism,* trans. Talcott Parsons (New York: Charles Scribner's Sons, 1958), p. 221. The deterministic ethos of the time colored Weber's presentation, but did not significantly distort it, as with many lesser commentators.

84. The so-called Gestalt therapy of Frederick Perls, by now a relic of the mellow, "me-generation" period, used the term to denote what, in our terminology about the complexes, we would call overcoming dissociation. To have less autonomous complex activity is to achieve more wholeness. But there is scarcely anything in Perls' work about what sort of being the human is or how he is prestructured. Legally speaking, I believe there was a time when the genuine Gestaltists or their heirs could have prevailed against Perls in an "unfair competiton" suit, the gravamen of which is sale of a commodity deceptively similar to an established one, deceiving the buyer into thinking he is dealing with the party who built the established product's reputation.

More recently, Kenneth R. Pelletier's *Mind as Healer, Mind as Slayer* (New York: Dell Publishing Co., 1977) has been making the rounds, offering a "holistic approach to stress dis-

nomenon by reducing it to it smallest elements or components, the holist seeks to study groupings of elements, the *Gestalt* (literally, form, shape, or configuration) having its own characteristic properties, its own information to convey that cannot be found from studying the smaller component parts outside the context wherein they participate. The phrase "the whole is more than the sum of its parts" is often heard in connection with Gestalt psychology: as a Gestalt composed of smaller parts is also, from the standpoint of a larger context, an element, the whole can sometimes be said to be less than the sum of its parts. At any rate, what should be noted is that the whole is different from the sum of its parts.

The reader with some psychology background will be familiar with many of the illustrations used in classical Gestalt psychology (and may wish to review them in a psychology text or dictionary).[85] These include: (1) The Gestalt "laws" of grouping, where properties implying relations of parts to one another (proximity, similarity, "closure," figure, and ground) operate to determine what bunches of elements will be perceived as a whole, and which wholes will be perceived as more clear, complete, and resolved than others. (2) Max Wertheimer's principle of closure, where a set of elements that is not so complete or harmonious initiates psychological tension in the perceiver, requiring resolution. The tension experienced when a melody is only partly played or when a task has been partly done is an example. (3) The figure and ground relationship of Edgar Rubin, wherein a configuration of elements will constitute a figure, against the rest of the perceptual field, the ground. The separation of a field into a figure and ground is related to the differentation of psychic energy taking the form of a symbol, which we encountered in Jung. Gestalt psychology can be seen as the study of such differentiations at a conscious level, and Jung's psychology as the study of the same at an unconscious one. (4) The "phi-phenomenon," in which two alternately blinking lights within certain limits of distance from one other and blink frequency, are seen as one light traveling back and forth, because the perceptual apparatus constitutes motion from a succession of relations of stimuli. The perception of motion reposes in the relations of elements, not in their "substance." (5) The "insight" or "aha" phenomenon connects the attainment of *Gestalten* with creative thought. Suddenly, as an all-or-nothing event, a new relation among the elements comprising the problem is revealed.

While the foregoing high points of classical Gestaltism are quite familiar, they are customarily presented in a way that makes them seem innocuous and does not bring out how different its implications are from those of other schools. For our limited purposes, it will serve to point out that the rest of psychology, tacitly if not expressly, employs mechanistic models and looks to analogies of human neurophysiology and some man-made device for understanding of psy-

---

orders." It covers biofeedback and transcendental meditation. The psychology in it is stimulus-response, and it is reductionist from the outset. Alas, *holistic* has become a buzz word to be invoked whenever healing-arts professionals have a vague, general, superficial gimmick to sell.

85. A particularly good short treatment of classical Gestaltism can be found in Edna Heidbreder, *Seven Psychologies* (New York: Appleton-Century-Crofts, 1933 and 1961), pp. 328-75.

chological processes. Wolfgang Köhler, one of the originators, stated the Gestaltist position on the differences between man-made systems and the biological substructure:

> In a physical system events are determined by two sorts of factors. In the first class belong the forces and other factors inherent in the processes of the system. These we will call the *dynamic* determinants of its fate. In the second class we have characteristics of the system which subject its processes to restricting conditions. Such determinants we will call *topographical* factors. In a conducting network, for instance, the electrostatic forces of the current represent its dynamic phase. On the other hand, the geometrical pattern and the chemical constitution of the network are topographical conditions which restrict the play of those forces. It will at once be seen that, while in all systems of nature dynamic factors are at work, the influence of special topographical conditions may be at a minimum in one case and predominant in another. On an insulated conductor electric charges are free to distribute themselves in any way which respects the boundaries of the conductor. If actually the charges assume a particular distribution which represents an equilibrium, this happens for dynamic reasons. In a steam engine, on the other hand, the piston can move only in one fashion, which is prescribed by the rigid walls of the cylinder.[86]

From Descartes' comparing the neurons to tubes in the hydraulic machines that were the most interesting technological devices of his day, to the use by John Watson (the pre-Skinner American proprietor of the term *behaviorism)* of analogies to the great dial-telephone exchanges that were the state of the art in communication technology in his day, to our present wonderful array of miniaturized electronic devices, the impulse to think of human psychology in terms of the current premier technological device is a historical constant in psychology. But even though the latest devices are tremendously intricate and their workings cannot be discovered by taking off the back and looking inside with the naked eye, all our man-made information-processing devices depend on rigid topographical organization, and only within very narrow, intensively defined conditions can they work. In contrast, what we know about information processing in the absurdly slow neurons and other tissue of the human nervous system does not follow the structural boundaries we are able to discover particularly faithfully, and the big successes of neurophysiology in recent years have been in identifying and manipulating brain chemistry. Even in that discipline, however, finding particular physical loci of the chemicals' operation has proven to be a very doubtful endeavor. While we raise no objection in principle to the possibility that a man-made device may one day process information "dynamically" and approach the flexibility of a biological system in adaptation to its surroundings, that device will be as different from the ones we know today as those are from the dial-telephone exchanges that so impressed Watson.

The application of this sort of "dynamic" or "organismic" thinking to humans and to clinical situations was achieved with great brilliance by the neurol-

86. *Gestalt Psychology* (New York: Liveright Publishing Co., 1947), p. 64.

ogist Kurt Goldstein, who was able to combine the academic lore of the Gestaltists with his experience as a physician treating traumatic neurological injuries in World War I. Although Gestalt psychology has all but disappeared from university psychology departments and laboratories, it is through Goldstein that authentic Gestalt concepts and terms remain alive, and part of the everyday parlance of the neurological ward and clinic and of the psychodiagnostics employed for neurological injury or impairment. Time has done nothing but enhance my appreciation of Goldstein's importance: I now realize that he has come closest to what is needed in the Jungian context—to put in place of the personal religious quest for a general statement about human nature or motivation.

Goldstein's understanding of the functioning of intact organisms came from noticing what was lacking in injured ones. He noticed the following: (1) The damaged individual reacts more strongly to isolated stimuli than does the intact one. This is true for sensory stimuli encountered in the environment under ordinary conditions, as well as the reflexes routinely tested by the neurologist. (2) Reactions to stimuli subside less quickly in the impaired individual. There continue to be the reverberations from them that the clinician accustomed to psychological testing refers to as "perseveration." (3) The neurologically injured person has much more difficulty resisting the impulse to continue to pay attention to a stimulus. He cannot detach himself from it and is said to be "stimulus bound." Translating this into Jungian terms, we would say that the impaired person exhibits lessened ability to withdraw projections and reconstitute them to fit the stimuli. (4) Inflexibility in reactions to stimuli takes the form of stereotyped reactions in some instances, and vacillation in others, as the individual is unable to resolve by conscious choice the conflict between two mutually exclusive responses elicited by a given stimulus. (5) The responses of the impaired are more "isolated" than in the normal, i.e., less of the total organism is involved in them. The qualitative difference between the total coordination of the intact individual and part of the impaired organism responding without the cooperation of other parts is immediately recognizable.[87]

The sine qua non of the intact organism is the pervasive interrelatedness of its parts. Stimulation or change in one part brings about compensating change or adjustment in practically every other part. The entire organism is involved even in relatively simple adaptations to the environment. While a man-made machine may be a thing of elegance performing a particular set task, it is nothing like an animal or human, able to exhibit elegance in many different tasks, including ones that are newly discovered—ones that were not part of the lives of any of their ancestors, for which their inherent capacities and capabilities nevertheless fit them. Looking at intact, adapting organisms in action, Goldstein saw one overall, teleologically constituted drive—self-actualization—defined as *adequate, adaptive behavior, in accordance with the capacities and capabilities of the organism.*

---

87. Kurt Goldstein, *Human Nature in the Light of Psychopathology* (New York: Schocken Books, 1963), pp. 16–19.

In opposition to all those psychological theories involving lists of basic biological drives seeking complete discharge of the tension concomitant to them (Freud's being such a theory, with two drives in his list), Goldstein made the one drive of self-actualization the centerpiece of his thinking. Unlike the multiple drives of other psychological theories, self-actualization is satisfied not by reduction of tension but by maintenance of an optimum level of tension,[88] and psychological tension has its pleasant, gratifying eventuality in Goldstein's view. Unlike other psychological subschools using the term *self-actualization,* such as those of Jung and Maslow,[89] with Goldstein the term does not necessarily imply continual growth or development. Animals using their species-specific, instinctive behaviors to survive in the wild and humans living and behaving normally in a slow-changing, tradition-directed society are self-actualizing in the sense contemplated by Goldstein.

The unimpaired human adapts to his surroundings principally through what Goldstein called the "abstract attitude." The person is able to detach his mental processes from the immediate draw of the stimulus before him and see its spatial, temporal, and causal implications in perspective. Goldstein understood the abstract attitude to depend on attainment of figure/ground differentiations and on the ability voluntarily to keep these stable or reorganize them, as the situation demands. Voluntariness of behavior—the ability by free will to decide on a course of behavior, tuning out stimuli not relevant for the purpose of the moment, avoiding being forced to vacillate under the influence of stimuli prompting conflicting behaviors equally strongly—is the key to the abstract attitude.

> In "concrete" performances a reaction is determined directly by a stimulus, is awakened by all that the individual perceives. The individual's procedure is somewhat passive, as if it were not he who had the initiative. In "abstract" performances an action is not determined directly and immediately by a stimulus configuration but by the account of the situation which the individual gives to himself. The performance is thus more a primary action than a mere reaction, and it is a totally different way of coming to terms with the outside world. . . . There is no gradual transition from the one to the other. The assumption of an attitude toward the abstract is not more complex merely through the addition of a new

---

88. Among mental-health professionals, one will often hear W. B. Cannon's term, *homeostasis,* used loosely and technically incorrectly to mean maintenance of an optimum or moderate level of psychological tension. The term's correct technical application is to mechanisms for maintaining chemical equilibria in the body within certain vital ranges, and it has no theoretically coherent wider application. If one examines the mental-health professional attempting to apply the term to psychological processes, one will find that at most, the single feedback loop of pure drive reduction has been replaced with the equally mechanistic concept of the double feedback loop, and the thinking reflected is not genuinely organismic.

89. Maslow used the term *self-actualization* to denote lust for change and progress, and tacitly supposed that full living is possible only with the restlessness of modern Western culture. He also grafted the term onto a nonorganismic, multidrive, tension-reduction model. Maslow extolled Goldstein as a major influence on him (he dedicated *Toward a Psychology of Being* to Goldstein), yet he discarded the essentials of Goldstein's contribution. It was like deliberately wrecking a fine classic car and keeping only a few nuts, bolts, and the hood ornament.

> factor of determination; it is a totally different activity of the organism. . . . Abstraction represents . . . a preparation for activity. . . . Real action is never abstract; it is always concrete.[90]

While the intact individual is able to use both the abstract and concrete attitudes, the organically damaged one is limited in his ability to utilize the abstract attitude in proportion to his neurological impairment. The impaired individual uses the concrete attitude in a compensatory fashion, to do what the unimpaired would do, with immensely more facility, by the abstract attitude. Up to a point, an outward appearance of normality can be affected.

Consider the following composite example of a neurologically damaged patient, such as the ones Goldstein described and I have observed myself in a rehabilitation hospital setting. The patient looks relatively normal and can answer routine questions as to his name, background, and other "overlearned" details. He may have intact short-term memory and know what date and time it is and what events he has experienced that day, although impairment of short-term memory is often observed in such patients. He finds his way around those parts of the hospital that are familiar to him, and nothing about his demeanor gives him away. But once he gets off the elevator on the wrong floor, where the basic layout is the same but the furnishings, decor, and other details are unfamiliar to him, there is a problem. The normal individual could apply his "cognitive map" of the floor plan with no difficulty. But our patient is completely thrown by the unfamiliar details, ceases to behave in any productive manner, and is noticeably upset emotionally. Noticing details and concentrating on what to do or which way to turn at each point where a "cue" detail came into view was the manner whereby the impaired patient had previously navigated in a seemingly normal way. He differed fundamentally from the normal individual in what aspects of the surroundings were functionally significant to him and how he used the information to direct his behavior.

Goldstein's view—that a psychic field is differentiated into figure and ground so that a pattern for action may be formulated—has its strong parallel to Jung's view that a psychic field is differentiated into symbols and divided into complexes so that the balanced rhythm of making and withdrawing projections will give order to what is received from outside. Looking at the two conceptualizations side by side gives us some idea of a potentially very fruitful area for further progress in psychological theory after more than a generation of neglect. The writings of Goldstein and of Jung are each bare of any mention of the other writer. Apparently, Goldstein thought of Jung as a mere offshoot of Freud and did not see that beneath all that distracting surplusage about personal religious quest was a teleological, one-drive, substantive theory like his own. And apparently Jung was too far into his third phase to be interested when mature works in Gestalt psychology appeared, although we are safe in supposing that such works would have excited him tremendously had he encountered them

90. Goldstein, *Human Nature,* pp. 59–61.

when he was younger. What should be noted is that the more mature organismic-teleological theory or subschool of psychology of the future will stress the manifoldness of the relations between the individual and its surroundings and will respond in some way to the part of those relations that has its locus outside the time, space, and causality bounds of our consciousness.[91] That psychology will patiently sort out the indirect indications of the relations we cannot directly reach, and not be looking to crash the barrier, as Jung and his followers were. But that psychology will not limit itself to the mundane, as Goldstein did.

Understanding the highest kinds of psychological functioning in terms of the abstract attitude has far-reaching implications. Indeed, the resistance to organismic thinking on the part of American psychologists becomes easier to understand when we note that it was hard for Gestalt-psychology criticisms of older psychological functionalism or behaviorism to be gently presented. The criticisms were unavoidably, by their intrinsic nature, harsh and sweeping. Consider all the laboratory experimentation with animals (as well as humans) that places a subject in a situation totally unlike any encountered ordinarily, and one requiring some artificially defined choice or response *that requires the concrete attitude only.* In the case of an animal, such a situation bears no relation to the species-specific instinctive behaviors that account for all animal adaptation and survival, except for domesticated or wild zoo animals, which really do not adapt in any active way and are totally dependent on their human innkeepers. Imagine some intelligent beings from another planet having human specimens to study, knowing nothing of human language or culture, and imagine that they only observed those specimens hung up by their heels or floated in sensory-isolation tanks. How much would the extraterrestrials learn about humanity that way? If they compared the humans with other earth species, would they for a moment think that the humans were the highest form of earthly life? Would they not wonder what these ungainly, weak, hairless creatures were doing among other magnificent specimens like panthers or cockroaches?

Seeing that reductive study of concrete-attitude responses can lead us entirely away from what is most essential about the human creature, we notice that there are some dearly held psychological notions that we must reexamine and apply more discriminatingly. Our notion that pathology in the adult human will resemble the normal behavior of the immature human (i.e., be "regression") or infrahuman behavior is such a notion. In the child, we observe all sorts of expressions of the abstract attitude exhibited in play, but only with maturation and experience do these become serviceable for serious adaptation. (In Jungian terms, we would say that the child makes fantastic projections and will withdraw and reconstitute them many times before they will fit experience well.) In the behavior of the child or unimpaired animal, we see the total organism in this or that activity and in response to relevant stimuli and tuning out irrelevant ones.

91. Wolfgang Köhler did investigate the implications of modern physics for Gestalt psychology in *The Place of Value in a World of Facts* (New York: Mentor Books, 1966), expanding on his presentations in the William James lectures at Harvard University in 1934–35. This is summarized in my earlier book, *C. G. Jung,* pp. 129–33.

The normal child and the animal are not distinguished from the normal human adult by Goldstein's five clinical criteria that distinguish the normal adult human from the impaired.

The habit in psychology of emphasizing similarities of human psychology to that of lower animals or the functioning of machines, thereby minimizing the uniqueness of human nature, is revealed as a bad one and needs to be broken. Only feebly and in specialized circumstances do we see infrahuman organisms utilizing the abstract attitude. (Köhler got his famous insight about insight, or the "aha" phenomenon, watching chimpanzees manipulate sticks to bring bananas within their reach.) Only by defining language in a manner that obscures the flexible process of symbol formation behind the structural sign-code regularities do we reach the conclusion that infrahuman organisms have "language." When the study of certain infrahuman species-specific behaviors, such as pair bonding in some birds or social hierarchies in primate colonies, yields some insight, the analogy to human behavior should not be carried too far.[92] And particularly, it needs to be kept in mind that present-day digital electronic-data-processing devices operate entirely within the realm of the concrete attitude.[93]

An implication of Goldstein's views that remains almost totally uninvestigated is its pertinence to what has been called nervous breakdown or, more contemporarily, "burn-out." The view made famous by Hans Selye—that the effects of stress are general regardless of whether the stressor is psychological, environmental, or biological, leading to the general-adaptation syndrome—and the Freudian view that depression and mourning follow the loss of an object to which libido has been cathected together pretty well exhaust the mental-health professions' current stock of concepts about psychological fatigue. Goldstein addressed only those instances where the organism finds itself in an environment for which its inherent capacities and capabilities do not fit it, and it cannot make

---

92. The best balanced study of infrahuman, species-specific behavior has been by German-speaking ethologists, of whom the best known is 1973 Nobel prizewinner Konrad Lorenz. Particularly good as an example of incisive study of animal behavior coupled with avoidance of the hasty conclusion that outwardly similar human behavior is "nothing but" what is observed in animals is *On Aggression,* trans. Marjorie Kerr Wilson (New York: Harcourt, Brace & World, 1966).

93. Organismic or dynamic functioning is not digital; I hesitate, however, to call it "analog," not knowing to what I would have it be analogous. It should be pointed out that electronic data-processing devices that recognize patterns "holographically," or transpose and section in three-dimensional space from scan data, do so by a very precise and methodical program of trigonometric calculations for each element of data, and in so doing, they resemble our hypothetical patient, compensatorily associating small "cue" details in the microcosm environment of the ward, much more than they resemble an intact organism coping.

A phenomenon that illustrates the difference is *idiot savants,* the very rare occurrence of highly developed, specialized abilities in neurologically impaired people who are mentally retarded by conventional reckoning. The specialized abilities make their appearance spontaneously, as the individuals are incapable of the normal discipline of a training situation. Cases with prodigious ability for musical performance, graphic-arts rendition, and performing chain calculations, such as telling on what day of the week a remote date fell, have been widely publicized. The conventional mental-health professions are completely baffled by them. However, if we look at *idiot savants* as compensatory development of a totally concrete attitude activity when the abstract attitude is impaired, some insight and a basis for comparing those rare individuals with the rest emerges.

any adequate response. Our hypothetical impaired patient's cessation of productive behavior, and his emotionality, illustrate what Goldstein called a "catastrophic" response.[94] Goldstein saw coping as an all-or-nothing affair and did not address himself to subtle, gradual, or cumulative thwarting of the one drive of self-actualization. As he never turned his scientific attention to patients without marked organic impairment, we cannot know what sort of views on less dramatic failures at adaptation he might have developed.

If we proceed from the view that the relation between psychic energy and the metabolism or physical vitality is indirect, it follows that the relation between mental or emotional fatigue or exhaustion and bodily fatigue or impairment of vitality is also indirect. Thwarting of self-actualization, in the sense described by Goldstein, will lead to a compensation of some kind. This can be coming to terms with the surroundings through new feats of abstraction or labored preoccupation with concrete-attitude activities. The labored concrete-attitude activities may be preparation for a new creative, adaptive abstraction eventually coming together. Thwarting could also lead to passivity, to taking those avenues in human society that let one be like a domesticated animal, with only suboptimal coping required. Such thwarting of the individual's life destiny is subtle, and is discernible only in a very long-term perspective. Harmful thwarting of self-actualization might go on and never produce the undermining of general physical vitality and premature aging, for which Selye has taught us to look.

Since Goldstein, advances in holistic thinking have taken place only outside the mental-health professions and academic psychology. Philosopher Michael Polanyi[95] has written on the attainment of *Gestalten* in perception and cognition and on the hierarchical organization of *Gestalten,* wherein one Gestalt becomes an element in a higher-order Gestalt.

The most interesting contributor to psychology and adjacent fields—and not a credentialed member in any of them—was Arthur Koestler (1905–1983). Of his several books on holism, *The Ghost in the Machine*[96] is the most pertinent to our topic. We have savored a bit of its analysis of human aggression.[97] The evidence against gradualistic views of evolution is also covered, leading to

---

94. *Human Nature,* pp. 57 ff. Goldstein described the catastrophic reaction, when in a situation with which the organism cannot come to terms, as a confrontation with nonbeing, and he went so far as to define anxiety as dread at the threat of nonbeing, in contradistinction to fear of some specific threat (pp. 92 ff). In this respect, I find Goldstein's views at variance with clinical experience, particularly with the earnestly suicidal. Goldstein apparently took the existential philosophy in vogue in his time too much to heart.

95. See p. 102, n. 65.

96. (New York: Macmillan, 1967).

97. Crucial to Koestler's analysis of human aggression was physiologist Paul MacLean's work on the human cortex, indicating that the "neocortex" evolved so rapidly that its integration with the evolutionary "older" parts of the brain is incomplete. Koestler referred to this dissociation within the human brain as "schizophysiology." He closed his otherwise superlative book with the absurd recommendation that world leaders take tranquilizing drugs to curb their otherwise uncontrollable aggressive impulses. In 1971, psychologist Kenneth B. Clark, famous for his studies of the effects of school segregation on black children, which informed the justices of the U.S. Supreme Court in the 1954 school-desegregation decision, made a similar recommendation of

the conclusion that the descent of one species from another, if such a thing occurred, went in sudden, purposeful shifts, repeating the same basic forms for different adaptations and often overshooting the environmental task needing a new adaptation. Particularly, man's intelligence, present in the form we know long before the full extent of its power was apparent, overshot whatever environmental tasks were before its first possessors. Koestler saw the basic unit of complex life as the "holon," a sort of biological Gestalt, with holons assembling themselves into hierarchical structures with ever more levels. Similar fixed rules and flexible strategies govern both individual adaptation and the evolution of new biological structures to cope with the environment. Both Koestler and Polanyi stressed hierarchical organization as the mode of relation of one element to another in a complex system, and neither advanced the vital theme of dynamic interrelation outside the apparent vertical ordering in such a system beyond the Gestaltists' handling of it. The question of unexpected systematic connection between events not apparently connected, outside the "chain of command," is just where Jung, Köhler, and Goldstein left it.

Several biblical issues integral to the nativism/empiricism issue are also integral to the other psychological issues that follow, and we shall come to them presently. What should impress us here is the telling sensitivity and perspicacity of the New Testament authors on the issue. Where the best present knowledge justifies no strong, one-sided stand, we find that the Bible authors have taken none. While the scientific mind of the last century could be cocksure that a reductionistic view would be the final one and would dismiss Bible observations about human nature out of hand, an informed contemporary—such as myself—might be so impressed by the Bible's intimations as to be tempted to buy the whole scheme. Those who learned to play upon human psychological vulnerabilities with such unexcelled virtuosity so long ago must have known a thing or two.

In 1 Corinthians 12:12–26, Paul reflects a fully developed organismic understanding of the human body and of social organization. He applies the naturally appealing organismic analogy to the organization of believers (which, as we shall see, turns out to be anything but organismic in practice). Our notion of manifold interrelatedness beyond our one-sided consciousness finds its striking expression in 1 Corinthians 13:10–12 and Romans 8:20–22. (While Platonism is one source of Paul's ideas about an existence beyond mortality, the Bible's notions about bodily resurrection on judgment day and creation of new heavens and a new earth are neither Platonic nor Old Testament, but a novel synthesis of the two.)

Whereas the heredity/environment or nativism/empiricism dichotomy remains an issue, even with holistic thinking, the mind/body issue loses its currency altogether. We learn that the experiences we call mind and body, each with its different properties and rules, arise because of the limitations of our con-

---

tranquilizers for world leaders, in his presidential address to the American Psychological Association. Both men were ridiculed, not unfairly, by the intellectual community and the press. Koestler rapidly lost interest in holism after that.

sciousness, and we infer that a totally alien reality underlies it. The classical psychological positions—materialism, psychophysical parallelism, subjective idealism, epiphenomenalism, etc.—will interest us little. With the prominence of the mind/body dichotomy in older psychologies came a particularly heavy infusion into theology of secular notions subdividing the human experience. Some potential for confusion will arise, if we do not sort them out.

Very few readers with an Evangelical background will have had religious teachers so astute as to have noticed that tripartite divisions of the human phenomenon—such as body, mind and spirit, or body, soul, and spirit—have no biblical basis.[98] I surmise that since the Bible very clearly makes God tripartite, comprising the three persons of the Trinity, and also teaches that man is made in God's image, the theologians have looked for some biblical tripartite nomenclature for man. Laying aside these old habits of thought, we come to be impressed how unified a totality the Bible portrays man to be. When separate components, such as body, flesh, mind, soul, or spirit are discussed, it is with some particular piece of theological business in view.

Even in that most drastic division of a personality, death, the most we can make out of the Bible's teachings is that physical death causes a temporary division, with a future reunificaiton in view. For the saved person who dies before Christ's return, the body remains to await resurrection on the last day, and some aspect or semblance goes to be "present with the Lord" in the meantime.[99] Finally, the saved are to be resurrected in new, spiritual, incorruptible bodies,[100] their totality not merely restored but better than ever, to inhabit the new heavens and new earth. As to the unsaved who die before the Christ returns, the Bible is unclear as to the status of their immaterial aspects pending resurrection.[101] But clearly their bodies and nonbodily aspects are to be reunited

98. The only biblical support for a doctrine of human tripartiteness is 1 Thess. 5:23, ". . . *I pray God* your whole spirit [*pneuma*] and soul [*psuche*] and body [*soma*] be preserved blameless unto the coming of our Lord. . . ." Because the Greek word *psuche* is the root for the modern term *psychology*, the tendency is to convert the typology into "body, mind, and spirit," although the underlying concepts of soul and mind overlap only trivially in the Bible's context. Note that the New Testament words that have to be translated "mind" are *nous* and *phronema*. The Greek word translated "flesh" is *sarx*. As to the relation of one integument to another, cf. 1 Cor. 15:44 and Heb. 4:12.

99. John 6:39–40, 44, 54; 11:24; 12:48; 1 Thess. 4:16–17 (body awaits last day); 2 Cor. 5:6, 8; and Rev. 20:4 (nonbody goes to be "with the Lord").

100. 1 Cor. 15:42–56. Cf., Gen. 5:24; 2 Kings 2:11; and John 3:13.

101. The only allusion to the manner of existence of the unsaved between bodily death and judgment day in the New Testament is the parable of the rich man and Lazarus (Luke 16:19–31). It seems to indicate that the unsaved person goes directly into eternal torment. That offends the Anglo-Saxon mind, since it means that the rich man has been sentenced before he has been judged. The parable makes conspicuous reference to the rich man's eyes and tongue, and we wonder how these can be present if his body is in the grave. Because the rich man has five brothers still on earth, the parable is definitely set in a time prior to judgment day. If we are to ignore these implications because it is a parable, we tacitly reproach the parable's author for its lack of craftsmanship for its purpose.

The Old Testament, in Ps. 115:17, informs us that the dead go to a place of silence. If the parable is not informing us differently, and we consider the references to being dead prior to judgment day as "sleep" (John 11:11; 1 Cor. 11:30; 15:51; and 1 Thess. 4:14) the picture emerging is of the unsaved being unconscious, so that the first thing they will know after physical death is

on the last day, so they can be judged and sentenced to the "second death," eternal life in pain and torment.[102] All those who are still in mortal life when Christ returns skip the step of body/nonbody fragmentation. Unity and totality of the human personality are the rule, and division and fragmentation are exceptional and relatively transitory conditions in the supernatural salvation plan.

The components, mind and flesh, are also fashioned with ultimate unity in view. The body, or flesh, of the saved person, prior to its transformation to its new, spiritual, incorruptible form, remains sin-tainted, does not partake in the spiritual renewal of the nonbodily aspects of the person's being, and continues to cause the saved person trouble, while he remains alive on earth.[103] The mind,[104] however, apparently occupies a position in between the flesh and the nonbodily aspects of the person, which include the spirit (*pneuma*) and soul (*psuche*)—differentiated little, if at all, from each other.

The issue as to whether man's intrinsic nature is good or evil is fundamental in the Bible, as well as being the issue where academic students of human behavior have utterly failed to arrive at any consistent or convincing position. The scholars' attempts to reduce the moral nature of man to a theory will be incomprehensible to us if we try to understand them outside the context of reaction to older religious views that gave rise to them.

It is on the moral nature of man that the Bible takes its most demonstrably false stand, and it does so for self-serving purposes. The Bible takes the most negative possible stand on the moral nature of man. Were it any more negative, it would be too obviously untenable as an explanation of man as we find him. Then, the all-out assault on individual self-esteem and self-confidence to which it

---

the proceedings of judgment day. Remember, discontinuity between the Old and New Testaments points to a mind-control purpose. We shall take up this point further, in the next chapter.

102. John 5:28–29; Rev. 20:5–6, 12–15. Note that the word *hell* in verses 13 and 14 is the Greek word *hades,* in contradistinction to *gehenna* and *tartarouo,* used where the context indicates eternal punishment.

103. Rom. 7:14–8:13. Note that continuing to meet with inner resistance and inner conflict in trying to live in accordance with good intentions remains the lot of the saved person, consistent with negative Bible promises, such as John 16:33, 1 Cor. 10:13, and Heb. 12:6. The particular restiveness of the flesh to renewal is also conveyed by the remarkableness and awe attending the transfiguration of Jesus' physical body (Matt. 17:1–13; John 6:53–58; and Gal. 5:24). The much-quoted transformation of a heart of stone into a heart of flesh, of Ezek. 11:19 runs counter to the usage of *flesh* generally throughout the Bible.

Although there have been many special-doctrine renditions of Christianity simply equating the flesh with evil, the Bible itself is much more subtle. We note that Adam and Eve were briefly untainted by sin, yet of flesh and blood. Also, there are quite favorable references to being "of one flesh," pertaining directly to the marriage relationship (Eph. 5:31) and indirectly to the relationship of Christ to the believers (Eph. 5:29–30).

The *heart* in the Bible (remembering that the Bible authors did not know of the circulation of blood) is broadly used, pertaining both to body and nonbody. The term seems to apply to what is authentic or true, as opposed to affected or self-deceiving, about the person. The Jewish expression "heart of hearts," connoting ultimate candor, is broadly representative of the way *heart* is used throughout the Bible. In the first instance, the heart is portrayed as just as bad as the flesh (Jer. 17:9; Matt. 15:19; and Mark 7:21). Yet the operation of salvation on the heart seems equivalent to its operation on the soul or spirit (Acts 16:14; Rom. 2:29; and 2 Cor. 4:6).

104. The mind, in the Bible, is spoken of as renewed by salvation (Rom. 12:2 and 1 Cor. 2:16), and yet vulnerable as the spirit, soul, and heart are not (2 Thess. 2:2 and Heb. 12:3). A person of wavering or insufficient faith is referred to as "double-minded" (James 1:8 and 4:8).

amounts would not work.

The following are representative of the Bible's teaching on human moral nature:

> The wicked are estranged from the womb: they go astray as soon as they be born, speaking lies.[105]

> . . . [F]or we have before proved both Jews and Gentiles, that they are all under sin; As it is written, There is none righteous, no, not one: There is none that understandeth, there is none that seeketh after God. They are all gone out of the way, they are together become unprofitable; there is none that doeth good, no, not one. Their throat *is* an open sepulchre. . . . [106]

> For all have sinned, and come short of the glory of God; Being justified freely by his grace through the redemption that is in Christ Jesus. . . . [107]

The taint or guilt contemplated by the passages is universal and not a function of the individual's transgressions or the lack of them.[108] Good works do not cure it.[109] Outside the religious program, the person is to find no source of self-esteem.[110] To put more than secondary emphasis on one's own adaptive or creative devices, to do more with the things of this life than is needed to further one's own and others' preparations for the next life is to lack trust in God.[111]

An objection to the thesis that "*there is* none good but one, *that is* God,"[112] so serious that the whole salvation scheme would become clearly indefensible were it not answered, is the obvious occurrence of goodness and decency in many individuals not following the biblical salvation program. The biblical answer to the objection is:

> For when the Gentiles, which have not the law, do by nature the things contained in the law, these, having not the law, are a law unto themselves: Which shew the work of the law written in their hearts, their conscience also bearing witness, and *their* thoughts the mean [i.e., intervening] while accusing or else excusing one another. . . .[113]

The unsaved person is capable of experiencing inner conflict over bad deeds, very much as the saved person experiences conflict between his renewed, spiritual nature and his fleshly nature.[114] By the absence of a way to tell the saved

105. Ps. 58:3.
106. Rom. 3:9–13.
107. Rom. 3:23–24.
108. Rom. 5:12–14.
109. Isa. 64:6; Eph. 2:8–10.
110. 1 Cor. 4:3–4; Gal. 6:3; Phil. 4:13.
111. Luke 16:11–15; John 15:19; 1 Tim. 6:17–19; 2 Tim. 3:2; and James 4:4.
112. Mark 10:18.
113. Rom. 2:14–15.
114. See footnote 103. Paul states that he derives a good feeling from knowing that he has a clear

from the unsaved, a semblance of correspondence of the scheme to humans as we find them is preserved, and the individual's uncertainty about which category he falls into is kept unresolved.

Both the saved and the unsaved have *conscience (sunekdaimos,* literally, coabsentee from home, fellow traveler) operating in the same way, according to the Bible. Deficiencies of conscience in the unsaved are said to arise from the person's rendering his conscience inoperative through "defiling" or "searing" it.[115] Conscience is seen as a secondary indication of God's law, the Scriptures being the primary indication. Never is conscience portrayed as a means of knowing what one could not otherwise learn from the Scriptures. Knowing right from wrong intuitively is for unbelievers; the believers are portrayed as receiving what defines conscience for them through instruction.[116] The point of quite a few of the biblical allusions to conscience is that the Scriptures should define what is of good conscience and what is of bad conscience for the believer. *At no point does conscience become a source of relief from Bible prescripts that the modern sensibility finds repugnant, such as absolute obedience to the secular state except where the dissemination of Christian doctrine is affected, or condemnation of all secular culture as "unprofitable."*

What is corrupt in human nature is innate in the individual, owing to original sin. At least some good in humans is innately "written in their hearts." And yet outward influences are crucial to the development of both the corrupt and the good in human nature.[117]A totality that cannot be meaningfully discussed in terms of hereditary or environmental factors in isolation is always in view. So far, the biblical psychology is well balanced and astute. The place where the biblical teaching on human moral nature takes leave of what the thoughtful modern observer can accept is in bifurcating its emphasis, stressing relation of inward, intrasubjective experience to man's negative side, but outward, socially shared experience to his positive side. To be inward-looking is to be wicked. To be "other-directed" toward the Christian community and the Scriptures is to be righteous. To be other-directed in relation to secular, civil masters, and fellow servants is not unrighteous. "Don't trust your feelings; don't

---

conscience, intimating affirmative knowledge that he is saved and that his very considerable past sins (Acts 22:19–20) have been forgiven (Acts 23:1; 24:16; Rom. 9:1; 2 Cor. 1:12; and 2 Tim. 1:3). Of course, the rest of the believers could enjoy a similar assurance only if they knew they were saved, and they could know that only if, at the end of life, they had always persevered in keeping the commandments. Note the possibly disingenuous allusion in Heb. 10:1–2 and 22.

In the King James version, John 8:9 portrays the men preparing to stone the woman taken in adultery as "being convicted by *their own* conscience," and those words have become standard Evangelical jargon for a subjective experience culminating in salvation. Contemporary Bible scholars agree that the phrase is not genuine, and reputable modern translations omit it.

115. 1 Cor. 8:7; 1 Tim. 4:2; and Titus 1:15.

116. Rom. 13:5; 1 Tim. 1:5; 1 Pet. 2:19 and 3:16. The rest of the biblical references to conscience pertain to tactfully avoiding offending the "weak" or uninformed consciences of those who still feel obligated to follow the rescinded provisions of the Jewish ceremonial law, such as refraining from eating certain meats. Note that references translatable as *conscience* appear only in the parts of the Bible attributable to Luke, Paul, and Peter.

117. 1 Cor. 15:33; Rom. 10:17.

trust your faculties, trust the Book!"[118]

The premise that man lacks free will in morally significant or longer-term aspects of living thoroughly permeates the Bible's teaching on the moral nature of man. The unfreedom contemplated by the Bible is not determinism in the sense familiar to modern psychology. Rather, the Bible has in view man as a creature with no major trend in his life not animated by some spirit (*pneuma,* literally, breath, breeze). This "spiritual" view of man, with "non-I" participating more intimately with "I" than would seem normal to modern man, comes through in these examples:

> So the [Holy] spirit lifted me up, and took me away, and I went in bitterness, in the heat of my spirit; but the hand of the LORD was strong upon me.[119]

> Watch and pray, that ye enter not into temptation: the spirit indeed *is* willing, but the flesh *is* weak.[120]

> Now we have received, not the spirit of the world, but the spirit which is of God; that we might know the things that are freely given to us of God.[121]

> For God hath not given us the spirit of fear; but of power, and of love, and of a sound mind.[122]

Even negative, entropic manifestations, such as deafness, dumbness, and bondage, are "spirits."[123] The gist or sense of a thing is its "spirit."[124] God's spirit is strongly emphasized as one of the three personifications in which he appears, and the Holy Spirit comes through as the master spirit, among the myriad of spirits that can be in concert with, or absent from, the individual person's spirit.[125] Indeed, spirits in the Bible behave much as complexes do in Jungian psychology.[126]

The presupposition that man neither is very much nor does very much but for the influence and animation of "spirits" is behind the narrow, insignificant scope given to human free will in the Bible. The illusion of separateness and unity of the ego-personality, with which modern man is so "ego-involved," was not de rigueur in Bible times. People did not take pride in thinking themselves more independent-thinking and objective than they really were, as we do in our culture. When the Jews had their spirits, the rest of mankind had their polytheistic gods, muses, furies, etc.

---

118. Gal. 5:16–25; Col. 2:8; and James 1:21.
119. Ezek. 3:14.
120. Matt. 26:41.
121. 1 Cor. 2:12.
122. 2 Tim. 1:7.
123. Mark 9:25; Rom. 8:15.
124. 2 Cor. 3:6.
125. Ps. 51:11; Rom. 8:16.
126. We noted the anticipation of psychological complexes by the biblical authors in our discussion of free will on pp. 108–111.

Thus, a biblical view of man's nature becomes a study of the exterior influences declared to be operating on him. His starting point is as a tainted creature, on account of Adam's fall. The world in which the human finds himself belongs to Satan by right of conquest, and if the human is comfortable or happy in it, that is by virtue of his taintedness, his spiritual blindness.

> Wherefore, as by one man sin entered into the world, and death by sin; and so death passed upon all men, for all that have sinned. . . . For as by one man's disobedience many were made sinners, so by the obedience of one shall many be made righteous.[127]

> *And* we know that we are of God, and the whole world lieth in wickedness.[128]

> . . . [K]now ye not that the friendship of the world is enmity with God? whosoever therefore will be a friend of the world is the enemy of God.[129]

> If ye were of the world, the world would love his own: but because ye are not of the world, but I have chosen you out of the world, therefore the world hateth you.[130]

If one is a member of God's elect, one gives evidence of it by being an obedient bond-servant of God. By process of elimination, all others are slaves of Satan.

> Know ye not, that to whom ye yield yourselves servants [slaves] to obey, his servants ye are to whom ye obey; whether of sin unto death, or of obedience unto righteousness? But God be thanked, that ye were the servants of sin, but ye have obeyed from the heart that form of doctrine which was delivered you. Being then made free from sin, ye became the servants of righteousness.[131]

> Enter ye in at the strait gate: for wide *is* the gate, and broad *is* the way, that leadeth to destruction, and many there be which go in thereat: Because strait *is* the gate, and narrow *is* the way, which leadeth unto life, and few there be that find it.[132]

> Mortify [deaden, subdue] therefore your members [limbs, bodily extremities] which are upon the earth; [to] fornication, uncleanness, inordinate affection, evil concupiscence, and covetousness, which is idolatry: For which things' sake the wrath of God cometh on the children of disobedience. . . .[133]

Although commanded to obey civil authorities (and given the option of having a

---

127. Rom. 5:12, 19.
128. 1 John 5:19.
129. James 4:4.
130. John 15:19.
131. Rom. 6:16–18.
132. Matt. 7:13–14.
133. Col. 3:5–6.

family, with additional strict duties attaching in that event), the alienation and disaffection of the believer from this world is to be total.

> These all [Old Testament patriarchs held up as models] died in faith, not having received the promises, but having seen them afar off, and were persuaded of *them,* and embraced *them,* and confessed that they were strangers and pilgrims on the earth. For they that say such things declare plainly that they seek a country. And truly, if they had been mindful of that *country* from whence they came out, they might have had opportunity to have returned. But now they desire a better *country,* that is, an heavenly: wherefore God is not ashamed to be called their God: for he hath prepared for them a city.[134]

> For our citizenship is in heaven. . . .[135]

> In the world ye shall have tribulation: but be of good cheer; I have overcome the world.[136]

The biblical view, then, contemplates humans starting from complete permeation by evil, in an evil world. When the world seems to be a nice place, that only goes to prove how deceitful it is.[137] By setting his sights on an existence different from and subsequent to earthly existence, "[r]edeeming the time, because the days are evil,"[138] doing a precise discipline set out for him in the Scriptures, a man gets over his earthly life. He is to enlarge the gap between his "fleshly" and acquired "redeemed" nature as much as he can. Interrelatedness with the natural creation around him is not his concern. Early in the Bible, man is told to "subdue" the creation, or exercise "dominion" over it.[139] The topic is not broached again until Paul describes the earthly creation as "subject to futility."[140] Man is to go through this life in an uncomfortable state of fragmentation, looking to judgment day for restoration to unity. Poor, benighted unsaved man is more unified than God's elect temporarily, because his mind and spirit essentially agree with the flesh. Apparently the unsaved have the rudiments of God's law "written in their hearts" only for the protection of the saved, to prevent them from being made entirely extinct through persecution.

Human Moral Nature

All modern views of the nature of man have the stringent, biblical view as their point of departure. After the stifling reign of terror conducted by Calvin in

134. Heb. 11:13-16.
135. Phil. 3:20; *New American Standard Bible.*
136. John 16:33.
137. Prov. 14:12; 16:25; Mark 4:19; Eph. 4:22; and Heb. 3:13.
138. Eph. 5:16.
139. Gen. 1:26, 28; 9:1 and 2.
140. Rom. 8:19-23. *Vanity (mataiotais)* is better translated "futility" or "depravity."

Geneva, it took nearly two centuries for another great man of letters to arise there. That was Jean Jacques Rousseau (1712–1778). Intolerance for creative thinkers forced Rousseau into a life of itineracy. He was persecuted and his books were burned by both Protestant and Catholic ecclesiastical authorities (Genevan and French, respectively).

Rousseau's philosophical writings were extensive and subtle. Reasonable philosophers can disagree as to what the main, seminal ideas in them are. But clearly, the fulcrum of his thinking was his polemic against the doctrine of original sin and his portrayal of what might be called man's "original goodness." Rousseau saw man in his natural state as having been nobly benign and decent but corrupted when the rise of rank and property in society upset his natural equality with his fellows. Rousseau advocated not a return to nature but a reordering of society as a "social contract," based on popular sovereignty. Besides influencing many later luminaries familiar to us, his writings stimulated widespread reform in child-rearing methods.

Rousseau retained a strong, sentimental attachment to Christianity and did not inveigh against its basic supernatural premises. He advocated, as a term of the "social contract," *civil religion,* a few affirmative religious essentials everyone could agree on with doctrinal specifics left out.[141] His notion of man in the state of nature drew heavily on the biblical account of Adam and Eve before the fall for its inspiration. But this time, mankind was to undertake the responsibility for statecraft and no longer be put off by the claim that God actively places civil authorities in their positions and those authorities need account to no one but him.[142] Only to the higher, natural law—of divine origin in Rousseau's view—was man to be unconditionally obedient. All education would ultimately be religious education, inasmuch as fostering self-knowledge, self-understanding, and, thereby, the discovery of the existence of God in one's own existence is its true purpose.[143]

Modern theories that take a stand on the broad issue of man's moral nature all have their roots in the earlier polemic between Rousseau and orthodox Christianity. When we encounter extreme and adamantly expressed views in favor of permissive rearing of children, nonpunitive handling of criminals, political ideologies based on the belief that an elite who are "enlightened" by some set of ideological beliefs could be trusted with absolute power, Rogerian therapy, etc., then it is the notion that man's good nature will spontaneously emerge if not spoiled by negative experiences imposed from without that is tacitly being presupposed. Interestingly, the same individuals who hold such views (except for Rogerians and proponents of other "existential" views) tend also to subscribe to deterministic psychological schools, such as behaviorism, or a later derivative of Freudianism. I know of no inherent intellectual reason for such an affinity of views. Can it be that the old-time-religion pastors did such a good job of

141. See p. 17, footnote 11.

142. Job 12:18; Ps. 75:6–7; Dan. 2:21; Rom. 13:1–2.

143. Ernst Cassierer, *The Question of Jean Jacques Rousseau,* trans. Peter Gay (Bloomington: Indiana University Press, 1963).

instilling the impression that the old religious ways were intertwined with the notion of free will that people implicitly expect a secular theory of man's moral nature to be deterministic?

Likewise, we find a tacit aversion to the view that there are absolutes in the structure of human experience, expressed in the unpopularity in the United States of all those psychological positions we have labeled nativistic. Can it be that the intellectual community is composed of individuals still personally too close to the stifling restraint of artificial religious absolutes to face the prospect that surrender to *natural* absolutes will be needful for them? The intellectual community has come so far with the one-sided twentieth-century experience of mastering nature that it is unprepared to deal with man's corresponding need—to master himself in order to live in harmony with nature where possible. Leaving aside the immense topic of the difficulty of humanizing technology, we have yet to see resolved the polemic between Rousseau and orthodox Christianity in productive seeking after the natural absolutes. Historically, we are not finished breaking the bondage of that great, premature attempt to find absolutes in nature and hold them close, which orthodox Christianity deserves some respect for having been, so that we can take the next big step.[144]

Incomplete liberation from, and continuing bondage to, reaction to the old religious views on the parts of those who are now the older generation of American social scientists and mental-health professionals may also explain the persistence of the notion that good and evil are either simple concomitants of pain and pleasure, or else are relative to learned standards and limitlessly plastic. Thus, it follows, all negative human behavior will supposedly disappear if provision is made for the gratification of those few, simple needs that are genuinely instinctive,[145] and, through enlightenment and education, the failures of communication from which all other outcroppings of negative behavior supposedly

---

144. Our incompleteness in figuring out what should be our goals at the highest level of generality and abstraction is due, in part, to the extremely short historical time in which our mastery over some aspects of nature has arisen. If anything, we Americans are better off than others, for the short-range practicality that has dominated our approach. We have referred to some of the splendid, but more introverted, intellectual approaches to higher-order issues that the German-speakers pursued before Hitler, and the eventual impoverishment of our own intellectual surroundings tracing back to the disruption of those pursuits. In that culture, it was widely regarded as desirable to be "private" or "unpolitical" and to rely on unseen, mandarinlike authorities to look after matters economic and governmental. Thomas Mann's supremely wrong-headed classic, *Reflections of an Unpolitical Man,* sets out vividly the attitudes that prompted many of the best Germans—including Jewish Germans—to be uninvolved when their body politic was in critical condition. In hindsight, we can see the biblical holdover in those attitudes. The biblical attitude of complete obedience to secular civil authorities was carried over intact, and a perilously fragile cultural, intellectual, and artistic discipline and order supplanted ecclesiastically mandated discipline and order in their private lives. In a way, the religious among those intensely private Germans suffered the consequences of relying on God to pull one's political and social chestnuts out of the fire.

145. Arising from a Freudian context, the notion that easy instinct gratification, specifically sexual gratification, will reverse the causes of neurosis, has been followed by Wilhelm Reich to the point of advocating sexual promiscuity. That view has, in turn, been stood on its head by Herbert Marcuse, mixing Freudianism with Marxism. Marcuse complained that by making instinct gratification too readily available, Western capitalist societies make their populations docile and uncritical, and he coined the term *repressive desublimation* for the soporification of mass populations by too easy instinct gratification. In addition to Reich's and Marcuse's own writings, see

arise, are resolved. Since the underlying premise is that good and evil are relative, this sort of thinking defeats itself, by implying that higher-order definition of the positive or desirable behavior being advocated is not possible. Members of that generation were offended if one pointed out that, even though the most clever cannot satisfactorily define good and evil, all but the least clever know them and can readily distinguish them on encounter. That generation tacitly accepted the false dilemma that either the old religious notions of good and evil are valid or else no immutable principles of good or evil can be valid. That generation could not see that the old religious notions can be a caricature of true absolutes and can reflect an element of validity with the spirits of times past and a manipulative hidden agenda overlying and obscuring it.

The prevailing tendency of theorists of human nature has been to make taxonomies or lists of drives. Leaving aside the objections of organismic or holistic thinkers to such theories, we find that their disagreement with one another and their crude fit to the phenomena make them unimpressive. The simplest of these focuses on general autonomically mediated arousal, preparatory for fleeing, fighting, or propagatory (mating, rearing the young, etc.) behavior, in that order of priority. Many others consist of different lists of drives and prioritizing relations among them. Freud's list of two drives—a "good" drive, *eros,* and a "bad" drive, *thanatos*—finally turned out to resemble the biblical notion, after Freud's long effort to make his system function with the erotic drive only.

A particularly admirable attempt to reconcile the "original goodness" of man with the constancy of his aggressive behavior, very popular in American behavioral-science circles in the forties and fifties, was the *frustration-aggression hypothesis.* It took ". . . as its point of departure the assumption that *aggression is always a consequence of frustration* . . . . that the occurrence of aggressive behavior always presupposes the existence of frustration, and, contrawise, that the existence of frustration always leads to some form of aggression."[146] Man was seen as having "legitimate" creature needs and as being a benign creature except when the frustration of those needs forced him to be otherwise. A social program to avoid need-deprivation frustrations would let man be the benign creature he, supposedly, really is. The presence of other reactions to frustration, such as regression, apathy, hyperemotionality, and creative problem-solving, along with nonfrustrating instigators of aggression, discredited the theory and made a museum piece of it by the end of the sixties.[147] The field of study of the negative in human nature has gone by default to views derived from Freud (with two natures, a "good" drive and a "bad" drive in contention), views based on

---

Philip Rieff, *The Triumph of the Therapeutic* (New York: Harper & Row, 1968) and Paul A. Robinson, *The Freudian Left: Wilhelm Reich, Geza Roheim, Herbert Marcuse* (New York: Harper & Row, 1969).

146. John Dollard, Neal E. Miller, Leonard W. Doob, O. Hobart Mowrer, and Robert R. Sears, *Frustration and Aggression* (New Haven, Conn.: Yale University Press, 1939), p. 1.

147. See Leonard Berkowitz, ed., *Roots of Aggression: A Re-examination of the Frustration-Aggression Hypothesis* (New York: Atherton Press, 1969).

analogies to infrahuman species-specific behavior, and views seeking to declare the issue nonexistent, as the behaviorists do.

Despite all the progress in our knowledge in other areas, we remain enigmatic to ourselves as regards our moral nature. Beyond the realm of behavior discernably related to survival or self-interest lie immense occurrences of altruism, on the one hand, and gratuitious cruelty and destructiveness, not benefitting the perpetrators at all, on the other, that we cannot explain. The generalizations about human nature we can confidently make are humble. Primarily, we are creatures equipped to cope with our environment, and we wither and become sick if it is too hard or too easy. We come in two sexes having different and interdependent biological destinies. We readily acquire inhibitions against using the means so near to hand for each of us to harm ourselves and others grievously. Secondarily, we are creatures equipped to deal with what is contrary to fact, to exhibit intelligence and creativity. Our ignorance as to the origins and purpose of our secondary symbolic equipment is vast, and the latter-day creation myth of random mutation and natural selection that comforted us during the preceding century dies hard. No schematic or reductive rendition of ourselves that we attempt rises higher than patent falsification.

Our problem of self-understanding is further complicated by the integral rôle misperception of our own moral nature plays, in lending that nature its character. Having a distorted view of our own moral nature or condition, usually in the adverse direction, is part of our nature. James implicitly recognized this when he characterized the religious-converison experience as the change of a subjective condition of being "wrong, inferior and unhappy" into one of being "right, superior and happy." Later psychologists recognized it also, in their continual emphasis on self-esteem, or the subjective feeling of being "o.k.," as an effect to be sought for, and a determiner of the individual's general mental health, to be manipulated.

One comes to appreciate the innateness of feeling "wrong, inferior and unhappy" in human experience, when one serves as a defense attorney. In my fairly extensive experience defending street criminals, generally I found the criminals to have good information as to the punishment risk entailed by their crimes. They had weighed the risks realistically and made the conscious decision that the benefit was worth it. The comments one often hears from criminologists about the supposed ineffectiveness of deterrence against crime ring false to those who have dealt with criminals on an individual basis. The sole gaping exception to the rule that criminals exhibit quite a functional approach to their own self-interest is in the area of confessions and admissions. Because self-disserving admissions can be used as evidence against one in court and the suspicions or inferences of the police based on the person's silence or lack of cooperation cannot be so used, it is never in the self-interest of one suspected of a common crime to cooperate with police, except with the participation of the defense attorney in circumstances indicating plea bargaining or some other negotiation with the prosecution. Every criminal knows this from his street education, from his past experiences with defense attorneys, and from the Miranda ritual that must precede any police interrogation accompanied by impairment of freedom of movement. And yet, one never ceases to be amazed at the substantial proportion of convictions that would have been unobtainable had the defendant not convicted himself out of his own mouth. The typicalness of the compulsion to confess[148] and the underlying sound but guilty conscience indicated by it are clear and impressive to all who work with common criminals.

Not only criminals experience the compulsion to confess. Joost A. M. Meerloo, a social psychiatrist who has written refreshingly and relevantly on mass psychology, suicide, aggression, and other complex social problems, recounted his own experience as a member of the Dutch Resistance in Nazi prisons:

> As soon as man is alone, closed off from the world and from the news of what is going on, his mental activity is replaced by quite different processes. Long-forgotten anxieties come to the surface, long-repressed memories knock on his mind from inside. His fantasy life begins to develop and assume gigantic proportions. He cannot evaluate or check his fantasies against the events of his ordinary days, and very soon they may take possession of him.
>
> I remember very clearly my own fantasies during the time I was in a Nazi prison. It was almost impossible for me to control my depressive thoughts of hopelessness. I had to tell myself over and over again: "Think, think. Keep your senses alert; don't give in." I tried to use all my psychiatric knowledge to keep my mind in a state of relaxed mobilization, and on many days I felt it was a losing battle."[149]

> To the horrors the accused victim suffers from without must be added the horrors from within. He is pursued by the unsteadiness of his own mind, which cannot always produce the same answer to a repeated question. As a human being with a conscience he is pursued by possible hidden guilt feelings, however pious he may have been, that undermine his rational awareness of his innocence. The panic of the "brainwashee" is the total confusion he suffers about all concepts. . . . The enemy knows that, far below the surface, human life is built up of inner contradictions. He uses this knowledge to defeat and confuse the brainwashee.[150]

Probably the most crucial blind spot in the mental-health professions has been in their widespread failure to understand the constructive rôle played in our makeup by the universal and pervasive tendency to feel "wrong, inferior and unhappy." Do we really want our self-esteem and self-confidence to forge so vigorously ahead, when the means to do grievous harm to others and ourselves are always so near to hand for each of us? Would we not come rapidly to harm without our constant, nagging doubts in much the same way that we would if deprived of pain sensitivity? In criminology, the consensus of opinion,

---

148. The standard orthodox Freudian statement is Theodor Reik, *The Compulsion to Confess* (New York: Farrar, Strauss and Cudahy, 1959). The underlying lectures were originally presented in 1925, when Reik was Freud's approved surrogate; the work mimicks Freud's style.
149. *The Rape of the Mind* (New York: Universal Library, 1961), p. 78.
150. Ibid., p. 29.

well supported by research, is that criminals whose self-esteem remains high because they always put the blame elsewhere than on themselves are the most likely to be recidivists and the least likely to benefit from rehabilitation. Is a bland, untroubled state of mind, without poignancy, contrast, or memorableness, what we would call fulfilling? Do mental-health professionals do us a favor by teaching us that a bland, untroubled state of mind, accompanied by coolly efficient performance, is possible, in some sense is normal, and is available to those who purchase their services and medications? Are the mental-health professionals and the Evangelicals ultimately competitors in marketing false promises on how to make life run on an even keel?

We have already established that the Bible takes the most negative plausible stand on the moral nature of man, and it is from the pervasive, innate human tendency to feel "wrong, inferior and unhappy" that the teaching of original sin gains its plausibility. For its own mind-control purposes, the Bible exploits that tendency and aggravates and distorts it enormously. Nevertheless, along with its broadside attack on human self-esteem and its promises of subjective stability for those who follow its program,[151] the Bible offers sound, avuncular advice on the management of the subjective sense of inner discord. The psychological astuteness of the Bible authors, dwarfing much contemporary psychotherapeutic wisdom, is reflected in the following:

> Bear ye one another's burdens. . . . For if a man think himself to be something, when he is nothing, he deceiveth himself. But let every man prove his own work, and then shall he have rejoicing in himself alone, and not in another. For every man shall bear his own burden.[152]

> There hath no temptation [trial, adversity] taken you but such as is common to man: but God *is* faithful, who will not suffer you to be tempted above that ye are able; but will with the temptation also make a way to escape, that ye may be able to bear *it*.[153]

> . . . [W]e glory in tribulations also: knowing that tribulation worketh patience; And patience, experience; and experience, hope; And hope maketh not ashamed. . . .[154]

> In the world ye shall have tribulation. . . .[155]

By presenting their hearers with realistic expectations about the experience of feeling troubled and by giving them to expect the untroubledness promised them to be, at best, bittersweet and poignant, the Bible authors protected themselves against losing credibility with their hearers, as would have quickly ensued

151. Phil. 4:7; Gal. 5:22; Luke 8:22–25.
152. Gal. 6:2–5.
153. 1 Cor. 10:13.
154. Rom. 5:3–5.
155. John 16:33.

had the promises been simply of life on an even keel. In orthodox church circles, there are no great numbers of ex-subscribers complaining of the emptiness and ineffectualty of their experience as we, today, encounter at every hand in former psychotherapy clients who have been misled by the tacit promise of an altogether untroubled life.

We can benefit from the Bible authors' penetrating insight into their people, in assessing the self-esteem issue for our own time. They expressed very clearly their low appraisal of it. They tacitly supposed that low self-esteem was not at the root of people's problems, and never suggested manipulation of self-esteem as a cure. They implied that man naturally has high self-esteem, perhaps like our rehabilitation-resistant, recidivism-prone criminal.

> He [Jesus] said unto him [the lawyer], What is written in the law? how readest thou? And he answering said, Thou shalt love the Lord thy God with all thy heart, and with all thy soul, and with all thy strength, and with all thy mind; and thy neighbor *as thyself* [italics added].[156]

> For no man ever yet hated his own flesh; but nourish and cherisheth it, even as the Lord the church. . . .[157]

It may well be that just as people in Bible times were not so convinced of the separateness and autonomy of their ego-personalities as we are, and were more aware of "spirits" partaking of the "non-I" animating them than we are, so also were they less self-conscious than we about the reality of lives failing to live up to prescribed aspirations. They would learn that sort of self-consciousness from the Bible authors. And just as the Bible authors would begin by giving their hearers good insight into the relation of native and learned influences in their experience, but then tell them, for ulterior reasons, that they must become entirely other-directed and not look within themselves in distinguishing right from wrong, so would those authors mount a broadside attack on their hearers' natural self-esteem. And after giving them psychologically sound advice on the management of self-doubt, they would tell them that they are to receive their self-esteem only from an exterior, monopolistic source:

> We love him, because he first loved us.[158]

> For I know that in me (that is, in my flesh,) dwelleth no good thing: for to will is present with me; but *how* to perform that which is good I find not.[159]

---

156. Luke 10:26-27. Cf. Lev. 19:18, 34; Matt. 19:19; 22:39; Mark 12:31; Rom. 13:9; Gal. 5:14; and James 2:8.
157. Eph. 5:29. Cf. Phil. 2:3.
158. 1 John 4:19.
159. Rom. 7:18.

> I am crucified with Christ: nevertheless I live; yet not I, but Christ liveth in me: and the life which I now live in the flesh I live by the faith of the Son of God, who loved me, and gave himself for me.[160]

> For I know nothing by myself. . . .[161]

> I can do all things through Christ which strengtheneth me.[162]

We can see the same pattern unfolding in the biblical authors' approach to each of our nature-of-man issues. They begin with some sound insight—often tacitly expressed but always unmistakable—about their people. They carry that insight far enough for some useful practical advice to arise from it. Then, in each instance, they veer off into something contrived and artificial. When the issue of free will versus determinism arose, we found that the Bible authors paralleled our psychodynamic concept of complexes, producing inner inertia against the good intentions of human will and preventing each individual from being truly the master of himself. But then they veered off, claiming that humans have no proclivity for good that is truly characteristic of them. When the issue of nativism versus empiricism (or heredity versus environment) arose, the Bible authors anticipated organismic thinking. But then they veered off in peculiar forms of fragmentation of the human experience, particularly pertaining to the time between earthly death and judgment day, portraying the saved person as being more fragmented than the unsaved during earthly existence. When the mind/body problem arose, to our astonishment the Bible authors transcended all secular philosophy, anticipating the view held by the most sophisticated late-twentieth-century thinkers, namely, that the awareness of discrepancy between mind and body is an artifact of the one-sidedness of our consciousness, pointing to a consciousness-alien underlying reality. But then they veered off, misrepresenting the alien reality as a place of threat and menace, a club to hold over their believers' heads. And when the question of man's moral nature arose, the Bible authors manifested the insight that, in Meerloo's words, "human life is built up of inner contradictions." But then they veered off, denigrating the inner man as something entirely negative, counseling as complete an alienation of the individual from his own inner being as possible, and representing the good in man as only coming in from the outside.

In each instance where the Bible authors began with a penetrating psychological insight but then veered off into pronouncements that—when we compare them with the best psychological information available to us—are revealed as contrived and artificial, a mind-control purpose is being served. However sorry a figure the Bible may cut as a didactic model of man or of human experience, it has succeeded and endured like nothing else in human history! The New Testament authors were not trying to create an intellectually correct didactic model.

---

160. Gal. 2:20.
161. I Cor. 4:4.
162. Phil. 4:13.

They were trying to do just what they did do: to create a human organization that could get started without social power, prestige, or acclaim on its side, eliciting total loyalty from its members and becoming self-perpetuating. Their aim was not education, but indoctrination. The debate has always been between parties complaining that the Bible indoctrination does not make rational sense and parties who answer that the Bible indoctrination, by its own terms, is not supposed to make rational sense. That debate has always left the crucial question unanswered: How can the biblical scheme be so wrong intellectually and yet have registered such unexcelled success in organizing and managing people? We shall proceed to answer that question and, by understanding the most successful assault on human psychological vulnerabilities ever devised, bring into focus some indirect indicators whereby psychological insights pertaining to human concerns more fundamental than religion may be tested.

For we have not followed cunningly devised fables. . . .—2 Pet. 1:16

. . . I should not be ashamed: That I may not seem as if I would terrify you by letters.—2 Cor. 10:8-9

And I went unto the angel, and said unto him, Give me the little book, And he said unto me, Take *it,* and eat it up; and it shall make thy belly bitter, but it shall be in thy mouth sweet as honey. And I took the little book out of the angel's hand, and ate it up; and it was in my mouth sweet as honey: and as soon as I had eaten it, my belly was bitter.—Rev. 10:9-10

Talking to a preacher,
'Said God was on his side.
'Talking to a pusher,
They both was selling highs.
—Contemporary Country Song[1]

Today's religion is tomorrow's bondage.—Bob Dylan[2]

Chapter 3

The Two Kinds of Mind-Games

It is awfully late in the history of Bible studies to come forward with startlingly new insight about it. How can it be that generation after generation of commentators incorrectly thought that if the Bible is not what it claims to be, then it must be a premature attempt at understanding the origins of the surrounding world or else a means of keeping people honest by making them think that the eye of a great, omniscient judge is always on them? With devices such as separating the believer from competing sources of influence, or providing ready rationalizations for discrediting sources of influence the believers cannot be kept entirely away from, or threatening the believer with retribution in a life to come—so obviously presented, and so easily seen through—how can there be room for new insight about the Bible as a manipulation tool? Can it really be that intelligent people today, with all their experience on the receiving end of

1. Neil Young, "Are You Ready for the Country?" (BMI). The hit version, circa 1976, was sung by Waylon Jennings.
2. *Philadelphia Inquirer,* Nov. 14, 1983, p. 5-E.

hype of every kind, can fall victim to a hype so old and so exhaustively exploited, if the Bible is that?

The short answer to all those questions is *synergism.* Several different devices—some that would not function well in isolation because they would be too obvious and transparent and others so subtle that, in isolation, their effects would be fleeting and quickly subside—are involved. The effect of all of them working together is immensely more powerful than the sum of their effects would be outside their synergistic relation with one another. The Evangelical mind-control system is more like a recipe than like an equation. It must have been through experience that the Bible authors learned just what combination of terrifying threats, illusory promises, arcane symbolism, and double talk would best manipulate the people and manage the cult.

The subject of our study is at once a literary masterpiece and a masterpiece of applied psychology. The unerring sense of people reflected in the Bible may well be what contemporary church leaders, even the liberal ones, have tacitly in mind when they reaffirm doctrinal statements characterizing the Bible as infallible or inerrant. When angry antireligionists from Thomas Paine to Madalyn Murray O'Hair have triumphantly pointed out contradictions and absurdities in the Bible, the implication has always been that its stupendous historical success happened for no reason, or ought not to have happened. The great apostles of rational cause and effect end up proponents of the view that something can be a sustained and repeated success by accident. One cuts a sorry figure arguing with success in our culture, which may be the reason why we hear so little of the organized atheists today.

The keys to sorting out the nonobvious features of the Evangelical mind-control system are its *indirect indicators.* For a century, the American religious debate has emphasized the Bible's cosmology and the contrast with modern attempts to explain mankind's origins. In the last analysis, the Bible was found to contain relatively few specific cosmological statements, and ways could be found to harmonize them with the relatively few strong conclusions that science can substantiate without speculating too broadly. In the previous chapter, we brought ourselves nearer to the pertinent questions by noting the way basic issues regarding human nature are treated by the Bible as compared to the best available insights of psychology and related fields. Although the current disarray and malaise in the psychology discipline hampered us and we fashioned our own psychological positions in the absence of ones representing broad scientific consensus, we were able to show that the Bible authors were astute psychological observers who consistently got remarkably close to the truth midway in their inquiry but then veered quite deliberately away, into artificialities.

The first major category of indirect indicators of mind-control purposes underlying biblical teachings is just this type of artificial psychological pronouncement. When we encounter a biblical author making penetrating observations about his people and then making a psychological statement that accords neither with the common sense of his own day nor with the scientific knowledge of ours, we are alerted. As I am unable to find a fitting term for this category of clue without an unfortunately strident ring to it, I shall refer to manipulative biblical misstatements about human psychology as *biblical pseudopsychology.*

The second kind of indirect indicator is a New Testament departure from tradition, particularly the one claimed as its root, namely, the Old Testament. Seminary professors have long told their students, "the Old [Testament] is by the New explained: the New is in the Old contained," and, "the New is in the Old concealed: the Old is in the New revealed." If well-enough indoctrinated, seminarians who are not unintelligent can read the Bible and preach all their lives without noticing the crucial instances where those slogans prove false.

Consider the phrase "Thou shalt love thy neighbor as thyself." It has already figured prominently in our consideration of the supposed biblical mandate to the church to undertake charitable relief for the creature needs of the unsaved and in the implicit biblical stand on the modern question of self-esteem. We find that in the whole Old Testament, the phrase makes only two obscure appearances,[3] with nothing to intimate that it is to become the second greatest commandment. But the phrase appears in the New Testament seven times, and very prominently.[4] We shall observe and analyze the operation of three distinct and manipulative psychological devices in it.

Less frequently, we find that the New Testament authors have ignored a very striking Old Testament verse that does not suit their purposes. For instance, nothing at all like Psalm 51:17, "The sacrifices of God *are* a broken spirit: a broken and a contrite heart, O God, thou wilt not despise" appears anywhere in the New Testament. We will see that the intrasubjective emphasis of this verse, which has made its teaching central for much of American old-time-religion Christianity, conflicts with the purposes of the New Testament authors.

The third important category of indirect indicator is the hypersensitivity of Bible authors or later proponents of biblicism. When they are unduly defensive in explaining something, using too much hyperpole, too many rhetorical questions in lieu of direct assertions—when they "protest too much"—we know we may be onto something psychologically interesting. When we encountered John Wesley stridently proclaiming Calvinism "blasphemy" because it offended his common sense,[5] we knew the point was a sore one. The first three of the epigraphs to this chapter are examples, although we would be less than fair were we to accept them as such without further explanation. If we neglect to substantiate the mind-control purpose we suppose underlies a peculiarly intense outburst, our

---

3. Lev. 19:18, 34. Actually, the exact phrase "thy neighbor as thyself" appears only in verse 18, and the latter, cognate verse pertains to the protection of sojourning foreigners. Nowhere else, in all the statutory portions of the Pentateuch, does the phrase or anything like it appear. Once, and once only, the Old Testament believer is told to love his compatriot as himself, and then to place the foreigner on the same level as his compatriot.

4. Matt. 19:19; 22:39; Mark 12:31; Luke 10:27; Rom. 13:9; Gal. 5:14; and James 2:8. The Lucan passage where the phrase occurs contains the only biblical information about the meaning of the term *neighbor*. See pp. 59-60.

5. See p. 24.

reliance on the outburst as an indicator will tend to *argumentum ad hominem.*[6] Indirect indicators are only clues, showing us where to look further.

The synergistic, mind-control program we seek is embedded in the New Testament. The indirect indicators are the preliminary way whereby we can distinguish the operative features from the camouflage and distracting surplusage. When the New Testament instructs us explicitly in how it is to be interpreted, we may safely infer that our real insight will come from circumventing that instruction. In presenting the system's separate devices, we will be following roughly their time sequence. It suits our didactic purposes to recapitulate both the historical sequence that gave rise to the system originally and the sequence it follows in taking hold of an individual person who comes under it.

Historical Context of the New Testament

The viewpoint of the New Testament as we know it is that of the strategically located, early Roman church, which prevailed over a wide and confusing variety of views then current and attributed to Jesus. The canonical books relegate some very significant history to oblique, seemingly innocuous references. Our treatment of that history will be confined to the very narrow purpose of showing main trends that distinguish the contents of the canon from other early writings that were first considered sacred but subsequently declared heretical.

We covered a bit of the situation of the Jews in Israel at the time of Jesus, in introducing the New Testament teachings on the believers' rigid duties with

---

6. Our method of explaining in psychological terms why people hold certain religious views can easily degenerate into *argumentum ad hominem* if used improperly.

The most impressive Christian apologetic argument for believing things that cannot be verified as propositions in other fields are verified is that Christianity's long history of attracting and holding the loyalty of people of good will must reflect that its truth and beneficiality was manifest to those people, even if it cannot be explained, or appreciated within the narrow breadth of the individual's perspective. That argument, and the history behind it, is the crucial datum for which social scientists studying religion have never accounted. Our purpose, which has never been undertaken before, is explanation of the psychological attraction that has given Christianity such a tenacious hold on people, despite the unverifiability or wrongness of its ideas. In so doing, we make no statement about Christians more derogatory than that they possess normal human psychological vulnerabilities. It is perfectly consistent with our approach to concede that nearly all Christians are sincere and bona fide, and that many of them are intelligent.

The key to distinguishing *ad hominem* argument from fair criticism of psychological bias in holding any given view, is to keep track of who should have the burden of proof. The proponent of a position that is neither self-evident nor supported by intelligible argument, or the one attacking a point that has been made and supported by some proof, must draw on substance, or else we are entitled to suppose it is only subjective motives and desires that account for the views expressed. If a Christian comes at me, saying that my failure to believe as he does indicates my lack of the Holy Spirit, or my having received a spirit of blindness, it is up to him to prove it. If he believes for no articulate reason, then it is fair for me to try to explain away his belief psychologically. Behind his biblical pseudopsychological analysis of me necessarily lies an indirect attack on my character. If my psychological analysis fails to make sense and fit the facts, then it is no better. The end result hopefully will be observables brought together and made intelligible by my analyses. The Christian, unable to make the facts and his doctrines cooperate, will finally be heard to say that his view is right because it follows biblical teaching, and the Bible is right because it says it is.

respect to secular civil authority.[7] In the first century, when the power of Rome was reaching its zenith, there was already a large Jewish diaspora, Jewish communities scattered throughout the Empire and in Rome itself. Those communities were prominent in the economic and civic life of the places where they were found, and they were at pains to demonstrate their civic desirability and lack of subversive or seditious potential. They were greatly respected, and the Jews came to be the only ethnic group exempted from participation in the state cult, at first by custom and later by law. Interspersed with that respect was out-group prejudice, much as occurred later under Christianity. The Jews' earnestness, practical success, and great antiquity of tradition as compared with the Romans, served to foster belief by the Romans in exalted, supernaturalistic claims made for the Jews. The Romans were an inordinately superstitious people, and the study of pre-Christian, anti-Jewish prejudice sensitizes one to the close affinity between tacit acceptance of the supernaturalistic premises of Judaism and prejudice against it.

The Roman church, in the second and third centuries, leading up to the closure of the canon, was in a position much like unconverted Jewish communities outside Israel, and, likewise, its leaders were at pains to show themselves and their flocks to be loyal citizens, without subversive or seditious potential. For reasons we will explain presently, the composition of the Roman church became increasingly Gentile, and its concerns diverged rapidly from those of Jewish nationalists after the fall of Jerusalem, A.D. 70. The canonical books, particularly the Acts of the Apostles, reflected the need to avoid saying ill of the Roman state and the Gentiles who were sought as proselytes. Accordingly, where the events in the ministries of Jesus and the disciples are described in the synoptic Gospels and Acts, the Jewish population's daily distress under Roman oppression recedes into the background and, understandably, the insular concerns of the Christian group loom large. Initially, we see Jesus as a popular leader, and no reason or explanation is given for the turn of the tide of Jewish public opinion against him, as portrayed in the Gospels. No indication is given of the unpopularity of the Sanhedrin, which was the Vichy government of its day. Hugh J. Schonfield[8] commented on the false ring of the Gospels in this respect:

---

7. See pp. 61-65.

8. Schonfield is a valuable resource for the historical background of the New Testament period, getting at the human motives underlying the events but not lapsing into rosy historical fiction. But readers of Schonfield must correct for his bias, which is against the early Jewish proponents of Jesus having intended to found a new religion, discard the keeping of the ritual law, or contaminate the sublime, "wholly-other" monotheistic God with pagan philosophical ideas. After *The Passover Plot* (New York: Bernard Geis Associates, 1965), in *Those Incredible Christians* (New York: Bernard Geis Associates, 1968), he traced the events from the crucifixion through the fall of Jerusalem, with nothing more said about a resurrection falsified by the use of a drug. In *The Jesus Party* (New York: Macmillan Publishing Co., 1974), he explained the secular history affecting the New Testament history and demonstrated the irreconcilability of biblical chronology with the well-established dates of certain events. Also, in *The Politics of God* (Chicago: Henry Regnery, 1970), he portrayed Jewish Messianism as resembling and converging with contemporary, Tillichian views and as highly relevant to modern man's search for meaning. He avoided dealing with the negative implications of obsessive concern with ritual purity, and passed very lightly over the Gnostic materials, with which he was quite familiar, that show the proliferation of sects in Israel composed of Jews and espousing intensely foreign theological ideas.

> Quite clearly, as the Gospels allow, the common people of Jerusalem regarded Jesus as empathically on their side. If the Evangelists had set down that Pilate, by some stratagem or display of force, had succeeded in getting Jesus into his power, but that then the people in their thousands had flocked to the governor's residence to clamor for his release, their account would have been in harmony with the people's known attitude. But that they should be represented as shouting to their enemy to crucify their champion is utterly incongruous. Only persons antagonistic to the Jews, writing long afterwards to placate the Romans and for Gentile believers unfamiliar with Pilate's character and the history of his administration,[9] could have been guilty of striking such a grossly false note. For Christian spokesmen still to talk of popular disillusionment, and of fickle mobs, is in this instance absurd.[10]

Also, if Pilate's purpose in having Jesus crucified were to please the Jews, then why did he put the inscription so derisive toward them, "Jesus the Nazarene, the King of the Jews," on the cross with Jesus?[11] And if the elimination of Jesus were so popular locally, why then did Pilate's superior, Vitellius, remove him from his post, send him to Rome to answer charges brought against him by the Jews, and force Caiaphas from the post of high priest shortly afterwards?[12] We find the preoccupations of later times superimposed on all accounts of Jesus and his ministry. While we can be reasonably sure that the most salient and frequently discussed features remained, their emphasis and implications were surely much altered. We simply can never know what the "cause of Christ" really was.

Another probable instance of biblical history refashioned to meet the political needs of the Roman church in a later time is the biblical rendering of the polemic between Paul and the "Judaizers," those who thought that becoming a Christian required first becoming a Jew and living in full compliance with Jewish ceremonial law. That way, the requirements of circumcision and keeping the complicated dietary laws remained as obstacles to the recruitment of Gentile converts. The New Testament presents us with the image of Paul presenting his streamlined rendition of ceremonial and moral righteousness to the Council in Jerusalem, and suggests that afterwards only a few misguided stragglers failed to come along. Is this reconcilable with what is known historically?

Schonfield summarizes what can be gleaned from all the sources about the church in its earliest times:

---

9. Pilate was a notorious brigand in his relations with the Jews. According to Josephus (*Antiquities of the Jews,* Book 18, chap. 3), when Pilate was first installed as procurator of Judea, contrary to his predecessors' practice of respecting the Temple, he had guards with insignia displaying the emperor's image, posted near the Temple. The insignia violated the prohibition of Jewish law against graven images. A crowd of Jews came to Caesarea to protest, and Pilate had his guards surround them with swords drawn. The Jews lay down on the ground and bared their necks. His bluff called, Pilate had the offending images taken away from the Temple.

10. *The Jesus Party,* pp. 74-75.

11. John 19:19. Note how the Gospel accounts of the inscription on the cross conflict with one another (Matt. 27:37; Mark 15:26, and Luke 23:38). A popular theme of discussion, deflecting attention from the practical, historical implications of this event, is the notion that God directly intervened in Pilate's mind to cause him to make the inscription for the believers' edification. The way for such a theme is prepared by the device of Mrs. Pilate's prophetic dream (Matt. 27:19.)

12. Josephus, *Antiquities,* Book 18, chap. 4.

> The irreducible minimum of knowledge . . . [is] that there had sprung up after the death of Jesus a Jewish organization centered on Jerusalem which claimed him as the Messiah and the prophet foretold by Moses. This organization was commonly described as Nazorean. It might fittingly be called an Israel Loyalist Movement, since it emphasized loyalty to God and His Law and devotion to the king of Israel of God's choice. The king, namely Jesus, after having been raised from the dead was now in heaven, but would soon return to earth in judgment to punish the wicked and deliver the faithful remnant of his people from their enemies and oppressors. Thereafter he would reign over a world converted to knowledge of God and obedient to His commandments.[13]

The Nazoreans, a "party" in Israeli life, as were the Pharisees, Sadducees, Zealots, and Essenes, centered around individuals who had known Jesus, particularly his relatives. For its first quarter century or so, their Council was presided over by Jesus' brother, James, who was succeeded by Simeon, Jesus' cousin.[14] The Nazorean leadership formed what was, in its own estimation, a loyal, legitimate underground Sanhedrin, in opposition to the illegitimate, collaborationist, spurious Sanhedrin mandated by the Romans. The Nazoreans never put into practice the abrogation of the ceremonial law proclaimed by Paul. It is not likely that they ever subscribed to the virgin birth or to the elaboration of Jesus' resurrection into a saving mystery, as these elements are borrowings from pagan mythology, with elements of the worship of Dionysus, Adonis, Mithras, and Perseus—just the sort of influence from which Jewish loyalists wanted to keep Israel separate and pure. They set great store by Jesus' baptism by John, as the point of his transformation from ordinary manhood to prophethood. The Nazoreans are known to have continued as a Jewish party into the fourth century A.D., and were known as such to Jerome and Epiphanius.[15] The disappearance of the Nazoreans may well have coincided with the promise of Jesus' speedy return not being fulfilled and hence becoming untenable.[16]

Seeing the Council Paul had to appear before in this light, and not as the more informal group of elders or participants in the Jerusalem church that it seems to be in Acts[17] and in Paul's own account,[18] the events make more sense.

---

13. *The Jesus Party,* p. 14.
14. Jules Lebreton, S.J., and Jacques Zeiller, *The Emergence of the Church in the Roman World,* trans. Ernest C. Messenger (New York: Collier Books, 1962), pp. 201–05.
15. *The Jesus Party,* p. 286.
16. It is striking to look at the biblical promises of a speedy second coming—Mark 13:30, Luke 21:32, John 21:22–23, Rev. 22:7, 12 and 20—and see that their unfulfillment after nearly two thousand years completely vitiates the Bible's supernaturalistic claims. (Matt. 16:28, Mark 9:1, and Luke 9:27 make a similar promise: "some standing here . . . shall not taste of death, till they see the Son of man coming in his kingdom." This can be rationalized as having been executed by the transfiguration, which comes immediately after in each of the synoptic Gospels and is seen by Peter, James and John, who had been standing with Jesus when he made the promise.) The authors of our college history text believed that the failure of the second coming had been one of the causes of the ascendancy of Paulinism, since "belief in an immediate Second Coming began to prove an embarassment after the first generation or so, and had to be spiritualized into a theological doctrine of salvation." Brinton, et al., *A History of Civilization,* vol. 1, 2nd ed. (Englewood Cliffs, N.J.: Prentice-Hall, 1960), p. 145.
17. Acts 15:1–35.
18. Gal. 2.

Paul is portrayed as having been most diplomatic and assuasive, in advocating changes so extreme as to bring danger of schism. We may have an indirect indicator of the third kind, in the author of Acts dwelling at considerable length on the conversion of the Gentile Roman centurion Cornelius, and putting into the mouth of the uneducated Jewish fisherman Peter, instead of the hellenized highbrow Paul, the vision mandating the discard of the Jewish dietary laws.[19] It is simply unthinkable that these Jewish loyalists could have been switched so easily from their intense concern with keeping the ceremonial law. Almost certainly, the real events must have included less success for Paulinism in Paul's own lifetime than the Bible portrays, and the ascendancy, or perhaps rehabilitation of Paulinism later, in response to an increasingly Gentilized church, and the relegation of Jewish loyalism to the periphery of provincial life, after the fall of Jerusalem.

While discrepancies between the biblical account and what we can verify historically are not, in themselves, indicators of underlying psychological devices, and it is our purpose to avoid following the long, dark groove of discussion about Christian-Jewish relations all too easily evoked by these topics, the Judaizer-Paulinist polemic points toward an insight essential for us. Christianity became gentilized. Although early Christian communities were necessarily set apart from others, pagan as well as Jewish, the Jewish Christians were assimilated by the Gentiles, and not the reverse. After the fourth century, we lose track of Christian groups with Jewish ethnicity and customs. Rather, surviving Jewish groups became firm in preserving their Jewishness as before, despite persecutions in some periods and overtures and pressures to become assimilated, in others. This occurred consistently enough to justify the conclusion that the psychological devices we seek worked well on Gentiles, but something about Jewish ethnicity spoiled their effect.

What was it about the biblical presentation that made so different an impression on the Gentile from that on the Jew? A different historical datum from another period relates. In each of the great historic manifestations of Christianity in the West, Roman Catholicism and Protestantism, once and once only has a work of fiction so poignantly expressed what the religion was about as to gain general recognition and acclaim. In the case of Roman Catholicism, it was Dante Alighieri's *The Divine Comedy,* which made concrete and tangible the cosmic system of politics, rules, rewards, and punishments that was the preoccupation of the individual Catholic at the zenith of the church's influence. For Protestantism, it was John Bunyan's *The Pilgrim's Progress,* which expressed in allegory the typical emotions and experiences of the Christian pilgrim in his alienated journey through this life on his lonely, desperate way to the next. It captured the genius of truly biblical, orthodox Christianity. The essence of that genius, coming into its own contemporaneously with the Renaissance, is, after all, allegory, that is, the use of allegory to convey its true message. *Making the events portrayed in the Bible into a subtle allegorical prescription for the in-*

---

19. Acts 10:1-23. See Schonfield, *Those Incredible Christians,* pp. 112-18.

articulate inner life of the believer is what Protestantism is all about. That is the innermost of the psychological, manipulative devices we are uncovering. Interpreting the allegory is the central task of this work.

The allegory with Jewish figures works well only on the Gentile, for whom the biblical figures remain alien, two-dimensional, stereotypic and fantastic. For the Jew, the figures are his forebears, of flesh and blood, rooted in the realm of the concrete. The Jew is on too-familiar terms with them for them to seem so close to God's own ethereal realm, as the Christian experiences them. Burdening the biblical characters with human reality and historicity militates against native, spontaneous response to them. The exclusively abstract, symbolic sense of relation to those figures, which can arise only for one to whom they are completely extramundane, is a necessary ingredient of the mind-control recipe, and for the Jew, it is either absent or more fragile than for the non-Jew.

The Nazoreans, whose claim to legitimacy derived from personal contact with Jesus and the other figures in the allegory, produced very little in the way of sacred writings. Still having the ceremonial law, perhaps they did not need a devotional relationship with a sacred writ, as did the early Paulinist Christian, who had only a few abbreviated ceremonial observances to keep. They are known to have had a Hebrew or Aramaic forerunner of the Gospel of Matthew and to have made a strong point of rejecting other gospels.[20] They probably had a historical document rivaling Acts. The surviving fragments of Nazorean writings tend to reflect knowledge of the other Gospels and Pauline epistles, indicating reaction against what was to the Nazoreans, the Pauline heresy, after it had taken root in the West.[21]

Pauline Christianity overcame its other significant competitor, Gnosticism, more easily than it overcame Nazoreanism. Where Nazoreanism had been a relatively conservative movement, trying to remain in mainstream Judaism, the assortment of splinter groups that scholars have designated as Gnostic were elite, educated, and individualistic. A plethora of purported sacred writings were produced by Gnostics. Some were preserved, or at least reported on, by ancient church scholars, and a large cache of them was discovered at Nag Hammadi, Egypt, in 1945.[22] Besides the interest naturally generated by the Nag Hammadi find, and the discovery of the Dead Sea Scrolls coming in close succession,

---

20. One may get a very rough idea of Nazoreanism by contrasting the canonical Matthew with the other parts of the Bible. The rendition of Christianity as the raising of the spiritual and moral standards required of the Jew, and predictions of the end-time, taking up where Daniel left off, is more prominent than in the other Gospels. In it, the quotation of Jesus most in disharmony with the premise that a new religion was intended, or that the ceremonial law was to be abrogated, survives: "Think not that I am come to destroy the law, or the prophets: I am not come to destroy, but to fulfil. For verily I say unto you, Till heaven and earth pass, one jot or one tittle shall in no wise pass from the law, till all be fulfilled. Whosoever therefore shall break one of these least commandments, and shall teach men so, he shall be called the least in the kingdom of heaven: but whosoever shall do and teach *them,* the same shall be called great. . . ." (Matt. 5:17-19). The Paulinists got around this by making out Jesus' atonement to be the "fulfillment," so that the ceremonial law could remain, yet not need to be kept.

21. See Schoenfield, *Those Incredible Christians,* pp. 144-62.

22. For English translations of the surviving Nag Hammadi documents, see James M. Robinson, ed., *The Nag Hammadi Library* (San Francisco: Harper & Row, 1977).

contemporary scholars of religion have been keenly interested in Gnosticism because—to make a long story very short indeed—it can be viewed as constituting an ancient forerunner or precedent to the twentieth-century attempt, culminating with Tillich, to find something modern and gratifying for Christianity to stand for.

The Gnostic writings bear titles such as *The Gospel of Truth, The Gospel of Thomas, The Apocryphon of John,* and *The Dialogue of the Savior.* They are amenable to such diversity of interpretation that Zoroastrianism, Eastern mysticism, neo-Platonism, and practically every other religious or philosophical idea abroad in the ancient world have seriously been suggested as having influenced their authors. Whereas the Nazoreans were antipathetic to foreign influences and the Pauline Christians who prevailed were discriminating and purposeful in their incorporation of non-Jewish influences, Gnostics were heterodox and insatiably curious. Gnostic writings make an impression strikingly different from canonical ones. A contemporary expert on Gnosticism explains:

> What is it which binds all this literature together and makes it possible for us to speak of its authors and devotees as Gnostics? After all, in antiquity the adherents of the Gnostic systems did not usually call themselves "Gnostics," and the Church Fathers spoke of them as members of various sects, often named after their founders [i.e., Manichaeism, Mandaeism, etc.]. Moreover, the word "gnosis" was used among Christians in speaking of the saving knowledge of the Christian faith. But there is one element which binds all the various systems together. This is the doctrine, to a considerable extent shared with Jewish apocalyptic writers of the period, that the world is bad; it is under the control of evil or ignorance or nothingness. It cannot be redeemed; indeed, for some Gnostics the world is the equivalent of hell. Only the divine spark, which somehow is imprisoned in some men, is capable of salvation. It is saved when, by divine grace, it comes to know itself, its origin, and its destiny.[23]

Gnostics saw the events and figures depicted in the sacred writings as symbolic, pointing beyond themselves to hidden meanings, and not literally true on their own terms. Whereas the orthodox Christian was to accept meekly the fragmentedness looking to literal reunification at judgment day that we earlier analyzed,[24] the Gnostics looked for clues to follow to attain personal wholeness earlier. They changed the metaphors and often elaborated fantastically on the themes of the orthodox Gospel. Elaine Pagels describes a typical Gnostic rearrangement of an orthodox theme:

> The *Gospel of Truth* . . . tells how Jesus, "nailed to a tree," was "slain." Extending the common Christian metaphor, the author envisions Jesus on the cross as fruit on a tree, a new "fruit of the tree of knowledge" that yields life, not death:
>
> ". . . nailed to a tree; he became a fruit of the knowledge [*gnosis*] of the Father, which did not, however, become destructive because it (was) eaten, but

23. Robert M. Grant, ed., *Gnosticism: A Sourcebook of Heretical Writings from the Early Christian Period* (New York: Harper & Row, 1961), p. 15.
24. See pp. 121-22.

> gave to those who ate it cause to become glad in the discovery. For he discovered them in himself, and they discovered him in themselves. . . ."
>
> Contrary to orthodox sources, which interpret Christ's death as a sacrifice redeeming humanity from guilt and sin, this gnostic gospel sees the crucifixion as the occasion for discovering the divine self within.[25]

The main feature of Gnosticism for us to note is its inward-looking, intra-subjective emphasis. The striking difference in a first impression between canonical writing and Gnostic writing is due to the permeation of the latter with inward looking and sensitization of the individual to the contents of the inner recesses of his own mind, in contrast to the complete absence of that orientation, except for being branded as wicked, in the former.

By looking to see what aspects of Gnosticism aroused the wrath of the orthodox church, we can identify other issues pertinent for us. These are indirect indicators of the third kind. They give us an additional bearing on distinguishing what drew and held people from what did not, the Gnostic sects having demonstrated little power to survive as institutions.

The first issue wherein the Gnostic sects characteristically dissented—and the church was diligent in persecuting them—was the literal historicity of miraculous events, such as the immaculate conception, resurrection, healings, multiplication of foodstuffs, walking on water, etc. The usual historical explanation is that the authority of the Roman church depended on these. How, precisely, was that supposed to work? We recall that the authority of the Jerusalem church had depended on its leaders' proximity to and personal knowledge of Jesus in person. Paul had not personally known Jesus, and the Holy Spirit came into the foreground because this was the device whereby it could be explained why persons who had not known Jesus had more authority to speak about him than those who had, and who even had the authority to contradict Jesus. If the Holy Spirit did not do that, then neither the closed canon nor the pope has any more patent on speaking for God than anyone else. To deny the miracles, so the argument goes, is to be on the way to the Gnostic "insight" that the meaning of the miracles is to be understood symbolically, and not taken at face value.

To place the issue of miracles in perspective, we should keep in mind that their possibility was not controversial to the average person in ancient times. Schonfield explains:

> . . . [T]he isolation of the New Testament, in the minds of Christians, from the literature of the ancient world familiar to scholars, puts a false value, in point of what are regarded as Divine interventions, on what is apprehended as being of the order of the miraculous. We have to accept that miracles and wonders were part and parcel of contemporary beliefs, whether credited to the gods or to the powers of sage and holy men. The accounts are so widespread and often circumstantial in narration that it is fruitless to argue whether they are true or untrue. What is relevant is that men's minds were attuned to the reception of such reports as accurate and in accordance with their understanding of the ordering of things.[26]

---

25. *The Gnostic Gospels* (New York: Vintage Books, 1981), p. 114. Footnotes omitted.
26. *Those Incredible Christians,* p. 47.

Clearly, small groups of highbrows inveighing against the genuineness of miracles cannot have represented so great a challenge to the church's authority as to account for its vehemence against Gnosticism. I believe some light is shed by comparing it with doctrinal conflict in a much later time.

The Roman church grew, gaining official toleration and finally establishment, as the state religion. Internally, it could indoctrinate its people from a very early age, and externally, it could ride the waves of secular political change and military conquest. Among the forms suited to those conditions, but not mandated by the Bible, are the exclusive hierarchy of clergy, the additional sacraments of confession and marriage, a more complicated and legalistic system of rewards and punishments beyond the grave, and authoritative, extrabiblical doctrine. Some of its forms were positively contrary to the Bible, such as celibacy of the clergy,[27] one-way confession to a priest,[28] and calling priests "Father."[29] It relied on architectural props and theatrical special effects and incorporated the forms and general superstitiousness of the preexisting pagan religions, having saints and the cult of the Virgin instead of polytheistic gods. Its modal mental image of the supernatural became much more concrete than it had been earlier, and the fragile biblical allegory was made to compete with all sorts of extraneous features. The Bible itself came to be kept secret and known only to the clergy who were fully committed to and surrounded by their church. With competing influences kept away all through the lives of the believers and the clergy living out their lives in surroundings of particularly intense indoctrination, an indoctrination psychologically less powerful and less stable than the biblical one could be maintained. With that indoctrination, had it needed to do so, the church would never have been able to cope with conditions requiring it to come from behind, or attract people in a vacuum. It became a psychologically far less interesting and remarkable phenomenon than the early church, the Reformation, or the contemporary resurgence we have called the mini-Reformation.

In the Reformation, no one in the Western world—and not even Rousseau two centuries after the dust had settled—challenged the epistemological premises of Christianity. Doctrinal arguments centered generally on papal authority and in particular on the church's mandate to sell indulgences. Yet we find Calvin, whose intellectual command of the Bible's doctrinal implications was unsurpassed and who had nothing but contempt for the Roman church, rising to the height of his vehemence over the Trinity (which is not mentioned in the Bible but is a fair rendition of all biblical statements about how God is manifested) and making it the apparent issue in the burning of Servetus. Calvin had no need to defend the authority of the Bible, because in his time that premise had no detractors of any consequence. Calvin, and Reformationists generally, shied away from miraculous manifestations such as personal revelations and healings,[30] and they had no incentive to defend them. Why, then, was Calvin just as

27. I Tim. 3:2.
28. James 5:16.
29. Matt. 23:9.
30. We touched on the biblical reasons for the orthodox believer in modern times to hold himself aloof from purported miraculous manifestations. See p. 49, footnote 88.

extreme and ruthless as his "Romanist" forerunners about defending the doctrine of the Trinity and its third person, who sent the revelations and made the miracles?

The real reason for orthodox Christians to have defended the doctrine of the Trinity so vigorously, and to defend it still, is its indispensability as an ingredient of the allegory that shapes the inner mental arrangement of the Christian. We shall see why the Christian must be presented with a God who is One but at the same time divided and fragmented, in order to take on the artificial inner dividedness and fragmentedness, emulating God's supposed image, that are part of the Christian's frame of mind. Also, the Christian needs a supernatural principle of his elusive, seeming understanding of what does not intellectually make sense and of his unusual emotional experiences. If the Trinity is attacked, the mental equilibrium, the relationship of the complexes to the conscious attitude, is thrown out of balance; the Christian is then subjected to an unsettling invasion of his consciousness by unconscious mental contents. Delete the Trinity from the recipe, and the new participant will not come under that condition of artificial, intrapsychic dividedness we call mind-control.

The other issue wherein the symbolic reinterpretation of the Gospel by the Gnostics brought out revealingly hyperintense ire in the orthodox was martyrdom. Very consistently, orthodox Christians regarded being put to death for the faith as the sine qua non of Christianity. The outward calm and equanimity with which Christians faced death always profoundly impressed outsiders to Christianity who observed it, and outsiders were drawn into Christianity wanting to achieve that state. When martyrdom was described in ancient historical works, typically the cheerfulness and confidence of the Christian about what awaited him after death was stressed. Later, we will see that if the Bible is a fair representation of the indoctrination the martyrs had received, their state of mind cannot have been so pleasant as has usually been supposed. The typical Gnostic position was that exposing oneself to martyrdom was the result of taking literally, on account of ignorance, what should have been understood symbolically.[31]

If we add to these historical triangulations, the observation that Jung, for whom orthodox Christianity was at the root of many profoundly negative early experiences, embraced Gnosticism and let it supply the direction for the entire third phase of his work, we bring ourselves into a position to identify what the psychological interior of orthodox Christianity is not. We become able to see what the psychological opposite of orthodox Christianity is. We become able to foresee with what the mind rebounding from Evangelical mind-control will overreact and overcompensate. That is a different matter, working at a more subjective level, than logical or intellectual antitheses of Christianity, such as evolution or "secular humanism." While natural-science knowledge can, for the most part, be accommodated to orthodox Christianity,[32] in Gnosticism we

31. See Pagels, *Gnostic Gospels,* pp. 84–122.

32. Some Evangelicals are to be found in the more microscopic and applied fields of science. The Evangelical habit of unreflectiveness may be conducive to concentration on the technical details of such a scientific specialty. But it is much more difficult for a theoretical physicist, astronomer,

encounter attitudes that cannot be so accommodated and that lead to deterioration of Christianity's hold on its people, if not suppressed.

Taking all its features together, we find that Gnosticism represents a radical shift in epistemological approach from orthodox Christianity, albeit camouflaged to a large extent by similarity of mythic content. The way to truth for the Gnostic was through his own mind, to that inner part of his personality made in God's image but subsequently overlain and obscured by confusion and ignorance.[33] Not confined to the terms of a received, authoritative revelation, he could change the premises and reinterpret the revelation. He could have the "insight" that the Gospel story was not to be taken literally, that the transformation through death to life is really a symbolic picture of personal growth occurring in this life.

The orthodox Christian has a much lower opinion of the mind. For him, the means to truth is wholly beyond its capacity. At most, he hopes to make his mind over to conform to Christian specifications, and use it—if at all—to make explicit the implications of the received revelation, on the revelation's own terms.[34] He accepts what the Bible presents as literally true, and his search for symbolic meaning at different levels in it is restricted thereby. His sources of truth are the scriptural rules, other believers keeping him under doctrinal surveillance, and his intimation that the Holy Spirit gives him some fleeting, inarticulate understanding of what he cannot understand intellectually. For him, all but a few aspects of earthly life are reduced to unimportance, and the next life is "where the action is."

To recapitulate: from our selective and fragmentary examination of church history, we have identified the distinctive, psychologically operative features of the kind of orthodox, biblical Christianity that came out of obscurity and prevailed, reasserted itself in the Reformation after having been refashioned into something substantially different—Roman Catholicism—and reasserts itself again today after having been substantially refashioned into old-time religion and religious liberalism. We indicated, but have not yet substantially explained, how the immediate, human identification that Jewish people have with the Jewish protagonists of the Bible blocks in them the receptivity that much of mankind has to the Bible's allegory. This practical approach to explaining the

---

or other macroscopically oriented scientist, who must be flexible about shifting his frame of reference and questioning premises, to be an Evangelical. Although such an individual might be able to keep his specialized knowledge out of conflict with the Bible by construing each as restrictively as possible in relation to the other, he would still be apt to notice lack of convergence, harmony, or dovetailing of implications between them. If such an individual does exist, I suspect that his facility for not seeing discrepancies he does not want to see makes him a most unpleasant individual to know.

33. Jung, when asked by John Freeman in a BBC television interview in 1959 whether he believed in God or not, answered, "I do not believe, I know." Clarifying this later in the interview, he said, "I don't believe. I must have a reason for a certain hypothesis. Either I know a thing [or I don't], and when I know it, I don't need to believe it." His statement captured well the Gnostic construction of the word *gnosis.*

34. Rom. 1:21-22; 1 Cor. 3:18-20; Eph. 4:17-19; Col. 2:6-8 (futility of human processes of knowledge); Rom. 12:2 and Eph. 4:22-24 (making the mind over).

resistance of Jews to conversion, and the frequency of untoward results in the lives of Jews who do convert, may become crucial in the future, if Evangelicals' expectations of contemporary, national Israel fail to materialize and the Evangelicals begin to rediscover the condemnation of national Israel and the Jews implicit in the New Testament. We will explore more of this in Chapter 5.

Whereas the interaction of early Christians with Jews more conservative than themselves brought to our attention the rôle of abstract allegory as a psychologically crucial feature of biblical Christianity, the interaction of early orthodox Christians with Jews more liberal and attuned to the cultures of other peoples than themselves brought to our attention the psychological necessity of denigrating the individual critical mind, for orthodox Christianity to take root. Early Christian groups that encouraged their people to be inward-looking, critical thinking, and self-conscious exhibited none of the powerful social cohesiveness of the orthodox Christians. The Gnostic sects simply never extended their influence beyond the time and geographic place of the various sects' founder-leaders.

There emerge two distinct kinds of religious activities, one involving intense intrasubjective preoccupation and the other having as its hallmark a discipline suppressing the natural tendency to be so preoccupied, and supplying a full complement of other preoccupations to take its place, indeed, to *dis*place it. Why would anyone want to keep such a discipline? What benefit do people derive or think they derive from it? Where does the human proclivity we infer—to submit to such a discipline—fit into the larger picture of human nature? With our historical clues in mind, we shift our focus back to the plane of psychology.

The Two Kinds of Mind-Games

Because there has been no consensus in the behavioral sciences as to what constitutes full, whole, "healthy" human psychological functioning, there has been little opportunity to discuss the relation of religion to such functioning—or to psychopathology or malfunction in the human organism. We have covered the neglected approach that focuses on one teleologically expressed tendency, "self-actualization," in preference to multidrive theories with implicit mechanistic and deterministic premises. The reader is asked, if not to accept such an approach, to tolerate it as a provisional benchmark for the sake of discussion.

We encountered two one-drive approaches, saying much the same thing in different terms. One was Goldstein's self-actualization, stressing intact organisms seeking to function according to their inherent capabilities. The organism's ability to build up and let go mental figure-and-ground representations of the features of its environment relevant to its functioning was stressed, and the importance of the unimpaired organism's ability voluntarily to react to a stimulus or ignore it was highlighted. In the other one-drive approach—Jung's—once we learned how to distinguish the substance from the context and correct for Jung's personal Christianity complex, we found that he also had in mind latent capabilities working themselves out teleologically. He spoke of symbols and complexes instead of figures and grounds and of a continuous ebb and flow of projecting and withdrawing projections, becoming attached to and detached from features of the environment, tangible and intangible.[35]

The individual finds himself in an environment consisting not only of tangible features within space and time but also of intangible, intrapsychic ones, affected by and in some way touching a physical reality to which time, space, and causality are irrelevant attributions, and affected by and in some way touching other persons' psyches. Earlier, we called that reality, tangible and intangible, *nonfantasy,* to avoid begging the question of what "reality" is. The true object of our one, teleological drive is to come to terms with nonfantasy. Of the essence for the one drive to find its true objective is the cyclic, almost dialectical[36] ebb and flow of projections emanating from those inner structures that Jung called archetypes, that Gestaltists called *Gestalten,* and that Kant called categories—that we cannot know in their purely noumenal or standing state, but know in action, by their wakes or trails, in their intercourse with nonfantasy. Our knowledge and our fantasy are found suspended between the unknowable noumena within and the equally unknowable "reality" outside. To simplify and provide something to hold onto through the rest of this discussion, we can say that the hallmark of whole, "healthy," sane human psychological functioning is *productive use of fantasy to come to terms with nonfantasy.* We can extend Jung's complex theory and build a framework with enormous facility for accounting for the various species of psychological malfunctioning. We can shed valuable light on every kind of psychopathology by analyzing and comparing how the fantasy has failed to respond to the nonfantasy.

What does our humble, short-form definition of mental health imply that frequently heard commonplaces in the mental-health professions about "adjustment," "adaptation to the environment," "reality contact," and the like do not? It implies far less plasticity than the usual nonnativistic approach does. Part of our intangible environment is the prestructured innermost part from which the projections emanate. It is like a searchlight caught in its own reflected beam. It is immutable, and corresponds hand-in-glove to the equally immutable "reality" without. With such equipment, the greater part of our native responses in terms of value—including what is mentally healthy and what is perverse—is universal and not culturally relative.

Accordingly, our definition of mental health cuts through endless discus-

35. The ebb and flow, or regression and progression of psychic energy, do not correspond to introversion and extraversion, or to any of Jung's other attitude types. Introversion and extraversion are individual styles of mental functioning, and presuppose regression and progression occurring in the normal manner. The attitude types cease to fit in a situation so unbalanced that one pole of the regression-progression oscillation has broken down and the other become correspondingly exaggerated.

36. As the corrective for the withdrawn and resynthesized projection is not necessarily its "antithesis" in the Hegelian sense, our formulation stops far short of declaring the dialectic to be a psychological principle or a principle of logic. Still less have we reason to declare the dialectic to be a principle whereby change in a dynamic external "reality" might be predicted. Marxism and all other prescriptive political ideologies are amenable to diagnosis as mind-games of the second kind.

sions about the need for some criterion of normality other than averageness, or whether the terms *illness* or *sick* should be applied to psychological malfunctioning. We have no trouble understanding why we consider the artist or author who lived long ago, was reviled, abused and thought to be a misfit in his own time but whose work retains its merit, ultimately to have been sane, while the well-adapted, leading member of an evil society, like an inquisitor or a Nazi, we do not. If our responsiveness does reach down into an unconscious realm of relatedness to other psyches and the cosmos, then being highly developed and conscious can imply compassion and decent regard for our fellow beings. Our definition allows for society to be civilized and become more decent without the cosmic policeman the Evangelicals claim is necessary.

When fantasy ceases to adjust to the requirements of nonfantasy and becomes oriented toward some fictitious objective—defined in terms of and consisting of fantasy, i.e., of itself—then the individual becomes engaged in what we shall call a *mind-game.* In a mind-game, a fictitious, illusory objective or purpose displaces the true, natural and prime human motive of coming to terms with nonfantasy and substituting understanding for puzzlement, mastery for helplessness, compassionate concern for callow not-knowing-better. Since much of what will be a motive, reward, "reinforcer," or unconditioned stimulus for the individual is determined within the mind-game, it will not prove useful to attempt to analyze mind-games in terms of game theory.[37]

There are two distinct mind-game processes or kinds of mind-games. We shall find that all religions, in their inception and apart from the socially useful institutions they may eventually foster, are mind-games. In their inception, they perform no practical, useful function, and they amount to individual and social pathology. We shall see that while not all mind-games are mental illnesses, all mental illnesses manifest themselves (symptomatically, at least) as mind-games. While the great majority of individual mind-game manifestations are mixtures of the two processes, our analysis will enable us to see quite clearly where one leaves off and the other takes up in any given individual case, and how the two processes interact.

Mind-games of the first kind, the rarer of the two, we identify as *autochthonous,* utilizing a term that has long denoted spontaneously generated fantastic mental content such as often accompanies schizophrenia. The object of the mind-game of the first kind is to get in touch with the most remote depths of one's own personality, to find the most poignant, sublime "truth." Gnosticism is the prototype of this type of mind-game. Jung, in defining individuation in terms of personal religious quest for the master symbol, made of his school a mind-game of the first kind. Producing states of mind altered through a medita-

---

37. Game theory requires definitions of the benefits being allocated among the players according to the game's rules or "parameters." While there can be a formal game where the quantity of benefits is not fixed—a "non-zero sum" game—there can be none reaching beyond its own defining premises and changing the definition of the benefits, the operating rules, and the number and identity of the players, while it is played. Unlike a formal game, a mind-game has contradictory rules and fictitious players as part of its repertory of psychological devices. Game theory cannot accommodate this.

tive discipline or drugs is a mind-game of the first kind, which finds its most characteristic expression in hallucinogen use. The essence of mind-games of the first kind is narcissistic. They consist of one-sided emphasis on regressive flow, on the greatest possible degree of detachment of the inwardly prestructured projection from its nonfantastic referent.[38] The mind-game player of the first kind is completely self-involved.

The power of the concept of two kinds of mind-games begins to be evident if we consider its implications where there is an even more unbalanced preponderance of regressive flow over progressive, than in the Gnostic or the Jungian analysand. Earlier, in the parliament analogy, we pictured the energetics of some of the diagnostic categories in terms of the alignments and affinities of the members of a parliament. A schizophrenic person corresponded to a parliament in which no party is strong enough to form a government, and a neurotic one, to a parliament where the ruling party (the ego-personality) is headed toward stalemate with other factions. We can expand the underlying idea, by looking at the diagnostic categories in terms of the oscillating projective knowledge process as well.

The distortion of the knowledge process characteristic of the mind-game of the first kind—too much detachment of fantasy from nonfantasy, carried to still further extremes—is fundamental to those disorders conventionally classified as psychoses. For the schizophrenic, autochthonous fantasy, detached from what goes on outside the sufferer, is so dominant that it isolates him terribly from the natural environment and other people. In affective-disorder cases so extreme as to be classed as psychotic, where moods, emotions and feelings are far detached from the external events appropriately evoking them, understanding is to be gained and empathic communication with the sufferer facilitated by conceptualizing the problem in terms of too much detachment of psychic energy from object. The true paranoiac—rare as a case, but pertinent to our topic—literally overflows with ideation too detached from its object, and out of hand. While the application of the parliament analogy to the true paranoiac is rather attenuated,[39] we can easily see that for him a projected fiction seems more real than fact does. Part of the paranoiac wrestles with nonfantasy, working out clever rationalizations to keep his delusions and the evidence of his senses out of conflict. But another part of him lives out the fantasy, tuning out the nonfantasy with such facile selectivity as to give the game away and reveal that at some hidden inner level he knows better, knows the cherished fantasy is untrue.

What should be noted about the mind-game player of the first kind is the

---

38. The reader should remember that the archetypal or noumenal realm is not known in its pure essence, and must be alloyed with contrasting, nonfantastic stuff to be experienced. The nonfantastic content of autochthonous mentation is torn out of its context, fragmented. Paucity of connectedness with the nonfantastic is what gives autochthonous or "schizy" mentation its characteristic quality.

39. The true paranoiac can be likened to a parliament where the plurality party has formed a coalition with a fringe, extremist party, with which it has nothing ideologically in common. But the analogy is strained. The analogy works best within the normal ranges of neurosis and depression.

originality, or at least idiosyncrasy, of the inner fantasy with which his awareness has good contact, but which itself has poor contact with the nonfantastic. His inner fantasy is detached, in that he fails to get his projections to make solid contact with their objects. He either is unable to make his projections attach, or has some motive not to. The Gnostic or gnosticlike navel contemplator simply doesn't want to. The true paranoiac satisfies some inner desire, gingerly and purposefully having the projections pertinent to the cherished fantasy miss their mark. Very few individuals have enough access to their own unconscious to play a mind-game of the first kind, and enough relatedness to communicate it well to others. The true paranoiac is the only outrightly psychopathological type able to do both. For the others to whom it is communicated, the mind-game ceases to be of the first kind, because inner structuring other than their own has lent it its form.

Anyone can be, and everyone is, a participant in mind-games of the second kind. Whenever any set of ideas or views ceases to respond to the pressures of experience and has a proprietor or proprietors with a vested interest against making the changes those pressures indicate, a mind-game of the second kind has arisen. The object of the mind-game of the second kind is defense of an imposed, prescribed doctrine against rationality, against indications why it should change. Standardization plays the rôle in mind-games of the second kind, corresponding to that played by idiosyncrasy in mind-games of the first kind. Accordingly we identify mind-games of the second kind—or more particularly, their mental content—as *heterochthonous,*[40] since all that pertains to it is funnelled in from outside and is foreign to the individual personality and intelligence of the player. The mind-game player of the second kind is totally other-directed.

The distortion of the knowledge process in mind-games of the second kind consists of one-sided emphasis on progressive flow of psychic energy. Instead of being able to become detached from its nonfantastic referent when it should, the projection persists unchanged. It sticks to its referent like flypaper. The relative rigidity and unresponsiveness of perception in a mind-game of the second kind resembles the stimulus-boundness of one of Goldstein's brain-injured patients. If discrepancies between projections and their objects go unnoticed and if withdrawal, resynthesis, and redispatch of the projection are not triggered, the individual cannot notice and cannot respond to new or previously unappreciated

---

40. *Autochthonous* and its antonym, *heterochthonous,* are borrowed from the earth sciences and refer, respectively, to species found where they are indigenous, and species found where they have migrated, moved, been transplanted. The term *autochthonous idea* came into psychiatry before the days of Freud or Janet, through the pioneering German psychiatrist Carl Wernicke, who called mental content experienced as delusion, and yet encountered with critical insight by the person experiencing it, *autochtoner Idee.* When I have heard older mental-health professionals use the term, the context indicated they understood it to mean any bizarre, dissociated mentation. English-language dictionaries and glossaries typically make out *autochthonous idea* to mean the same as "obsessive idea," missing the point as to its alienness to the individual's experience and reflecting the antinativist bias that all mental content results from learning. To my knowledge, no psychologist has previously borrowed the term *heterochthonous.* To an empiricist or tabula rasa thinker, *all* mental content is necessarily heterochthonous, so there could be no need for a term to distinguish transplanted mental content from native.

attributes of the object of knowledge. The doctrine, and not the evidence of the senses, controls what is perceived. The mind-game player of the second kind, by a variety of devices more elaborately worked out in some games than in others, avoids allowing anything from his own unconscious to correct the rigidified projection.

The healthy, non-mind-game knowledge process progresses from the greater to the lesser fiction, never reaching the end of the process of correcting what does not fit, and adding what is missing. Any intellectual endeavor that begins as an honest search for truth is in danger of becoming a mind-game of the second kind. As with the early Gnostic sects and Jungian analytical psychology, a search for truth that depends on the unique intuitive gifts of one individual cannot but become a mind-game after that individual is gone. All the disciples can do is imitate the founding genius. Alas, outside the hard sciences, limited success or dying out of a truth-seeking movement are a sign of the sincerety of its originator. To set in motion a movement that attracts followers far and wide, one must deliberately promote those ideas that effectively manipulate and manage, and not be fastidious about incorporating what one believes ultimately to be true.[41]

The focus of the mind-game of the second kind is the collective rather than the individual; such a mind-game has its inception at the point where a group ceases to cooperate to achieve goals that make sense for all and some member or members indoctrinate the others in seeking after a fictitious goal. Authentic give and take among the members gives way to transference-like projections, distorting and rigidifying relations among people. A group based on a mind-game of the second kind may present an outwardly harmonious appearance and yet have much less depth to the human relationships in it than another group, outwardly appearing disorderly and fractious because authentic, human give and take are not squelched, and the individual is not afraid to say inadvertently a true thing inveighing against the group's cherished fiction. No matter how advanced a human group may become, *to think it has any concern more important than the perishable individuals it comprises is* always *pseudosophistication,* indicating the operation of a mind-game of the second kind.

We find the reflection of the social indoctrintion aimed at making the individual's projections rigidified, stultified, stuck to their objects with the glue of misrouted psychic energy, in the individual disorders conventionally classified as neuroses. The normal run of physical symptoms, unreasonable fears, undifferentiated anxiety, mild to moderate depression because the complexes have

41. Freud was quite unashamed of being interested in indoctrination, not information, in organizing the psychoanalytic movement. The mental-health fields have suffered from his bad rôle model, in that respect, ever since. This attitude is clearly shown in a colloquy between Freud and Jung in 1910: ". . . Freud said to me, 'My dear Jung, promise me never to abandon the sexual theory. That is the most essential thing of all. You see, we must make a dogma of it, an unshakable bulwark.' He said that to me with great emotion, in the tone of a father saying, 'And promise me this one thing, my dear son: that you will go to church every Sunday.' In some astonishment I asked him, 'A bulwark—against what?'" Jung, *Memories, Dreams, Reflections* (New York: Vintage Books, 1965), p. 150.

too much psychic energy and the ego-personality too little, etc., all arise from some indoctrination that has dissociated the ego-personality from the inner roots of the person's being. Instead of cooperating with the ego-personality and providing all it might by way of intellectual insight and empathic and feeling relation to what is there to be known, the unconscious is estranged from the ego-personality. Instead of being continually integrated into the conscious attitude, so the ego-personality can grow, what is in the unconscious finds expression blindly, in the form of manifestations at cross-purposes to the conscious attitude, i.e. neurotic symptoms. Lack of conscious insight of the person in whom such symptoms are manifested is the sine qua non of neurosis.

The insight that neuroses are a species of mind-game of the second kind enables us to put in perspective Freud's comment that "devout believers are safeguarded in a high degree against the risk of certain neurotic illnesses; their acceptance of the universal neurosis spares them the task of constructing a personal one."[42] The individual neurosis is not necessarily more extreme or "worse" than the collective one; it simply is not shared. For it, less social support is available than would be were the game a communal one. The fortunes of the neurotic individual, and of the group based on a mind-game of the second kind, are comparable. In the short run, the game becomes increasingly complicated and convoluted to accommodate those pressures of nonfantasy too clear to be misperceived or tuned out. The neurosis or game will, in the long run, either be punctured by insight into the matter it was conceived to evade, or the neurotic or group will collide catastrophically with the truth.

Three features of the psychology of mind-games of the second kind, including individual neuroses—already alluded to, but so crucial for what follows as to bear reiteration—are:

Firstly, when part of the truth is excluded from the conscious attitude, it is not bolstering of self-esteem but rather *evasion of conscience* that is being attempted. All of us who have received our education where the influence of the American mental-health professions was felt, have been indoctrinated through endless repetition in a premise that now turns out to have been quite empty: that the ego-defense mechanisms underlying the neuroses have for their aim the avoiding of loss of self-esteem, or spuriously increasing it.

The classic ego-defense mechanisms described by Freud—repression, sublimation, projection, reaction formation, introjection, etc.[43]—are a part of his legacy that retain their validity and remain indispensable in the clinical setting. They do not depend on the specifics of the rest of the Freudian theory and are compatible with a wide range of personality theories. Our declaration that dissociation, not repression, is the general case, the common denominator of the

42. See p. 6.

43. For those who may wish to use a dictionary or glossary to review the ego-defense mechanisms, the list has grown to include denial, fantasy (suffering and conquering hero), rationalization (sour grapes and sweet lemons), undoing (atoning), regression, fixation, identification, compensation, displacement, isolation, intellectualization, sympathism (manipulating others into expressing sympathy), and acting out. Note that in general psychology, the Freudian habit of equating dissociation with the narrow, specific realm of emotional isolation or intellectualization survives.

other defense mechanisms, does not detract at all from the explication of case material in terms of the mechanisms. For the same historical reasons that made the views of Carl Rogers so popular, the conventional wisdom of those who wrote mental-health textbooks in the forties and fifties gravitated toward the view that instead of protecting the conscious mind from the supposed insight that incest and self-annihilation were the true motives, the defense mechanisms had to have as their aim, making the conscious attitude compatible with self-esteem. No alternative to the Freudian explanation of conscience in terms of a reified structure called the superego has ever been widely discussed, much less gained acceptance, in the mental-health disciplines.

For the same reason that not much can be said about emotion in a nativist psychology, not much is to be said about the structure and dynamics of *conscience.* Like emotion, conscience is part of the specific structure of the experience to which it pertains. It is evoked or, as Jung would say, "constellated" in a different way each time. The study of emotion and of conscience is somewhat like organic chemistry, in which the properties of each compound are catalogued; it is unlike mechanical branches of science, where a relatively few general principles are applied to a myriad of specific cases.[44] Both emotion and conscience figure in the cyclical knowledge process. They are part of the symbolism whereby we make the indicators of a set of circumstances around and in us intelligible. Perhaps the most destructive thing that popularized psychology can do is to tout to us states of mind where conscience and emotion are muted and dulled (life on an even keel!), to tell us such states are in some sense "normal" or characteristic of those individuals who function best, and to make us afraid to experience fully and savor our emotions and the promptings of conscience. We do not function at our best without the full information of both of these.

Conscience, in our view, is manifested along a continuum, with the universal and immutable at one extreme and the conventional and culturally relative at the other. At the one extreme, conscience is noumenal, and we cannot experience it except in its intercourse with the nonfantastic. (Hopefully, we will experience it in a productive, related way and not in the fragmentary and unrelated manner of the mind-game of the first kind.) At the other extreme, conscience converges with and becomes a mind-game of the second kind. Not only the following of ethically neutral mores that conveniently regularize conduct in the group but also compromise with group mores that substantially offend the pristine conscience is necessary. Compromise that leaves unresolved, tension between the collective and the continually growing, healthy individual conscience, and no far-reaching synthesis or resolution of the tension, is the lot

44. Hence, emotion and the promptings of conscience are not reducible to general arousal, to the activity of the reticular activating system, or to stress-producing stimuli, in the sense contemplated by Selye. The relation of the specifics of emotion and conscience to general arousal is complementary. Note that our view of conscience and emotion localized as to meaning but not mechanism could have predicted what has happened in neurophysiological research: anatomical centers of specific emotions and a catalog of emotions guided by anatomical topography have not been forthcoming.

of the fully functioning human.[45]

Multiple influences inform the conscience, including societal influences, the four Jungian functions, and a transcendental sense of right and wrong that permeate from deep within our knowledge-gaining apparatus. We may envision conscience as not merely heterochromatic but also multilayered. Conscience can be divided against itself. If strong indoctrination from without makes the conscious attitude dissociate the promptings of the lower layers of conscience so that they become the nucleus of a complex, then we have a socially induced neurosis. Others so indoctrinated will not see it as such, and its symptoms will be part of the "normal" condition shared by those under the indoctrination. (Such a thing has been written about as an *existential neurosis,* although that term has not gained such acceptence that one would expect to see it used in a patient's diagnosis or on a health-insurance form.) We shall see that setting native good conscience over against indoctrination imposed from without and a resultant condition amounting to neurosis are the inevitable result when a contemporary person with intelligence and integrity attempts to be a biblicist Christian.

How does such a view of conscience relate to our old debate about the moral nature of man? In our provisional personality theory centered on the knowledge process, we do not reach the conclusion that human moral nature is originally good, but we do strongly suspect that compassionate concern is an achievement of maturity. We alluded to man's built-in blind spot regarding his own moral nature and the practical utility of having man be prestructured, as we have declared he is, to misperceive his own moral nature as worse than it really is, so that doubt and hesitation will always counterbalance his impulsiveness. The second psychological feature of the mind-game of the second kind for us to note specially, is that it preys upon man's universal prejudice against himself and *indoctrinates its people in a pseudopsychology misrepresenting human nature as more empty, more inadequate, and more contemptible than it really is.* To prevent individual conscience from undermining the imposed collective indoctrination, the individual must be made to distrust and disparage his own conscience.[46] Having the Christian believer think in terms of the biblical

45. Our notion of conscience is adapted from Jung, "A Psychological View of Conscience," in *Civilization in Transition* (Princeton, N.J.: Princeton University Press, 1964), pp. 437-55, pars. 825-57. Jung thought in terms of mores coming into tension with duty (in the Kantian, a priori sense) and an ethical synthesis (in the Hegelian sense), a third standpoint, arising. Endowed with the wisdom of hindsight, we shall take care not to imagine we see a dialectical process at work where there is merely a cyclical one. That is why it is important to distinguish between a compromise, leaving tension unresolved, and a synthesis that resolves old tensions, clearing the way for new ones.

46. Note that in the mental-health professions, Freud has stood alone, towering above the competition for loyalty of following while so doing, in espousing a view of man's moral nature as disparaging to man as is the Christian doctrine of original sin. Freud postulated two drives, each seeking a devastatingly antisocial fulfillment. He also created a whole mythology of how man supposedly got to be painfully divided against himself in order to be able to live in civilized society with others, set forth in *Totem and Taboo* (1913) and *Civilization and Its Discontents* (1930). Mental-health professionals apparently have the same vulnerability as other people for being convinced that any tendency to do straight thinking for themselves is to be attributed to "resistance," to their being bereft of the "insight" that the precious doctrine supposedly supplies.

pseudopsychology we covered in the preceding chapter, with its misdefinition of the term *conscience,* is only one of the formidable array of biblical devices cooperating for this purpose.

The third special feature of mind-games of the second kind is that *they are ultimately inseparable from and dependent upon* what I call *the relative impartiality of the unconscious.* Earlier we made reference to the inherent limitations of the conscious attitude to the modalities of space, time, and causality, much as our eyes are limited to the spectrum consisting of radiant-energy wavelengths longer than ultraviolet but shorter than infrared. Consciousness has great difficulty transcending its proclivity to think in linear relationships and to segregate the field of experience into manageable small bits. The underlying "reality" or "truth" is not limited to space, time, and causality; dynamic interrelation, not merely linear relation, exists between each feature and every other feature. When a contrived indoctrination is imposed on consciousness, either socially or neurotically by the individual upon himself, deep down in the person's being, "in his heart of hearts" as the ancient Jews put it, he knows the indoctrination is not true. He has some inarticulate intimation of what the truth is, and his conscious belief does not correspond to it, does not harmonize with it. The more his unconscious tries to supply some compensating piece of insight, the more psychological energy he must divert, to keep that insight and what pertains closely to it dissociated from conscious awareness.

What can we observe of that underlying intimation of the truth, contrasting with the conscious attitude? Consider a typical-case scenario, repeated constantly in combat situations, a favorite demonstration for ward psychiatrists, and one I have witnessed: The patient has been in combat and perhaps been superficially wounded in a battle incident where a buddy has been maimed or killed. The patient has every reason to doubt he did all he could have to avoid the tragic harm to another. The patient, shortly after, complains of being blind, has the sincere conscious experience of inability to see, but there is no physical disfunction to account for the symptom. He is brought into the classroom, where the psychiatrist will "demonstrate" his symptoms to the assembled trainees. The person on whose arm the patient is led into the room steers him where a low stool is in his way. Unerringly, and in a way that could not occur without the guidance of the visual sense, the patient avoids stumbling over the stool. Deep down, he can see, knows he can see, and the whole strategy of avoiding return to combat, of self-punishment, of sympathy arousal, etc. makes out a premise without which the symptomology would have no point of departure, no set of unconscious motives around which to organize. Just as the patient must know, at some level, the whereabouts of the stool in order to avoid it, so does some sort of knowledge of his still intact visual apparatus need to exist, for the symptomology of blindness to be affected.

Eugen Bleuler, the kindly mentor of Jung's days as a staff psychiatrist at Burghölzli Hospital, observed the same curious persistence and resilience of the truth underlying and directing the psychopathological obfuscation in schizophrenics. Later textbooks on psychopathology have not equaled Bleuler's sensitivity of observation and refinement of descriptive shading:

> In schizophrenia, orientation in time and place is always present, often even better than normal, if not hindered by secondary influences, delusions and hallucinations. One who believes he is Christ will usually think he is 1900 years old; for artificial reasons, the calendar is often directly falsified; the surroundings are nearly always correctly perceived by the conscious schizophrenic. On the other hand, at least with hospitalized schizophrenics, in most cases orientation to the circumstances is incorrect: patients cannot understand that they are considered sick, believe they are unjustly imprisoned, etc.
>
> Moreover, orientation in all its ramifications can be falsified by hallucinations and illusions: if the sick person perceives hell instead of the hospital room, and the devil instead of an orderly, then he cannot comprehend that he is in a mental hospital. It is remarkable that in such schizophrenic conditions—hardly at all in other psychoses—the correct orientation parallels the false one; what occurs is a *double orientation.* Depending on his frame of mind, the patient uses one, then the other, often both conglomerated.[47]

I have often heard mental-health professionals express the same insight, saying that beneath the surface of the insane person's symptoms is a sane person trying to come out. The sane one remains somehow off to the side, clearly appraising the same matters outwardly made subject to delusions and distortions. With many kinds of abnormal persons, e.g. neurotics, psychopaths,[48] and criminals, one is impressed at how the dream life, the indirections, the things said in unguarded moments contain a correct appraisal of the person's situation, factually and ethically, without which the person's illusions could not be maintained, could not be continually adjusted so as to remain tenable for the person. Organically impaired individuals excepted, the cyclic, coming-to-terms process we have described goes on, but instead of being central and leading to a more authentic relation of the person to all the circumstances of his existence, it is relegated to the periphery, imprisoned or enslaved in a manner of speaking, put to the inferior purpose of self-deception management.

The aim of the self-deception, and of defense of the group doctrine against conflicting individual experience and conscience, is solidarity with the group. One trades off individual authenticity for the support of the collective. If one has the proclivity toward individual authenticity in large measure, then maintenence of the prescribed self-deceptions becomes an extravagantly energy-consuming, vitality-sapping operation. Often, those mind-game players of the second kind in whom an illusion-puncturing personal insight is most disturbingly near the surface are the ones most exercised to try to force circumstances to imitate the illusion, by proselytizing or persecuting those who do not share it.

This pervasive vulnerability of the human being to become inveigled into preferring fiction to truth and contrivance to authenticity is among the most paradoxical aspects of his psychological makeup. The paradox goes to the underlying meanings of "truth" and "belief," for which there is no clear intellectual consensus. We shall shortly formulate our own provisional definitions of

47. *Lehrbuch der Psychiatrie,* 3rd ed. (Berlin: Verlag von Julius Springer, 1920), pp. 83–84. My translation of the passage.

48. The attentive reader will note that we have not yet integrated several important categories of psychopathology into our conceptualization of mind-games: the cyclic, coming-to-terms knowledge process, complexes, etc.

these, to have benchmarks for comparing and contrasting the biblical ones that so litter our unexamined presuppositions about such terms in our culture.

What psychological capabilities do we have that we could not have without our vulnerability to mind-games of the second kind? We are able to use our fantasy to compare and contrast conditions that are different at different times. The reader should have little problem agreeing that past and future partake heavily of nonfantasy, even though they are not "here-now." All of us stake everything every day, on our feeble ability to infer the future from our mental synthesis of the past. To be able to deal with what is contrary to present fact, we need to be able flexibly to detach ourselves from the stimuli, as Goldstein taught us. Of the essense of such flexibility is the ability to formulate the contrary-to-fact in more than one way. Ability to rise above the here-and-now necessarily requires ability to be wrong. Breaking the truth up into segments small enough for our minds to handle necessarily falsifies it, distorts its proportions like a fun-house mirror. Our limitations of time and place make it necessary for us to utilize secondhand accounts of fact—fact which our own, personal coming-to-terms apparatus has not participated in gathering. We are vulnerable to disinformation. What is a mind-game of the second kind, after all, but a program of disinformation with its own appealing internal self-consistency and seductive aesthetic attractiveness?

What should be noted about double orientation and the normal tendency to be oriented rather than disoriented is that the very features of the mind-game of the second kind that lend it its defining character are secondhand, remain flat, lack vitality and retain an aura of unreality if not corroborated and complemented by firsthand experience. That aura of unreality limits the extent to which its player "believes" it, and also limits the intensity of disorientation or psychopathology that involvement in such a mind-game can produce. In the case of the Christian mind-game of the second kind, we find that only a few individuals have the combination of intelligence, imagination, and dissociative proclivity enabling them to work themselves into a state such as we have observed in Jonathan Edwards, John Wesley before Aldersgate, and Bunyan's pilgrim. What makes the biblically authentic, mini-Reformationist game more compelling and stable than other mind-games of the second kind is the way it anticipates the aura of unreality it will necessarily have for the believer. A devotional program perfectly crafted to get the believer to misinterpret, distrust, and disparage his natural, healthy tendency to disbelieve the artificially imposed set of views, and dissociate all that pertains to that tendency, is set up. With this in mind, we are at last ready to explain away the Bible as the most artful, most devious, and most durable program of disinformation ever devised!

Summing up: We have established the knowledge process in its broadest sense, the cyclical process of coming to terms with every part of the experience wherein we find ourselves, as the measure of "sanity" or "health" in human psychological functioning. We look to the process, not an end state, for the principle distinguishing healthy from unhealthy, fully functioning from impaired. For a key word to hold onto, denoting what the psychologically fully functioning individual strives for, I suggest *relatedness.* Such an individual primarily seeks to clarify his relationship with the various facets and features of his existence. He prefers what is relevant to him to what is not, and he knows better what his own coming-to-terms apparatus has participated in than what he knows secondhand. Pathology, or deviation from full functioning, is of two kinds: (1) mind-games of the first kind, which detach fantasy from its object too much for the fantasy to serve its true purpose of mediating the person's relation to nonfantasy; and (2) mind-games of the second kind, wherein it is made taboo for the individual's knowledge process to transcend a shared fiction, a chimera exalted over the only reasonable desideratum of human existence—human welfare.

The Notion of Mind-Control

The notion that being a conservative religious buff involves a mental state that is somehow diminished and unhealthy is widely held. I have often heard the acquaintances and coworkers of such people say so and describe the vacuousness and mindless euphoric calm[49] they exhibit as due to some sort of hypnosis. The observation typically comes from one who does not relate personally to and cannot imagine being in such a frame of mind. To mental-health professionals, the question may have seemed too obvious, and not interesting when it was commonly taken for granted that it was just a matter of time until supernaturalistic religion would die out in Western culture, and the dwindling Protestant clergy they knew personally were liberals, who supported the aspirations of the mental-health movement.

Besides declarations by behavioral scientists that conservative religion is a topic needing study—and that they intend to study it—there has been some indication that the intellectual climate is moving toward our insight. In her deservedly acclaimed book on Gnosticism, Elaine Pagels let drop some important clues that must surely have made some subconscious impression on me when I first read them:

> Contemporary Christianity, diverse and complex as we find it, actually may show more unanimity than the Christian churches of the first and second centuries.[50]

> Gnosticism and orthodoxy . . . articulated very different kinds of human experience; I suspect that they appealed to different types of persons.[51]

> For ideas alone do not make a religion powerful, although it cannot succeed without them; equally important are social and political structures that identify

49. The term *euphoric calm,* will recur in our discussion and become a term of art. It has been used with the meaning we have in view by Robert Jay Lifton, in *Thought Reform and the Psychology of Totalism: A Study of "Brainwashing" in China* (New York: W. W. Norton & Co., 1963), p. 118.
50. *Gnostic Gospels,* p. xiii.
51. Ibid., p. 171.

and unite people into a common affiliation.[52]

> IT IS THE WINNERS who write history—their way. No wonder . . . that the viewpoint of the successful majority has dominated all traditional accounts of the origin of Christianity.[53]

There has been no focused commentary about mind-control pertinent to Evangelicalism in the serious social-science literature that I can find. A popularized commentary of that kind, *Holy Terror: The Fundamentalist War on America's Freedoms in Religion, Politics, and Our Private Lives,*[54] by Flo Conway and Jim Siegelman, of "snapping" fame,[55] has been by far the most conspicuous of such books in recent years. Besides fulfilling my obligation to give due credit to a book with its main seminal idea akin to this work's, I have an opportunity to point out a product of our time's intellectual malaise, especially in the behavioral sciences, revealing its own relation to the resurgence of Evangelicalism, with its seeming provision of the answers secular intellectualism has failed to provide and its camouflaged and slickly repackaged reintroduction of the same sorts of intolerance and antiintellectualism that have given us history's most unhappy chapters.The resurgence is an understandable but misdirected attempt to compensate for the malaise.

In their earlier work on cults, which included interviews with many individuals personally experienced in extreme, sequestered religious groups, Conway and Siegelman noticed:

> Of forty-eight groups in our study . . . more than thirty . . . had emerged out of fundamentalist or other branches of conservative Christianity. Moreover, these thirty Christian sects combined ranked higher than the most destructive cults we studied in terms of the trauma they inflicted upon their members. Long-term effects included emotional problems such as depression, suicidal tendencies and feelings of guilt, fear and humiliation, and mental disorders such as disorientation, amnesia, nightmares, hallucinations and delusions. The anguished comments we received in personal replies only added to our concern over the effects of some fundamentalist practices on individuals and families in America.[56]

Leaving aside Conway and Siegelman's bellowing mode of expression and their dizzying misuse of behavioral-science terminology, I note that they identify the concern that is also my primary one in bringing out this work: the negative mental-health consequences of conservative Christianity for its own participants.

The initial intuitions of Conway and Siegelman are quite sound. The title of the book correctly points to the manipulation of the deeply involved believer by

52. Ibid., p. 169.
53. Ibid., p. 170.
54. Updated edition (New York: Dell Publishing Co., 1984).
55. See pp. 73–74.
56. *Holy Terror,* p. 6.

fear. But they do not follow that initial impression through to any productive result.[57] They also indicate the condition we are coming to know as mind-control, as the "syndrome of ideological fundamentalism," which they say is manifested in the individual believer in three steps: (1) surrender of the will, (2) intellectual control (looking to the Bible, not personal conscience for rules by which to make life decisions), and (3) emotional control (for which I am unable to fashion a definition from the contents of their book). There are several case histories but precious little application of this "syndrome" to the facts.[58] The main thrust of the book is an attack on politicized conservative Christianity, which Conway and Siegelman regard as a superlatively organized and coordinated political conspiracy. As soon as they depart from their first impressions and proceed to analysis, their work speedily goes downhill. The bulk of the book consists of blatant, card-stacking reportage of facts and stereotyping and scapegoating of the Evangelicals.

An essential thing these authors and others, including trained social scientists, fail to appreciate is the long tradition and refinement in asking tendentious questions and making tendentious statements that the Evangelical has behind him. In sermon after sermon, the Evangelical has taken in a distillation of renditions of the biblical message calculated from time immemorial to deflect the hearer from the more vulnerable and questionable assumptions of that message. When secular commentators encounter a religious matter, they are too readily inveigled into relegating to the periphery of their thinking, and tacitly accepting, the key premises of the Evangelicals' positions—just the premises that ought to be challenged and subjected to focused thought. As I take note of media coverage of the public-policy issues conservative Evangelicals are interested in,[59] I am saddened and grieved to see how nearly every time the Evangelicals have the initiative in shaping all parties' perception of the issue; the splendidly credentialed liberals are backed into a reactive position, one artificially made hard to defend, where there is too much heat and too little light.

Particularly subversive to their purpose of debunking Evangelical spokesmen on public-policy issues is Conway and Siegelman's tacit acceptance of the premise that those spokesmen's positions are truly biblical. *It is of the utmost importance to understand that current Evangelical positions on various public-policy issues are, with no significant exception, quite unbiblical. By holding*

57. Instead of following through on the biblical-terror message, Conway and Siegelman define rightist political lobbying and propaganda as terrorism: "It is a system of *terrorism by communication,* a plan of social and political control using, not guns, bombs or other physical implements, but *information:* symbols, statements, images, myths, coded messages and other meanings. It works, not by violence, but in casual exchanges between individuals, in private encounters and in expressly public media, marketing and mass-communications campaigns. The instruments of Holy Terror may be as hard as copper wires and computer consoles, as remote as satellite parking spaces on the road to the moon. But their impact is as soft as a touch, and as fleeting as a picture in the mind's eye, as intangible as a quiet suggestion slipping undetected through a barrage of noise." Ibid., pp. 240-41. So much for an open marketplace of ideas, and the competence of free people to choose! By such blatant abuse of words, Conway and Siegelman emulate another of the techniques of those they abhor, a technique, we shall shortly term *logocide.*
58. Ibid., pp. 241-71.
59. This was written six weeks before the 1984 presidential election.

Evangelicals to their own declarations about biblical authority, one can make them take their turn to be the ones backed into a corner and forced to take absurd, indefensible positions. What should be noted is that becoming mentally ill from a biblically authentic, personal-devotional regimen on the one hand and being sold a political bill of goods through the fraudulent pretense that the bill of goods is biblically authentic on the other are two different social problems, affecting different, albeit overlapping, groups of people.

The tendentious bad habit now current in commentators viewing conservative Christianity as a form of mind-control (including Conway and Siegelman) is taking the believers' declarations regarding surrender of control, or self-abandonment, at face value.[60] If one proceeds from a psychological viewpoint that excludes the possibility of mental activity going on intact outside conscious awareness or that views too restrictively and exclusively what the character of such activity can be, one's alternatives for understanding someone's declaration that he has surrendered control of his life to Jesus are quite limited, and the double orientation manifested in that person's behavior will be misinterpreted or go unnoticed altogether. A few years ago, when the focus of this sort of commentary was on eccentric, sequestered religious groups alleged to be cults, it was reasonable to focus on the individual's ceasing to think for himself and letting the leader or others in the group's hierarchy do his thinking for him and to call that the distinguishing feature. But when we are confronted with people who report having given over their wills but who still function economically and socially in the free, unsequestered community as before, and who participate intensively in religious groups that do not subject them to any particular monitoring or censorship, what do the reports mean? To what, are we to think, have they abandoned their wills, and from what do they get the guidance whereof they "testify"? Even if we narrow the self-surrender notion to mean merely following teachings or precepts, what of people who participate in groups where Bible knowledge is meager, personal guidance, equivocal and timid, yet, nevertheless, the ethos of self-surrender comes on loud and clear? To accept the believer's subjective report of self-surrender as an objective account of what has

---

60. David F. Gordon in "Dying to Self: Self-Control Through Self-Abandonment," *Sociological Analysis* 45 (1984), pp. 41–56, uses ultrarelativist symbolic interactionist sociology to study self-abandonment in two Jesus-people groups, about 1973–75. Proceeding from the premise that "identity" or perceived "me" is nothing but the result of external influences, Gordon refrains from making overt value judgments as to the narrowly prescribed new "identities" Jesus-people inductees took on, and in a disclaimer footnote at the end of the paper, says: "This analysis should not be seen as an endorsement of the Jesus People groups or of any other new religious groups. It is merely an attempt to establish that participation helped members to achieve self-goals which they believed were desirable." How "objective" can you get?

Michael Scott Cain's "Psychic Surrender: America's Creeping Paralysis," *Humanist*, 43, no. 5 (Sept./Oct. 1983), pp. 5–12, is written from the vantage point of a college English teacher, who sees a rising tide of vacuous, religious-enthusiast students, talking *at* him in biblical clichés, rather than with him, and "testifying" as to the idyllicness of their lives since they gave their wills over to Jesus, or whatever Eastern or pop-psychology guru, as the case may be. Cain describes it as "a kind of creeping zombiism." Most interesting about this article is the undertone Cain does not explicitly address, namely, the students grudging presence to complete their academic requirements, but rejection of him and the collegiate, liberal tradition he represents as a source of ideals or a rôle model.

happened to him is tacitly to acknowledge the objective existence of something for his will to be surrendered to, exercising control over his life in his stead. As a nonsupernaturalistic explanation, the self-surrender idea collapses, and we are put on notice that a more sophisticated explanation is needed.

Our multilayered system of biblical devices—at their best persuasive and at their worst disinforming—are our response to that need. The differences among manifestations of mind-controlling religion are as interesting as the things they have in common, and the aspiration of commentators of the past, to have a one-size-fits-all theory of religions generally, was too ambitious. For our particular time and circumstances, the place for us to gain our first foothold is the Bible itself, since it is the sole common denominator of the conservative Christian groups I allege to be mind-controlling. It, alone, remains constant as the personnel change and as individuals migrate from one group to another. Most importantly, the inarticulate impressions the Bible is designed to make are present, or in prospect, as the involvement and participation of each individual progresses. While our descriptions will often depict a purity of mini-Reformationism in contrast to the opposite, old-time-religion pole of the continuum we fashioned, such as is seldom reached in actuality, the effects often reach a high intensity in the deeply involved believer in every conservative Christian group.

Chapter 4

The Evangelical Mind-Control System

Satan never attacks believers with a more grievous or dangerous temptation, than when he disquiets them with doubts of their election, and stimulates to an improper desire of seeking it in a wrong way. . . . when miserable man endeavors to force his way into the secret recesses of Divine wisdom, and to penetrate even to the nighest [i.e., most remote] eternity, that he may discover what is determined concerning him at the tribunal of God. Then he precipitates himself to be absorbed in the profound of an unfathomable gulf; then he entangles himself in numberless and inextricable snares; then he sinks himself in an abyss of total darkness. For it is right that the folly of the human mind should be thus punished with horrible destruction, when it attempts by its own ability to rise to the summit of Divine wisdom. This temptation is the more fatal, because there is no other to which men in general have a stronger propensity. For there is scarcely a person to be found, whose mind is not sometimes struck with this thought—Whence can you obtain salvation but from the election of God? And what revelation have you received of election? If this has once impressed a man, it either perpetually excruciates the unhappy being with dreadful torments, or altogether stupefies him with astonishment. . . . no error can affect the mind, more pestilent than such as disturbs the conscience, and destroys its peace and tranquility towards God. Therefore, if we dread shipwreck, let us anxiously beware of this rock, on which none ever strike without being destroyed. But though the discussion of predestination may be compared tc a dangerous ocean, yet, in traversing over it, the navigation is safe and serene, and I will also add pleasant, unless any one freely wishes to expose himself to danger. For as those who, in order to gain an assurance of their election, examine into the eternal counsel of God without the word, plunge themselves into a fatal abyss, so they who investigate it in a regular and orderly manner, as it is contained in the word, derive from such inquiry the benefit of peculiar consolation. . . . [Saint] Bernard. . . . says . . . "A tranquil God tranquilizes all things; and to behold rest, is to enjoy repose." —John Calvin, c. 1536[1]

If we are mentally unbalanced because of spiritual despondency—and a lot of mental imbalance comes from this—the fear of hell and mental imbalance can be an escape mechanism to escape the reality of having to face the judgment throne . . . anything of this nature still leaves man a sinner. . . . —Harold Camping, 1985

1. *Institutes of the Christian Religion,* trans. John Allen, vol. 2, 6th ed. (Philadelphia: Presbyterian Board of Publication, n.d.), pp. 182-83 (Book 3, chap. 24, par. 4).

> I pray that God will fuck you up. —Respected local pastor and "nouthetic" counselor to the author.

We shall now take up the interlocking, layered psychological devices—seven in number—embodied in the Bible. They are arranged roughly from the more obvious to the more hidden and from the more prominent in the experience of the newcomer to the more prominent in the deeply involved, intensively indoctrinated believer.

Device 1: The Benign, Attractive Persona of the Bible

The best things in the Bible are superficial. Another way of understanding the kindly, philanthropic, and surprisingly tolerant old-time religion we described earlier is to note that its proponents took the lovely surface impressions of Jesus in the Gospels and built a whole new religion out of them alone. This had been attempted from time to time earlier in history, e.g., by Saint Francis of Assisi, but never before had Christianity so expanded its sphere of influence, and at the same time effected such a measure of warmth and humanity, as in the United States. Besides the great variety of denominations and sects in constant competition and an ill-educated, "people-person" clergy until very recent times, the Elizabethan English of the King James version lent the Bible an air of harmless quaintness and kept its finer *nuances* embedded in a code few could decipher. This made it possible for a few hand-picked fragments of the biblical message to stand for the whole. Of course, people on the American frontier who had had the short end, in one way or another, in the places from which they had come, were glad to hear that they could live forever, that their pasts could become irrelevant, that the old games of nationality and class distinctions which had oppressed them would be supplanted by a new one with new rules, that they could receive something for nothing, and that they would not be thought crazy or made vulnerable to too great exploitation if they wanted to give away something for nothing, to benefit the less fortunate. This was and is a lovely folklore tradition.

Not so long ago, the image of Billy Graham, taking his followers through the exaltation of accepting Jesus for the umpteenth time once and for all, and pretending his "crusades" were filled with people who had not been Christian enthusiasts before, was the one most familiar to non-Evangelicals. This has changed; we now have an image of politicized, conservative television preachers, receiving more and more respectful attention from secular journalists. That image, in turn, conceals the individual human problems at the grassroots level.

The outside observer currently can see only the bare beginnings of the effects to be expected when the protective superficiality gives way to deeper indoctrination. I have already indicated how the new wide acceptance of contemporary translations of the Bible (accompanied by the opportunity to deepen comprehension by comparing and contrasting different renditions of any given passage) radically facilitates involvement in the Bible experience. Also, I have shown part of what there is to wean the believer away from the surface notion that ministry to assuage physical want and suffering is called for, toward the view that only ministry of the salvation message is proper, to bring the huddled masses of the world into bliss in the next life so as to make irrelevant whatever they may have suffered in this one, and away from the notion that *freedom* in the Bible means political freedom, toward the "insight" that there is no such thing as freedom, except from the bondage of sin.[2] We shall shortly see that the believer must be weaned away from the come-on notion that healing of his own or his loved ones' physical illnesses—or this-worldly personal success or prosperity—is in view, or else practical experience will conflict with the religious scheme and discredit it. Innocent of the historical lessons of old-time religion, and its successor, the liberal-modernist approach, the more deeply indoctrinated convert softens himself up to be sold some reactionary political teaching, and if he gets well enough indoctrinated to know that teaching to be unbiblical, he goes on doing his discipline relentlessly and ends up despising nothing so much (or so defensively) as genuine human spontaneity and cheerfulness.

What I mean by the *persona* of the Bible, then, is an apparent relevancy of teaching and promise of benefit that finally turn out to have totally different meanings from what the new inductee was led to think. We will encounter it many times, as our analysis unfolds. Little by little, newcomers are brought along to understand the teachings to mean something altogether different from what appeared on the surface—and oriented toward the next life, not this one. But one kind of promise, the kind that indicates a tranquilized, soporific, guilt-assuaging state of mind will be experienced, is kept, albeit by a means with a net detrimental effect on mental health.

Ironically, the liberal preachers of the mainline denominations, by talking themselves and their followers into the notion that they had found something contemporary and gratifying for the Bible to mean, set their people up to become recruits for the new, conservative Christian hucksters. Between the attempted liberal redefinition of the Bible message and the host of distracting features to be observed in conspicuous manifestations of incomplete biblical indoctrination, the present-day non-Evangelical American simply does not know what he is looking at, when he encounters a conservative Christian group. If one is not part of it (and therefore, not under it), one will not get to see enough of mini-Reformationism to appreciate the depth of the problem.

The misleading biblical surface impressions are not inadvertent. Initial recruitment contacts could not succeed without them. A short description of Device 1, the most external of the seven, is that a colossal bait-and-switch sales pitch is worked on the new believer!

---

2. See pp. 109-27.

Device 2: Discrediting "The World"

We earlier covered representative biblical teachings requiring the believer to distrust and to disparage reliance on his own mind for knowledge. Only through the teaching does he get whatever murky indications of the life more real than this one, beyond the grave for God's elect, as his earthly, incompletely redeemed, fragmented condition will permit. When he gets himself to imagine that some sort of energy is coming into him from outside, so that he sort of understands the teachings (but they sort of elude him as well), then things are going according to the believer's Bible-authentic expectations.[3] Obviously, such a state of mind is elusive, and much more is needed to make of it the formidably stable and compelling illusion we have indicated it to be. To the discrediting of his own conscience—indeed the discrediting of all four of the Jungian functions—the discrediting of people other than believers and of the environment itself is added, to make the indoctrination more comprehensive.

In the New Testament, we find that explicit instructions about conduct are relatively rare, in contrast to the detailed ceremonial instructions that are integral to Judaism but which disappeared from Christianity with the ascendancy of the Paulinists. Explicit New Testament instructions for conduct, together with related ones in the Old Testament not abrogated by the New Testament, we shall refer to as the biblical *devotional program.* There is not a shred of such explicit instruction without a mind-control purpose clearly behind it. However, the main operative devices, the ones toward the end of this list, work not through the devotional program but through the allegory, toward which the believer is brought into the desired posture by following the devotional program. Were the most essential behaviors wanted of the believer to be spelled out, the mind-control system would become transparent. Only about peripheral matters, ones merely preparatory to the object to be achieved, does the Bible venture to be explicit. The devotional program sets the stage, but the Bible is scrupulously bare of mention of what is to take place there.

For the believer, there are three kinds of people, and the devotional program prescribes a clear-cut mode of conduct toward each. There are: (1) ordinary unbelievers, (2) believers, and (3) missionaries of a conflicting or competing "false" gospel. The Bible presupposes relatively little depth of contact between believers and ordinary unbelievers. The objects of evangelism, unbelievers are often referred to collectively as "crops" of various kinds to be "harvested," or "fish" to be "netted." Precious little is said on handling contacts with them. One very crucial specific instruction on evangelization is given by Jesus to the apostles: "And whosoever will not receive you, when ye go out of that city, shake off the very dust from your feet for a testimony against them."[4] The context of the instruction indicates peripatetic movement of the apostles from one place to another, spending little time in any one place. Abundant numbers of evangelistic

---

3. See pp. 56-58.
4. Luke 9:5. Cf. Matt. 10:5-15 and Mark 6:7-13. See also Acts 5:42. Note also the example Jesus sets in eating with the publicans and harlots, in Matt. 9:10-12; Mark 2:15-17, and Luke 5:30-35.

contacts, not depth, are being mandated. If one does not get an immediate positive response, one is not to persist. When the believer is in the presence of an unbeliever, it is to preach and "witness," not to listen.

The only other nugget of explicit advice for relating to unbelievers comes in the unexpected context of believers with unbelieving spouses:

> . . . [Y]e wives, *be* in subjection to your own husbands; that, if any obey not the word, they also may without the word be won by the conversation [i.e., behavior, conduct] of the wives; While they behold your chaste conversation *coupled* with fear. Whose adorning let it not be that outward *adorning* of plaiting the hair, and of wearing of gold, or of putting on of apparel; But *let it be* the hidden man of the heart, in that which is not corruptible, *even the ornament* of a meek and quiet spirit, which is in the sight of God of great price.[5]

Taken together with less direct mention of unnatural self-restraint and outward appearance of freedom from negative emotions in the face of provocation,[6] a principle of conduct is established that serves two purposes at once. It puts the believers in the presence of unbelievers in a frame of mind that closes them off to anything the unbelievers might have to say. The object of the game is to don a mask and prevent the unbeliever from seeing through it at all costs. To the unbelievers is presented a very odd state of euphoric calm, the deeper causes of which we are coming to, that gets the unbeliever's attention and invites misinterpretation as a spiritually higher, happier state than the normal, not the dulled and divided one, masking artificially induced inner turmoil, that it really is. The more natural (if not actually obnoxious) mein of the unbeliever is distasteful and unsettling to the believer, who practices at remaining aloof and oblivious to whatever the unbeliever might have to say and developing the defensive knack for having that obliviousness be mistaken for tolerance.

In his churchly life, the believer hears about how he is to be a stranger and pilgrim in a world and among people that, although they are God's creation, are under Satan's rule. The rules mandating a closed off and stereotyped mode of relation to ordinary unbelievers simply ensure that no message contrary to their doctrine will wake up the believers' minds. The rules for relating to other believers have the same end in view. In surroundings that protect him against any competing indoctrination, the believer can be permitted to open up—to a precisely limited degree. The following passages are highly representative of the surroundings believers are instructed to provide for one another; they savor richly of the deeper devices to which we are coming.

> If ye then be risen with Christ, seek those things which are above, where Christ sitteth on the right hand of God. Set your affection on things above, not on things on the earth. For ye are dead, and your life is hid with Christ in God. When Christ, *who is* our life, shall appear, then shall ye also appear with him in glory. Mortify therefore your members which are upon the earth; fornication, uncleanness, inordinate affection, evil concupiscence, and covetousness, which is

5. 1 Pet. 3:1-4.
6. See Luke 6:29-31 and 1 Pet. 2:23.

idolatry: For which things' sake the wrath of God cometh on the children of disobedience: In the which ye also walked some time, when ye lived in them. But now ye also put off all these; anger, wrath, malice, blasphemy, filthy communication out of your mouth. Lie not one to another, seeing that ye have put off the old man with his deeds; And have put on the new *man,* which is renewed in knowledge after the image of him that created him: Where there is neither Greek nor Jew, circumcision nor uncircumcision, Barbarian, Scythian, bond *nor* free: but Christ *is* all, and in all. Put on therefore, as the elect of God, holy and beloved, bowels [lit., "gut" feelings] of mercies, kindness, humbleness of mind, meekness, longsuffering; Forbearing one another, and forgiving one another, if any man have a quarrel against any: even as Christ forgave you, so also *do* ye. And above all these things *put on* charity, which is the bond [lit. "tie" or "sinew"] of perfectness [completeness, unity]. And let the peace of God rule in your hearts, to the which also ye are called in one body; and be ye thankful. Let the word of Christ dwell in you richly in all wisdom; teaching and admonishing one another in psalms and hymns and spiritual songs, singing with grace in your hearts to the Lord. And whatsoever ye do in word or deed, *do* all in the name of the Lord Jesus, giving thanks to God and the Father by him.[7]

If *there be* therefore any consolation in Christ, if any comfort of love, if any fellowship of the Spirit, if any bowels and mercies, Fulfil ye my joy, that ye be likeminded, having the same love, *being* of one accord, of one mind. *Let* nothing *be done* through strife or vainglory; but in lowliness of mind let each esteem other better than themselves. Look not every man on his own things, but every man also on the things of others. Let this mind be in you, which was also in Christ Jesus. . . . That at the name of Jesus every knee should bow, of *things* in heaven, and *things* in earth, and *things* under the earth; And *that* every tongue should confess that Jesus Christ *is* Lord. . . .[8]

So much for Christian liberals, laying claim to biblical authenticity of lifestyle, basing the claim on a few Bible fragments in isolation or restricting the application to some but not all areas of life. Complete immersion is the idea. The human surroundings are to be devalued, "deprioritized," and any really heartfelt investment of psychic energy in them is to be withdrawn. Other people are no longer to count as ends in themselves, but biblical procedures, which the believer is to trust are helpful even though his sin-clouded mind cannot see how, are to be followed. Accordingly, the constant big-lie repetition from the Evangelicals—an example of Device 1—that the biblical program is synonymous with family values, goes glaringly against the grain of the Bible. (As we shall see, Jesus and Paul did not hesitate to divide families over religion, and the biblical program for conduct within the family is unrelievedly hierarchical, militating much more strongly against than for spontaneous human give and take.) Intolerance for individuality of personality is at the core of what is inculcated. While differences in function as organs in the "body of Christ,"[9] and differences

7. Col. 3:1-17.
8. Phil. 2:1-11.
9. 1 Cor. 12:12-31.

in "gifts"[10] are lauded as having their appointed purposes in the biblical plan, individuality of personality is irreconcilable with Bible authenticity. The Bible does *not* teach, "Be yourself!"

Device 2, then, is the place where our analysis touches the question of values, often such a stumbling block for the behavioral sciences. We have indicated that behavioral scientists in the past deluded themselves in aspiring to be value-free or objective, and we aspire more modestly to be imitators of William James, evincing fairness, honesty and humaneness in dealing with contending viewpoints, whereupon no one is to have the last word. The social psychologist Kurt Lewin expressed it durably in a paradox, advocating a basic principle: "intolerance against intolerant cultures."[11] When we confront the intense atmosphere of conformity and uniformity mandated by the Bible, we must relate it to other available psychological atmospheres, to the alternatives that exist for individuals who might fall within it.

If, as I have suggested, the epitome of mental health is productive application of the cyclical knowledge process, so that the individual becomes progressively better related to and in his surroundings, and decency and compassion may be achieved with maturity, through the realization that we share the same destiny and same sad finale with other living beings, then the lack of freedom to investigate, participate and experience, which is prescribed in the Bible, is sick. I hasten to point out that the reasoning would be circular, and its application unfair, were I to present that idea more strongly than as a suggestion. I formulated it as an answer to the tendentious question, "What is it that was sick about my own behavior and that of others in my experience in orthodox Christianity, when nearly all that was done, was done with good intentions, much of it seeming quite attractive at the time?" Does my picture of what human psychological functioning ought to be partake too much of individualistic elitism and camouflage my intolerance toward the great mass of mankind, who are not able to supply much structure for their own lives and thus fall victim to all sorts of deceptions and temptations unless directing structure is imposed from without? Have I forgotten how quickly, after the best days of the hippie counterculture in the sixties, that positive attempts to create alternative life styles for those who wanted to evade the more negative aspects of life in the mainstream disappeared, but how durable that time's negative proclivities, such as scruffy personal grooming and drug abuse, have turned out to be? Do I, or does anyone, really understand the causes and viscissitudes of the decay and debasement of scholarship in the behavioral sciences, which I complain of so bitterly at every opportunity, and the broader ideological confusion and malaise of which it is symptomatic? Do I fail to notice how remarkable it is that our contemporary culture fails to provide a more constructive outlet for tender idealists who do not want to participate in the coarseness, meanness, and general socially approved craziness with which the mainstream supplies us all so richly, than the sequestered, religious cults?

---

10. Eph. 4:1-16.
11. *Resolving Social Conflicts* (New York: Harper & Row, 1948), p. 36.

That the biblical plan for life, without more, fails to correspond to human life at its best, raises a powerful intellectual objection to that plan's exalted claims. That objection may or may not be relevant to the plan's practical implications. The questions worth asking, where people live or attempt to live according to the biblical plan, are, "What are the alternatives and what are their implications?" and "What harm, if any, does it do?"

From the group pressure experiments, we can infer that peer pressure alone would be enough to keep most of the people in any given religious group in line. We here reach a transition point, where we begin to get behind externalities, and encounter features more characteristic of active participants and leaders than of rank-and-file believers. At the point where the believer is in jeopardy of encounter with persons or natural phenomena in discord with his doctrine, the more complex proposition of an *active* devotional discipline, its proponents would say, to equip the believer to interpret what cannot be rightly interpreted in the natural, and we would say, to trick the believer into misinterpreting, misperceiving, and distorting the evidence of his own faculties, according to fictitious criteria, comes into play.

The category of "ordinary unbelievers" blends gradually into that of believers, since the large numbers of persons who are accepted in the religious community but cannot articulate much of its doctrine and generally have little to say partake of both. These present little challenge to the believer's indoctrination. But persons bringing ideas with other supernaturalistic premises represent such a hazard that a plurality of the Bible's carefully rationed explicit instructions pertain to them.

In ancient times, the premise of some sort of supernaturalistic dimension was universally assumed. In Paul's encounter with the intelligentsia of Athens on Mars Hill,[12] we see the permeation of the philosophers' thought with the polytheism that would ultimately prove so inferior in depth and poignancy to the Jewish monotheism and its progeny. Rationalized denial of the operativity of one or more gods would not come until modern times, and precious little in the Bible lends itself to application for defense against rationalized or scientific challenge to itself. That lack, undoubtedly, had much to do with the extreme vulnerability of mainline clergy, during the rise of modernism, to a critique based on the natural sciences.[13]

Besides passing references to atheism in the Psalms, e.g., "The fool hath said in his heart, *There is* no God,"[14] one passage in the New Testament might be taken as addressing secular antireligion, or "secular humanism," in a modern context:

> For the wrath of God is revealed from heaven against all ungodliness and unrighteousness of men, who hold the truth in unrighteousness; Because that which

---

12. Acts 17:16-29.

13. The famous religious controversy over astronomy, wherein the Roman Catholic church persecuted Galileo for espousing a heliocentric theory of the relations of the planets to the sun, had little to do with Protestantism; it took place primarily for doctrinal reasons exterior to the Bible.

14. Ps. 14:1; 10:4 and 53:1.

may be known of God is manifest in them; for God hath shewed *it* unto them. For the invisible things of him from the creation of the world are clearly seen, being understood by the things that are made, *even* his eternal power and Godhead; so that they are without excuse: Because that, when they knew God, they glorified *him* not as God, neither were thankful; but became vain [foolish, wicked, idolatrous] in their imaginations, and their foolish heart was darkened. Professing themselves to be wise, they became fools, and changed the glory of the uncorruptible God into an image made like to corruptible man, and to birds, and fourfooted beasts, and creeping things. Wherefore God also gave them up to uncleanness through the lusts of their own hearts, to dishonour their own bodies between themselves: Who changed the truth of God into a lie, and worshipped and served the creature more than the Creator, who is blessed for ever, Amen. For this cause God gave them up unto vile affections: for even their women did change the natural use into that which is against nature: And likewise also the men, leaving the natural use of the woman, burned in their lust one toward another; men with men working that which is unseemly, and receiving in themselves that recompence of their error which was meet.[15]

Paul's equation of whatever is not the prescribed religious program with homosexuality, like any latter-day Bible-thumper might make, will have more significance for us later on. While the context elsewhere more clearly indicates competing supernaturalistic religions, the implication is that anything passing for learning that is not the biblical religious program is to be opposed, whether it arises within the religious community or comes from outside, and if it cannot be "corrected," its proponents are to be ostracized:

For many deceivers are entered into the world, who confess not that Jesus Christ is come in the flesh. This is a deceiver and an anti-christ. Look to yourselves, that we lose not those things which we have wrought, but that we receive a full reward. Whosoever transgresseth, and abideth not with the doctrine of Christ, hath not God. . . . If there come any unto you, and bring not this doctrine, receive him not into *your* house, neither bid him God speed [i.e., give him no greeting]: For he that biddeth him God speed is partaker of his evil deeds.[16]

In a different place, the historical context of the instruction can be seen:

For there are many unruly and vain talkers and deceivers, specially they of the circumcision: Whose mouths must be stopped, who subvert whole houses, teaching things which they ought not, for filthy lucre's sake. One of themselves [i.e., the "Cretans"], *even* a prophet of their own, said, The Cretans *are* always liars, evil beasts, slow bellies [gluttons]. This witness is true. Wherefore rebuke them sharply, that they may be sound in the faith; Not giving heed to Jewish fables, and commandments of men, that turn from the truth. Unto the pure all things *are* pure: but unto them that are defiled, and unbelieving *is* nothing pure; but even their mind and conscience is defiled.[17]

---

15. Rom. 1:18-27. Cf. Col. 2:8 and Heb. 13:9.
16. 2 John 7-11.
17. Titus 1:10-15.

While an intellectually competent effort to apply the implications of the Bible's teaching to the present day will inevitably lead to the conclusion that secular humanists—i.e., educators, mental-health professionals, liberal politicians, etc.—fall within a biblical definition of false prophets bringing a death-dealing false gospel, no image or personality negatively presented in the Bible resembles any of them. Without a process of reasoning, the believer will not see those classes of persons as inimical to his beliefs, but a guided process of reasoning, entirely true to its biblical premises, will lead him to what approaches paranoid fear of them. All of the superior human types the Bible warns against come with a religious gospel resembling, both in idea content and devotional practice, the "true" Gospel. The following are conspicuous and representative examples:

> For there shall arise false Christs, and false prophets, and shall shew great signs and wonders; insomuch that, if *it were* possible, they shall deceive the very elect.[18]

> Let no man deceive you by any means: for *that day* [i.e., the second coming] *shall not come,* except there come a falling away [i.e., apostasy] first, and that man of sin be revealed, the son of perdition; Who opposeth and exalteth himself above all that is called God, or that is worshipped; so that he as God sitteth in the temple of God, shewing himself that he is God. . . . For the mystery of iniquity doth already work: only he who now letteth [i.e., restrains] *will let,* until he be taken out of the way. And then shall that Wicked be revealed, whom the Lord shall consume with the spirit [or breath] of his mouth, and shall destroy with the brightness of his coming: *Even him,* whose coming is after the working of Satan with all power and signs and lying wonders, And with all deceivableness of unrighteousness in them that perish; because they received not the love of the truth, that they might be saved. And for this cause God shall send them strong delusion, that they should believe a lie: That they all might be damned who believed not the truth, but had pleasure in unrighteousness. But we are bound to give thanks alway to God for you, brethren beloved of the Lord, because God hath from the beginning chosen you to salvation through sanctification of the Spirit and belief of the truth: Whereunto he called you by our gospel, to the obtaining of the glory of our Lord Jesus Christ.[19]

A crucially important practical insight to be derived here is that the political preachers and religious hucksters with whom our culture is littered are the people who most nearly fit the negative types depicted in the Bible as coming in the end-times! Secular commentators have not scratched the surface of the possibilities for discrediting conservative Christian agitators in the eyes of their following by holding them closely to the Bible they say they espouse. Concomitantly, the kind of churches we have characterized as mini-Reformationist and transitional generally retain a certain stability and resistance in the face of attempts to exploit them politically or commercially, because they are able to

18. Matt. 24:24.
19. 2 Thess. 2:3-14.

discern—often without articulating it well—what is unbiblical. Although the leaders may hesitate to speak ill of another Christian group, they do not want to go "down the tubes" with a false gospel. As a historical matter, the tendency of Protestant groups to suspect one another of being under false gospels—while it fosters any given group's cohesiveness and sense of specialness—has discouraged them from forming a unified front on public-policy issues or otherwise co-operating regularly.

The active phase of the devotional process of discrediting "the world" begins with the rearrangement of perception to confirm the expectation or tacit presupposition that there is an ulterior purpose behind everything that is not part of the religious program—not that the individual bringing the extraneous teaching personally has a bad motive but rather his lack of the "truth" entails his inability to have any good motive. How can a human, whose fleshly little mind is sin-cursed, whose heart is innately wicked and corrupt, and who has come from his mother's womb preprogrammed to speak lies, have a good motive unless it is inspired in him by the Holy Spirit? And how can anything not permeated by the biblical teachings be permeated by the Holy Spirit? One becomes uncritical as to what is in the religious program and hypercritical as to whatever conflicts with it, ready to jump at any refutation of an extraneous view, and not looking too closely at the refutation's substance. One has "faith" that the refutation will come later or that some religious leader who knows more would be able, if present, to refute the view with which one is confronted. The subjective appeal of the view clashing with the doctrine is interpreted as a form of temptation. That one does not succumb to such temptation is a sign of good Christian character, an evidence of salvation. If one's mind tells one otherwise, that only goes to prove how deceitful the fleshly human mind is and how right the Bible is to hold it in such low esteem.

The substance of the nonbiblical view confronting the believer becomes completely irrelevant. Inasmuch as all merely human views are inherently defective, the *argumentum ad hominem* becomes a fair argument, and the blow is softened by that argument's equal validity and "impartial" applicability against all, including the Christian if he weakens and lets his thinking stray outside biblical premises. Critical thinking about human affairs is simply dispaired of as futile. While the Bible does not explicitly say that independent thinking is the cardinal sin—to do so would give the game away—we shall soon see that it is the crux of any biblically authentic definition of sin, one particularly incompatible with doing the devotional program. The technological successes of modern, unsaved man only go to prove how God can use the wicked to work his inscrutable will. Did he not even deign to speak through the mouth of Balaam's donkey for just such a purpose?[20]

The way discrediting of natural phenomena works in the mental life of the well-indoctrinated Bible-believer may well be the area of conservative Christianity wherein outsiders are most misinformed. Quite conspicuous to outsiders are

20. Num. 22:21-35; 2 Pet. 2:15-16.

those peripheral and minority enterprises that offer personal economic prosperity through will power applied to prayer and the having of faith, faith healing of bodily illness, reception of personal marching orders from God through mental telepathy, etc. Except for the very unintelligent, listeners to these eventually catch on, and conclude that their own failure to become wealthy was not because they failed to pray hard enough or have enough faith, that unexplained remissions of physical disease, like the sunlight and the rain, fall on the just and the unjust in equal proportions,[21] and that God seems all too agreeably inclined to tell people to do the very things they want to do anyway. The purveyors of these sorts of "gospels" are the most commercialized of the conservative Christians, hence, the most conspicuous to outsiders. Their activity can often work as Device 1, resulting in someone's migration to a more Bible-authentic group, and leaves many a disillusioned victim along the way.

In the churches we identify as mini-Reformationist, we find not only no trace of but also express aversion to expectation of physical manifestations of the supernatural. In the ones we identify as transitional, we find the topic artfully contained, deemphasized, the occasion for a certain embarrassment, and waning. Every attempt to find in everyday experience divine supernatural manifestations demonstrably occurring in ways depicted or intimated in the Bible flies in the face of that experience. The honest, not unintelligent believer is forced into unbelief, unless a more sophisticated approach be taken to reconciling the Bible with the fact that unbelievers fare successfully in the world. In the Reformation of old and the mini-Reformation, belief in the Bible could not have reasserted itself had it depended on holding to beliefs jarringly disconfirmed by everyday experience.

In the connections that most often come up—prosperity, health and direct miraculous manifestations or revelations—there are clear biblical implications. Unless some sectarian commitment required otherwise, the studious Bible-believers I have known did gravitate toward the same understandings of them. Based on my own study and, more importantly, what the more articulate Bible-believers took them to mean, they can be summarized as follows:

On the topic of prosperity: one is first confronted with Jesus' constant praise of poverty and disparagement of wealth. He has come "to preach the gospel to the poor." He declares them "blessed" in the Sermon on the Mount, and it "is easier for a camel to go through the eye of a needle, than for a rich man to enter into the kingdom of God."[22] The disciples leave behind their livelihoods (and apparently, their families) to follow him. Consequently, the applicant to whom Jesus responded with the hyperbole about the camel and the eye of the needle could not become his follower because it grieved him too much to give up his possessions.

Several times, Jesus constructs intricate paradoxes out of the arithmetic, cause-and-effect relations of business transactions.[23] On the surface, these are

21. Matt. 5:45.
22. Matt. 19:24; Mark 10:25; and Luke 18:25.
23. Matt. 13:44-46; 17:24-27; 20:1-16; 25:1-30; Mark 12:41-44; Luke 7:40-50; 16; 19:11-27; and 21:1-9.

attractive, in that they invite the believer to disdain the pressures and frustrations of the marketplace and imagine he rises above them. A person being pressured to overachieve or strive for things he really does not want, may use Christianity to compensate, or to evade whoever is pressuring him. At a deeper level, if these paradoxical stories do not point to the futility and unprofitableness of having one's heart in worldly business, they are unintelligible.

This early approach turned out to be too severe for good church management, and even Jesus needed a rich patron, Joseph of Arimathea, to provide him with a shroud.[24] Paul took a much more expedient approach than Jesus, in counseling disciples on the care and feeding of wealthy people in the church.[25]

Regarding healing of physical illness: occasionally in the Old Testament, under intensely poignant circumstances, someone was healed of a physical illness.[26] Such healings always appeared as a demonstration of God's special interest in the business at hand. Quite significantly, the only male who came into the body of believers by conversion after Abraham, Naaman, was miraculously healed of leprosy. The far larger number of healings in the New Testament and the indiscriminate way they are handed out represent a great departure.

During Jesus' ministry, a great number of healings are portrayed, as well as multiplication of foodstuffs and displays of telekinetic power over water, apparently for the purpose of proving their author's claims. No consistent trend is evident as to whom Jesus chose to heal, what they were healed of, or whom they told or what they did after being healed. After Jesus' crucifixion, the apostles and two favored deacons went on healing for awhile. But the healings become less frequent, less dramatic, and the emphasis on them after Acts is very slight. Clearly, if Jesus went to the cross to give the believers whole bodies in this life, he was wasting his time. Also, all the teaching about judgment day and its transformations is reduced to unintelligibility if the biblical mentions of "healing" contemplate something other than salvation and preservation of candidacy for heaven.

The topic of direct revelations and signs is a matter of unending controversy in the kinds of churches we term transitional. These often have very striking, and to outsiders bizarre, manifestations, such as glossolalia,[27] prophesying, being "slain in the spirit" (falling over backwards in a state of ecstasy), etc. These features alienate them thoroughly from mini-Reformationist churches. They have grown up almost entirely in the present century. Protestantism had left that sort

24. Matt. 27:57.
25. 1 Tim. 6:17-19.
26. Exod. 4:6-7; Num. 12:10-15; 1 Kings 13:4-6; 2 Kings 5:10-14; and 20:7. Note that all Old Testament healings are of dermatological disease; except for Naaman's, all consist of God gratuitously inflicting the disease to make a doctrinal point, and then relenting.
27. On glossolalia, the kind of "speaking in tongues" that consists of outbursts of ideomotor gibberish, there are strikingly conflicting biblical signals. The believer is told they will cease but is not told when (1 Cor. 13:8). Pastors are explicitly instructed not to forbid them (14:39), but when they are allowed, it is not to be without someone gifted to interpret them (14:27). Letting someone interpret the glossolalia exposes the church to the danger of false prophecy deceitfully imitating true prophecy. The rulers of the church are confronted with a no-win situation. The more literate Bible-believers usually resolve it by not having glossolalia in their church, inferring that tongues ceased with the completion of the canon.

of thing behind in Roman Catholicism; it was only through Christian Science and an early, popularized, liberal theological movement called "New Thought" that they reentered. Conservative Protestant groups identifying with older historical movements, such as Machen-denomination Presbyterians and Southern Baptists, generally shy away from such manifestations. In Pentecostalism, such overt manifestations turn out to have profound ameliorative effects on mind-control and make for some genuinely new and unexpected psychological subtleties. The Pentecostal pays attention to inner thoughts and feelings, diluting and interrupting the devotional discipline we are exploring.

For the deeply indoctrinated and not unintelligent believer, the whole question of direct manifestations of God's power, articulately or by gesture, is fraught with preoccupation about the dangers of false prophets in the end-times and the testing program for believers, to which discerning the "true" Gospel from false ones mimicking it and competing with it, amounts. For the mini-Reformationist, the place where purported wondrous manifestations of God are flying about is a good place not to be, since participation in false prophecy is the one thing that will bring the nonelect added punishment in Hell![28] The "Word" is where the believer is to seek God and from where God's spiritual "nourishment" is to be received. The only kind of prophet it is safe to be is a "bread-eating prophet," whose declarations of God's word remain confined to the contents of the Bible, "rightly dividing the word of truth."[29] As we shall see while analyzing the Bible's statements on "faith," a large and integral part of the Bible's doctrine would be reduced to surplusage if its "truth" could be proved by events in the natural world. Harold Camping expresses it by saying that in the end-times God will not "break the silence" between the natural and the supernatural, but he permits Satan and his emissaries to do so. So far as I can find, nothing in the Bible fails to harmonize with that view. This means that if the believer witnesses, or thinks he witnesses, genuine occult or parapsychological phenomena, he should attribute them to Satan's working and be glad that being God's child affords protection against them. That such phenomena do not follow any pattern depicted in the Bible is perfectly in accord with correct biblical expectations. Brought together, the range of ungodly events capable of fulfilling biblical expectations is so wide that no sequence of events could fall outside it.

How, then, do events in the surrounding world relate to the believer's total experience? He prays, as he is instructed to do, for what he wants to take place. He is not to pray for a sign, "tempting" God and putting him to the test.[30] If the thing prayed for does not come to pass, that only goes to prove that God's answer is no. Was that not his answer to Paul regarding the thorn in his flesh and even to Jesus himself, praying in the Garden of Gethsemane not to have to go to the cross? When bad things happen to good people and good things happen to bad people, it only goes to prove how far beyond our sin-cursed, wicked little minds God's wisdom, justice, and foresight are. Any set of events,

28. See pp. 56-57 and p. 49, note 88.
29. 2 Tim. 2:15. See also Gal. 1:6-9.
30. Matt. 12:39; Luke 4:12.

no matter how absurd, takes on an aura of purpose, of being under control, in the light of that "insight." The deeply indoctrinated believer ceases entirely to look for confirmation of his beliefs in the surrounding world.

In short, Device 2 consists of placing a favorable, self-satisfying construction on unshakable and unashamed prejudice. Toward other persons who bring anything but the biblical teaching, the believer is to remember privately teachings ridiculing them, while outwardly evincing endless patience and self-restraint. To be sure, the believer rationalizes that contempt, reminding himself that he is not to judge the unbeliever, whose heart only God can know and whose destiny, to salvation or eternal punishment, is God's business alone. Toward the natural environment, the biblical teaching amounts to an all-encompassing, nondisprovable hypothesis. Whatever happens, that it does proves it is God's will.

Device 3: Logocide

How far is it possible to go in misusing words—planting them in contexts that distort their meanings and draw their feeling tones and connotations too far into the foreground—to mislead people, confuse them, and mount a campaign of disinformation against them? Is anyone really misled by the use of the phrase *protective reaction strike* for the napalming of helpless Vietnamese civilians, or by the other premier world power naming one of its conquered vassal states the German Democratic Republic? Does it demonstrate the triviality of the technique or, on the contrary, the insidiousness of its working that we have elected to a second term as president of the United States a man whose job it used to be to intone to us, over black and white television, the slogan "Progress is our most important product"?

The proposition that totalitarian control over people could be facilitated by the debasement of the language itself has been most articulately expressed by George Orwell in the Appendix to *1984,* "The Principles of Newspeak." He explains the use of such a technique in the novel's fictional setting, Oceania, as follows:

> The purpose of Newspeak was not only to provide a medium of expression for the world-view and mental habits proper to the devotees of Ingsoc, but to make all other modes of thought impossible. It was intended that when Newspeak had been adopted once and for all and Oldspeak [i.e., English] forgotten, a heretical thought—that is, a thought diverging from the principles of Ingsoc [a contraction of "English Socialism," Oceania's prescribed ideology] should be literally unthinkable, at least so far as thought is dependent on words. Its vocabulary was so constructed as to give exact and often very subtle expression to every meaning that a Party member could properly wish to express, while excluding all other meanings and also the possibility of arriving at them by indirect methods. This was done partly by the invention of new words, but chiefly by eliminating undesirable words and by stripping such words as remained of unorthodox meanings, and so far as possible of all secondary meanings whatever. To give a single example. The word *free* still existed in Newspeak, but it could only be used in

> such statements as "This dog is free from lice" or "This field is free from weeds." It could not be used in its old sense of "politically free" or "intellectually free," since political and intellectual freedom no longer existed even as concepts, and were therefore of necessity nameless. Quite apart from the suppression of definitely heretical words, reduction of vocabulary was regarded as an end in itself, and no word that could be dispensed with was allowed to survive. Newspeak was designed not to extend but to *diminish* the range of thought, and this purpose was indirectly assisted by cutting the choice of words down to a minimum.[31]

Even in Oceania, the aim of remolding humanity to the ideological specifications of Ingsoc (a take-off on the Soviet aspiration to create a "new soviet man" by applying Pavlovian principles) is not achieved—only its outward semblance by coercion and force. None of the political totalitarianisms of our times lastingly achieved anything approaching thought control. No totalitarian government's program of brainwashing has ever remolded anyone along the lines intended. All that has really been learned from our century's experience with such techniques (no matter how carefully their application is managed), we could have guessed at once: human beings are damaged in direct proportion to the amount of cruelty and brutality to which they are subjected. And cruelty and brutality can be entirely mental.

Every deeply indoctrinated believer I have known has shared the experience of finding the Bible hard to read, with passages studied many times before seeming unfamiliar and surprising. In the Bible, instead of paradoxical *déjà vu,* one experiences *ne déjà vu pas.* Something about the verses eludes their adherence to memory: they are teflon coated. The believer ascribes this quality, which distinguishes the Bible from other writings in ancient languages, to the process of the understanding coming through the intervention of the Holy Spirit, qualitatively unlike the way earthly ideas are understood. Only to a very limited degree is that elusiveness due to hyperbole and plays on words we are hindered from appreciating by the cultural and language barriers separating us from those who lived in Bible times and lands. The attachment of ungainly meanings to often repeated, key words, different from, but confusingly contaminated with, the meanings of the same words as found in contexts other than the Bible, accounts for the slippery, unassimilable quality of the most psychologically significant passages. Frustration of communication, and of thought inconsistent with the churchly enterprise's purposes, is the end served by the resulting terminological confusion. *I submit that the New Testament was designed that way.* Paul knew what he was doing, and building on the Pharisaic tradition of putting an interpretive gloss on the Scriptures, he deliberately made his terminology confusing. He may even have been mocking the believers when he said, "crafty fellow that I am, I took you in by deceit."[32]

A distinction must be made between cases where multiple meanings or multiple levels of meaning enhance the artistry and communicative power of a

31. (New York: New American Library, 1961), pp. 246-47.
32. 2 Cor. 12:16. *New American Standard Bible.*

passage and cases where crossed meanings and contrived ambiguities confound and confuse. The Bible has the former richly in common with all other great literature. The latter, it has in common with contemporary advertising, propaganda, and hype techniques, all of which it incomparably surpasses in artfulness.

At least once, a double meaning in the Greek is used simultaneously to express two aspects of a straightforward doctrine. *Anagenao,* translated "born from above" or "reborn," depending upon the choice from the meanings of the prefix *ana,* while clever, is not confusing or misleading.[33] Elsewhere, we encounter Jesus speaking of a "kingdom," meaning a spiritual kingdom, when the mind-set of his hearers makes them understand a political kingdom; Jesus also speaks of a temple torn down and rebuilt in three days, which his disciples later took to mean his atoning death and resurrection.[34] Such literary uses of semantic double meanings merely help establish that sensitivity to subtlety of word expression is wanted of the believer. Our culture's whole approach to secular literature grew from that. But the more covert biblical manipulations of words operate differently.

Another mode of biblical expression to be distinguished from the disinforming kind we pursue is *hyperbole.* Jesus said that it is harder for a rich man to enter into Heaven than for a camel to go through the eye of a needle; hyperbole also occurs in allusions to the moving of mountains or believers doing greater miracles than Jesus himself.[35] Hyperbole is used by Paul to reinforce his point against false prophets; incidently, this point comes as close as the dour Bible gets to levity:

> But though we, or an angel from heaven, preach any other gospel unto you than that which we have preached unto you, let him be accursed.[36]

To understand these passages, making the necessary allowances for biblical hyperbole,[37] it is necessary to understand the pervasive Semitic custom of using hyperbole in activities ranging from worship to bargaining in the marketplace. As this is being written, in a Middle Eastern city, Teheran, there stands a billboard in a major square, put up by the Islamic fundamentalist government, with a motto on it in Persian and in English that illustrates such hyperbole: "America is worse than Britain. Britain is worse than America. Russia is worse than both of them. And each one is worse than the others."

Obviously, no great philosophical wisdom, contravening logic or breaking

---

33. 1 Pet. 1:23.
34. John 2:19-22.
35. See p. 58.
36. Gal. 1:8.
37. In exegesis of the Bible, particularly of the extravagant promises about faith moving mountains, nothing being impossible, and believers being empowered to do greater miracles than Jesus himself, it is acceptable, indeed, merely part of translating from the ancient languages in which the text is supposed to be "inspired," to allow for hyperbolic expression. To make such allowances as to the *form* of expression is much different from discarding *content* alleged to be anachronistic and hence uninspired, as the liberals do. The former can be done preserving the integrity of the text, but the latter cannot.

new philosophical ground, is in view. The paradoxical, incongruous relations are for the purpose of emphasis. They serve a purpose comparable to that of colorful adjectives in our Western political rhetoric. Neglecting that insight, some pedantic philologists could have a merry time "interpreting" the motto. I suspect that the growth of the theological parties of Jesus' time out of the earlier, less self-conscious Hebraic religion—and the sequel to that development, Gentilized Christianity—included quite a lot of inflation of such hyperbole into ponderous, pseudoprofound intellectual lore. Because our modern intellectual environment conditions us to expect every paradox to point beyond itself to some lofty concept or at least to express an entertaining conundrum (such as a Cretan telling us that all Cretans are liars), we do not expect a paradox to be empty or pretend it expresses something substantial when it is really just a ploy. After Tillich, especially, we always look for some sublime and ineffable thing being symbolized, and for the elusive master symbol standing for the referent of our ultimate concern. But in the Bible, an absurdity is often just an absurdity, put there to keep us busy and distract our attention from other things.

After taking into account the plays on words, other translation problems, and use of hyperbole in a way foreign to Western literature, there remain the calculatedly confusing biblical usages of words, making them take on conflicting or even contradictory definitions. The believer cannot articulate or relevantly discuss the ponderous ideas and menacing implications impinging on him; nevertheless, they register at a subconscious level. His attempts to articulate and discuss them result in his discourse becoming filled with time-consuming casuistry. Dialogue with the deeply indoctrinated goes in circles.

To load a word (including synonyms, cognates and other contextually related words) so that it is no longer serviceable for making an idea conscious, just the right posture of artificial meaning for the word under attack, in relation to its established usages in the language it is part of, must be struck. In the key words of Christianity—which are also key words in human experience generally—we shall shortly see how words are so artfully overburdened that they are put out of commission entirely as vehicles for articulate thought or communication. The biblical assault on key words, loading them with ponderous, contrived, dissonant meanings I call *logocide,*[38] the killing of words. I fully intend the

38. In fashioning the neologism *logocide,* I mean to emulate Joost A. M. Meerloo, *The Rape of the Mind* (New York: Universal Library, 1961), p. 27, who coined the term *menticide* for the manipulation of confusion, fear, and the latent inner contradictions and sense of guilt in every person, for political ends. The term was intended for wider application than *brainwashing,* which is an intensive and custodial affair. *Menticide* includes what happens to those who listen to a demogogue, when their society is in turmoil. Meerloo had in mind the United Nations' then-recent coining of the term, *genocide.* My apologies to classical purists for mixing a Greek root with a Latin one.

A notion midway between menticide and logocide, on the debasement of language for manipulative purposes, has been advanced by George Steiner, who connects the Hitler phenomenon with the death of the German language itself. (His most vigorous statement on it, from which the quotation below is taken, was made in 1959, before "God is dead" theology.) Steiner overstated the case and retracted much of what he had written, when he learned his writings were having a detrimental effect on younger German literati, trying to bring German literature back to life after World War II. It is fitting, in the midst of our exploration of Eastern hyperbole, to set

sinister connotation I hope the term conveys. It stands for the Bible's success at what the most vigorous political and commercial exploitations of our century have tried and failed.[39] Language is resilient. Only in that unique transplantation and hybridization of traditions, from defeated Israel to Rome, was it perfected. One might well become convinced that its genius is beyond human capability. But the guile is all too human.

We shall examine what key terms (such as *life, death, truth, wisdom, righteousness, justice, liberty, bondage, love, hate, will, grace, witness* and *word*) refer to in the Bible and in the intrapsychic life of the Bible-believer. (Later, we shall analyze the most significant terms, *sin, faith* and *belief,* in the major devices to which they pertain.) Our object, in each instance, will be to make articulate the otherwise inarticulate ideas behind each term. It should be kept in mind that we have yet to address the *causes* of the unarticulated ideas' remaining so. The answer to that vital question will come in the deeper devices.

Also, it will be noted that within each instance of logocide Devices 1 and 2 also operate. Always, the inarticulate meaning is a more somber and intimidating one than the apparent meaning that had helped attract the new recruit into participation. The new inductee is weaned away from the ordinary meaning of each key term, baited and switched to the "deeper" meaning. Also, the terms come to have meanings so different for Christians than for others that they serve as stumbling blocks to Christians' and outsiders' attempts to communicate with one another. The outsiders are "protected" from knowing pertinent things about their prospective religion that would discourage them from wanting to know any more. The believers are "protected" by their eventual inability to understand what the unbelievers are talking about. Being closed off to outsiders' influence and conditioned to disparage them as foolish, inconsequential slaves of Satan are both facilitated in the process.

---

out Steiner's artfully hyperbolic statement of his thesis: ". . . the German language was not innocent of the horrors of Nazism. It is not merely that a Hitler, a Goebbels, and a Himmler happened to speak German. Nazism found in the language precisely what it needed to give voice to its savagery. Hitler heard inside his native tongue the latent hysteria, the confusion, the quality of hypnotic trance. He plunged unerringly into the undergrowth of language, into those zones of darkness and outcry which are the infancy of articulate speech, and which come before words have grown mellow and provisional to the touch of the mind. He sensed in German another music than that of Goethe, Heine and Mann; a rasping cadence, half nebulous jargon, half obscenity. And instead of turning away in nauseated disbelief, the German people gave massive echo to the man's bellowing. It bellowed back out of a million throats and smashed-down boots. A Hitler would have found reservoirs of venom and moral illiteracy in any language. But by virtue of recent history, they were nowhere else so ready and so near the very surface of common speech. A language in which one can write a 'Horst Wessel Lied' is ready to give hell a native tongue." "The Hollow Miracle," in *Language and Silence* (New York: Atheneum, 1967), p. 99.

39. For a fictionalized account (but representitive of true events) showing the Soviet style of brainwashing to obtain raw material for propaganda, with no thought of the future of the victim, see Arthur Koestler, *Darkness at Noon,* trans. Daphne Hardy (New York: Macmillan, 1941). For a thorough case analysis of victims of the Chinese Communist variety, intended to remold the person into the desired ideological image and premised on a very materialistic and reductionistic pseudopsychology, see Robert Jay Lifton, *Thought Reform and the Psychology of Totalism: A Study of "Brainwashing" in China* (New York: W. W. Norton & Co., 1963). Of particular interest are the complexity and destructiveness of the ramifications of the so-called reeducation experience for its victims.

The first impression received by the prospective convert is apt to involve the terms *life* and *death.* Since man, for obvious reasons, is prestructured to fear physical death, to associate it with pain, and to strive to survive, avoiding death as long as possible, the topic is charged from the outset. Of course he is interested in anything that promises to postpone or avoid that sad finale. An evangelist comes along, and confronts his audience with statements like these:

> And as Moses lifted up the serpent in the wilderness, even so must the Son of man be lifted up: That whosoever believeth in him should not perish, but have eternal life. For God so loved the world, that he gave his only begotten Son, that whosoever believeth in him should not perish, but have everlasting life. For God sent not his Son into the world to condemn the world; but that the world through him might be saved.[40]

> And every one that hath forsaken houses, or brethren, or sisters, or father, or mother, or wife, or children, or lands, for my name's sake, shall receive an hundredfold, and shall inherit everlasting life. But many *that are* first shall be last; and the last *shall be* first.[41]

These, and numerous similar verses, make it look as though God is making an open offer that anyone may accept, thereby gaining much and standing to lose only much less. Since we have looked at the rivalry between Arminian and Calvinist theology[42] and established how an Arminian view can be maintained only through ignorance of the Bible or cultivated superficiality and obtuseness in studying it, we know that some pretty short strings are attached to these apparent promises. We shall see not only that Arminianism amounts to a doctrine fashioned out of the calculatedly misleading biblical surface impressions but also that discourse sounding Arminian to the casual listener may actually have a totally different meaning for the well-indoctrinated person reciting it, and be understood accordingly by the well-indoctrinated other hearing it, because the inarticulate meanings of the key terms permeate the tacit understanding of them both. Calvinism, by making the deeper content of the Bible more plain, did not lend itself to a Device-1-oriented approach to new converts. Hence, religious fervor ebbed from the time of the Great Awakening to the Revolutionary War period. People could see too easily how unattractive the implications of the Bible were, compared with humanist learning. John Wesley showed the Christians how to repackage the old merchandise, restoring the operation of Device 1. After all, Jesus never told the believers not to put *old* wine in a *new* container!

By alerting us to the dangers of putting new wine in an old container, Jesus prepares us for the indirectly indicative and sharp departures from the Old Testament he was about to introduce.[43] What was being departed from? In the

40. John 3:14-17.
41. Matt. 19:29-30.
42. See pp. 12-25.
43. Matt. 9:17; Mark 2:22; Luke 5:37-38.

Old Testament, there were only vague indications that punishment for wickedness would occur[44] and only the most fleeting and fragmentary references to reward for righteousness[45] after earthly death. Nowhere in the Old Testament is such reward juxtaposed to "life": all Old Testament mentions of that term point to biological life, the lifetime or duration, or vitality or thriving. Once, in the Old Testament, living persons even descend into Hell.[46] Old Testament references to Heaven and Hell are further marred for the modern reader by constant identification of Heaven with the sky, the location of Hell beneath the earth, and the depiction of the earth as flat and four-cornered.[47] Not enough information about reward and punishment after death is presented for a formulation of an Old Testament doctrine of them to be possible, and we see the result in the proliferation of theological parties in Israel in Jesus' time, each with its own such doctrine, not inconsistent with the canon but hotly in contention with one another.

In contrast to the Old Testament authors, who were quite commendably restrained in their treatment of natural human fears and superstitions about death, Christianity was quick to exploit those superstitions to the fullest. In an environment of massive pagan encroachment on Hebrew culture—at that time in a civilized and often attractive way rather than in the brutish, culturally inferior way of such encroachments before the Greeks—one could get away with heavy-handedness in manipulating people by their fear of death. Indeed, the soberness of the Hebrew religion in that regard may have enhanced the respect of Gentiles for the Jewish diaspora communities in their midst. To offset the diminished plausibility of an appeal presupposing wild ideas about the consequences of death, in the eighteenth century and after, the pitch had to be softened. The advent of Wesleyanism, reassuring people that the key to their salvation from such terrors was safely in their own pockets, sufficiently reduced the incentive to pick at the flaws in the scheme, discredit it, and throw it off entirely.

Hence, Jesus could be very direct about his new interpretations of *life* and *death* even though they departed greatly from his traditions. The following representatives of that reinterpretation permit us to sample both its articulate and its indirectly expressed features:

> Then said Jesus unto his disciples, If any *man* will come after me, let him deny himself, and take up his cross, and follow me. For whosoever will save his life shall lose it: and whosoever will lose his life for my sake shall find it.[48]

---

44. Deut. 32:22; Ps. 5:5-6; 6:5; 9:16-18; Prov. 8:35-36; 15:24; Isa. 38:18; Hos. 13:14. Note that reference to punishment of the wicked (or of Israel's military enemies) is much more frequent and less unclear in the Old Testament, than reference to punishment taking effect after physical death. Physical death is usually the horror in view, and nowhere in the Old Testament except Dan. 12:2, does the context justify interpreting *death* or *perishing* to contemplate anything else.

45. Prov. 11:18; Isa. 26:19; Ezek. 37:12 and Hos. 10:12. Also, note well Dan. 12:2, the only verse in the Old Testament that can fairly be taken as implying a New Testament style salvation plan. These verses, like those possibly contemplating punishment after earthly life, are heavily outweighed by others indicating reward, justice, or judgment upon Israel's foes on earth.

46. Num. 16:30-33.

47. Deut. 32:22; Job 11:8; 38:4, 13; Ps. 86:13; 139:8; Prov. 15:24; Isa. 11:12; 55:9 and Ezek. 32:27.

48. Matt. 16:24-25. Cf. Matt. 10:39; Mark 8:35; Luke 9:24-25; 17:33, and John 12:25

And these shall go away into everlasting punishment: but the righteous into life eternal.[49]

And if thy hand offend thee, cut it off: it is better for thee to enter into life maimed, than having two hands to go into hell, into the fire that never shall be quenched: Where their worm dieth not, and the fire is not quenched. And if thy foot offend thee, cut it off: it is better for thee to enter halt [i.e., lame] into life, than having two feet to be cast into hell, into the fire that never shall be quenched: Where their worm dieth not, and the fire is not quenched. And if thine eye offend thee, pluck it out: it is better for thee to enter into the kingdom of God with one eye, than having two eyes to be cast into hell fire: Where their worm dieth not, and the fire is not quenched. For every one shall be salted with fire. . . .[50]

And fear not them which kill the body, but are not able to kill the soul: but rather fear him which is able to destroy both soul and body in hell.[51]

But Jesus said unto him [to the defecting Scribe who wanted to bury his father before departing with Jesus], Follow me; and let the dead bury their dead.[52]

God is not the God of the dead, but of the living.[53]

. . . [T]he dead shall hear the voice of the Son of God: and they that hear shall live.[54]

He that heareth my word, and believeth on him that sent me, hath everlasting life, and shall not come into condemnation; but is passed from death unto life.[55]

If we had only the sayings of Jesus to go by, the new, alternative meanings of *life* and *death* would be neither difficult to unravel nor confusing. From the references to the last becoming the first and the saving of life by losing it, we receive the clue that the dichotomy of life versus death is employed in two distinct senses depending on the context, one pertaining to continuity or discontinuation of biological life, and another pertaining to salvation or the lack of it. As Harold Camping puts it, the important "death" the Bible has in view is eternal damnation. Even the phrase *from death unto life* and the accompanying imagery about seeds dying in the ground so that fruit might be brought forth lend themselves, with only minor bending, to such an interpretation, earthly life and death serving as types and figures to instruct us about their spiritual namesakes. To the Old Testament expert or the pagan philosopher, it must have seemed far-fetched and unconvincing. But Paul added embellishments fore-

49. Matt. 25:46.
50. Mark 9:43-49.
51. Matt. 10:28.
52. Matt. 8:22. Cf. Luke 9:60.
53. Matt. 22:32. Cf. Mark 12:27 and Luke 20:38.
54. John 5:25.
55. John 5:24.

closing such a two-dimensional analysis and introducing the all-important ingredient of confusion masquerading as profundity, to take in open-minded, not unintelligent people:

> Wherefore, as by one man sin entered into the world, and death by sin; and so death passed upon [i.e., spread to] all men, for that all have sinned:[56]
>
> For the wages of sin *is* death; but the gift of God *is* eternal life through Jesus Christ. . . .[57]
>
> . . . [R]eckon ye also yourselves to be dead indeed unto sin, but alive unto God through Jesus Christ. . . .[58]
>
> O wretched man that I am! who shall deliver me from the body of this death?[59]
>
> For none of us liveth to himself, and no man dieth to himself.[60]
>
> . . . [T]hough our outward man perish [decay, deteriorate], yet the inward *man* is renewed day by day.[61]
>
> . . . [T]o me to live *is* Christ, and to die *is* gain.[62]
>
> But sin, taking occasion by the commandment, wrought in me all manner of concupiscence [*epitheumia,* longing, desire]. For without the law sin *was* dead. For I was alive without the law once: but when the commandment came, sin revived, and I died. And the commandment, which *was ordained* to life, I found *to be* unto death. For sin, taking occasion by the commandment, deceived me, and by it slew *me.* Wherefore the law *is* holy, and the commandment holy, and just, and good. Was then that which is good made death unto me? God forbid. But sin, that it might appear sin, working death in me by that which is good; that sin by the commandment might become exceeding sinful.[63]

Paul moved the tremendous statements about the relationship of death and sin of Genesis 2 and 3 (about which we shall have much more to say) toward resolution. The rest of the Old Testament had merely reduced that relationship to a call to ritual purity and good works. Jesus let drop only hints, indecipherable in themselves, that he heralded anything other than a simple amnesty that would be *euangelion* (good news) for his Father's unilaterally and, to all appearances, arbitrarily chosen elect, and bad news for all others. Neither was re-

56. Rom. 5:12.
57. Rom. 6:23.
58. Rom. 6:11.
59. Rom. 7:24.
60. Rom. 14:7.
61. 2 Cor. 4:16.
62. Phil. 1:21.
63. Rom. 7:8-13.

sponsive to the loose ends of Genesis 2 and 3, left dangling so long. But Paul was brilliantly responsive to them.

Of all the purposes served by the form that responsiveness took, making the terms stand for many dimensions rather than two, with a host of disagreeing implications, is the most basic. We can quickly say enough to enable the reader, if he wants, to follow them through. A device I shall repeatedly use for that purpose, when contrasting the biblical use of a term with its conflicting, ordinary language use, is denoting the biblical usages with a prime (′).

Bringing together the usages we have sampled, of *life, life′, death* and *death′*, we notice some unexpected things. If one is elect, then at some time during his life, while still living, he dies′. Before dying′, he had been one of the living dead′. Inasmuch as he has died′, he is, by definition, still dead′. But also, by biblical definition, to be dead′ is to be truly alive′. This apparent contradiction is resolved by taking into consideration that two biblical dimensions of aliveness versus deadness come through, one relative to sin and the letter of the law, and the other relative to the Holy Spirit. To be dead′ to one is to be alive′ to the other, and vice versa. So during life, each person is only partly alive′, and which part it is depends upon whether the person is saved or not. At death, the person's life′ status does not change: he remains alive′ or dead′ as the case may be in his soul existence, but since the disposition of his corporeal part is not to occur until judgment day, his body, although dead and perhaps decomposed or dispersed, apparently remains alive′ to the flesh′! After judgment day, the saved person at last becomes fully alive′ in his resurrected, glorified body—hence, for the first time, entirely dead′ to sin—and the unsaved person, in his putrid old body, which somehow still exists even though the old, unglorified Heavens and earth have been destroyed, remains in the deadly′ state of life′ to the flesh′, cast into Hell, where his soul and body are eternally to undergo destruction but, we infer, also always preserved so that the destruction can grind on sadistically forever.

In addition to the one-way transformations of biological life to death and from nonsalvation to salvation, an additional kind of transformation is implied, which cannot be articulately discussed without the insights of depth psychology. Life′ comes to denote mental activity and consciousness (i.e., light′), and death′ comes to denote unconsciousness or anesthesia (i.e., darkness′). Death′ (to the flesh′ and the law or to the Holy Spirit, as the case may be) entails life′ continuing to occur, but outside conscious awareness (i.e., in darkness′). *Life′* and *death′* become part of a vocabulary of sorts for making some very limited and predetermined statements about the relationship of the conscious attitude to mental activity going on unbeknown, at a deeper level. It is not a vocabulary for reducing the adversity between conscious and unconscious, and not for depotentiating that adversity through insight, but a vocabulary for harnessing (or in King James lingo, "yoking") the tension arising from that adversity and making it serve a churchly purpose. Device 2, in this connection, interlocks with Device 5, Dissociation Induction. More on this later.

Little did the believer know when he was first recruited that the Christians were talking about eternal life′, not eternal life. Everyone, saved or not, has eternal life in the Christian view; yet that does not solve any problem but adds instead a new problem created out of whole cloth by Christianity, so that the prospective believer can be sold the supposititious solution for it. Never does the Christian bring the various constructions of the terms together so concisely as we do. They remain portentously ambiguous for him. Conversations using them, made exponentially more confusing by their interaction with other fractured terms, rather resemble Abbott and Costello's old "Who's on First" routine. Except it isn't funny. It's a matter of life′ and death′.

Terms ascribing value to their referents, such as *truth, wisdom, righteousness* and *justice,* are used in the Bible in a way that invites coloration by the more abstract meanings of such terms, which is second nature for the modern reader. That coloration has aided the liberal-modernist approach and the management of surface impressions to make it appear that something pertinent to our times and circumstances was anticipated by the Bible authors and is to be found in the Bible. But when we get deeply enough into the Bible to make out the context of each individual statement taken from it, we find that value terms take on a much more primitive, one-sided construction. *Truth,* in the epistemological sense of Plato's rhapsodic rendition of it, or in an ethical or aesthetic sense, is never explicitly in view, and even the practical, common-sense standpoint implicit in Proverbs' avuncular advice recurs only piecemeal as the rest of the Bible unfolds. Of the Bible content pertinent to mind-control, the value terms are the tendentious device most fully formed in the Old Testament, and they undergo the least abrupt change in usage in the New Testament.

The principal observation to be made about biblical statements on value is that they are completely arbitrary, divorced from all active human processes of knowledge. What is true′ or righteous′ always relates back to a premise not disprovable except by the Bible. The Bible knows nothing at all about ethics, and its morals[64] always relate back to a commandment given by one with legitimate authority to command. Ultimately, the commandments depend for their legitimacy on the notion that the creation is God's rightful property and a rightful owner may dispose of his property as he pleases. Much of the contemporary affinity of conservative Christianity with political views exalting the right to private property over balancing that right with the common good is to be understood in terms of the appealing analogies of God and created beings to owner and chattels that pervade the Bible:

> . . . O man, who art thou that repliest against God? Shall the thing formed say to him that formed *it,* Why hast thou made me thus? Hath not the potter power over the clay, of the same lump to make one vessel unto honour [i.e., dignity, economic value], and another unto dishonour? *What* if God, willing to shew *his*

64. The only Bible passage translatable to include *morals,* is 1 Cor. 15:33: "'Bad company corrupts good morals [*ethos*].'" *New American Standard Bible.* The words *moral, morals, ethics, ethical,* and related words are absent from the King James version. While customs or "manners" are spoken of, the topic of good standards for human conduct of human authorship is not addressed.

wrath, and to make his power known, endured with much longsuffering the vessels of wrath fitted to destruction: And that he might make known the riches of his glory on the vessels of mercy, which he had afore prepared unto glory, Even us, whom he hath called. . .?[65]

But I would have you know, that the head of every man is Christ; and the head of the woman *is* the man; and the head of Christ *is* God.[66]

What? know ye not that your body is the temple of the Holy Ghost *which is* in you, which ye have of God, and ye are not your own? For ye are bought with a price: therefore glorify God in your body, and in your spirit, which are God's.[67]

Know ye that the LORD he *is* God: *it is* he *that* hath made us, and not we ourselves; *we are* his people, and the sheep of his pasture. Enter into his gates with thanksgiving, *and* into his courts with praise: be thankful unto him, *and* bless his name. For the LORD *is* good; his mercy *is* everlasting; and his truth *endureth* to all generations.[68]

Wisdom′ and *wise′*, substantially interchangeable with *righteousness′* and *righteous′* in the Bible, are also used so as to exclude any basis except divine commandment. Human wisdom is disparaged as "foolishness" and equated with wickedness. *Wisdom* and *wisdom′* are treated as mutually exclusive.

There is a way which seemeth right unto a man, but the end thereof *are* the ways of death.[69]

For it is written, I will destroy the wisdom of the wise, and will bring to nothing the understanding of the prudent [i.e., clever, sagacious]. Where *is* the wise? where *is* the scribe? where *is* the disputer [debater, sophist] of this world [age, world of a certain period]? . . . For after that in the wisdom of God the world by wisdom knew not God, it pleased God by the foolishness of preaching to save them that believe. For the Jews require a sign, and the Greeks seek after wisdom: But we preach Christ crucified, unto the Jews a stumblingblock, and unto the Greeks foolishness; But unto them which are called, both Jews and Greeks, Christ the power of God, and the wisdom of God. Because the foolishness of God is wiser than men; and the weakness of God is stronger than men. For ye see your calling, brethren, how that not many wise men after the flesh, not many mighty, not many noble, *are called:* But God hath chosen the foolish things of the world to confound the wise; and God hath chosen the weak things of the world to confound the things which are mighty. . . .[70]

65. Rom. 9:20-24.
66. 1 Cor. 11:3.
67. 1 Cor. 6:19-20. See also 1 Cor. 7:22-23.
68. Ps. 100:3-5.
69. Prov. 14:12 and 16:25.
70. 1 Cor. 1:19-27.

Instead of the more instrumental meanings the value terms have in other contexts, in the Bible, when referring to a person's behavior, they become code words for following the commandments and being mentally saturated with the teaching. The value terms lend themselves to superficial reading as attributions about individual character or conduct, but close and comparative reading either relates them back to the commandments, or renders them unintelligible:

> Hear thou, my son, and be wise, and guide thine heart in the way.[71]

> And that from a child thou hast known the holy scriptures, which are able to make thee wise unto salvation through faith which is in Christ Jesus.[72]

> And the foolish [virgins] said unto the wise, Give us of your oil; for our lamps are gone out. But the wise answered, saying, *Not so;* lest there be not enough for us and you: but go ye rather to them that sell, and buy for yourselves. And while they went to buy, the bridegroom came; and they that were ready went in with him to the marriage: and the door was shut. Afterward came also the other virgins, saying, Lord, Lord, open to us. But he answered and said, Verily I say unto you, I know you not.[73]

> And he [John the Baptist] shall go before him . . . to turn the hearts of . . . the disobedient to the wisdom of the just; to make ready a people prepared for the Lord.[74]

> Mine eyes fail for thy salvation, and for the word of thy righteousness.[75]

> Know ye not, that to whom ye yield yourselves servants to obey, his servants ye are . . . whether of sin unto death, or of obedience unto righteousness?[76]

> By faith Noah, being warned of God of things not seen as yet, moved with fear, prepared an ark to the saving of his house; by the which he condemned the world, and became heir of the righteousness which is by faith.[77]

Particularly revealing is the transformation of the concept of justice in the Bible. The Old Testament is rich in substance pointing to a philosophical concept of justice in human affairs, with reciprocity and balancing of the parties' interests and with God assisting in seeing to it that the individually righteous are rewarded and their enemies and the enemies of national Israel are punished. But the New Testament believer is to give up on expecting or striving to establish fairness in this world. This transformation is quantitatively evident in the

71. Prov. 23:19.
72. 2 Tim. 3:15.
73. Matt. 25:8-12.
74. Luke 1:17.
75. Ps. 119:123.
76. Rom. 6:16.
77. Heb. 11:7.

frequent and instrumental usages of words translated as *justice, equity, uprightness,* and *integrity,* in the Old Testament, in contrast to their conspicuous absence from the New Testament. In the King James version, *justice* appears twenty-eight times and *injustice* once in the Old Testament, and neither occurs in the New Testament. Note that *just* and *justified* become New Testament code words for salvation. *Equity* occurs ten times in the Old Testament, and nowhere in the New Testament. Neglecting those occurrences of *upright, uprightly* and *uprightness* that refer exclusively to physical posture, those words are found ninety times in the Old Testament but only once (Gal. 2:14) in the New Testament. *Integrity* appears sixteen times in the Old Testament and not at all in the New Testament.[78] *Honour, respect* and *esteem* as the Bible unfolds, undergo a transformation from something earned or voluntarily bestowed to something bestowed by God arbitrarily, or by humans by commandment. A similar word study of any other reputable Bible translation would not produce materially different results.

Jesus taught instead relinquishment of rightful interests in pursuit of higher spiritual values, and he set out instructions for the settling of disputes between his followers, placing all the emphasis on letting go of personal interests for the sake of harmony within the group.[79] Whereas the Old Testament places a high value on vindication of grievances on earth, the New Testament looks forward, with a certain smugness the Christian does not admit to himself, to the believers' unbelieving oppressors getting their comeuppance in the eternal death′ in life′ beyond the grave.

> Seeing *it is* a righteous thing with God to recompense tribulation to them that trouble you; And to you who are troubled rest with us, when the Lord Jesus shall be revealed from heaven with his mighty angels, In flaming fire taking vengeance on them that know not God, and that obey not the gospel . . . Who shall be punished with everlasting destruction [away] from the presence of the Lord, and from the glory of his power; When he shall come to be glorified in his saints. . . .[80]

Letting the justice-related words fall into disuse but leaving undisturbed the residual impressions from their Old Testament usages, and letting the believer suppose that the secular culture's concept of justice somehow squares with the Christian teaching, serves the purposes of both Device 1 and Device 3. The prospective believer coming from an advanced secular culture is falsely reassured that Christianity will not be at cross-purposes to his civic values. He does not see how he is gradually weaned away from those values. If pressed to articulate the relationship of Christianity to justice, he thinks his inability to do so is due either to ignorance his pastor could quickly clear up or to the great mysteriousness and profundity of the teaching, which is beyond mere human understanding. Because he harbors a tacit assumption radiating unarticulated contradictions, he will

78. See *Strong's Exhaustive Concordance.*
79. Matt. 5:21-48; 18:15-35; Luke 17:3-4 and 1 Pet. 2:23.
80. 2 Thess. 1:6-10.

become puzzled and confused if he tries to think the matter through. Paul goes right to the brink of exposing the game, and we can see an indirect indicator of the third kind in these tendentious questions:

> What shall we say then? *Is there* unrighteousness [injustice, wrong] with God? God forbid.[81]

> But if our unrighteousness demonstrates the righteousness of God, what shall we say? The God who inflicts wrath is not unrighteous, is He? (I am speaking in human terms.)[82]

These questions initially suggest to the believer that he has heard them answered, with answers so elementary that he ought to be able to recall them easily. If he reflects more deeply, it will appear to him that the answers might be a sublime mystery. Many huge tomes have been written over the centuries about that supposed mystery. Giving ourselves permission to consider that there may be no mystery at all but only a psychological ploy, we make a liberating discovery: the responsive answer to the questions is a mere sterile tautology. Things God does that seem wrong to man are "good," "just," "wise" and "righteous" simply because those are attributes of God's doings, by definition. God is defined in terms of all those words, and they are all redefined in terms of him. Whatever intrinsic meanings those words may have is forced from them the moment they are attributed to eternal sadistic tormenting of people held to *responsibility* for what they were put in this world for without the *ability* to avoid. The same is true of eternal bliss for others who are no better, but have been arbitrarily chosen to be favored! And if all those who have enriched our lives with art, science, and viable political institutions were "foolish," "wicked," and "unrighteous" because they brought something other than the Christian gospel, then those words are dead and cannot speak to us any more.

The New Testament demise of justice and the debasement of the other value-related words, uprooting them from the human experience they pertain to and denaturing their meanings, is particularly symptomatic of the historical situation of Israel in the first century A.D. We must pause to consider the overwhelming calamity to which the Jewish authors of the Evangelical mind-control system were subjected, lest we overstate the deliberate, malign, cynical appearance their work, in retrospect, takes on. They experienced the total devastation of their social surroundings and the extensive, if not total, devastation of their physical surroundings. Even the victims of the Nazi concentration camps had the benefit of knowing that life was still going on sanely elsewhere in the world, and their calamity did not drag on decade after decade. But for the Jews in Israel, the events leading up to, including, and following the seige of Jerusalem in A.D 70 were like the end of the world. How oppressed must they have felt for their long nourished aspirations to civic justice and political freedom to disappear so

---

81. Rom. 9:14.
82. Rom. 3:5. *New American Standard Bible*

completely? How bleak must the world surrounding them have been for them to withdraw so far into a world of fantasy, only to have the fantasy, resonating as fantasy will, to real life, become even more ugly and terrifying than reality? It makes complete sense that the best Jewish minds in such a situation would be stimulated to fashion a scheme that would make Gentiles and Jews think alike and make it possible to build around themselves a stable, comforting, protective human network out of alienated Gentiles and Jews. Those Jewish geniuses cannot have foreseen that they were doing their work so much too well that the symptoms of the calamity would long outlive their historical context and become a socially shared, obsessive-compulsive neurosis that would stifle human creativity for a thousand years, from the fall of Rome to the Renaissance. When the early Christians got themselves off the hook with the Roman authorities with that fable about the Jews, suddenly and for no apparent reason, having turned upon and demanded the death of one of their more eccentric favorite sons, Jesus, those Christians could hardly have foreseen how that expediency would become the pretext for untold persecutions of Jews, until the twentieth century would provide a pseudoscientific, racial-eugenic pretext for it instead. Likewise, they can hardly have foreseen how their work would provide a prevalent symptomology for a time when all mankind would be threatened with nuclear catastrophe, approaching the magic-numbered year, 2000 A.D..

It is in the context of a world so terrible that something in one's better nature resists appraising it as "real" that the biblical redefinition of *truth* and related words is to be understood. In the Pentateuch, the predominant constructions of *truth* and its cognates are the basic and natural ones, the existence, nonexistence, occurrence or nonoccurrence of a fact, and loyalty or sincerity of a person or of God himself. A different meaning comes through strongly in the Psalms, reflecting the preoccupations of nationhood and adversity with other nations:

> He [God] shall cover thee with his feathers, and under his wings shalt thou trust: his truth *shall be thy* shield and buckler.[83]

> Judge me, O God, and plead my cause against an ungodly nation: O deliver me from the deceitful and unjust man. For thou *art* the God of my strength: why dost thou cast me off? why go I mourning because of the oppression of the enemy? O send out thy light and thy truth: let them lead me; let them bring me unto thy holy hill, and to thy tabernacles.[84]

> Thy word *is* true *from* the beginning: and every one of thy righteous judgments *endureth* for ever.[85]

Truth had a decidedly proprietary and xenophobic character for David.

83. Ps. 91:4.
84. Ps. 43:1-3.
85. Ps. 119:160.

For the balance of the Old Testament, the usages of *truth* in the conventional senses coexist with an additional one, wherein *truth* becomes a code word for the believers' ideological viewpoint. And in the New Testament, the conventional usages of *truth* not only drop out, leaving the field to *truth* as a label for the believers' beliefs, but there are strong clues that the other usages are irrelevant to the believer. To an extent astonishing for a document laying claim to sempiternal comprehensiveness, the epistemological question is evaded.

Only three fleeting times is the question of the truth of a proposition by any criterion other than scriptural revelation addressed in the New Testament. Each time, the question is addressed by disparaging it, not answering it.

The first is John's account of Jesus before Pilate:

> Pilate therefore said unto him, Art thou a king then? Jesus answered, Thou sayest that I am a king. To this end was I born, and for this cause came I into the world, that I should bear witness unto the truth. Every one that is of the truth heareth my voice. Pilate saith unto him, What is truth? And when he had said this, he went out again unto the Jews, and saith unto them, I find in him no fault *at all.*[86]

No answer is given, or even expected, to the unrighteous man's rhetorical question. A saved man would never ask such a question. Although Pilate has heard Jesus' voice, clearly he is not "of the truth." He heard Jesus' voice but not his voice′.

The second instance is the short and unhappy tenure of Ananias and Sapphira as believers. They committed the ecclesiastical equivalent of tax evasion in underreporting to the church authorities the amount realized from a sale of property, at a time when church members were to contribute to the church all proceeds of such sales. All the onus is removed from the factual lie about the amount of money and placed on the intrapsychic condition of the persons:

> . . . Peter said, Ananias, why hath Satan filled thine heart to lie to the Holy Ghost, and to keep back *part* of the price of the land? Whiles it remained, was it not thine own? and after it was sold, was it not in thine own power? why hast thou conceived this thing in thine heart? thou hast not lied unto men, but unto God. And Ananias hearing these words fell down, and gave up the ghost: and great fear came on all them that heard these things.[87]

We shall not risk stripping our intellectual gears trying to figure out how the transaction can have been free of a lie to men (an earlier verse says the two laid the partial proceeds at the apostles' feet). The contradiction strips the outward events of their factual value, and the reader or hearer is thereby directed away from his natural curiosity as to whether the thing is factually true or not.

The third instance is highly significant, because it is the only one wherein Paul is reported to have addressed himself to the factual truth or falsity of a

---

86. John 18:37-38.
87. Acts 5:3-5.

proposition with any disprovable terms. On the one occasion when Paul discussed the truth value of a factual statement—as opposed to simply narrating events declared to have occurred, or speaking in generalities too broad to be verifiable—he affirmed the truth of a classical paradox inherently incapable of being true or false:

> One of themselves, a prophet of their own, said, "Cretans are always liars, evil beasts, lazy gluttons." This testimony is true.[88]

If the Cretan Paul quoted was a truth-teller, then what the Cretan said, i.e., that all members of the class he belonged to are non-truth-tellers, cannot be the truth. If the Cretan was a liar, then, for the thing he said to be a lie, the Cretan would have to have been a truth-teller. Either way, the proposition contradicts itself, and is incapable of being simply true or false. But Paul declared it to be simply true, and did so purporting to speak inerrantly for the God who cannot "lie."[89] For the one and only time Paul committed himself on a question of fact to turn out to be a piece of semantic trickery, gives us an indirect indication of the third kind, that our leg is being pulled.

The contradiction can, with perfectly good intellectual consistency, be resolved by adopting a biblical definition of lying that is totally spiritual and not pertinent to this world. Under such a definition, *truth* and its cognates refer to correct scriptural doctrine, and *lie* and its cognates (besides descriptions of physical posture) refer to any communication derogating from such doctrine. That way, the teaching involving the Cretans and the story of Ananias and Sapphira converge. Both seek to tear the matter of *truth* away from the realm of facts, to incline the believer to dissociate them from one another, considering them as pertaining to wholly separate planes. In that way, a far-reaching intellectual modus operandi for spiritually superior disdain for the here and now can develop. Applying these definitions, all the mentions of *truth* and its opposite in the New Testament are harmonized with one another. Consider the following examples:

> As the truth of Christ is in me, no man shall stop me of this boasting in the regions of Achaia.[90]

> You heard of this hope through the message of truth, the gospel, which has come to you, has borne fruit, and has continued to grow in your midst, as it has everywhere in the world. This has been the case from the day you first heard it and comprehended God's gracious intention through the instructions of Epaphras, our dear fellow slave, who represents us as a faithful minister of Christ.[91]

---

88. Titus 1:12. *Revised Standard Version.* We encountered the King James rendition of this verse on p. 177.
89. Heb. 6:18.
90. 2 Cor. 11:10.
91. Col. 1:5-7. *New American Bible.*

> But if I tarry long, that thou mayest know how thou oughtest to behave thyself in the house of God, which is the church of the living God, the pillar and ground of the truth.[92]

> Of his own will begat he us with the word of truth, that we should be a kind of firstfruits of his creatures.[93]

> For I rejoiced greatly, when the brethren came and testified of the truth that is in thee, even as thou walkest in the truth.[94]

> Ye [Scribes and Pharisees congregated on the Mount of Olives, where Jesus was holding forth] are of *your* father the devil, and the lusts of your father ye will do. He was a murderer from the beginning, and abode not in the truth, because there is no truth in him. When he speaketh a lie, he speaketh of his own: for he is a liar, and the father of it [i.e., lying]. And because I tell *you* the truth, ye believe me not. Which of you convinceth [rebukes, convicts] me of sin? And if I say the truth, why do ye not believe me? He that is of God heareth God's words: ye therefore hear *them* not, because ye are not of God. Then answered the Jews. . .[95]

Frequently *truth* and its cognates are juxtaposed to *lie* or its cognates in a way that seems curiously redundant, if one thinks "truth" in a more familiar sense is meant. Passages where that occurs make more sense, when we realize that Christian doctrine, as opposed to other gospels, is in view:

> Wherefore God also gave them up to uncleanness through the lusts of their own hearts, to dishonour their own bodies between themselves: Who changed the truth of God into a lie, and worshipped and served the creature more than the Creator, who is blessed for ever. Amen.[96]

> Who is wise and understanding among you? Let him show by good conduct that his works are done in the meekness of wisdom. But if you have bitter envy and self-seeking in your hearts, do not boast and lie against the truth. This wisdom does not descend from above, but is earthly, sensual, demonic.[97]

From time to time, Paul would protest too much as to his truthfulness′, like many a contemporary of ours whose speech includes too frequent repetition of such phrases as "trust me" or "to be honest with you."

> . . . I am ordained a preacher, and an apostle, (I speak the truth in Christ, *and* lie not;) a teacher of the Gentiles in faith and verity.[98]

---

92. 1 Tim. 3:15.
93. James 1:18.
94. 3 John 3.
95. John 8:44-47.
96. Rom. 1:24-25.
97. James 3:13-15. *New King James Bible.*
98. 1 Tim. 2:7.

> I say the truth in Christ, I lie not, my conscience also bearing me witness in the Holy Ghost.[99]

> The God and Father of our Lord Jesus Christ, which is blessed for evermore, knoweth that I lie not.[100]

> Now the things which I write unto you, behold, before God, I lie not.[101]

> For if the truth of God hath more abounded through my lie unto his glory; why yet am I also judged as a sinner?[102]

At one point, there is even an express statement of the biblical definition of liar′:

> Who is a liar but he that denieth that Jesus is the Christ? He is antichrist, that denieth the Father and the Son. . . . But the anointing which ye have received of him abideth in you, and ye need not that any man teach you: but as the same anointing teacheth you of all things, and is truth, and is no lie, and even as it hath taught you, ye shall abide in him.[103]

What the biblicist means by *truth,* then, is the operating rules of another dimension, different from and transcending the here and now. To be reassured that he is one of God's elect, he wants that dimension to seem more real than real, so real that it seems unreal. The question of truth in a factual sense is displaced far into the background of the believer's awareness. The attractive connotations of *truth* in a mundane context are seen as types and figures of "real" life′ beyond the grave. Christian "truth" is, by its own terms, "truer" than other kinds. How could pertinence to the tangible do anything but contaminate the truth, and make it less true? And in a mean, ugly, dangerous, and chaotic world, is not the "truth" necessarily somewhere else?

In the biblical treatment of "truth," we can see the purposes of the more outward devices being served. As with eternal life′ the outsider hears much appealing discussion of "truth." Who, on first impression fails to respond favorably to that word? Little does the prospective believer know that Christian party line, company policy, or the order of events of a place that is somewhere else or nonexistent is meant. Having all else come under the opprobrious word *lie* certainly helps to foster estrangement from other people and the surrounding natural world. Since truth′ has several usages—i.e., doctrine, the regularities of the supernatural, and a gift from the Holy Spirit—plenty of semantic confusion is injected whenever believers, who of necessity remain interested in the factual truth of information they receive about mundane things, discuss "truth."

---

99. Rom. 9:1.
100. 2 Cor. 11:31.
101. Gal. 1:20.
102. Rom. 3:7.
103. 1 John 2:22, 27.

In the more inward devices, we shall see several additional purposes served by the biblical fracturing of *truth.* What should be noted now is that these usages together effect the same sort of artful juxtaposition of unity and fragmentation that we earlier noted in the unity and fragmentation of human personality in the Bible, emulating the image of a God who is unitary and fragmented at the same time. Truth′ is dissociated from fact, yet there is no other truth than truth′! More on this later.

If asked to choose the most misleading phrase in the Bible, my selection would be the one where *truth′* and *freedom′* interact to express something utterly opposed to what the words, in their ordinary meanings, express: "And ye shall know the truth, and the truth shall make you free."[104]

Some additional quotations can serve to refresh our recollection as to the biblical meaning of *freedom′*:

> They [the Scribes and Pharisees on the Mount of Olives] answered him, We be Abraham's seed, and were never in bondage to any man: how sayest thou, Ye shall be made free? Jesus answered them, Verily, verily I say unto you, Whosoever committeth sin is the servant of sin. . . . If the Son therefore shall make you free, ye shall be free indeed.[105]

> But thanks be to God, that you who were once slaves of sin have become obedient from the heart to the standard of teaching to which you were committed, and, having been set free from sin, have become slaves of righteousness. . . . For just as you once yielded your members to impurity and to greater and greater iniquity, so now yield your members to righteousness for sanctification.[106]

> So speak ye, and so do, as they that shall be judged by the law of liberty.[107]

> For the sake of the Lord, accept the authority of every social institution: the emperor, as the supreme authority, and the governors as commissioned by him to punish criminals and praise good citizenship. God wants you to be good citizens, so as to silence what fools are saying in their ignorance. You are slaves of no one except God, so behave like free men, and never use your freedom as an excuse for wickedness.[108]

> For, brethren, ye have been called unto liberty; only *use* not liberty for an occasion to the flesh. . . . For the flesh lusteth against the Spirit, and the Spirit against the flesh: and these are contrary the one to the other: so that ye cannot do the things that ye would.[109]

---

104. John 8:32.
105. John 8:33-34, 36.
106. Rom. 6:17-19. *Revised Standard Version.*
107. James 2:12.
108. 1 Pet. 2:13-16. *Jerusalem Bible.*
109. Gal. 5:13, 17.

We have already analyzed the biblical statements pertaining to human freedom or the lack of it;[110] what should be noted from that analysis is that the strident, unending theological controversy as to whether the Bible comes down on the side of free will or of determinism draws attention from the more subtle message, irrelevant to that modern philosophical issue, really being conveyed. The Bible avoids confrontation with the universal human apprehension of having some space for free movement, wherein choices are made. As with *justice, freedom* in that sense falls into disuse as the Bible progresses, and the biblical statement on it is ultimately made by omission rather than articulation. We can see it quantitatively. In the King James version, we find the word *freewill,* connoting voluntariness or spontaneity, used in the Old Testament sixteen times, all but one of them pertaining to offerings. For obvious reasons, those passages come up frequently in American entrepreneurial Evangelicalism. The notion of free will never comes up in the New Testament. In a way parallel to conscience, where we found out that individual, intuitive discernment of right and wrong is regarded as something for an unsaved person, to be replaced by Scripture-directedness in the saved person, strength or courage of *will,* lauded repeatedly and rhapsodically in the Old Testament, is replaced by strength or courage of *faith,* in the New Testament.[111]

We have observed two strategies of logocide in operation, the first working by burdening the words with a profusion of abstruse meanings and the second, by phasing out the unwanted words—those with implications deleterious to mind-control—and letting them disappear. In both of these the words are deflated, their value in articulate speech reduced. There are also instances where words are inflated, vested with artificial, "dummy" meanings, usually with loaded emotional or sentimental connotations. This reduces the value and dilutes the context of other words that do refer squarely to nonfantastic things. The inflated words relate closely to the operation of the more inward devices, to which we are coming.

The process of inflation is most readily observable in the progress of the term *grace.* Since the Reformation and Luther's rehabilitation of the notion that good works occupy a posterior position in salvation, grace′ has been regarded as a Christian mystery, a concept defying full explication. Grace′ has seemed integral to Protestantism for a very long time; yet when we look at the ancient-language texts of the Bible, we find *grace′* to be largely an artifact of translation. The words translated as "grace" can just as aptly be translated as "favor" or "preference." (The New Testament word *charis* is also occasionally translated as the predicate nominative "joy.") Only the context determines when the latter-day translator inserts the term of art, *grace.* If not for the inflation of the term *grace,* the passages containing it would more clearly impart the

110. See pp. 108-27.
111. The only reference to strength or courage of will I can find in the New Testament is the ambivalent, and, to the unbeliever, rather comical mandate of 1 Cor. 7:36-37, for a father to be as capricious and arbitrary as he pleases in granting or denying his spinster daughter permission to marry.

bestowal, from the human point of view, arbitrarily, of eternal life'. Consider some New Testament verses as they must have appeared to the pre-Reformation reader:

> For by . . . [preference] ye are saved through faith; and that not of yourselves: *it is* the gift of God: Not of works, lest any man should boast.[112]

> Now our Lord Jesus Christ himself, and God, even our Father, which hath loved us, and hath given *us* everlasting consolation and good hope through . . . [preference].[113]

> Thou therefore, my son, be strong in the . . . [favoritism] that is in Christ Jesus.[114]

By using the term *grace,* the contradiction of the passages containing it and others stating "there is no respect of persons with God"[115] is made less obvious.

The term that is most inflated without becoming the keystone of any of the more inward devices is *love.* The promise that the believer will become the object of a love greater than mere, human love is among the most powerful inducements of Device 1. Disdain for supposedly inferior, human love serves the purposes of Device 2. We shall see how attempted compensation for negative personal experiences with the frailty and fickleness of human love (as well as sexual maladjustment) figure importantly in the attraction of people into Christianity.

In the New Testament, the notion of love undergoes the most radical transformation imaginable, compared with its precedents. The word *eros,* so familiar to us because of Freud, and extensively used in classical Greek literature, is absent. Positive characterization of erotic love, such as frequently occurs in the Old Testament, does not occur in the New Testament. New Testament direct references to erotic love are disparaging, e.g., *lust* and *burn. Storgē* and its cognates, the standard, classical Greek words for intrafamilial love, occur only once in the New Testament.[116] *Phileo* and its cognates, expressing brotherly love, are used occasionally in the New Testament. But the principal New Testament word for love, *agapē,* was unknown prior to the New Testament and apparently was invented for it. Christians think of *agapē* as one of their faith's most significant mysteries, and believers know that Greek word, who know no other.

Terminology indicating love as we experience it in our own natures falls into disuse in the New Testament to make way for the negative, biblical, pseudo-

---

112. Eph. 2:8-9.
113. 2 Thess. 2:16.
114. 2 Tim. 2:1.
115. Rom. 2:11. Cf. Eph. 6:9 and Col. 3:25. There is no more intrinsic reason to regard the Greek word *charis* as different in meaning from the ones translated as "respect," e.g., *prosopolepsia,* than there is to regard the English word *favor* as different in meaning from *preference.*
116. Rom. 12:10.

psychological rendition of human nature that we earlier covered.[117] The believer is to perceive himself as incapable of any motive or impulse other than a misbegotten or wicked one, except where he puts his own personality aside and makes himself a conduit for God's love:

> Love not the world, neither the things *that are* in the world. If any man love the world, the love of the Father is not in him. For all that *is* in the world, the lust of the flesh, and the lust of the eyes, and the pride of life, is not of the Father, but is of the world. And the world passeth away, and the lust thereof: but he that doeth the will of God abideth for ever.[118]

> Beloved, let us love one another: for love is of God; and every one that loveth is born of God, and knoweth God. He that loveth not knoweth not God; for God is love.[119]

> . . . [W]e glory in tribulations also: knowing that tribulation worketh patience; and patience, experience; and experience, hope; And hope maketh not ashamed; because the love of God is shed abroad in our hearts by the Holy Ghost which is given unto us. For when we were yet without strength, in due time Christ died for the ungodly.[120]

If we look for attributes of *agapē* as manifested in the saved, we find that it is placid, stolid, and not associated with strong or troublesome emotions:

> Love suffers long and is kind; love does not envy; love does not parade itself, is not puffed up; does not behave rudely, does not seek its own, is not provoked, thinks no evil; does not rejoice in iniquity, but rejoices in the truth; bears all things, believes all things, hopes all things, endures all things. Love never fails. . . .[121]

> But thou, O man of God, flee these things [false gospels and the love of money]; and follow after righteousness, godliness, faith, love, patience, meekness.[122]

An explicit biblical definition of love is given: "love *is* the fulfilling of the law."[123] Also, "And this is love, that we walk after his commandments."[124] We begin to suspect that this new kind of love, this exalted mystery, touted to be so much superior to our own decisions and tastes as to what we are to want or to care for, is nothing but a very strict and obsessive species of self-discipline. Just

---

117. See pp. 106 ff.
118. 1 John 2:15-17.
119. 1 John 4:7-8.
120. Rom. 5:3-6.
121. 1 Cor. 13:4-8. *New King James Bible.* Note that the King James version used *charity* interchangeably with *love,* as a translation of *agapē*. The King James word for tangible gifts to the needy is *alms.*
122. 1 Tim. 6:11.
123. Rom. 13:10.
124. 2 John 6.

as truth′ is torn away from the realm of fact, love′ is torn away from the realm of human affections.[125] A renowned Bible commentator confirms this suspicion for us:

> *Agapē* has to do with the *mind:* it is not simply an emotion which rises unbidden in our hearts; it is a principle by which we deliberately live. *Agapē* has supremely to do with the *will.* It is a conquest, a victory, and achievement. No one ever naturally loved his enemies. To love one's enemies is a conquest of all our natural inclinations and emotions.[126]

The commentator goes on to explain how the prescribed discipline of "love" is intrinsically so hard that no one could ever manage it unless he or she had given up direction of his or her life to the Holy Spirit. We shall see that by doing the devotional program one brings about the illusion that one's attitudes toward others are not a part of oneself, but flow in from outside. Being out of touch with one's own feelings and emotions will prove to be a prerequisite of *agapē.*

The one useful concept about true, altruistic love afforded us by the psychologists—object relations, the energetics of investment of libido outside oneself—can come to our aid in understanding *agapē.* Probably the most conspicuous direction to the believer as to where his libido is to be invested is found in that relatively obscure Old Testament teaching that receives no less than seven pointed and emphatic repetitions in the New Testament:

> And Jesus answered him [a Scribe], the first of all the commandments *is,* Hear, O Israel; the Lord our God is one Lord: And thou shalt love the Lord thy God with all thy heart, and with all thy soul, and with all thy mind, and with all thy strength: this *is* the first commandment. And the second *is* like, *namely* this, Thou shalt love thy neighbor as thyself. There is none other commandment greater than these.[127]

In the Old Testament dispensation, the prescribed obsession with God looked for resolution in rituals that, if perfectly kept, would ensure salvation. Immediately following the first occurrence of the Old Testament teaching that Jesus was quoting, the instruction was given:

> And these words, which I [God speaking through Moses] command thee this day, shall be in thine heart: And thou shalt teach them diligently unto thy children, and shalt talk of them when thou sittest in thine house, and when thou walkest by the way, and when thou liest down, and when thou risest up. And thou shalt bind

---

125. Besides disparaging references to lust, wickedness, concupiscence, etc., biblical allusions to human affection are few and mixed. Twice, there is indirect acknowledgement that there is something good about human affection, by decrying the supposed lack of "natural affection" in bringers of false gospels (Rom. 1:31 and 2 Tim. 3:3). Instructions of the devotional program include voluntary control and redirection of affection (Col. 3:2). Affections are explicitly stated to be part of what dies in salvation. (Gal. 5:24).

126. William Barclay, *New Testament Words* (Philadelphia, Westminster Press, 1974), p. 21.

127. Mark 12:29-31. See also p. 139.

> them for a sign upon thine hand, and they shall be as frontlets between thine eyes. And thou shalt write them upon the posts of thy house, and on thy gates.[128]

These instructions (incidentally, the basis for the wearing of phylacteries and the placing of mezuzahs on doorposts by observant Jews, together with a host of more specific ceremonial instructions codified by the Halakah) amount to a comprehensive plan for living, through which love for God is to be expressed. But the plan is so hard and complicated that full compliance with it is impossible. Obsessive concern with the mythic content and compulsive structuring of all behavior to uphold ritual purity cannot resolve the tension, and one is impelled to look to the coming of the Messiah to resolve it.

Then, by the official account, Paul came along and streamlined the literal aspect of compliance with the commandments. He told the Council at Jerusalem, "Now . . . why tempt ye God, to put a yoke upon the neck of the disciples, which neither our fathers nor we were able to bear?"[129] Apparently he was bringing to fruition the expectation aroused by Jesus when he said, ". . . my yoke *is* easy, and my burden is light."[130] Baptism would be substituted for circumcision, money contribution for blood sacrifices, and a simple, summary communion observance for the immense catalogue of halakic observances. The sign bound on the hand and the frontlets between the eyes would now be understood as types and figures for an inward, psychic condition.

Before, one had always known just where one stood. If one was born a Jew, that was a good start, and by following all the rules diligently, one could perfect one's salvation. Now, one would be told that one can be saved only by God's unilateral and inscrutable choice, and that choice can only be thought to be running in an individual's favor if he expresses love for God in the new dispensation's spirit:

> If ye love me, keep my commandments. And I will pray the Father, and he shall give you another Comforter [intercessor, advocate], that he may abide with you for ever; *Even* the Spirit of truth; whom the world cannot receive, because it seeth him not, neither knoweth him: but ye know him. . . . He that hath my commandments, and keepeth them, he it is that loveth me . . . and . . . shall be loved of my Father, and I will love him, and will manifest myself to him.[131]

With the burden of ceremonial observances so reduced, the Christians needing only to abstain from food animals that had been sacrificed to idols or strangled, blood and fornication,[132] and having only to decide to ride Jesus' bandwagon to be saved, it would seem that the tension of Judaism was greatly relieved. But what would keeping the commandments now mean? Apparently it means having one's heart be right,[133] having one's mind be one with those of the

---

128. Deut. 6:6-9. See also Ps. 1:1-2.
129. Acts 15:10.
130. Matt. 11:30.
131. John 14:15-17, 21
132. Acts 15:29.
133. Acts 8:21.

other believers,[134] "[c]asting down imaginations [*logismos,* processes of reasoning] and every high [lofty] thing that exalteth itself against the knowledge of God, and bringing into captivity every thought to the obedience of Christ,"[135] and being unnaturally free of intense or troublesome emotions.[136] Formerly, outward obedience and faithfulness had been enough, and there was no great emphasis on management of one's psychological apparatus. But now, the commandments would be expressed in arcane symbolism, in language so confusing that reasonable experts would disagree until the end of time about what it means. The Christian walk would be through a minefield of false-gospel booby traps and false preachers who seem like angels of light. The reduced strictness of what outward discipline that remained required, belies the staggeringly more strict, ambiguous, and uncertain inner, intrapsychic discipline of Christian love′. While the Christian rendition of love′ for God may superficially appear to consist of a shift in emphasis from doing and onto a condition or state of being, doing is no less strongly emphasized in the new dispensation.[137] But where the requirements of doing were explicitly set out and straightforward in the old dispensation, they are obscure and shrouded in confusion, while being subtly imparted through parable, symbolism, and indirection, in the new.

So by an active process on the part of the believer, but not understood by him to be so, libido is primarily to be cathected toward God, away from this world, and necessarily away from those other persons the believer is commanded, nevertheless, to love with a special, godly kind of love. What kind of object, or "other," is this God, to be a fulfilling partner in so special and jealously monogamous a relationship? The character of his love is a wholly different question from that of the kinds of love he commands of humans (a matter we shall take up when we discuss the next device). In the person of the Father, although the supposed positive nature of his love is lauded constantly, his actions manifesting it are often negative, reflecting more petulance and tyrannical senility than righteousness or lovingkindness. His deputy angel leads a rebellion against him, the quelling of which is promised but not yet accomplished. He creates humans in his image in order to have some company, gives them the means—the fruit of the tree of the knowledge of good and evil—to fulfill their nature after his image, tells them not to eat of it, but lets another of his creatures inveigle them into doing so. Moses requests him to show his face, and he shows his rump.[138] When his people prove unable to follow his impossible rules, he lets others who are not his people conquer them. At all times, he screams for attention, deference, and reassurance, like some senile human incumbent of a powerful office with lifetime tenure. In Hosea, in a way not so different from the male middle-aged crazy of our own day, God makes plans to

134. Rom. 15:5-6; 1 Cor. 1:10; 2 Cor. 13:11; Phil. 1:27; 2:2; 4:2 and 1 Pet. 3:8. Also, contrast Rev. 17:13.
135. 2 Cor. 10:5.
136. 1 John 4:18 and Phil. 4:6-7.
137. James 1:22-25; 4:11; Rom. 2:13.
138. Exod. 33:18-23.

divorce his chosen people and take for his bride an exotic, new spiritual elite, called out of all the nations and stations of the world. With no hereditary claim, individuals can no longer know whether they really have his favor or not, and for them everything depends on having it. How obvious a projection of the entrenched, human authority figures, under whose dead hands younger generations have always labored, God is!

Since one could hardly work up much affection for the furious, terrifying bundle of contradictions God the Father is portrayed to be, it is oddly reasonable for the love′ for him to which man is exhorted to consist of obedience, not affection. Be he real or imagined, God is not amenable for the individual to come to terms with him through the four Jungian functions, to develop or to enhance a condition of relatedness to him. He cannot be known and one cannot interact with him as with phenomena providing evidence for our senses. In psychodynamic terms, God is a complex, siphoning off libido, depriving the ego-personality of it, and upsetting the vital balance between progressive and regressive flow of libido. Since he is a product of convention, and the clashing impressions of him that lend him his mysterious, "numinous" quality will decay if not maintained through continuing repetitious indoctrination, he cannot exist—at least, not in a form that agrees with and serves the group fiction—as an autochthonous idea. Rather, he must be projected onto the surrounding environment, and the believer must not be permitted to attend to those discrepancies between the projection and its object that would, in the normal course of events, prompt the fully functioning individual to withdraw his projections and reorganize them. On one level (we shall come to the others later) the homogenization of language as the medium for thought corresponds to *diffusion* of libido, opposing the proclivity of libido to organize itself purposefully, to flow in some direction, and to make brisk enough contact with its objects that the serviceable features of the projection and those features needing to be altered can be sorted out. By gaining the insights (1) that the Christian substitution of collective discipline for individual affection in love serves the mind-control purpose of valuing non-correction of the group's prescribed projections more highly than the natural potential recipients of the person's affection and concern and (2) that the depotentiation of libido is wanted so that libidinal energy will not go for any mental activity fostering unwanted insight into the group's proprietary fiction, we make our first real progress toward explaining the dynamics of the collective neurosis Freud declared Christianity to be.

Our conceptualization of love′ for God as a siphoning off of libido, undermining the individual's good and natural tendency to enhance his relatedness to the natural environment and other persons, agrees with our previous observations about biblically mandated alienation from the natural world and other people, except under biblically defined and prescribed circumstances. Under further analysis, the principal biblical statements about the believer's love′ for other people will also fit right into place. Consider the following:

> But I say unto you which hear, Love your enemies, do good to them which hate you, Bless them that curse you, and pray for them which despitefully use you.

> And unto him that smiteth thee on the *one* cheek offer also the other; and him that taketh away thy cloke forbid not *to take thy* coat also. Give to every man that asketh of thee; and of him that taketh away thy goods ask *them* not again [i.e., do not demand it back]. And as ye would that men should do to you, do ye also to them likewise. For if ye love them which love you, what thank [grace, blessing] have ye? for sinners also love those that love them. . . . But love ye your enemies, and do good, and lend, hoping for nothing again . . . and ye shall be children of the Highest: for he is kind unto the unthankful and *to* the evil.[139]

> I therefore, the prisoner of the Lord, beseech you that ye walk worthy of the vocation wherewith ye are called, With all lowliness and meekness, with long-suffering, forbearing one another in love; Endeavouring to keep the unity of the Spirit in the bond of peace. . . . But [instead of futile, chaotic human thinking] speaking the truth in love, [you] may grow up into him in all things, which is the head, *even* Christ. . . .[140]

> If *there be* therefore any consolation in Christ, if any comfort of love, if any fellowship of the Spirit, if any bowels [lit. intestines, fig. natural affection] and mercies, Fulfil ye my joy, that ye be likeminded, having the same love, *being* of one accord, of one mind. . . . let each esteem other better than themselves. Look not every man on his own things, but every man also on the things of others.[141]

> . . . [B]eing reviled, we bless; being persecuted, we suffer it. . . .[142]

The focal point of love′ for others is not the persons themselves but rather acting toward them so as to comply with the commandments. Where God's love′ seems to be privileged to be selective as to its object—he, after all, supposedly makes and is in charge of the rules that man's love′ consists of obeying—man's love′ is not permitted to be selective as to its object. Where the question "And who is my neighbour?" was so relevant to the question of the nature of God's love′ that Jesus had to evade it, human love′ is to be the same for all comers, be they brothers′, neighbors′ or enemies′. Man is to be no respecter of persons, even if he cannot fathom how it is that the God he is to emulate is an elector of persons but no respecter of them. The believer is to respond to no provocation and to refrain from entering into the spirit of any human interaction not following a biblical script. If an unbeliever spits in a believer's face, the believer is to behave as if it were raining. The Bible acknowledges the impossibility of these commandments in practical life by providing for an intrachurch mechanism for resolving disputes between believers and by allowing believers to take unbelievers or excommunicated believers before the secular courts.[143] Even while our attention is being deflected to a meaning of the teaching on other than the literal or practical level, we receive

---

139. Luke 6:27-32, 35.
140. Eph. 4:1-3, 15.
141. Phil. 2:1-4.
142. 1 Cor. 4:12.
143. Matt. 18:15-17 and 1 Cor. 6:1-8.

the clue that the teaching is a practical impossibility. Our leg is being pulled. We shall explore the psychological implications of believers attempting to live up to a teaching even harder than Halakah.

The secondary significance of human others in the love′ the believer is exhorted to manifest toward them, shows through in the rule-boundness and revealing overemphasis on prescribed dominance-submission requisites in all the primary human relationships:

> Giving thanks always for all things unto God and the Father in the name of our Lord Jesus Christ; Submitting yourselves one to another in the fear of God. Wives, submit yourselves unto your own husbands, as unto the Lord. For the husband is the head of the wife, even as Christ is the head of the church: and he is the saviour of the body. Therefore as the church is subject unto Christ, so *let* the wives *be* to their own husbands in every thing. Husbands, love your wives, even as Christ also loved the church, and gave himself for it; That he might sanctify and cleanse it with the washing of water by the word, That he might present it to himself a glorious church, not having spot, or wrinkle, or any such thing; but that it should be holy and without blemish. So ought men to love their wives as their own bodies. He that loveth his wife loveth himself. For no man ever yet hated his own flesh; but nourisheth and cheriseth it, even as the Lord the church: For we are members of his body, of his flesh, and of his bones. For this cause shall a man leave his father and mother, and shall be joined unto his wife, and they two shall be one flesh. This is a great mystery: but I speak concerning Christ and the church. Nevertheless let every one of you in particular so love his wife even as himself; and the wife *see* that she reverence *her* husband. Children, obey your parents in the Lord: for this is right. Honour thy father and mother; (which is the first commandment with promise;) That it may be well with thee, and thou mayest live long on the earth. And, ye fathers, provoke not your children to wrath: but bring them up in the nurture and admonition of the Lord. Servants [*doulos,* slaves], be obedient to them that are *your* masters according to the flesh, with fear and trembling, in singleness of your heart, as unto Christ; Not with eyeservice, as menpleasers; but as the servants [*doulos*] of Christ, doing the will of God from the heart; With good will doing service, as to the Lord, and not to men: Knowing that whatsoever good thing any man doeth, the same shall he receive of the Lord, whether *he be* bond or free. And, ye masters, do the same things unto them, forbearing threatening: knowing that your Master also is in heaven; neither is there respect of persons with him.[144]

So, no primary relationship with another can have legitimacy or a raison d'être in itself. All such relationships are to be filtered through a haze of transference-like projections about an incomprehensible mystical relationship of individual and church. If the haze be dispelled, then the only way one can know that one knows God is taken away, since the presence of the haze amounts to a commandment. The biblical pseudopsychological premise has it that humans are incapable of truly caring for one another without a God-obsession in the forefront of consciousness, and what may seem like lovingkindness from an

---

144. Eph. 5:20-6:9.

unbeliever is really God, unseen, jerking his strings. And what may seem to the believer to be a good motive on his own part toward another person is really a deception of his sin-cursed, wicked little mind—a deceitful lust of the flesh. He is to avoid that assiduously and remain in the haze. Unjust earthly servitude is given the full dignity of a godly project and is not to be resisted, just as evil-doing by others is not to be resisted.[145] And note well that nothing resembling the notion that one can improve one's capacity to love others by loving oneself more is intimated. Loving′ oneself is to be on a par with loving′ significant others, inferior in priority to loving′ God, and any tendency to esteem oneself more than that is to be remedied. One may not even permit oneself to view oneself, except through a distorting filter.

Exhortations to refrain from investing affection except in the God-complex, and to split emotion and affection off from each other, clearly would not be enough in themselves to produce so radical a disturbance of the normal flow of libido as we portray love′ to be. The believer must be made pervasively to experience his affections as ambivalent, as "wrong, inferior and unhappy," and as a matter of bad conscience, for such an effect to be achieved. Flatly to tell the believer that he is subjectively to experience affection for none but God, would give the game away. Much of the message as to fragmentation of affection is imparted through camouflaged contradictions. We must digress from our analysis of the energetics of love′, to make some general observations about the use of inconsistencies and contradictions in the Bible.

There are a few instances of unrelieved factual contradictions in the Bible, mostly in the Old Testament.[146] These have little bearing on the hortatory content of the Bible, and emphasis in the past, on the part of organized atheists, on them and on apparent contradictions that can be explained away, has protected believers from hearing antibiblical criticism well-targeted to their vulnerabilities and latent doubts. The uncamouflaged contradictions are all strategically placed, safely away from the consequential issues. For the believer, such contradictions can always be explained away as scribal errors not material to the spiritual teaching, as testing devices put there to help cull out the unfaithful from the faithful, or lofty teachings whose meanings the Holy Spirit is not yet ready to reveal.

The usual form taken by biblical inconsistency is not contradiction, but dissonance and tension among statements with modifiers and expressive features different enough that a way can be found for them not to be in contradiction. The inquisitive proselyte can be drawn in by the absorbing activity of reconciling them. The most frequent subject of statements in tension is the openness or

145. Matt. 5:39.

146. E.g., Gen. 1:25-26; 2:18-20 (time relation of creation of lower animals and man); Gen. 16:16; Gal. 4:22; Heb. 11:17 (number of sons Abraham begot); Num. 33:37-39, 41; Deut. 10:6-7 (place of Aaron's death); 2 Sam. 6:23; 21:8 (number of Michal's children: some ancient manuscripts substituted Merab for Michal in the latter verse); 2 Kings 24:8; 2 Chron. 36:9 (age of Jehoiachin when he began to reign); 2 Kings 8:26 and 2 Chron. 22:2 (age of Ahaziah when he began to reign: some ancient manuscripts have it as twenty or twenty-two in the latter verse, instead of forty-two).

closedness of election to salvation, and we shall have much more to say about the psychological implications of keeping the believer perpetually off balance about that crucial question. The other frequent subject of statements in tension is the believer's affections; hence our consideration of the inconsistency topic at this point. Consider the following superficially similar statements, from each of the synoptic Gospels:

> He that is not with me is against me; and he that gathereth not with me scattereth abroad.[147]

> . . . [H]e that is not against us is on our part.[148]

> . . . [H]e who is not against you is for you.[149]

The first statement is part of a different incident from the latter two. The *us* refers to Jesus and the disciples—the church, the "body of Christ"—and the *you* to the disciples alone. Only the very studious believer ever notices the difference in the statements, which are often indiscriminately paraphrased to sound a xenophobic note ("If you're not for us, you must be against us"), or a tolerant one ("If you're not against us, then you're for us), as fits the needs of the moment. The statements restate the dilemma as to whether those who are indifferent to the Gospel, neither saints of the church nor bringers of a false gospel, to whom we earlier referred as "ordinary unbelievers," are in or out. If there is a mystical identity of Christ and his church, then there is a problem about the middle group being excluded as to the former, but included as to the latter. If we approach the question intellectually, our admiration will be aroused for the condensation of such relatively complex issues into so few words. The privilege of God to love′ only his elect, while the believers are to love′ all comers and resort to ostracism only very deliberately against one who clearly brings a false gospel, is concisely and artfully expressed. The uncertainty of the individual believer as to whether or not he is one of those predestined to persevere until the end is reiterated and reinforced in the process. Unless there is an active effort to bring the statements together and study them comparatively, the tension among them will remain latent and unarticulated. Of such things, complexes are made that need no individual personal conflicts to energize them.

Although mini-Reformationist leaders are well aware that they are not to superimpose ideas on Scripture that are not intrinsically there, some inconsistencies fairly cry out for the formulation of hypothetical constructs, as is natural, and properly done in any other field of knowledge when there is occasion to try to make sense of observations in the natural. The key verse limiting the use of such constructs says, ". . . I testify unto every man that

147. Matt. 12:30. See also Luke 11:23.
148. Mark 9:40.
149. Luke 9:50. *New American Standard Bible.*

heareth the words of the prophecy of this book, If any man shall add unto these things, God shall add unto him the plagues that are written in this book. . . ."[150] And if too much interrelating of biblical information is allowed to take place, a point will be reached where the ponderousness and incongruity of the concepts strains credulity, as it did for us when we articulated the implications of life and life′. But if kept in limits, hypothetical constructs interrelating biblical statements in a way that appeals to the modern mind does not damage the effect: the mind works on one thing, and the dissonant implications of the statements do another thing in the unconscious. Consider the following statements:

> And the LORD said unto Moses, Whosoever hath sinned against me, him will I blot out of my book.[151]

> He that overcometh [has victory, endures to the end], the same shall be clothed in white raiment; and I will not blot out his name out of the book of life. . . .[152]

> . . . [A]nd they that dwell on the earth shall wonder [marvel], whose names were not written in the book of life from the foundation of the world, when they behold the beast that was, and is not, and yet is.[153]

> And whosoever was not found written in the book of life was cast into the lake of fire.[154]

As is typical where there is noticeable tension between two biblical statements, salvation doubts are being subtly aggravated. The images of a book including one's name, but wherefrom it might be erased, and a book that might or might not include one's name, to remain undisclosed until the end of time, are in ominous discord. Harold Camping tries to explain this contrast with the notion that one book is from the standpoint of creation (with the names of all those who God, "looking down the corridors of time," knew would be alive on the earth at some time), and the other, from the standpoint of salvation (with only the names of those predestined to election). That really does not work. For the erasable book to be a "book of life" in the sense of earthly life, the names of the saved as well as the unsaved, except possibly for those who are still here when Christ returns, would have to be blotted out anyway. If "book of life" refers to the elect, then there is overwhelming other biblical indication that a name, once written there, is never to be erased. I doubt that there is a hypothetical construct to resolve them that does not greatly distort the metaphor.

Such instances, where an inconsistency or even a contradiction can be made plain by the juxtaposition of two biblical statements, are neither the most

150. Rev. 22:18. See also, Deut. 29:20, 21, 27.
151. Exod. 32:33.
152. Rev. 3:5.
153. Rev. 17:8.
154. Rev. 20:15.

interesting, psychologically, of biblical uses of inconsistency, nor the ones that contribute most to the frustration of the normal, healthy human proclivity to invest libido in other persons, in objects, in ideas, in goals to be accomplished, and in oneself. Camouflaged inconsistencies, involving more than two biblical statements, do a larger part of the psychological task. In a single stroke, we shall analyze a deeper level of manipulative inconsistency in the Bible than the foregoing, and do so with more precision, adding less extraneous meaning to the biblical statements as we find them, than any orthodox exegete could possibly achieve. If we really go the last mile in rigor as to biblical statements, shocking results that no orthodox believer could ever countenance are produced. Absurdities are revealed that orthodox claims as to the supposed textual integrity and divineness of purpose in the Bible cannot withstand.

What we will do amounts to a whole new method. Since the more literate mini-Reformationists of our day have their shibboleth, "presuppositional apologetics," we shall have ours: *triadic antiapologetics.* It is through the interaction of groups of three statements (these sometimes derived from and implied by more than one biblical passage) that the inconsistencies best calculated to stick in the believer's unconscious are impressed upon him.

Consider these three biblical statements:

> . . . [E]very creature of God *is* good, and nothing to be refused, if it be received with thanksgiving. . . .[155]
>
> *Let* love be without dissimulation. Abhor that which is evil; cleave to that which is good.[156]
>
> Love not the world, neither the things *that are* in the world. If any man love the world, the love of the Father is not in him.[157]

From the first two statements (assuming everybody agrees it is biblical that the world and the things in it fall within the category of creatures of God), a third, to the effect that man is to love the world, cherish it, take good care of it, try to alleviate its ills, etc., would logically follow. The statements lend themselves to arrangement as a syllogism, with a major and minor premise, but a conclusion that is the contradictory of what follows from the premises. That is the essence of the triadic antiapologetic. It follows the form of the invalid syllogism, "All men are mortal, Socrates is a man, therefore Socrates is *not* mortal." If we are fair about the statements or implications we allege to be the common elements of the biblical passages we bring together in this way, taking only those naturally understood to be expressing the same thing and actually understood by believers "in the field" as meaning the same thing, then we can make it dramatically clear that in the most humanly relevant things, the Bible speaks in mere rhetorical

155. 1 Tim. 4:4.
156. Rom. 12:9. See also, Amos 5:15.
157. 1 John 2:15.

absurdities, not in sublime mysteries, not in genuine paradoxes pointing beyond themselves to otherwise inexpressible lofty insights. What the apologist would have pass unnoticed through the periphery of one's attention, the antiapologist strives to bring dramatically and focally into the foreground.

The component statements of a triad occur removed from one another in the text, are embedded in different topical contexts, and thus do not draw conscious attention to themselves as belonging together. They are quite familiar to the well-indoctrinated believer, having been impressed on his mind by frequent repetition. Asking him the right questions would reveal that he has no trouble discerning the common elements in the diverse biblical statements. That a common element may be represented by synonyms rather than the same word, and a general statement may occur extraneously in the midst of discussion of a special topic (e.g., "every creature" coming after a discussion against Judaizing prohibitions of acts permitted by Christianity), does not change the underlying logic, and even less does it change how people characteristically use and understand language. People fed on contradictions in this way, so that they do not consciously recognize it, develop a vague, diffuse, unarticulated sense of bad conscience, unease and apprehension toward the matters the contradictions pertain to. By loading all nonfantastic potential recipients of investment of libido with contradictory counsel as to what valence of affect toward them the believer is to have, all investment of libido except in the God-complex is rendered tentative, ambivalent and forbidden, but demanded and commanded, all at once. The exigency of keeping the contradictions camouflaged, at least three scattered biblical statements needing to be compared to sort any one of the contradictions out, is greater when the topic is the believer's affections than when the believer is being diddled as to whether the salvation plan be closed or open.

The topic of our first example of an antiapologetic triad, investment of libido in "the world," represents the most general and diffuse of the levels on which investment of libido is disturbed by inducing ambivalence. Since we proceed from the psychological premise that "relatedness" to "the world" is the most fundamental of human motives, and the antithesis of psychopathology, we infer that the Bible can be expected to affirm love for "the world" relatively infrequently. People are natively drawn in that direction anyway. Conversely, we expect the Bible to be very elaborate about expressing the alienation-from-the-world' horn of the dilemma. These expectations turn out to be so, and the pertinent Bible passages we earlier encountered in our examination of the Bible's negative pseudopsychology of human nature are representative.[158]

Two additional antiapologetic triads on the topic of the believer's prescribed affective ambivalence toward "the world" are self-explanatory, and take us as far along that line as is useful for us to go:

> . . . [T]he earth *is* the Lord's, and the fulness thereof.[159]

158. See p. 123.
159. 1 Cor. 10:26, quoting Ps. 24:1.

He loveth righteousness and judgment: the earth is full of the goodness of the LORD.[160]

And . . . the whole world lieth in wickedness.[161]

. . . [B]ehold, I come quickly; and my reward *is* with me, to give every man according as his work shall be.[162]

But the day of the Lord will come as a thief in the night; in the which the heavens shall pass away with a great noise, and the elements shall melt with fervent heat, the earth also and the works that are therein shall be burned up.[163]

Blessed *are* the meek: for they shall inherit the earth.[164]

We find similar uses of camouflaged contradictions inducing ambivalence in every one of the believer's primary human relationships. We earlier noted the draconian posture of the Bible as to the believer's obligation to obey secular civil authorities except in the narrow special case where promulgation of the Christian message is interfered with. Now, note the way that commandment is brought into collision with the commandment of love′:

Know ye not, that to whom ye yield yourselves servants [slaves] to obey, his servants ye are to whom ye obey; whether of sin unto death, or of obedience unto righteousness?[165]

. . . [*T*]*here is* none good but one, *that is,* God. . . .[166]

Let as many servants [*doulos,* slaves] as are under the yoke count their own masters worthy of all honour, that the name of God and *his* doctrine be not blasphemed. And they that have believing masters, let them not despise [disparage, have disrespect for] *them,* because they are brethren; but rather do *them* service, because they are faithful and beloved, partakers of the benefit.[167]

Also,

. . . [W]e have had fathers of our flesh which corrected *us,* and we gave *them* reverence: shall we not much rather be in subjection unto the Father of spirits, and live? For they verily for a few days chastened *us* after their own pleasure; but he for *our* profit, that *we* might be partakers of his holiness.[168]

160. Ps. 33:5.
161. 1 John 5:19.
162. Rev. 22:12.
163. 2 Pet. 3:10.
164. Matt. 5:5.
165. Rom. 6:16.
166. Matt. 19:17.
167. 1 Tim. 6:1-2.
168. Heb. 12:9-10.

> No servant [*oiketes,* domestic, menial] can serve two masters: for either he will hate the one, and love the other; or else he will hold to the one, and despise the other.[169]

> Slaves [*doulos*], obey your earthly masters in everything. . . .[170]

If "the whole world lieth in wickedness," then the unsaved, including the slavemasters, military commanders and political chiefs who are unsaved lie in it too, and submitting oneself to obey them makes one partaker in the wickedness. Nevertheless, that is precisely what is being commanded. The whole essential human project of living with conflicting loyalties, of compromising, of prioritizing, of trading off the lesser violation of pristine conscience against the greater, runs headlong into biblical teaching, requiring one not only to serve two (or more) masters, but to serve totally and exclusively each of the mutually exclusive objects evoking loyalty. Of course, nobody can or ought to try, to do that. Where some superior individual might conceivably keep the laws of Halakah perfectly from Bar Mitzvah to death, Christianity raises the standard from one of mere extreme impracticability to one of logical and necessary impossibility: the sumultaneous keeping of conditions predefined to be mutually exclusive. The idea of investment of all one's libido in one object is communicated by all this, pointing in turn, to investing all one's libido in the God-complex, displacing all other libidinal investments, and reducing them to the status of derivatives or secondaries.

Now, the God-complex is not a very good receptacle for investment of libido. For the orthodox believer, all knowledge of God is second-hand or hear-say. One cannot interact with him through the four Jungian functions, and one's own, personal coming-to-terms apparatus has not participated in gathering whatever information one has or thinks one has about him. Such a receptacle for libido requires a constant, energy-consuming mental activity to keep it constituted in mind. Direct stimulation such as one receives from persons, objects and events in the natural world, constantly refreshing and enhancing the information that constitutes them in our minds, is absent for him who goes about developing a relationship with God in a Bible-authentic manner. (We neglect, for the time being, the additional complexities of the Bible-inauthentic believer who claims to receive direct new message transmissions from God.)

The psychological condition resulting from the effort to make the God-complex the focus of libido, then, is not a resolution or synthesis of the latent contradictions through which the condition is in part brought about, but rather an unstable resultant of contending forces. On the one hand, one tries to invest one's affection in something illusory, something that, so far as one's knowledge-mediating faculties are concerned, is not there.

---

169. Luke 16:13.
170. Col. 3:22. *New International Version.*

> Set your affection on things above, not on things on the earth. For ye are dead, and your life is hid with Christ in God.[171]

On the other hand, one tries to invest one's libido absolutely, totally and exclusively, in each of those civil, church and family institutions and members one is commanded to love′ at close range. One is suspended betwixt wholeness and fragmentedness, divided and undivided loyalty, tacitly emulating the image of a God who is one, but of whom there are three faces.

Some finer *nuances* of the technique of pulling libido away from its normal, natural recipients to redirect it to the churchly enterprise's purposes can be seen in the devotional program instructions as to close family members, i.e. spouses, parents and children. When the Bible commands, "Children, obey *your* parents in all things: for this is well pleasing unto the Lord,"[172] and ". . . ye wives, *be* in subjection to your own husbands; that, if any obey not the word, they also may without the word be won by the conversation [conduct] of the wives. . . ,"[173] those commands can be substituted for the exhortations to slaves to obey their masters in the preceding two antiapologetic triads, manifoldly increasing the latent conflicts attending loyalty and affection. Husbands are repeatedly told to love their wives.[174] But that commandment is always covered in a haze of mystical symbolism, burdening the relationship of husband and wife with the distracting spiritual task of typifying the union of Christ with his church. We gain more insight into the attitudes being coaxed into place, by the things not said in the instructions. Fathers are never told to love their children, only not to provoke them.[175] Interestingly, the talent for keeping his children "in subjection" is set out as one of the qualifications of a pastor.[176] Wives are never directly instructed to love their husbands. Once, passing reference is made to older women teaching younger married women to love their husbands and children, carefully setting the scene so that married women will not hear that through more "official" sources, such as their pastor or husband.[177] One is commanded to love strangers, neighbors, brothers (in contexts pointing to brothers and sisters in Christ, i.e. fellow church participants) and wives. One is not commanded to love parents or children (although manifold duties of obedience and care are commanded), and loving husbands is deemphasized. What is going on here?

An additional antiapologetic triad, composed entirely of sayings of Jesus, enables us to sort out those subsequent places where the Bible appears to "go soft" on love:

> As the Father hath loved me, so have I loved you: continue ye in my love. If ye keep my commandments, ye shall abide in my love; even as I have kept my

171. Col. 3:2-3.
172. Col. 3:20. Cf., Eph. 6:1.
173. 1 Pet. 3:1. Cf., Eph. 5:22 and Col. 3:18.
174. Eph. 5:25; Col. 3:19 and 1 Pet. 3:7.
175. Eph. 6:4 and Col. 3:21.
176. 1 Tim. 3:4.
177. Titus 2:4.

> Father's commandments, and abide in his love. . . . This is my commandment, That ye love one another, as I have loved you.[178]

> He that loveth father or mother more than me is not worthy of me: and he that loveth son or daughter more than me is not worthy of me.[179]

> If any *man* come to me, and hate not his father, and mother, and wife, and children, and brethren, and sisters, yea, and his own life also, he cannot be my disciple.[180]

His love for his elect, we are justified in concluding, constitutes a limit that the believer's, for him or for his creatures, could only approximate. The believer is to love′ his fellows to the absolute extent of his capability, but love him even more. While the second statement gives the believer qualified permission to love′ father, mother, son or daughter less than fully—how nice of Jesus to do that!—it stops short of commanding the believer to do so, or even commending it, should the believer exercise his option. Note that the first statement commands only love′ for other believers ("one another"). Unbelieving fathers, mothers, sons and daughters are not necessarily included in any of the other categories of persons the believer is commanded to love′, i.e., strangers, neighbors and enemies. What remains is permission conferred on the believer to love his parents and offspring, provided it be not too much, and due care be taken to hate them at the same time. Also, note that nothing in the context or usage of the word *hate, miseo,* justifies the excuse pastors typically offer, that the term is used in a Semitic, hyperbolic way, intended merely to convey detachment, distance or indifference: the imagery or rhetorical flourish of the genuine hyperbole is absent. (All words for attitudes attended by strong emotions, e.g., *hate, anger, fear,* and *anxiety,* are handled in the Bible by permitting the attitude to be harbored in isolation, under certain prescribed circumstances, but requiring the emotion to be split off from the experience of the attitude. We defer our discussion of these words to Device 5, since their biblical usages are not so completely divorced from their respective ordinary language usages, as to constitute logocide.) Most probably, the followers of Jesus and the earliest Christians were not family oriented, since being his follower necessitated rejecting the family's existing Jewish theological party affiliation, and there would be no need to procreate new members, if the end of the world were immanent.

Taken together, the devotional instructions seek to make all affections for others equal. The more casual ones are elevated in importance, and the more humanly significant ones, downgraded. It is easier for affections to be ambivalent when they are equivalent, and if they are both ambivalent and equivalent, then they can also be homogeneous and undifferentiated. The primary relations to significant others lose their distinctiveness: they become relative to the God-complex, and are no longer to seem important in or for themselves. Together

---

178. John 15:9-10, 12.
179. Matt. 10:37.
180. Luke 14:26.

with these, in the passages containing them, are other instructions stressing obedience, discipline, prohibition of emotional spontaneity, and generally the same sort of stereotyped, closed-off interaction toward significant others as we earlier encountered governing relations among believers. Pseudocommunity, with seeming immediate acceptance of newcomers, is fostered by such an approach to affection, and not genuine, *gemeinschaftlich* community. If acted out well as prescribed, the scene is picture perfect.

Making human affections for one another equivalent and shallow creates an outwardly attractive condition aiding Device 1, and of some genuine benefit as regards dying, death and grief. When a member of an Evangelical church community dies, one immediately notices that the impact of the grief, even on those closest to the deceased, is less than for other people. The same remarkable mein of euphoric calm often noticed in the well-indoctrinated Evangelical becomes, by contrast, even more pronounced, and lends an aura of dignity and control that cannot but impress an outsider observing it for the first time. The outsider will quickly hear all about how the deceased has "gone to be with the Lord." The conventional wisdom of mental-health professionals is that denial of death, simply avoiding coming to terms with the fact that the loved one has died, accounts for the relative absence of negative emotions. If that were a sufficient explanation, then there would be times when a loved one died who was thought to be unsaved, and the community would be stricken and driven to hysteria by the apprehension that the next thing the departed would know, he would be being arraigned at judgment day, seeing God at last face to face, perhaps scowling or petulantly banging his gavel. But Evangelicals practically never make that connection. On closer reflection, we realize that without more, the thought of the loved one being in a better place would not offer particularly great relief to family members still sorely needing his or her comfort and care. What has really happened is that subordination of the relationship with the loved one to the God-complex has made the relationship less intense than it would normally have been. Less libido was invested in that relationship than would otherwise have been the case, so loss of the relationship was less of a loss than it would otherwise have been. The God-obsession, and preoccupation with preservation of one's own salvation candidacy, leave precious little room for such things.

In the rule-bound regularization of affectional relationships of Christian love′, we can see a microcosm of the larger relationship of Evangelicalism and the surrounding society. The kind of love′ Evangelicalism offers is a big improvement for someone coming out of mean, chaotic surroundings, neglect, substance abuse, anomie, etc. Love′ can well be an improvement, for someone for whom love has been too unruly, turbulent and poignant. Love′ can be a supporting framework for someone with too few good traditions to draw upon, and (employing devices we have not yet covered) be an effective and physiologically harmless means to kill the pain of a psychic wound that is too deep to heal, and would otherwise render the one who has suffered it inconsolable. But for the whole, sound person, one not so deprived, love′ is an invitation to refrain from the satisfactions of truly loving, of living passionately, of caring enough about things wrong in *this* world to exert all the force of one's personality to help correct them. Improving the quality of life socially and technologically, curiosity, yearning to increase understanding and reduce confusion and mystification, are second-rate concerns at best, from a biblical point of view. It is entirely consistent that precious little contribution to the use of human intelligence to improve the quality of human life has come from the religiously conservative. (Fervent religious revisionists, hungry for change, have made great contributions in their time, but never those whose emphasis has been on turning the clock back!)

Summing up, we can formulate a definition of Christian love′, *agapē,* harmonizing all that the Bible has to say about it. Leaving aside the question whether there be such a thing as Holy Spirit intervention or not, or whether the subjective experiences attributed to that intervention are an illusion for which we can fully account or not, Christian love′ is biblically defined as *Holy Spirit-aided self-discipline in internalizing Christian doctrine and performing the devotional program.* As manifested in and by the believer, Christian love′ has hardly anything to do with passion or affection. Notice how the the poetry of Paul's rhapsodic description of Christian love′ collapses, even while the meaning of the words becomes clearer, if we substitute descriptive, neutral words for the toned code words:

> [Spirit-aided self-discipline] . . . suffers long and is kind . . . [Spirit-aided self-discipline] does not envy . . . [Spirit-aided self-discipline] does not parade itself, is not puffed up; does not behave rudely, does not seek its own, is not provoked, thinks no evil; does not rejoice in iniquity, but rejoices in . . . [Christian doctrine]; bears all things, believes all things, hopes all things, endures all things. [Spirit-aided self-discipline] . . . never fails. . . .[181]

The words *witness* and *word* take us into the realm of biblical metalanguage. They are words about the knowledge process itself, attempting to rise above the context whereof they are part. Confusing the believer about that process is crucial, for the disparaging biblical pseudopsychology to retain its plausibility for the believer, for the believer not to have words articulately to express whatever he might observe in himself that is different from and better than what the pseudopsychology dictates.

The course of *witness* through the Bible parallels that of *truth.* Up until the New Testament, *witness* refers to presence to take events in through one's natural senses, and the sin of bearing false witness consists of reporting events otherwise than as one experienced them. Sometimes, an object that was present when events occurred is described as a mute "witness." In the Gospels, false witness in the conventional sense continues to be condemned. But its significance is muted, and the status of factually true witness as a specially Christian virtue is clouded, when the Pharisees trying to orchestrate purjury against Jesus do so with such bad conscience that they bungle it, their suborned perjurers unable to

181. 1 Cor. 13:4-8. *New King James Bible.* See p. 206, footnote 121.

get their stories straight.[182] Apparently witness tampering was not of the essence of the arch-evil represented by the Pharisees.

In the Gospels, "witness" also continues in the Old Testament sense of announcing prophetic messages received from God. This, in itself, is not contrary to "witness" in the familiar sense. But right off the bat, in Acts, when the remaining eleven apostles fill the vacancy left by Judas Iscariot, we are confronted with something radically new. From two candidates, Barsabbas and Matthias, neither of whom do we know to have been present for any events involving Jesus, the eleven choose by lot which one shall fill the office, and become *ex officio* a "witness," as Jesus had conveniently redefined it in terms of the Holy Spirit, during one of his appearances in the forty days after his death.[183] And Paul, who had not been around for any of those events, and whose rendition of them depended entirely on the Holy Spirit, became the key such chosen "witness."[184] After that, the mentionings of "witness" become very obscure, hard to pin down, and encrusted in arcane symbolism. But if we sift through them patiently, it becomes clear that parroting the doctrine while cultivating that elusive sense that the Holy Splrit strengthens one in the intimation that it rings true, even though one's "fleshly" intellectual faculties resist it, is true witness′. Witness′ is the testimony of sights one has not seen and sounds one has not heard. The Book, not the evidence of one's senses and faculties, becomes the criterion of witness′. What would have been false witness in the Old Testament becomes the highest kind of true witness′ in the New. What that entails comes through most clearly in these passages:

> The Spirit itself beareth witness with our spirit, that we are the children of God. . . .[185]

> This is he that came by water and blood, *even* Jesus Christ; not by water only, but by water and blood. And it is the Spirit that beareth witness, because the Spirit is truth. For there are three that bear record [i.e., witness, the underlying Greek word is the same] in heaven, the Father, the Word, and the Holy Ghost: and these three are one. And there are three that bear witness in earth, the spirit, and the water, and the blood: and these three agree in one. If we receive the witness of men, the witness of God is greater: for this is the witness of God which he hath testified of his Son. He that believeth on the Son of God hath the witness in himself: he that believeth not God hath made him a liar; because he believeth not the record that God gave of his Son.[186]

Once, probably indirectly criticizing the Gnostics, Paul negatively defines *witness′*.

182. Matt. 26:59-60 and Mark 14:55-63.
183. Acts 1:8, 22, 23.
184. Acts 22:15 and 26:16.
185. Rom. 8:16.
186. 1 John 5:6-10.

> . . . [I]f Christ be not risen, then *is* our preaching in vain, and your faith *is* also vain. Yea, and we are found false witnesses of God; because we have testified of God that he raised up Christ: whom he raised not up, if so be that the dead rise not. . . . If in this life only we have hope in Christ, we are of all men most miserable.[187]

As truth′ continues to seem to have something to do with truth, and love′ continues to seem to have something to do with love, for the believer who does not find his way out of the semantic labyrinth, witness′ seems to endow faith and belief with some of the tough-minded authority of legal proceedings.[188] Witness′ has extensive further ramifications, to be explored in the next two devices.

The usages of *word* in the Bible open up an extraordinarily hard intellectual issue, where the academics who study it have reached no consensus: the issue of the relationship between thought and language. Factions contending that human thought can be reduced to cybernetics, to logic, to ordinary language, to "semantics," and to connections between mental elements, all still have their respectable proponents, as do those contending that language can be reduced to grammers, either of the formal kind or the more empirical, phrase-structure kind. This present work is definitely biased, in finding considerable merit in the symbolic approach of Cassierer, Jung and Tillich, and in viewing the other available approaches as unsatisfying and contrived. The symbolic approach is the only one of the lot that is genuinely holistic, rather than reductionistic.

Some generalizations, that to me seem incontestable, can help us in our present, relatively nontechnical purposes. Language is a necessary but not sufficient condition of all but the most rudimentary thought, i.e., mental representation including contrary-to-present-fact circumstances. (The internalization of actual, present stimuli is merely an extension of sensation.) When a human grows up without language, as in the case of Helen Keller or feral children (who grow past the age where language is usually acquired, without human contact), there is a dramatic and sudden transformation of their behavior when language is introduced. No longer only concrete, aimless and undifferentiated, the behavior becomes purposeful, and the deprived individual rapidly begins to come to terms with the surroundings. Yet, facility in language can be a misleading indicator of the underlying quality of thought, and of the quality of application of a personality to that which is outside itself. There are many people with a gift

187. 1 Cor. 15:14, 15, 19.

188. An often recounted incident, that led up to John Wesley's Aldersgate experience, hinged on witness′. Under the tutelage of the German pietist, Peter Böhler and looking for relief from his salvation-doubt suffering and finding none in the Scriptures, Wesley decided that if he could hear the testimony of two or three witnesses as to a sense of inner certainty of victory over sin (2 Cor. 13:1; Matt. 18:16), he would gain the peace of mind he sought. Böhler brought three other pietists to Wesley, each of whom "witnessed" to just such an intrasubjective experience. What Wesley and those who retell the story always fail to notice is that each of the three had a different, albeit similar discrete experience. Their "testimony" was of three experiences with one witness each, not three witnesses "testifying" as to one and the same experience. Perhaps Wesley's conversion fails for want of proper biblical procedure. John Wesley's *Journal,* May 24, 1738.

of talk, who are not good at turning intention into a tangible result. There are others, whose talk makes them seem dull, but who reveal a very high quality of thought in the tangible results they achieve. Especially with intuitive-type people, we are apt to receive a negative first impression of someone who turns out to be an inarticulate genius.

Facility in language (including specialized, ultraexplicit mathematical language) and the human capacity for relatedness apparently are complementary rather than correlative in relation to one other. The relation parallels that of particular emotional states to general arousal.[189] A neglected and important insight of holistic thinkers about human thought, directly pertinent to the mystery of human thought and only indirectly pertinent to language, is the opposites dichotomy of *abstraction* and *empathy*. That dichotomy is similar to, but not the same as, Goldstein's abstract and concrete attitudes. Abstraction, as we shall employ the term, is the analysis of impressions, separating out from them the properties, principles, schemata at work in the phenomena behind the impressions. And empathy is the synthesis—and assimilation to ourselves—of impressions, the mental manipulation of them in space and time, in relation to one's bodily position and posture, and in terms of one's feelings, emotions and intimations. Both are implicated in human activity at its best, at the point where it deserves to be called by the much abused word *creative*. Language facility does, to be sure, always help, and the tangible result of important kinds of creative activity does, indeed, consist of language. But refinement of language expression and refinement of the human activity attending it often do not coincide. My definitions of *abstraction* and *empathy* are tailored to fit the provisional, "relatedness" psychology we have been using, and depart from those of the terms' originators.[190]

The psychological literature provides us with little information and less consensus on the topic of empathy and its ethical consequence, *compassion*. Again, we compensate for the deficiency by hastily fashioning a "for the sake of discussion" view. The impressions that empathy consists of synthesizing, partake partly of three-dimensional space and the juxtaposition of things in it, partly of feeling and emotion, partly of imagining oneself as a personality other than one's own familiar ego-personality, and partly of intimations of a realm beyond the jurisdiction of time, space and causality. Empathizing makes one vulnerable, since one leads with the more tender, immature, undifferentiated elements of one's personality. The mind-games we have described are, without exception, too-costly attempts to shield that vulnerability from being hurt or overtaxed. The mind-game player (of either kind) is ultimately a cop-out in the face of the frontier challenges of full living.

Where empathy is our starting place for appreciating what there is besides articulate thought or reasoning in the human knowledge process, compassion is

---

189. See p. 158, footnote 44.

190. For a discussion of the abstraction-empathy dichotomy, leading back to the seminal contributors, Wilhelm Worringer and Theodor Lipps, see C. G. Jung, *Psychological Types*, trans. R. F. C. Hull (Princeton, N.J.: Princeton University Press, 1971), pp. 289-299, pars. 484-504.

our starting place for understanding how human relatedness necessarily leads to sympathy and generosity toward our fellow living beings. What else is there for us to do, we ultimately must conclude, when it dawns on us that our own lives go down to the same sad finale, regardless? Just as our innate tendency toward self-doubt, toward a jaundiced view of our, to us, enigmatic moral nature evidently works for our collective, mutual protection, ingeniously designed to inhibit us from making ourselves and our posterity extinct, so does our innate tendency to form a bond with our fellow living beings, exercised to aid them in their plight, serve those ends. It can be seen in the experience of those who must deal with hostage-taking situations, who have learned, no thanks to the mental-health professionals, that manipulating an episode to drag on long enough for the terrorists to develop a sense of human relatedness to their victims, reduces the risk of a tragic outcome. We see in ourselves how a presentation drawing us into the first-hand experience of one who suffers arouses our sympathy and elicits assuasive action from us far more readily than statistics proving the suffering to be widespread, or pictures of human devastation so terrible that something in our better nature resists appraising it as nonfantastic. We are more moved by *The Diary of Anne Frank* or *Sophie's Choice* than by pictures of gaunt-faced, concentration-camp survivors still behind barbed wire, or the tortured bodies of those who did not survive, stacked like cordwood. We catch ourselves getting involved, in the invented life of a figment of some storyteller's imagination, and just as unreasonably unmoved by massive but mute evidence of the real thing! This was written a few weeks after the first public showings of ultrasound scan pictures of a human fetus about twelve weeks after conception being aborted. A recognizable human form could be seen, struggling convulsively against the force of the suction upon it. Clearly it was not the passive blob of tissue portrayed in the doctrine of the mind-game our generation has played with itself, to obscure the native, human implications of the abortion issue. I predict that the rest of society will come around to much of the view against the trivialization of abortion that the Evangelicals now take, albeit so rigidly and for the wrong reasons. Even a clock that has stopped is right twice a day!

How did we come to have a proclivity for compassion as native to us as our capacity to acquire language? How did we get that way? I do not know. I was not there. My ignorance, if I confront it fairly, will no longer tempt me to regress into fables about those tendencies having resulted from "selective pressures" in evolution, or about the God of the Bible having engraved those tendencies on my heart for the protection of his children, of whom I am not one. It is highly dangerous for people of learning not to come fairly to terms with the boundaries of their own ignorance. While being "enlightened" and in touch with their inner selves may well create problems of decadence and malaise in people, it does not, in itself, lead to callousness or lack of ethics. "Enlightenment" may lead to paralysis of action (as does a mind-game of the first kind), but a mind-game of the second kind, pressuring people to repress both the constructive and the destructive in their individual personalities, is behind every active social pathology. From the empathic deficiency of the common criminal in the midst of our society to the "normal" stormtrooper or death-squad member, whose group norms approve what amounts to criminal behavior, empathy has to be neutralized by some psychological stratagem, for humans consistently to oppress and victimize others. Much more will be said about this in Chapter 5. What we should remember now is that the stock Evangelical pseudopsychological dogma, holding that only fear of retribution can induce people to behave decently, is full-fledged Big Lie!

We shall return several times to the biblical effort to neutralize genuine empathy by estranging the believer from the emotive and creative roots of his own personality, and giving him instead the sterile obsession with the God-complex, to siphon away from those roots their nourishment. While empathy is a concept foreign to the Bible, compassion (with its King James synonyms, pity and mercy) is superficially very prominent in it. The Old Testament is rich in instances of compassion, both by God and by man, in a tacitly empathic and overtly sentimental human sense.[191] In the New Testament, active compassion becomes entirely the prerogative of Jesus, and except for the Good Samaritan, a figure of Jesus, no portrayal of genuine human compassion is to be found in it. The compassion, pity and mercy repeatedly attributed to God in the New Testament do not partake of any bond or obligation growing out of one being's participation with and empathic knowledge of another, but only by his fiat, bestowed helpfully or hurtfully, for reasons known only to him:

> For he [God] saith to Moses, I will have mercy on whom I will have mercy, and I will have compassion on whom I will have compassion.[192]

> Therefore hath he mercy on whom he will *have mercy,* and whom he will he hardeneth.[193]

> Shouldest not thou also have had compassion on thy fellowservant, even as I had pity [same Greek word as *compassion* in this sentence] on thee? And his lord was wroth, and delivered him to the tormentors, till he should pay all that was due unto him. So likewise shall my heavenly Father do also unto you, if ye from your hearts forgive not every one his brother their trespasses.[194]

Because the ordinary-language understanding of *compassion* is fairly ambiguous, its debasement as the Bible progresses never becomes so clear a departure from ordinary language as to constitute fully developed logocide. It does not impart, explicitly or implicitly, any mind-control instruction. *Compassion* and its synonyms partake almost entirely of Device 1. They do lose their emotive rootedness, and become overly disciplined, rule-bound and inhibited, as Chris-

191. E.g., Exod. 2:6; Ruth 1:16.; Job 19:21; Ps. 25:10; 51:1-12; 78:38; 103:13; Isa. 54:7-8; Lam. 3:22-23; Jon. 4:10-11 and Zech. 11.
192. Rom. 9:15.
193. Rom. 9:18.
194. Matt. 18:33-35.

tian love′ does. They also parallel Christian love′ in losing their right to be bestowed unequally, on recipients unequal in value to the individual.

Feuerbach, whose work went far toward what we are doing, but without the benefit of depth psychology, anticipated much of the foregoing in discussing the question whether morality depends on religion:

> Wherever morality is based on theology, wherever the right is made dependent on divine authority, the most immoral, unjust, infamous things can be justified and established. I can found morality on theology only when I myself have already defined the Divine Being by means of morality. In the contrary case, I have no criterion of the moral and immoral, but merely an *un*moral, arbitrary basis, from which I may deduce anything I please. Thus, if I would found morality on God, I must first of all place it in God: for Morality, Right, in short, all substantial relations, have their only basis in themselves, can only have a real foundation—such as truth demands—when they are thus based. To place anything in God, or to derive anything from God, is nothing more than to withdraw it from the test of reason, to institute it as indubitable, unassailable, sacred, without rendering an account *why*. Hence self-delusion, if not wicked, insidious design, is at the root of all efforts to establish morality, right, on theology. Where we are in earnest about the right we need no incitement or support from above. We need no Christian rule of political right: we need only one which is rational, just, human. The right, the true, the good, has always its ground of sacredness in itself, in its quality. . . . If morality has no foundation in itself, there is no inherent necessity for morality; morality is then surrendered to the groundless arbitrariness of religion.[195]

Several of the strands needing to be brought together run through Feuerbach's work. The rôle we have ascribed to compassion in the grounding of ethics radically psychologizes the question. The need for a discoverable underlying rational scheme to ethics is eliminated. Our approach agrees well with our human experience that situations constellating compassion in humans do so in myriad ways, all too readily misperceived as exhibiting so little consistency as to imply ethical relativism. The neat, comprehensive ethical system so long sought by philosophers is not to be found. But human experience does, nevertheless, admit to closely prestructured limits. Experiments in regulating human conduct do have necessary outcomes foreseeable by wise people. We do not need for some set of absolutes or givens to be imposed on us to save us from chaos. Philosophical ideas about ethics were much more prominent in the intellectual foreground of Feuerbach's time than in that of our own. They were not so stale and played out, as now. Feuerbach's thinking did not stand apart from the conventional learned thought of his day, in this respect. The notion that compassion is a principle in itself, and a concomitant of maturity in personality development, has been in the forefront of German literature from *Parzifal* through *Joseph and His Brothers*. It would probably have seemed to Feuerbach like too familiar and obvious an idea to use to solve so exalted a philosophical

195. *The Essence of Christianity*, trans. George Eliot (New York: Harper & Row, 1957), p. 274.

problem. How sad that our political discussion in the United States in the 1984 elections reverted to the low *niveau* of Feuerbach's time and circumstances!

The strands that run through Feuerbach's work to the modernist theologians, culminating in Tillich, have their origin in the insights on the relation of thought to language embedded in a few biblical statements, mostly attributed to John. The idea that words are symbols with powerful latent meaning and energy locked up in them is intrinsically to be found in the Scriptures, and that is why it struck such a responsive chord with the mainline pastors, who were glad to find a new, nominally biblical focus, relegating the anguishing dilemmas of the salvation plan to the periphery. Feuerbach had simply put down Christian rhapsodizing about "the Word" to a holdover of primitive ideas that philosophical analysis would entirely displace.[196] Twentieth-century students of symbolism as a human thought process rightly saw that there was useful insight to be gleaned from the Bible, even though they did tend to excesses in their neo-Gnostic religiosity. Tillich arrived at his views, while trying to create a theology that would justify the further existence of Protestant churches, and at the same time fully respond to Feuerbach's challange, removing every feature of the old ways that Feuerbach had criticized. The new views worked well enough that it took more than a generation for it to become evident that the rank and file mainline Protestants had not assimilated them, that the improvement in vitality was temporary or even illusory, and even that the decently decadent liberal churches may yet turn out simply to have served to keep some human "fish," "sheep" and "sheaves of wheat" tended, so that neoconservative Christian hucksters might "harvest" them! The sheer durability of the Bible and the variety of its historical *sequelae* "bear witness" that the biblical authors had some substantial insight for us to sift from the manipulative artificialities with which we find it conglomerated, and explicate it.

The main passages conveying an expansive and exalted view of the power and significance of the Word are:

> In the beginning was the Word, and the Word was with God, and the Word was God. . . . In him was life; and the life was the light of men. And the light shineth in darkness; and the darkness comprehended it not.[197]
>
> And the Word was made flesh, and dwelt among us, (and we beheld his glory. . . ,) full of grace and truth.[198]
>
> For there are three that bear record [witness] in heaven, the Father, the Word, and the Holy Ghost: and these three are one.[199]

196. Ibid., pp. 74-79.
197. John 1:1, 4-5.
198. John 1:14.
199. 1 John 5:7.

> . . . [Y]e have purified your souls in obeying the truth through the Spirit unto unfeigned love of the brethren, *see that ye* love one another with a pure heart fervently: Being born again, not of corruptible seed, but of incorruptible, by the word of God, which liveth and abideth for ever. For all flesh *is* as grass. . . . But the word of the Lord endureth for ever. And this is the word which by the gospel is preached unto you.[200]

> And I saw heaven opened, and behold a white horse; and he that sat upon him *was* called Faithful and True, and in righteousness he doth judge and make war. His eyes *were* as a flame of fire, and on his head *were* many crowns; and he had a name written, that no man knew, but he himself. And he *was* clothed with a vesture dipped in blood: and his name is called The Word of God. And the armies *which were* in heaven followed him upon white horses, clothed in fine linen, white and clean. And out of his mouth goeth a sharp sword, that with it he should smite the nations: and he shall rule them with a rod of iron: and he treadeth the winepress of the fierceness and wrath of Almighty God.[201]

The universal human experience of awareness and articulate thought at the frontier of disparate material and intrapsychic realms, where the jurisdiction of one set of principles leaves off and another takes effect, is richly expressed. (The ultimate clashing of the principles of the two jurisdictions keeps Christianity and Platonism from being reconcilable.) Monotheism expressed a higher plateau of self-awareness and integration of the individual personality than had the more chaotic and naïve outlook of its polytheistic forerunners.[202] This more modern, more "tightly wrapped" self-awareness is particularly evident in the foregoing "Word" passages. Essentials of what later came to be perceived as distinctive attributes of mind—the light of awareness contrasting the darkness of unawareness, individual personality, imperishability, the equation of individual personality with name, that had made one's name a sacred mystery to primitive religious sensibility—are epitomized by the "Word." All inchoate or latent things are hidden in their "Words" in this view.[203] The tacit notion that the existence of a thing depends on, or is at least interdependent with, the existence of a personality to comprehend it, is also implicated. And so is the sense of wonder, at insight

---

200. 1 Pet. 1:22-25.

201. Rev. 19:11-16. Note the inconsistency of the King James translators, about capitalization of *word.* See also Rev. 2:27; 12:5.

202. We earlier speculated that the average person in ancient times experienced himself as a ground where autonomous "spirits" bumped together and penetrated one another. See p. 134.

203. The Greek word for *word, logos,* in classical metaphysics, had meant a pervasive, impersonal ordering force in the universe. Heraclitus and the Stoics had philosophized on its nature in the fourth century, B.C., and some tinge of their views undoubtedly is present in the New Testament. The term carries over to modern social scientists, including Freud and Jung. Freud, in the last few paragraphs of *The Future of an Illusion,* used the term loosely and patronizingly, intending to describe the principle underlying science, but really only restating his notion of the "reality principle," said to work in opposition to the "pleasure principle." Jung used the term at times, most typically for the principle governing his thinking type. From the scant and indirect figurative usages of *logos* in the Bible, it is impossible to determine how much of the term's philosophical gloss is really there. Remember, the Book is constructed for psychological effect: its purpose is not didactic.

transcending conventional ways of looking around one, and at intimations of a dimension more real than what is real, so real that it seems unreal. That the forerunner and inspiration of Cassierer's, Jung's and Tillich's understanding of human cognition in terms of symbolism happens also to be the most successful piece of psychotechnology in all human history, is indicative of their views' merit.

The sharp, menacing sword coming out of the mouth of the Word of God, Jesus, in ominous tension with other biblical images of Jesus as a benign, agreeable companion or caregiver, exposes John's tacit awareness what a powerful implement the apostles had in their Word. Its instrumental power, and that of words and what go with them, is expressed in other, scattered passages:

> Hide me [David] from the secret counsel of the wicked; from the insurrection of the workers of iniquity: Who whet their tongue like a sword, *and* bend *their bows to shoot* their arrows, *even* bitter words. . . .[204]

> . . . [T]he tongue is a little member, and boasteth great things. Behold, how great a matter a little fire kindleth! And the tongue *is* a fire, a world of iniquity: so is the tongue among our members, that it defileth the whole body, and setteth on fire the course of nature: and it is set on fire of [by] hell.[205]

> . . . [H]e hath made my [Isaiah's] mouth like a sharp sword; in the shadow of his hand hath he hid me, and made me a polished shaft; in his quiver hath he hid me. . . .[206]

> Repent; or else I will come unto thee quickly, and will fight against them with the sword of my mouth. He that hath an ear, let him hear what the Spirit saith . . . To him that overcometh will I give to eat of the hidden manna, and will give him a white stone, and in the stone a new name written, which no man knoweth saving he that receiveth *it*.[207]

> . . . [T]he word of God *is* quick [vital], and powerful, and sharper than any two-edged sword, piercing even to the dividing asunder of soul and spirit, and of the joints and marrow, and *is* a discerner of the thoughts and intents of the heart.[208]

The notion of division, or "dividing asunder" in a violent manner with a mouth-borne sword, we shall explicate further in Device 5. What or who gets killed by all these mouth-borne swords? In real life, it is the words that are killed by the Word![209]

---

204. Ps. 64:2-3.
205. James 3:5-6.
206. Isa. 49:2.
207. Rev. 2:16-17.
208. Heb. 4:12.
209. Note how fortuitously in English the words *sword* and *word* are the same except for the first letter. This visual similarity may lead to some subconscious association of the two, particularly in individuals tending to eidetic imagery. Cf. Jer. 12:12 and 47:6, and the many occurrences of the phrase "word of the Lord" in the Bible, e.g., Gen. 15:1 and Exod. 9:20.

Concluding our study of logocide, the biblical debasement of words so as to undermine articulate thought and communication by the believer, we return to our original comparison of biblical logocide and Orwellian Newspeak. Consider the three slogans emblazoned on the "Ministry of Truth": "War is peace. Freedom is slavery. Ignorance is strength." Clearly, the second slogan is good biblical doctrine, since willful freedom is slavery to sin, and spiritual freedom, from "the law of sin and death,"[210] requires being an obedient slave to God. Is war peace? Consider the following Scriptures on the subject:

> . . . [T]he weapons of our warfare are not of the flesh, but divinely powerful for the destruction of fortresses.[211]

> Finally, my brethren, be strong in the Lord, and in the power of his might. Put on the whole armour of God, that ye may be able to stand against the wiles of the devil. For we wrestle [struggle] not against flesh and blood, but against principalities, against powers [forces, authorities], against the rulers of the darkness of this world, against spiritual wickedness in high *places.* Wherefore take unto you the whole armour of God, that ye may be able to withstand in the evil day, and having done all, to stand. Stand therefore, having your loins girt about with truth, and having on the breastplate of righteousness; And your feet shod with the preparation of the gospel of peace; Above all, taking the shield of faith, wherewith ye shall be able to quench all the fiery darts of the wicked. And take the helmet of salvation, and the sword of the Spirit, which is the word of God: Praying always with all prayer and supplication [petition] in the Spirit, and watching thereunto with all perseverance and supplication for all saints. . . .[212]

> Be careful [i.e., anxious] for nothing; but in every thing by prayer and supplication with thanksgiving let your requests be made known unto God. And the peace of God, which passeth all understanding, shall keep your hearts and minds through Christ Jesus.[213]

Christian warfare and "the peace of God, which passeth all understanding" occur together, as consequences of wearing that ponderous, restrictive uniform of Christian love′. While war and peace are not exactly the same thing in the Bible's contemplation, neither are they opposites. They become kissing cousins. Two more of the most momentous concerns of life in this world become equivalent, flat and detached from their true affective significances, thereby. Note that devotional program instructions are the items being likened to pieces of military equipment, and the premise that the program is to be done militantly

---

Also, the question of what unit of verbal expression is contemplated by *logos,* arises in this connection, since, ". . . the letter killeth, but the spirit giveth life." 2 Cor. 3:6. Often, *logos* is employed in the sense of an entire thought or message being conveyed. Cf. Acts 4:4; 12:24; Rom. 9:6 and 1 Cor. 12:8. Occasionally, *logos* apparently indicates a single grammatical sentence. Acts 28:25 and Gal. 5:14.

210. Rom. 8:2.
211. 2 Cor. 10:4. *New American Standard Bible.*
212. Eph. 6:10-18.
213. Phil. 4:6-7.

comes across. The peace—which "passeth" not our depth-psychology understanding—ultimately is caused by the doing of the program. How that occurs, and the answer to the question whether "ignorance is strength" or not will come after we have laid some more theoretical foundation.

Device 4: Assaulting Integrity

There is no group around, whose people as a rule are more sincere, well-meaning, generous, natively tolerant if no one inveigles them into being otherwise, and free from saying one thing while intending another than the conservative Evangelicals. It will seem incongruous and even mean to claim that impairment of integrity has to do with their believing as they do. The reader versed in the mental-health professions will note drawing a blank as to technical understanding, there having been little written, and no consensus, on what is meant by *integrity*.

Of what does integrity consist? To what extent is it a moral or ethical concept? Does lack of consciousness of duplicity or deception, without more, amount to integrity? Does a benevolent motive in entertaining a conscious purpose that is duplicitous or deceptive preserve integrity? Is a deliberately misleading half-truth worse than a complete lie? Our shared, common-sense understanding of integrity would suffice for a basic, implicit understanding of the stratagems we shall call "assaulting integrity"; however, we shall find we can order them better, and enhance our understanding, by making *integrity* a term of art in our provisional "relatedness" psychology.

Integrity in its most fundamental form has no ethical significance. It acquires such significance in action, as it is a precondition of compassion. That is because the most basic kind of integrity is biological. A person whom Goldstein would have diagnosed as impaired could not manifest integrity. Interrelatedness, and functioning in accordance with innate capacities are preconditions of integrity.

At a higher level, with the complex model and the varieties of psychopathology in mind, we perceive that all psychological conditions other than integration and relative cooperation of the ego-personality with the other complexes involve impairment of integrity. An ego-personality with control over its own boundaries, communicating with and continually integrating what lies in those reaches of the psyche beyond those boundaries, has a measure of integrity that the "psychotic" or "neurotic" lacks. One who can use his capabilities to come to continually better terms with the circumstances of his existence we would say has integrity.

To manifest progress in relatedness, then, is to manifest integrity. To have both one's articulate abstractions and one's empathy cooperate to enrich one's knowledge, including self-knowledge, is to have integrity. We implicitly think of one who is honest with himself about himself, as having integrity.

The process most significant in impairing integrity (assuming absence of the further complication of organic impairment) we earlier encountered as "double orientation": the utilization of the cyclical knowledge process to direct, manage and stabilize self-deceptions, rather than make the conscious attitude as well informed as possible. The knowledge process, in that case, is in the periphery of consciousness, rather than in the forefront. The knowledge process becomes like a journalist who uses his information selectively to make propaganda seem credible, rather than representatively to communicate fairly to others a set of circumstances. While our hysterically blind soldier patient was as sincere as he could be about not seeing the stool, we would not say he had integrity. And if someone were consistently a truth-teller, because he was so organically impaired that he could not think to lie or because he was struggling to avoid making tenuous "reality contact" even more so by confusing himself with misinformation or because he believed that an all-seeing God would sadistically torture him forever unless he told the truth, we would not say his truth-telling derived from integrity. Even without sophisticated ideas on the topic, we would implicitly want to know quite a lot about the circumstances and motivations of truth-telling or untruth-telling before forming an opinion as to the degree of integrity reflected in it.

The topic of integrity leads us to the question of belief. We detect impairment of integrity in one who believes what, based on the information of his faculties, he ought to disbelieve. The behavioral sciences do not inform us what belief is. Once more, we shall supply ourselves hastily with concepts, where our forerunners have let us down.

We can gain some useful insight about the human process of belief formation functioning well from the schematization of it implicit in the rules of evidence used in the courts of common-law countries (i.e., Great Britain and her former colonies). Just as the colossal failure of the mental-health professions to provide the legal system with a better approach than it had evolved without their help, to the issue of mental condition as an excuse for criminal acts, points to something drastically and fundamentally amiss with the stock of ideas in those professions, the good working of the rules of evidence, particularly where evidence is presented before juries of laypeople points to the presence of essentially sound insight underlying those rules, which is worth studying.

The key idea of the rules of evidence is that testimony of a live witness from recollection in his mind as he tells it, is the primary source of information about matters in question. The witness is to be under oath, not only because he supposedly fears God's wrath if he lies but also to subject him to criminal penalties in case of perjury, and to enhance the damage to his reputation and credibility should the other evidence make a liar of him. The opportunity for the hearers to observe the tone and demeanor of the witness and the right of the opposing side to cross-examine (or "confront") him are to give the finder of fact as much information as possible, explicit and implicit, from which to discern the truth from the falsity in what he has heard. Physical evidence is admissible only with live witness testimony to connect it with the matters in question, and explain and demonstrate it. The witness is to tell what he has seen, heard, etc., and (except in circumstances that need not concern us here) it is not proper for the witness' opinions or subjective reactions to be heard. After the testimony, the finder of fact may look at, touch, handle, etc., the physical evidence. The object of the process is to provide factual information as well separated from the subjectivities of the witnesses as possible and to give the finder of fact the benefit of as much nonverbal information about the witnesses as possible, from which an intuitive feel for their credibility—their integrity—may be derived.

The prime general rule embodying that key idea is: evidence is not admissible and may not be heard if it is *hearsay*—i.e., it has been said out of court, it was not said under oath, its opponent has no opportunity to cross-examine the declarant, and whoever said it is not present to be observed as to tone and demeanor. The additional distorting filter of a second person retelling what someone with first-hand experience of the events in question said is what the rule against hearsay evidence is intended to avoid. There are important exceptions to the rule against hearsay, each describing a characteristic situation militating in favor of the outside statement being reliable, and contemplating a public-interest reason why the information to be gained is thought to be so useful as to overcome the reluctance to hear hearsay. Among these exceptions are statements (admissions, confessions) against the interests of the person making it, exclamations by one in the midst of an extreme situation, and the last words of a dying victim of violence. Other more technical exceptions, important because of the recurring, routine matters they pertain to and the large amount of actual courtroom time given to them, become overemphasized, obscuring the essentials for the nonlawyer and putting them out of perspective for lawyers and judges embroiled daily in the process. For me, participation in trials before some judges and with some opposing counsel who tacitly appreciated the *genius* of the system were the most satisfying experiences of my sojourn in the legal profession.

The main thing that the Anglo-American court system does right (when it works as it is supposed to) is seeking to put the events in question and the cyclical knowledge process of the finder of fact in as close proximity as possible. Where the finder of fact cannot be brought into direct contact with the pertinent events and objects, then the effort is to bring out what is immediate in the testimony of the witness and keep what is subjective or "mediate" in what he might say from being heard. The finder of fact's knowledge process is given the opportunity to take in as much relevant immediate stimulation as possible. When the cyclical knowledge process cannot go to work on first-hand experience, then it goes to work on the circumstances wherein the second-hand information was received, to try to interrelate it and to assess it. In that respect, what goes on in court imitates real life's more lucid moments. The courts jealously guard and supervise the framing of the issues, knowing well how easily the result can be skewed if they are framed tendentiously. Restrictions as to relevance are applied, hopefully to prevent one side from inveigling the finder of fact into tacitly and thoughtlessly assuming just that premise that ought to be explicitly challenged and subjected to focussed thought.

Note how we, as our founding fathers before us, structure that institution which, if it malfunctions, can take our property, our liberty, even our life away.

As nearly as may be, an airtight seal is maintained to join the realm of truth to the realm of fact. We want words to be used precisely and for quantitative relationships to follow the rules of arithmetic. No room for casuistry, hyperbole or tricky plays on words here. Not all things are, can be, or should be of equal affective significance for us. Where our own ox is at risk of being gored, counsel that the realms of truth and fact are to be separated by as much void, empty space as possible, as our religious friends imply they should, fall flat.

The Anglo-American rules of evidence provide us, then, with a model of the mature, "related" person's process of coming to belief. Much more than his conscious attitude is involved in believing. If some datum does not fit, that will register unconsciously before he is ever able to put his finger on what is wrong and adjust what he believes to harmonize with all his impressions. Since important news comes through second-hand accounts, he is all the more on his mettle to notice dissonant clues, and to discern which, of the propositions he is asked to believe, should be doubted. Information that does not engage the receiver's personal knowledge process and does not participate in a context with other information against which it can be tested is believed only in a very shallow way. Apart from religion, there is no occasion for any appreciable investment of libido in such beliefs. The unintelligent, the organically impaired and, to some extent, children believe in that way. Such beliefs are easily changed, without much mental rearrangement.

Besides providing us with a useful model of the information process in the mature, "related" person, court proceedings are a bad analogy for human behavior. In the crucial functions of issue framing and principle application, the legal system is designed radically unlike the individual psyche. A schematic system cannot have empathy or compassion. Yet empathy and compassion are crucial to individual ethical behavior. If these are faulty, adherence to and application of abstract moral "principles" can serve, at most, as an inadequate, limping compensation. Subjective sensibilities run far ahead of the legal system. Individuals can like, dislike, obey with misgivings, engage in political activity to change, or in the extreme case, conscientiously disobey the governmental system's laws. Also, the legal system presupposes, and in our country often admirably achieves, motive and emotive disinterest on the part of the decision makers. As soon as a judge or jury is confronted with some potential perquisite connected with a win for one of the parties before them, the integrity of the system falls off rapidly. The legal system really can approach the ideal of treating all equally. But the individual is best advised to discard the self-deception that he can treat all comers equally in matters that touch him personally, and get on with the essential human project of making a virtue of the inequality of his preference and investment of libido. If one occupies a formal decision-making rôle, integrity lies in intellectual consistency. Outside such a rôle, no substitute has been found, nor do I foresee any, for a highly developed, seasoned subjective sensitivity, not amenable to explication, always obscured by our inherent blind spot as to our own moral nature, not intrinsically "irrational," but always running ahead of our "reason," eluding reason's grasp. Explication pertains to the history of human sensibilities, not to their current events!

There emerge, then, two kinds of healthy, nondisordered belief: The higher kind engages the whole personality, not just the conscious part, is continuous in development over time, and is so interrelated that many related beliefs may have to shift when new impressions render an existing belief untenable. That kind of belief is an active, discerning process. Alas, for most of humanity, that process gets lost in carrying out conventional routines. For most of humanity, psychological limitations discourage genuine relatedness, and in the line of least resistance lies the mind-game of the second kind.

The lesser kind of nondisordered belief is essentially limited to the conscious attitude. It serves in practical, immediate situations where one must receive and act upon the kind of information that becomes unimportant once it has been acted upon. Provisionally, one believes a hearsay report that thunderstorms are coming, and as soon as one has closed the windows and brought the wash in off the clothesline, all questions about whether or not the report and the circumstances of its reception ring true and fit in with other impressions are moot. In the healthy, "related" person, such beliefs can be shifted, discarded, altered with great facility. The lesser kind of belief is short-term, and acts as a filter or buffer for those impressions that need to be taken in, assimilated, digested, employed to adjust the *Gestalten* one attains, the projections that will flow out to meet new stimuli.[214]

The mature, "related" person, then, is economical and parsimonious about what he believes. What "rings true," what fits together, what works is what he believes. What fails those tests, or is insufficiently exposed to them, is tentatively, provisionally, skeptically held. Perishable, flesh-and-blood people get the benefit of doubts, but not propositions capable of being true or false. Only what one has taken in and responded to with one's whole being can be a proper object for higher-order belief. William James' advice that bad human outcomes are a reason not to believe a thing despite intellectual considerations in its favor is indispensable in engaging a proposition with one's whole being. The person who cannot bring the inarticulate stuff beyond the boundaries of consciousness to the question of what is worthy of belief, even though he be intellectually bright, well-educated and competent in a certain habitat, will be confused about belief. That is a characteristic "tender-minded," thinking type failing. But on the other hand, the person who cannot bring self-conscious, intellectual discipline to bear on questions of belief had better structure his life so that the ethical implications of his acts are simple.

---

214. The psychology-oriented reader will note the parallel and relevance of higher-order and lower-order belief to long-term and short-term memory. Clinicians have noticed that memory for events that have just occurred, i.e., what one had for lunch, what the state of the weather is, etc., behaves much differently from memory for more lastingly pertinent information and significant events that have not newly occurred. Short-term memory is erased while long-term memory remains intact in a patient who receives electroconvulsive therapy. The capacity for short-term memory becomes impaired sooner and more dramatically than long-term, at the onset of senility. Mental-health professionals widely hold that the two kinds of memory reflect different underlying physiological processes, affected differently by e.c.t. and by age.

The question of disordered belief brings us back again, albeit from another direction, to mind-games. Whenever the data of experience is glossed over, distorted, ignored or suppressed, to evade an emerging need to change ideation to fit it, then there arises a mind-game (usually of the second kind), integrity is impaired, and disordered, hypertrophied belief is present. That insight is not so homely or obvious as it may seem. At every hand in learned fields outside the natural sciences, we find specialists bickering about whether they accept or reject this or that leading contributor's proprietary position. If not engaged in defending such a position, they call themselves eclectic. Eclecticism, like pragmatism, began from sound insights, about which we shall have more to say. But as pragmatism has degenerated into short-term expediency, so has eclecticism degenerated into stringing together fragments of ideas past, without appreciating their differing, even conflicting implications. We see it in the vandalization of Gestalt psychology by American pop-psych hucksters. When not defending a proprietary position against experience counter to the position's expectations, and incoherently mixing up stray ideas, the academics look to some method—usually statistics—to solve problems untouched by human minds. At the root of the malaise in the behavioral sciences is the tacit assumption that ungrounded belief is somehow legitimate. A faulty notion of belief was also at the root of the disastrous enthusiasms of large numbers of people for our beleaguered century's discredited "isms." I believe that the problem has its roots in bad habits of thought carried over from religious men of the past, in people who have shaken off the destructive content of the old religion but have neither clarified nor resolved the issue of the hold its style of thinking still exerts on them. Where Max Weber contemplated "the Protestant ethic and the spirit of capitalism," we, for the needs of our intellectually disillusioned, possibly post-literate time, now contemplate "the belief ethic and the spirit of ideological hyperenthusiasm"! Perhaps the simultaneous heating up of religious fundamentalist hyperenthusiasm and dying away of secular ideological hyperenthusiasm in the current period are related.

Because the cyclical knowledge process is resilient, belief continually grounded only on peer-group pressure meets with inner resistance. The knowledge process keeps on trying to work properly. Removing its promptings from conscious awareness and keeping its working from being realized in articulate thought require energy. Conscience is evaded: avoiding the pain that goes with bad conscience is an inducement to expend that energy. With the part of him that, were he in touch with it, would belie the deprecating pseudopsychology of the heterochthonous mind-game kept out of awareness, the person's conscious mind can go to work mastering the doctrine and distorting whatever would discredit it. With sufficient indoctrination and a conducive psychological makeup, one can work oneself into full-fledged double orientation, unconsciously making selective use of the gleanings of the knowledge process to defend the doctrine and to prevent too many of its dissonant implications from troubling the conscious mind at once.[215]

---

215. A psychological makeup particularly conducive to keeping what is inconsistent with the heterochthonous mind-game out of awareness would be a Jungian thinking type, who was also

What does the Bible do that so encourages groundless belief to get out of hand and so successfully displaces the good, natural tendency of the person to be grounded and rooted in experience to the periphery of awareness? We analyzed in Device 2 the clever, logically tenable way that the doctrine places itself beyond the reach of the knowledge process by making everything it has to say about the moral condition of people and about expectations of events in the natural world nondisprovable. The existence of a tremendous, perilous realm transparent to all human modes of inquiry except a divine, written revelation is not inherently illogical, only far-fetched.

If the believer were ever to notice that his belief takes place in a vacuum, that nothing in his direct experience supports or augments it, and that its purport to be more real than reality, so real that what is real, by comparison, seems unreal, deteriorates if not constantly refreshed with more repetitions and exercises in the hearsay information that is its sole source, then he might begin to imagine how his world would be without it. He might explore the possibility that when his beliefs sometimes seem fantastic, that is because they *are* fantastic. The moment he begins to think over how living a limited span of years (or even immanent physical death) without the impending jeopardy of taking sadistic torture forever, or how having back the right to entertain in mind something other than the same old prescribed thoughts and images, that do get boring after a while, might be more pleasant than constant Christian warfare against his own flesh', he is on the way to being one acutely miserable Christian, or else an ex-Christian.

The next thing needed to forestall such a collapse of indoctrination, after the three devices we have covered, is building up the habit, little by little, of repressing any tendency to think critically about the beliefs. This, in part, is done by confronting the believer with calculated absurdities, some of them quite extreme, and each loaded with some lurid, perverse or scatological feature, to gratify the repressed, shadow side of the believer's personality. An integral part of the Christian experience is intensely taboo Scripture content passing right under one's nose, not consciously recognized but producing a perceptible titilating rush all the same.

The point of the stratagem of assaulting integrity is inducing the believer, for the sake of obedience, to affirm teachings that are inherently incredible, not

---

inclined toward the sensation and introversion functions. A thinking type is not necessarily intelligent, and it would be a not particularly intelligent thinking type who would try to navigate the Bible's semantic labyrinth, but never find his way out. Emphasis on the explicit, characteristic in one who favors the sensation function, would lead to haziness about the more remote features of his surroundings, resembling the innocence of worldly knowledge in the Bible. The introvert's preoccupation with helplessness, and finding the environment irritatingly overstimulating, would find compensation in biblical withdrawal. And all these types favor sharper conscious discrimination, making contrast with the unconscious and alienation of the conscious attitude from it more pronounced. While a feeling type may find an agreeable set of people to be devoted to in a conservative church community, the finer *nuances* of the mind-control system, like water on a duck's back, will not penetrate. Feeling-type styles ultimately lend "old-time religion" its most salutary features, and characterize individuals who thrive and do not suffer mental-health damage in the conservative church experience.

germane to, and in discord with, the rest of the Bible. He violates his conscience, his common sense, his good inclination to tell the truth as it occurs to him, to call things as he sees them. He does as he is commanded, and stifles the still, soft inner apprehension he has that he is doing something shameful. The Evangelical enthusiast has no idea how close he comes to the real issue, when he describes himself as "sold out to the Lord."

The most extreme integrity-assaulting passage in the New Testament, and the one most clearly making no positive contribution to its theological teaching, comes from Luke:

> And he [Jesus] spake a parable unto them *to this end,* that men ought always to pray, and not to faint [shirk]; Saying, There was in a city a judge, which feared not God, neither regarded [cared about] man: And there was a widow in that city; and she came unto him, saying, Avenge [vindicate, bring punishment in behalf of] me of mine adversary. And he would not for a while: but afterward he said within himself, Though I fear not God, nor regard man; Yet because this widow troubleth me, I will avenge her, lest by her continual coming she weary me. And the Lord said, Hear what the unjust judge saith. And shall not God avenge his own elect, which cry day and night unto him, though he bear [suffer] long with them? I tell you that he will avenge them speedily. Nevertheless when the Son of man cometh, shall he find faith on the earth?[216]

The passage follows the rule we earlier laid down, that *unjust* and its cognates are code words for salvation status, and relate to no notion of ethics. Nevertheless, to take the hard edge off the passage, all of the widely used contemporary translations have *bring justice for,* or the like, instead of *avenge,* lending an ethical connotation to the widow's petition that it lacks in the underlying Greek text. Like her modern counterparts, of whom I have represented not a few, she did not want "justice." She wanted to win.

If this passage were not in the Bible, a believer encountering it would find it an offensive, blasphemous parody of the Bible's major teachings. God is likened to a wicked judge, who is lazy or infirm, and tires easily. The believer is exhorted to pray for completely selfish reasons. Pray to stick it to your enemies—but be sure to bless them too! Making prayer an occasion for vigorous, marathonlike expenditure of effort, and juxtaposition of such prayer to faith, will become meaningful to us when we consider the next device.

Even though the passage is a parable and contains nothing it taxes credulity literally to accept, the believer's critical mind needs to be shut off for him not to wonder why his general notions about the perfection and faithfulness of God, and the selflessness the believer is to strive for, are stood on their heads in this passage. By passively, tacitly and with vague misgivings acknowledging the enhancement of those notions for him by the instruction of this passage, he relinquishes a little of his integrity. My speculation—conveniently nondisprovable—is that this passage developed in the early church as a test of candidates

216. Luke 18:1-8. Luke 16:1-13 is amenable to a similar analysis.

for inner-circle membership, on whom one would have to depend not to betray those circles to the persecuting authorities. The defensiveness as to the soonness of the second coming gives the passage away, indicating the concern of a time well after the apostolic age. If the novice receiving instruction in the passage showed no sign of caviling at its incongruity but instead dropped unhesitatingly to his knees and went into fervent, wailing prayer, then the church father knew he could be trusted.

The relative unimportance, to the working of the passage's stratagem, of literal belief that some particular fact existed directs our attention to a crucial point. The angry antireligionists of the past have always assumed that literal belief in past events contrary to familiar natural principles was the central issue to all religious questions. That is one reason why the Tillichian revolution, entirely discarding the question of literal truth while supplying something portentous and exciting for Christianity to mean, seemed to be the answer to all the Christian liberals' problems. But, as we analyze the passages, we find that assault on individual integrity not only can occur but can reach its height where no demand is made for literal belief in implausible hearsay facts. And since we live in a time when modern physics has opened our minds to the possibility of other realms, places, and times where the laws evinced in the phenomena we know do not apply, we really have no business being more than mildly put off by reports of a special dispensation where those laws were suspended and events contrary to them occurred. In our provisional "relatedness" psychology, when one is bidden to believe propositions based entirely on hearsay, where the cyclical knowledge process has no opportunity for first-hand experience, and the proposed beliefs are transparent to all natural modes of investigation, "belief" in them is superficial, and integrity has little bearing on it. But when there is something for the knowledge process to work on, including the assertion that there was some component of personal experience in the thing to be believed when there was none, the presence of content pertinent to the person's empathic, ethical and aesthetic sensibilities—and it is doctrinally required to be falsified—then integrity is being assaulted. It is in the act of witnessing' to something whereto one has been no witness, contrary in some way to what one has witnessed, that the undercutting of one's own integrity lies. When one has done that repeatedly, he is subtly degraded and made untrustworthy in his own eyes. The appeal of the negative biblical pseudopsychology of man's moral nature is bolstered thereby.

Another example, extreme enough to be clear, is the purported post-crucifixion encounter of Cleopas and Simon with Jesus, on the road to Emmaus:

> And, behold, two of them went that same day to a village called Emmaus. . . . And they talked together of all these things which had happened. And it came to pass, that, while they communed *together* and reasoned, Jesus himself drew near, and went with them. But their eyes were holden [stayed, held fast] that they should not know him. And he said unto them, What manner of communications *are* these that ye have . . . as ye walk, and are sad? And the one of them . . . said unto him, Art thou only a stranger in Jerusalem, and hast not known the things

> which are come to pass there in these days? And he said unto them, What things? And they said unto him, Concerning Jesus of Nazareth. . . . Then he said unto them, O fools, and slow of heart to believe all that the prophets have spoken: Ought not Christ to have suffered these things, and to enter into his glory? And beginning at Moses and all the prophets, he expounded unto them in all the scriptures the things concerning himself. And they drew nigh unto the village . . . and he made as though he would have gone further. But they constrained him, saying, Abide with us: for it is toward evening. . . . And he went in to tarry with them. And . . . as he sat at meat with them, he took bread, and blessed *it,* and brake, and gave to them. And their eyes were opened, and they knew him; and he vanished out of their sight. And they said one to another, Did not our heart burn within us, while he talked with us by the way, and while he opened to us the scriptures?[217]

This passage, too, makes no demand on literal credulity. Its language does not require the disappearance of Jesus concomitant to the others' realization of his identity, to have been other than by ordinary, pedestrian means. (The requirement of *abaissement de niveau mental* as a condition of Jesus' fellowship will become intensely significant for us in the next device.) The passage probably has basis in fact, reflecting the catastrophic loss that Jesus' crucifixion must have meant to his followers. It parades before our eyes an obvious and simple thing that it violates the rules of the mind-game to say: the man Cleopas and Simon encountered and listened to was not Jesus. They saw what they desperately wanted and needed to see. The Bible speeds the believer past the point where he ought to come to that conclusion. The subject is abruptly changed, to one rubbing a very raw nerve in the believer well enough indoctrinated to suffer from salvation doubt. Simon and Cleopas are indulged in what the church-age believer is not to expect: a wondrous occurrence engaging the senses, probative of "in all the scriptures the things concerning himself." Then, assuming that their "heart burn" does not refer to a case of indigestion caused by excitement, they receive another benefit denied the latter-day believer: an inner, emotional experience, calming their fears and doubts, and somehow probative of their salvation. Taken in the context of the entire Bible, that is a tantalizing and confusing thing. The next sequence of events aggravates that tantalization further:

> And they told what things *were done* in the way. . . . And as they thus spake, Jesus himself stood in the midst of them, and saith unto them, Peace *be* unto you. But they were terrified and affrighted, and supposed that they had seen a spirit. And he said unto them, Why are ye troubled [agitated]? and why do thoughts [*dialogismos,* ambivalent ponderings, ruminations] arise in your hearts? Behold my hands and my feet, that it is I myself: handle me, and see. . . . And he took . . . [some broiled fish and honeycomb] and did eat before them. . . . Then opened he their understanding, that they might understand the scriptures. . . . And ye [the group Jesus was addressing] are witnesses of these things.[218]

---

217. Luke 24:13-19, 25-32.
218. Luke 24:35-39, 43, 45, 48.

Here, the man preaching, and whose mere presence alive and well amazes the onlookers, clearly is Jesus. This time, the hearers' incredulity must be suspended.[219] Where the earlier encounter could be a faithful report of what Cleopas and Simon saw, so presented that the hearer is group-pressured into ignoring what the facts imply, this encounter is probably an embellishment. If so, its author could not have contrived it better had he had the benefit of *this* book. The description of events one can natively relate to, on an empathic, physical level, is so vivid, that one can easily forget one was not there and did not actually see it. The basic matter of knowing a thing by touching and handling it and the multisensory activity of eating foods that have distinctive textures and tastes are strongly emphasized.[220] That emphasis comes just in time, abruptly to change the subject away from that of negative emotions and thoughts. The thwarted longings of the believer for supernatural signs and inner signals, stirred up and briefly aggravated in the preceding passage, find their church-age palliative in this one: immersion in the Scriptures, where one learns that one has somehow "witnessed" that for which one really has only mute, two-dimensional hearsay evidence. Since that is a supernatural mystery, it "makes sense" for it not to make sense. One is constantly to saturate one's conscious mind with the material to be believed in that way. We begin to understand why Evangelicals are so defensive and bellicose about the trustworthiness of the Bible.

That saturation serves the purposes of the next device, and pertains to faith—a different phenomenon from belief, as we shall see. Much as an oyster, trying to assuage the irritation of a grain of sand, makes a pearl, the believer tries to assuage the inner awareness that, deep down, he really does not believe his cherished beliefs, and puts himself under mind-control. We shall see if the state of mind-control is really of any more use to the believer than the pearl is to the oyster.

The passages setting out the devotional program instructions for immersion of consciousness in the prescribed content, and evacuating all else to the periphery of consciousness or to the unconscious, we shall cover in the next device. The foregoing examples, although extreme in the plainness of the discrepancies they train the believer not to notice, are relatively mild in the loaded or scandalous latent concerns they express. The taboo and ambivalent features pertain to longing for some tangible basis for the prescribed beliefs, and without the Bible, would not even be taboo. "An evil and adulterous generation seeketh after a sign; and there shall no sign be given to it. . . ."[221] These examples particularly stress the component of assaulting the belief process, seeking to confuse the believer as to what basis he has for belief, and do not

---

219. The ancient manuscripts are not consistent as to whether Jesus' parting from this group at Bethany (Luke 24:51) included a spectacular ascension or not.
220. The emphasis on touching and handling the resurrected Jesus is further elaborated in the encounter with Thomas. John 20:24-29. But note the unexplained or possibly sexist ambivalence of the resurrected Jesus toward being touched or handled by Mary Magdalene. John 20:17.
221. Matt. 12:39.

stress the component of assaulting the believer's personal conscience and the empathic sensibilities arising from it. Where one component is at work, the other is always at least discernably present. With these examples still fresh in mind, we digress to look specially at some of the vicissitudes of the belief component of the "integrity assaulting" process.

Earlier, mention was made of believers' becoming especially exercised to evangelize others, to protect themselves against experiences threatening their indoctrination. Time after time, intelligent men trying to be believing men of integrity have agonized in print over the terrifying mein God takes on, for one who knows one's Bible too well. We observed it in Jonathan Edwards and John Wesley. Frequently, in the lives of such men, some mentor recommended that they go out and teach others as a means of getting themselves to believe. Pivotal in the career of Martin Luther was such counsel from his mentor, Dr. Staupitz.[222] Wesley described his encounter with such advice, in his journal entry for March 5, 1738:

> Immediately it struck into my mind, 'Leave off preaching. How can you preach to others, who have not faith yourself?' I asked Böhler whether he thought I should leave it off or not. He answered, 'By no means'. I asked, 'But what can I preach?' He said, 'Preach faith *till* you have it; and then, *because* you have it, you *will* preach faith!'

Note how a self-deception that would instantaneously be identified as illegitimate in any other setting was freely accepted by these otherwise highly intelligent and decent men. How beleaguered one's thought processes must be to do such a thing! Within a mini-Reformationist church, the suspension of incredulity is apt to take the form of a crude, uncritical *abaissement de niveau mental.* For me, visiting such churches as an ex-believer, the atmosphere is obvious, almost palpable. I am appalled how I was oblivious to it while I was a believer.

One of the persons answering to the description "religiously disillusioned" whom I interviewed described a critical incident. The penetrating insight in it is hers, not mine. For nearly all her adult life, she had been an active participant and Sunday school teacher in a highly visible, conservative church in a large city. One of the few such churches with a long history, it was what we have called an atypical church in a liberal, mainline denomination. She was articulate

---

222. Luther described his state of mind, before arriving at his partial solution of making a mystery of "grace":

"Is it not against all natural reason that God out of his mere whim deserts men, hardens them, damns them, as if he delighted in sins and in such torments of the wretched for eternity, he who is said to be of such mercy and goodness? This appears iniquitous, cruel, and intolerable in God, by which very many have been offended in all ages. And who would not be? I was myself more than once driven to the very abyss of despair so that I wished I had never been created. Love God? I hated him!"

Seeing that argument and consolation were doing no good, Staupitz arranged for Luther to preach, and to succeed to the former's university chair of Bible. Roland H. Bainton, *Here I Stand* (Nashville, Tenn.: Abingdon Press, 1978), pp. 44-45. For a psychohistorical rendition of these events, see Erik H. Erikson, *Young Man Luther* (New York: W.W. Norton & Co., 1958), pp. 36-40, 165-69. See also 1 Tim. 4:15-16.

and well educated, a teacher by profession. Being the main source of emotional support for her mother had been a strong influence in her being a churchy person, and in her not marrying. She fell into the outward stereotype of the silent, sexless spinster, so often taken for granted around churches.

Frequently, she would be a guest in the home of one of the church's elders and his wife. He was elderly, and his visitor, by then, middle-aged. A flirtation between them grew up, making for awkwardness in one another's presence obvious to both. Neither could overcome the reticence and embarrassment enough to approach the other and go through the declarations of repentance and mutual forgiveness that would ideally resolve such a situation between two church members.

The minister in that church was fairly young, academically prodigious, ambitious, a fine pulpit performer, and well on his way to being a big celebrity in the conservative Evangelical subculture. He had artfully conveyed the impression that counseling parishioners was a major activity and *forte* of his. She made an appointment to see him. After two weeks' wait, she was at last ushered into the minister's office, an ornate, stagy affair, where he sat behind a huge desk, and she sat on a low chair, looking up at his splendidly framed personage. This contrivedly intimidating, intelligence-insulting set-up scene caused to well up in her a rage that she had never before known she felt.

When the problem was laid out before him, the minister acted as if it were something tremendous and stunning to him. He could hardly bring himself to say anything responsive to facts, and yet to her his resentment and condemnation came across. How dare she trouble the great man to respond to anything other than the compliant, selfless, spinster stereotype, on the fringe of his awareness! He wavered between denying that there was any problem and agreeing to speak with the elder and then speak with her again. She never received any communication from the minister again. But the elder and another of the minister's confidants, in separate incidents, very soon approached her and coolly, without batting an eyelash in either instance, invited her to terminate her relationship with the church that had consumed her youth and untold thousands of her dollars.

This hatchet-wielding response to so minor a plea for help upset her profoundly. Where were all those pretty sentiments she had heard from these people for all those years? She lost sleep, occasionally experiencing a kind of panic, "an almost physical sensation of having . . . [her] mind split." That feeling of inner division centered on and was resolved through this insight:

> It was beginning to fit a pattern of people not being aware that they didn't believe what they said they believed. And I don't think they are aware that they don't believe it. . . . I think they have themselves fooled, and it was just so apparent to me.

A major crisis in that church, that may have helped position it for such a collective effort to create a latter-day Hester Prynne, was the minister's decision to have his church secede from the liberal denomination and join a conservative one. It seems the liberal denomination had rendered itself "apostate" by ordaining a minister who denied the deity of Christ. The secession would entail litigation between the church and the denomination over title to the building housing the church. In the last few weeks before handing in the resignation requested of her, she made a point of asking elders and prominent members how they could so eagerly anticipate litigation with brother Christians, and whether the Christian thing for them to do would not be to walk meekly and humbly away from the property and begin again. "Why do ye not rather take wrong? why do ye not rather *suffer yourselves to* be defrauded?"[223] Each time she would do this, the person would be momentarily stunned and then recover, saying that this was one of those Scriptures reflecting the cultural bias of other places and times past, not one of those that is still good for instruction, reproof or training in righteousness. None had such presence of mind as duly to remind her that she was, after all, a woman who was supposed to be silent in church anyhow.[224]

This burlesque demonstration of how blind the believers were to obvious inconsistency when it suited them made it possible for her own inner division—that had enabled her also to avoid making unwanted intellectual connections—to be healed. She has since progressed in making a humanly authentic life for herself, in those areas where it is not too late.

Her penetrating insight that churchy people, in a crucial sense, really do not believe their cherished supposed beliefs and fail to understand that they do not believe provides us a useful point of departure. It made me think of a constantly repeated slogan of one of the major television evangelists: "You'll know that you know that you know."[225] The slogan, although not biblical, never fails to sound a responsive chord in the evangelist's fans. It points to a three-layered psychological process of believing. Belief is a tacit opinion about the grade of knowledge one has of any given premise: the tacit opinion, the knowledge about the premise, and the premise itself are each different and severable components of the complex psychological process of higher-order belief. We can alternatively define belief as a kind of knowledge about knowledge about knowledge. In any mind-game of the second kind, religious or otherwise, the first layer of knowledge is put out of mind and ignored. One deceives oneself that one knows that one "knows" that one "knows," when one really has obligingly and conveniently forgotten that one knows one does not know! Subjectively, the double negative seems to make a positive. A corresponding definition of disordered belief is unknowing that one knows that one lacks sufficient basis for belief.

The insight that belief is three-layered affords us an opportunity to improve our grasp of "integrity," with an alternative definition. Basis for belief is a major component of that about which we have said the person of integrity is honest with himself. He calls things as he "sees" them, not as mind-game doctrine or peer-group pressure prescribe he should. He calls them as the promptings of

223. 1 Cor. 6:1-8.
224. 1 Cor. 14:34.
225. The slogan is a take-off on 1 John 2:3, departing strikingly from the verse's right meaning. The evangelist's other "signature" slogan is a correct statement of 1 John 4:4.

what we have called the lower levels of conscience indicate, not as the heterochthonous norms of the upper levels of conscience predefine them. The person of integrity accepts the stress of being out of harmony with those others who are the source of peer-group pressure, as he accepts the distress of having his familiar, guiding ideas undermined, and need for their revision made evident. His lack of peace of mind and the failure of his life to proceed on an even keel in bad times are indications of his human soundness. A more important kind of distress he accepts is from the empathic, compassionate, "moral" promptings of conscience. Being in touch with those puts him in "bondage" to them, where the person who can dull or insulate them with self-deception is "free." Oh yes, like Christianity, our provisional, "relatedness" psychology admits to a vital and positive sense of being in bondage! Our alternative definition of *integrity* is being well in touch with the promptings of the unconscious, but from a deliberate, conscious standpoint. That standpoint corrects the conscious attitude against inundation by the unconscious, as in the mind-game of the first kind, and against the opposite excess, impoverishment, as in the mind-game of the second kind.

The insight that belief is three-layered also affords us an opportunity to clarify the relationship of belief to consciousness and to discover how exclusively it is that disordered belief is a conscious attitude phenomenon. Earlier, we noted how emphasis on separateness, on elements, on one static frame of reference at a time in the limited but useful ruts of time, space and causality, are properties of consciousness, in contrast to the unity and dynamic interrelatedness of all the contents of the unconscious. When we referred to the "one-sidedness" of the conscious attitude, we were really referring to a specialized psychological organ unlike the rest of the psyche. When we refer to man's blind spot as to his own nature—not only his moral nature—we contemplate avoiding the mistake of depending too much on understanding the unconscious in terms of similarity to the familiar, conscious experience. If all the latent relations among psychic contents affect one another in our unconscious life, then our unconscious mind knows very well what things have impressed us with the depth of the relations and implications of the things we know about them, and which are incoherent, shallow and need no response. While the surface ideas of the Bible do intrigue, and entice us to expect something with depth, we have seen how cumbersome and incoherent the overall view, or *Weltanschauung,* based on it is, and how shallow its impact, without more, on our unconscious mind is apt to be. After the considerable effort needed to take it all in, one would normally notice that one has taken in nothing whereby to appraise its truth or falsity, and lose interest in it. The mind-control stratagems working together keep the conscious attitude weakened and fooled, so that the corrective, welling up from the unconscious—which is never fooled—is not received. We can characterize disordered belief in still another way: when conscious belief is at variance with what has registered and resonated deeply in the unconscious, then for that state to be maintained, division in the personality against itself must occur, and psychological energy must be consumed to maintain the divided state and to effect the double orientation that makes it possible for the presence of the divided state to evade conscious notice. "Assaulting integrity" and the question of belief apart from the larger question of faith are but the conscious aspect of a process also having an integral but qualitatively much different unconscious aspect.[226]

All the while that the believer is "witnessing" and "testifying" to the effect that his religion has given him something to hear, see, touch or handle, or something even better in lieu of those, he is stifling the inner apprehension that he has had no such thing. The more he stifles it, the worse the irritation of nagging bad conscience gets, since stifling that sense of bad conscience without coming consciously to terms with its cause is inherently a dishonest thing to do. So he stifles it all the harder, to keep the apprehension down, out of awareness. This self-generating, "vicious cycle" is greatly amplified by the presence of lurid, scandalous implications in the pertinent biblical content. By having the biblical content implicate not only otherwise neutral matters made taboo by biblical prohibitions but aspects of one's own personality that would be taboo in any civilized society as well, an immensely powerful dissociation (or repression) pertaining to those ideas, avoiding unsettling conscious confrontation with their implications, can be triggered. Hence, much of what follows belongs just as much to the next device as to this one.

The memorable events depicted in the Bible are such familiar fixtures in our culture that we do not react to their bizarre features as we would, on first impression, to equally bizarre accounts of other pedigree. Others around us are similarly hardened, so that the subtle signals of others' alarm without which most people apparently are very slow to be upset by hearsay information are not evoked. For those infrequent occasions when someone has other than a stock, mild reaction to a Bible story, there is always some mild, stock explanation that the true meaning is something else symbolic, with tradition and expert opinion underlying it, beyond the ken of the mere layperson.

A theme where the surface implausibility and taboo content are relatively balanced is Jesus' various contacts with lewd women. We encounter these prepared with the knowledge that Jesus' ministry to outcasts sometimes made it nesessary for him to present an outward appearance of impropriety genuinely misunderstood by some, and exploited to his detriment by others.[227] Yet, these Scriptures are crafted to let unmistakable embarassment about Jesus and the lewd women show through, contrary to our usual experience with accounts by

226. Our notion that the unconscious is relatively unresponsive to purely hearsay information is relevant to the issue of unconscious suggestion, ubiquitously covered in college psychology courses and texts. In the early experiences of the depth psychologists, posthypnotic suggestion was used to relieve neurotic symptoms, with the result that if there were still an active unconscious conflict, the conflict would simply crop up again in different symptoms. Attempts to reach the problem with suggestion in various forms were typically unsuccessful. Various claims have been made over the years—but not substantiated—for influencing behavior with communications in the form of subliminal written messages embedded in movie images or disguised verbal messages embedded in sound presentations, and effortless learning by means of didactic sound recordings played during sleep, to teach the sleeper. Our premise that response to hearsay is characteristically a conscious-attitude activity agrees well with the equivocal trend of these findings and provides a perspective for it that is lacking in the other available theories.

227. Matt. 9:9-12; 11:19; Mark 2:16-17; Luke 5:27-32; 7:34-35 and John 4:27.

lieutenants loath to mention the revered leader's personal peccadilloes.

Each time he encounters it, Jesus waxes "soft" toward heterosexual sin, as he does toward no other kind. Neither Paul nor John carry his liberalization through: they revert to the old way, railing just as vehemently against heterosexual sin as other kinds. When Jesus encounters the Scribes and Pharisees about to stone the woman who has been caught in the act of adultery (but not the man, whom they must have had just as good an opportunity to catch), he reacts in an extraordinary, and from the standpoint of the rest of the Bible, inexplicable way.[228] The entire incident is absent in the most ancient manuscripts, and found in a different place in some others, alerting us that it may well be a later, purposeful interpolation.[229] If rescission of the Old Testament death penalty for adultery is being effected then and there, why are those devout Jews brought up so short by Jesus' suggestion that they should have a bad conscience about correctly enforcing it, as they had, so long ago, been duly commanded?[230] If rescission of that particular death penalty is of the essence, then why are the death penalties for murder, idolatry, sorcery, male homosexuality, bestiality and disrespect to a parent left in place?[231] And why is any revision of a Jewish death penalty important, if the criminal laws and administration of criminal justice are going to be the business of secular, nonecclesiastical civil authorities, at least until the end of the age of the Gentiles, and the rapture of the church? It cannot be that Jesus is advocating universal mellowness and nonjudgmentalness, as many liberal clergy like to make out, because of the precisely enunciated double standard as to humans judging other humans that we earlier covered.[232] The only interpretation harmonizable with the rest of the New Testament statements on sexual sin, judging others, and response to sinful acts in this life generally is that Jesus is commanding, and giving a theological rationale for, letting the secular legal system take its course, and no longer following those portions of pentateuchal law calling for individuals to take the law into their own hands. That observation leads us to the reason why I conclude that the whole incident is a Gentile interpolation, added to please the Roman authorities at some later time, and not the work of anyone of Jewish origin: no Jew would have pronounced the venerable Jewish ways illegitimate so heavy-handedly and sweepingly. I prefer to believe that the enormous impression Jesus evidently in his time made was due in part to his wise counsel against suicidal confrontations with the Romans, and in favor of sublimation, putting life on a higher spiritual and moral plane instead. But I cannot believe it could ever have lain in the mouth of any believing Jew to imply that justice was all present with the Roman colonial administration but absent entirely from the Jews. Still less can I believe that even he could have sold an angry mob of Scribes and Pharisees on such a premise!

---

228. John 7:53-8:11.
229. See pp. 124, footnote 114 (2nd paragraph).
230. Lev. 20:10-12; Deut. 22:13-29.
231. Exod. 21:12; Lev. 24:17 (murder). Deut. 13 (idolatry). Exod. 22:18; Lev. 20:27 (sorcery). Lev. 20:13 (male homosexuality). Exod. 22:19; Lev. 20:15 (bestiality). Exod. 21:15-17; Lev. 20:9; Deut. 21:18-23 (disrespect to a parent).
232. See pp. 106-08.

If indeed the story of Jesus and the woman caught in adultery was designed as camouflage for an extra, politically convenient shot to slant the Gospel in favor of Roman authority and to dump the onus more and more onto Judaism, then the sexual issue was an artful choice of connotation for distracting features. The incident adds to the untoward impression already made by dubious women ministering to Jesus and his reactions to their ministrations:

> Now when Jesus was in Bethany, in the house of Simon the leper, There came unto him a woman having an alabaster box of very precious ointment, and poured it on his head, as he sat *at meat.* But when his disciples saw *it,* they had indignation, saying, To what purpose *is* this waste? For this ointment might have been sold for much, and given to the poor. When Jesus understood *it,* he said unto them, Why trouble ye the woman? for she hath wrought a good work upon me. For ye have the poor always with you; but me ye have not always. For in that she hath poured this ointment on my body, she did *it* for my burial. Verily I say unto you, Wheresoever this gospel shall be preached in the whole world, *there* shall also this, that this woman hath done, be told for a memorial of her.[233]

Here, we receive the clear indication that good works to the benefit of the poor are not to be understood as primary to the Gospel message, beyond the failure we earlier noted, of symbols expressed in terms of such works, such as feeding, giving drink, clothing the naked and releasing captives from prison, to retain that meaning when the same images are found in other contexts.[234] And what can he mean, "me ye have not always," when the last thing he says in the same Gospel is, ". . . lo, I am with you alway[s], *even* unto the end of the world. Amen."?[235] Why do the disciples focus on the waste of the expensive ointment, when elsewhere Jesus' appearance of impropriety with harlots, tax gatherers and the like (from whom he also cheerfully received money contributions[236]) had been a sore spot? Was this an isolated instance?

> And one of the Pharisees desired him that he would eat with him. And he went into the Pharisee's house. . . . And, behold, a woman in the city, which was a sinner, when she knew that *Jesus* sat at meat in the Pharisee's house, brought an alabaster box of ointment, and stood at his feet behind *him* weeping, and began to wash his feet with tears, and did wipe *them* with the hairs of her head, and kissed his feet, and anointed *them* with the ointment. Now when the Pharisee . . . saw *it,* he spake within himself, saying, This man, if he were a prophet, would have known . . . what manner of woman . . . toucheth him: for she is a sinner. And Jesus answering said unto him, Simon. . . . There was a certain creditor which had two debtors: the one owed five hundred pence, and the other fifty. And when they had nothing to pay, he frankly forgave them both. Tell me therefore, which of them will love him most? Simon answered . . . I suppose that

223. Matt. 26:6-13. See Mark 14:1-9 for a parallel account.
234. See pp. 58-61, especially footnote 117.
235. Matt. 28:20.
236. Luke 8:1-3.

> *he,* to whom he forgave most. And he said . . . Thou hast rightly judged. . . . I entered into thine house, thou gavest me no water for my feet: but she hath washed my feet . . . and wiped *them.* . . . Thou gavest me no kiss: but this woman since the time I came in hath not ceased to kiss my feet. My head with oil thou didst not anoint: but this woman hath anointed my feet with ointment. Wherefore I say unto thee, Her sins, which are many, are forgiven; for she loved much: but to whom little is forgiven, *the same* loveth little. And he said unto her, Thy sins are forgiven. . . . Thy faith hath saved thee; go in peace.[237]

Even the parable is in violent contrast to others. Wherever arithmetic concepts were involved, Jesus denegrated the natural, arithmetic rules and made a paradox.[238] But here, he lets sin depravity, forgiveness, and the love or faith of the one forgiven stand in direct arithmetic proportion. Are debtors grateful in proportion to the amount of debt they go free of? Is the amount of obsequious fawning before an authority figure a trustworthy measure of love? Nowhere else in the Bible is the believer given pseudopsychological premises so fatuously contrary to common human experience as these. If all humans are equal before God in the totalness of their depravity, and salvation is by grace′ through faith′, and not subject to what the individual does, why then must the one who has sinned more, demonstrate more? The tension of the passage with the general tendencies of the New Testament in these regards puts us on notice that our leg is being pulled.

Doing the devotional discipline and following the examples of other believers, one pretends one does not see and brings oneself along to the point where consciously one is no longer aware of seeing how wildly implausible these events are, and how the suggestion of some sort of illicit erotic contact between Jesus and these women bellows from off the page. One thinks pure thoughts, and perish the thought of such a thing! The latter passage is practically a blueprint for a clergyman to ensure that his philanderings will go unnoticed by the believers, even if their signs are obvious. Love′ "believes all things."

There is a contrasting lurid implication in the alchemical symbolism wherein Christ is depicted as a bridegroom, and the believers his bride, he being the head of each man as the man, if married, is head of his wife, and each man is supposed to have his conscious thoughts filled with the nonimages of this human male, Jesus, whom the Renaissance painters have made us think of as a taffy-haired sissy. How can a man's head be filled with that, without some homoerotic constellation of that exalted relationship he is supposed to have with Jesus

---

237. Luke 7:36-48, 50. Despite the host having the common name Simon in each instance, the anointing of Jesus' head in the first instance and his feet in the second, the apparent continuity of the second with a sequence of events taking place at Nain, nowhere near Bethany, the different *dénouements,* the apparent absence of disciples from the second, and the unlikelihood that a leper would have been tolerated in the ranks of those obsessive ritual puritans, the Pharisees, weigh overwhelmingly in favor of two different incidents. Note the contradiction of the woman's knowing of Jesus' presence and approaching him only after he entered and had been seated, and his declaration that she had kissed his feet unceasingly since his arrival.

238. See p. 180, footnote 23.

arising in his maundering thoughts and needing to be repressed immediately because it is so taboo and blasphemous?

The inveigling of the believer in luridness reaches its height in the sadistic and masochistic vicarious activities wherein the believer is to participate. These are very plain, and the scriptural transactions where they occur are so well known that our treatment of this distasteful topic can be mercifully, but disproportionately to its importance, brief. Yet, we are all so hardened to these images by constant and repeated exposure that we must reflect deeply to get in touch with their significance. Beyond its more plainly gruesome features, such as its use of a Roman terror and intimidation instrument for its main symbol, its incessant preoccupation with dominance-submission relationships, and its muted, sordid anticipation of retribution against despised outsiders in the afterlife, in whose condemnation the believers are to expect to participate—perhaps like a jury in a court where Christ will sit as judge[239]—two pervasive sado-masochistic aspects of Christianity stand out as illustrative of assaulting integrity.

The *communion ritual,* the only sacrament recurrently required of the Bible-believer, combines the most solemn devotion and the most direct confrontation of the believer with luridness in one event. It reverts to thc underlying idea of ritual incorporation with a totem animal or enemy by ingestion, and belongs to a religious sensibility far more primitive than Judaism. I have repeatedly been told by sensitive friends of Christian origin, and used to misunderstand with particularly lamentable obtuseness, how their realizing that the meaning of the communion amounted to cannibalism alienated them from supernaturalistic religion and helped prompt their development toward radicalism. Here, perhaps more than in any other place, we can observe how the turgid, "normal" sensibility apparently shrugs off offending stimulation, so long as reference others fail to register telltale cues of alarm or offense. But the bright, sensitive, inner-directed child's sensibilities are intensely overstimulated, cauterized by it. To such a child, it makes an essential difference that he is badgered to appraise this horror as real, in crucial contrast to the premise tacit in the presentation of all the gruesome content taken in from fairy tales or television, ultimately helping all but a psychologically deficient fraction of children to sort out what is real from what is imaginary and not to be feared or acted out. The biblical image of ". . . having their conscience seared with a hot iron"[240] is an ironically apt description of the believer's condition, desensitized to the obvious, unappetizing implication of eating Christ's flesh and drinking his blood. Mislabling that "psychic numbing" as a mystery, or as deep spiritual understanding, does not change its true character. Having tried to work the matter out each way in turn, in my own religious life, I conclude that real understanding lies in retaining the sensibility to be disgusted and embarrassed by the communion ritual, not in mutilating that sensibility so badly that it no longer functions. Alas, past generations have witnessed the ugly consequences of repressing the communion ritual's

---

239. 1 Cor. 6:2-3 and Rev. 20:6. See also Matt. 19:28 and Luke 22:30.
240. 1 Tim. 4:2.

gruesome implications, leading to their projection in the form of the "blood libel," the belief of European peasants that Jews kidnapped Christian children to perform cannibalistic rituals on them. From where else can the peasants have carried over such an idea?

The element of implausibility becomes obscure, and the tender root of the sensibility that makes it possible for a thing to be experienced as lurid, most exposed, in the Christian notion of the *substitutionary atonement,* Christianity's supposed remedy for the supposed sin affliction. Here, we meet the topic that, more than any other, dominates the worship services and all other outwardly observable manifestations of conservative Christianity. The believer and the sophisticated outside observer are readily misled by all the unending talk about the substitutionary atonement and its ramifications in two respects. Firstly, one is misled to appraise it as central or essential. We shall find out that its only function is to distract. It is an irrelevancy put there to keep the mind busy, occupied with empty paradoxes, and off the scent of the real issues, so that impressions utterly alien to what appears on the surface can work in the unconscious, untrammeled by insight. Like the self-surrender notion, the substitutionary atonement notion beguiles the observer to mistake the more conspicuous features, the ones the believer himself thinks important, for the ones actually operative. Secondly, both believer and would-be analyst of religion are misled into accepting the Bible's self-serving declarations that guilt, expiation, satisfaction of some obligation, spiritual renewal, etc. are pertinent to sin. We shall find out that the core of all that the Bible has to say about "sin" has precious little to do with those things. The next device, Dissociation Induction, depends on penetrating the true, depth-psychological issue hidden in the biblical obscurities that arrange themselves around the notion of sin. In order to do that, we shall have to be able to separate the substitutionary atonement notion from it.

If we put aside the thought habit of being intimidated by the substitutionary atonement, and look ahead, anticipating social concerns so serious as to override our desire not to trespass on the sensibilities of our religious friends and neighbors, we find that that atonement offers little resistance to reductive critique.

The premise of the atonement is that man, in the "wrong, inferior and unhappy" state of original sin is devoid of good spirits and has nothing to give that could possibly please God. In the Jewish, Roman Catholic and Wesleyan traditions, man gives a partial *quid pro quo* in the form of contrition, self-affliction and good works, but always remains off balance, knowing he can never bring the debt fully current. God, for reasons known only to himself, requires propitiation for sin, with which man comes into the world totally saturated, yet somehow becomes supersaturated by his inevitable bad deeds. So God, in his love′, has to propitiate himself for the sin(s) of his elect, or else these will go unpropitiated. The Bible-authentic believers too, are to desire to give a *quid pro quo* for the propitiation, but this time, to all spiritual intents and purposes, the *quid pro quo* is not merely deficient or inadequate, but a necessary and vital complete nullity. It has no substance. It is like a reflection in a mirror. He is not to take any comfort in belief that his good works make it better, as someone in one of the said other traditions can. Something more is required, and the only definite reassurance he receives is that the nature of that "something" is not to be penetrated. The repentant "sinner," looking desperately to have his behavior contain reassuring evidences of salvation, ultimately is no participant in the transaction. At best, he is a third party to a self-dealing transaction between God the Father and God the Son, who are one person. Instead of a participant in an inferior rôle, he is a mere bystander. Instead of being able to esteem himself a substantial contributor looking for a matching contribution from God, the Bible-authentic believer cannot hope to do more than satisfy a few formal, nonsubstantive prerequisites.

By making the ideas pertinent to the issue of whether or not the believer can do something about his condition so much more complicated and convoluted than they had been in Judaism, and by making the assault on whatever natural tendency toward self-esteem the believer may have had more devastating, an absurdly simple, underlying strategy is obscured. The huckster of our own day seeks to instill in the prospective customer apprehension of a problem he was previously unaware of having—or possibly a nonexistent problem—like b.o., halitosis or the "heartbreak of psoraisis," to sell him a product to remedy it. The religious huckster seeks to instill the idea that his prospective client has a "sin" problem, about the nature and dangers of which impenetrably confusing "information" is cheerfully furnished, and a remedy proposed, entailing payment of money, under some guise or another. The ultimate commodity in view is God's love′, incomparably greater and better than mere fickle, frail human love, the prospect is given to understand.

Of what does that love′ consist, if we look at it fearlessly? Like a manipulated child who is taught to feel guilty and do as he is told whenever the parent tells of all the pain and sacrifice that has taken place on the child's account, the believer is to feel guilty and to want to obey whenever he hears about the enormity of Christ's sufferings in his behalf—should that believer turn out to be one of the lucky ones.[241] What, indeed, are those sufferings, whereby the love′ may be appraised? For the Father aspect of God, it is the sacrifice of his "only begotten son." Unlike a mortal father who loses a son, God had him back safe and sound in three days. For Jesus, it is the suffering concomitant to the crucifixion, beginning with his anxiety attack in the Garden of Gethsemane. That, and the death on the cross, no more gruesome, after all, than similar crucifixion deaths suffered by many another Jewish patriot of the time, are apparently all there is to it. The Bible hedges so adroitly as to Jesus' post-death experience that it is not even clear he had any conscious awareness again, until he was resurrected![242] Pretty puny stuff, to equal all the sins of God's elect!

---

241. The Bible does explicitly teach that God hates sinners, and does *not* merely hate the sinful acts while continuing to love′ the sinner. Ps. 5:5 and Rom. 9:13.

242. Note that one of the crucial tenets of the Apostles' Creed, "he descended into hell. . . ," has less than sufficient biblical basis. The only affirmative statement as to Jesus' wherebouts in that period is Matt. 12:40, where Jesus predicts his own future, saying, ". . . so shall the Son of man be three days and three nights in the heart of the earth." The phrase "heart of the earth" appears nowhere else in the Bible. Similar phrases had been used twice as pleasant images, not connected

Indeed, the Gospel accounts so underplay the content of the atonement, as compared with subsequent Christian traditions, that we must suspect its usefulness as a conscious preoccupation for the group became evident only as the failure of Christ to return quickly made it necessary to shift the focus. What makes this and the other "integrity assaulting" Bible stories work, is their resonance with the inferior, shadow side of each person's personality. The shadow of the natively decent, thoughtful person—as Evangelical enthusiasts in our time characteristically are—is gullible, stupid, perversely fascinated by erotic gratification and pain. Our relative unconsiousness of the shadow side, and our propensity ego-defensively to project it, are closely related to our inherent blind spot as to our own moral nature, to our vulnerability to topical confusion, appraising our own moral nature and condition as worse than it really is. The inherent, and for the sake of the survival of the species, necessary tendency of people not to give their own moral nature or condition the benefit of the doubt, brings with it the negative side-effect of insatiable apetite for stimulation pertaining to the nagging, endemic tendency to feel guilty. The "integrity assaulting" stories seem well aimed at the soft spots, and arrest attention like a blow to the solar plexus. Ultimately, the "integrity assaulting" exercises are effective for the same reasons why criminals, who know full well why they should not confess, do so anyway, and why a psychiatrist, as intelligent and well integrated as Dr. Meerloo, would develop a sense of guilt, wrongdoing, and the impulse to confess his resistance activities, when in the hands of the Gestapo.

Special care must be taken, to avoid misunderstanding *assaulting integrity* to be mere assault on self-esteem. An earlier generation of liberal pastors, and their psychologist contemporaries, more familiar with churchiness than those who are now active, understood the negative core of the old religious ways to be attack on self-esteem. They knew of case histories where a constant refrain drummed in during early life, which could be paraphrased "But for your position

---

with Hell (Ps. 95:4 and 139:15), and once as a hellish image (Ezek. 26:20). Interpreting "heart of the earth" to mean Hell as opposed to a grave seems entirely unjustified. The matter comes up only twice, after the fact. Acts 2:31 tells us "that his [Jesus'] soul was not left in hell," suggesting but artfully avoiding declaring that his soul had ever been there. Eph. 4:9 puts its suggestion in the form of a rhetorical question, coming through more clearly in the modern translations, such as *The New American Standard Bible,* which renders it: "Now this *expression,* 'He ascended,' what does it mean except that He also had descended into the lower parts of the earth?" The believer is left to supply his own answer, and is no more enlightened than before as to the meaning of "lower parts of the earth." The hesitance of two New Testament authors to commit themselves as to Jesus' descent into Hell is curious. Also, events fail to bear out Jesus' prediction that his subterranean sojourn would be "three days and three nights." The descriptions of the events following after the crucifixion generally, and explicit statements such as Matt. 16:21;17:23; 20:19; Mark 9:31; Luke 9:22; 24:7 and Acts 10:40, have Jesus rising the third day, after spending only two nights, the latter part of Good Friday, all of Saturday, and a small portion of the morning of Easter Sunday wherever he was between death and resurrection. Still another complication arises, when Jesus, hanging on the cross, tells the thief being crucified with him, who is one of the elect, "Today thou shalt be with me in paradise." How could Jesus be in Paradise, and in Hell at the same time? When he was hard at work on his assignment, to atone for the sins of the elect over three days and three nights, was he, as the Boss' Son, privileged to arrive for work late, leave early and go home for lunch with the thief? (Note also the discrepancy between Mark 15:25 and John 19:14 as to the time of day of the crucifixion.)

in Christ, you are a worthless worm, and even if you had died in infancy before you could do anything bad, you would still deserve to go to Hell and be infinitely tormented forever," had appeared to be an agent causing psychological injury. Hence, there were many takers for Rogers' naïve psychological approach based on doing the perceived opposite, i.e., pumping the "client" full of empty, disingenuous affirmation. What was never noticed is that with the constant attack on individual self-esteem, which more modern conservative pastors have learned to soften by talking more about the benefits of being in the fold, and making their personal style more gentle in contrast to their message, goes the more broad attack we have been analyzing, amounting to an attack on the Jungian "rational" functions, thinking and feeling. The promotion of disordered belief, which we earlier encountered as the uprooting of the realm of truth from its ground of fact, in logocide, is really also an assault on the thinking function. And desensitization of conscious sensibility to what ought to revolt it, which we earlier encountered as the uprooting of the realm of love from its ground of affection and the promptings of the lower levels of individual conscience, is really an assault on the feeling function. As we have tried to emphasize in our provisional, "relatedness" psychology, these functions are far more essential to human well-being than self-esteem, or relief from the discomfort of diminished self-esteem.

The attack on self-esteem and the manipulation of people by promoting guilt feelings are such prominent external features of the conservative Christian experience that overestimating their psychological significance in making it powerful over people is a logical mistake. I stumbled over it repeatedly while working out these ideas, until it dawned on me that in spite of all the Christian declamation I had heard about the resolution of guilt being a *forte* of Christianity, from my extensive exposure I knew of no instance where Christianity had helped anyone handle a truly weighty burden of guilt. Neither in first-hand experience, including an ongoing criminal-defense law practice, nor from the media had I encountered it! I know of plenty of cases where someone had a *shame* problem—Charles Colson is a conspicuous and typical example—and wanted to demonstrate to himself and to society the turning of a corner in life. Persons who are genuinely helped over a substance-abuse problem, with a shame problem embedded in it, are a special case, whose main features have fairly little to do with guilt or insufficient self-esteem. Of people whose act or neglect caused terrible human harm, people for whom experiencing compassion for their victim or victims would cause anguish, one hears extraordinarily little in Evangelical circles. Evangelicals are guilt dilettantes, not people who really know about the vicissitudes of substantive, realistic causes for remorse. Being "delivered" from a vague, background sense of guilt with insignificant causes, or no cause at all, is a pastime of theirs. If there are any who do have heinous things on their consciences, they do not "witness" about them. Not all such people could have current, practical reasons for keeping quiet about their former guilt problems, disobedient to the applicable devotional program instruction.[243] If

243. James 5:16.

conservative Christian groups typically do have persons whose pasts include heavy guilt, their consistent failure to "witness" about it points at least to the failure of religion to help them resolve it.

What should be noted as we close our discussion of "assaulting integrity," with necessary pieces of the puzzle yet unprovided, is that the ultimately unbelievable premises that the believer, perforce, strives to believe, and with difficulty deceives himself into thinking he believes, are always accompanied by latent taboo content. That way, those premises are always partly in the blind spot, and focussed thought about them is rendered more difficult and less likely. The stratagem depends on having the individual regard his experienced resistance to the belief as part of his supposed negative, corrupt nature that he is to seek to suppress, to overcome, to "crucify." Actually, that resistance is of the essence of what is most positively, distinctively and creatively human and honest about him. When Christianity comes on with the figure of the man in whose words the echoes of the best human achievements of the far distant future must have resounded, being tortured, mutilated, killed early in what should have been the prime of his life, for its central emblem, it is telling us plainly what it proposes to do to the corresponding tendencies in ourselves, and we are too desensitized to turn away in nauseated disbelief! That emblem is, itself, an "integrity assaulting" piece of business, seen in that light. ". . . I am come . . . that they which see not might see; and that they which see might be made blind."[244]

The practical working of the "assaulting integrity" stratagem can be observed in an extract from Harold Camping's call-in program. The caller, inferring from his voice, was a man, not old, reasonably literate, and of no distinctive ethnicity. The exchange is vintage mini-Reformation.

> Caller: The big question: You see, I'm listening to Family Radio for about three years, because, as I read in the Bible that faith comes by hearing.[245] But say that I feel that I still haven't come to salvation, would it be a good idea to quit listening if I don't believe?
>
> Camping: Well, but, all right, now, let's look at the alternatives. I finally begin to trust the Bible sufficiently so when it says that he who knows the way and doesn't turn to Christ will be beaten with many stripes but he who does not know the way will be beaten with few stripes[246] if he does not become saved. So, I've been listening to the Word, for many years, and I'm still unsaved, maybe I'd better not listen any longer because I don't want to be beaten with many stripes, that is, I don't want to have the greatest punishment in Hell. Well, what are your alternatives? Your alternatives then are either I'm going to go to Hell and be a little less punished, or I'm going to Hell and I'm going to be a little more greatly punished. But, in either case, the alternatives are absolutely unacceptable, because you're going to Hell! In either case, you're still going to Hell. But there is a third alternative, and the third alternative is, all right, I've been listening for three

244. John 9:39.
245. Rom. 10:17.
246. Luke 12:47-48.

> years; I'm still unsaved, and it's probably because I have not come to the moment of truth yet, I am not broken before God as yet, I have not really seen my sins as they are. I have not really leveled with myself and with God, and so, and yet I know I don't want to go to Hell, and so I begin to beseech the Lord, I begin to cry out to him, I begin to beg of him, "Oh, Lord, Oh, Lord, give me that faith in the Lord Jesus. I know I don't want to go to Hell." Again, we can't read enough of this publican that Jesus spoke of,[247] that stood afar off. He had no pretentions of any kind, of any personal holiness, and he smote his breast, and his only cry was, "Oh, God, have mercy on me, I'm a sinner. Oh, God, have mercy on me." And God says that he went home justified, because he had come to the moment of truth, where he recognized that he was going to Hell, he recognized that only the God who should send him to Hell is the one who could be his salvation, who could have mercy on him, and we just keep agonizing before the Lord. That's our only hope, our only hope is to cry to God that we might not go to salvation [*sic*] uh, go to Hell. Because whether we're going to be punished less or greater, it's still Hell![248]

Now, the caller had begun with a question about degrees of punishment in Hell, and tipped Camping off that fear of Hell was, for this caller, a button that would give him a jolt when pushed. Camping then swiftly moved the focus of the discussion away from the question of what is worthy of belief, over and beyond the fairly broad overlap between the devices, into Device 7, Holy Terror. Seeing that subtle distraction with understated luridness would not work, Camping, most effectively, fired off Christianity's heaviest artillery in the caller's face, to make him too upset to follow through with his straight thinking, that could have led the caller (or perhaps, Camping) to the dangerous insight that things in the Bible may seem absurd because they are absurd, and not for the convoluted, Device 2 reasons the Bible itself gives. The caller quickly changed the subject, with a question about Camping's own testimony about how he knows he is saved, and Camping assuasively indulged him for a few minutes. The pattern of Device 7 operating in the caller, despite the failure of 4 and 5, may well indicate unresolved early experiences where God was depicted as a bogeyman for parental control.

Of interest is the way both parties to the discussion tacitly equate belief in what in the "natural" is unbelievable, with salvation. What does it take, to get a person to believe that he believes? What does it take to efface, as for Jonathan Edwards, the differences between "horrible" and "exceedingly pleasant, bright and sweet . . ."? For that, we must take up what, perforce, remains unconscious in the believer.

Device 5: Dissociation Induction

Dissociation Induction is at the core of this work, the matter where, at last, depth-psychology insight gets intensively applied to explaining the Bible's power

---

247. Luke 18:9-17.

248. Generally, "uhs," "ums," words for which the next word is clearly a substitution in the extemporaneous speech, and other immaterial distractions are deleted in transcriptions of conversations used in this work. Where utterances with any savor of intelligibility in context are deleted, an ellipsis is used.

over people. The more outward devices we have covered serve to create the conditions for this one to work. The subsequent ones depend on this one, and primarily serve to stabilize or to ingrain it. We have touched on various aspects of this present device in limited contexts, such as the devotional program, the use of allegory, the provision of ideational busy work for the conscious mind so that the operation of contrasting pieces of ideational business in the unconscious will go consciously unnoticed, and no conscious insight into them will be gained. Now these are to be brought together, and our focus readjusted to a wider angle of vision.

We shall have need for one additional insight as to the relation of the conscious attitude to the unconscious, complementary to our earlier contemplations about belief. Belief is mainly a conscious-attitude activity, and disconnected, second-hand information penetrates the relatively more objective unconscious only with difficulty or not at all. But implication and interrelation of particulars, first-hand and hearsay is mainly an unconscious matter, and the conscious attitude (or ego-personality) is the more resistant and dense of the two media, where products of the synthesis of particulars are concerned. Information, experiences and impressions are gathered, and a gestation process invisible to the conscious mind occurs, before conscious insight emerges. Humans use logic not to solve problems in the first instance, but to check the work and put it in presentable order after the insight has been attained. It is very characteristic of people, including religious people, tacitly to understand and correctly to apply implications and principles they cannot (or cannot yet) articulately explain. With Evangelicals, it is manifested by living out and correctly applying the implications of the biblical teachings, even though these are not consciously understood, discussion and articulate thought about them are impeded by terminological confusion, and slogans contrary to and less retrograde than the correct implications have been well learned, and can be recited on demand.

How different things would be, if the unconscious were not so differential in its receptivity, requiring what amounts to overwhelming redundancy to appraise a thing as present, extant fact, and yet ultrasensitively responsive in putting together the relations and implications of a premise that might or might not fit present facts. That differential receptivity goes with the resilience of the knowledge process. Our minds, if healthy, want to keep reworking ideation that does not fit the evidence of the senses. Our century's efforts at planned personality change—from political brainwashing to commercial manipulation to reshaping the outlook of a mental patient or criminal—would not have been such a grand flop had conditioning techniques worked on the unconscious as they do on the conscious mind. And the terrifying stuff in the Bible would produce intense, acute religious "hysteria" or "mania," rather than the chronic, relatively low-grade problems of fear, anxiety, depression and socially destructive opinions we find.

We have painted a very drastic picture of the condition of mind prescribed for the believer. His conscious thoughts are to be obsessed with God and God's thoughts as expressed in the Bible, and all others are to be avoided, lest they get out of hand and involve the thinker in a death-dealing false gospel. The feeling area of the believer's life is to be the amorphous, numb peacefulness of Christian love′. What we have seen of it so far leaves us bewildered, unable to understand how anyone could keep up such a discipline, or why anyone would want to, except for that old superstition about avoiding hellfire. Even after we have gotten wise to the practice of "testifying" about the benefits of being in the fold not because the "witness" is convinced they are true, but as an exercise to convince himself, the convincingness depending on the acting ability of the "witness," we sense much is still missing from our understanding, and we have not gotten far past the surface.

The core of the Bible-authentic, Christian experience is *dissociation.* The supposed renewal of the mind so that it thinks only godly thoughts, the fatuous peace and tepid joy of the person exhibiting euphoric calm, the apparent absence of friction with other people, these are all side-effects of a dissociated state of mind. To penetrate it, we must once more remind ourselves that the beginnings of estrangement of the conscious attitude from the rest of the personality lie neither in the specific problem areas of sexuality and aggression (as Freud taught) nor in maintenance of self-esteem (as a generation of post-Freudian clinicians tacitly assumed but could not say in so many words because it would have sounded hollow, even to them). Such ideas kept psychologists from understanding religion in the past, and could confuse us still, if we remained bound to them. In a sense, each instance where impressions are differentiated, segregated, some aspects ignored so that others may be subjected to focussed thought, and applied to a particular purpose at a particular time, is a kind of dissociation. Without dissociation, the ego-personality would have no boundaries, and the result would be an extreme and totally disabling psychosis.[249] The pejorative, diagnostic jargon sense wherein we will tend to use the term contemplates mind-games. What is a mind-game of the first kind, if not hypertrophied, malignant dissociation? What is a mind-game of the second kind, if not the dispossession of the evidence of one's own faculties by the commands of others, or peer-group pressure, as the touchstone of dissociation? "Relatedness" is healthily flexible and responsive dissociation. A mind-game is marked by disordered dissociation; i.e., either too rigid or too pliant (or both at the same time) relative to what it ought to be, to its operating specifications, so to speak.

The notions of "sin" and "faith," both by our reckoning and conventionally, are essentials of Christianity. In contrast to other topics that occupy much communal devotional time, like the substitutionary atonement, the seeming mystery of Christian love′, and the seeming profundity of Christian truth′, having less to them than first meets the eye, we shall find underlying the misleading biblical and theological conceptions of sin and faith, meaty psychological stuff, with dissociation at its root. There is no assuasive way to go about uncovering it. It has to be *dys-angelion;* i.e. "bad news" for those with heavy libidinal investments in churchly enterprises.

---

249. That is, schizophrenia. See p. 97, footnote 61.

What of the notion of sin? One passage undertakes a biblical definition of sin, and reflects all the main concerns the believer understands to pertain to it:

> Whosoever committeth sin transgresseth also the law: for sin is the transgression of the law. And ye know that he [Christ] was manifested to take away our sins; and in him is no sin. Whosoever abideth in him sinneth not: whosoever sinneth hath not seen him, neither known him. Little children, let no man deceive you: he that doeth righteousness is righteous. . . . He that committeth sin is of the devil; for the devil sinneth from the beginning. . . .[250]

The explicit definition agrees with the great majority of mentionings of "sin" and "sins" in the Old Testament, contemplating "sins" as episodes of disobedience to scriptural rules, such as formerly could be made good by sacrifices and atonements. Then there is an abrupt shift, to the notion of sin unconnected with individual behavior, poignantly portrayed in Genesis 2 and 3, then let lie dormant until Paul would, at last, take it up. "Sin" in that sense, is original sin, and individual sins somehow only add to a sinful condition that was already total from the outset. Nowhere does the Bible indicate that the deportment of his saints will be perfect, and the obvious fact of their imperfection is accommodated by fragmenting them into redeemed and unredeemed parts, in Christian life′. While the saint is permanently at pains to clean up his act more and more, we are put on notice that something other than a cleaned-up act is required, but whatever that is will be kept mysterious, or communicated by indirection.

Genesis 3 lets drop some clues as to the character of the original sin, a sin so great that it is imputed to all those born of nonvirgins until the end of time. In the Garden of Eden, God has planted two remarkable fruit trees, the Tree of Life, and the Tree of Knowledge of Good and Evil. Before Eve is created, God commands Adam not to eat the fruit of the latter tree, or else he will die that day. Since Adam did not physically die the day he ate the fruit, we must assume that God already had death′ in mind. Having no basis in experience for knowing what physical death is all about, Adam could not have been misled by it anyhow. Eve comes along, and the serpent tells her—entirely truthfully—that she will not die (at least, not physically) if she eats it, and that she will become like God, that she will gain an exciting prerogative heretofore limited to God (and the serpent): knowing good and evil. She, herself, indicates knowing she is commanded not to eat the fruit of the tree in the middle of the garden. Her memory seems a bit vague, as she does not know the name of the tree, and has embellished the commandment, having it that merely touching the fruit will bring dreaded death—whatever that is.

Eve takes the forbidden fruit, eats it, and instigates poor Adam to do the same. Their eyes, figuratively speaking, are opened. They know good from evil, and become self-conscious about their nakedness. God rebukes Eve, and pronounces the curses under which she and all subsequent females will labor. Then he rebukes Adam, and pronounces the curses under which he and all subsequent

250. I John 3:4-8.

males will labor. God then excludes them from the Garden of Eden, closing off access to the other remarkable tree, by eating the fruit of which they might defeat his purpose. Death has become a reality. No longer are all the plants and animals to be benign. There will now be carnivores, thorns and thistles. Post-ubescent sexuality has arrived. The transition from childish idyll to adult care, and from naïveté to critical self-consciousness is expressed with incomparable artistry in the allegory.

Each time the great fathers of the church take this story apart and put it back together again, they have more pieces left over afterwards than with other Bible stories. For them, what was wrong with the First Parents' behavior was simply their failure to obey God. Since these events occurred before the law was laid down, it is thought to make no difference that the supposed prototype of all wrongdoing violates none of the Ten Commandments, nor the Golden Rule. The notion that usurping a prerogative of God, in an activity such as judging unbelievers, or judging a fellow believer in an area where oneself is deficient, offers a limited opportunity to develop that line of thinking. If the church fathers want to be Victorian about it, they can say that sexuality is part of the curse, that sexuality is somehow central to transgressing against God. But the First Parents apparently were more interested in hiding their nakedness from God, than from each other or the animals. There is no indication that having sex as married people was unknown before the fall, or a consequence of the newly acquired knowledge. The plain implication that the essence of transgression against God is in desire for knowledge, in self-awareness, in the development of a sensible, conscious standpoint toward what lies deeper and hidden within gets lost. The First Parents' interest in covering up their genitals can just as well pertain to the propensity of genitals to remind one that there is powerful responsiveness in one's being, outside the boundaries and control of consciousness. And, moreover, "sin" is never mentioned in Genesis accounts of Adam and Eve.

A few more indications of the nature of "sin" come out in the first eleven chapters of Genesis, before the Bible gets down to the Jewish business of cataloging diverse sins, and setting up the halakic structure that is later to define the "sin" problem and prescribe an obsessive-compulsive ritual solution for it. The first mention of "sin" involves the first member of God's nonelect, Cain. For no apparent reason, God rejects his offering, then bawls him out for getting angry and failing to keep a stiff upper lip.[251] Noah gathers together a tiny, chosen group of people and animals, to be concentrated in a very small place of safety, while a deluge sweeps the rest into oblivion. The last thing before Genesis departs from the realm of the purely mythic and becomes a chronicle is the Tower of Babel. Besides containing what may have been the inspiration for the New Testament authors to invent logocide, the story apparently indicates that the march of human science and technology, and the aspiration for mankind to cooperate as a single global community, usurp God's prerogatives. The enlarge-

---

251. Gen. 4:7.

ment of man's range of outlook from an architectural tower and the unity of man in one community threaten God, who is obliged to take defensive measures.

Actually, most of what is in the first eleven chapters of Genesis can be fruitfully understood as an allegory of human coming to consciousness.[252] The division of the primordial chaos into an upper and lower part by a firmament is followed by the segregation of an area of dry land, the creation of an innocent and naïve male, the creation from out of him an *anima* figure to whom the desiderata of his strivings occur before they occur to him, and the appearance of a shadow figure, Cain, who remains under God's curse, and yet, essential to all later developments as grandfather to Enoch and great-grandfather to Noah. Next, consciousness gets constricted to Noah's claustrophobic little menage, while all the rest of human and animal imagoes are swept into unconsciousness. The ego-personality rides on the immense, complex-laden sea of unconsciousness, like a boat rides on troubled water. And after that is over, the unity and concentration of human energies symbolized by Noah's descendants, with their universal language and nationality, is short-lived. They are fragmented into divers language groups, i.e., complexes.

There is no way that people of that day could explicate, articulately discuss or mange the insight of the first eleven chapters of Genesis. Indeed, we in our time can barely do it. The manifest understanding of "sin" rapidly degenerated into the facile notion of disobedience to rules lain down by the One with inherent authority to make rules. Outward obedience was the essential thing for the Old Testament believers, and they had little to say—of systematic or general import, nothing to say—about the inner condition corresponding to it. But the die was cast, pitting God against individual self-consciousness and self-realization.

Of what, then, does the sin principle really consist? To lack self-consciousness, as before the fall, was to be pure and pleasing to God, but gaining it or at least the proclivity toward it made one corrupt and hardened in a posture of rebellion against him. Only the painful and socially destructive implications of individualistic self-consciousness are touted: it can lead only to personal depravity and running after barbaric, stupid, idolatrous religions. One must never give oneself permission to apply all the force of one's own personality to some heroic, principled, individualistic purpose. Having one's energies unified and focussed for such a purpose is the essence of what the bible abhors. One is to

---

252. Jung frequently brought up Genesis and other similar and related creation myths as recapitulations of coming to consciousness, on a phylogenetic as well as an ontogenic level. The following is representative:

"Not for nothing did the Bible story place the unbroken harmony of plant, animal, man, and God, symbolized as Paradise, at the very beginning of all psychic development, and declare that the first dawning of consciousness—'Ye shall be as gods, knowing good and evil'—was a fatal sin. To the naïve mind it must indeed seem a sin to shatter the divine unity of consciousness that ruled the primal night. . . .

"And yet the attainment of consciousness was the most precious fruit of the tree of knowledge, the magical weapon which gave man victory over the earth, and which we hope will give him a still greater victory over himself." "The Meaning of Psychology for Modern Man," in *Civilization in Transition,* trans. R. F. C. Hull (New York: Pantheon Books, 1964), pp. 139-40 (pars. 288, 289).

"believe" that nothing of oneself worth getting in touch with lies hidden deep within. In Jungian terms, the shadow is supposedly all there is to the unconscious, and there is nothing positive to do but bring the shadow in check.

Psychological integration, being in touch with the inner depths, and able practically to make use of the energies usually locked up in complexes are of the essence of sin. That is what lies behind the idea that original sin makes one totally sinful, leaving nothing for sinful acts quantitatively to add, no significance for them to assume, except as outward emanations of the abhorrent inner condition, frosting on the poison cake. Immorality or unethicalness of behavior or thought is not even a prerequisite for sin, not even of its essence. The facially apparent opposite premise is the biggest distracting irrelevancy in the whole business. And to throw us off even more, great emphasis is placed on Christ being without sin,[253] despite his high degree of self-awareness and inner-directedness. The gravamen of sin, both in our perspective and conventionally, is appropriating God's prerogative when one is not God. God cannot "sin" for the same reason he cannot lie′.

Never, after the Garden of Eden, does the Bible explicitly associate "sin" with salutary manifestations of individualistic self-awareness. The Old Testament is full of "sinful" heroes in this respect, who chafe at the halakic constraints. For the Jews, individual shortcomings became the whole problem, and overcoming or compensating for them, the remedy. In the New Testament, individual shortcomings are reduced to the occasion for putting up a smokescreen, and the wide array of stratagems directed primarily against integrated self-awareness, and only indirectly and obliquely against individual rule infractions, are camouflaged with unsurpassed care and artfulness.

While we shall not be able to establish conclusively from the New Testament's express language that a concept of "sin" divorced from ethics or morals is being promulgated, much less the particular one we propose, we shall establish that such a concept fits and makes better sense of the biblical language than any conventional theological conception, or any attempt to save something ethical or moral for the term to mean. Consider Paul's interpretation of the events in Eden:

> Therefore as by one man sin entered into the world, and death by sin, and thus death spread to all men, because all sinned—(For until the law sin was in the world, but sin is not imputed when there is no law. Nevertheless death reigned from Adam to Moses, even over those who had not sinned according to the likeness of the transgression of Adam, who is a type of Him who was to come. But the free gift is not like the offense. For if by the one man's offense many died, much more the grace of God and the gift by the grace of the one Man, Jesus Christ, have abounded to many. . . .)[254]

---

253. 2 Cor. 5:21; 1 Pet. 2:24 and 1 John 3:5.
254. Rom. 5:12-15. *New King James Bible.*

And on it goes for six more verses, contrasting *one* and *many,* obliquely intimating a separate, distinctive mystery corresponding to each.

Even though Eve was the first to do what would bring about the fall, Paul puts all the blame and all the spiritual significance on Adam. Paul's crass sexism and uncharacteristic lapse in scholarship are revealing. While he did require their passivity and subjection in the family and church situations, even he never taught that women were so spiritually inferior that their sins did not count, or were to be imputed to their husbands or fathers, or some such thing. By injecting a discrepancy so obvious to anyone who knows his Bible well, was Paul setting up a credulity test, like the parable of the unjust judge? Would it have spoiled the symmetry of his big idea about Christ as the second Adam,[255] to let Eve remain the conduit whereby sin came into the world? Paul's viewpoint was intensely and onesidedly masculine. He relegated femininity to deep unconsciousness. His observations about actual women were pedestrian and practical, tending toward the trivial. There was no room in his imagining for a female personification of wisdom or compassion, or a sacred virgin. No wonder the Holy Spirit is masculine.[256] When femininity did find its way into his spiritual teaching, it was formless and alchemical, e.g., the invisible church as Christ's bride. He was less in touch than other men with the normal projected images and his own sexuality. Hence, his tendency to drastic bifurcations—dissociations—of God's kingdom and Satan's, sin and salvation, flesh and spirit, "law" and "grace," etc.

The counterposition of *one* and *many* is a good example of the Bible's practice of employing paradoxes and latent contradictions in strategic places where those drastic bifurcations need camouflaging, lest a more plain expression of the underlying idea expose how far-fetched it is and give the game away. We encountered it in Jesus' disparaging this-worldly problems in his parables, by making paradoxes of the number concepts occurring in them, in the complete lack of biblical information indicating more than a finite and relatively minor sacrifice to the atonement, and in the confusion of unity with triunity, of wholeness with fragmentation, in the personality of God. Logocide, where truth is untruth, life, death and wisdom, foolishness, depending on the usage, complements this stratagem.[257] The sense wherein sin exists apart from rule violation (Paul tells us plainly that sin somehow existed before there was any law to transgress against) is the most crucial embedded concept masked by the paradoxes and latent contradictions.

---

255. I Cor. 15:44-49.

256. While the masculinity of the Holy Spirit is implicit in Paul's teaching, it may just as well have been an existing feature he found agreeable, as an innovation of his. The Holy Spirit's gender is explicitly stated in John 14:16-17.

257. One of the official slogans of Oceania, in *1984,* is "two and two make five." Just as the political apostasy of Winston and Julia is discovered, they cling to the secret, subversive doctrine, "two plus two make four." I have a fantasy of a mini-Reformation church service where the hymn whose chorus ends, "every knee shall bow, every tongue confess, that Jesus Christ is Lord," adapted from Rom. 14:11, is being sung. But instead, the words are sung, "every knee shall bow, every tongue confess, that two and two make five!"

How do sins, with their inevitable tendency to recur, relate to the condition of sin, with its once-and-for-all remedy? Consider the following passages, purporting to inform the believer as to their relation:

> If ye fulfil the royal law according to the scripture, Thou shalt love thy neighbour as thyself, ye do well: But if ye have respect to persons, ye commit sin, and are convinced of [i.e., shown up as to] the law as transgressors. For whosoever shall keep the whole law, and yet offend in one *point,* he is guilty of all. For he that said, Do not commit adultery, said also, Do not kill. Now if thou commit no adultery, yet if thou kill, thou art become a transgressor of the law. So speak ye, and so do, as they that shall be judged by the law of liberty. For he shall have judgment without mercy, that hath shewed no mercy; and mercy rejoiceth against judgment.[258]

> For there is no respect of persons with God. For as many as have sinned without law shall also perish without law: and as many as have sinned in the law shall be judged by the law; (For not the hearers of the law *are* just before God, but the doers of the law shall be justified. . . .)[259]

> If we say that we have no sin, we deceive ourselves, and the truth is not in us. If we confess our sins, he is faithful and just to forgive us *our* sins, and to cleanse us from all unrighteousness. If we say that we have not sinned, we make him [God] a liar, and his word is not in us. My little children, these things write I [John] unto you, that ye sin not. And if any man sin, we have an advocate with the Father. . . .[260]

> Whosoever is born of God doth not commit sin; for his seed remaineth in him: and he cannot sin, because he is born of God.[261]

So, there is a kind of "sin" that the born-again believer does not and cannot commit any more, and another that he not only can but inevitably will commit. These disparate senses of "sin" correspond to the "one" and the "many," respectively. "Sin," in the latter sense, clearly contemplates disobedience to so much of the law as has not been revoked in the New Testament, i.e., by setting aside Jewish ceremonies as completed or fulfilled, or by abdicating civic functions to the secular state. No longer being under the law does not mean it need not be obeyed. When qualities like "just," "justified," "righteous" and "merciful" are attributed to the believer, nothing is really added, because no criterion of any of these except, tautologically, being a believer, is ever given. Indeed, "sin" boils down to being an unbeliever. By definition, "sin" is the quality that the believer lacks and the unbeliever has. As to the character of this quality, the Bible is silent.

Having exhausted the biblical information about "sin" in the former sense,

---

258. James 2:8-13.
259. Rom. 2:11-13.
260. I John 1:8-2:1.
261. I John 3:9

we turn to the proposed remedy for it. In our perspective, and in the conventional one to the extent it interests itself with individual conduct, the proposed remedy for "sin" is *faith.* Since "sin" is the condition that faith is designed to counteract, we wlll be able to make powerful inferences as to the unstated nature of "sin" by analyzing faith. The Bible contains superabundant, albeit camouflaged information as to the psychological nature of faith, although its explicit statements on the topic are sparse, self-serving and misleading. Practically everything that devout theologians traditionally have puzzled over in the Bible pertains to it, and will become transparent and plain of purpose, to our depth-psychological analysis. Looking back, we can discern how, symptomatically, conventional theologians have always tended to borrow more from outside their "revealed" information to formulate a doctrine of faith than for any other purpose.[262] We shall find that "faith" is the touchstone of the Bible's psycho-

---

262. Tillich's rendition of "faith" (*op. cit.,* see p. 37 ff.) actually ends up calling the same thing "faith" that we (and the orthodox theologian, also) would call "sin." The whole notion that man's paramount problem is "sin," and the remedy, salvation, is conveniently forgotten.

Machen's *What Is Faith?* (*op. cit.,* see p. 30) is probably the only conservative Christian elaboration of "faith" with enough to it, possibly to seem credible to an intelligent unbeliever. Written largely in response to the "historical Jesus" theologians, who stressed Jesus as teacher and model, sidestepping his teachings as to who he, himself was, as well as the implications of sin and the exclusive salvation remedy for it, Machen depicted faith as having two indispensable components: (1) trust and reverence for Jesus, and through him, the other persons in the Godhead, and (2) subscription to the intellectual content, i.e., the doctrine of the Bible. Machen was quick to point out the shortcomings of the secular psychology and philosophy of his day, particularly logical positivism and Dewey's kind of pragmatism. The malaise in these in the intervening years powerfully vindicates Machen's views in this respect. Machen attributed the bad repute orthodox Christianity had come into, to faulty biblical scholarship. "The depreciation of the intellect, with the exaltation in the place of it of the feelings or of the will, is, we think, a basic fact in modern life, which is rapidly leading to a condition in which men neither know anything nor care anything about the doctrinal content of the Christian religion, and in which there is in general a lamentable intellectual decline." Ibid., p. 23. Machen's main attractive idea about faith was that by coming to know the sublime personality of God through the Scripture, one could come to trust, revere, be consoled and have one's loneliness relieved thereby. ". . . [T]he Bible is found to be true to the plainest facts of the soul; whereas the modern separation between faith in a person and acceptance of a creed is found to be psychologically false." Ibid., p. 48. "The transcendence of God [i.e., his separateness and distinctness from the cosmos, which he created and upholds by his power]—what the Bible calls the 'holiness' of God—is at the foundation of Christian faith. The Christian trusts God because God has been pleased to reveal himself as one whom it is reasonable to trust; faith in God is based on knowledge." Ibid., p. 65.

This approach responds very sensitively and ingeniously to a major scriptural problem. Conservative Christians generally, like Machen, have had the notion that "relationship with Jesus" is a crucial feature of their religion. But that "relationship" has undergone an evolution. From the beginning of the Bible until the promised land is reached, at least some of God's people have literal dialogues with him. After David, these clearly turn into one-way proclamations from God, delivered under more and more adverse circumstances, and to even unlikelier people, i.e., Paul who had been a sort of Pharisee Yuri Andropov, and Psychedelic John the Divine. What a come-down, for the God who would not let Moses enter the promised land because he had struck the stone, and only let him view it from the mountain top, who would not let David build the Temple because he had shed too much blood, and who delighted in leaving 7,000 in Israel who had not bowed to Baal! Except for the one sensual image of Jesus and an unnamed future believer having a friendly dinner together (Rev. 3:20), the New Testament has precious little to indicate a familiar or mutual relationship between the believer during the church age and Jesus! Alas, when one gets steeped in the Bible, the personality, if any, one gets to know is the volatile and monstrous One who terrified Edwards and whom Luther had hated. The test Machen laid down, and seemed to be "testifying" that the Bible had passed, it fails.

logical objective, and is implicated in every salient thing in the New Testament. Exposing it is tantamount to the destruction of conventional theology!

The conscious idea answering to the term *faith* is drastically different from the psychological condition to which all mentionings of it, taken together, point. The conscious idea boils down to a special kind of belief—we would say, disordered belief. The psychological condition, the unconscious component of the phenomenon, is a special kind of dissociation. The believer is guided into the posture that will make it possible for him to exclude from his conscious mind those thoughts, attitudes, emotions and feelings incompatible with the ones prescribed for the believer. That vacuous, pain-relieving *abaissement de niveau mental* that we have called euphoric calm is ultimately what we shall understand "faith" to contemplate. We shall analyze the conscious component, then the unconscious, and then go systematically through the stratagems whereby the inducement of the dissociated state for which *faith* is a euphemism is effected.

The Bible contains only one meaty statement of what the believer is intellectually to understand as "faith":

> Now faith is the substance [confidence, assurance, lit. undergirding] of things hoped for, the evidence [conviction, lit. showing up] of things not seen. For by it the elders [men of old] obtained a good report [commendation]. Through faith we understand that the worlds [aeons] were framed by the word of God, so that things which are seen were not made of things which do appear [are visible].[263]

So, "faith" is belief in that for which one has no direct evidence, only hearsay evidence, i.e., from the revealed sources.[264] Our world emanates from, and is subordinate to, a source on the other side of the boundary between the natural and the supernatural. The ultimate hope/fear conflict is subtly intimated by the characterization of the realm beyond the boundary as "hoped for." The ultimately subjective nature of "faith" is intimated less subtly.

Will the biblical information allow "faith" to rest on belief other than in a vacuum? Can we get around the implication that "faith" rests on intellectually objectionable belief, by making of "faith" some sort of noble, supersensitive, but still human faculty of intuition? Such a notion has been a cornerstone of "old-time religion" and liberal, "modernist" attempts at a humane and livable rendition of the biblical message. But the clear, biblical language will not allow it.

The most informative of the other fragmentary explicit statements about faith is purposefully embedded in a different topical context:

> . . . [*W*]*e are* always confident, knowing that, whilst we are at home in the body, we are absent from the Lord: (For we walk by faith, not by sight [*eidos*, appearance, percept]:) We are confident, *I say*, and willing rather to be absent from the body, and to be present with the Lord.[265]

263. Heb. 11:1-3.
264. Heb. 1:1-2.
265. 2 Cor. 5:6-8. Note the King James translation of *eidos* as "appearance," in 1 Thess. 5:22, "fashion," in Luke 9:29, and as "form" or "shape," in Luke 3:22 and John 5:37.

Faith is associated with the supernatural dimension, and disassociated from "fleshly," human psychological faculties, that pertain only to life this side of the boundary. The juxtaposition of faith to life after death again implicates the hope/fear conflict. Other fragmentary allusions, declaring faith to be a "mystery,"[266] and a supernatural "gift,"[267] rule out continuity between "faith" and any modern conception of human intuition.

If "faith" is completely detached from even the most subtle and least explicit or apparent bases of nondisordered belief, then close scrutiny of the Bible's handling of "faith" and "belief" should be revealing. To do that, we must first separate out the usage of cognates of *faith,* such as *faithful, loyal, true, keeping the faith,* etc., that denote consistency of character of a person, and lend *faith* much of its sanguine connotation, but typically do not implicate those psychological processes *faith* denotes. (Remember, being the servant of a spirit or spirits is the only kind of human faithfulness the Bible has in view. We lose the biblical truth′, by ascribing anything intrinsically positive to humans in themselves, or by superimposing anachronistically modern or functional psychological ideas on the biblical language.)

The most fundamental of all shifts in biblical agenda, and the most striking indirect indicator of the second kind, is the sudden appearance of concern with "faith" in the New Testament, after the complete absence of such concern, in the pertinent sense, in the Old Testament. It is striking to look at the King James translation, and find that the word *faith* is found only twice in all of the Old Testament![268] Even those usages do not involve *faith* in the epistemological sense that becomes central in the New Testament. The modern translations have taken more opportunities to use the word, with regard to a person's character. By that means, without making the language too awkward, a translator could increase its frequency to twenty or thirty occurrences in the Old Testament. Even that would be dwarfed by the 238 times *faith* occurs in the King James New Testament. Likewise, *doubt* and its cognates appear only three times in the King James Old Testament, never in a context associating doubt with wrongdoing or "sin," while *doubt, unbelief* and their cognates appear 37 times in the New, and always in a context implicating "faith" in the exclusively New Testament sense.[269] And much of what was written to impart "faith" never mentions that word.

The distinguishing features of "faith" in the sense that was novel in the New Testament are not so obvious as the quantitative, word-study data at first lead us to suppose. Right from the Garden of Eden, we find concern expressed about God's children's failure to get it through their heads that God means what he

---

266. I Tim. 3:9.

267. I Cor. 12:9 and Eph. 2:8.

268. Deut. 32:20 and Hab. 2:4. The latter, "the just shall live by his faith," was a battle cry during the Reformation.

269. *Unbelief* never appears in the King James Old Testament. Excluded from these word counts is *doubtless,* which is used occasionally in both the King James Old and New Testaments, always as a synonym for *certainly.*

says, that they are to suffer when they neglect to take him at his word, and if they keep it up flagrantly enough for long enough some foreign aggressor will be empowered by God to bring them under captivity. From Noah, and particularly in the later prophets who become opponents of the Jewish political chiefs, people doubt which purported prophets are actual witnesses to a revelation received from God, and which are phonies, trying to pull their leg. Whether he be obeyed or not, whether or not a particular purported prophet be genuine or self-styled, there arises no widespread doubt that the God of the Bible is real and active in national Israel's history. At least, no such doubt is recorded in any appreciable depth in the Old Testament.

The Old Testament reflects a mentality innocent of Greco-Roman philosophy, innocent of the beginnings of natural science, and unaffected by any form of polytheistic religion sufficiently appealing to turn many heads. However harsh life may have been under the heel of one or another neighboring oppressor nation, God would relent, send his people a prophet, and bring them home again. Despite the captivities, Israel remained a proud nation. But the blandishments of Hellenistic culture and the overwhelming military might of Rome finally crashing down on Israel, brought the Jews profound discouragement, confusion, and a spoliated sense of who they were. For those Jews attracted to the Nazorean party, that naïve, provincial Old Testament innocence (not to be equated with the lively evolution of the Jewish tradition that remained alive and even flourished in the Diaspora) was spoiled.

The difference in mentality of the New Testament from the Old brought about a profound transformation in cosmology. The Old Testament lacked any sharp distinction or fundamental qualitative difference, between the natural and supernatural realms. In it, God was up in the sky, and highly ambulatory. Occasionally, he took someone up to be with him in bodily form, like Enoch, Elijah or Moses. There was a murky place below the earth, and people had been known to descend into it alive, as well. What plan there was to this arrangement, what happened to a person after death, what the postdeath implications of one's actions were, and all related questions were passed over lightly and left ambiguous. This life, one's nation and one's posterity were "where the action is." Nobody had taught those people to ask the critical questions that it is our second nature, due to our polyglot background, to ask.

With Hellenistic culture came alternative ideas about the extramundane. Most conspicuous (and also tacitly relevant to a modern's approach to Christianity) was Platonism, with its ideal realm of autonomous ideas and forms, to which what is best in the natural world is like shadows on the wall of a darkened cave, or as fuzzy carbon copies are to an original impression. Informed by the contrasting perspective of Hellenistic culture and enveloped in a political and social situation so oppressive that one's own integrity made something in one's inner being resist appraising it as real, and desperately desire for something else to supersede it and be real instead, the mind could be prepared for a viewpoint entailing spectacular clash and discord between incommensurable worlds or realms. The real versus the ideal, cosmopolitan Hellenism versus aloof, dogmatic Judaism, and the military might of Rome versus Zealotry each provided an example for a thought-principle involving incommensurable realms hostile to one another, separated by a boundary that it is inherently hurtful to breach, so that one's object becomes, perforce, keeping it unbreached. The notions of God's realm differing drastically from the earthly realm, where Satan had obviously gotten the upper hand, a world to come in stark contrast to the present, looking forward to total segregation of God's people from all the others, who are to wait in line for their eternal comeuppance, the existence of two mutually exclusive kinds of psychological life separate and apart from biological life—all express the terrible alienation and personality fragmentation of the individual caught up in the political and military madness attending the fall of Jerusalem and the destruction of the second Temple, A.D. 70.

Such events, after all, evoked ambivalence about God himself: Did the turning of the tide so forcefully and finally against national Israel indicate an extraordinary outpouring of his wrath, or his weakness, infirmity, inability to influence events? If he had gone away, beyond the boundary into another dimension, how would one's prayers reach him anymore? How would one propitiate him if he were off in a dimension where one's sacrifices, offerings and ritual purity had no more meaning? How would one come to terms with the heightened sense of wrongness and cursedness such ominous signs of his displeasure evoked? When God had last spoken, four hundred or so years earlier, had he not closed his Old Testament with the words, ". . . lest I come and smite the earth with a curse"? But if the calamity occurred because of God's powerlessness or his aloofness, then what was the point of all that Jewish tradition and history in back of one? The foreign incursion had brought with it the very modes of thought and expression, in whose terms all these poignant, bipolar adversities could be shared. And the intensity and poignance of it all would stimulate some Jews to express it in a way that would psychologically grip and arrest people entirely removed from and ignorant of the circumstances that had shaped and called into being the product of its expression. But for those to whose background was added the restoration of perspective and regaining of balance attained by Judaism in the Diaspora after the catastrophe, the bulk of the arresting and gripping to arise from that product would not be psychological.

The main bipolar adversity, to which all the others point, is that between the conscious mind and the unconscious. That is at the core of the unconscious component and true psychological meaning of *faith,* and the ultimate meaning of all New Testament allegory. When the separation of the conscious attitude from the unconscious is best maintained, one is not to have insight that those of one's projections that pertain to the group's shared fiction are projections. If one ceases to perceive them as literally real, if one dares to withdraw them, one is on the slippery slope to upsetting one's carefully managed self-deceptions, to a breaching of the boundary that will let in an unsettling invasion of what one has been keeping out of consciousness, and on one's way to a wrenching, and possibly survival-threatening alienation from those to whom one's relation is mainly based on the shared fiction. So, whenever the topic of "faith" is explicitly discussed, it will have to be couched in terms of, and articulately thought about in no other terms than, literal belief.

Only when the *Zeitgeist* has progressed so far that intellectual objections to literal belief are known and unbelief in conventional supernaturalistic premises has become thinkable can "faith" or belief become problematical, and unbelief, as opposed to mere insubordination, a temptation. Hence, the lack of occasion for the King James translators to employ the word *faith* in their rendition of the Old Testament. The abundant use of that word in their New Testament ultimately worked to camouflage the telling overinsistence on literal belief, in much the same way that their usage of *grace* worked to camouflage the lack of an articulable difference of *grace,* from *favor, preference,* or *respect of persons.* The King James translators must tacitly have sensed that "faith" was a novel, New Testament phenomenon, to use it so as to make of it a term of art, comtemplating more than mere belief. They usually used the English word *faith* (from the same Latin root as *fidelity*) to render the prevalent Greek word for belief, *pistis,* a noun. Where the cognate verb *pisteuo* occurs, the King James translators usually employed *belief* or its cognate. The related usages partaking of character attribution are typically adjectives or adverbs. A few King James near-synonyms, such as *trust* and *obedience,* straddle the categories. The advent of *faith* as a special term served the purposes of Device 1 as the underlying Greek could never have, and conveniently insulates the modern prospective believer from confrontation too soon with a ploy so obvious as to give the game away.

The New Testament authors' indirectly indicative self-consciousness about their incessant harping on a nontraditional issue crucial for their purposes, like we encountered before in the early church's vehemence against the skeptical Gnostics, in extravagant disproportion to those sects' actual success or influence, is also plain on the surface of the main biblical pronouncements about faith, earlier quoted. In the more informative of those,[270] at the same time while grounding "faith" in the fleshly, human psychological faculties is being ruled out, and the specification of "faith" to intend another life after physical death, and the hope/fear conflict is being unequivocally declared, great store gets set on the claim that "faith" is the paramount virtue of the heroes of the Pentateuch. Instead of revealing anything more to satisfy our curiosity about "faith," the passage goes on:

> By faith Abel offered unto God a more excellent sacrifice than Cain, by which he obtained witness that he was righteous, God testifying of his gifts: and by it he being dead yet speaketh. By faith Enoch was translated that he should not see death; and was not found, because God had translated him: for before his translation he had his testimony, that he pleased God. But without faith *it is* impossible to please *him:* for he that cometh to God must believe that he is, and *that* he is a

270. See p. 269, footnote 263.

> rewarder of them that diligently seek him. By faith Noah, being warned of God of things not seen as yet, moved with fear. . . .[271]

And on it goes for 34 more verses, reconstituting the actions of Abraham, Issac, Jacob, Sarah, Joseph, Moses and Rahab, the harlot.

Actually, the only one of those persons who exhibited anything at all resembling New Testament "faith" was Rahab, also the only one who came into the body of believers in a manner resembling New Testament conversion. All the rest of them had animated dialogues with God, leaving them no cause to doubt that "he is." With none of them had there been any mention of a future unearthly life. The notion of God as rewarder strikes a rather sour note regarding Moses, since entry into the promised land was the reward contemplated, and he was denied it for the misdemeanor of striking the water stone at Meribah, in violation of no particular instruction the Bible records. The first instance in the list, the comparison of Cain and Abel, will prove to be the only one affording a nonmisleading clue to the nature of "faith." Cain's failure to keep a stiff upper lip bears some relation to the absence of "faith" and the presence of "sin." This passage, and the one defining "sin," play so fast and loose with the underlying Pentateuchal accounts, as to alert us to consider the possibility that they are long postapostolic in origin, for the consumption of a predominantly Gentile audience. There is little possibility that knowledgeable Nazoreans would have stood for such mangling of their beloved Jewish history!

The excessive protesting about the essentialness of literal belief to New Testament Chrsitianity takes a different form in this unique fragment:

> Now if Christ be preached that he rose from the dead, how say some among you that there is no resurrection of the dead? . . . And if Christ be not risen, then *is* our preaching in vain, and your faith *is* also vain. Yea, and we are found false witnesses of God; because we have testified of God that he raised up Christ: whom he raised not up, if so be that the dead rise not. . . . if Christ be not raised . . . ye are yet in your sins. Then they also which are fallen asleep in Christ are perished. If in this life only we have hope in Christ, we are of all men most miserable.[272]

No doubt, Paul would have had occasion to polemicize against Gnosticism,[273] and that, in itself, is not a signal of anything amiss. But why would the companions of people who had directly experienced the miraculous events connected with Jesus—and must have told others much more about them than is recorded in the Bible, including Paul himself, who "testified" to having been prostrated by the miraculous events that made him a believer—have found the proposition that the sacred events were unhistoric, all that appealing or worthy

271. Heb. 11:4-6.
272. 1 Cor. 15:12, 14, 15, 17-19.
273. See also 1 Cor. 2:4-8. Yet see how admiration for Gnostic ways (i.e., the hidden wisdom) peeks through in Col. 2:2-4 and Rev. 2:17. Could the creators of these passages have been closet Gnostics who publicly did the mind-control number to keep the proles in line?

of discussion? Is that not much more a problem for people trying to come to terms with those events after the direct witnesses have died, and the evidential trail is cold? The passage can fairly be paraphrased as saying about belief, "If it becomes discredited—and indeed the threat to it is great enough—then your world collapses." Whenever I have known a believer to begin to be able to entertain such an idea, he would immediately hedge his position with the claim that being a Christian could still be of benefit, because it afforded a better way of life than could be found in the surrounding secular world. But the passage expressly eliminates that possibility. Whoever fashioned the passage must have been far too self-insightful to be under mind-control himself, and, I think, must have been motivated much more by considerations of personal safety, comfort and social standing gained from manipulating others than is reported of Paul. (This plain display of a negative outcome of being a believer partakes of Device 4, and also exemplifies what we shall soon come to know as "reverse suggestion.") The passage appears to be the work of a later period's cooler, more expedient manipulator. The author of the statement that happens to paraphrase it, by the way, is Sigmund Freud.[274]

The next most significant of the explicit "faith" fragments point toward defining "faith" in terms of its biblical opposites:

> . . . Verily I [Jesus] say unto you, If ye have faith, and doubt not, ye shall not only do this *which is done* to the fig tree [finding no fruit on it to satisfy his hunger, only leaves, Jesus curses it and causes it to wither], but also if ye shall say unto this mountain, Be thou removed, and be thou cast into the sea; it shall be done.[275]
>
> . . . [N]o man is justified by the law in the sight of God, *it is* evident: for, The just shall live by faith. And the law is not of faith: but, The man that doeth them shall live in them. . . . before faith came, we were kept under the law, shut up unto the faith which should afterwards be revealed. Wherefore the law was our schoolmaster *to bring us* unto Christ, that we might be justified by faith. But after that faith is come, we are no longer under a schoolmaster. For ye are all the children of God by faith in Christ Jesus.[276]
>
> Hast thou faith? have *it* to thyself before God. Happy *is* he that condemneth not himself in that thing which he alloweth. And he that doubteth *is* damned if he eat [the foods forbidden by Halakah], because *he eateth* not of faith: for whatsoever *is* not of faith is sin.[277]

So, on the one occasion where Jesus indulged in a fit of nasty pique—also the occasion most instrumental in committing Christianity to special enmity toward unconverted Jews, the fig tree supposititiously symbolizing national

274. *The Future of an Illusion,* p. 54.
275. Matt. 21:21.
276. Gal. 3:11-12, 23-26.
277. Rom. 14:22-23.

Israel—absence of (conscious) doubt was the way to accomplish a phenomenal result of some kind. Regardless whether or not the secular philosophical concern with literal belief occurred to the thoroughly unhellenized Jesus, or was put in his mouth retroactively, the exhortation to believe is right up front. Then Paul shifts the gears, aligns "faith" with salvation, and makes it, instead, the theological opposite of sin. That is to be the only express statement for us to find of the opposing, problem/solution relationship of "sin" to "faith," albeit, corroborated by a host of implicit and camouflaged clues. Note how well the rule we earlier laid down holds up: a basic shift from efficacy of obedience to rules to efficacy of some other principle, entirely different and undefined, but assuming nevertheless obedience to a greatly truncated and simplified set of rules, is always contemplated. The biblical purpose of obscuring the discontinuity of the two senses of "faith" is given away by the psychologically understandable but illogical disconnection of "faith" and the law. It takes the form of an anti-apologetic triad, composed entirely of sayings of Paul:

> . . . [W]hatsoever is not of faith is sin.[278]
>
> And the law is not of faith. . . .[279]
>
> Is the law sin? God forbid. Nay. . . .[280]

This unique instance, where the syllogistic relations of the inconsistent assertions are not even obscured by convolutions of phrase, brings out the fine craftsmanship of the mind-control system. To other items contrived to keep the conscious mind occupied, diverted and off the trail of the genuinely relevant essentials is added another, couched in terms of itself, and acquiring an added air of mystery and portentousness through the confusing mixing of levels. Elsewhere, the believer has been given to attempt to understand how it is that he can invest one hundred percent of his psychic energy in the God-complex and still have more for the mandated earthbound recipients of Christian love′ and how it is that he can give all his loyalty to God and still be heartily and unswervingly loyal to ungodly earthly masters. What is it that is so good about God's choosing some for eternal bliss while others intrinsically no worse, he has created lacking any resource to avoid dispatching themselves to Hell? How is it that not knowing whether one is predestined to eternal bliss or not, until one has persevered to the end (the law written on the unsaved person's heart being able to counterfeit the saved person's Spirit-aided desire to obey God, and the hard-hearted insouciance of the unsaved person being able to mimic the sublime joy and peace of the believer, leaving no biblically approved subjective indicant

278. Rom. 14:23.
279. Gal. 3:12.
280. Rom. 7:7. The import of *law, nomos,* is further obscured by enigmatic usages besides the general one. Cf., Rom. 7:22 ("law of God"); Rom. 3:27 ("law of faith"); Rom. 9:31 ("law of righteousness"); Rom. 7:23 and 25 ("law of sin").

of salvation) is encouraging and reassuring? Now, added to all those, the believer is to meditate on the puzzle of how it is that it is good to believe that for which the psychological raw materials of nondisordered, intellectually honest belief are entirely absent (that belief itself, in turn, part of the called-for field of belief), and how it is that the catalogue of particular sins is linked to the other, general, faith-remediable species of sin, when the basis for any such link is not evident, and has been studiously omitted from the sourcebook of truth′. Just as divers "sins" and general, faith-remediable "sin" apparently move in different dimensions, cannot interact with one-another, and become aligned only by the activity of God, who is master of both dimensions, so does the Spirit-aided-belief notion of "faith," upon which the conscious attitude is to remain fixated, move in a different dimension than the hidden principle of "faith" we are exposing. Whatever intimation the believer may have of his "faith" being bound up in activities quite unlike his articulable notions about "faith" is chalked up to the flesh′, against which the believer is to wage continual Christian warfare′. The two dimensions, separated by their dense boundary, correspond, among other things, to consciousness and unconsciousness. That correspondence, the mind-control system does not seek to fragment, detach, or dissociate!

The common denominator of all the explicit biblical statements, i.e., ones capable of being part of a theological doctrine, is lack of voluntary control. Without the Spirit, one does not believe the unbelieveable, one does not receive intimations from across the impenetrable boundary, and one has no remedy for "sin," the wages of which is, curiously, death′ for the sinner, despite his having never been alive′, in the sense contemplated by that death′.[281] Yet, all of the New Testament occurrences of "faith" and nearly all of "belief" present these as somehow laudable. These blend imperceptably into outright exhortations to believe or have "faith." Such exhortations pervade the New Testament. We encountered the same exhortations earlier, and noted how they implied the existence of some limited range for the working of free will. In the same way that the exhortations to "faith" and "belief" set themselves over against the express biblical statements about "faith," so do they set themselves over against all the biblical statements indicating the fortunes of people to be predestined, foreknown and spiritually animated.

Why exhort people to do something, if their doing it makes no essential difference? We touched fleetingly on the answer: the things the believer is to do are cleverly arranged so that the connection between them and the subjective effects experienced goes unrecognized, and the believer thinks something wondrous and supernatural is taking place. As our analysis moves toward the periphery of the conscious aspect of "faith" toward those features whereof the believer remains entirely unsuspecting, we shall find a few instances where exhortations to do are juxtaposed to the term *faith*. Thereafter, we shall become able to identify a much larger number of exhortations and allegorical models for the believer's mental life, not mentioning "faith," but having the same

281. Rom. 6:23.

intents and purposes as the ones that do. Having declared our purpose to respect the integrity of the Bible text more faithfully than the Bible-believer faced with the task of maintaining his own and others' mental equilibrium can dare to, we shall take up the ones containing explicit reference to "faith" first, and then relate them to others lacking such a reference.

The items effecting dissociation will fall into four categories: (1) *Explicit Devotional Program Instructions.* These are concrete acts the believer is commanded to do. Under this heading, we shall treat the devotional program instructions systematically, many of which we have already encountered piecemeal. (2) *Implicit Devotional Program Instructions.* Often, the believers are exhorted to do an act not meant to be done literally, i.e., in figurative terms. (3) *Direct Suggestions.* Much biblical allegory, particularly that having to do with bodies of water, really serves to illustrate the mental state wanted of the believer. This we can decode in terms of the complex model. (4) *Reverse Suggestions.* Much other biblical allegory, particularly that involving animals, demons and disasters, really serves to illustrate the negative psychological consequences of being a believer, some, manifest and some others, closely impending. The reverse suggestions provide the believer with feedback, that he is "on target."

What we are uncovering could not have remained hidden so long, if any explicit instructions had been associated with "faith." Yet, just as Jesus explained in nonparabolic language how the disciples were to go about unraveling his parables, he is depicted as having carefully let it be known that some unexplained, glorified kind of extracurricular activity was part of "faith," or at least distinguished its possessor from its nonpossessor:

> And the apostles said unto the Lord, Increase our faith. And the Lord said, if ye had faith as a grain of mustard seed, ye might say unto this sycamine [mulberry] tree, Be thou plucked up by the root, and be thou planted in the sea; and it should obey you. But which of you, having a servant [*doulos,* slave] plowing or feeding cattle, will say unto him by and by, when he is come from the field, Go and sit down to meat? And will not rather say unto him, Make ready wherewith I may sup, and gird thyself, and serve me, till I have eaten and drunken; and afterward thou shalt eat and drink? Doth he thank that servant because he did the things that were commanded him? I trow [suppose] not. So likewise ye, when ye shall have done all those things which are commanded you, say, We are unprofitable servants: we have done that which was our duty to do.[282]

How quaint, that the honorable institution of slavery should receive another commendation. The notion of "faith" growing from a tiny, almost nonexistent

282. Luke 17:5-10. Note that the Gospel of Luke, attributed to a Gentile physician to whom Acts is also attributed, conveniently ties in what would otherwise remain theological loose ends, through Jesus' pronounciation of the law as fulfilled in the synagogue at Nazareth, and the nonanswer to the lawyer's question, about the parable of the Good Samaritan. This may reflect the position of the Roman church somewhat later, polemicizing against the Nazoreans, and approving or rehabilitating Paulinism.

nucleus, a mustard seed, suggests a psychological complex in this context, and connects with other occurrences of the same symbol, where the proliferation of the body of believers is in view.[283] Note the repetition of the concrete example of an inanimate object made to go jump in the water, exemplifying the kind of miracle a believer is to be able to perform: rearranging consciousness by making some conscious content disappear into the unconscious. The point is made that something above and beyond following rules is required, the doing of something not stated, only hinted at. The trick is to carry out the hidden agenda without being let in on what it is. The normal, endemic human sense of wrongness is aggravated: one is to deem oneself "unprofitable" for having done right.

Some fragmentary hints as to the unknown quantity in the psychological makeup of the faith-possessor are found in the three persons to whom Jesus commented, after healing their respective physical diseases, that each had been made "whole" (or "well," or "delivered") by his or her "faith." One is a blind beggar, Bartimaeus, whose sight is restored and who becomes Jesus' follower.[284] Since elsewhere we learned, ". . . Jesus said, For judgment I am come into this world, that they which see not might see; and that they which see might be made blind,"[285] we take into account that becoming sighted in one sense means becoming blind in another, just as coming alive′ in one sense means becoming dead′ in another. We have no trouble "seeing" that we are to equate "faith" with receiving spiritual "sight" to perceive the truth′. The second is a Samaritan, one of ten lepers Jesus heals to impress the Temple priests and the only one who turns back to thank him.[286] Apparently not everyone Jesus healed of physical disease also got saved, and the behavior of worship becomes implicated in the unknown quantity. The most detailed account, spread through all three synoptic Gospels, is of a woman who had suffered from chronic menstrual bleeding for twelve years.[287] To get healed, she approaches Jesus from behind and touches the edge of his robe. Jesus, although he does not see who touched him, feels energetically drained or depotentiated, as the vitality (*dunamis*) flows out of him and into her, ostensibly to effect the healing. Since the physical healing so evidently comes from him, here also salvation is quite possibly that which her "faith" has accomplished. The flow of vitality from him to her suggests complexes, albeit the direction and result of this reinvestment of libido is misleadingly the reverse of what actually occurs: a prominent God-complex siphons off libido and impoverishes the ego-personality, rather than bolstering it. Most interesting about her are the implications of this healing. We must not view it in terms of our superior, modern understanding of the medical facts. Chronic menstrual bleeding was ritually unclean, taboo, shame-shrouded stuff for the Jews of that day. A division of the upper part from the lower, anesthesia against troublesome stimulation from regions below the waist, restriction of the range of the conscious attitude, is the "wholeness" or "deliverance" being touted.

283. Matt. 13:31; 17:20; Mark 4:31 and Luke 13:19.
284. Mark 10:46-52 and Luke 18:35-43.
285. John 9:39.
286. Luke 17:11-21.
287. Matt. 9:20-22; Mark 5:25-34 and Luke 8:43-48.

Besides these, all New Testament situations where behavior is lauded as demonstrating "faith" relate back to cognitive belief. Of them, only the centurion commended by Jesus for believing he could miraculously heal just as well at a distance as in his immediate presence, is at all remarkable.[288] The three "faith" cases tell just enough to provide a framework for making related implicit devotional instructions intelligible. From the case of Bartimaeas, we can "see" that some distinct, qualitative, preferably sudden change in perception is wanted. From the case of the elect Samaritan ex-leper, the implication is of requirement for worshipful, ultimately prayerful activity, particularly on the part of the non-Jewish convert. And from the woman with the issue of blood, the desired disappearance or drying up of one's inner self-awareness, so distastefully mischaracterized in the story, is implicated. These indications fall far short of supporting our interpretations conclusively. Related symbolic material will, however, thoroughly and redundantly corroborate them.

What should be noted about the perceptual transformation accompanying "faith" is the ambivalence with which it is handled. The believer is led to assume "faith" to be a sensitization of faculties that earlier would have been too crude and too "fleshly" to receive the new perceptions. Yet, where it really counts, wherever a hint drops that the believer could implement, or make some motion toward implementing, other-directedness toward the Word, and despising and distrusting anything else, are implied. Compare these Scriptures with those explicitly describing "faith":

> . . [F]aith *cometh* by hearing, and hearing by the word of God.[289]

> If thou put the brethren in remembrance of these things, thou shalt be a good minister of Jesus Christ, nourished up in the words of faith and of good doctrine, whereunto thou hast attained.[290]

> O foolish Galatians, who hath bewitched you, that ye should not obey the truth, before whose eyes Jesus Christ hath been evidently [i.e., explicitly] set forth, crucified among you? . . . Received ye the Spirit by the works of the law, or by the hearing of faith? . . . He . . . that ministereth to you the Spirit, and worketh miracles among you, *doeth he it* by the works of the law, or by the hearing of faith?[291]

---

288. Matt. 8:5-13 and Luke 7:1-10. The story of the centurion is so distinctive that the two accounts must surely be of one and the same incident. Yet there is a clear contradiction between the Matthean account, with the centurion approaching in person, and the Lucan one, with the centurion as an apparently lofty personage, who deigns to communicate with Jesus through intercessory third parties only. The Lucan account seems at pains to rationalize such unlikely behavior for a Roman centurion in occupied Palestine. Jesus' gushing praise for the centurion's authoritarian, rulebook mentality and his invidious slap at his own people who, at that point, had neither rejected nor betrayed him, may well be the later interpolations of a fine Italian hand.
289. Rom. 10:17.
290. I Tim. 4:6.
291. Gal. 3:1, 2, 5.

Despite the constant adumbration of some mysterious way that one perceives truth′, saturation of the conscious mind with Scripture is the only solid clue we get about the active ingredient of "faith."

The theme of scriptural saturation of the conscious mind identifies some further clues to the behavioral unknown quantity in "faith." If scriptural saturation is so fundamental, then the Scripture-oriented one-mindedness we have elsewhere encountered must figure in the attainment of "faith":

> *There is* one body, and one Spirit, even as you are called in one hope of your calling; One Lord, one faith, one baptism, One God and Father of all, who *is* above all, and through all, and in you all. . . . [and God has different individuals performing different organic rôles in the body] Till we all come in the unity of the faith, and of the knowledge of the Son of God. . . .[292]

> . . . [W]e have the mind of Christ.[293]

> I beseech you therefore, brethren, by the mercies of God, that ye present your bodies a living sacrifice, holy, acceptable unto God, *which is* your reasonable service. And be not conformed to this world: but be ye transformed by the renewing of your mind. . . . For I say . . . to every man that is among you, not to think *of himself* more highly than he ought to think; but to think soberly, according as God hath dealt to every man the measure of faith.[294]

The ambiguity as to whether a quantity or ration of "faith" is meant, or perhaps a "faith" standard against which each believer is to be measured, is not an artifact of translation. Neither is the believer permitted to clarify whether the "unity" or "measure" is to be an immediate mystical participation with the other constituents of the body of Christ or merely faithfully following the biblical script in this life, looking forward to something more satisfying to be hoped for in the next life. What is clear is that the conscious attitude is to have a shared common denominator, and be emptied of all that is not biblically approved, uniform and regulation. In various contexts, we pick up many an instruction designed to produce such a conscious condition.

Since love′, under analysis, turned out to consist of following the rules, it is to be expected that some informative if oblique statements about "faith" will relate to love′:

> . . . [F]aith . . . worketh [*energeo,* is active, has effect] by love.[295]

> Ye are all the children of light, and the children of the day: we are not of the night, nor of darkness. Therefore let us not sleep, as *do* others; but let us watch and be sober. For they that sleep sleep in the night; and they that be drunken are drunken in the night. But let us, who are of the day, be sober, putting on the

292. Eph. 4:4-6,13.
293. I Cor. 2:16.
294. Rom. 12:1-3.
295. Gal. 5:6.

> breastplate of faith and love; and for an helmet, the hope of salvation. For God hath not appointed us to wrath, but to obtain salvation by our Lord. . . .[296]

> . . . [Y]our work [*ergon,* expenditure of energy] of faith, and labour [*kopos,* toil, wearying oneself] of love, and patience of hope in our Lord Jesus Christ, in the sight of God. . . .[297]

> . . . [W]e pray always for you, that our God would count you worthy of *this* calling, and fulfil all the good pleasure of *his* goodness, and the work [*ergon*] of faith with power [*dunamis*]: That the name of our Lord Jesus Christ may be glorified in you, and ye in him, according to the grace [*charis*] of our God and the Lord Jesus Christ.[298]

> Fight the good fight of faith, lay hold on eternal life, whereunto thou art also called. . . .[299]

> Peace *be* to the brethren, and love with faith, from God. . . . Grace [*charis*] *be* with all them that love our Lord Jesus Christ in sincerity. . . .[300]

Even though we are not told what it is, besides steeping himself in the Word, that the believer is supposed to do, we are duly notified that it is something effortful, labored, difficult and adverse. Behind the biblical authors' having hit on the same Greek words that would later provide the roots for key technical terms in Newtonian mechanics (*energy, erg* and *dynamic*), a tacit notion of psychic energy quite close to our modern, depth-psychological ones evidently lay almost near enough to the surface to be formulated explicitly. The biblical relating of love′ to "faith" with an energetic notion gives some good cause for the modern convention of interpreting *charis* energetically (viz. "charismatic"), and doing so also serves the Device 1 purpose of evading confronting the distasteful implication of godly arbitrary preference or favoritism that goes with the term of art, *grace.* Apparently "faith" entails a constant outpouring of energy, and whatever "peace" and "joy" there are to it do not necessarily bring respite from the drudgery of it. Obsessive conscious concentration, resembling nothing so much as insomnia, is lauded, and mental relaxation, flight of fantasy, and anything at all resembling ecstasy are devalued and negatively characterized. The prescribed preoccupations for consciousness are deemed "light," and all else, benighted debauchery. Let your guard down, and that may be just the moment when Christ returns like a "thief in the night," to whisk you away to Hell![301] Expenditure of energy in the "faith" activity is also juxtaposed to "Christ . . . glorified in you, and ye in him," suggesting investment of libido in the God-complex. The energy is seen as emanating from God in the first instance,

296. 1 Thess. 5:5-9.
297. 1 Thess. 1:3.
298. 2 Thess. 1:11-12.
299. 1 Tim. 6:12.
300. Eph. 6:23-24.
301. 1 Thess. 5:2,4; 2 Pet. 3:10; Rev. 3:3 and 16:15.

and indications about the circumstances of the believer's expending it (which comes under the heading of "works," and so cannot appear to the believer as the determining factor) are equivocal. Yet, the believer is subtly made out to be the repository of "faith," the one of whom "faith" is an attribute, as opposed to its "author" or "finisher,"[302] as the persons of the Godhead in his own right never are. It is taught that God loves and that he is love, but never is it taught that he evinces "faith" in the New Testament sense.[303]

The tense, on-guard, "breastplate of faith and love" model of "faith" is further elaborated:

> Finally, my brethren, be strong in the Lord, and in the power of his might. Put on the whole armour of God, that ye may be able to stand against the wiles of the devil. For we wrestle not against flesh and blood, but against principalities, against powers, against the rulers of the darkness of this world, against spiritual wickedness in high *places*. Wherefore take unto you the whole armour of God, that ye may be able to withstand in the evil day, and having done all, to stand. Stand therefore, having your loins girt about with truth, and having on the breastplate of righteousness; And your feet shod with the preparation of the gospel of peace; Above all, taking the shield of faith, wherewith ye shall be able to quench all the fiery darts of the wicked. And take the helmet of salvation, and the sword of the Spirit, which is the word of God. . . .[304]

This passage receives a great deal of attention, because it lends itself readily to superficial misreading in liberal quarters to justify disobedience to secular civil authorities in the name of Christianity, and in conservative ones to justify subjecting the flock to some extreme "discipling" program of regimentation. The biblical pseudopsychological cynicism about human nature, supposing man to be innately incapable of rising higher than passive follower, and whose thoughts cannot be his own in any worthwhile sense, is less than subtly expressed in the passage. The believer's "Christian walk" is to be in uniform and cumbersome military attire, that submerges his individuality, insulates him from all but a few approved kinds of stimulation, restricts his freedom of movement, and generally is good for making war, not *love.*

---

302. Heb. 12:2.

303. While the King James version frequently uses the phrase *faith of God* (cf. Rom. 3:22; Gal. 2:16, 20; Eph. 3:12; Phil. 3:9 and Rev. 14:12), the context clearly indicates an activity primarily of the believer and secondarily from God. This is made more clear in the modern translations.

Machen, as an engaging way of fending off the anti-Jewish churchly prattle of his day about whether Jesus was to be counted as a Jew or as a Christian, used to remark:

"Many persons hold up their hands in amazement at our assertion that Jesus was not a Christian, while we in turn regard it as the very height of blasphemy to say that he was a Christian. 'Christianity,' to us, is a way of getting rid of sin; and therefore to say that Jesus was a Christian would be to deny His holiness." *What Is Faith?,* p. 110.

Accordingly, God would have no occasion for "faith," having no "sin" to overcome. Since he controls the rules, he would have no occasion for love′ either, so the same line of thinking exposes the attribution of love′ to him as disingenuous. *Faith* relates to the believer's distinctive condition apart from God's, while *love* somehow pertains to both conditions.

304. Eph. 6:10-17.

The "sword of the Spirit, which is the word of God . . . ," is, or course, none other than the mouth-borne sword wielded by Jesus from the back of the white horse, also the one ". . . piercing even to the dividing asunder of soul and spirit, and of the joints and marrow . . . a discerner [*kritikos,* judge] of the thoughts and intents of the heart."[305] Using it on others is the objective of the campaign, and avoiding being pierced by the point of any other dangerous insight, the purpose of the armor. Just as the witness′ goes to the unbelievers to talk and not listen, the Christian soldier is out to pierce others and not be pierced himself. He cannot be pierced, because all that pertains to being pierced is safely outside his little armor-plated shell of consciousness. His "faith" is a "shield" or "breastplate," i.e., a boundary or barrier keeping out extraneous stimulation. If someone had a dream like this, any analyst worth his salt would ask, "What is the dreamer so defensive about?"

The themes of dividing asunder and of applying psychological energy in some unseen process to produce a result or maintain a state of "unity" or "measure," but subjectively experienced as a state of peace or rest,[306] culminate in this passage, also the one coming closest to giving an explicit instruction labeled as bearing on "faith":

> And straightway Jesus constrained his disciples to get into a ship, and to go before him unto the other side, while he sent the multitudes away. And . . . he went up into a mountain apart to pray: and when the evening was come, he was there alone. But the ship was now in the midst of the sea, tossed with waves: for the wind was contrary. And in the fourth watch of the night [3-6 A.M.] Jesus went unto them, walking on the sea. And when the disciples saw him walking on the sea, they were troubled, saying, It is a spirit; and they cried our for fear. But straightway Jesus spake unto them, saying, Be of good cheer; it is I; be not afraid. And Peter answered him and said, Lord, if it be thou, bid me come unto thee on the water. And he said, Come. And when Peter was come down out of the ship, he walked on the water, to go to Jesus. But when he saw the wind boisterous, he was afraid; and beginning to sink, he cried, saying, Lord, save me. And immediately Jesus stretched forth *his* hand, and caught him, and said unto him, O thou of little faith, wherefore didst thou doubt? And when they were come into the ship, the wind ceased. Then they that were in the ship came and worshipped him, saying, Of a truth thou art the son of God. [They disembark, and some men at the destination are healed of unnamed maladies by touching the hem of Jesus' robe, like the woman with the issue of blood.][307]

This story contains the central psychological paradigm of the Bible. It is as central in our view as the substitutionary atonement is in any conventional theological view, or "ultimate concern" in a Tillichian, revisionist view. We must digress at length to analyze it, and show its supporting context.[308]

From this story, the believer learns that besides making a mountain or

---

305. See p. 232, footnote 208.
306. Heb. 4:1-11 and Phil. 4:7.
307. Matt. 14:22-33.
308. To do this, the directly suggestive symbolic passages expressed in terms of water are treated out of the sequence of my outline.

mulberry tree go jump in the lake, he can, by "faith," develop a knack for investing libido into the boundary of surface tension between the conscious and unconscious realms of the mind, reinforcing that boundary so that what otherwise would support no more than the weight of a leaf or mosquito larva will now support a man's weight. But if his concentration is diverted, as with Peter's failure at tuning out natural stimuli and impressions, and his own emotions, then the effect is spoiled, and the boundary reverts to its usual permeability. The biblical moral of the story is that failing to have one's mind obsessively on Jesus will rapidly and disastrously result in the deterioration of "faith," in the letting down of the "shield" that "faith" represents. Then, one will have to come to terms with one's unconscious, characteristically mischaracterized in Christianity as a stormy sea in which to drown. But, we answer, it only seems that way when one bottles it up, forces it to express itself too turbulently, and in terms of the shadow side. Evangelicals need to be reassured by us, "Come on in, the water's fine!"

Giving due respect to the incomparably artful camouflage job that has so long kept the true meaning of the walk-on-the-water story suppressed, and the drastic and unsettling shift in *Gestalt* here being asked of religious professionals, we must look to whatever clues the story may afford as to its history before we look at it in terms of related biblical symbols. Here, as before, we wonder why "faith" in terms of belief should be a problem for anyone with the benefit of first-hand experience with Jesus and the events surrounding him. We wonder particularly why it would be a problem for an uneducated Jewish provincial, innocent of Hellenistic objections to the Jewish supernaturalistic status quo. The anachronistic prominence of the issue may indicate that whatever actual events are included in the story have been filtered through the minds of later people, removed from the pertinent places and to whom the live witnesses were no longer available.

I detect more similarity in the story to an individual's dream than to an episode of collective folklore. My experience with modern dream analysis prompts from me the conveniently nondisprovable speculation that this was the nightmarish dream of some first-century convert, under the exhortations and social pressures of the Christian group, having trouble turning off his integrity or believing the unbelievable stuff required of him. I wonder, but can find nothing to indicate, whether the dreamer was a Gentile making a fresh, first-impression response to the Old Testament symbols, or a Jew in whom the political and military catastrophe cried out for their radical reinterpretation. It hardly seems that the New Testament cast of characters and end to the story could be the authentic ones, from that individual's actual dream.

All of the major symbols in the story do have their Old Testament precedents. In both New and Old, a body of water corresponds to the unconscious; high, dry ground, to particularly lucid, we would say "related," consciousness; meteorological disturbance, to passion and emotion; and after going down into murky depths, coming up ready for some psychic accomplishment for which the sojourner had been unready, to psychological or "spiritual" growth.[309] The essential difference lies in the choice of persons qualified to experience individualistic psychological growth. In the Old Testament, godly people undergo the transformation and then do things that, in turn, foster national Israel's fortunes. In the New Testament, however, the transformation becomes the jealously held, exclusive prerogative of God Incarnate, and mankind is to gush with gratitude at being granted even the slightest, most heavily diluted, vicarious connection with it. In the Old Testament, to be sure, such a transformation is only for a few, chosen spiritual elite, and the modern, "humanist" project of making such growth widely available lacks biblical precedent, Old Testament or New. Jung and Tillich correctly perceived the resurrection story to have to do with psychological growth, but they ignored and obscured for their followers the crucial prohibition and dire condemnation against such growth for the individual believer, doctrinally required throughout the New Testament. They could never have faced up to the implication that their most prized value emerges as the true, biblical meaning of "sin," arising inescapably from the few fleeting, direct biblical statements about it, and from the massive, methodical program of opposition to such growth that the New Testament "faith" project turns out to be.

Every time that Old Testament protagonists brave the waters, they go from one set of circumstances to another quite different and better, are "translated," in King James lingo, or undergo psychic transformation or growth, in ours. When God originally divides the heavens from the earth and the dry land from the waters by firmaments, the emergence and differentiation of human consciousness are expressed. From our knowing perspective, we understand some kind of division of the psyche to be necessary, and the best that can be hoped for in the finite, human condition is that the boundaries will be permeable, and may be rearranged from time to time. When Old Testament protagonists brave the waters, the boundaries of their lives are much changed, and for the better. The linearity of the process, and the impossibility of return to an undifferentiated, naïve, Adamic state are always evident. The remedy now proposed for the distress attending the disequilibrium and tensions of human psychic dividedness is a new departure. Return to the original, undivided state is never in view.

---

309. "Old-time religion" Christianity, through the notion of salvation as a kind of mind-cure, placing strong emphasis on sudden, ecstatic subjective conversion experiences as the Bible, itself, does not, and where no historical commitment prevents it, making an emotional, transformation experience out of baptism by immersion, circumvents the austerity of the Bible's position on psychological growth. The popularity of baptism by immersion, and making such baptism a deliberate act by one of sufficient age to be deliberate, has arisen since the seventeenth century, and specifically out of the Baptist tradition. It is not clear that baptism (*baptizo*) contemplates immersion, although the baptisms of Jesus and the Ethiopian eunuch suggest it. I have noticed that the more articulate contemporary mini-Reformationists favor infant baptism, and think that sprinkling more accurately reflects the Bible's intent than immersion, after Ezek. 36:25. There are numerous references to ritual sprinkling of blood in the Old Testament, and the notion of believers being "sprinkled" among the more numerous doomed unbelievers of the earth ties in (Isa. 52:15), as does the notion of believers being the "salt of the earth" (Matt. 5:13). Note the inconsistency of Jesus, the sinless One, partaking of baptism, if its significance is remission of sins, and John the Baptist's theologically astute reluctance to baptize him (Matt. 3:13-15).

The transformation works the same way in each of its three most impressive Old Testament occurrences. When mankind rises to the hybred vigor of the "men of renown,"[310] jealous old God cannot tolerate it, so the purview of mankind is temporarily restricted to the pious confines of Noah's Ark. Consciousness is compressed and floats on the surface, fifteen cubits above the highest mountain top. All not included in that small preserve of consciousness are swept away, and all that are to be descend from the little conscious menage. The moral of the story is: to put out of mind all outside influences, all that detracts from the obsessive purity of Jewish ideology is to put them out of existence. The Bible commits itself at that point to the underlying premise of all neurosis, namely that relegation of troublesome thoughts to the unconscious gets rid of them, kills them, insures that they can never return, never manifest themselves again. Instead of recognizing that thoughts cannot be killed as living beings can be, man is condemned to live them out in the form of symptoms, or projectively to imagine that they come back from the dead in the form of ghosts or spirits.

When Moses and the fleeing slaves reach the Red Sea, there is an impressive dividing of the waters.[311] Moses and his followers share the momentary privilege of descending to the solid bottom normally obscured underneath the murky depths, and they come out on the other side, at the beginning of the trail leading to the promised land. The Egyptian outsiders to the proprietary way of thinking attempt the same descent, and are swept away. Many further travails lie ahead for Moses and his followers. He is permitted a mountain-top experience, but the finitude of the human condition is poignantly expressed by an entry into the promised land being denied him. And the recurrent nature of the transformation process is hinted at by marking the eventual crossing over the Jordan into the promised land with another, somewhat less impressive dividing of the waters.[312]

All of the distinctive features of the watery adventures of Noah and Moses are repeated in Jonah. Jesus himself attests to its significance, saying, "An evil and adulterous generation seeketh after a sign; and there shall no sign be given to it, but the sign of the prophet Jonas: For as Jonas was three days and three nights in the whale's belly; so shall the Son of man be. . . ."[313] The story is one of those rare, poignant instances, as with Rahab the harlot, Ruth the Moabitess, and Naaman the leper,[314] where God's Old Testament people have favorable,

---

310. Gen. 6:4.
311. Exod. 14.
312. Josh. 3.
313. Matt. 12:39-40.
314. The relatively few, remarkable instances of foreigners becoming part of normally exclusive, xenophobic Israel partake of veiled, diplomatic language, or the symbolism of a political cartoon. Rahab the harlot, in whose house Joshua's spies are harbored (Josh. 2) may be a figure of Egypt, and the fish that swallows Jonah is often interpreted as a figure of Babylon taking the Israelites into captivity. The story of Naaman (2 Kings 5), depicting the admirable extravert Naaman going through a dramatic and untroubled transformation by carrying out Elisha's instruction to bathe seven times in the Jordan River, may pertain to some unusual incident of diplomatic breakthrough in relations with the Aramaeans. But note well how even Naaman's affliction does not simply go out of existence, but is converted over to the crafty servant, Gehazi.

portentous contacts with outsiders. Jonah, trying to get away from God and away from a hard assignment he does not realize he is on the threshold of growing into, finds himself on a boat with a bunch of Gentiles, albeit sensible and decent ones. When God brings the storm and the heavy seas, the sailors first throw their excess baggage overboard to lighten ship. How we wish their modern counterparts could more often be induced to do that! Even when it has been conclusively established that their peril is on Jonah's account, they remain loath to incur guilt by harming him. Like Noah's menage and the Israelites crossing the Red Sea, consciousness and a conventional point of view are synonymous, or nearly so. But it is in a cosmopolitan, rather than an obsessive, theologically orthodox frame of mind that the stormy psychic crisis comes on Jonah, and the occasion for his regressive, transforming experience comes about. The intimate association with so primative a form of life as a fish (which Jesus embellishes into the phylogenetically higher, mammalian whale) conveys the regressive quality of the experience. Even after he has done God's will, and, astonishingly, received better treatment from the pagan, Ninevite recipients of his prophetic message than Amos, Isaiah or Jeremiah ever received from their purebred Jewish audiences, the dense, conventional-minded Jewish nationalist Jonah can only be disgusted with himself for having shared the exclusive, spiritual riches with outsiders. God has to chastize him still further with the lesson of the gourd (or castor-oil plant) to make him understand that disseminating the gospel of obsessive, spiritual orthodoxy—and neither becoming assimilated to cosmopolitan ways nor hoarding the truth′ for the Jews alone—is the name of the game.

The main protagonist undergoes his watery transformation in each instance, and comes out into circumstances much changed for the better. For Noah and Moses, their mundane companions simply remain with them: the shared attitudes do not change, but find a place more favorable for them. But for Jonah, a splitting of the ego-personality takes place. The outward, conventional, cosmopolitan aspect of Jonah's awareness continues on its course without the inner, creative part, which goes down into the water, to the ordained rendezvous with the fish and arrival in alien Nineveh. Even after Jonah has done well what he was supposed to do, he remains obtusely uncomprehending of its meaning. The creative disruption of a conventional point of view can temporarily be quelled by submerging it in unconsciousness, but it neither dies nor stays lost. It goes on, and manifests itself somewhere else.

The story of Jonah can just as well be seen as a picture of modern individualism becoming possible, just as Jewish monotheism can be seen as a picture of unity emerging in the individual personality, the accruing of libidinal energy to one awareness, so that its force can be directed to some thoughtful, individualistic purpose, or at least to a collective one, individually assented to. But that is not what the New Testament makes of it, at all.

The "sign of the prophet Jonas" is taken completely away from the water and expanded to cosmic proportions, and any hope that individual personality integration is its portent is removed in the New Testament. Jesus' descent is into the "heart of the earth," well beyond the human domain, and his majestically slow ascent, to Heaven. With the vastness of those proportions goes vagueness, enabling the story to remain intelligible even though cosmological ideas become more sophisticated. By a salvation scheme so elaborate and pervasive that the New Testament becomes unintelligible if one neglects its details, it is made clear to the believer that he is to experience nothing like the personal transformation of Jesus or his precursors while in this life, is indeed not to experience any ever, except within the bounds and rules of the biblical program. He is to look for fragmentation, estrangement and pilgrimhood only in this life, leading to another mode of existence in the next life so unimaginably different that he can know it only in terms of a few fragmentary clues.[315] If there is a growth or transformation process to Christianity, it is not for the individual believer but for the "body" of which the individual believer is to consider himself but a small, dependent component part.

The other images of bodies of water in the New Testament are carefully drawn to have nothing at all to do with psychological growth. When boats and water occur, it is usually on the Sea of Galilee, with navigation on a manageably small, tame scale.

On another occasion than the walk on the water, Jesus and the disciples go to cross the sea. A late afternoon gale arises, while Jesus, in the stern, lies asleep on a cushion. The disciples become afraid and awaken Jesus, who orders the sea to be still, and rebukes the disciples for their lack of "faith."[316] Here also, the fluid boundary is smoothed over, and troublesome emotions are safely out of the way when there is "faith," which seems to be facilitated if Jesus is in the forefront of attention, i.e., awake. This time, the boat is accompanied by other boats on the water, and the episode ends with the conscious attitudes of all the witnesses fixated on the magical, divine authority that has brought these events to pass.

Other references to boats pertain to fishing, and to the casting of nets. The identification of the boat with the individual believer, who is to become a "fisher of men," is clear. Paul's experiences with voyages and shipwrecks receive more than passing attention: he survives two shipwrecks, and describes erstwhile believers' loss of "faith" as "shipwreck."[317]

The Matthean story of the walk on the water brings all these allusions together. It begins with Jesus separating himself from his disciples—sending

315. The character of life beyond the grave for the believer is conveyed more in terms of statements as to what features of earthly life are to be absent, than characteristic or distinctive features to be present, in the other life. We are told there is no marriage (Matt. 22:30), and by implication, no gender, nationality, or social distinction (Gal. 3:28). The other life is simply different, e.g., 1 Cor. 15:35-56; Rev. 7:16-17 and 21:4-5, and the inference is fair that the believer will no longer care about what preoccupies him in this life, because the resurrection of the flesh' part will so alter his point of view. The positive aspects of that life are alluded to only vaguely. Luke 15:7,10; Rom. 8:18; 1 Pet. 1:4; Rev. 7:16 and 14:13. The believer must further infer that the relentless, insomniac, rather boring impression conveyed by the hints given about heavenly life, e.g., Rev. 7:15; 21:25 and 22:5, will not adversely affect the changed persons who are to experience it.

316. Matt. 8:23-27; Mark 4:35-41 and Luke 8:22-25.

317. 1 Tim. 1:19.

them into a situation less conscious than his own at that point—and only then extricating himself from the multitudes—the complexes—so that he can go up on the mountain top to pray. Leaving the star without security protection from the mob is as unusual for the disciples as it would be in our own day: practical reference is made elsewhere to awareness of need for security precautions when Jesus worked the crowds.[318] Here, as at the transfiguration, a certain awed distance, not so apparent at other times, comes between Jesus and the disciples. Like Moses, Jesus goes to the mountain alone to commune with God. Since standing on the mountain is not for the mere believer, now we know why the taking away of a mountain or a mulberry tree—both objects one might stand on to enlarge one's range of view, to raise one's consciousness—and submerging it in the sea is a miracle to which the believer may aspire. God forbid that, in his thoughts, he should take the high ground!

The same sort of splitting of the personality as in Jonah—the focussed, creative aspect going in one direction and the conventional, other-directed aspect in another—takes place. But this time, the hearer's attention is directed to the fortunes of the conventional, socially shared part.

The impressions the believer is to receive of the disciples in the boat when Jesus walks on the water are camouflaged by the abrupt cut to the boat in midstream, in Matthew, but supplied elsewhere, by fragments in Mark and John.[319] (Interesting that Luke, the Gospel from a Roman, Gentilized point of view, skips these events entirely.) The following of all the Gospel accounts of Jesus walking on water immediately upon the highly distinctive feeding of five thousand tourists with five loaves and two fish militates in favor of one incident behind all three accounts. Also, there is no way that seeing Jesus walking on the water could have retained its terrifying novelty for the disciples through three separate occurrences. Yet there are integrity-assaulting inconsistencies. The theme of personality fragmentation is subtly expressed by the same boatload of disciples having a different Galilean seaside destination in each account: Gennesaret in Matthew, Bethsaida in Mark, and Capernaum in John. Also, Jesus apparently never completely climbs into the boat before it reaches its destination in John, as he does in the other two accounts.[320] Most importantly, Mark and John make no mention of Peter's watery walk, strong evidence that it is a later embellishment.

Both Mark and John supply the missing image of the disciples' circumstances while in the boat before Jesus' return. Tensely and laboriously, they row against the wind on a troubled sea, furnishing another energy-expending image of the "faith-work." If "faith without works is dead," then so are "works" without work![321]

---

318. Mark 3:9.

319. Mark 6:45-52 and John 6:15-21.

320. The question whether Jesus got into the boat or not, in John 6:21, turns on the subtlety of translating *lambano*. The consensus of the reputable modern translations is that he did not. *The Jerusalem Bible* has: "They were for taking him into the boat, but in no time it reached the shore at the place they were making for."

321. The notion that "rest" and "peace" correspond to the special kind of energy expenditure to keep the barrier between conscious and unconscious energized enables the following passage to

If the desired end state is keeping the membrane between conscious and unconscious energized, stiffened and smoothed over, then perhaps solidification of the membrane, so that proscribed mental contents are kept down, without need for a constant energetic outpouring to keep the boat bailed, would constitute an image of heaven for the believer. A passage that conventional theologians have always stumbled over furnishes just such an image:

> And I saw another sign in heaven, great and marvelous, seven angels who had seven plagues, *which are* the last, because in them the wrath of God is finished. And I saw, as it were, a sea of glass mixed with fire, and those who had come off victorious from the beast and from his image and from the number of his name, standing on the sea of glass, holding harps of God. And they sang the song of Moses the bond-servant of God and the song of the Lamb. . . .[322]

While the passage does relate back to another of John's visions—of a glazed ceremonial laver in God's throne room,[323] and to various ceremonial lavers not reported to have had glazed surfaces—the features of admixture of the surface with fire, and the possibility of persons standing on the solidified surface, are unique. In a rather alchemical way, the paradox of gaseous, active fire and solid, inert glasslike material where liquid had been expected is presented. The incipiently contradictory conscious experience of a peaceful, restful state, yet one taking constant energy to maintain it, is vividly expressed. One other time, the pious aspiration to experience "faith" as a solid feature in relation to others more movable, just at the moment when conscious attention is taken up with Jesus, occurs:

> . . . [T]he trial of your faith, being much more precious than of gold that perisheth, though it be tried with fire, might be found unto praise and honour and glory at the appearing of Jesus Christ. . . .[324]

Summing up, the biblical "faith" project, the aggregate of the statements and images allowed by the biblical language itself to be connected with that term, has as its central feature the idea of *division*. Radical separation of one realm from another, usually an upper from a lower, recurs much more consistently

---

make more sense than it does in its usual guise, as a teaching on Sabbath observance:

"Let us therefore fear, lest, a promise being left *us* of entering into his rest, any of you should seem to come short of it. For unto us was the gospel preached, as well as unto them: but the word preached did not profit them, not being mixed with faith in them that heard *it*. For we which have believed do enter into rest, as he said [Christ, quoting Psalm 95:11], As I have sworn in my wrath, if they shall enter into my rest: although the works were finished from the foundation of the world." Heb. 4:1-3. Cf., Matt. 11:28.

322. Rev. 15:1-3. *New American Standard Bible*. Whether the unidentified, probably human harp holders stand on the glazed surface or not turns on the translation of the preposition *epi*. While the King James also has it so, and has thus made it so for the Anglo-American world, reputable modern translations (besides the above quoted) generally, and also Luther's German, have the harp holders standing at the glazed sea's edge.

323. Rev. 4:6.

324. 1 Pet. 1:7. Cf., p. 334, footnote 437.

than anything else. The faint outline of "sin" as a traducement of the sort of individualistic personality integration always prized in the humanist tradition—and lauded by us as "relatedness"—becomes more distinct, as we establish that the program touted to remedy "sin" is organized about the central purpose of defeating individual tendencies toward "relatedness" and fostering instead a narrow, compressed, totally conventional conscious attitude at cross purposes to the rest of the individual's personality, that adversity to be experienced as Christian warfare′ against the flesh′. All the while, my approach accounts for more of the Bible's contents and explains them in a more elegant and intellectually satisfying way than any proponents of supernaturalistic claims for the document can possibly attain to. I shall not stop, however, at proving my case by a preponderance of the evidence. Immensely more of what the Evangelical is fed is organized around the objective of psychic dividedness than is traceable to the term *faith.* We can usefully continue on, to prove our case beyond a reasonable doubt. We shall selectively cover enough further devotional instructions and suggestions to establish that the dividedness—i.e., dissociation—project is the most ubiquitous feature of the Bible. We will not attempt to catalogue them exhaustively.

The Bible, preferring to use suggestion and indirection, closely rations statements explicitly instructing the believer to do, or refrain from doing. Earlier, we observed that most such statements deal with the paramount concern of shielding the believer against all possible sources of extraneous religious teaching, by counseling opposition to those who bring it, or ostracism of them. The only topic of explicit advice, besides adversity towards heresy or apostasy, which occurs in more than isolated fragments, deals with discipline of the conscious mind. Earlier, we also set out the meatiest passage describing the conscious attitude prescribed for the believer, Col. 3:1-17. It will now be more intelligible for us because we know the biblical definitions of the key terms. The reader may desire to reread it, on pp. 173-74. The following is a companion passage.

> This I say . . . and testify in the Lord, that ye henceforth walk not as other Gentiles walk, in the vanity [futility] of their mind, Having the understanding darkened, being alienated from the life of God through the ignorance that is in them, because of the blindness of their heart: Who being past feeling have given themselves over unto lasciviousness, to work all uncleanness with greediness. But ye have not so learned Christ; If so be that ye have heard him, and have been taught by him, as the truth is in Jesus: That ye put off concerning the former conversation [i.e., conduct] the old man, which is corrupt according to the deceitful lusts; And be renewed in the spirit of your mind; And that ye put on the new man, which after God is created in righteousness and true holiness. Wherefore putting away lying, speak every man truth with his neighbour: for we are members one of another. Be ye angry, and sin not: let not the sun go down upon your wrath: Neither give place to the devil. Let him that stole steal no more: but rather let him labour, working with *his* hands the thing which is good, that he may have to give to him that needeth. Let no corrupt communication proceed out of your mouth, but that which is good to the use of edifying, that it may minister grace

> unto the hearers. And grieve not the holy Spirit of God, whereby ye are sealed unto the day of redemption. Let all bitterness, and wrath, and anger, and clamour, and evil speaking, be put away from you, with all malice: And be ye kind one to another, tenderhearted, forgiving one another, even as God for Christ's sake hath forgiven you.[325]

The key phrases are *put on* and *put off*. The notion that the prescribed attitudes are to be "put on" and all others "put off" is repeated several times. The modern, colloquial sense of those words is ironically apt: not only is one to "put on" a biblical attitude like military apparel. One is to "put on" disciplined affectation of the biblical attitude, to seek to make it part of one by practicing it, by acting it out, by deliberately and methodically applying it to life situations as they occur. The Christian's behavior is to be premeditated at all times, and the doctrine puts a negative, fleshly′ value on all spontaneous behavior. (The well-acted appearance of spontaneity might, however, be in order for making a favorable impression on prospective converts, and thus constitute a "good witness.") "Putting on" the prescribed attitude looks ahead to making it eventually authentic if not in this life then in the next! In this respect, the Bible approves changing what is, by wishing very hard, by having the mind or will prevail over the flesh′. The biblical *put on* is another expression for Christian love′.

Notice what things the Bible explicitly states are to be "put on": the "new man," "incorruption," "immortality," "bowels of mercies," "love," "armour of light," "whole armour of God," and "Lord Jesus."[326] When we come to more meaty passages describing what all is to be "put on," even if those words are not used, we find two purposes intended: (1) The believer's psychic energy is to be taken up in the attempt to internalize and make his own an attitude that is psychologically inauthentic, false and maladaptive. The very strangeness of what is commanded, and its contrariness to common sense, simulate profundity if that be one's mind set. The natural, healthy inclination to use common sense is the occasion for the Christian to feel pangs of bad conscience, and to perceive need of a remedy for those pangs. (2) Behavior is called for, that, were it really carried out without tempering rationalization or hypocrisy, would render the believer incompetent to cope with life away from the Christian fold. Dependency on the fold (obliquely expressed in much talk about dependency on God) is fostered.

> . . . [L]et your communication be, Yea, yea; Nay, nay: for whatsoever is more than these cometh of evil. . . . it hath been said, An eye for an eye, and a tooth for a tooth: but I [Jesus] say unto you, That ye resist not evil: but whosoever shall smite thee on thy right cheek, turn to him the other also. And if any man will sue thee at the law, and take away thy coat [tunic], let him have *thy* cloke [outer garment] also. And whosoever shall compel thee to go a mile, go with him twain [two]. Give to him that asketh thee, and from him that would borrow of thee turn not thou away. . . . it hath been said, Thou shalt love thy neighbor, and hate thine enemy. But I say unto you, Love your enemies, bless them that curse you, do good

325. Eph. 4:17-32.
326. Eph. 4:24; Col. 3:10 (new man); 1 Cor. 15:53-54 (incorruption, immortality); Col. 3:12 (bowels of mercies); Col. 3:14 (*agape,* love, charity); Rom. 13:12 (armor of light); Eph. 6:11

to them that hate you, and pray for them which despitefully use [i.e., slander, falsely accuse] you, and persecute you. . . . For if ye love them which love you, what reward have ye? do not even the publicans the same? . . . Be ye therefore perfect, even as your Father . . . in heaven is perfect.[327]

Give to every man that asketh of thee; and of him that taketh away thy goods ask *them* not again.[328]

I have been crucified with Christ; it is no longer I who live, but Christ who lives in me; and the life I now live in the flesh I live by faith in the Son of God, who loved me and gave himself for me.[329]

Wherefore laying aside all malice, and all guile, and hypocrisies, and envies, and all evil speakings, As newborn babes, desire the sincere milk of the word, that ye may grow thereby: If so be ye have tasted that the Lord *is* gracious [kindly]. To whom coming, *as unto* a living stone, disallowed indeed of men, but chosen of God *and* precious. Ye also, as lively stones, are built up a spiritual house, an holy priesthood, to offer up spiritual sacrifices, acceptable to God by Jesus Christ.[330]

Finally, brethren, whatsoever things are true, whatsoever things *are* honest, whatsoever things *are* just, whatsoever things *are* pure, whatsoever things *are* lovely, whatsoever things *are* of good report; if *there be* any virtue [*arete,* gallantry, manly virtue], and if *there be* any praise, think on these things.[331]

For I determined not to know any thing . . . save Jesus Christ, and him crucified.[332]

The explicit list of things to be "put off" is relatively understated: the "old man," "anger," "wrath," "malice," "blasphemy," "filthy communications," "deceitful lusts," and "works of darkness."[333] In context, what is to be "put off," particularly the last two of the categories just mentioned, turns out to include all creative use of human intelligence to solve human problems, all spontaneous human compassion untrammeled by prejudice, and all naturalness and cheerfulness in human conduct. The process of "putting off" is rather intricate, its ramifications, extensive and crucial.

(whole armor of God); Rom. 13:14 and Gal. 3:27 (Lord Jesus).

327. Matt. 5:37-44, 46 and 48.

328. Luke 6:30. This passage clearly commands the believer to part with his property on the request of any person. Having its reference memorized enables one to give street "witnesses" and the like a bad time, and occasionally to obtain their watches, pocket money, Bibles, etc. from them. See Conway and Siegelman, *Holy Terror,* p. 215.

329. Gal. 2:20. *Revised Standard Version.*

330. 1 Pet. 2:1-5.

331. Phil. 4:8-9.

332. 1 Cor. 2:2.

333. Eph. 4:22; Col. 3:9 (old man); Col. 3:8 (anger, wrath, malice, blasphemy and filthy communications); Eph. 4:22 (deceitful lusts) and Rom. 13:12 (works of darkness).

Their context overwhelmingly indicates that "putting on" and "putting off" occur together, are aspects of one and the same process, and are reciprocal. That salvation implies becoming alive′ to the Spirit but dead′ to the flesh′, that receiving sight′ or hearing′ as to truth′ implies becoming blind′ or deaf′ to all else, that the contrast between light′ and darkness′ is always so sharp and clearcut, and that spiritual regeneration is an all-or-nothing affair, as we have encountered in numerous connections, all point to the tantamountness of "putting on" a biblical way to "putting off" fleshly′ ways.

The notion that changing human personality by getting rid of detrimental features alone does not work, and that the successful approach to planned personality change must necessarily supply new ways to compensate somehow for the old ones being extinguished or depotentiated—so successfully implemented by Christianity—seems to me the key neglected insight for the mental-health professions. The infrequency with which mental-health treatment regimes even attempt to provide people with an affirmative, alternative focus, and the failure of theories that have been current to aid those involved to find such foci, are crucial clues both to the failure of those professions in the present and to the successes they can still have some day. Just as we must anticipate that something will be required to fill a psychological "vacuum" created by getting rid of what is detrimental in an individual's activity, we must anticipate that the vacuum created by the disappointing showing of the mental-health professions in our day will be sought to be filled by various purported remedies. While "old-time religion" Christianity can sometimes do rather well as an alternative lifestyle replacing another that was negative, it blends imperceptibly into mini-Reformationism, where the psychotechnology we are perusing ultimately fosters manipulation, control and group solidarity, brutally and at the expense of the individual's mental health and well-being. The substantive failure and poor general reputation of those secular intellectuals in our time who ought to be providing advice for living based on knowledge and rationality gives the mini-Reformation, with its facile promise of the one and only ideal lifestyle, a dangerous opportunity.

The most explicit devotional-program instructions pertinent to the "putting on/putting off" process deal with *prayer*. The Bible is very specific about the sort of prayer it requires. Noncomplying prayer practices are particularly informative clues to the psychological "atmospherics" of any particular religious group.[334] The *sine qua non* of biblical prayer is intelligible content, engaging the believer's conscious mind. Formalistic, rote-repetition prayer is discouraged.[335] Prayer in "tongues" or "mysteries in the Spirit" is characterized as secondary or inferior, and the related issue as to whether or not glossolalia ceased with the apostolic age makes it very doubtful that such prayer belongs in a church trying

334. That is, a church with much prewritten or rote prayer is very likely rooted in traditions that once enjoyed comprehensive indoctrination, and needed neither to be psychologically subtle, nor to attract believers competitively. Mystification of believers with liturgy in a foreign language not understood by many of the worshipers has not been a Protestant device, although pretended scholarship and abuse of genuine scholarship in the Bible's ancient languages is heavily emphasized in the circles I call mini-Reformationist.
335. Matt. 6:4-8.

to be true to the Bible.[336] Liturgy in languages not understood by the worshipers, familiar in Roman Catholicism and Judaism, will generally not be found in a biblicist environment because it defeats the purpose of occupying the conscious mind with prescribed content.

An interesting feature of biblical prayer is its direction, always toward God the Father. Even Jesus, God the Son, prays to God the Father, who denies his prayer request in the Garden of Gethsemane not to have to go to the cross. The believer finds himself in the best of all possible company, if God does not fulfill his prayer requests in the short run! Beyond the absurdity of its being outside God's will to grant his own prayer request of himself, the emphasis on the unitary aspect of the God who is both unitary and triune, as recipient for the believer's focussed attention in prayer, is revealing. The Father is the most contradictory and difficult to imagine of the three aspects and also seems to be the most powerful. As an imagined receptacle for the believer's concentration, the most vague, "wholly other" outline but with the most compact, power-packed affective nucleus, is wanted. In a context other than prayer and for an altogether different psychological purpose from complex formation, we shall find the triune aspect brought, in its turn, into the foreground.

As purposeful as its direction are the manner and content prescribed for believers' prayer. These Scriptures are broadly representative:

> These all [the disciples] continued with one accord [unanimously, with one mind] in prayer and supplication [petition, request], with the women, and Mary the mother of Jesus, and with his brethren.[337]

> Continue [persevere, be constant] in prayer, and watch [be vigilant, remain awake] in the same with thanksgiving; Withal praying also for us. . . .[338]

> For it [every creature of God] is sanctified by the word of God and prayer.[339]

The great preponderance of positive examples of prayer in the Bible are requests or petitions.[340] Space apparently is made for the believer to care about himself and what he prefers. However, there are inescapable, albeit understated indications that one is to pray for some things, but not for others.[341] And it is subtly but firmly reiterated that prayer is to partake of the commanded one-mindedness with other bellevers, that in their prayer life the believers are to march in step with one another, Jesus and the Holy Spirit.[342] The heavy burden of participa-

---

336. 1 Cor. 14:13-19.
337. Acts 1:14.
338. Col. 4:2-3.
339. 1 Tim. 4:5.
340. E.g., Matt. 24:20; Mark 11:24; 13:18; Luke 16:27; Eph. 6:18; Phil. 4:6; 1 Tim. 2:1 and 5:5.
341. John 17:9, 15, 20; Acts 8:20-24; Rom. 8:26; 10:1; 2 Cor. 13:7; Phil. 1:9 and James 4:3. Note how the Lord's Prayer (Matt. 6:9-15 and Luke 11:2-4) is presented as a model or example, not a rote formula.
342. 2 Cor. 1:11; 5:20; 9:14; Col. 4:3; 1 Thess. 5:25; 2 Thess. 1:11; 3:1; 1 Tim. 2:8; Heb. 13:18 and James 5:14, 16.

tion and communion with Jesus and the Holy Spirit in prayer to the Father, is on the believer, even as he is reassured that their eloquence makes up for the believer's shortcomings in expressing what he should, in prayer.[343] The ostensible purpose of prayer is to get godly things done. Collectively, prayers are somehow to give the omnipotent God needed help in accomplishing his purposes. Actually, prayer is an endless exercize in internalizing the group ethos and forcing the conscious mind to conform to it. Prayer comes down to self-brainwashing. The obsessive, insomniac quality of prayer, if it is truly biblical, is rather plainly expressed in some passages.[344]

The initial purpose of prayer is simply to displace, to crowd out of consciousness, what does not harmonize with what is prescribed. Every pastor knows the manipulation technique of suddenly asking those present to pray with him when a meeting of believers is not going to his liking, and changing the subject or administering a veiled rebuke, by what is said in the prayer. As a disciplining of consciousness, more advanced private prayer resembles the sort of exercises that enable one to concentrate, to relax, to make one's mind a blank, or to achieve control over vegetative processes not innately under conscious control, as in yoga or biofeedback. Likewise, such prayer resembles self-hypnosis or autosuggestion. The acquired knack for putting mental contents out of consciousness, like the mountain or mulberry tree in the parable, parallels the acquired ability to control otherwise involuntary psychological phenomena in those other mental disciplines. Christian prayer diverges drastically from those other disciplines of consciousness in two crucial respects: None of them provides an elaborate or intelligible substitute conscious content, as Christian prayer does. More importantly, Christian prayer is set up so as to keep its practitioner in the dark as to its true purpose. Going on the pretext that communication with God is taking place, the believer does not realize that by couching his prayer in what he supposes to be good doctrine, by trying constantly to tell God what he thinks God wants to hear, by continually "renewing his mind" to want what he is supposed to want, he indoctrinates himself. And since a psychological complex, if vested with enough libido, takes on its own splinter personality, as when neurotic symptoms become so well organized that their sufferer hears voices representing their combination, or in an extreme case, develops a multiple personality, the believer experiences the illusion that a presence possessing personality is there. Since the God-complex lacks the intrinsic, personally relevant incompatibility with the conscious attitude that enables a personal neurotic complex to constellate itself, constant effort by the ego-personality is necessary to keep it constituted. By prayer, the believer keeps the God-complex energized. It disappears like a balloon with the air let out of it, if that effort is not kept up. Hence, the need of the inarticulate mind-controlled believer for church twice on Sunday, constant private devotion, and perhaps the constant drone of a religious radio station, to keep his God-complex pumped up.

---

343. Rom. 8:34; Heb. 7:25 and 1 John 2:1 (intercession by Jesus). Rom. 8:26 (intercession by the Holy Spirit).

344. Matt. 26:41 Mark 13:33; 14:38; Luke 18:1; 21:36; Acts 6:4; 10:2; 12:5; Rom. 12:12; Eph. 6:18; Col. 1:9; 1 Thess. 5:17; 2 Thess. 1:11; and 1 Pet. 4:7.

Explicit advice with a consciousness-altering objective is also given for dealing with negative emotions. Although these are quite sparse, their practical importance ensures that they will be well known to believers and often discussed. Consider the most important ones:

> Be ye angry, and [yet] sin not: let not the sun go down upon your wrath: Neither give place to the devil.[345]

> Be careful [i.e., anxious, distracted] for nothing; but in every thing by prayer and supplication with thanksgiving let your requests be made known unto God. And the peace of God, which passeth all understanding, shall keep your hearts and minds through Christ Jesus.[346]

> There is no fear in love; but perfect love casteth out fear: because fear hath torment [i.e., expectation of punishment]. He that feareth is not made perfect in love.[347]

> Rejoice in the Lord alway: *and* again I say, Rejoice.[348]

> As sorrowful, yet alway rejoicing; as poor, yet making many rich; as having nothing, and *yet* possessing all things.[349]

> Bless them which persecute you: bless, and curse not. Rejoice with them that do rejoice, and weep with them that weep. *Be* of the same mind one toward another.[350]

> Is any among you afflicted? let him pray. Is any merry? let him sing psalms.[351]

The emotions of anger, anxiety (or worry) and fear are to be handled in the manner known to abnormal psychology as "emotional isolation." The affective charge of the emotion and the apperception evoking it are to be split apart. One is permitted to be aware of having those emotions, but is not to be (or is to pretend not to be) touched by them. Falsifying one's emotions, trying to convince oneself that negative situations immediately evoke positive emotions is a major project to which the believer devotes energy. Much as love′ is torn away from the realm of affection in logocide, the believer's emotions are torn away from the apperceptions that appropriately evoke them. The ability of the believer to utilize empathy to help him come to terms with the complexities of his social surroundings—as well as his ability to get in touch with his true feelings about the discipline to which he subjects himself—are consequently impaired.

---

345. Eph. 4:26-27.
346. Phil. 4:6-7.
347. 1 John 4:18.
348. Phil. 4:4.
349. 2 Cor. 6:10.
350. Rom. 12:14-16. Cf., Matt. 5:10-12.
351. James 5:13.

An interesting question is raised by the selection of anger, worry and fear as emotions whereof the believer may retain some truncated conscious vestige, while others are to be banished from consciousness without a trace:

> Ye have heard that it was said by them of old time, Thou shalt not commit adultery: But I say unto you, That whosoever looketh on a woman to lust after her hath committed adultery with her already in his heart.[352]

> Whosoever hateth his brother is a murderer: and ye know that no murderer hath eternal life abiding in him.[353]

> You have heard that it was said to the men of old, 'You shall not kill; and whoever kills shall be liable to judgment.' But I say to you that every one who is angry with his brother shall be liable to judgment; whoever insults his brother shall be liable to the council, and whoever says, 'You fool!' shall be liable to the hell of fire. So if you are offering your gift at the altar, and there remember that your brother has something against you, leave your gift there before the alter and go; first be reconciled with your brother, and then come and offer your gift.[354]

The apparent contradiction as to whether the believer is permitted to be angry or not is easily resolved by taking note that anger against a "brother," i.e., a fellow believer, is forbidden, even though self-righteously muted anger is in order in some situations. One is allowed to be angry at Satan, and John the Divine's incoherent fulminations against any and all deviation from correct Christian doctrine that take up most of Revelation, amount to a rôle model for the kind of anger the believer may harbor and yet not sin. Note Jesus' masterful evasion of going too deep into the question of anger against a brother. To feel anger at the brother is tantamount to actually killing him. And just when it sounds as if Jesus is about to give advice on handling one's own angry thoughts and feelings he instead redirects the hearer's attention to what the other has against him, to judging the other's attitude and remaining unreflective about one's own, and by implication, to being duly subject to other believers' judgments about oneself. That Jesus does, notwithstanding his disclaimer elsewhere, about the "mote" in the other's eye and the "beam" in one's own.[355] Biblical counsel on anger comes down to permitting anger but not admitting it to oneself.

---

352. Matt. 5:27-28.
353. 1 John 3:15. Note the implications if one interprets this verse in the light of Luke 14:26: "If any *man* come to me, and hate not his . . . brethren . . . he cannot be my disciple;" and 1 John 4:20: "If a man say, I love God, and hateth his brother, he is a liar: for he that loveth not his brother whom he hath seen, how can he love God whom he hath not seen?" The propositions "only he who is a murderer and does not have eternal life abiding in him can be Jesus' disciple," and "he who *says* he loves God and *is* worthy to be Jesus' disciple is a liar" emerge as correct statements of good biblical doctrine.
354. Matt. 5:21-24. *Revised Standard Version.* Footnotes omitted. The phrase *without cause* is found after *angry with his brother* in some ancient manuscripts. The phrase is present in the King James, absent in Luther's German, and typically left out of the text but indicated by a footnote, in the reputable modern translations. Apparently, the pious men of long ago had problems with the idea of being all that free of anger!
355. See p. 100, footnote 63.

The preconditions for the believer to be full of bottled up tensions induced by the hobbling Christian constraints and to vent those tensions on out-group scapegoats, congratulating himself all the while for being so exemplarily meek and benign and affecting the appropriate persona, fall into place.

The specification of what amounts to semiconsciousness as the proper status for anger, and its uneasy reconciliation with absence of sin turns out to be quite purposeful, for occupying the conscious mind with angry content not relevant to, and diverting the believer from, the real sources of conflict in his life.[356] The author of Revelation, shut up in a Roman prison on the island of Patmos, instead of seeing his oppressors realistically, vents his anger on the irrelevancy of the seven apostate churches and has no insight at all as to how much his state of mind is worsened by his self-imposed theological obligation to regard his nightmarish reveries as true. With each of the other emotions for which semiconsciousness is specified, fear and worry, a corresponding purpose of providing irrelevancies for consciousness to work on is in view. No such purpose is connected with those emotions commanded not to be conscious: lust and hatred. All the human emotions mentioned, and by implication all strong human emotions, are to be the occasion for bad conscience in the believer. Putting them out of consciousness relieves the pangs of bad conscience. The emotions themselves are sins, and merely experiencing them makes the believer beholden to be forgiven, and constitutes evidences of lack of salvation in his life. This stratagem is so crucial that the express teaching that worry and fear are sins is a hallmark of heavily mind-controlling, mini-Reformationist churches. With the additional impetus from being made afraid of being afraid, anxious about being anxious, and worried about being worried, the acquired knack for dissociating away the emotional charge is practiced, enhanced and perfected. If one has that knack down well, one gets the peace of mind experienced as the immediate benefit of being a believer, and outwardly, one evinces euphoric calm. It all has the same appeal as a chemical soporific—hence Christianity's famed successes as a substitute for drug or alcohol dependence. The dampening of unpleasant emotions is rewarding, so as to prompt the believer at an intermediate level of indoctrination to continue, and is sufficiently impressive and unfamiliar as a subjective experience to make the believer think something supernatural is happening to him. The biblical scheme that the believer does not yet understand (or may never advance to understanding) to be transparent to experiential corroboration, is seemingly corroborated. This soporific secondary gain of dissociation is the key, indispensable psychological factor in conservative Christianity's contemporary renewed popularity.

The same sequence, aggravating the pain of a normal emotion by making

---

356. Both in ordinary language and in biblical usage, anger denotes a transitory, locally reactive sort of hostility, and hatred, a more active, ongoing, deep-seated hostility. Note how it is the transitory emotion that the Bible qualifiedly approves: "let not the sun go down upon your wrath. . . ." The approved "angers," at Satan and at the bringers of other doctrines, are, however, ongoing. The nature of human hostility itself is consequently falsified. The believer is further confused by what amounts to a tacit biblical pseudopsychology of human hostility.

the emotion, itself, besides the situation to which it responds, an occasion for the psychic pain of bad conscience, is intended by biblical counsel about worry or anxiety (and about fear, a special case we defer until Device 7). Note what follows immediately upon a particularly troublesome verse we have encountered before, on the commanded alienation of the believer's earthly affections:

> If any *man* come to me, and hate not his father, and mother, and wife, and children, and brethren, and sisters, yea, and his own life also, he cannot be my disciple. And whosoever doth not bear his cross, and come after me, cannot be my disciple. For which of you, intending to build a tower, sitteth not down first, and counteth the cost, whether he have *sufficient* to finish *it?* Lest haply [perhaps], after he hath laid the foundation, and is not able to finish *it,* all that behold *it* begin to mock him, Saying, This man began to build, and was not able to finish. Or what king, going to make war against another king, sitteth not down first, and consulteth whether he be able with ten thousand to meet him that cometh against him with twenty thousand? Or else, while the other is yet a great way off, he sendeth an ambassage, and desireth conditions of peace. So likewise, whosoever he be of you that forsaketh not all that he hath, he cannot be my disciple.[357]

This passage, as the Marxist "liberation theologians" never tire of pointing out, dispenses in one bold stroke with every conceivable expression of capitalism. Rational planning to accomplish anything in this world is directly condemned, adding to the impression already received from Jesus' use of paradoxes taking off from the arithmetic relations of worldly transactions, in discrediting "the World."[358] But this time, instead of being encouraged to feel good about failing to cope with life's realistic pressures, the believer is traduced into suffering bad conscience when he copes with those pressures successfully, and for doing what is basically good and blameless in human nature: planning and building things. The passage has its historical dimension: it subtly compares the Temple preoccupation (edifice complex?) of the Jews of Jesus' day with the Tower of Babel, and follows that comparison with what can well be a reference to avoiding the impending suicidal military confrontation with the Romans, that may have been essential to Jesus' historically unascertainable true purposes. In several other places, Jesus directly teaches that making practical arrangements and plans for this life, even in the short run, is forbidden, taboo and sinful.[359] All passages that superficially seem to hedge on the antipracticality commandment, and at least tolerate thoughtful management of the Christian group's communal resources, turn out to make more sense and fit the context better when understood to be about spiritual resources, laid up in the world to come.[360] From the itinerant, homeless, familyless vagrants waiting for the immanent end of the world, the

357. Luke 14:26-33. Cf., Luke 18:29-30, promising to the believer, in return for alienating his affections as commanded, "manifold more in this present time, and in the world to come life everlasting." Unless the supposed subjective gratification of being a believer is meant, this is a demonstrably false promise, threatening to bring down the whole scheme.
358. See p. 180, footnote 23.
359. E.g., Matt. 6:25-34; Mark 10:17-31 and Luke 12:13-34. See also, James 4:13-16.
360. Cf., Luke 12:33-34 and 2 Cor. 12:14.

examples progress to family-oriented, churched believers who have tightly controlled, modest households, and support their family and church by being the obedient hirelings of unbelieving go-getters, or the secular state. At no point are there explicit instructions as to the rational, economic management of anything. The only kind of Christian entrepreneur or go-getter the Bible ever mentions is the Christian slave owner! Alas, the ingrained "old-time religion" custom of interpreting these teachings to discourage only excessive anxiety or worry about speculative, unlikely problems ("borrowing trouble"), or else futile worry about the unchangeable or inevitable, stretches the words beyond their elastic limits.[361] The context indicates that Jesus truly meant, "So do not worry about tomorrow: tomorrow will take care of itself. Each day has enough trouble of its own."[362]

After having been attracted with the prospect of encouragement to feel good about his worldly failures, even to esteem himself spiritually superior on their account, when the believer becomes more advanced, he finds himself conscientiously on the defensive for doing what is right and natural for him to do, what he must do, especially if called to a leadership rôle. As with the commandments to invest more than one hundred percent of his libido, and to give one hundred percent of his loyalty to each of more than one master, the believer struggles to make sense out of contrived paradox, to put in practice that which has been predefined and set up to be impossible. By rendering the individual's adaptive proclivities ambivalent in this way, sometimes a frenzy of effective, practical management as a volunteer for the church is stimulated. But even that is part of what is ultimately forbidden, and the frenzy of work for the church and the affirmation it elicits from the church's rulers help keep that realization and its attendant psychic pain out of mind. Very clever, these originators of Christianity, who, by making it taboo, stimulated practical getting things done!

The equating of the mere thought of sexual lust and internecine hatred to their respective actual deeds is a crucial feature of the mind-control system. The general theme of confusing nonfantasy and the Bible's prescribed heterochthonous fantasy is explicitly, if fleetingly, expressed in the idea that the difference between imagining a thing and actually doing it is morally unimportant. The theme of making all things affectively equal, so that the commandments and not the unequal affective significances of people and things will govern the believer's thought and behavior finds its most extreme expression in the instruction to esteem thinking a thing the moral equivalent of doing it. Woe to him who tries to be true to the Bible, but who does not have such a talent for dissociation as to become blissfully oblivious to whatever lustful or violent stirrings go on, pressed down beneath the threshold of his consciousness. That person will be condemned to the continual pain of bad conscience and to ominous salvation doubt, because of his inability to "get victory" over those thoughts, his failure at

---

361. Pastors, particularly in connection with fund-raising, like to refer to a few passages revolving around "stewards" or managers. Cf., Matt. 20:8; Luke 12:42; 16:1-18; 1 Cor. 4:1-2; Titus 1:7 and 1 Pet. 4:10. None of these can fairly be read to be in praise of earthly practicality.
362. Matt. 6:34. *The Jerusalem Bible.*

"bringing into captivity every thought to the obedience of [i.e., to] Christ."[363]

The biblical assault on the healthy, "related" process of distinguishing the consequence of doing a thing from the inconsequence of merely thinking it—and the interesting express juxtaposition of the matter to the same two issues that seemed so important to Freud that he named them *eros* and *thanatos*—has humanly important implications. What should be noted here is that the mental-health professions have been entirely right in these bits of conventional wisdom: Failure clearly to distinguish action from mere thought, and bad conscience coupled with felt need to censor conscious thought rigorously because mere thought is perceived to be occasion for guilt, are premises of mental illness. Also, the mentally healthy person feels free to experiment with whatever thoughts may occur to him. With those ideas, the mental-health movement did correct a benighted, retrograde, pervasive Christian practice.[364] It is impossible to be serious about following the Bible and dispense with that practice. That is the most serious reason why biblical counselors ought never be considered competent or desirable helpers of people with psychological problems. That is the most compelling reason for branding mini-Reformationist churches a public mental-health menace.

Continuing with our immediate topic, we conclude our tour of the realm of explicit instructions conducive to the biblically desired dissociation, and take up less direct, symbolically expressed teachings that induce dissociation more by suggestion than by exhortation. Our four-fold typology of explicit and implicit devotional instructions and direct and reverse suggestions becomes particularly clouded at this point by the convolutions of biblical language. Some of the suggestions are phrased as exhortations, and the difference between them and teachings actually entailing some behavior the believer can perform, or a knack he can acquire, is worth noting if only to help us overcome the overlearned conventional interpretations we bring to them.

Two nonbiblical analogies illustrate by exaggeration the way biblical suggestions work. Recently I heard a television preacher talk about faith, using the analogy of a person floating on water. To float, one must suspend the normal, reflexive tendency to assume an upright posture when one feels off balance, and relax, letting one's mouth and nose point up, making no effort to lift them out of the water. Trying to lift them out makes one go under, and unless one can support oneself on something solid, or go into some quite different, active swimming mode, a person will drown. That faith be blissful relaxation after complete self-surrender was the preacher's message.

The preacher's analogy accurately portrays how faith seems from the subjective viewpoint of the believer. In its better moments, it seems effortless. But we understand that is only because the part of the process involving expenditure of energy is hidden from conscious awareness. An alternative analogy, including

363. 1 Cor. 15:54, 57; 1 John 5:4 (victory); 2 Cor. 10:5 (thought captivity).

364. Note the similarity between the censoring activity contemplated by the equivalence of some taboo thoughts and their corresponding deeds, and *crimestop,* the remedy for "thought crime," in Orwell's *1984,* pp. 19, 174.

what the floating analogy is so well chosen to leave out, would liken faith to riding a bicycle. To one who has never done it, it seems amazing that the bicyclist can remain upright on such a narrow footing. When one first tries it, one is afraid to go fast enough for the underlying physical principle, centrifugal force making the wheels act as gyroscopes, to take hold and stabilize machine and rider. Perhaps the learner is not well-coordinated enough at first to pedal fast enough while keeping his weight evenly distributed. The more energy the rider can transmit through the pedals, the faster he can go, and the uprightness of the bicycle, depending on the mass of the wheels, becomes so stable that it would take relatively great force to tip it over. And while the bicyclist does sometimes get to coast effortlessly down hills, he must pedal laboriously up others.

To make the bicycle analogy work for Christian faith, a feature contrary to the ordinary experience of riding a bicycle must be added. Even the most immature young bicyclist sees a cause-and-effect relationship between his input of energy by pedaling and the forward motion of the bicycle: this will be understood even though the lateral stability of the bicycle after a certain threshold speed has been reached remains a mystery. The bicyclist who understands that his pedaling is translated into forward motion is more analogous to someone who does one of the other consciousness-altering disciplines, such as self-hypnosis, bio-feedback, or yoga. If the bicyclist could become fixated on some more strange and exotic notion of the relation of the effort he expends to the result produced, e.g., that the feeling of tiredness in his limbs produces an anti-gravity effect, or the forward motion is produced by his will power, leaving the pedaling only to serve to keep the tires inflated and prevent them from going flat, or that the discomfort and self-affliction of the tiredness propitiates the motion god, then he would be more like the Christian, whose own efforts produce the illusions that there is vague, mysterious other personality there, that his negative emotions and thoughts have been supernaturally washed away by the blood of Christ, and that his being has become divided into one set of components that has been supernaturally regenerated and into another that has not. If one could convince the bicyclist that the heretical thought that his pedaling both moves the bicycle forward and provides the energy that makes the bicycle stable through the gyroscopic effect of the turning wheels could be detected by some omniscient inquisitor, who would send the bicyclist off to an eternal uphill climb with demonic tormentors in hot pursuit, snapping bloodthirstily at his rear reflector if he so much as dared to form the offending thought in mind, then we would succeed in making the bicyclist a true image of the Bible-authentic Christian. What the biblicist bicyclist must do is pedal consistently enough to be sure that his potential offending thoughts spin at or above escape velocity, kept away from the focal axis of consciousness by the psychic equivalent of centrifugal force, but deliberately enough not to tire himself out. The pedaling might alternatively be pictured as bailing a leaky boat faster than it fills, or adding air to a leaky balloon faster than the air escapes.

The rest of the biblical dissociation-inducing images we have to investigate resemble these, but are more subtle, oblique and quaint. The image of the person floating can be our prototype for the direct suggestion, portraying something of how awareness is supposed to appear to the well-indoctrinated believer. The image of the assiduous, deluded bicyclist can be our prototype for the reverse suggestion. The negative consequences, the concomitant, adverse symptoms caused by the biblical faith activity are permitted to show just enough, that the believer's peripheral awareness of manifesting them is anticipated and acknowledged, and the believer given thereby to know that he is on the right track. All the while, he takes up the doctrinal ploys provided to help him misinterpret the symptoms, as his flesh′ warring against his regenerated spirit, or fulfillments of the Scriptures, "In the world ye shall have tribulation . . . ," and ". . . the trial of your faith . . . [is] more precious than of gold. . . ."

Since putting out of mind what does not suit the doctrine is their point, we would expect to find images and express statements together, imparting the idea that cleansing consciousness is tantamount to, or at least the starting place for, spiritual renovation or "sanctification" of the person. Explicitly stated, that would come down to the pseudopsychological principles that a clean consciousness bespeaks a clean body, mind, soul and spirit and that refraining from thinking about problems is a salutary way to handle them.[365]

Our expectations are met, with far-reaching biblical, pseudopsychological implications, in the following:

> Not that which goeth into the mouth defileth a man; but that which cometh out of the mouth, this defileth a man. . . . whatsoever entereth in at the mouth goeth into the belly, and is cast out into the draught [defecation]. . . . But those things which proceed out of the mouth come forth from the heart; and they defile the man. For out of the heart proceed evil thoughts, murders, adulteries, fornications, thefts, false witness, blasphemies: These are *the things* which defile a man. . . .[366]

This is presented as Jesus' polemic against the Jewish principle of salvation by ritual purity, the dietary laws in particular. Of the occasions when Jesus is portrayed to have rebelled against the Jewish status quo, this savors least of a philosophically appealing, higher standard partaking of, yet improving on and somehow completing, the old. This time, he simply overthrows the old standard and goes off into a categorical pronouncement on the negative pseudopsychology of human moral nature that would seem more at home coming out of the mouth of Paul. We are alerted to a probable later interpolation, and a particularly self-conscious mind-control purpose, when the departure from Old Testament ways is so drastic. (This is rather like the paradox of the Cretans: since Jesus was as fully a man as he was fully God, and this statement proceeded out of his mouth, it

---

365. Coupled with the antipracticality commandment so clearly enunciated by Jesus, a very good biblical argument can be made for a wide variety of practical problems, perhaps all those for which there are no explicit love′ directives, to be biblically "solved" by putting them out of mind and keeping them out. Perhaps Scarlett O'Hara was not quite biblical when she said, "I'll think about it tomorrow," but she could have become so by saying instead, "I won't ever think about it."

366. Matt. 15:11,17-20. See also Mark 7:15,18-23, and Heb. 13:9.

follows that the statement itself must be an "evil thought," a "false witness" or a blasphemy, defiling Jesus.) Man is encouraged to rate his creative capacities equal in value to indigestion. The myriad depictions of Scripture as solid or potable nourishment, as "bread," "meat," "milk" or "water," enhances the view that permissible mental content is ingested only from outside.[367] Any kind of thought he might form in mind, except the scriptural, heterochthonous ones "put on," defile the believer.[368] Sanctification requires not entertaining them in one's mind any more!

The notion that the remedy for the pollution of the foul secretions of the inner man, besides the cleansing by the Holy Spirit, the blood of Christ, etc., is the evacuation of noncomplying thoughts from consciousness, is expressed by using the eye as a figure of consciousness:

> No man, when he hath lighted a candle, putteth *it* in a secret place, neither under a bushel, but on a candlestick, that they which come in may see the light. The light of the body is the eye: therefore when thine eye is single [unified, homogenous], thy whole body also is full of light; but when *thine eye* is evil [malignant], thy body also *is* full of darkness. Take heed therefore that the light which is in thee be not darkness. If thy whole body therefore *be* full of light, having no part dark, the whole shall be full of light, as when the bright shining of a candle doth give thee light.[369]

367. Note that biblical references to wine are slightly more ambivalent than for other comestibles, associating it with the Holy Spirit, but not the Word. Drunkenness is condemned, and in Revelation, the wine of "wrath" (14:8,10;18:3) and "fornication" (17:2) are spoken of. Yet, Timothy is given leave to take a little, for his digestion (1 Tim. 5:23). What is really being avoided is the premise that the scriptural program is a soporific substitute for wine.

368. Only once is Jesus portrayed as departing from his bleak view of man's inner resources, but with striking implications:

"He that believeth on me, as the scripture hath said, out of his belly shall flow rivers of living water. (But this spake he of the Spirit, which they that believe on him should receive: for the Holy Ghost was not yet *given;* because that Jesus was not yet glorified.)" John 7:38-39.

This, like Ps. 51:17 and Ezek. 11:19, has provided a point of departure for "old-time religion's" expedient humanization of the Gospel message. But note how the interpretation is immediately furnished, that whatever it is that the verse refers to is to be fulfilled and executed at Pentecost, leaving no promise of such dramatic inner experience still owed to the believer during the church age. The parenthetic interpretation also neatly disposes of the potentially disruptive prophecy of Joel 2:28, ". . . your sons and your daughters shall prophesy, your old men shall dream dreams, your young men shall see visions. . . ."

An important clue to the puzzle of this atypical saying of Jesus is its purport to be an earlier, i.e., Old Testament, scriptural quotation. There is no Old Testament verse juxtaposing "living" or flowing waters to any part of a human body, although there are important ones dealing with miraculous production of water out of dry earth. (See Exod. 17:1-7; Isa. 12:3-4; and Zech. 14:8.) Jesus is here depicted as uttering a spurious Scripture verse! I suspect that this saying, with its obvious Gnostic leanings, was too salient a part of the contemporary, unwritten lore about Jesus for the earliest proponents of the mind-controlling rendition of his teachings to suppress. To foster the position that theirs and not the Gnostics' was the true rendition of Jesus' teaching, they must have had to go ahead and acknowledge its authenticity, but then explain it away and put the blame on the Jews' Scriptures for good measure. At a minimum, we can be sure that the suggestion of rivers of living water flowing from the believer's inner being must have been a very sore point, for the verse containing it to have been handled in such an extraordinary way.

369. Luke 11:33-36. Cf. Matt. 6:22-23.

Jesus goes on for the rest of the chapter in a tirade against the outward appearances affected by the Pharisees and lawyers, complete with an ambiguous allusion to almsgiving.[370] In context, the thrust of the teaching is clearly that policing conscious contents comes ahead of deeds in Jesus' devotional priorities.

While a less literal word, like *clear* or *pure* could arguably be used where the King James uses *single,* the figure of a single eye for the monomania being urged occurs again:

> . . . But I say unto you, That whosoever looketh on a woman to lust after her hath committed adultery with her already in his heart. And if thy right eye offend thee, pluck it out, and cast *it* from thee: for it is profitable for thee that one of thy members should perish, and not *that* thy whole body should be cast into hell. And if thy right hand offend thee, cut it off, and cast *it* from thee: for it is profitable for thee that one of thy members should perish, and not *that* thy whole body should be cast into hell.[371]

Substantially the same image of self-mutilation appears in two other places, with more elaborate descriptions of the terrors of Hell.[372] Note the important clue as to the still-mortal bodily condition of the inmate of Hell. We receive an important clue as to how people handle symbolism, in the absence of Christians in history who actually mutilated eye, hand or foot as an act of faith. While the most important theologian of the third century, Origen, did castrate himself in order to achieve the purity he thought was required, and themes of self-mutilation are fairly prevalent in Renaissance religious painting, history records no order of one-eyed Christians going around wearing holy eye patches. Clearly, psychic self-mutilation and fragmentation are in view.

Another image of division comes in a passage parallel to "I came not to send peace, but a sword":[373]

> Suppose ye that I am come to give peace on earth? I tell you, Nay; but rather division: For from henceforth there shall be five in one house divided, three against two, and two against three.[374]

Jesus goes on to tell which family members, some of whom are elswehere commanded to be in specified dominance-submission relationships, are to form these factions. Can it be that when he also said, ". . . a house . . . divided against itself . . . cannot stand . . . ,"[375] He meant that the "house" so divided—or dissociated—is to be under mind-control?

---

370. Luke 11:41. Underlying ". . . give alms of such things as ye have . . . ," is the unusual word *eneimi,* translated as "have," but connoting what one has *within:* spiritual possessions rather than physical.
371. Matt. 5:28-30.
372. Matt. 18:8-9 and Mark 9:43-48.
373. Matt. 10:34.
374. Luke 12:51-52.
375. Mark 3:25.

The other end of the Christian range of experience that runs from pure, monochromatic one-mindedness to inner division and fragmentation is expressed in Paul's description of his own experience of inner dividedness:

> . . . [W]e know that the law is spiritual: but I am carnal, sold under sin. For that which I do I allow not [i.e., do not understand]: for what I would, that I do not; but what I hate, that do I. If then I do that which I would not, I consent unto the law that *it is* good. Now then it is no more I that do it, but sin that dwelleth in me. For I know that in me (that is, in my flesh,) dwelleth no good thing: for to will is present with me; but *how* to perform that which is good I find not. For the good that I would I do not: but the evil which I would not, that I do. Now if I do that I would not, it is no more I that do it, but sin that dwelleth in me. I find then a law that, when I would do good, evil is present with me. For I delight in the law of God after the inward man: But I see another law in my members, warring against the law of my mind, and bringing me into captivity to the law of sin which is in my members. O wretched man that I am! who shall deliver me from the body of this death? I thank God through Jesus Christ our Lord. So then with the mind I myself serve the law of God; but with the flesh the law of sin.[376]

What a "testimony"! So much for the peace that passeth understanding, the inability of the believer to sin any more, and "Casting all your care upon him; for he careth for you."[377] All that comes in the next life. For the Christian who really does the devotional task set out in the Bible, alienation from the world, from people outside of the strictly structured, intrachurch interactions, and from oneself, are the right expectations. One acts out the "put on" program, and is to be so out of touch with the rest of one's being that in all other behavior one experiences oneself as a puppet whose strings are being jerked by someone else.

The tacit realization by the Bible authors that putting noncomplying mental content out of consciousness does not really get rid of it, addressed in Paul's pseudopsychological explanation that the outer shell of the old nature remains until one gets one's new, glorified body on judgment day, also underlies two crucial symbolic biblical themes that conventional theology has had most difficulty handling: the question of evil spirits and the Trinity.

Nothing in secular literature illustrates so well as the biblical lore on spirits the clinical insight that people, if they do not integrate what wells up from the unconscious to the conscious attitude, if they do not depotentiate negative manifestations of the unconscious through insight, must live out their implications blindly, or experience them as baffling neurotic symptoms, expending energy that could be put to much better use instead to keep them down, to combat the agitation for their expression inevitably following from the attempt to handle them by repression or dissociation only. That the Christian, who tries to make the gap of inner dividedness so wide that what is on the other side is too far away to perceive, will continue to have trouble with what he dissociates, is vividly, perhaps mockingly expressed, in this reverse-suggestive passage:

376. Rom. 7:14-25.
377. 1 Pet. 5:7.

> When the unclean spirit is gone out of a man, he walketh through dry places, seeking rest, and findeth none. Then he saith, I will return into my house from whence I came out; and when he is come, he findeth *it* empty, swept, and garnished [tidied]. Then goeth he, and taketh with himself seven other spirits more wicked than himself, and they enter in and dwell there: and the last *state* of that man is worse than the first. Even so shall it be also unto this wicked generation.[378]

The idea that dealing with proscribed mental content by repression or dissociation leads to return of the same kind of content seven times worse is all too psychologically valid. Perhaps the proportion is geometric, and after another devotional exercise of smoothing the boundary over, one would be invaded by 64 unclean spirits (the original eight, plus seven more recruited by each of them). The pastors tend to find excuses for interpreting the passage's negative consequences to apply only to the unsaved. That tact works well with relatively advanced mind-controllees in a mini-Reformationist setting, who then work all the harder to cleanse their minds of the natural thoughts and feelings that would, to them, signify jeopardy of lack of salvation.

Not until the third verse does the hearer even find out whether the subject of the sentences in the first two verses was the man or the unclean spirit. The impression of a curious split in viewpoint is conveyed. The behavior of psychological complexes, potentially manifesting themselves as obsessive thoughts, unruly feelings, hysterical medical symptoms, or in the most extreme case, a splinter personality experienced as entirely separate and apart from the ego-personality, is artfully condensed in the allegory. (We must keep in mind the snare of circularity in identifying the sources of the analogies: the originators of our ideas about psychopathology, particularly Jung, were influenced by these same cultural fixtures as well as by their clinical experience—with patients also influenced by the same cultural fixtures.) The believer is not merely encouraged but required to appraise projections of facets of the dissociated shadow side of his own personality as real, as so powerful in the natural world as to appear to have the upper hand generally, and as definitely having the upper hand in the lives of the unsaved. Note how the biblical devotional program creates the fragmentation problem, by alienating the person from his inner roots so thoroughly that their manifestation can only take place divorced from insight as to their true nature and origin. The devotional program then supplies just the wrong solution: constant escalation of the effort devoted to dissociating the contents, to preventing their constructive resolution to the conscious attitude. The biblical devotional program does best at seeming to solve problems that it, itself, has created!

---

378. Matt. 12:43-45. Luke 11:24-26 is an almost identical parallel. Note how, in each instance, Jesus uses this hard-hitting picture of the hyperreligious person's symptoms hastily to change the subject after delivering a rebuke to proponents of some variety of supernaturalistic superstitiousness other than his own. Also, he follows it in each instance, correcting people whose comments indicate that they have misunderstood him to be a proponent of familial values. This may be an accurate composite picture of Jesus' technique when he worked the crowds, which many contemporary pastors successfully imitate.

The splitting of viewpoint, the paradoxical superimposing of the man's and the unclean spirit's respective viewpoint is one of several pieces of biblical information that, put together, yield up a rather clear biblical doctrine of unclean spirits or demons. The tacit perspicacity of the Bible authors about the activity of the unconscious is impressively demonstrated in it. The Bible itself does not require wholesale incorporation into Christianity of the pagan lore of demons, as occurred in Roman Catholicism. To the modern assumption that seeming manifestations of the negative supernatural are merely figments of people's imaginations can be added the qualification "nearly all," and the result can readily coexist with the biblical premise that some demonic or Satanic manifestations are real and particularly to be expected accompanying end-times bringers of spurious gospels. To be Bible-authentic, the believer must necessarily maintain a hefty respect for the negative supernatural. For the modern, non-ignorant believer, maintenance of that respect entails additional exercises in assaulting his integrity. The resulting partial return to childish fears, otherwise inappropriate for a grown-up, heightens dependency on the church group and alienation from all others. We shall have more to say about the execrable effect of belief in evil spirits on believers' attitudes. (Too casual an attitude toward the negative supernatural is, in my opinion, the most prevalent symptom of a pastor who no longer personally believes, who "fakes it.")

All descriptions of unclean spirits dwelling in and being cast out of people in the Bible occur during Jesus' ministry. Only passing mention is made of them after that, and along with miraculous healings of physical diseases, they peter out rapidly after Pentecost.[379] The thwarted spirit possessions and miraculously cured physical diseases in the New Testament bear little resemblance to modern conversion hysterias or other psychopathologies. The biblical accounts are too stylized to support psychological commentary on whatever historical events may underlie them. They describe neither outward symptoms, nor an individual's dream or productive fantasy. They savor of shared, collective folklore, or at least a good counterfeit of such folklore, adapted to harness the real thing's appeal.

The unclean spirits represent the unconscious as experienced from the individual conscious standpoint. The attribute most clearly so identifying them is their sagacity: they know much more about Jesus than do his human onlookers. The appearance is put up, as if it were Jesus, striking a responsive chord in the hearer's unconscious:

> . . . [W]hen he was come to the other side [after one of the Sea of Galilee voyages] into the country of the Gergesenes [Gadarenes], there met him two possessed with devils [demons], coming out of the tombs, exceeding fierce, so that no man might pass by that way. And, behold, they cried out, saying, What have we to do with thee, Jesus, thou Son of God? art thou come hither to torment us before the time? And there was a good way off from them an herd of many swine feeding. So the devils besought him, saying, If thou cast us out, suffer us to go away into the herd of swine. And he said unto them, Go. And when they were come out, they went

379. Acts 5:16 and 8:7.

> into the herd of swine: and, behold, the whole herd of swine ran violently down a steep place into the sea, and perished in the waters.[380]

Consistently, the demons are characterized as numerous, or "legion."[381] Yet they speak with one voice and apparently have perfected that unity of mind whereto Christians are exhorted. That the demons do not cease to exist, but must go somewhere else when cast out, is indicated by their transfer to an infrahuman host—one negatively symbolizing a lower, more primitive level of the human psyche.[382] The animal side of human nature may seem to perish in the waters of the unconscious; however, it does not take great imagination to anticipate what the decaying carcasses would do to the water. The possibilities in the biblical statements about them—that the demons are finite in number, are none other than the fallen angels, and continue to exist to prey upon successive generations of mortals—all point to the demons' transpersonal or archetypal nature. What should be noted is that only negative allusions to the individual's unconscious or fantastic inner life are conveyed, and that there is biblical acknowledgement and seeming explanation that the peace that passeth understanding and the casting of one's cares on Christ will not be all that untroubled or free from inner turmoil, stress and strain. There is an immediate, apparent ring of truth to the psychological half-truth imparted by the passage, and that is misused to lend credence to the larger manipulative stratagem.

There is a fascinating incident, following immediately upon the transfiguration of Jesus, where he cures a boy of demon possession. In each of the synoptic Gospels it has a different dénouement, each tying some aspect of demon exorcism securely into the larger dissociative "faith" project. Mark's version is:

> . . . [O]ne of the multitude . . . said, Master, I have brought unto thee my son, which hath a dumb spirit; And wheresoever he taketh him, he teareth him [i.e., causes him to convulse]: and he foameth, and gnasheth with his teeth, and pineth away: and I spake to thy disciples that they should cast him out; and they could not. He answereth him, and saith, O faithless generation, how long shall I be with you? how long shall I suffer you? bring him unto me. And they brought him . . . and . . . straightway the spirit tare him; and he fell on the ground, and wallowed foaming. And he asked his father, How long is it ago since this came into him? And he said, Of a child. . . . but if thou canst do any thing, have compassion on us, and help us. Jesus said unto him, If thou canst believe, all things *are* possible to him that believeth. And straightway the father of the child cried out, and said with tears, Lord, I believe; help thou mine unbelief. When Jesus saw that the

380. Matt. 8:28-32. The relative omniscience of the demons is also evident in Mark 1:23-28; 3:11 and Luke 4:33-35. Another incident of the use of swine as an alternative vehicle for demons is described in Mark 5:1-15 and Luke 8:26-36.

381. Mark 5:9 and Luke 8:30.

382. Note that all references to swine in the Bible are negative. Cf. Prov. 11:22; Matt. 7:6; Luke 15:15, and 2 Pet. 2:22. Historically, swine, dietarily forbidden to the Jews, are associated with disparaging references to non-Jews. The raising of swine in Israel in Jesus' day must have been for food for the foreign oppressors, lending an extra dimension of symbolism to the story.

people came running together, he rebuked the foul spirit, saying unto him, *Thou* dumb and deaf spirit, I charge thee, come out of him, and enter no more into him. And *the spirit* cried, and rent him sore [i.e., made him convulse terribly], and came out of him: and he was as one dead; insomuch that many said, He is dead. But Jesus took him by the hand, and lifted him up; and he arose. And . . . his disciples asked him privately, Why could not we cast him out? And he said unto them, This kind can come forth by nothing, but by prayer. . . .[383]

Apparently when the disciples received their exorcism commission from Jesus, they neglected to read the fine print.[384] Jesus looks to be sure he has a crowd before performing the exorcism, thereby instructing rustic preachers for all times that they should always have a crowd whose presence exerts psychological pressure toward the desired result on the individual whose symptoms are to be "miraculously" altered. The business of the father's ambivalence about believing, besides tagging the passage to a postapostolic time, almost gives the game away: it is not a question of believing because there is evidence, but believing or else not getting the goodies. Believe, and then the prerequisite basis for the belief will be added. Finish building the house, and then he will give you the bricks for it. Do that trick, and your demons, or those of your alter-ego, will go away!

The paradox of the "deaf spirit" hearing Jesus and being obliged to obey him is a variation on the theme that sensitivity or life′ to the natural is inconsistent with sensitivity or life′ to the biblical supernatural. The Lucan account of the demon-possessed boy and his father concludes with another variation on the same theme:

But while they [the crowd] wondered every one at all things which Jesus did, he said unto his disciples, Let these sayings sink down into your ears: for the Son of man shall be delivered into the hands of men. But they understood not this saying, and it was hid from them, that they perceived it not: and they feared to ask him of that saying.[385]

A host of theological issues are raised, diverting the thoughtful mind from the psychological stratagem being worked: Often enough, God is portrayed figura-

---

383. Mark 9:17-29. The last omission is of the words *and fasting*, which are not found in the most ancient manuscripts and are usually removed to a footnote in the reputable modern translations. Apparently an interest in fasting developed later, after a period of disinterest beginning while the apostles were still alive. Perhaps early church fathers perceived the need to camouflage the link between demon exorcism and prayer.

The question of fasting is ambivalently treated in the New Testament. Cf., Matt. 4:2; 6:16-18; 9:14-15; Mark 2:18-20; Luke 5:33-35; 18:12 and Acts 13:2-3. It seems to be a holdover from the ceremonial law, used later as a figure for instruction in the new inner condition of mind that is to supersede ritual purity. The most thoughtful Bible expositors and most fully realized mini-Reformationist groups in my experience see a tendency toward trying to earn salvation by a work of self-affliction in the practice of fasting, and do not advocate it for present-day believers. More transitional and rustic groups tend to make fasting an occasion for disciplining their people to tune out inner, bodily sensations.

384. Matt. 10:1.

385. Luke 9:43-45.

tively blinding an eye, deafening an ear, or hardening a heart. The careful Bible reader cannot escape the conclusion that God takes full responsibility, and God-controlled attainment of hearing′ and sight′ as to the Gospel, and the loss of the same as to the flesh′, are essential in salvation. The believer seeks to cultivate such sight′ and hearing′ sensitivity, and without them he is exposed to salvation doubt. Particularly during Passion Week, such insensitivity is reflected in the disciples' bickering about "who is the greatest" among them, Peter's denials of Jesus, Judas' betrayal, and Jesus' revocation of his earlier instructions to the disciples to go out two by two without provisions of food or clothing, telling them instead to take provisions and even a couple of swords.[386] Those events can be reconciled with the rest, for all conventional theological purposes, as a special figure of the headless, temporarily dead church between the epochs. The exhortation to compensate for the difficulty of taking the more unbelievable beliefs in with devotional exercise—"Let these sayings sink down . . ."—is more germane. The conscious experience attending the *abaissement de niveau mental* wanted of the believer is the psychologically pertinent feature. It is expressed plainly. Being oblivious to some highly consequential matters, but nevertheless sufficiently aware of them peripherally to be afraid to ask, talk, or think about them, is a rule of the game. As regards the believer's difficulty in getting the "spiritual" truth′ to register, that is, of course, really due to its intrinsic artificiality and absurdity, and the believer's innate integrity persisting. By connecting the perceived, ominous failure of the supposititious, "holy" kind of inner perception (which would lead, were it to progress, to failure of the dissociation, and reversion to normal psychological integrity) to an image evoking the tense, unsettled, claustrophobic atmosphere of Passion Week, the unease that really originates from the dissociated contents' continuing agitation for expression is acknowledged and seemingly accounted for.

The Matthean account of the demon-possessed boy and his father ends with a truncated rendition of a theme now familiar to us:

> Then came the disciples to Jesus apart, and said, Why could not we cast him out? And Jesus said unto them, Because of your unbelief: for verily I say unto you, If ye have faith as a grain of mustard seed, ye shall say unto this mountain, Remove hence to yonder place; and it shall remove; and nothing shall be impossible unto you.[387]

So, even the disciples, who have all seen him perform miracles and performed them themselves, pursuant to their commission, have a problem coming to the conclusion urged, before seeing the evidence, just as the father did, in Mark. Aha! And note how the theme is not completed here. Its resolution is withheld until it recurs, four chapters later.[388]

---

386. Luke 22:24-38.

387. Matt. 17:19-20.

388. Matt. 21:21. See p. 275, footnote 275. See also Luke 17:6, p. 278, footnote 282. In the King James version, after the above account, there is a verse not found in the most ancient manuscripts, and put in brackets or removed to a footnote in the reputable modern translations: "Howbeit this

Like the walk on the water, the several Gospel accounts of the story of the demon-possessed boy and his father clash, if brought together and compared. It turns out that everyone in the story except Jesus and the poor, zonked-out boy has grave problems with belief, even though they got to see, hear, touch and handle the evidence. In one version, the exhortation is to take in ("hear") the indoctrination passively and patiently, in another, to pray or actively indoctrinate oneself, and in the third, to alter one's interior, imaginative landscape, putting the mountain in a different place, and in striving to make the altered interior landscape seem more real than the real one, convince oneself that it is real. Now we see the true purpose of having several Gospels. Each overstates some aspect of the larger message of devotional exercise and effort to force oneself to believe the unbelievable. Were it all put together in one account, the events would not go together smoothly and the true purpose of the self-disinformation drill being urged might be exposed. By interweaving several operative themes and some distracting irrelevancy and separating the parts so that one will not be covered while another in discord with it is fresh in mind, the message is successfully gotten across without the one to whom it is communicated catching on. The "hidden persuasion" that contemporary psychologists have attempted, and for all practical purposes failed to achieve with tachistiscopically presented visual messages and masked auditory ones, can be achieved if the camouflage is at the level of *ideas* rather than the level of *sensory transmission.* The artistry and craftsmanship needed for it seldom occur. But the effects are positively epidemic when they do.[389]

The most important of the subtle operative themes interwoven in the Gospel narratives and embedded in other themes is that of the contrast between unity and plurality, between wholeness and fragmentation, in individual personalities. In the story of the demon-possessed boy and his father, it comes through in the "legion" number, yet singleness of purpose and voice, of the demons. It is more subtly expressed in the alter-ego relationship of the father and the boy. Since clear, explicit commandments provide that a pious father will not "respect" his son more than others, and not make so undiluted an investment of affection in

---

kind goeth not out but by prayer and fasting." Matt. 17:21. Apparently the early church fathers did still more of the kind of tampering which I noted on p. 312, footnote 383. I would speculate that the early church fathers found the Matthean account just quoted too subtle for their people, and in need of some more facile resolution.

389. The contageous, epidemic nature of the spread of Bible belief is acknowledged and anticipated by the recurrent theme of rapid, sinisterly magical multiplication of foodstuffs, connecting in turn with others, symbolizing the Word and the flesh of Christ as bread. Those images are reverse-suggestive on a social, rather than an intrapsychic level, adumbrating what the believer is to expect, going on around him. Jesus miraculously feeds five thousand restless tourists with five loaves and two fishes. Cf. Matt. 14:13-21; Mark 6:30-44; Luke 9:10-17 and John 6:1-14. Later, he feeds four thousand with seven loaves and "a few" fish. Each time, he has baskets of broken pieces left over. Cf. Matt. 15:32-39 and Mark 8:1-9. (In neither case are the people poor, nor does the feeding have the character of almsgiving.) Afterwards, he asks his disciples incomprehensible rhetorical questions, culminating in warning against the "leaven of the Pharisees." Notwithstanding, the Gospel has just been demonstrated *a fortiori* to have no little leaven of its own. There is a certain cynicism in depicting the growth of the movement so, also conveyed by depicting the believers as sheep, or fish to be netted.

him as to displace others or weaken his obsession with God, overidentification of a human father and son with one another cannot be what is being urged. Yet, the father's belief is the only human activity depicted as having had any effect on the exorcism. A less detailed biblical account of a demon exorcism has a Gentile woman approaching Jesus, to have her daughter exorcised of a demon.[390] Jesus speaks to the woman of having come only for the lost sheep of the house of Israel, and of not throwing bread to dogs when the children have not been fed. The woman, in contrast to the other persons present, responds with the unexpectedly sagacious image of crumbs falling from the master's table, showing she understands that God's elect, not national Israel, are meant. Having answered the quiz question correctly, she collects the prize of her daughter's exorcism. The parallel of the correct mental behavior effecting the exorcism of the same-sex child is what should be noted.[391] As in the earlier story, where Jesus had a dialogue with the demons before he cast them out, authentic folklore is imitated, and the false impression is transmitted, that the business involving Jesus resonates in the unconscious of the hearer.

The personality fragmentation sought in the believer is illustrated by biblical themes of body fragmentation or division. The waist and the midline demarcate the desired, imaginary psychic boundaries. We get an early hint of it in the desire of Adam and Eve to conceal their genitals from God after the fall, their attempt to do so with fig leaves, and God's furnishing them with more sturdy "skins," to cover the offending areas. The notion of getting rid of pelvic awareness by faith comes through clearly in the story of the woman with the issue of blood. Jesus raises it again when he says:

> For there are some eunuchs, which were so born from *their* mother's womb: and there are some eunuchs, which were made eunuchs of men: and there be eunuchs, which have made themselves eunuchs for the kingdom of heaven's sake. He that is able to receive *it* [i.e., this saying], let him receive *it*.[392]

While Origen, alone, understood this to call for self-castration, the evolving Roman Catholic church, contrary to the rest of the Bible's teachings on marriage, found its purposes better served by celibate clergy, disciplined to keep erotic awareness out of mind, billeted together in intensely group-pressuring, group-living situations. The affinity of erotic awareness and general receptivity to one's inner thoughts and feelings is demonstrated by the evident historical experience that dissociating the former helps draw attention away from the psychic implications of dissociating the latter. The same result is fostered by

390. Matt. 15:21-28 and Mark 7:24-30.

391. Having it be an alien female figure who utters an unexpectedly profound, explicit statement is, considering the onesidedly masculine perspective of the Bible, a manifestation of a Jungian anima imago. The same theme recurs, with the strangeness of the female figure heightened by her Samaritan ethnicity, in the story of the woman at the well (John 4:7-30). Her giving of water, her plural husbands (animus figures often occur plurally, and in a particularly archetypal individual dream or fantasy, an anima often has its own animus), and her unnatural sagacity are very much reminiscent of authentic, collective folklore.

392. Matt. 19:12.

rustic fundamentalist groups, having their people discipline themselves to fast and to tune the resulting hunger pangs out of conscious awareness. Note how being "able to receive" the teaching aligns with election, and the corresponding inability, with evidence of lack of salvation, placing the subject in jeopardy.

The Bible is more adamant about fostering a subjective sense of inner dividedness along the midline of the body, i.e., the axis across which the body is bilaterally symmetrical. We noted how pointedly the believer is confronted with the choice either to go to hellfire, or to have a figurative single eye, single hand and single foot in earthly life. Our contemporary understanding of the division of labor in the brain, with speech and articulate thought apparently concentrated in the left hemisphere, inarticulate motor skill in the right hemisphere, and local exterior bodily sensitivity reversed relative to the brain, because the neural pathways cross at the midline, makes it reasonable that a suggestion-induced, empathic sense of one side of the body separated and experienced differently from the other, would be consistent with dissociation. ". . . [W]hen thou doest alms, let not thy left hand know what thy right hand doeth. . . ."[393]

Since the portentous theological benefits that the believer receives from the breaking of Jesus' body and that he repeats that act, eating his flesh and drinking his blood each time he takes communion prepare the way for it, we would expect the fragmentation of Jesus' body to be implicated in the message of psychic fragmentation. We find the theme of midline division powerfully asserted in these passages:

> When the Son of man shall come in his glory, and all the holy angels with him, then shall he sit upon the throne of his glory: And before him shall be gathered all nations: and he shall separate them one from another, as a shepherd divideth *his* sheep from the goats: And he shall set the sheep on his right hand, but the goats on the left. Then shall the King say unto them on his right hand, Come, ye blessed of my Father, inherit the kingdom prepared for you from the foundation of the world: For I was an hungred, and ye gave me meat: I was thirsty, and ye gave me drink: I was a stranger, and ye took me in: Naked, and ye clothed me: I was sick, and ye visited me: I was in prison, and ye came unto me. Then shall the righteous answer him, saying, Lord, when saw we thee an hungered, and fed *thee?* or thirsty, and gave *thee* drink? . . . And the King shall answer . . . Verily I say unto you, Inasmuch as ye have done *it* unto one of the least of these my brethren, ye have done *it* unto me. Then shall he say also unto them on the left hand, Depart from me, ye cursed, into everlasting fire, prepared for the devil and his angels. . . . And these shall go away into everlasting punishment: but the righteous into life eternal.[394]

---

393. Matt. 6:3. Interestingly, the commandment not to let the left hand know what the right hand is doing is in conjunction with a Device I activity that the Bible superficially pretends to be about, but does not turn out on closer study to value highly—almsgiving. Untold generations have been required as part of their upbringing to "testify" that they understood modesty and unassumingness in good-doing to be taught by the verse. But is not the operative effect of the words to restrict almsgiving to those situations not requiring cooperation or coordination? Does it not rule out major coordinated involvement of the Body in that activity?

394. Matt. 25:31-37, 40-41, 46. Cf. Matt. 7:13-23.

> Then were there two thieves crucified with him, one on the right hand, and another on the left.[395]

> And I saw another mighty angel come down from heaven, clothed with a cloud: and a rainbow *was* upon his head, and his face *was* as it were the sun, and his feet as pillars of fire: And he had in his hand a little book open: and he set his right foot upon the sea, and *his* left *foot* on the earth. . . .[396]

The refinement of emphasis in the usage of the right side/left side theme is unsurpassed. Twice, when a passage's true drift is most near the surface of the language, the Bible leads with the extraneous, surface issue of almsgiving.[397] The conscious mind is diverted from the real business of the passages thereby. The two thieves argue about Jesus, and one ends up going to heaven (to be with Jesus there at the same time that Jesus is supposedly in Hell, atoning for all the sins of the elect). The other thief, by implication, goes to the place of silence to "sleep" until the day of arraignment. The Bible studiously avoids the dead giveaway of telling which thief was on which side. The theme of consciousness and goodness associated with one side of the body and with one another, set over against the same for unconsciousness and unrighteousness, with all the premium on increasing the separation between the poles, is clear. The angel with the book, which the context requires be understood to be a Bible—placing his weight on the surface of the water first, before distributing his weight between the land and the sea—brings many images we have encountered poignantly together, and tends to corroborate our interpretation of them.

The negation of the right side/left side theme marks the place where the most plainly psychological kind of inner division first appears:

> Then came to him [Jesus] the mother of Zebedee's children with her sons, worshipping *him,* and desiring a certain thing of him. And he said unto her, What wilt thou? She saith unto him, Grant that these my two sons may sit, the one on thy right hand, and the other on the left, in thy kingdom. But Jesus answered and said, Ye know not what ye ask. Are ye able to drink of the cup that I shall drink of, and to be baptized with the baptism that I am baptized with? They say unto him, We are able. And he saith unto them, Ye shall drink indeed of my cup . . . but to sit on my right hand, and on my left, is not mine to give, but *it shall be given to them* for whom it is prepared of my Father.[398]

395. Matt. 27:38.

396. Rev. 10:1-2.

397. We earlier covered the failure of the Scripture to follow through on the theme of caring for the physical needs of the unsaved, and the tendency of those steeped in Scripture to understand the giving of food and drink, the clothing of nakedness and the visitation of prisoners (who may be the "goods" referred to in Matt. 12:29 and Mark 3:27), as figures of the sin affliction and its remedy. See pp. 58-61. Now, we further understand the food and drink to relate to the Gospel's ability to proliferate unnaturally. Hiding the human body, insulating its more sensitive zones, and visiting those who are in bondage to Satan become symbolically intelligible as intimating evangelization.

398. Matt. 20:20-23.

The passage goes on about the jealous dissention the request causes among the disciples and culminates in the familiar non sequitur of servanthood as the greatest virtue and Jesus as the supreme example of servility. Note the self-seeking prayer-rôle model, as in the parable of the unjust judge. In Mark's parallel account, it is James and John, not their mother, who take the initiative in asking superior rank for themselves, and Jesus emphasizes predestination as having long since determined who shall hold what rank, instead of passing the buck to another person in the Godhead.[399] The only elements with any appreciable thematic affinity for one another are the two images of personality fragmentation. The collapse of the notion of right side/left side division occurs just before the introduction of the notion that God, in whose image the believer is to esteem himself to have been created, has more than one discrete conscious awareness and more than one volition.[400] The location of this passage earlier in the text than the ones conveying the right side/left side notion helps camouflage the operative elements.

A most startling picture emerges, if the passages most strongly asserting the multiple personality of the Godhead are viewed together:

> Thinkest thou that I [Jesus] cannot now pray to my Father, and he shall presently give me more than twelve legions of angels? But how then shall the scriptures be fulfilled, that thus it must be?[401]

> And he [Jesus in the Garden of Gethsemane] said, Abba, Father, all things *are* possible unto thee; take away this cup from me: nevertheless not what I will, but what thou wilt.[402]

> . . . Jesus . . . said, I thank thee, O Father, Lord of heaven and earth, because thou hast hid these things from the wise and prudent, and hast revealed them unto babes. . . . All things are delivered unto me of my Father: and no man knoweth the Son, but the Father; neither knoweth any man the Father, save the Son, and *he* to whomsoever the Son will [i.e., intends to] reveal *him*.[403]

> Jesus saith . . . I am the way, the truth, and the life: no man cometh unto the Father, but by me. If ye [Thomas] had known me, ye should have known my Father also: and from henceforth ye know him, and have seen him. . . . Believest thou [Philip] not that I am in the Father, and the Father in me? the words that I speak unto you I speak not of myself [i.e., on my own initiative]: but the Father that dwelleth in me, he doeth the works.[404]

> I [Jesus] and *my* Father are one.[405]

---

399. Mark 10:35-45.
400. Cf. the right hand/left hand image is juxtaposed to the armament image, inappropriate, love' emotions and other opposites paradoxes, in 2 Cor. 6:4-10.
401. Matt. 26:53-54.
402. Mark 14:36.
403. Matt. 11:25, 27. Cf., Luke 10:21-22.
404. John 14:6-7, 10.
405. John 10:30.

. . . [H]e that sent me is true; and I [Jesus] speak to the world those things which I have heard of [i.e., from] him.[406]

Jesus cried and said, He that believeth on me, believeth not on me, but on him that sent me. And he that seeth me seeth him that sent me. . . . For I have not spoken of myself; but the Father which sent me, he gave me a commandment, what I should say, and what I should speak. . . . whatsoever I speak therefore, even as the Father said unto me, so I speak.[407]

But of that day and *that* hour [the second coming] knoweth no man, no, not the angels . . . neither the Son, but the Father.[408]

. . . [I]f any man sin, we have an advocate with the Father, Jesus Christ the righteous. . . .[409]

The servant is not greater than his lord; neither he that is sent greater than he that sent him.[410]

. . . [W]hen he, the Spirit of truth, is come, he will guide you into all truth: for he shall not speak of himself [i.e., on his own initiative]; but whatsoever he shall hear, *that* shall he speak. . . . He shall glorify me: for he shall receive of mine, and shall shew *it* unto you.[411]

When they deliver you up, do not be anxious how you are to speak or what you are to say; for . . . [it] will be given to you in that hour; for it is not you who speak, but the Spirit of your Father speaking through you. Brother will deliver up brother to death, and the father his child, and children will rise against parents and have them put to death; and you will be hated by all for my name's sake. But he who endures to the end will be saved. When they persecute you in one town, flee to the next; for truly, I say to you, you will not have gone through all the towns of Israel, before the Son of man comes.[412]

So, with God also, the left hand is not to know what the right hand is doing. So it was Jesus, not God, who determined which people would receive saving knowledge of God. And God, in turn, determined which of those will hold what ranks in the pecking order of heaven. Yet, Jesus and the Holy Spirit serve only as parrots, in declaring God's Word. But even so, they *are* God's Word, were with him from the beginning, and are not reported to have been created by him.[413] Perhaps Jesus would be entitled to plead, to the accusation that his oft-repeated promise to return quickly has been broken, ignorance as to

406. John 8:26. Cf., John 5:26-27, 30-31.
407. John 12:44-45, 49-50.
408. Mark 13:32.
409. 1 John 2:1.
410. John 13:16.
411. John 16:13-15.
412. Matt. 10:19-23. *Revised Standard Version.*
413. Gen. 1:2, 26 and John 8:58. Note that the first pronouns referring to God are *us* and *our.*

the time of his own second coming. While all three persons of the Godhead are expressly represented to be endowed with God's power, apparently the Father is more omnipotent than his colleagues.[414] Viewed from the standpoint of personality fragmentation, little of the exalted nature we expect of God shows through. The interaction of the three persons of the Trinity resembles nothing so much as the interaction of the splinter personalities in that especially sick human case, the multiple personality. The personalities are not mutually co-conscious. Eve Black knows all about Eve White, but Eve White does not know of the existence of Eve Black, and is puzzled by the mute evidence of her activities. Eve White and Eve Black want characteristically different things, and manifest themselves at different times. Our notion of God turns out to have some all-too-human, psychopathological inferiority mixed in it. We receive the signal that something is radically amiss, with the notions of God's nature that have always been touted to us!

We can expose the true, psychological raison d'être of the Trinity and all other paradoxically expressed doctrines about the nature of God, and dispose of their alleged substance, by analyzing the suggestions of personality fragmentation they impart to the believer. The truth claims made for the doctrines expressed as paradoxes all depend on the premise that the paradoxes point beyond themselves to profound insights of which earthbound humans are not capable, that the humans will only be let in on beyond the grave. That makes the doctrines transparent to all human modes of inquiry, like the biblical statements as to how things are on the other side of the boundary between the natural and the supernatural. Since expectations for the paradoxes can rise no higher than that, they will seem intellectually absurd and empty "in the flesh," just as the biblical statements about the supernatural are contrived so as to mandate no unlikely expectations about the unfolding of mundane events, the presence of profound, poignant, inexpressible truth behind the paradoxes is conveniently nondisprovable. It cannot be explored. To the mind that wants to have something to test, the criterion of what the scriptural language will allow takes on great appeal. Hence the mini-Reformation. Ultimately, the source of the continuing attraction of the paradoxically expressed doctrines, besides their intrinsic rhetorical artfulness, is the circumstantial evidence that sincere people continue to take keen interest in them. The insight that a psychotechnical manipulation is involved—also circumstantial as regards the truth claims made for the doctrines—is needed to account for the doctrines' presence in the religious scheme, to show what they are really for, and to demystify them.

The psychological significance of the Trinity, behind the biblical language that gives rise to the doctrine, is further obscured by successive layers of theological gloss, put on it over the centuries. The Bible contains no term that is translatable as *Trinity,* and biblical statements indicating God to have a threefold nature are cryptic and scarce.[415] The Old Testament contains some raw

414. Cf., Matt. 28:18; Luke 1:35; Acts 10:38; Rom. 14:9; 1 Cor. 15:28 and Phil. 3:21.

415. Isa. 6:3; Matt. 28:19; John 14:26 and 15:26. A passage about three witnesses, 1 John 5:7-8, appears differently in various ancient manuscripts. Apparently it underwent later embellishments,

materials, including God referring to himself in the first instance as plural, a "Spirit of God" who emanates from him but is never endowed with any particular personality attributes or specialized functions, and a messiah to come. Historical events in the Christian Era, not the Old Testament, are the likely sources of the threefold conception of God. After having the claim to chosenness by the one and only God, who would one day send a vindicating messiah, so long be the Jews' unique, identifying distinction, in a time of unprecedented distress, a theologically original and personally impressive aspirant messiah appears. His pointed claim to be the equal of God is an integral part of his message.[416] Although the aspirant messiah dies the usual honorable death of the conspicuous Jewish patriot of that day, that death belies his exalted claims for himself. Too much time passes for his followers' expectation of his victorious return to remain credible. Finally the Paulinist interlopers need a rationale to confute their Nazorean competitors, who boast unbroken lineage back to Jesus, his companions and relatives, and the earlier, fragmentary lore of the "Spirit of God" provides a convenient legitimizing device—and a third person to the Godhead. To such potentially subversive notions as prior, ancestral claims to godly favor, and preferring evidence to credulity when settling historical questions, the new masters of Christianity would react with telling vehemence for all time to come.

The biblical statements implying a Trinity work out so that any coherent summarization one tries to make of them will be wrong. If one focuses on Scriptures indicating that God is "one" and describing the personality attributes of God the Father, then one runs counter to others, indicating the deity of Jesus and the Holy Spirit, making Jesus the ultimate judge, and conferring on the Holy Spirit such dignity that blasphemy against him is a special, unforgivable class of sin. If one focuses on the different consciousnesses and volitions of the three, then one neglects his oneness and the commandment to "have no other gods before Me"—not "before Us." If one tries to make the Trinity one God with three faces or aspects, then the ability of one to be present when another is absent and of one to be literally dead while the others remain alive go unaccounted for. No matter what the novice may understand of God's quantity, the initiate can always force him to be wrong, correct him, and admonish him to be less proud of his sin-cursed, wicked little mind, and more dependent. Having a doctrine flatly stating the contradiction seems to explain the matter. In the development of the Trinity into an express doctrine, there must have been some analogical contamination from the political triumvirates that governed Rome during two crucial periods in the years leading up to the fall of Jerusalem.

The most recent cycle in the continual, historic confrontation of the biblical program and developments in secular learning, the one involving Feuerbach, Jung and Tillich as its major figures, implicated the Trinity more directly than the intervening ones. Repeatedly, the religious leaders of various periods were overeducated and passed their religious experience through more and more

---

some sounding more trinitarian than others. (See p. 230, footnote 199.) The Scriptures establishing the Holy Spirit's deity (Acts 5:3-4) and masculine gender (John 14:16-17) do so obliquely.

416. John 5:18 and Phil. 2:6-7.

elaborate filters that ordinary church participants lacked. It is reasonable to suppose that the confrontation with secular learning characteristically brings church leaders increasingly out of touch with those to whom they minister. This most recent cycle can be traced back to the superimposing of Hegelian philosophy on the biblical allegory.

G. W. F. Hegel (1770-1831) described nature as unfolding dialectically, realizing itself through the confrontation and synthesis of opposites. Each reality, or *thesis,* calls into being its opposite, or *antithesis.* The result, or *synthesis,* is a new step in the inevitable world process, constituting, itself, the thesis for the next cycle. Marx's historical determinism is based on the overplaying, perhaps caricature, of Hegelianism. Hegel, whose personal views were rather conservative, saw Christianity as symbolizing the unfolding of human consciousness, the incarnation of God in man standing for the upward unfolding of man. Hegel saw nature, symbolized by God, as realizing itself in man's unfolding realization of it. The influence of Hegel is as central to the modernist theologians as it is to the rise of communism.

Feuerbach and Jung, the only significant past psychological commentators on the Trinity, saw in the Trinity the thesis, the monotheistic God, whose intercourse with man calls into being the incarnate antithesis, Jesus; they come into creative collision with one another, giving rise to the synthesis, the Holy Spirit. Neither Jung nor Feuerbach found himself in such circumstances as would call attention to the biblical information opposed to such an idea, the innocuous but clear indications of the Holy Spirit's activity at various junctures throughout the Old Testament,[417] and his rôle in conceiving Jesus. In Middle Europe in the nineteenth century, anyone steeped in the Bible was also steeped in the theological conventional wisdom of the day. Feuerbach was confronted by staid, powerfully inertial clergy, albeit less convinced than they pretended, and more ready to cave in to his criticisms than he could ever have imagined. Jung saw the influence of the churches fall off rapidly during his early adulthood, and became, himself, a source for educated churchmen frantically looking for something new to have their religion mean. Neither had opportunity to observe or even cause to anticipate an episode of resurgent conservative Christianity, like our mini-Reformation. They never expected legions of upstart pastors to arise, who know their Bible intimately, truculently aspire to know nothing else, and have less than no use for a dialectical reinterpretation of their precious Trinity. The churches Jung and Feuerbach knew were hierarchical and uncompetitive, and in them the occasion to look to the Bible rather than the church hierarchy's proprietary doctrines to settle theological questions no longer arose, as it had, during the Reformation.

Feuerbach, who had been Hegel's pupil, did not carry on his teacher's effort to find positive philosophical implications in the Trinity. For Feuerbach, God was a projected hypostasis of the good human qualities that believers, because of their indoctrination in the supposed total depravity of themselves, were not

---

417. Gen. 1:2; 6:3; Exod. 31:3; Job 33:4; Ps. 51:11; 139:7; Isa. 32:15; 61:1; Joel 2:28-29 and Zech. 12:10.

permitted to attribute to themselves. Breaking up that projection into three persons was merely a failed or thwarted attempt to understand the human qualities so projected: the requirement of eventual unity in the Godhead stood in the way of the natural tendency to hypostasize a whole pantheon of gods, as ancient pagans had done. Feuerbach thought that endowing the Godhead with a variety of personalities had initially met a psychological need of celibate Roman Catholic clergy, whose lives he perceived to want for real, human relationships. Consequently, he thought the Trinity had little relevance for Protestantism.[418]

Jung, although he disliked Hegel's writings, did more than anyone else to foster Hegel's purpose of affirmatively reformulating Christianity. While Jung would not have disagreed that ideas about God are, necessarily, projections, he thought that archetypes of mankind's innermost essence, not mere dissociated mundane human qualities, provide the content of the projections. For Jung, fixation of the projection would indicate failure of the ongoing religious process, whose full functioning would include continual cyclic withdrawal, reconstitution and renewed application of the projected religious archetypes. To become more and more conscious would be to emulate the God after whose image man, a creature prestructured to seek after self-knowledge, must have been fashioned. Although Jung rejected what he regarded as the naïve projection (or hypostatization) of transformation through the synthesis of opposites onto exterior, inanimate nature by Hegel and his left-wing disciples, psychological growth or "individuation" did consist of inner, intrapsychic transformation through such synthesis, in Jung's view.[419] In the Trinity, Jung perceived a sublime symbol of that elusive inner synthesis:

> The Trinity and its inner life process appear as a closed circle, a self-contained divine drama in which man plays, at most, a passive part. It seizes on him and, for a period of several centuries, forced him to occupy his mind passionately with all sorts of queer problems which today seem incredibly abstruse, if not downright absurd. . . . Even theologians often feel that speculation on this subject is a more or less otiose juggling with ideas, and there are not a few who could get along quite comfortably without the divinity of Christ, and for whom the role of the Holy Ghost, both inside and outside the Trinity, is an embarassment of the first order. . . . This, so far as the revealed archetype is concerned, is an inevitably retrograde step: the liberalistic humanization of Christ goes back to the rival doctrine of homoiousia [i.e., that the Father and Son are like in kind but different in substance] and to Arianism, while modern antitrinitarianism has a conception of God that is more Old Testament or Islamic in character than Christian.[420]

418. *The Essence of Christianity*, pp. 65-73.

419. Personality change through the synthesis of opposite or, at least, disparate integuments of the psyche does, I am convinced, occur occasionally. See *C. G. Jung and the Scientific Attitude*, pp. 53-69. But those occasions are important turning points in the lives of those who experience them, not everyday occurrences. The pervasive effort in Jungian analysis to force every little event into the mold of transformation through the synthesis of opposites works to transform such analysis from a productive, life-affirming activity to a mind-game of the first kind.

420. "A Psychological Approach to the Trinity," in *Psychology and Religion: West and East*, pp. 152-53 (par. 226).

Jung analyzed the Trinity in terms of its archetypal symbolism, particularly the interplay of unity, triunity and quaternity, which he tied in with the four psychological functions. His comparative exposition of the religious symbols is not immediately relevant for our purposes, and we shall avoid the terrible injustice a summary treatment would do to it. The essay from which the preceding quotation is taken once impressed me as giving credence to the proposition that profound, inaccessible truths were behind the symbols and semantic paradoxes, and that build-up attracted me and helped inveigle me into laying myself open to the rest of the Christian pitch. My view of the matter is, accordingly, jaundiced. The essay does, I still think, contain valid insight as to the reception of the symbolism by the sensitive religious connoisseur and as to the way the originators of Christianity probably arrived at the symbols. The symbols' archetypal nature does bear on their innate appeal. But that is equally true for any symbolism that seems poignant or exerts aesthetic appeal. Jung saw no calculating or manipulative purpose in the Christian rendition of the universal religious symbols, whose non-Christian parallels he so ably demonstrated. He entirely missed the point that the symbols are tools for the workaday task of subjugating ordinary people, not playthings for elite narcissists.

It is in conjunction with two other seemingly unconnected perennial theological issues that the Trinity works its psychological purpose. These are the dichotomy of *transcendence* versus *immanence,* and the problem of the moral nature of God. Tremendous though they seem, we can readily account for these issues psychologically and render further attention to their theological lore unnecessary and uninteresting. They only provide vocabulary for interminable, circular discussion about the contradictory personality traits attributed to God in the Bible. To the mountain of theological books that have been written about them, we can inwardly say, "be removed," and mentally watch them disappear into the water.

The notion of God's transcendence (not to be confused with transcendentalism or transcendental meditation) stresses his humanly unknowable, "holy" attributes. Because modernity needs reasons for holding that there is something to an entity whose existence cannot be empirically proven, whose nature eludes us and is expressed in absurdities and contradictions, there have been many prominent transcendentist theologians. Karl Barth, with his notion of God as "wholly other," Rudolf Otto, with his notion of the *numinosum,* and Paul Tillich, putting God far off as the referent of the symbol of human ultimate concern, belong in this category. Their work provides seeming justification for repressing the horrid suspicions that God's jealousy is a mere projection of the petulance of elderly men in authority who lived long ago, that the unavailability of an image of God is due to his emptiness rather than his gloriousness, or that the absence of any discoverable criterion for his bestowing favor amounts to arbitrariness or caprice. (These theologians provide us with lesser justification for repressing the equally horrid suspicion that their elaborate assertions of the existence of a sublime, transcendent insight beyond the pale serves to call our attention away from their failure to let us in on the insight.) Although there are no notable, current immanentist theologians, the widely current, liberal-church and old-time-religion notions that God and nature coincide, that Eastern religions impart the same essential message as Christianity, and that control over the natural environment can be taken through concentration or willpower are, at their root, immanentist. Immanentist ideas conflict with biblicism more dramatically and obviously than transcendentist ones do. Conservative theologians typically criticize immanentist views as "pantheist."

In the personality traits portrayed in the three persons of the Trinity and arrayed along the transcendentist-immanentist continuum, we can apprehend no consistent patterns emerging. The "revealed" traits cover, indeed conduce toward saturating, the field. Despite the unequivocal implications of the biblical language on many matters that Evangelicals find inconvenient and struggle to ignore, on the attributes of God, we run into equivocation and outright ambiguity. Man is to construct no image of God (even though he is taught that he *is* such an image, right down to those features betokening masculine gender), and could not do so anyway because he is given what amounts to contradictory specifications for such an image.[421] Man is to draw not a blank but a blur in imagining God!

In managing the ordinary believer, the problem posed by the irremediable blurring of his image of the perfect is most often avoided by bringing one aspect clearly into focus while others that clash are not fresh in mind.[422] They are for some other Sunday. A skillful pastor can almost entirely avoid bringing the dissonant implications of the Trinity and the traits partaking of transcendence and immanence to focal awareness in this way. The wise pastor avoids too frequent resort to the explanations that dissonant pieces of biblical information seem so because humans, trapped in their vile, half-dead bodies, cannot understand them correctly, see them only "through a glass darkly," and are to regard them as elements of a testing program to see how well salvation candidates can trust and obey. The believers' potential irritation at their inability to bring the God-image into focus is most acute as regards his moral nature. Whenever the

421. An analogous development of biblical images of God's glory, with contradictory specifications so that no artisan could faithfully render them, is found in Ezek. 1:4-28 and 10.

422. The question of God's image and the specifications for it is what really lies behind Anselm's and Descartes' ontological proof of God, which we can paraphrase, "I think: I have conscious experience; therefore, I am. And since, thinking, I can conceive of a perfect being, whose perfection entails existence, I know that a perfect being, i.e., God, exists." With equal logical force, although less support from historical precedent, we may argue that a perfect being, like a pure geometric figure or a Platonic ideal form, would have by virtue of its "perfection" a clear, sharp, replicable, universal image. What is wrong with the ontological proof—as Descartes' coeval, Pascal, pointed out—is that it uses secular philosophical semantics, irrelevant to the supposedly revealed sources, to get its specifications for God. The intermediate historical layer of secular gloss obscuring the Bible represented by the ontological proof is as far removed from the mentality of the Bible itself as it is from the Hegelian-toned, modernist theological mentality dying out in our day. Useful for our purpose of understanding the mini-Reformationist point of view is the clue we receive here, to look at the development of the idea of "perfection" within the confines of the Bible. Never does the Old Testament describe God as perfect, although it does state that his ways and laws are perfect. While God is portrayed to be "perfect" in the New Testament (e.g., Matt. 5:48), notions of completeness or fullness of development fit the words better than any later, scientifically or mathematically toned concept of "perfection" does.

negative qualities of God—his wrath, his jealousy, his passivity in letting his evil created beings have their way, his fickleness, his tantalizing secretiveness as to the criteria for bestowing his favor, etc., are expounded (and they must be expounded for the mind-control psychotechnology to work efficiently)—it becomes necessary to tell the believer that those qualities are reconciled in a sublime mystery that he cannot penetrate with his sin-cursed, wicked little mind. While it may have worked well to let the matter remain vague in a premodern culture, the characteristic modern practice is to state the paradox expressly, and hammer home by endless repetition the proposition that behind the paradox lies some supreme insight, the profundity of profundities.

The most familiar form of the paradox, standard fare throughout the spectrum of occidental religious groups ranging from Unitarians to mini-Reformationists, contrasts the "lovingkindness" specified to be an attribute of God, with the presence of evil, physical as well as moral, in a world where he is also specified to reign omnipotently. "If God is God, he is not good; if God is good, he is not God." Since many readers will have had early, formative exposure to teaching that tries to cheat the paradox by portraying God as not omnipotent, we must state the obvious, namely that the scriptural language will not permit such a solution.[423] The scriptural information is deliberately arranged not to permit the dilemma to be defeated so easily. The solution the Scriptures will allow is a variation of those biblical arguments that prevent any act of God from being a sin and any saying of God from being a lie′: what he does is, by biblical definition, righteous′, and what he says, by biblical definition, true′. The believer's sin-cursed, wicked, unredeemedly humanistic ideas must give way, ipso facto!

The strongest statement of ulterior specifications for the God-image, albeit making its ominous impression subtly enough that the New Testament can cover it over with others more agreeable, is Job.[424] With all due respect to its genuine drama and a sophistication of form astonishing in a work so early, Job shows its age if we view it without the cerulean filter of Sunday school. Job is completely unequivocal about making God fully responsible for evil. Whether he actively brings down evil on his enemies and those of his chosen or passively

---

423. Cf. Gen. 28:3; Jer. 32:17, 27; Matt. 28:18; Rom. 14:9; 1 Cor. 15:28; Phil. 3:21; 1 Tim. 1:17 and 6:15; Heb. 1:3.

424. Isaac Asimov has written about Job: "The original legend must be ancient (there is even a form of it existing in Babylonian literature) and the writer of the Biblical Book of Job includes it as a prose introduction and a prose ending to the book. In between that beginning and ending, however, he inserts his own deep poetic probing of the relationship between God and man, allowing it to be carried like rich cargo within the simple and sturdy vessel of the well-known Job legend."

"In the original story, the constancy of Job was rewarded by a return of his prosperity and a growth of new happiness—as is, indeed, recorded at the end of the book. Between the beginning just described and that ending, however, the writer has put in a series of speeches by Job and answers by his friends (plus a final answer by God) that hold the meat of the book. In these speeches, Job is anything but patient and uncomplaining, and seriously questions the justice of God. Nevertheless, this has not, for some reason, altered the common conception of Job as a patient, uncomplaining man." *Asimov's Guide to the Bible.* (New York: Avenel Books, 1981), pp. 474, 479-80.

permits evil angels he has created to persecute his chosen, it amounts to the same thing. Job, a wealthy entrepreneur, is celebrated for his piety. Satan and the "sons of God"—apparently the same curious beings who took the daughters of men as wives and begat the men of renown before the Noachian flood—come before God, and tell of their recent wanderings on earth. Satan asks God to ruin all that Job has, and God volunteers that Satan may do so himself. Satan ruins all Job's property and kills all Job's children. When all this fails to elicit from Job the curse against God that Satan had predicted he would utter, Satan asks God again, and receives from him an additional mandate to go against Job's person. God grants Satan permission to spoil Job's physical health, but not to kill him. While poor Job, courtesy of Satan, sits scraping his boils, his wife (whom it apparently would have fallen within Satan's mandate to kill, but it suits him better to let Job keep her) tells her husband, "curse God and die."

This hand-in-glove cooperation of God, Satan and Satan's surrogates, absolutely crucial to the impression received by the Bible-steeped believer, has an important precedent:

> And the king of Israel said to Jehoshaphat, Did I not tell thee *that* he [Micaiah] would not prophesy good unto me, but evil? Again he [Micaiah] said, Therefore hear the word of the LORD; I saw the LORD sitting upon his throne, and all the host of heaven standing on his right hand and *on* his left. And the LORD said, Who shall entice Ahab king of Israel, that he may go up and fall at Ramoth-gilead? And one spake saying after this manner, and another . . . after that manner. Then there came out a spirit, and stood before the LORD, and said, I will entice him. And the LORD said unto him, Wherewith? And he said, I will go out, and be a lying spirit in the mouth of all his prophets. And *the LORD* said, Thou shalt entice *him,* and thou shalt also prevail: go out, and do *even* so.[425]

So, God casts *in* unclean spirits, as well as casting them out! He is, after all, best at solving problems he himself creates. Note the early occurrence of left hand/right hand division, and spirits behaving much like pathogenic complexes in our Jungian energetic model. Far from being aloof from Satan and his surrogates, God cultivates them as his intimates, courtiers and lackeys. This image carries over in the prominent New Testament Scripture, ". . . God shall send them strong delusion, that they should believe a lie."[426] And when Jesus says, ". . . fear not them which kill the body . . . but rather fear him which is able to destroy both soul and body in hell. . . ," there is no competent reason for concluding that he refers to Satan and not himself.[427]

The dire resistance and ambivalence of all but the most stalwart, true believer to the notion that God is all so deeply implicated with the morally evil beings through which he works to bring physical evil as well as spiritual blindness to prevent members of the nonelect from attaining a saving knowledge of

425. 2 Chron. 18:17-21. Cf., 1 Kings 22:20-23, a nearly identical parallel account.
426. 2 Thess. 2:11.
427. Matt. 10:28. Cf., 2 Sam. 24:1 and 1 Chron. 21:1.

truth′, permeate Job. Enter Job's three purported friends, Eliphaz, Bildad and Zophar, solid, conventional thinkers all. They are so sure that God rewards piety and goodness and punishes sin in the short run that, for them, Job is guilty prima facie of some secret or hypocritically unconfronted sin. They exhort him to confess and to repent of it. They look coldly askance at his wounded denials and rebukes. A young know-it-all, Elihu, comes along, and claims to have new insight to contribute: his peroration is mostly a differently phrased repetition of what the other three had already said, but he does originate the hypothesis that God sends chastisement to bring a person to his spiritual senses, to prod him to confess and to repent. All through Job's interchange with the others, he whines, complains, pities himself, and reiterates his desire to die and be out of his misery quickly. Then, God interrupts Elihu, to regale Job with a lurid, detailed description of all the havoc he can wreak with natural phenomena (actually rather tame by atomic-age standards), and to praise Job for having come through the ordeal without sin. All along, over the protests of the four interlocutors and his wife, Job has stuck by his doctrine that it is God who brings the evil, even to a pious, righteous man who does not deserve it. To have succumbed to the others' wrong doctrine would have been the sin, and however deficient Job's conduct may have appeared by New Testament standards of self-control and mental self-discipline, his dogged adherence to that hard doctrine won the day for Job that time!

The more practical implications of Job's doctrine we defer until Device 7, so that we can savor the implications of God revealing murky, ulterior depths to his personality. How does that fit in with the three persons of the Trinity, so antiseptically severed from personality contrasts such as better self versus shadow side, or admixture of one's own gender with undertones of the other gender, yet oscillating mercurially between the poles of transcendence and immanence? What does it accomplish psychologically to have the God-image so cluttered up? If the God of Christianity is as messy and junk-filled as all that, then how is it that Christians can sincerely talk of a relationship with him and that a clear thinker like Machen could seriously liken knowing him to knowing an infinitely virtuous, trustworthy person?

The key clue is that despite the failure of the biblical information about God to support it, despite the superabundance of biblical information to the contrary, believers overwhelmingly perceive God to be good, kind, benevolent, affirmative, just, etc. Is this due to a preponderance of biblical surface impressions skewed toward the positive, prompting the believer consciously to think of God in that way, while more subtle, indirectly communicated impressions to the contrary are tacitly taken in and remain inarticulate? Does God's excellent public relations image arise from the favorable ordinary-language connotations of words denatured by logocide, e.g., *love′, truth′, righteousness′, freedom′*, etc.? Is it due to traditions that somehow get preserved and remain stable, separate and apart from the believers' relationship with their Bible? I contend that the evident subjective stability of the God-image, despite the overwhelming dissonant biblical information for it, is the most internally determined, that is to say psychologically conditioned, aspect of the phenomenon of Christianity.

The proposition that the God-image serves as a receptacle for projections of affirmative human qualities dissociated in the devotional program, returns us to Feuerbach, whose main idea was that the positive God-image resulted from indoctrinating the believers to deny that such qualities are attributable to themselves. That means that the biblical information bearing on the doctrine of original sin and biblical passages that portray the attributes of humans and not those portraying attributes of God are the operative biblical determinants of the believers' God-image. For us, Feuerbach's thesis does suffice for the more outward, accessible aspect of the psychology of the Christian God-image, and we shall shortly come to others he missed. Availing ourselves of psychological concepts that were not available to Feuerbach, we can specify how it is that the most successful religious manipulation must, as a matter of psychological necessity, displace all the positive qualities to its God-image.

When we could not arrive at a satisfying response to the perennial question of man's moral nature, we found it nevertheless significant that humans as we find them have a pervasive sense of being "wrong, inferior and unhappy" in deciding what to do, a blind spot as to their own moral nature, a consistent tendency to perceive that nature as worse than it really is—all apparently vitally important and necessary in enabling them to acquire such inhibitions as allow them, individually and collectively, to survive. That blind spot makes humans susceptible to doctrines wildly overplaying their negative side, as they are to no other systematically skewed doctrine about themselves. Any other would much more readily succumb to focussed thought and realistic reappraisal. If one affects a pompous and authoritative enough mein in telling naïve people that their hearts are hopelessly wicked and corrupt, that they came from their mothers' wombs speaking lies, that they ought to have no threshold expectation but that they deserve to go to the torture chamber of a loving God, to be infinitely tormented forever—one will be believed. Such a ploy would never work if self-esteem were so fundamental a human want as the popular psychologists claim.

The Evangelical experience, however, does not involve devoting all that much time to wallowing in one's personal sense of sinfulness, as Feuerbach, and Nietzsche more blatantly, caricatured it. From time to time, one does go through the exercise of "confessing" the supposed terribleness and persistency of one's remaining "fleshly" nature, but rapidly the pastor moves on to the prescribed, obsessive prayer content for the believer's conscious mind. The Christian message has an attractive element of realistic individual confrontation with the presence and activity of an unseen shadow side of the personality, but veers off into the displacement of that insight by the prescribed, artificial devotional content before that self-confrontation can progress very far. It is the general, endemic, nonspecific sense of guilt that the Christian program seeks to highlight; little more than a pretense of confronting an individual's actual guilt occurs in the skillfully managed church situation. Moreover, a controlled semblance of self-esteem is fostered. The day-to-day Christian experience of having more obvious sins out of his life, of progressively growing in self-discipline and gaining "victory" over other sins, of having the prescribed, biblical thoughts constantly occupying his mind and experiencing his more unruly emotions as gratifyingly blunted does let favorableness back into the believer's self-image. That favorable self-attribution is to be vicarious, diluted and insecure, but it is allowed. Indeed, it may be the very vagueness and derivativeness of the sense of self-esteem the believer is permitted that lends the God-projection its portentous, unclear, paradoxical quality. If believers intensively dissociated their personal better selves, then their resulting God-images would savor much more of a personal alter-ego than actually proves to be the case.

Evangelicals as we find them do not wallow in self-mortification, but rather steep themselves in a denatured, artificial, impersonal sense of sinfulness contrasted by an equally denatured, artificial and impersonal sense of self-esteem derived from their "position in Christ." Their sense of themselves reflects not so much the "slave morality" described by Nietzsche, but a "plastic mentality," obtuse as to its own best and worst features. Dissociation and projection of the shadow side continue much as in any other person, but somewhat changed in style and assimilated to the religious themes. Of course, Satan and the demons constitute a receptacle for the believer's shadow projections, and the constant Evangelical prattle about Satan having done this and that, Satan being the one behind all those "secular humanists" and other "demon-possessed," ungodly people, and even Satan being the reason why this or that happy expectation of the Christian profession fails to be fulfilled are all manifestations of the dismally familiar process of scapegoating hatred against out-groups, inseparable from an outlook conditioned by the Bible. Once the Christians hated the Jews for having supposedly murdered Jesus and for the supposed ritual slaughter and drinking the blood of Christian children. Later, it was supposedly because they were responsible for the "Communist-Jewish conspiracy of world domination." For the present, Jews as such are rarely mentioned: "secular humanists" and homosexuals are the prevalent receptacles for the contemporary conservative Christian's shadow projections.

If dissociation of the highest qualities is the way wherein the conscious attitude most readily impoverishes itself under devotional indoctrination, but dissociation of the lowest qualities is also implicated, should not the resulting projected God-image be one with the most exalted, positive qualities predominating, but with an evident, menacing, sinister depth to him, as well? Should not a devotional program such as we have gone over give rise to an idea of God that the believers explicitly understand to be morally bipolar, even as the information given in the Bible implies such a God? What in the biblical program prevents that, and what would be the difference in psychological implications of allowing such a God-image versus taking means to prevent its formation?

The church's early experience with Gnosticism, and its modern parallel, the rise of Tillichian theology, provide us some possible answers. In their attempts to harmonize dissonant information about God, the Gnostics came up with all sorts of notions other than the onesidedly benevolent, male God of the Trinity. The second-century heretic, Marcion, posed to himself our same riddle of God's goodness and omnipotence coexisting in a world full of evil, and came to the conclusion that there must be an almighty God of wrath who was superior, and that the benevolent, creator God, or "demiurge," was his inferior. After all, when God finds it necessary to give priority to the commandment to have no other gods before him and characterizes himself as "jealous," does he not protest too much, and inadvertently let the cat out of the bag that there is some other God above him in the hierarchy for him to be jealous of? Gnostic sects were also rife with ideas about the Godhead incorporating a feminine, "God-the-mother" aspect, and with organizational innovations giving women a much less unequal rôle than in the orthodox church. Proponents of such exotic religious ideas made them into privileged doctrines for elite, inner circles only, and disdained the orthodox doctrines as for the ignorant rank and file. The Gnostic ideas subverted the church fathers' claims of authority, so carefully interwoven in the orthodox canon.[428] Sects espousing such ideas, we noted, attracted elite individualists, evinced little solidarity or endurance, and lost out in the competition with the orthodox church for ordinary people's hearts and minds.

The early church's experience with alternative notions of God is remarkably recapitulated in the current, terminal decline of the older, mainline Protestant denominations. The advent of the German theologians really marked an end of serious struggle with the biblical information about God, in the old denominations. To Wesley's innovation that despite the Bible's absolute supremacy, common sense was to take precedence over it and mandate that Arminian theology would control one's reading of it, was added the further innovation that one would have to read the Bible so as to come to the conclusion that all the major religions are animated by the same humane message. That provided an additional dividing layer, containing the Book's harder implications, of which the pastors evidently were so very tired, and liked to imagine that their parishioners were, too. With such presuppositions, a layman or seminarian studying the Bible might never again be able to break its code, and the resulting extra measure of impenetrability and unintelligibility would even enhance the Bible's enticing mysteriousness.

When the one-dimensional loving and male God of the Trinity was taken out of its biblical context, mixed with some agreeable fragments from Eastern religions, and passed through Jung's and Tillich's comparative filter, the implications of humans being made in that god's image could become very silly indeed. That mixture made for two generations of pastors who could share their ideological pseudopsychology with Marxists, holding that the moral nature of man was basically loving, and that only mistreatment or miseducation—ultimately failure of communication—made him otherwise. Here, too, the religion broke

---

428. Pagels, *The Gnostic Gospels,* describes in detail the contention of the orthodox church and Gnosticism over the loving, unitary God (pp. 33-56) and the exclusively masculine God (pp. 57-83). Attuned to the political implications of the unitary God, justifying a hierarchical church headed by one exclusive bishop, Pagels has much to say about the different groups' notions as to God's gender, and the literal truth of the miracle stories. Pagels was not looking for specific psychological differences between orthodoxy and Gnosticism, and it may be indicative that she found barely any occasion to discuss orthodox insistence upon, and Gnostic resistance to, the Trinity.

up into an exotic version for inner circles of elite narcissists, and a debased, literal, conventional version for the rank and file. The pastors could mince their words, and the older people would not notice that something other than the lovely images and civic optimism of their earlier days was being preached. Alas, that kind of church is running out of older people. Also, we see the liberal churches recapitulating an important part of the substance of Gnosticism, in giving God a female nature as well and even making a big project of the publication of a bowdlerized, gender-neutered lectionary by the National Council of Churches.[429] Not only do they scourge him and nail him up: they castrate him as well! As with Gnosticism, the liberal church fails to hold onto its people because it tampers with too much of the information that must be received for the mind-control psychotechnology to work. To contain the harder features of the biblical message is to loosen or break its hold. The liberal church is historically unique: never before were historically older church bodies the ones for innovation, tolerance and heterodoxy, and the newer upstarts, the ones against new ideas and in love with a distorted, romanticized view of the older church's fairly recent past. Never before was it the historically older church bodies that backed down gladly from secular, intellectual criticism.

A rich vein of experience with a biblical but trinityless God-image, that would take volumes to treat adequately, is Judaism. The psychologically important differences between Christianity and Judaism are the absence from Judaism of a clear-cut negative pseudopsychology of man and of a clear-cut dichotomy between the natural and the supernatural, as are present in Christianity. For the Jews, God's mind has never had three compartments with semipermeable membranes separating them. Judaism never had godly personalities other than God the Father: he had angels under his control, and a curious, time-traveling high priest, Melchizedek, but their subordination to him, like the subordination of Satan and his surrogates to him, was always clear, and never expressed in terms particularly alien to human experience. Most importantly, the devotional practices of Judaism laid all their stress on outward actions and on required knowledge.[430] Even for the most orthodox, parochial Jew, entertaining thoughts freely and discussing them with other scholars is no sin. Judaism has no precedent for the policing and censoring of thought, the Orwellian "crimestop" of Christianity. While the pervasive communal and private ritual devotions of Judaism—usually not in the devotee's spoken language—is powerfully self-indoctrinating, the Jewish focus is never on an altered psychological state as a devotional objective.[431] The Jewish tradition of layer upon layer of theological

429. See Richard N. Ostling, "More Scriptures Without Sexism," *Time,* Oct. 29, 1984, p. 75.
430. From such Scriptures as, "My people are destroyed for lack of knowledge . . ." (Hosea 4:6), and ". . . if you listen obediently to my [Moses'] commandments . . . He will give the rain for your land in its season . . ." (Deut. 11:13-14, *New American Standard Bible*), a Midrashic tradition valuing knowledge of the law over performing it, and even implying that salvation is based on godly legal knowledge to which action is irrelevant, grew up and had proponents.
431. While Jewish liturgy is predominantly in Hebrew with a few key parts in Aramaic, the worship experience in the Diaspora has, perforce, typically contrasted that liturgy with a foreign national language or a separate Jewish local language such as Yiddish or Ladino.

gloss—Talmud, Midrash, and rabbinical commentaries on these as well as the underlying (Old Testament) Scriptures—fostered a lively and free tradition of study, disciplined active thinking, and discussion.[432] When Jews got the opportunity, that tradition converted readily into successful university study in the Gentile world. The shared history of the Jewish people replaced theology as the touchstone of Jewishness. With a God-image so closely akin to that of Christianity in all respects save for the Trinity, the supernaturalistic side of Judaism proves to be far less psychologically compelling and more apt to be undercut by secular learning than that of Christianity. Jewish people become some of the foremost proponents of secular ideas, and attempts to subordinate those ideas to the old theology, or to modify them to meet theological requirements, have proven neither popular nor durable in Jewish circles.

While many other uncontrolled factors (and our neglect of Islam) undermine our comparison of these three historical examples of the downhill progress of orthodoxy with a biblical but trinityless God-image, the proposition that the Trinity can somehow stabilize that woolly image, so much that its proponent, when he occupies himself with secular learning, will fracture the secular learning to conform to the theology, rather than fracture the theology to accommodate the secular learning, deserves to be explored. From all I have learned, I have the impression that the sum of the God-information in the Bible, if the Trinity idea be not held in the foreground and deliberately defended, implies a moral bipolarity to God too troublesome to evade destructive criticism. Were I an artisan, I would sculpt the nontrinitarian Godhead as Janus-faced. Facing forward, he would have a smiling, avuncular face, a sort of Santa Claus face with Semitic features. Facing rearward, and hidden in any two-dimensional picture of the sculpture featuring the first face, he would have a scowling, horned, red devil face like the logo on a leading American brand of glazier's putty.

Psychologically, the two absurd images, the Janus-faced, good cop/bad cop God and the trinitarian, three-faces-of-God God apparently cancel one another out. To conform to the image of them both, the impression of God must become unclear, slippery, teflon-coated. The purpose of the threeness seems to be to displace the troublesome twoness into the background. To avoid the terrible Two, trust in the Three! But the pull of the terrible Two keeps the Three out of focus, and the believer is somehow to relate to an indescribable, shimmering blob. There is something to contradict any attribution about it one might make! No picture you could draw, no essay you could write, no dream you might dream would bring you nearer to understanding it, synthesizing your impressions about it, getting the tension it creates out of your system! It neither is of the autochthonous stuff that lends the projections their structure, nor has it any distinctive, uncontradicted feature with which the knowledge process could make productive contact. That God-image is the ideal stumbling block for the "related" flow of psychic energy. In no other sense is it ideal. To escape the

432. The rôle of independence of thought, even in the most reactionary forms of orthodox Judaism, is richly portrayed in Chaim Potok's novel *The Chosen* (New York: Simon and Schuster, Inc., 1967).

terrifying implications of confronting his ulterior side, the believer is ready to understand God to be flatly, two-dimensionally good. By not reminding himself of the tension between better self and shadow side in his own personality, the believer avoids a kind of insight that would defeat the dissociating devotional activity. Also, to avoid confronting the own gender/other gender polarity in his own personality, which would also make dissociative restriction of the conscious attutude more difficult, the believer is glad to understand the shimmering blob to be male. For the female believer, the male blob and his human male manifestation can be an animus projection. That would help explain how crassly sexist, conservative Christian groups can thrive on enthusiastic female adherents right in the midst of the feminist ethos of North America in the eighties. For the believing men, the male blob with his human male manifestation as a supposed love object may help let off a head of homoerotic steam.

Ultimately, the God of the Bible is an all-purpose deflector of psychic energy. By that insight, the cryptic, biblical statements about God's substantive nature are cast in a different light:

> God *is* a Spirit: and they that worship him must worship *him* in spirit and in truth.[433]

> . . . God is light, and in him is no darkness at all.[434]

> God is love; and he that dwelleth in love dwelleth in God, and God in him.[435]

> In the beginning was the Word, and the Word was with God, and the Word was God.[436]

> . . . [R]eceiving a kingdom which cannot be moved, let us have grace, whereby we may serve God acceptably with reverence and godly fear: For our God *is* a consuming fire.[437]

When the biblical information about God does not consist of traits of a splinter-personality, it consists of metaphors for mental activity, mostly energetic. The God of the Bible turns out to be nothing but a psychological complex. All the difficulty throughout history of attempting to derive a philosophical or theological understanding of the God of the Bible turns out to have been in vain, and to have missed the point that psychological effects are all he has ever been about, since the Gentiles exiled him from his original ethnic context.

> Seeing then that we have such hope, we use great plainness of speech: And not as Moses, *which* put a vail over his face, that the children of Israel could not stedfastly look to the end of that which is abolished: But their minds were blinded:

---

433. John 4:24.
434. 1 John 1:5.
435. 1 John 4:16. See also verse 8.
436. John 1:1.
437. Heb. 12:28-29. Cf., p. 291, footnote 324.

for until this day remaineth the same vail untaken away in the reading of the old testament; which *vail* is done away in Christ. But even unto this day, when Moses is read, the vail is upon their heart. Nevertheless when it shall turn to the Lord, the vail shall be taken away. Now the Lord is that Spirit: and where the Spirit of the Lord *is,* there *is* liberty. But we all, with open face beholding as in a glass the glory of the Lord, are changed into the same image from glory to glory, *even* as by the Spirit of the Lord.[438]

When the Christian has gotten into the swing of putting his natural personality away from focal awareness, trading his actual guilt problems for a cosmic sense of sinfulness, and such actual grounds of favorable self-regard he may have for a derived, "positional" self-esteem based on being a member of the flock, then he has a God-complex with so much psychic energy devoted to it that his personal complexes are dwarfed, overwhelmed, drowned out. He seems to be free of them, but in actuality, he has covered over whatever individual psychopathology he may have with the shared, artificially induced one indicated by Freud.

But the natural man receiveth not the things of the Spirit of God: for they are foolishness unto him: neither can he know *them,* because they are spiritually discerned. But he that is spiritual judgeth all things, yet he himself is judged of no man. For who hath known the mind of the Lord, that he may instruct him? But we have the mind of Christ.[439]

Everything looks different when the point has been reached where the devotional practices, the acquired knack for dissociation, possibly the ability of the God-complex to attract psychic energy to itself and drain the ego-personality even as it drains the personal complexes, together efficiently evacuate the person's conscious awareness of the proscribed, "natural," "fleshly" thoughts and feelings, and those that get through to consciousness are so weakened that they have lost their sting. The Christians' claim to a transformed outlook is true. We earlier encountered the claims of that outlook to supersede the world, looking to a supernatural realm where different rules apply, to which some things in this world point as instructive types and figures, but to which events in the natural are transparent and "discredited." Those are complemented by distinct reverse-suggestive indications that the transformation in outlook achieved by perfecting the dissociation of the natural is contrary to, or an inversion of, an outlook conditioned by the natural.

The symbolism of the "glass" and the veil in the former passage conveys it very well. The distracting anti-Jewish defamation helps keep the reverse-suggestion from being scrutinized too critically. While the likening of the transformed outlook to the removal of a veil, or the falling of scales from the eyes, or the receiving of hearing after deafness is obvious, the image of one's own face with godly glory transposed over it powerfully expresses the ultimate intrapsychic origin of the God-obsession and the curious resemblance of the transformed

438. 2 Cor. 3:12-18.
439. 1 Cor. 2:14-16.

outlook to narcissism. Instead of relating to what is, one contemplates a distorted reflection of pieces of oneself in a mirror. It did not escape the awareness of the Bible authors that such an image is seen backwards.

> For if any be a hearer of the word, and not a doer, he is like unto a man beholding his natural face in a glass: For he beholdeth himself, and goeth his way, and straightway forgetteth what manner of man he was.[440]

> For now we see through a glass, darkly; but then face to face: now I know in part; but then I shall know even as also I am known.[441]

It is not for nothing that, in the New Testament, the "last shall be first," the church celebrates the Sabbath on the first day of the week instead of the last, the foolish change places with the wise, the deaf′ change places with those who hear′, the blind′ change places with the sighted′, the dead′ change places with those who are alive′, the "poor" become the heirs and the "rich" are disinherited, and the One who is without sin becomes sin for his people.[442] God vents the full force of his wrath on the one sentient being in the universe entirely innocent and undeserving of such treatment—himself. And the apostles are described as the men who turned the world upside down.[443] Legend has it that Peter aspired to be crucified head down, so that he might go out of this world seeing it as the unsaved supposedly do.

Summarizing, dissociation induction consists of stratagems to get a person inwardly to divide his awareness, so that biblically prescribed artificialities occupy his consciousness and all else in his psychological make-up is sought to be put away from him. The endemic human tendency to have a blind spot as to one's own moral nature and to err on the side of appraising that nature worse than it realistically is directs that one will be most susceptible to putting one's better self away, and projecting it onto the maze of contradictory information about God furnished in the Bible. That projection forms the nucleus of a psychological complex drawing energy away from and depotentiating the ego-personality and all the other personal complexes. That "God-complex" manifests itself symptomatically as obsession with God. But the individual shadow side, with all its painful relevance, is also put away, and a much less painful, non-specific sense of sinfulness is all that remains of it in conscious awareness. That put-away shadow side is projected onto the murky biblical information about the negative supernatural, and provides the impetus for attribution of the negative supernatural to all persons not in the narrower, "non-apostate" Christian fold. The putting away entails vitality-sapping expenditure of energy, but is not perceived so because the activity on which the energy is spent goes on mainly outside conscious awareness. The person in whom the Christian dis-

---

440. James 1:23-24.
441. 1 Cor. 13:12.
442. 2 Cor. 5:21.
443. Acts 17:6. Note that all references in the Old Testament to inversion are negative. Cf. 2 Kings 21:13; Ps. 146:9; Isa. 24:1 and 29:16.

sociation is successfully induced experiences the secondary gains of symptomatic relief from troublesome emotions and thoughts, and from the symptoms of personal neuroses—at least in the short run. We shall have more to say about the longer-term effects of the dissociative lifestyle mandated by the Bible, which admit to very great individual differences.

The American experience with the larger mind-control scheme whose most important component is dissociation induction, has principally been old-time religion and imported theological liberalism. These tone down and contain the blblical mind-control scheme by injecting just those ideas (e.g., Arminianism, the equivalence of Christianity and other religions, the superimposition of individualism and democratic customs on the Bible) that go most squarely against the Bible's true grain. That way, people could preserve Christianity's outward forms, but never sort out the Bible's true implications. The increasing activity in our time, of historically rootless new practitioners of the mind-control technology, meaning well but totally in the dark as to the true nature and implications of their activity, make the induced dissociative way of life a prominent feature on our psychological landscape for the first time since the days of Jonathan Edwards and George Whitefield. Those men accurately reflected what results when the Bible is taken seriously, and without dampening layers of secular academic gloss. There is, we admit, a certain degree of ambiguity to the Bible's language that one so disposed can mistake for profundity, and that furnishes a receptacle for projections shaped by seemingly unrelated aspects of the Bible's teaching. We reject the commonplaces—which are, themselves, ideas cutting against the biblical grain—that the genius of the Bible is its provision of an all-purpose justification for any and every humane or progressive, well-intended project, or that the Bible lends itself to any and all manner of interpretation, as some sort of spiritual Rorschach blot. Language does communicate. Pretend the words do not say what they say, and they will do one hell of a number in your subconscious mind!

Because it consists of so many diffuse and indirectly working components, it is difficult to observe very much dissociation induction in any one piece of Evangelistic or biblical counseling activity. One extract from Harold Camping's call-in program happens to bring it out, owing to the marvelous command of words this particular caller had. Even so, assaulting integrity is more conspicuous on the face of it than dissociation induction. From the caller's voice and speech, she was not young, of no distinctive ethnicity, and possibly from or in one of the industrial metropolitan areas of the northeastern U.S. In her voice, I sensed depression, woe, a sense of drudgery.

> Caller: My question, rather than being about a certain verse, is more about a problem of spiritual morale, you might say, and to try to be as concise as I can: For years I've been a believer; I've felt close to God; I've seen those around me and in my own life more of the grace of Spirit; I've just had every fine and good example that my study of the Word and my love of the Lord are effective and are meaningful. But I have something that occurs, that I just sort of need a little moral support. I don't believe I'm unique at all, that when I think I have finally

reached a plateau where all of that will be more like from the twenty-third Psalm, "still waters." Then I find, just as quick as a wink, it seems I'm back in the sense that there is still a, I call it, I nickname it, a "creature-self": part of me that is like the verse that says, "the fool that sayeth in his heart, 'there is no God.'" That part of me, in a sense it's as though it whips around like an animal would do with his tail, saying, "Ha! Ha! The world is still very much with you. Part of you just doesn't believe in that which we cannot see." I just sometimes think, "Am I the only one and will I ever, ever get to the point where that sort of haunting, almost choking sense of ungodliness will stop jolting me?" That's my question.

Camping: Yes, well, your question is handled very, very beautifully in Romans, Chapter Seven. Here we find, under the inspiration of the Holy Spirit, the aged Paul speaking, a dear man of God who loved the Lord tremendously, and what do we read about it? He says in verse 19, "For the good that I would I do not: but the evil which I would not, that I do." And so then he goes on in verse 21, "And I find then a law, that, when I would do good, evil is present with me." Verse 22, "For I delight in the law of God after the inward man. . . ." That would be in his soul or spirit-essence, where he has become saved. "But I see another law in my members, warring against the law of my mind, and bringing me into captivity to the law of sin which is in my members." That is, the potential to sin is still in his body. Why? Because he's not experienced the new life in his body as yet; he doesn't have his resurrected body. That's the one thing we believers are looking forward to. So he cries out just as you're crying out. In verse 24, "O wretched man that I am! who shall deliver me from the body of this death?" In other words, he aches for the time when this potential to sin is gone entirely. That's why the Bible encourages us to crucify the flesh and its desires.[444] The Bible encourages us to deny ourselves, and take up our cross and follow him.[445] And that's a figure to indicate that we are to put to death these evil things that are potentially within our body. And as we live out our Christian life, we will find that there is a growing in grace. Hopefully, the sin that is so close at hand today, or that was so close at hand a few years ago, we've gotten victory over. But when we got victory over one sin, we find it was covering up another sin. And actually this will go on throughout our lifetime. We never can get rid of our body. And therefore, we have to walk so humbly, and we have to keep our eyes on the Lord, Jesus, because if we take our eyes off Christ, we can slip into sin. And then we have all the distress that goes with that.

Caller: Oh, sir, you certainly did hit that correctly, and I was almost afraid to ask, as though I was going to sound foolish, and I so much appreciate that, really, as they say, [it] hits the nail on the head. Thank you so much.

The unique passage "explaining" the inner dividedness the believer will experience notwithstanding the monochromatic one-mindedness striven for, like that other unique passage "explaining" decent behavior in people who, by virtue of not being believers are "slaves of Satan," identifying its cause as God's law written on their hearts, is crucial because the biblical scheme as a whole would be untenable and beyond rationalization without it. With someone as thoroughly hooked as this lady, the ministering Christian may dare to let the cat out of the

444. Gal. 5:24. Cf., Rom. 6:6.
445. Matt. 10:38; Mark 8:34 and Luke 9:23.

bag, that all the bright hopes are for the life beyond the grave, and the most to be hoped for by the Christian in this life is partial minimization of the misery. The caller identifies the elusive, peaceful state as "still waters"! So much of her energy goes into stifling her authentic humanness, that her dissociated, natural side agitates to manifest itself as a nasty, masculine, lizardlike animal that talks. Now, she would probably be a perfectly nice person even without the Christianity, but she has been so sold on the negative pseudopsychology that she thinks she would be a monster if she were not struggling against herself this way. The more one forces stuff out of consciousness, the more negative and dangerous the forced-out stuff seems. Edwards, Luther and Wesley experienced it too. She is in good company. But is it really "a multitude of sins" that love′ covers?[446] Or is the induced state of *abaissement de niveau mental* of Christianity the real reason why it took so long for there to be a Renaissance after ruined Israel's psychological revenge overtook the decaying Roman Empire?

Device 6: Bridge Burning

Returning from the bottommost depths of our subject, we return to more familiar things. We are relieved that the major occasions to defy conventional wisdom are behind us. The substance of the last two devices does not cut so deeply against the grain of widely held notions about conservative religion, and, moreover, we have encountered most of it incidentally in the foregoing discussion. What remains is to put it in sequence and into our larger context. These devices, so obvious standing alone that neither could ever take in a modern person by itself, turn out to have a stabilizing and fixative rôle in the larger mind-control system.

At several levels, the New Testament seeks to make the gap between the believers in their tightly knit circles and outsiders so wide that the believer will not get out, even though outsiders should come in. The idea of a one-way spiritual transformation, so tied up with crossing rivers in the Old Testament, and with passing from earthly life irreversibly to the eternal grand prize or else the eternal booby prize in the New, subtly and repetitiously put the point across. It is no accident that those who read the Scriptures most carefully concluded that once salvation occurred, it could not be lost, and that seeming loss of salvation could take place only in one who had been subjectively deceived about having it in the first place.

The discrediting of outsiders, the express prohibition against considering the possibility that an outsider might have something to say worth heeding, and the intensely taboo aura of bad conscience accompanying any thought that might undermine the doctrine, combine to counteract the effects of outsiders in close proximity, with whom the believer may have business. If someone disagrees, that only goes to prove that God has some inscrutible reason for blinding him, and there is nothing to be done. If someone says something that seems reason-

---

446. 1 Pet. 4:8.

able or appealing, that only goes to prove how wily and deceptive Satan is. If the Christian experience seems or feels wrong, that only shows that one has not yet gotten victory over the flesh′. It is expected that what seems right to the saved is topsy-turvy for the unsaved, and vice versa.

The passages against family and against fraternization with unbelievers, those suggesting that believers are blind′, deaf′, and dead′ to worldly things, and all we have covered that militates against straight thinking about what disagrees with the Christian indoctrination, work powerfully and synergistically together to make the believer impervious to outside influences, even though he may continue to be exposed to them constantly and even though he may remain exposed to the same influences that were his whole cultural milieu before conversion. To keep people in line under such conditions requires something psychologically far more powerful than what suffices to attract a few susceptible people and keep them indoctrinated entirely within the ambit of the sequestered community's group pressure. The dissociated state of mind, so different from any other that it does make the surrounding world seem discolored and distorted, and so different from that of outsiders that the believer can no longer empathically relate to them, is that powerful.

Two passages we have not scrutinized for other purposes illustrate how the New Testament authors foresaw the gap would be managed:

> Be ye not unequally yoked together with unbelievers: for what fellowship hath righteousness with unrighteousness? and what communion hath light with darkness? And what concord hath Christ with Belial? or what part hath he that believeth with an infidel? And what agreement hath the temple of God with idols? . . . Wherefore come out from among them, and be ye separate, saith the Lord, and touch not the unclean *thing;* and I will receive you, And will be a Father unto you, and ye shall be my sons and daughters, saith the Lord Almighty.[447]

The reader from a mainline Christian background, which, at least up to the Viet Nam War tended to be rather patriotic and did not seek to follow through on the biblical project of alienating the believer from the surrounding civic community, will immediately respond that the passage focuses on prohibition against marrying outside the denomination. If you think so, read it again. Neither the context nor the thematic content nor the etymology pertain to marriage.[448] Muted disgust is to be the believer's reaction to the world outside the flock, notwithstanding the unrelieved duty of wholehearted obedience to secular civil authorities.

While the New Testament does forbid a believer to contract marriage with an unbeliever, the instructions to the convert with an existing spouse who does not come along reveal how intractable even the newly acquired indoctrination is to be:

---

447. 2 Cor. 6:14-18.

448. The expression *unequally yoked together* renders a single word that appears only once in the New Testament, *heterozugeo.* It means, literally, to link together things which are different, i.e., to mismatch them. It is unlike any expression used in the Bible to indicate marriage.

> Likewise [after Christ's example of patient suffering], ye wives, *be* in subjection to your own husbands; that, if any obey not the word, they also may without the word be won by the conversation [i.e., conduct] of the wives; While they behold your chaste conversation *coupled* with fear.[449]

In the earliest days of the church, as now, the woman would usually be the believer, of an "unequally yoked" couple. The instruction not to preach to the husband may relate to the stringent restriction of that office to males.[450] No special instruction is given to the believing husband for dealing with an unsaved wife. Also, although Jesus said one must hate one's wife, among others, to be his disciple, he never said one had to hate one's husband![451] What should be noted is that even in the close physical proximity of marriage, the indoctrination is expected to hold up. What the believer is to feel estranged from does not stop at the boundaries of the body. That body is the Spirit's as yet unregenerated earthen temple, and to be part of Christ's body means that "communion" with other believers is at the level of mind, i.e., being of one mind.[452]

Quite deliberately, the life′ of the "new creature in Christ" is described in terms of hating, with a special kind of muted godly hatred, those members of his earthly family who do not come along, of leaving them and all one's possessions behind to be his follower, and to expect and to have one's pseudopsychological rationalization ready for uncomprehending or hostile response of one's former family and friends, to the newly acquired viewpoint. One is to burn one's bridges behind one, to make it as hard as possible for oneself to return. Besides the censorious, group-pressuring Christian fold, one is to have no place to go.

The content of the teaching, as well as the form of the social relations, is set up so as to dig a psychological moat around the believers. We have seen it from the standpoint of entry into Christianity, symbolized as returning to babyhood and being reborn, and passing a camel through the eye of a needle, and in schematic, logical terms, in the father who needed to see his spirit-possessed son healed in order to be able to believe, but needed to believe first in order to obtain the healing. By making a consequence of some occurrence also its prerequisite, by making the occurrence, in effect, its own prerequisite, a paradox that produces intellectual deadlock or impasse escapable only by "bootstrapping" is set up. We recall how inability intentionally to disengage oneself from the pull of such a situation, being "stimulus-bound" by it, resulted when the abstract attitude was impaired in Goldstein's patients. Where straight or critical thought about religious issues is fraught with negative emotions and dissociation-induced *abaissement de niveau mental,* we might expect a corresponding impairment of an individual's ability to make himself stop fixating obsessively (i.e., "perseverating") on such a paradox or conundrum. If such fixations can be set up, one

449. 1 Pet. 3:1-2.
450. 1 Tim. 2:11-12 and Rev. 2:20.
451. Luke 14:26.
452. 1 Cor. 6:19.

more irrelevant thing to keep the conscious mind busy is added to the many others, to obstruct the Christian from breaking out of the semantic labyrinth.

If an indoctrinated Christian were going to notice how convenient for controlling him, how full of human guile in their own right, are the ideas that giving someone with disagreeing ideas a fair hearing is to give Satan the opportunity to deceive and to tempt, and that to have a dialogue with such a one is to offend by saying more than "yea, yea" and "nay, nay," he would first have to give himself permission to engage in forbidden thoughts. But he needs to entertain the forbidden thoughts first, to get to the place where he can give himself that permission. If he is given to intellectual consistency and integrity, he will not quite be able to bring himself to do either. The nondisprovability of the Bible's premises, and consequent absence of distinctive expectations about events in the natural world for one steeped in the intricately and meticulously hedged biblical language, are by the time he reaches such a level of indoctrination well known to the believer, and he can "explain" any unpleasant event away. And he does genuinely experience seemingly inexplicable and temporarily pleasant blunting of his negative emotions and discoloring of his perception, and interprets these as corroborating his theology. To see his position in perspective, he would have to clear all the distracting biblical irrelevancies out of his mind. And he would have to see his position in perspective already, in order to identify the distracting irrelevancies and clear them out. Any number of variations of the conflict that one must freely think forbidden thoughts in order to get to the premise that thinking them is all right, can be found in Christians' experiences. The miserable prelude to Jung's giving hmself permission to imagine turds falling from heaven and wrecking the bright cathedral is a variation of it.

The stratagem of creating an impasse in the believer's rational thinking is carried to its extreme in the issue of the unforgivable sin, also known as blasphemy against the Holy Spirit. Because it involves heavy fear manipulation, and the naïve superstitiousness of ignorant ages past is obvious on its face if one views it without the churchy filter, one will hear very little about it in churchy situations where persons who are not yet thoroughly and dependably indoctrinated may be present. In a good mini-Reformationist church, the subject will be passed over very lightly from the pulpit but hit on heavily in one-on-one contacts, small study groups and advanced Sunday school classes. The reader having a dear one in the early stages of being evangelized can make good use of the following study, to alert the person to the ugliness and absurdity lurking ahead in the later stages and to get the person to quit.

Each of the synoptic Gospels puts an ominous warning about blasphemy against the Holy Spirit in Jesus' mouth. Taken in order, they read:

> He that is not with me is against me; and he that gathereth not with me scattereth abroad. Wherefore I say unto you, All manner of sin and blasphemy shall be forgiven unto men: but the blasphemy *against* the *Holy* Ghost shall not be forgiven unto men. And whosoever speaketh a word against the Son of man, it

shall be forgiven him: but whosoever speaketh against the Holy Ghost, it shall not be forgiven him, neither in this world, neither in the *world* to come.[453]

Verily I say unto you. All sins shall be forgiven unto the sons of men, and blasphemies wherewith soever they shall blaspheme: But he that shall blaspheme against the Holy Ghost hath never forgiveness, but is in danger of [i.e., liable to, under penalty of] eternal damnation: Because they [Scribes from Jerusalem] said, He hath an unclean spirit.[454]

. . . Whosoever shall confess me before men, him shall the Son of man also confess before the angels of God: But he that denieth me before men shall be denied before the angels of God. And whosoever shall speak a word against the Son of man, it shall be forgiven him: but unto him that blasphemeth against the Holy Ghost it shall not be forgiven.[455]

These verses prompt endless, nervous discussion in Christian circles, and there are plenty of people today who go around worried that they may say the word or think the thought that will consign them to eternal torment. It is not clear that speaking the blasphemy aloud, as opposed to thinking it or expressing it by gesture, is the gravamen. Modes of expression other than verbalization are sometimes "speech" in the Bible.[456] For obvious reasons, the Bible authors would have wanted to squelch adverse elocution within the fold. Since it is hard to see where speaking against the Holy Spirit leaves off and speaking against other manifestations of the same triune God commences, the believer so admonished will be apt to take few elocutionary risks. The general trend for Christianity to stress inward compliance in contrast to Judaism's stress on outward compliance goes against having verbal externalization be the gravamen of the unforgivable sin. After all,

Not that which goeth into the mouth defileth a man; but that which cometh out of the mouth, this defileth a man. . . . But those things which proceed out of the mouth come forth from the heart; and they defile the man.[457]

The troublesome linkage of confessing Jesus, rather than denying him, to other people with some desired benefit may suggest that the issue of speech as opposed to other symbolization activities is a deliberate distraction. Since numerous other Scriptures indicate constant danger from false prophets and false brethren, how can merely affirming Christ verbally be the litmus test? Did we not elsewhere learn that it is Jesus who decided who shall attain saving knowledge of the Father?[458] Why is it important to have Christ as an "advocate with the Father" at some future time, if that be so? Were not the salvation

---

453. Matt. 12:30-32.
454. Mark 3:28-30.
455. Luke 12:8-10.
456. Cf., Ps. 15:2; Prov. 6:12-14; Rom. 10:6-11; 2 Cor. 13:3 and 2 Pet. 3:16.
457. Matt. 15:11, 18.
458. See p. 318, footnote 403.

decisions made before any of the people to whom they pertain were born, anyhow? The angels, God's little messengers and functionaries, certainly do not make such decisions. Perhaps Jesus is only offering to put in a good word for those that "confess" him to the secretaries and receptionists in the Boss' outer office, even though the word he puts in with the Boss himself will be something else again. The question whether any one sin can be forgiven or not implies threshold salvation, not degree of punishment to be meted out to him not all of whose sins are forgiven.[459] Perhaps the advocacy before God and his angels goes only to severity of sentence, aeons after the verdict is in. Just what constitutes blasphemy of the Holy Spirit, betokening impossibility of acquittal, is kept tantalizingly vague.[460]

There are two other accounts of sets of circumstances irreversibly foreclosing salvation:

> For *it is* impossible for those who were once enlightened, and have tasted of the heavenly gift, and were made partakers of the Holy Ghost, And have tasted the good word of God, and the powers [*dunamis*] of the world [age, aeon] to come. If they shall fall away, to renew them again unto repentence; seeing they crucify to themselves the Son of God afresh, and put *him* to an open shame.[461]

> For if we sin wilfully after that we have received the knowledge of the truth, there remaineth no more sacrifice for sins. But a certain fearful looking for [i.e., expectation] of judgment and fiery indignation, which shall devour the adversaries. He that despised Moses' law died without mercy under [i.e., on the testimony of] two or three witnesses: Of how much sorer punishment, suppose ye, shall he be thought worthy, who hath trodden under foot the Son of God, and hath counted the blood of the covenant, wherewith he was sanctified, an unholy thing, and hath done despite unto the Spirit of grace? For we know him that hath said, Vengeance *belongeth* unto me, I will recompense, saith the Lord. And again, the Lord shall judge his people. *It is* a fearful thing to fall into the hands of the living God.[462]

---

459. See p. 57, footnote 108.

460. Pastors have various rationalizations about blasphemy against the Holy Spirit, to avoid coming on too ominously or intensely, and to quell their own anxieties about forbidden thoughts. The least lame of these I have heard is the one Harold Camping uses on his call-in program. Camping, who is generally quite admirable about not dodging questions, deftly evades being drawn into a discussion about the Matthean or Lucan account, and focuses on the appended phrase in Mark, about Jesus having given the warning with the Scribes' attribution of his own activity to Satan in mind. For Camping, that makes attributing Jesus' acts to Satan, and not derogatory "speakings" about the Holy Spirit, the biblical criterion for blasphemy against the Holy Spirit. That way, one would have to buy into the whole biblical salvation scheme but take Satan's side against God within it to be a blasphemer against the Holy Spirit. For all practical purposes, nobody could blaspheme the Holy Spirit and get into a position where his salvation were certainly impossible. For Camping, the passages, like some others, are a "testing program," to confuse those whom God does not plan to save and give them the opportunity to confuse themselves, and cause themselves needless anguish by trusting their sin-cursed, wicked little minds too much.

461. Heb. 6:4-6.

462. Heb. 10:26-31. See also 1 John 5:16.

Both passages from Hebrews were most likely composed by some erudite, hellenized Jew other than Paul, before the destruction of Jerusalem.[463] The first boils down to the managerially astute policy that someone who leaves the fold may not be received back into it. Because that is so unfamiliar in our competitive, voluntary church environment, it takes an effort for us to imagine the viewpoint of someone to whom that would be a dire threat. After estranging oneself from other associations, including one's family, if one leaves the Christian fold, one will really be out in the cold. "Don't even *think* about backing out!" The second superficially seems to make "sinning" worse if one knows better than if one does not. Ignorance of the law, as we have seen, is an excuse in justice′, and the only particular sin punished more severely than others is false teaching. Whether punishments will fit their respective crimes or not is without spiritual relevance in Christianity. And see how the unspeakably unjust punishments meted out to the Christians by the Romans—whose authority the Christian was at all times admonished to respect and deem godly—are introjected! Disobeying after one knows better or has been admonished is made fraught with the greatest fear. Doing wrong while knowing better is made a biblical definition of treading on Jesus, calling the Holy unholy, and some unspecified manner of transgression against the Holy Spirit. I submit that these passages are the forerunners of the three synoptic Gospel renditions of blasphemy against the Holy Spirit, which, in turn, are simply the heaviest fear appeal that the early church fathers found got them a compliant response. By making people afraid that, through some unspecified, perhaps inadvertent, impious act or thought, the dreaded destiny might be set unstoppably in motion, the early church fathers, like contemporary mini-Reformationists, must have succeeded in eliciting paroxysms of obsessive, compulsive, reaction-forming behavior. Where Hebrews only incidentally hits on the fear of not being readmitted to the heaven-bound fold if one leaves, while generally cajoling Jewish believers not to slip back into earlier notions about sacrifices and ritual purity, thc synoptic Gospels bring on that fear as their heaviest piece of straight-thought-disrupting artillery. They bring it on in defense of ultraexaltation of the Holy Spirit. Why would that doctrine have so high a priority for Gospel authors? To justify their calling for their followers to accept Paulinist teaching, and to reject the Nazorean claim of legitimacy by association of the Nazoreans' forebears with the actual companions and family of Jesus. The Paulinists could compensate for the lack of historical continuity later, with cord upon cord of relics of the true cross and other wondrous products of ecclesiastical industry.

If we take the synoptic Gospel warnings against blaspheming the Holy Spirit at face value, we are left with Jesus supernaturally contemplating, and the

463. The differences from the other Pauline writings in general writing style, different way of using Old Testament quotations, and lack of Paul's usual greetings and salutations have led scholars to doubt the Pauline authorship of Hebrews from the earliest days of the church. However, the lack of any reference to the destruction of Jerusalem, the general warnings to the Jews against what seems more like worship centering on the Temple than like Jewish worship in the Diaspora, and the possible direct reference to worship in the Temple still going on, in 8:4, may indicate that Hebrews existed before the texts of the synoptic Gospels were settled.

apostles taking in appreciatively, things that were, as yet (i.e., prior to Pentecost), meaningless. We are left with the semantic contradiction wherein saying that Jesus was under the power of Satan—without ever even mentioning the third person of the Trinity—constitutes speaking against the Holy Spirit, but does not constitute speaking against Jesus. If we try to make the teachings about blasphemy against the Holy Spirit intelligible other than for their psychological effect, they are opaque. But as purposeful insertions into Jesus' mouth by later church fathers, the passages become historically and psychologically understandable.

What hold, if any, does the notion of an unforgivable sin, particularly one that could be committed merely by one's speech or private thought, have over the popular mind today? In the English language and the others familiar to me, expletives and exclamations still chastely avoid the Holy Spirit as content. In sharp contrast, the Father, the Son, and where she is deified, the Virgin Mary abound in expletives. Only intimate bodily functions occur as often. The Holy Spirit retains its mystique, and evidently a deeply ingrained taboo against cursing the Holy Spirit still operates. The high prevalence of Americans who profess belief in the religious scheme the Holy Spirit is part of, taken together with the low prevalence of action to give meaningful effect to the supposed belief, may indicate that the Christian religious scheme is still vaguely threatening to most people. They tacitly prefer not to learn more about it, lest they find out what they would rather not know, and have a worse conscience and heightened trepidation. So they "play it safe" and refrain from breaking the scheme's most ominously stated taboo. For once, the thing forbidden has little intrinsic attraction. It only becomes a problem for someone so religiously obsessed that the dissociated, forbidden thoughts form an unconscious complex, accumulate libido, and clamor for expression. Probably, some sensationalist will yet be able to tickle our jaded ears with some rock-and-roll song or lurid movie involving blasphemy of the Holy Spirit. Until the time comes when that arouses no more offense than any other dull, predictable, worn-out piece of profanity, one must presume that the Christian superstitions are alive, potentially robust and unpleasantly dormant in the subconscious minds of most Gentile Americans.

Apart from creating gridlock in the believer's beleaguered thought processes, the doctrine of the unforgivable sin has a modern, mundane aspect that the Bible authors must have understood very well. Crediting whatever power the Gospel evinces to Satanic or demonic forces is made part of the special, most condemned category in two of the five passages. A reductionistic, psychological assault on the Bible does not violate the letter of the prohibition. The Bible singles out false gospels, religious teachings deceptively resembling the true Gospel, as the danger great enough to give the true believer signal cause for concern. Simple denial of the supernaturalistic premises of the scheme, the Bible passes off as mere foolishness, something only an inconsequential fool would bother to do. Yet, we have noticed hints all along the way that the Bible authors knew that deception, psychological trickery, and sham were their stock-in-trade, and we cannot fathom how they could have accomplished what they did without being self-consciously well aware of it. The magic, sorcery, astrology, etc., that the Bible condemns from time to time, were well understood by their practitioners as well as critics, to be quite mundane and calculating. Then as now, making it taboo to think about negative supernatural true causes of the Gospel's power is a euphemism for making it taboo to think that this-worldly trickery, i.e., camouflaged applied psychology, is involved. A psychological anti-theology violates the spirit of the prohibition, if not the letter. Here, too, a hoary taboo still exerts its hold. We have seen it in the feinting, desultory investigation of Christianity by behavioral scientists. Allport almost said as much. The operation of such a taboo would explain why the emphasis, when conservative religion came under attack earlier in this century, was on the Bible's literal truth vis à vis evolution, and why there was so little follow-through on the preliminary insights of Feuerbach and Freud. Moreover, progressive forces were in the ascendancy in corporate Protestantism, and for earlier American psychologists to attack it focally would have been to attack strong allies on their own side. I would hardly be bringing out such a work as this, if that were still the case.

In sum, bridge burning extends the splitting up of the believer's psychological reality into dissociation induction's incommensurable realms, and severs connections and creates gaps in his natural existence that the believer cannot traverse. Whether it be by psychologically isolating him and poisoning his mind with suspicion against all those outside the fold, or putting logical conundrums in the way of his escape from the semantic labyrinth of the biblical scheme, or bluffing him with the supposed final and irreparable harm of that which would expel the Gospel's artificial dissociative intrusion into his normal and legitimate striving for psychological wholeness, the creation of gaps, of troubled psychological waters with no bridges over them is the objective. None of these stratagems could work, if the underlying induced psychological dissociation had not already made some headway. Bridge burning could not create the gap, but it keeps it open, like a wedge, after it has been opened. The stratagems we group together under this heading serve only to lend stability to an already existing condition of Evangelical mind-control.

Device 7: Holy Terror

What can be left for us to say about the use of fear in Christianity? However strongly the ignorant, superstitious people of centuries past may have responded to superstitious fear appeals, are not modern people immune from such a transparently manipulative, guileful device? I grew up in a nominally Jewish home and went to public schools in the last years before prayers and nominal Christian devotions in them were ruled unlawful by the Supreme Court. At age ten or eleven, I formed the opinion that those teachings, and what I learned in Hebrew school, had in common the bluff that God's mighty rewards and punishments ought to terrify me into compliance with the pedagogues' stupid little rules, and that these religions were nothing but a stupid, dishonest ploy. As an adult, I fell in with those who assured me that there is much more to it. I am persuaded that I was right the first time, wiser at ten than at forty!

The bottom line is that getting people to dance to its tune out of fear is what Christianity is all about. All else is evasion and obfuscation. Every other issue turns from what is first expected into arcane, abstruse dizzying stuff as the believer's indoctrination progresses. But the fear appeal, alone, retains its initial form, and is embellished and intensified as the indoctrination progresses.

Notice what has happened to all other salient matters Christianity purports to be about, under our scrutiny. Is Christianity meant to enhance mundane life? Consider these bright promises:

> . . . I am come that they might have life, and . . . have *it* more abundantly. . . ."[464]

> There is no man that hath left house, or brethren, or sisters, or father, or mother, or wife, or children, or lands, for my sake, and the gospel's, But he *shall receive an hundredfold now in this time*. . . . [stress added][465]

The first turns on the believer's failure consciously to put together what the Bible means by "life," and the second on the predictable failure of the believer to consider (and of the preachers to point out) the important little qualifying words *with persecutions* that follow immediately in the text. (Perhaps those words imply that the absence of anyone to persecute the believer should be taken to mean that he is not among the intended recipients of the promise, and should arouse salvation doubts.)

What of the promised remedy for the sin affliction? It went in a curious semicircle. The sin affliction started out overtly as any disobedience to the One inherently endowed with the right to demand obedience, and implicitly as usurping knowledge of good and evil, which God had reserved for himself and another class or classes of his created beings. Then, "sins" became a mixed bag of common criminal misdeeds and failure fully to perform halakic rituals. Finally, "sin" became divorced from all except ecclesiastical misdeeds, and all persons became equal in their imperfection, with all nonreligious crimes spiritually regarded as equal. The idea of the punishment fitting the crime came to be disparaged as spiritually naïve. The supposed biblical enlightenment as to justice, to which contemporary Evangelicals claim there is no alternative but confused, directionless relativism, turns out to do nothing but dwell on a few offenses that pertain only to keeping the indoctrination in place, ratify whatever any existing secular state decrees, and perhaps incorporate such prohibitions against stealing, maiming, killing, encroaching on another's familial relationships etc., as all human groups necessarily invent anyway. The magnificent rhetorical style only makes it seem like there is more to it. And the believer would never even have known that a "sin" problem was what ailed him had not some Christian brought him that supposititious information and the equally supposititious remedy.

After receiving the build-up that becoming a Christian would make one the recipient of a love consummated in the sacrifice of the redemptive atonement,

---

464. John 10:10.
465. Mark 10:29-30. Cf. Matt. 19:29 and Luke 18:29-30.

far better than the frail, fickle human kind, the believer neither finds nor notices that he has not found anything in the Bible really telling about the content of godly love or what it was about the alleged sacrifice that could have mattered so much to God. The matters of charitable works, of who are the poor, and of who are one's neighbors wind up entirely clouded. And what "hope" does the believer get? The Bible creates, out of whole cloth, the bogey of spending eternity being worked over in God's torture chamber. The only hope offered is some slight chance of escaping the bogey. It is as if a robber, who did not shoot his victim after taking the victim's valuables, were entitled to gushing gratitude at every hand, rather than prosecution. (My image is biblical, after references to God as a "thief in the night," and as the one to "spoil" [i.e., burgle] the "strong man's house."[466]) And the best the Bible does about bolstering the institution of the family is some profamily verses to cancel out its antifamily verses, the ones subordinating the family to the Christian fold and plainly requiring the believer, if forced to choose, to choose fold over family. But the fear appeal undergoes no comparable metamorphosis, as the believer's involvement and indoctrination deepen.

In other words, the fear appeal is unique among the issues overtly and prominently presented in the Bible, in that it is not subjected to the Device 1 process that starts with an appealing, superficial, calculatedly misleading stock interpretation, and then gradually weans the believer away from it, drawing him gradually along toward a more biblically integral rendition of the same issue, one that is hard, has teeth, and inverts common sense. It is true that, to deal with times less credulous than before, pastors have universally developed the habit of telling their people that the "fear" of God incessantly exhorted in the Bible, and declared to be the "beginning of wisdom,"[467] and the "fountain of life"[468] is really only reverence or awe. Like their custom of saying that the commanded hate for family is only psychological distance, or acknowledgment that love for God is to have priority, they do it without a shred of contextual, thematic or etymological justification. The custom does clumsily reflect the devotional pattern of selectively dissociating or emotionally isolating the affective charge from the idea that elicits it, and enjoying, as a result, a false conscious sense of peace and calm. Because one is commanded not to be afraid because being afraid is a "sin," one has to be afraid of being afraid, but unafraid of being afraid of being afraid, and be stimulated by fear to do whatever perfects Device 5 dissociation, so that one can fear without being afraid—as the Bible, when all is said and done, commands!

Of the three negative emotions not declared the moral equivalents of overt, antisocial acts, i.e., anger, anxiety (or worry) and fear, fear is attended, by far, with the most unrelieved ambivalance. For anger, scapegoating or displaced out-group enmity is provided as an outlet. The prohibitions against anxiety are

---

466. Matt. 12:29 and Mark 3:27. Note how the two images of God as the burglar of Satan's house are contextually interwoven with others now meaningful to us, namely Jesus' rhetorical question about whether a house divided against itself can stand, and the taboo matter of whether demons can be cast out by Satan's power.
467. Job 28:28; Ps. 111:10; Prov. 1:7 and 9:10.
468. Prov. 14:27.

neither emphasized nor put in a particularly threatening way. The believer experiences the muting of his anxiety as a benefit. But the believer is commanded to fear about as plainly, about as often, and in about the same circumstances as he is commanded not to fear.[469] No tenable distinction between situations where fear is commanded and where it is forbidden is available to the believer. The devotional instructions force him to fear, but arouse a sense of bad conscience about doing so. Whatever he does, he is wrong, and that makes him more "dependent" unless he finds his way out of the semantic labyrinth.

The devotional-program instructions pertinent to fear lend themselves particularly well to condensation in an antiapologetic triad:

> Hear, O Israel; The Lord our God is one Lord: And thou shalt love [*agapao*] the Lord thy God with all thy heart, and with all thy soul, and with all thy mind, and with all thy strength: this *is* the first commandment.[470]

> Having therefore these promises, dearly beloved, let us cleanse ourselves from all filthiness of the flesh and spirit, perfecting holiness in the fear [*phobos*] of God.[471]

> Herein is our love made perfect, that we may have boldness in the day of judgment: because as he is, so are we in this world. There is no fear in love; but perfect love casteth out fear: because fear hath [entails] torment [punishment]. He that feareth is not made perfect in love. We love him, because he first loved us. [*Love* is *agape* or *agapao*, depending upon whether it is a noun or a verb; *fear* and its cognates are *phobos* and its cognates.][472]

Loving God and fearing him, specifically as regards penal disposition in the next life, are both commanded, and by implication can coexist. Yet, love and fear are biblical contradictories, and one receives the impression that one is doing the devotional program properly, if by one's love′—which the believer at least tacitly understands to consist of doing what is commanded with self-discipline experienced as Spirit-assisted—one "casts out," or "puts off" the negative emotion of fear, and feels better. Perhaps the ultimate devotional accomplishment or level of spiritual "maturity" is becoming able to think on what is to be feared, but not feel the fear. That is the ultimate soporific. By irritating the conscious mind with anticipation of the worst thing imaginable, the ultimate in dissociation, expelling the anguishing content from consciousness and covering it over with a protective layer, the more viscous the better, is stimulated.

The passage apparently setting out the "promises" to which the believer is to

---

469. Cf., Matt. 10:28; Luke 1:50; 12:5; Acts 13:16; Rom. 11:20; 13:7; 2 Cor. 7:1; Eph. 5:21; Col. 3:22; 1 Pet. 2:17; Rev. 14:7; 15:4 (commandments or examples understood to be for the edification of the believer, to fear God); Matt. 10:31; 28:5; Luke 1:13, 30; 2:10; 5:10; 8:50; 12:7, 32; John 12:15; Acts 27:24 and Rev. 1:17 (commandments, or examples understood to be for the edification of the believer, not to be afraid).
470. Mark 12:29-30.
471. 2 Cor. 7:1.
472. 1 John 4:17-19.

respond by cleansing himself and "perfecting holiness in the fear of God" brings out the psychic energetics of the process, meaningful to us in terms of complexes:

> For we must all appear before the judgment seat of Christ; that every one may receive [own, take the consequences of] the things *done* in *his* body, according to that he hath done, whether *it be* good or bad. Knowing therefore the terror of the Lord, we persuade men; but we are made manifest [i.e., laid open] unto God; and I trust also are made manifest in your consciences. For we commend not ourselves again unto you, but give you occasion to glory on our behalf, that ye may have somewhat [something] to *answer* them which glory in appearance, and not in heart. For whether we be beside ourselves, *it is* to God: or whether we be sober, *it is* for your cause. For the love of Christ constraineth us; because we thus judge, that if one died for all, then were all dead: And *that* he died for all, that they which live should not henceforth live unto themselves, but unto him which died for them, and rose again. Wherefore henceforth know we no man after the flesh: yea, though we have known Christ after the flesh, yet now henceforth know we *him* no more. Therefore if any man *be* in Christ, *he is* a new creature: old things are passed away; behold, all things are become new. And all things *are* of God, who hath reconciled us to himself by Jesus Christ, and hath given to us the ministry of reconciliation; To wit, that God was in Christ, reconciling the world unto himself, not imputing their trespasses unto them; and hath committed unto us the word of reconciliation. Now then we are ambassadors for Christ. . . . For he hath made him *to be* sin for us, who knew no sin; that we might be made the righteousness of God in him.[473]

First comes the fear appeal. At this crucial juncture, a form of the fear appeal in ominous discord with the much more recurrent portrayal of salvation as general amnesty for the elect (and with this passage's own comments on "reconciliation") is employed. How is it that Christ took on and atoned for all the elect's sins, if even Paul and his devout hearers expect eventually to be arraigned for theirs? Does this mean Paul is to be arraigned for his persecution and killing of Christians before he saw the light on the Damascus road? Next comes the obligatory reminder that deep internalization of teaching emanating from Paul and his entourage, not from within themselves, is the source of truth' for the believer. One is to use it to land some snappy replies on the dreaded false brothers, but not hear whatever they might have to say in reply. There is a suggestion of some unspecified bizarre or unseemly apostolic behavior, which Paul intimates is a sign but if anyone else traffics in signs and wonders, that must be Satanic!

It is highly indicative that a fear broadside coupled with the teaching that godly ideation (the renewed mind, the mind of Christ) comes in from outside is alien to one's own, natural ideation, together comprise the prelude to a major statement about the radically transformed, inverted outlook the believer is to take on. Perhaps the juxtaposition of the transformed condition's onset with

473. 2 Cor. 5:10-21.

being "beside ourselves" helps prepare the believer for the radicalness of it. The contrast of "one" and "many," which we earlier encountered corresponding to sin as self-conscious integration of the ego-personality with the rest of the personality, and sin as commandment infraction, respectively, lets us know that a dissociation theme is about to be introduced. Then it comes. Being a "new creature" in Christ, for whom "all things are become new" states again the obliviousness or death′ to the natural, to be accompanied by coming alive′ to the God-complex and the elusive intimation that truth′ makes sense or rings true. To "hear" this passage tell it, the mature believer ceases entirely to engage in any of the human fraternization or camaraderie of people who are alive′ to the flesh′, and relates to other believers only in terms of the mystical participation that sharing the mind of Christ is supposed to be, "teaching and admonishing one another in psalms and hymns and spiritual songs," and praying without ceasing. One's new, godly knowledge of one's fellows apparently is to be irrelevant to mere human affection. Now we know why the "unequally yoked" Christian wife is allowed to stay with her unbelieving husband: the human relation is to be so attenuated that whom it is with does not matter. Now we know how far the believer is to go, in not preferring or "respecting" one individual person over another. The believer is alerted that even Christ is no longer to be known as before, perhaps intimating that the immature believer's notion of Jesus as a benign, beautiful pastoral young man is to be superseded by some more abstruse conception. What is really being described is divestment of the ego-personality of psychic energy, and investment of it in the God-complex instead. That transfer is apparently to be so major that the "new creature" lives only "unto" Christ, is in Christ—thus, outside or "beside"[474] himself—is reconciled to Christ, and not Christ reconciled to him. The process of "reconciliation" inverts the believer, turns him inside out. That is what is "new" about it.

The connection between obedience to the commandment to fear God and attainment of the dissociated state of mind identified as "faith" is reinforced in three passages, each often taught from the pulpit under the guise of a more pedestrian theological nonissue. One of these apparently emphasizes that being a good hireling is God's commandment:

> Servants [*doulos,* slaves], be obedient to them that are *your* masters according to the flesh, with fear and trembling, in singleness of your heart, as unto Christ; Not with eyeservice [*ophthalmodouleia*], as menpleasers; but as the servants of Christ, doing the will of God from the heart; With good will doing service, as to the Lord, and not to men: Knowing that whatsoever good thing any man doeth, the same shall he receive of the Lord, whether *he be* bond or free.[475]

Note the conjunction of obedience, "fear and trembling," and "singleness of heart," a proposition not unlike singleness of eye. One is to have an abstruse,

---

474. *Existemi,* lit., "to stand out of one's wits."
475. Eph. 6:5-8. Cf., the very similar companion verse we encountered in modern translation, p. 55, footnote 98, Note how the modern translation incorrectly renders *phobeo* as *reverence.*

theological notion in mind, all the time one is performing one's work duties. The inclination is clearly against a creative secular profession or occupation for the Christian, as this would require "this-worldly-mindedness." The duty to God, not care for the human or practical implications of what is done, is to be the motive keeping the Christian at the task. That way, the believer's mind is kept off of the "deceitful" notion that something he is ordered to do offends his innate conscience: that is not the believer's business, when obeying some master in authority. The verse speaks of reward to the believer for doing "good," leaving for another time the explanation or resolution of the fear issue. The passage steps back from risking giving the game away. The theme of a different dimension of slavery′ versus freedom′ obtaining beyond the pale of the natural serves to reinforce the tacit premise that reception of dual meanings of key terms is essential to proper hearing′ of the Word.

The passage connecting "sinning" after having "received the knowledge of the truth" with expectation of "judgment and fiery indignation" without hope of reprieve, which we encountered in our scrutiny of blasphemy against the Holy Spirit, makes the same point, seemingly innocuously, since the believer is unable to articulate "sin" in the crucial, operative sense.[476] At most, he can articulate that keeping certain classes of thoughts out of mind, particularly lascivious and pugnacious ones, is part of it. What should be noted is that avoidance of "sinning," i.e., institution or perfection of "faith" or dissociation, is sought to be stimulated by bringing to mind the most horrible biblical consequences.

The third passage, unsurpassed in artfulness of wording, presents itself and is very often preached on, under the guise of explaining why Christians "rest" on the first day of the week instead of the seventh:

> Therefore, let us fear lest, while a promise remains of entering His rest, any one of you should seem to have come short of it. For indeed we have had good news preached to us, just as they also [i.e., those who professed Christianity and fell away]; but the word they heard did not profit them, because it was not united by faith in those who heard. For we who have believed enter that rest, just as He has said,
>
> "As I swore in My wrath,
> They shall not enter My rest,"
>
> although His works were finished from the foundation of the world.[477]

This time, the fear appeal is understated, euphemistically expressed in terms of omission from the group appointed to enter "rest." The recurring theme of

476. See p. 344, footnote 462.
477. Heb. 4:1-3. *New American Standard Bible.* We encountered the King James rendering of this passage in footnote 321, p. 290. Some modern translations take the menacing edge off the passage by using *since* instead of *while,* suppressing the message that an opportunity for a limited time only is meant. Cf., 2 Cor. 6:2 and 1 Thess. 5:1-2. Also, the passage is often rendered to have it that voluntary activity is intended by *faith,* correctly conveying what "faith" is, but circumventing this particular passage's camouflage of that feature and injecting a spurious, if comforting, element of choice on the believer's part.

contradiction as to whether the salvation plan be closed or open and hence whether the believer has any control over the outcome or not is employed to lend a portentous air. Apparently the quotation from Psalms[478] is part of the "good news."

What is it about the fear that the Bible commands be apperceived but prohibits being deeply experienced that stimulates dissociation? What is it that the conscious mind finds so intolerable that the offending content must be covered in insulating layers to avoid its irritation, like an oyster making a pearl? I submit that the Bible authors, departing from the Old Testament's cautious vagueness about the matter, deliberately contrived the portentous New Testament statements about horrors in the afterlife to be the worst eventualities of which the mind—or at least the ordinary minds of those who would be rank-and-file believers—could conceive. I can almost imagine Paul and whoever actually wrote Hebrews sitting together in the shade of a fig tree, asking themselves what would be the most horrible outcome imaginable, with which to threaten people, and answering their own question: that the prospect of taking the utmost in corporeal punishment for infinite duration would, as a matter of sheer logic, be it. And for embellishment one could add some further atrocities done to other people and things one cares about, offensive to the sort of "natural affection" the Bible authors elsewhere disparaged and passed over lightly, to get the believers, pursuant to their "faith," to "put off" their natural reactions of revulsion. There is no need for an inquisitor, like O'Brien in *1984,* to find out and to arrange what the individual idiosyncratically fears, to threaten someone like Winston with a rat to eat his face in order to make him betray Julia and learn to love Big Brother.

To get at the biblical fear experience, it is crucial to separate out the varied, secular gloss on it, which conditions commonly held notions about its content. Biblical Hell bears little resemblance to Dante's Inferno, and involves no red-suited man with a tail, horns or a pitchfork. We have touched on some of its features in other contexts.[479] The following are representative:

> . . . [T]he hour is coming, in the which all that are in the graves shall hear his voice, And shall come forth; they that have done good, unto the resurrection of life; and they that have done evil, unto the resurrection of damnation.[480]

> . . . [A]nd I saw the souls of them that were beheaded for the witness of Jesus, and for the word of God, and which had not worshipped the beast, neither his image, neither had received *his* mark upon their foreheads, or in their hands; and they lived and reigned with Christ a thousand years. But the rest of the dead lived not again until the thousand years were finished. This *is* the first resurrection. Blessed and holy *is* he that hath part in the first resurrection: on such the second death hath no power, but they shall be priests of God and of Christ, and shall reign with him a thousand years. . . . And they [Satan and his gathered armies] went up on the breath of the earth and compassed [surrounded] the camp of the saints about,

478. 95:11.
479. See pp. 121-22, particularly footnotes 101 and 102; pp. 145-49; p. 228, footnote 194; p. 289, footnote 315; p. 307, footnotes 371-72 and p. 316, footnote 394.
480. John 5:28-29.

and the beloved city: and fire came down from God out of heaven, and devoured them. And the devil that deceived them was cast into the lake of fire and brimstone, where the beast and the false prophet *are,* and shall be tormented day and night for ever and ever. . . . And I saw the dead, small and great, stand before God; and the books were opened: and another book was opened, which is *the book* of life: and the dead were judged out of those things which were written in the books, according to their works. And the sea gave up the dead which were in it; and death and hell [*hades*] delivered up the dead which were in them: and they were judged every man according to their works. And death and hell were cast into the lake of fire. This is the second death. And whosoever was not found written in the book of life was cast into the lake of fire.[481]

These things saith the first and the last, which was dead, and is alive; I know thy [the Smyrna church's] works, and tribulation, and poverty, (but thou art rich) and *I know* the blasphemy of them which say they are Jews, and are not, but *are* the synagogue of Satan. Fear none of those things which thou shalt suffer: behold, the devil shall cast *some* of you into prison, that ye may be tried; and ye shall have tribulation ten days: be thou faithful unto death, and I will give thee a crown of life. He that hath an ear, let him hear what the Spirit saith unto the churches; He that overcometh shall not be hurt of the second death.[482]

If any man worship the beast and his image, and receive *his* mark in his forehead, or in his hand, The same shall drink of the wine of the wrath of God, which is poured out without mixture into the cup of his indignation; and he shall be tormented with fire and brimstone in the presence of the holy angels, and in the presence of the Lamb: And the smoke of their torment ascendeth up for ever and ever: and they have no rest day nor night, who worship the beast and his image, and whosoever receiveth the mark of his name.[483]

What should be especially noted is the inextricably interwoven relation of punishment of the nonelect to catastrophe at the end of the world, as the Bible unfolds. Instead of attributing an emotional, mental, moral or other psychic content to the punishment the individual believer is to fear for himself, it is couched exclusively in terms of corporeal punishment, so that the most dense sensibility will get the message. To the special meanings of death′, i.e., lack of election, transition into salvation, and unconsciousness, insensitivity or anesthesia, is added another meaning belonging to the eschatological schedule, and amounting to remand for eternal punishment. By far the most prevalent description of the punishment is bodily burns continuing to be inflicted eternally.[484] Fleeting reference is made to being fatigued and deprived of rest or sleep, and to being whipped.[485] The believer is also given to understand that whatever it is will take place in darkness, elicit weeping and gnashing of teeth, be worse than Sodom, and, in the case of a didactic offender, be worse than being drowned

481. Rev. 20:4-6, 9-10, 12-15.
482. Rev. 2:8-11.
483. Rev. 14:9-11. Note the contradiction as to the presence of God at punishment, with the passage at footnote 80, p. 196.
484. Matt. 25:41, 46; Luke 3:9, 17; 16:24; John 15:6; Heb. 10:27; Jude 7; Rev. 14:10; 19:20; 20:10 and 21:8.
485. Luke 12:47-48.

with a millstone around one's neck.[486] The Bible authors seem to have restrained their otherwise fertile imaginations, and left it to the believers' own unaided imaginations to fill in the lurid details. The implication that crucifixion—all too familiar in Israel in the first century A.D.—is a figure of God's wrath on those for whom Christ did not die, comes across clearly without needing to be stated. In all, the biblical punishment plan is nothing but a reflection and an introjection of Roman methods of colonial control, indeed, of every authoritarian regime's control, depending ultimately on the fear of corporeal punishment. That is the kind of "lord" the God of the Bible ultimately is. His nature is to have his concentration camp ready, where Satan and his cohorts are to be the unsaved humans' fellow-prisoner trustees or block captains.

The punishment's other dimension, witnessing the natural creation and unsaved people in whom one has some emotional investment destroyed, cuts across the devices. The believer is certainly induced to foster in himself a sense of alienation, and to avoid poignant attachments to worldly things and unbelievers. The separation of love′ from natural affection and human emotion is fostered by such unpropitous prospects for the objects of such affection and emotion. The radicalness of the separation to be effected between the natural and supernatural realms, and hence, the new mind being "put on" and the old, "put off," are also implicated. What with all the references to burning and to "searing" of conscience, perhaps a strip of scorched and smoldering earth, a sulphurous, volcanic no-man's land between the realms would be an apt image. And it certainly assaults one's integrity to be required to recite with a straight face how beautiful, hopeful, righteous and lovely one finds the plan, when the plan is really a sadomasochistic pervert's wet dream!

The preeminence of the theme of corporeal punishment in the salvation plan must be thought of in its historical context of persecution and martyrdom. In a situation where violent death was all around, early Christianity could serve to make such death as a martyr seem like an alternative preferable to continuing to live and going around in constant mental anguish, wondering which way of spending eternity had been appointed to one. Consciously deliberate suicide would be out of the question for the Christian, since that would ensure Hell. But to maneuver oneself into martyrdom would seem to ensure the opposite result, and shorten one's earthly misery in the bargain. One could not consider suicide in the manner of Judas, but not only could one consider, one was commanded to seek, disguised suicide after the fashion of Stephen, Peter, or Jesus.

> Forasmuch then as the children are partakers of flesh and blood, he also himself likewise took part of the same; that through death he might destroy him that had the power of death, that is, the devil; And deliver them who through fear of death were all their lifetime subject to bondage.[487]

---

486. Matt. 8:12 (weeping etc.); Matt. 11:24; Jude 7 (Sodom); Matt. 18:6; Mark 9:42 and Luke 17:2 (millstone).
487. Heb. 2:14-15. Cf. Rom. 8:13-15.

A ubiquitous fixture in the conservative church's Sunday-school experience is a compendium of accounts of martyred Christians from the first century to its own time (the reign of Bloody Mary), *Foxe's Book of Martyrs.* It has an innate, lurid, sadomasochistic appeal, holding the reader's attention while indirectly and obliquely putting across the message that the eternal penalties possible in Christianity are so terrible that temporal ones of the utmost grisliness are preferable. The following is representative:

> In the same persecution suffered the glorious and most constant martyrs of Lyons and Vienne . . . giving a glorious testimony, and to all Christian men a spectacle or example of singular fortitude in Christ our Saviour. Their history is set forth by their own churches, where they did suffer:—
>
> The whole fury of the multitude, the governor, and the soldiers, was spent on . . . [two stalwart men of the church] and lastly on Blandina, through whom Christ showed that those things that appear unsightly and contemptible among men are most honourable in the presence of God, on account of love to His name exhibited in real energy, and not in boasting and pompous pretences. For—while we all feared, and among the rest while her mistress according to the flesh, who herself was one of the noble army of martyrs, dreaded that she would not be able to witness a good confession because of the weakness of her body;—Blandina was endued with so much fortitude, that those who successively tortured her from morning to night were quite worn out with fatigue, owned themselves conquered and exhausted of their whole apparatus of tortures, and were amazed to see her still breathing whilst her body was torn and laid open. The blessed woman recovered fresh vigour in the act of confession; and it was an evident annihilation of all her pains, to say 'I am a Christian, and no evil is committed among us.'[488]

Undoubtedly, the assurance and dignity evinced by early Christians facing suffering, dehumanization and death, the euphoric calm concomitant to the perfected dissociation, made a deep impression on many onlookers. One could readily think that something supernatural, wonderful and happy was taking place. At the time for facing death, many such Christians must have felt great relief, no longer psychologically to have to walk on eggshells, and go around afraid of being afraid, worried about being worried, and anxious about being anxious, but commanded to "witness a good confession," to keep a stiff upper lip, nevertheless. Could Hell itself be any worse than its uncertain anticipation?

Our awareness that facilitating dissociation is a major objective likely to be at work at any juncture in the Bible enables us to put the fragments of biblical information about the afterlife together, and see why introducing the fear appeal at the conscious level is particularly effective to stimulate advanced, relatively stable dissociation in a person prepared by sufficient indoctrination. (The Bible authors indicated their awareness of the incrementalness of the indoctrination

488. John Foxe (Springdale, Pa.: Whitaker House, 1981), pp. 25-26. First published in its present form in 1570.

process, by comparing potential converts to soil to be sown.)[489] Quite deliberately, the Bible authors set it up that the unsaved are resurrected in their reconstituted earthly bodies, and although the present heavens and earth are annihilated in something resembling a nuclear catastrophe, it is definitely with their earthly psychological make-up that the unsaved are remanded to eternal torment. Where the destructibility of their bodies was characteristic of earthly horror, now the horror will lie in the indestructibility of the body, which the fire does not burn up and the whipping does not pound to pieces. Where death can give release in earthly concentration camps and gulags, there is no such possibility of relief from God's concentration camp. Its experience is to involve not only infliction of exquisitely intense pain, but denial of all creature comfort, to creatures still so constituted as to desire it. To eat, to drink, to make love, to hear music, to see beauty will apparently be desired still, but gone forever. The saved, whose resurrection even takes place at a different time,[490] get "incorruptible" bodies, and will supposedly inhabit the new heavens and new earth, to whose nature the Bible affords precious few clues. But it is clear that the heavenliness of the resurrected believers' existence consists mainly of release from creature wants and bonds of affection that had only seemed important.[491] The saved will be like the angels—those relentless, android, single-purpose creatures of God; they will have no gender, no intimate bodily functions, no ordinary human feelings or compassion, and although the Bible does not indicate that they will be like winged choir members with harps riding around on clouds, one does receive the impression that the contemplated heavenliness lies in the received ability to sit through an interminable church service without being bored or one's posterior getting tired.

> And before the throne *there was* a sea of glass like unto crystal: and in the midst of the throne, and round about the throne, *were* four beasts full of eyes before and behind. And the first beast *was* like a lion, and the second beast like a calf, and the third beast had a face as a man, and the fourth beast *was* like a flying eagle. And the four beasts had each of them six wings about *him;* and *they were* full of eyes within: and they rest not day and night, saying, Holy, holy, holy, Lord God Almighty, which was, and is, and is to come. . . . The four and twenty elders fall down before him that sat on the throne, and worship him that liveth for ever and ever, and cast their crowns before the throne, saying, Thou art worthy, O Lord, to receive [*lambano,* take] glory and honour and power [*dunamis*]: for thou hast created all things, and for thy pleasure they are and were created.[492]

489. Matt. 13:3-23 and Mark 4:2-34.

490. See p. 355, footnote 481. Apparently the saved and the unsaved are to be judged at different times, perhaps as if an earthly criminal court would decide it were going to try guilty people on Mondays, Wednesdays and Fridays, but innocent people on Tuesdays and Thursdays. Also, note the contradiction between verses indicating that the saved come into judgment (Rom. 14:10; 2 Cor. 5:10; Heb. 9:27; 1 John 4:17 and Jude 15) and others indicating that they do not (John 5:24; 1 Cor. 11:32-34). The seeming King James distinction between *judgment* and *condemnation* is not found in the Greek, where *krisis* and *krima* stand for either.

491. Matt. 22:30. For biblical information as to the heavenly condition of the saved, see p. 289, footnote 315.

492. Rev. 4:6-8, 10-11. Note how the four beasts representing the despised unconscious, three parts animal and one part human, and the fragmentation of whose awareness is further indicated

The stark biblical contrast between heavenly and hellish modes of existence in the afterlife—really in the psyche—turns out to be merely another way of setting the rarified, expurgated consciousness to be affected by the believer, over against a defamatorily negative rendition of the unconscious. By forcing every authentic product of the unconscious into the shadow side, the believer creates for himself the illusion that every such product is something negative and threatening. Since perfecting the separation between the realms is his goal, pictured for him in terms of heaven being way up and Hell way down, and by a hyaline barrier provided at last, so that constant, draining energy expenditure is no longer needed to keep the two media apart, it comes to seem oddly reasonable and even reassuring that the natural and the supernatural are so separate that the former reveals nothing whereby propositions about the latter might be proved or disproved. Fear of Hell doubles as a metaphor for fear of the supposed catastrophic consequences of letting the disparate mental realms communicate. Where full, "related" living involves mixing the realms, letting the mental serve to help the subject come to terms with what we have called the nonfantastic, Christianity boils down to so much destructive, wasted effort toward the undesirable end of keeping them estranged. It is because several pervasive issues converge in it, that contemplation of fear of Hell prompts such a redoubled effort within the believer, to perfect the dissociation. When the dissociation weakens, the activities that strengthen it kick into passing gear, so to speak. The believer prays more, turns Family Radio up louder to drown out the doubts, goes to a church service to get peer reassurance, reads the Bible to reinforce the allegorical suggestions of separation of the realms, etc.

The artfulness and craftsmanship of the interweaving of the fear appeal into the larger fabric of the biblically conditioned state of mind reach their greatest heights in the inclusion, and actual utilization for a mind-control purpose, of the

---

by a multiplicity of eyes throughout their bodies (or perhaps, only throughout all those wings indicating the creatures' airiness), representing nuclei of awareness, complexes, or splinter-personalities, both regard the throne and are superimposed on God the Father, who occupies the throne even while the four beasts occupy the "midst of the throne." Also, contrary to all biblical notions of energetics, but consistent with our notions about the transfer of libido among complexes, the God who is allegedly the source of all energy "receives" (and apparently craves) "power" from the twenty-four elders worshipping him. The intimation that the great "I am" is really pieces of oneself, projected and energized with one's own energy is again educed.

The same sort of reverse-suggestive image of a projected alter-ego on an official seat, exercising authority over the very one whose projection the alter-ego is, is embedded in the dilemma of whether or not the believers stand before the bar at judgment day. See p. 358, footnote 490. An ingenious attempt to resolve the dilemma (advocated by Camping, among others, and suggested in Heb. 9:26, 28; 1 Pet. 2:21 and 3:18) is to conclude that Christ's atonement for the sins of the elect entails his standing in their place, and the believers who have already been raptured or caught up in the air to be with him (1 Thess. 4:15-17), able to be in the jury box or spectators' gallery, instead of the prisoners' dock. Such a solution would work if God the Father were the judge's only guise. But the authors of the Bible were most deliberate in having Christ be specified as the guise of the judgment-day judge (John 5:22, 27; 2 Cor. 5:10., 2 Thess. 2:8 and 2 Tim. 4:1). Christ sits in judgment, but also stands before himself, as defendant, in the believers' stead. Perhaps that relates to his being an "advocate." It all adds up to the believer, at least by proxy, fearing to stand before a sitting judge, who is nothing but the believer's projection, formed and energized from within the believer.

very phenomenon that works most effectively against the fear getting out of hand: double orientation. It is crucial to keep in mind that, although the deeply indoctrinated believer unconsciously knows full well that he lacks any substantive basis for the beliefs exhorted and must, perforce, dissociate the awareness that his "testimony" about confidence in them or subjective certainty of them is untrue, neither he nor anyone else has any direct or affirmative basis for declaring the beliefs false. Accordingly, *unbelief* connotes a certain passivity and noncommittalness for us, distinguishing it sharply from active, affirmative "disbelief." The great genius of Christianity, wherein it is superior to every other indoctrination, lies in protecting itself with its intricately contrived nondisprovability. All the "isms" of modern times entailed expectations necessarily confirmed or disconfirmed in time—and always the result has been disconfirmation. Experience undermines the "isms," and if they cannot survive by raw, proprietary power, they wither. Their defenders ultimately cut a sorry figure in the eyes of the intellectually honest. But that which could disconfirm Bible doctrine is always tantalizingly (and for its defenders, conveniently) out of reach, beyond the pale. I can imagine a historical situation that may have been, where time and again, the Jews of the first century A.D. were told that Roman legions as numerous as grains of sand on the beaches they would land on would come and smash them and their country, and that after discounting and disbelieving warnings and false alarms, the Jews learned in shock and horror that it was all true. Then, when a sect came along with a religious revision based on dire warnings about remote but indescribably dreadful, prospective horrors, it would find many takers. Humans have no sure defense against the possible faultiness of second-hand information not amenable to independent corroboration.

Like the God-image constituted in mind by the believer, animated by content expelled from consciousness, perhaps invested with so much libido that it becomes a splinter-personality with which there can be the illusion of a dialogue, but never brought into clear focus because its biblical specifications clash, so does the entire biblical scheme hover in empty space, transparent to confirmation and disconfirmation alike. To try to dispel it is like trying to waft away what seems like a cloud of gas, when really it is a smudge on one's glasses that one sees. No matter how well inculcated, the indoctrination cannot elicit whole-hearted action and simply does not immediately get one's adrenaline secretions activated, as a natural situation, with palpable aspects and need for action, does. To respond emotionally to the religion's features requires an outcome of the devotional effort resembling nothing so much as Pavlovian conditioning. The activities of love′ are linked to and confused with affection for a natural person, propagandization is linked to and confused with ingestion of nourishment, and being in the fold is linked to and confused with the joy, sentimentality and latent prurience of a wedding. Not for nothing did Jesus for his first public miracle turn water into wine so that wedding guests could get soused! Such conditioned responses, however, extinguish easily and decay rapidly, if the sequences effecting the conditioning are not constantly repeated.

Another pertinent psychological analogy is Goldstein's observation that a fully functioning organism can actively break out of the vacillation brought on by stimuli evoking conflicting responses equally strongly, but an impaired one cannot. To act according to "faith" involves the competing inclination to dismiss what one is exhorted to do, because there is no natural reason for doing it. Quite deliberately, the Bible sets the requirements of love′ in opposition to perfectly decent, reasonable natural modes of behavior. With one's critical thinking selectively impaired by the dissociation, the person under mind-control is held in place, vacillating about his supposed convictions. Just in case they are true after all, he will not dare ignore what "faith" requires. The absurdity of that position is still another irritant to the conscious mind, prompting still more dissociation to assuage it.

Double orientation accounts not only for the fear remaining sufficiently remote and unreal not to get out of hand, to be merely nagging and irritating rather than exhausting or debilitating, but also for the mind's knowing, at some inner level, what to dissociate, by what criteria to expel contents from conscious awareness. What with so much exhortation to do what makes no sense in the natural, part of the believer is involved with keeping his behavior credibly within his and the other believers' notions of how a believer should behave, and another part copes with the still present natural and human surroundings. The awareness of tension and ambivalence between the demands of the religion and the demands of the natural serve to account for the general unease the believer often feels, in order that his mind be kept off the absurdity of devoting his entire energy to keeping the stringent, sterile Christian discipline, just in case, despite nagging, inescapable, well-grounded unbelief.

There is another consideration that ameliorates not only the impact of the fear appeal but all the previous devices. Its operation is most plain relative to the fear device; hence our postponement of our main consideration of it to this juncture. The fit of our analysis to real church experiences as they are presently being lived would be greatly impaired were we to neglect it. The consideration is the difference in effect of the mind-control system on inner-directed individuals as opposed to other-directed.

Hopefully, our earlier psychological discussion and the context have made it clear enough that by "inner-directed," we mean an individual whose relation to others and to situations is guided mainly by conscience, a person who is sensitive and responsive to the several layers of his own conscience. And by "other-directed," we mean an individual who takes his cues from peers and from generally approved points of view. He is capable of being confronted with what ought properly to disgust or outrage him but can accept it with feckless cheerfulness if others around him give off no cues to the contrary. Most people, we are warned, are really much more other-directed than appears on the surface, and it is terrible to contemplate what most of our friends and neighbors would blithely do were leaders and peers to turn malignant. Inner-directedness, particularly if accompanied by particular intuitive sensitivity or perspicacity, means that many an intrinsically admirable person must pass through life in conflict with the prevailing ethos.[493]

Internalization of the byzantine intricacies of the Evangelical mind-control system is much more a matter for the sensitive, the intelligent, the thoughtful, the individual possessed of integrity for the system to assault, than for the rank and file. The turgid, normal sensibility is protected from the sort of painful, anguishing confrontation with the system that we have observed in various famous heroes of faith of the past. Most people just go along with the flow, and apparently have a much more fragmentary and chaotic view of the implications of things than appears on the surface. For most believers, the atmospherics of the Christian group where they "fellowship," not the precise theological content of the teaching, determine their state of mind. The great danger for a churched person is to spend most of his life working himself into the position where the cosmetic, Device 1 commonplaces leave off and the true implications of the Bible take up, with anguishing effect.

Another example from Camping's call-in program illustrates the fear device in action and, I think, the most fundamental of the kinds of harm arising from renewed biblicism. This replicates many a "counseling" contact in private, between a believer and a mini-Reformationist pastor, where the gloves studiously kept on in the pulpit come off. From her voice and speech, the caller was a fairly young woman of no distinctive ethnicity:

> Caller: I am very confused. . . . The question I want to ask is: I've gone to a Christian Reform church for two years, and I found it excruciating. Now, I know a lot about systematic theology. My pastor is—was a systematic theologian, and I've been really confused because now I don't go to that church any more, 'cause I found it too hard to just practice Christianity in my life. I can understand it intellectually, but I felt really guilty inside, and I felt like I really couldn't do what they asked of me. My family isn't Christian, so I came to that church becoming a Christian, but now I have doubts about my whole Christian life today. I go to another church, but I'm so confused, that I don't even want [laughing lilt to her voice] to go to church any more.
>
> Camping: Well, let me make a suggestion, or let's discuss for a moment what is salvation. Is salvation simply learning systematic theology, learning certain

493. In using the terms, *inner-directed* and *other-directed* without stopping to define them, I took into consideration their self-evident connotations and their dictionary definitions, with which my usages agree. However, it should be pointed out that my usages do not entirely agree with those in the classic sociological work where the terms were first introduced: David Riesman, *The Lonely Crowd* (New Haven, Conn.: Yale Univ. Press 1950). That work dealt not in psychological individual differences, but in what it regarded as modal personalities corresponding respectively to three characteristic phases in a society's industrialization: (1) "tradition-directed" where custom, ritual, religion and kinship, with shame as the guiding emotion, define the individual to himself; (2) "inner-directed," where the inculcation of inner principles, goals, a psychological gyroscope, craft skill and guilt as guiding emotion so define the individual; and (3) "other-directed," where smooth assimilation into the group ethos, psychological radar instead of a gyroscope, manipulative skill with people instead of craft skill, and anxiety as the guiding emotion, so define the individual. Our usages do not harmonize with the historical-deterministic aspect of Riesman's work, but instead correspond much more to field independence versus field dependence, and to group-pressure resistance versus group-pressure susceptability. See pp. 67-71.

doctrines of the Bible and then trying as best as we can to live in accordance with the Word of God? Is that salvation? And the answer is, no! Not at all. That kind of "salvation" will lead us into Hell for sure. Salvation is this: that, first of all, we recognize that we're a sinner, that as we compare our life against the standard that God sets forth in the Bible, we know we do not measure up. However we look at our life, we do not measure up, and we are faced with that terrible fact of the Bible, that the wages of sin is death, and the death that God has in view is eternal damnation. And so, that is the first giant truth that we become aware of when we're on a path to salvation. Number two, we learn that in myself I cannot do anything. No matter how hard I try to live God's way, all I'm doing is digging my way deeper into Hell, because every time I miss the mark a little bit, I'm not quite as God-glorifying as God demands, the wages of sin is Hell, and any sin is going to send me to Hell. And so I know that trying to keep the law of God, trying to do it God's way is never going to save me. More than that, of myself I can never become saved, because no matter how hard I try, I'm always faced with the fact that I have not measured up. But I also come to the point where I learn that the only thing I can do is throw myself on the mercies of God. Like the Bible talks about the publican of old, who stood afar off, and he smote his breast, and he dared not look up, and he said, "O God, have mercy on me; I'm a sinner. Have mercy on me."[494] That is the cry of those who are recognizing their need of salvation. We don't deserve anything. All we know is that we're in trouble with God, and that only God can save us. And so we cry out to God for his mercy. Now, when God saves us, a marvelous thing happens: and this is God's action entirely. Before we are saved, both in body and soul, body and in spirit essence, we lust after sin. We want to do our own thing. But when we become saved, God gives us a brand new soul or spirit essence. He gives us a new, resurrected soul, in which we never want to sin again. And also, of course, he takes us out of the dominion of Satan, and he translates us, transfers us into the kingdom of the Lord, Jesus Christ, so that even though we have a body that still lusts after sin, that is balanced against a soul or a spirit essence, which is also an integral part of our lives, in which we never want to sin. And so, the struggle is entirely different. Now, as a saved person, I'm not saying, "Oh, I've gotta do it God's way, Oh, I've gotta live God's way, because otherwise I'm going to be threatened by Hell." And yet, its uphill work, because in every fiber of my being, both in body and soul, I don't want to do it God's way. I really want to go my own way, and I'm always longingly looking over my shoulder. "Oh, I wish I could live in the world, I wish I could do this, I wish I could do that." But once we become saved, there is this desire within us, an ongoing "want-to," to do the will of God, so that as a matter of fact, we are happiest when we are doing the will of God. We have learned that we have most contentment and most joy in our life when we are doing the will of God. And so the question is not how much theology have I learned; the question is not how well am I doing in keeping the law of God; the question is, "Am I saved? Have I really come to know Jesus as my Lord and Savior? Have I recognized that I'm a sinner? And have I asked the Lord for mercy, and has God indeed given me a new heart, so that I find in my life an implicit trust in Christ as my Savior and as my Lord, so that there is an ongoing, earnest desire to do the will of God?" And if that is not in your life, then, because it is still the day of

494. Luke 18:13.

salvation,[495] you can still cry out to God, "Oh God, have mercy on me!" And the Bible promises that if we seek him with all our heart, we will find him.[496]

Caller: Well, what does it mean, then, "work out your salvation with fear and trembling"?

Camping: You're quoting from Philippians, chapter two, verse twelve: "Work out your own salvation." It is not talking there about the matter of becoming saved. That conclusion would go contrary to everything else the Bible talks about, because the Bible is very clear that salvation is altogether of God. Now, God has saved us. Now we work out that salvation within our lives as we continue to study the Word, and as we begin to pray to God and communicate with him. But notice the next phrase; the rest of that sentence: "Work out your own salvation with fear and trembling, *for it is God who worketh in you to will and to do of His good pleasure.*" [italics indicate emphatic intonation] In other words, once we are saved, and [sic] that is totally the action of God in saving us. And now we find that earnest desire to do the will of God in our life, and we are increasingly desiring to do his will and to be pleasing to him. We know that we can't take any credit: it is God who is working this out in our life because we have become his children, and because he has given us a new, resurrected soul.

Caller: But there's a definite difference: it's not my will, but his will be done, but how do you—I mean—you say these things, and I just—I mean—I don't know if I'm saved or not. I keep—

Camping: Well, that's a good question, "Am I saved or not?" We all have to face that question, and don't [sic] take anything for granted, that, well, because I've been in the church a couple of years, or because I've learned some theology, or because of this or because I made confession of faith or was baptized, therefore I know I'm saved. You cry out to God and pray, "O Lord, I don't know whether I'm saved," and the Bible insists that if we say we know him, and that's a figure to indicate, if we say that we are saved and yet do not keep his commandments, then we *are* not saved; the truth is not in us. Remember, First John, chapter two teaches that. And so if you find that there is not that earnest, ongoing desire to do the will of God, then there is probably good evidence that you are not a child of God. But then it means that because it is still the day of salvation, you still can become saved as you really cry out to God for that salvation. And remember, "faith cometh by hearing, and hearing by the word of God," and one of the things we want to do is really study the Word. . . . [station break] We're talking to a caller who is really asking the big, sixty-four-dollar question, "What really is salvation? How can I know I'm saved?" And many, many people have gone through a certain action, they've followed a certain formula, they have invited Jesus into their heart, or they have prayed the sinners' prayer, or they have done some other action, and then they somehow believe that they were saved. But the fact is, if we *are* saved, the evidence is found in our life by the fact there's an ongoing, earnest desire to *do* the will of God, and there is a growing in grace, that is, an increasing desire to do the will of God, and an implicit trust that our sins have been paid for through the Lord, Jesus Christ. Now, if we're not saved, wonderfully it is still the day of salvation, and we can still really begin to beseech

495. 2 Cor. 6:2.
496. Matt. 7:8 and Luke 11:10.

the Lord for that salvation, because, remember, it is God who has to save us. We cannot save ourselves.

Caller: But then, if I have felt the love of God and the comfort of God in church, that doesn't necessarily guarantee that I'm saved. It just says I've felt his love and I've felt his comfort. And in this church, I was moved by the Holy Spirit.

Camping: Yeah, well, you see, the Bible says this, that he who endures to the end will be saved. Now what does that mean? That we are saved by our endurance? No, that can't be, but it is saying that the evidence of true salvation is that we do endure. Because, of course, when we are saved we have eternal life. Now the other side of the coin, or picking up exactly the same truths from a different perspective, we read about the sower that went forth to sow,[497] and some of the seed—and the seed is the Word of God and the land that it falls on is the heart of men—some of the seed fell on rocky soil, the Bible teaches, and so the plants began to grow up, and then, because there was no root, when the sun beat upon it these plants withered and died. And God says that's like those who hear the Word of God, and they believe for a while, but because they have no root in Christ, they don't have true saving faith, when other temptations come along, they fall away. And so one of the evidences of true salvation is that there is a continuing, a continuing desire for the things of God, a continuing interest in the Word of God, a continuing desire to do the will of God, and if that is not found in our life, if for a little while like a meteor, like a skyrocket, we were all enthusiastic about salvation, we thought we felt the power of the Holy Spirit, we felt so much at peace and all of that, and now we find that it's dead, we don't have that kind of interest, then we have to ask the question, maybe I wasn't saved at all. I simply intellectually or emotionally got involved with this, but I'm like the seed that fell on rocky soil.

Caller: Exactly, that's exactly my story. That's exactly what happened. And right now I'm saying, "Am I really saved?" I mean, I went to this church for two years, it's all intellectual, and I'm thinking that I'm saved, and here I come along, and I'm tempted beyond, you know[498]—

Camping: [sympathetically] Yes.

Caller: I feel, well, "I'm a weak Christian," but I'm not, I just, I don't really want to believe—

Camping: All right well now [voice cracks momentarily into high falsetto] you know, at least this you've learned, that the wages of sin is death, and the death that is in view in the Bible is eternal damnation. And you know that you have no guarantee that you're going to live through the night. Not one of us has that guarantee. As a matter of fact, every day around two hundred thousand people all over the earth die, and they die for a thousand different reasons, young and old. And if you die without being saved, you know that you're going—its guaranteed you'll spend eternity in Hell. Therefore, if you suspect that you are not saved, your situation is very, very precarious. Because, obviously you wouldn't want to die, through an accident or however, and die unsaved. And that's why the Bible also warns, "Now is the day of salvation." Or the Bible warns, "How shall

497. See p. 358, footnote 489.
498. Reference to the promise of 1 Cor. 10:13, to which we shall come presently. Camping obviously notices, and avoids addressing it.

ye escape, if you neglect so great savation."[499] And so, the wonder of it all is that, right now, even though you honestly confess, "I don't have any interest in the Bible right now, I don't have any interest in church right now, but I still know that if I die unsaved, I'm going to Hell." Now, face that for a while. Walk in those shoes for a while. And the next thing, you're going to be crying out, "O God, have mercy on me, I don't want to go to Hell. And forgive me for my sins, and give me a desire for your Word, and give me a trust in the Lord, Jesus Christ." And you begin to beseech the Lord, that there might be a complete change in your life.

Caller: Well, that's exactly what I've been doing. I've been saying, "I don't want to go to Hell, I just don't want to go to Hell." I don't know what it's like, but I'm afraid. So I just—

Camping: All right. Now the Bible promises, that if we seek him with all our heart, we will surely find him. And you keep beseeching the Lord, and because you're meaning business, and coming to salvation, or beginning to really face up to our real situation, [that] *is* the moment of truth. And if on the one hand you are praying, "Oh, God, help me to turn away from my sins, help me to have a love for the Lord Jesus, help me to read the Bible," and yet you make no effort to open the Bible, and you make no effort to turn away from your sins, then you know that what you're saying is true hypocrisy, because you know as well as I do, there's no force in Heaven or Hell that's keeping you from opening your Bible and beginning to read. But on the other hand, if you go to the Lord and say, "O Lord, in my heart I don't want to read the Bible, O Lord, I know I'm a sinner, and I see these sins in my life and I know they're sending me to Hell. O Lord, give me a desire to read the Bible. Give me a desire to turn away from my sins. Give me a trust in the Lord Jesus." Well then, because you're really agonizing before the Lord, and you mean business with him, then you're also going to open the Word of God, and as you open it you're going to pray, "O Lord, now I'm opening your Word, and now give me a desire to keep reading, and strengthen me as I read, and help me to want to be obedient to what I find there." Do you follow what I'm saying?

Caller: Yes, yes, yes, I understand.

Camping: All right, thank you so much for calling, and may God's grace come upon you, and many of us will be praying for you.

Caller: Thank you.

Camping: Good night.

The detail that must have tipped Camping off, that this caller would sit still for such a withering blast, is her having persevered so long in a Christian Reformed church. That denomination, to which Camping himself belongs, is atypical among conservative denominations, in having remained consistently Calvinist from its old-country roots, and not having been formed by conservative hold-outs from a larger denomination that went liberal within living memory. It remains strong because it manages to hold onto its young people and retains a remarkably homogenous Dutch ethnicity. When an outsider does come in otherwise than through marriage to an existing church member, it is usually a

499. Heb. 2:3.

well-indoctrinated Evangelical enthusiast who has found some other church insufficiently rigorous. Typically, in this denomination there is less self-consciousness about being part of a dissident, conservative minority than in other mini-Reformationist churches. Technique for bringing new converts along by Device 1 is not highly developed. When Camping heard that one not raised in it, in the "fear and nurture of the Lord,"[500] had remained so long, he knew she must really have been hooked.

Yet, if one would ask him, surely Camping would honestly say that he had been aware of no such purpose, that he was only trying to give the right biblical answer, and be in obedience to the Bible, himself, in the way he couched it. An analysis of the double orientation that reflects on the part of the practitioner could get quite complicated. At some level, the Christian practitioner must necessarily know that the representations he makes to the prospective convert or new believer are misleading, deliberately leaving the impression that cheerfulness, philanthropy, affection, making things in this life better, etc., are what the religion is about. One gets a glimpse of it, hearing pastors talk shop, about their obligation to give the "whole counsel of God," meaning the fear message and other unlovely features, along with the rest. Their conclusion is always the same: some degree of benevolent deception is considered proper and is no sin for the pastor employing it. The rustic pastors of the past carried that premise to extremes, setting up phony healings with shills or snake handlings with defanged snakes. Today, the typical practitioner is, himself, very much under mind-control, but wants to perceive himself as aboveboard. He is at pains to avoid the apprehension of something wrong about making a pitch that leads with deception. If his latent integrity and bad conscience about the mode of livelihood in which he has too much personal investment to give it up is eating him, that will usually show up in moodiness, remoteness, and lack of initiative—like Jung's father! The casual observer (and alas, most of the press) mislead themselves looking for Elmer Gantry on the contemporary conservative church scene. Today's mini-Reformationist practitioner, with a clientèle of constantly rising literacy, sophistication and socioeconomic class, avoids overtaxing credulity and salves his own conscience by confining himself to the misleading artifices built into the Bible, the uninterpreted symbolism of giving food, drink, release to captives, and the residual ordinary-language connotations of the key terms affected by logocide.

A few passages make reference to a different, less stringent line to be taken with the neophyte as opposed to the experienced believer:

> Him that is weak in the faith receive ye, *but* not to doubtful disputations. . . . Let us not therefore judge one another any more: but judge this rather, that no man put a stumbling block or an occasion to fall in *his* brother's way. . . . Hast thou faith? have *it* to thyself before God. Happy *is* he that condemneth not himself in that thing which he [i.e., God] alloweth.[501]

---

500. Camping's revealing, habitual misquotation of Eph. 6:4.
501. Rom. 14:1, 13, 22.

So also Christ glorified not himself to be made an high priest: but he that said unto him, Thou art my Son, today have I begotten thee. As he saith also in another *place,* Thou *art* a priest forever after the order of Melchisedec. Who in the days of his flesh, when he had offered up prayers and supplications with strong crying and tears unto him that was able to save him from death, and was heard in that he feared; Though he were a Son, yet learned he obedience by the things which he suffered; And being made perfect, he became the author of eternal salvation unto all them that obey him; Called of God an high priest after the order of Melchisedec. Of whom we have many things to say, and hard to be uttered [i.e., explicated], seeing ye are dull of hearing. For when for the time ye ought to be teachers, ye have need that one teach you again which *be* the first principles of the oracles of God; and are become such as have need of milk, and not of strong [substantial] meat. For every one that useth milk *is* unskilful in the word of righteousness; for he is a babe. But strong meat belongeth to them that are of full age, *even* those who by reason of use have their senses exercised to discern both good and evil.[502]

Nevertheless I [Jesus at the Last Supper] tell you the truth; It is expedient [advantageous] for you that I go away: for if I go not away, the Comforter will not come unto you; but if I depart, I will send him unto you. And when he is come, he will reprove the world of sin, and of righteousness, and of judgment: Of sin, because they believe not on me; Of righteousness, because I go to my Father, and ye see me no more; Of judgment, because the prince of this world is judged. I have yet many things to say unto you, but ye cannot bear them now. Howbeit when he, the Spirit of truth, is come, he will guide you into all truth: for he shall not speak of himself; but whatsoever he shall hear, *that* shall he speak: and he will shew you things to come. He shall glorify me: for he shall receive of mine, and shall shew *it* unto you. All things that the Father hath are mine: therefore said I, that he shall take of mine, and shall shew *it* unto you. A little while, and ye shall not see me: and again, a little while, and ye shall see me, because I go to the Father.[503]

The first passage ties tolerance for the stumblings of the beginner with the dual standard of judging others. At the one extreme, declared, experienced "brothers" who bring false doctrine are to be ostracized, and the "mature" believers are to keep one another under constant doctrinal surveillance, but refraining from administering reproof where they may also be derelict themselves, and, we infer, where they are not entirely sure of their doctrinal grounds. At the other extreme, what the unbeliever does is none of the believers' business, and they are to be radically nonjudgmental regarding it. In between, there is a gray area, necessarily vague because the boundary between the "household of faith" and ordinary unbelievers is purposefully kept so ambiguous that one does not even know on which side of it oneself falls. So, go easy on the weaker ones, including oneself, lest one discourage oneself with the harder teachings too soon. The context is the dispute that arose between believers who still felt bound by

502. Heb. 5:5-14.
503. John 16:7-16. See also John 14:26.

the Jewish dietary laws and those who did not. Its resolution was that whether disregarding those rules was sinful or not depended on the actor's state of mind. That serves to fuzz the issue as to the significance of discrete "sins" (inordinately overemphaszing the state of mind over the practical consequences of the wrong act), pointing from a different direction to the mystery of the once and for all remedy for the unitary "sin" affliction, which we have solved. As a practical matter, a pastor can trot out this passage whenever a disturbance over one member of the flock censoring another too zealously arises and needs to be quelled.

In the other two passages, it is no coincidence that the issue of different tacts mandated for different stages of indoctrination is found intertwined with some of the most artful and intense suggestive imagery in the Bible. In the first, attention is arrested by the poignant déjà vu evoked by the theophany, Melchisedec. I find it deeply ironic that the passage speaks of the Bible's "first principles": it compresses the other-directed, heterochthonous orientation intended throughout, but camouflaged so well that people have never before caught on, into fewer words than anywhere else. Parallel to Peter walking on the water replacing the substitutionary atonement as the Bible's main paradigm in our view, this passage can occupy in our view the place that John 3:16 conventionally occupies: the foremost example of the Bible's entire program condensed in a few well-chosen words. The passage hides the real "first principles" in plain sight!

The surprising information that the mature, meat-eating believer is to be skilled at discerning good from evil brings us full circle from the Garden of Eden, where no law had been laid down except that aspiring to discern good from evil was the prototypic "sin." Here lies a crucial suggestive clue that being spiritually on the right track to belief will not involve restoration in this life of the idyllic, whole state of man before the "fall" into self-consciousness, but something tentative, not looking for resolution until after earthly life. We receive the clue that the original kind of discernment of good from evil, having to do with individual conscience, is different from the kind the mature believer is to cultivate, consisting entirely of application of doctrine that has come in solely from without. Just as the believer is to emulate Jesus and the Holy Spirit in praying to God, incorporating some facets of him even while addressing him as other, the believer is to identify with both of them in lacking knowledge of God's will unless it is "heard," and repeating it only as it was "heard." With one stroke, those two suggestions, and the purposeful partitioning of the mind of God into three parts, are communicated, all merged together. And for good measure, an occasion for the believer to feel "wrong, inferior and unhappy," not knowing the ineffable, advanced spiritual lore when he is taught that it has been taught to him, being examined and flunking, is thrown in!

The third passage bears the telltale marks of Paulinist tampering. Literal belief somehow intrudes as a problem, even for the apostles at the Last Supper. The Holy Spirit as the giver of advanced-level revelations to come later, for which even the apostles were not yet ready, is legitimated out of Jesus' mouth. (That which cometh out of the mouth defileth the man!) Even Jesus goes easy on beginners who are not ready for the hard stuff.

The viewpoint of the practitioner, enabling him to rationalize soft-pedaling the fear appeal for general consumption while ensuring that he will administer it with a whip hand to the faithful inner circle, is as interesting to us as that of the receiver. More than anyone else in the flock, those "who labour in the word and doctrine"[504] put together and eventually understand that alienation from life, not its enhancement, is the main theme of the New Testament, and avoidance of the ugly concentration camp hereafter, its bottom line. As pastors progress, studying the Word to prepare their sermons week after week, to the point where they understand or ought to understand it, their way of escape lies in a further course of assaulting integrity, akin to the one wherein Luther and Wesley each received and implemented the advice to combat their own unbelief by making as fervent lying public declarations of their "faith" as possible. The pastor who has intellectual integrity is forced to disparage that integrity as his worldly fleshliness getting in the way of sight′ and hearing′ of the truth′, and for additional incentives to stifle that good quality, were he to give in to it, he might lose his livelihood, and disrupt all his relationships with flock and family, under mind-control but protected from the acute discouragement he feels by their inability articulately to put their religion's sour implications together. The pastor can go the "low" route, accepting that benevolent deceptions are all right because he must, perforce, operate in Satan's princedom, or find a higher form of rationalization, one sufficiently sophisticated to enable him convincingly to mislead himself while he misleads others. One way, the double orientation is obvious, the self-deception, crude, and the prospective steady clientèle limited to the unintelligent; the other way, the double orientation is subtle, and understanding it, we can relate to and feel sympathetically toward those enmeshed in it who fail to sort it out.

In this respect, Camping is not typical, and affords us an opportunity to observe the process of subtly rationalizing and obscuring the double standard of teaching built into the Bible, carried on with rare purity. When we hear him "counsel," it is no ordinary pastor depending on force of personality or the unintelligence of his hearers, but the most intellectually competent and honest Bible expositor I know of, living or dead, speaking off the cuff, revealing the workings of his mind. Were I still trying to proceed from the premise of paramount biblical authority, I would feel obligated to give substantially the advice he gives. Even Camping tacitly approves the double standard, in that the twenty hours or so of programming other than his teaching that go out each day over the domestic stations of Family Radio are the usual bland, soporific stuff. But Camping himself gives a much harder line than a church pastor would normally dare. There are pastors who give a hard line, but their churches (unless they draw on an unusual history, like that of Christian Reformed Church) are made up of "graduates" of less rigorous, "transitional" churches, and do not grow rapidly, like those employing the expedient of a "soft" line from the pulpit, coordinated with a harder one in hand-picked small groups. I gather that the

504. 1 Tim. 5:17.

real audience for the call-in program is not the slow-witted pew-sitters who call in and ask the same questions about speaking in tongues and baptism over and over, but pastors who would emulate Camping in their own practice but would not dare call in themselves lest one of their flock hear them asking Camping a question, exposing their ignorance or unbelief to gossip. From listening, and my own sampling visits to mini-Reformationist churches, I gather that never was a seminal thinker more plagiarized or more glad to be plagiarized than Camping.

To illustrate, let us listen to a woman caller, with no particular ethnicity of speech:

> Caller: . . . [garbled] 20:30. "The blueness of a wound cleanseth away evil: so do stripes the inward parts of the belly." Does that refer at all to punishing of children?
>
> Camping: Oh, I'm sure—where did you find that? In Proverbs? . . . [Finds the passage with uncharacteristic fumbling, and reads it aloud.] No, that has nothing to do with the—well, not anything directly dealing with the punishment of children. It really has to do wlth God's salvation plan. Who was punished, who was wounded in order that we might be cleansed from our sins?
>
> Caller: Uh, Jesus.
> Camping: The Lord Jesus. And because he was wounded, that cleansed the evil from us. Likewise, the stripes that he endured for us cleansed away [sic] the inward parts of the belly, and it's a figure there to indicate that the very essence of man is evil. . . .
>
> Caller: O.K., good, and one other thing: I have an eight-year-old and a five-year-old, and I've talked about Jesus and the Gospel. Tonight is an example of my five-year-old [who], after a series of disobediences, got a few swats, and I was holding her afterwards and comforting her and telling her I loved her, and telling her that God has commanded me to punish if there's disobedience, and that I want to obey him, and that I care about how she grows up, and so on and so on. And in the conversation to me—she's in tears—and she says to me, "Oh, I don't want to go to Hell." Am I hitting them too hard with the Gospel at this age?
>
> Camping: Is it possible that we can talk too much about the Gospel to a five-year-old? And the answer is, no. No, you can be grateful when your daughter gives you—or expresses herself in this way, because you can come right back to her and say, "Well, honey, you know it's so wonderful that if we trust in the Lord Jesus, and really put our whole life on him, he came so we don't have to go to Hell." In other words, I'm always grateful, I don't care if it's a child or an adult, if they really have come to a point where they begin to look Hell fairly in—squarely in the face, and recognize, it is super awful. Because that sets the—that is preparation for bringing the rest of the wonderful Gospel of salvation, that we can know the love of God, and we can be rescued from Hell by trusting in Jesus, and you can turn right around and say, "Honey, you know, that's what Jesus did for us if we believe on him. He endured Hell for you and for me and for all who will believe on him. All we have to do is ask the God to have mercy on us and to help us to trust Jesus, and we're going to spend as much time as we can reading the Bible together and getting to know more about this Jesus."

The caller's lead-off, with a particularly gory and wrathful biblical image, is a gambit I have frequently observed in conservative church circles. It may possibly express some anger or hostility that she cannot give herself permission to address relevantly, and may possibly give her some slight sadomasochistic gratification. Corporeal child abuse (rare in Evangelical circles) is not what this is about: it is a more devious, compensatory, vicarious expression of the same impulse, however, that prompts the caller to come on as she does. The image of an irritated or ever-bleeding wound, often found in secular mythology of the Christian era (e.g., Amfortas in the Parzifal legend) may well be rightly understood as pointing to the inner psychic dividedness not allowed to become whole in the obedient believer, and biblical references to salt may even pertain to that substance's propensity to irritate wounds, if this caller's intimations are as typical as I think they are.

The caller knows very well that she has gone too far in using God as a bogeyman for parental control. She may well be recapitulating some similar cruelty inflicted on her by parental figures. And while other children in our day only have to worry that a poisoned environment or nuclear holocaust will render adulthood irrelevant for them, this little girl has on top of those worries, the worry that the next thing after such a catastrophe may be God's no-exit concentration camp, and still on top of that, when (and if) she is a little older and better indoctrinated, the worry that the act of worrying may be the "sin" that will send her there. The caller's conscience tells her she is doing something absurd and wrong, but Camping's counsel is to ignore her conscience and keep her eyes on the doctrine. No wonder Pat Benatar gets such a response from teenagers when she sings "Hell Is For Children."

The way the call threw Camping, forcing him to temporize for many awkward seconds to collect his wits, was most striking, standing out from that particular evening's performance and his performance generally. Usually, when he backs up and rephrases what he is saying, nothing of interest is revealed. But this answer is littered with his near slips of the tongue. He draws back from being so crass as to say "when your daughter gives you the opportunity," or "sets the stage." He stumbles over looking at Hell "fairly," and transmutes the cleansing of the inner parts of the belly into a radical evisceration.

In the substance of his suggestions for approach to a child, something he knows as the father of seven now-grown chlldren, six of them daughters, he departs from his usual standard in two striking ways. Firstly, this arch-proponent of salvation by God's unilateral election, not necessarily following in a family, lets himself sound as if salvation were something the individual could choose, and lock up with nominally good, obedient behavior. That is just the kind of doctrine of which Camping lives to disabuse adults. Secondly, emulating a strategy the Bible follows at several crucial junctures, what seems like a bright, sugar-coated promise turns out to be a threat in disguise, a propitious place to inject a suggestion as to what the believer is to have a bad conscience about, and stir up savation doubt. He did the same thing with the former caller.

With the former caller, although he knew her knowledge level was high,

Camping used the prosaic, harmless-sounding parable that compares the true believers, who are predestined to persevere to the end, with good soil for planting seeds of "faith," and others, to various adverse botanical conditions. The tone of it is benign enough, and in the text, Jesus uses it as an elementary training example in the interpretation of parables. The imagery is tied in with the imponderables of agricultural life, and it invites the inference that one's own job of crop tending plays some rôle. But other symbolism in the same vein is not so kindly, and Camping did well to divert the caller's attention from it. Elsewhere, the elect and the nonelect are represented respectively as sheep and goats, lambs and wolves, transformed creatures and dogs returning to their own vomit or sows returning to the mire after a futile effort to wash them, wheat and tares, good seeds and bad seeds, good fruit and bad fruit, and fruit and leaves. If one starts with the parable of the sower and follows the related symbolism through, things of different kind from their inception are the rule. One starts out thinking one is promised that aspiration to be a sheep, lamb, transformed creature, grain of wheat, good seed or good fruit will surely be rewarded. One ends up in desperate suspense for the day when one can at last find out in which class one falls. One obeys to avoid Hell. But that, one is told, is not permissible motivation for obeying, and one can never get a straight answer as to what is permissible motivation. All that one can pin the Bible down to is "He who perseveres to the end shall be saved."

Early on, in discussing Calvinism[505] and in our discussion of the biblical uses of contradiction,[506] we saw how pervasively the Bible gives off conflicting signals as to the openness or closedness of the salvation plan, to keep the believer off balance and mystified as to that most consequential of theological issues. We also noted how rarely the Bible yields up a promise capable of being disconfirmed, and how the few demonstrably literally false ones, dealing with moving mountains by "faith," surviving untreated snakebites and healing the sick by laying hands on them serve to force the thoughtful believer to think parabolically.[507] Proceeding from the threshold expectation that a promise will be a portentously slippery commodity, we can see the reverse suggestion and salvation-doubt aggravation embedded in some of the Bible's most popular and seemingly cheerful promises:

> And we know that all things work together for good to them that love God, to them who are the called according to *his* purpose. For whom he did foreknow, he also did predestinate, *to be* conformed to the image of his Son, that he might be the firstborn among many brethren. . . . What shall we then say to these things? If God *be* for us, who *can be* against us?[508]

> And ye have forgotten the exhortation which speaketh unto you as unto children, My son, despise not thou the chastening of the Lord, nor faint when thou art

505. See pp. 11-25.
506. See pp. 213-219
507. See p. 58.
508. Rom. 8:28-29, 31.

> rebuked of him: For whom the Lord loveth he chasteneth, and scourgeth every son whom he receiveth. If ye endure chastening, God dealeth with you as with sons; for what son is he whom the father chasteneth not? But if ye be without chastisement, whereof all are partakers, then are ye bastards, and not sons.[509]

> Let your moderation [mildness, gentleness] be known unto all men. The Lord *is* at hand. Be careful [i.e., anxious] for nothing; but in every thing by prayer and supplication with thanksgiving let your requests be made known unto God. And the peace of God, which passeth all understanding, shall keep your hearts and minds through [in, throughout] Christ Jesus.[510]

> There hath no temptation [trial, adversity] taken you but such as is common to man: but God *is* faithful, who will not suffer you to be tempted above that ye are able; but will with the temptation also make a way to escape, that ye may be able to bear *it*. Wherefore, my dearly beloved, flee from idolatry.[511]

Once one penetrates the high sound of the passages and reads the fine print, one finds that the promises are illusory, i.e., concrete events neither confirm nor disconfirm them. It may be farther in the future than one can foresee, or beyond the grave that all things will finally work together for good. If they seem not to be working out, then that just confirms the expectations of the believer to receive chastisement, and in this world, to have tribulation. One is promised only subjective, soporific relief from the pain of living, and for the believer any pain is, by definition, within his capacity to endure. But note the back-hand implication of each of the promises. If not all things work together for one's good, that may indicate that one is not called according to God's purpose after all. If one is not subjected to chastisement and tribulation (the context, when this topic occurs, is usually praise for martyrdom), that may be evidence of lack of salvation. If one does not experience the subjective soporific relief, that too may be evidence of lack of salvation, although the Scriptures never say so. And if one gets thrown a "temptation" that is just too much, that too may foreshadow the award of God's booby prize.

The devotional-program instructions in the last two quotations and their implications are by now familiar except for the references to escape and flight. The theme of fleeing from proscribed thoughts and feelings—doing what is appropriate to them if they evoke fear—and symbolizing again the separation of mental contents from one another—recurs:

> Flee fornication [*porneia*]. Every [other] sin that a man doeth is without [i.e., outside] the body; but he that committeth fornication sinneth against his own body.[512]

> Flee also youthful lusts. . . .[513]

---

509. Heb. 12:5-8.
510. Phil. 4:5-7.
511. 1 Cor. 10:13-14.
512. 1 Cor. 6:18.
513. 2 Tim. 2:22.

> Submit yourselves therefore to God. Resist the devil, and he will flee from you. Draw nigh to God, and he will draw nigh to you. Cleanse *your* hands, *ye* sinners; and purify *your* hearts, *ye* double minded. Be afflicted, and mourn, and weep: let your laughter be turned to mourning, and *your* joy to heaviness.[514]

Alas, the plight of the Christian, kept in desperate suspense and required to find beauty and encouragement in what amounts to the ultimate obscenity, can be reduced to an antiapologetic triad:

> . . . [H]ast thou not known me, Philip? he that hath seen me hath seen the Father; and how sayest thou *then,* Shew us the Father?[515]

> Beloved, do not imitate evil but imitate good. He who does good is of God; he who does evil has not seen God.[516]

> No man hath seen God at any time; the only begotten Son, which is in the bosom of the Father, he hath declared *him.*[517]

The working of the biblical fear stratagem in individuals' lives is normally difficult to observe, and to get behind the commonplaces that direct questions about it will typically elicit, one must necessarily rely heavily on inferences from indirect indications. My own view, wherein the fear device becomes central only in the context of a relatively complete and advanced biblical indoctrination, is colored by my own experience. I think it best to present the impressions that condition my view in narrative form, and exhort the student of these matters to be skeptical as to surface impressions, to keep in mind that this matter especially awaits future systematic study.

My preliminary interview study of persons answering a newspaper ad soliciting the religiously "disillusioned" could easily have led me to a wrong conclusion based on the interviewees' unremarkable responses. I interviewed a total of fifteen persons, five of whom had experienced the pattern in which I was most interested, that of a personal crisis precipitated by advice received in a conservative church, followed by intellectual rejection of Christianity. The five had all had favorable experiences with psychotherapists in the aftermath of the personal crisis, undoubtedly accounting for their distinctive (and self-selecting) willingness to answer such an ad and talk openly to me. Yet the people I interviewed had only the most ordinary things to say about the rôle of the biblical fear appeal in their experience, and then, only as an example of what had seemed too absurd to continue to defend, when they had stepped back and looked at their religion in perspective. These were all people on whom the fear appeal had never made a strong impression, who left before ever going through the mandated process of meditating and focussing on the fear appeal because the God who is wiser than humans said they ought to.

---

514. James 4:7-9.
515. John 14:9.
516. 3 John 11. *Revised Standard Version.*
517. John 1:18.

In contrast to my interviewees' lack of pertinent experience with the fear appeal, I recall a visit to a highly successful, independent church in the northern Virginia suburbs of Washington, D.C., where the fear appeal was most strikingly in evidence. That church, which I do not classify as mini-Reformationist because of some conspicuous doctrinal pecularities[518] and the uncharacteristic, overbearing cult-leader style of influence of its pastor over the flock, attracted nearly a thousand civil servants and military every Sunday to hear lurid descriptions of the terrors of Hell, delivered with wild eyes and the same, peculiar finger-wiggling gestures as Ayatollah Khomeini gives in his public performances. Unlike any other church I have ever visited, during the sermon the people sat stock still, and one could easily observe their far slower than normal eye-blink rate, as they sat in a trance-like state under that hysterical preaching. In my state of mind at the time, I took it as proof that the darkest of evil was to be found in apostate churches mimicking the true ones. For the only time ever, that day I visited a church without leaving an offering. I felt disappointed that Evangelical friends whom I had highly regarded had known all about that church and when it came up as a topic of conversation had said nothing about its peculiarities. Later, I talked at length with a woman who had been propelled into deep depression by that church's atmosphere, and had partly relieved it by participating in a Pentecostal church with a very cheerful tone to it.

The involvement of the fear theme at the end of my espousal of Christianity illustrates, I think, the deeply buried but pervasive implications of that theme in the indoctrination. My entry into Christinity was atypical, in that it occurred long after childhood and against the resistance arising from growing up with an attitude vacillating between xenophobia and envy toward Christians, particularly the genteel WASPs my parents emulated. My Jungian period had enhanced the influence of, and widened my contacts among, liberal, mainline pastors, of whom not a few have regarded me as someone to whom to confess what they could confess to no one else. I had bought the Jungian premise that mankind has a religious need, yet being drawn in repeatedly as a helper of troubled, disturbed, drifting liberal clergy gradually engraved the impression on my mind that something was basically amiss with them.

I think that a crucial but perilously thin protection against the involvement of larger numbers of educated people in conservative Christianity has lain in the pervasive tacit presumption that some expert somewhere understands and is in a position satisfactorily to explain away whatever impressive and seemingly salutary things one may observe among conservative Christians. When I encountered the Christians, I knew well what had been written about the matter, and realized that nothing in my academic background accounted for the manifestly changed

518. For instance, that church required the women's heads to be covered in the sanctuary, and most of them wore quaint little veils on their heads during the service, in supposed obedience to 1 Cor. 11:5. The good Bible student knows that since that verse specifies, ". . . every woman that prayeth or prophesieth with *her* head uncovered dishonoreth her head . . . ," and women are required to be silent in church (1 Cor. 14:34), the verse cannot be referring to behavior in church as opposed to other settings, and must be speaking more figuratively of the requirement that women always be in subjection to their "heads," i.e., fathers, husbands, pastors, elders, etc.

personalities and heightened sense of community I perceived. These people were neither the downtrodden subjects of "slave morality" of Feuerbach and his disciple, Nietzsche, nor Freud's evaders and obfuscators of aching Oedipus and Electra complexes. Neither did my background prepare me with any satisfying explanation for the evident superior vitality of their churches, compared with those where the project of giving symbolic meaning and raising consciousness about "ultimate concern" was receiving deliberate attention. If that were the true, affirmative core of meaning of the world's religions, then why did not enlightenment about it make for something better than dying religious communities? No thanks to those who had undertaken to write about the psychology of religion—I was on my own as to those issues. And the way most of my nonreligious contemporaries lived seemed and continues to seem ugly and alienating to me.

I was so fascinated with the Christians that I no longer even noticed how unsatisfactory the ends I pursued daily in my law practice ultimately were, and instead of tending to my emerging need for a new direction there, I looked to my newfound Christian affiliation to supply it. I decided to go and study at the seminary Machen had founded. But in the year or so between that decision and my arrival there, I learned much more of the Bible, without realizing that I had gotten to that stage of Bible understanding beyond which the believing Christian dare not go, lest the game be exposed. At the seminary, all I heard were the same, by then tiresome clichés that I had heard over and over in the churches, and the rigid, vacant demeanor of the people at the seminary troubled and irritated me. The technically excellent job done with the ancient Bible languages there, I realized, served not to deepen understanding of the Bible's content as pretended, but was in lieu of such deepening.[519]

Also, in the weeks leading up to my beginning the seminary, there came in close succession some memorable instances where I was exposed for the first time to displays of extreme, offensive, meanly reactionary social views expressed by church people, and others, instead of being taken aback, would cheerfully agree. Paralleling the undergraduates viewing Freeman's film, the church people saw nothing wrong with various and sundry kinds of indecency, so long as it

519. Westminster Theological Seminary was founded by J. Gresham Machen with the dissident, conservative faculty from Princeton Theological Seminary after it went liberal. Machen had put great emphasis on the teaching of Koiné Greek to the incoming first-year class himself, and the textbook he wrote for that purpose is still in use. After overcoming the rigors of Greek and ancient Hebrew, study there for upperclassmen is downhill. Very few of the graduates retain very much of their hard-won facility in the languages, which deteriorates much as undergraduates' modern-language facility does when the courses involving it are over. Also, I noticed that even the most accomplished exegetes there, in their scholarly work, seldom went any deeper than one can readily go without even knowing the underlying ancient languages of the Bible, with the aid of the exhaustive secondary reference works that have accumulated over the years. It dawned on me that in the absence of any sound educational reason for so much emphasis on the Bible languages, that emphasis served to divert the minds of the seminarians from the idea content and implications of their program of study, while putting them through an initiation ritual to deepen their personal investment in their illusions. The ancient-language study also served to enhance the graduates' professional mystification value. The whole curriculum was designed around indoctrination, for erecting an additional layer of irrelevancy to keep the conscious minds of the seminarians busy, lest unwanted insight intrude. That observation helped me on toward the conclusion that the gravamen of the Bible itself is indoctrination, not information.

were properly denominated "Christian." I found myself giving advice when asked, duly modeled after the harder scriptural teachings, but the words stuck in my mouth.

In my program of applying the scriptural teachings in my own life, I had reached a stage where I meditated more and more deliberately on the fear teachings, and experienced the kind of awareness change that the Christian seeks. I could get to where I was sort of peripherally perseverating some prescribed, biblical thought, and felt calm, insulated, protected, confident in a sort of invisible supernatural barrier erected between me and the world around me. But I had the feeling that I had to move very gingerly to avoid upsetting that state of mind, which would deteriorate noticeably if I did not get my "fix" of prayer, Bible reading, and "encouragement" in church surroundings. That altered perception, I now realize, is the conscious concomitant of the dissociated state of mind, and the crux of the distinction between saved people and unsaved, adumbrated but never explicitly stated in the Bible. That state is sensed by one Christian in another, and accounts for the notion in even the most knowledgeable Christians that they know if a person is saved or not, notwithstanding the lack of an approved biblical criterion for making such a determination. The incessant gossip in church circles about who is truly saved and who is not all relates back to that distinction. I attributed the instability and fragileness I perceived as the state of that state in myself, to my relative newness and immaturity as a Christian. Also, I did not notice that maintenance of that state was costing me continual, vitality-sapping effort, that it all was beginning to seem stifling and boring, and that avoidance of the penalty had gradually but entirely replaced any affirmative elation or "joy" as the reason for keeping up the effort. Had the occasion arisen, I would have "testified" in the most effusive, expansive terms about the benefits of Christianity in my life, that passed understanding, to which justice could not be done in mere, human words.

In my third week at that seminary, with the prospect yawning before me of never again having a good conscience about genuine enjoyment of normal, human activities, of being supposed to be incapable of lively interest in worldly history or politics, in no longer enjoying any but suitably watered-down literature or music, of only going around obsessively preoccupied with God all the time, and thinking about whether this or that prospective behavior broke any of the rules or not, I felt more and more trapped and became more and more depressed. I got up one morning and followed the custom of beginning the day in prayer I had set up for myself, when an extraneous thought powerfully intruded. The thought was, "The door to paradise stands open, and now I'm going to close it." Where had I heard that before? I imagined it spoken in Orson Welles' voice, and that enabled me to place it as coming from *The Trial* by Franz Kafka (1883-1924), which Welles had made into a rather bad movie that I had long ago seen. Then I realized an essential thing: the God of the Bible, toward whom I had labored so hard to cultivate the right relationship of fear and Bible marination, and the spirit of absurd, oppressive, antihuman, killing authority pervading all of Kafka's writing *are one and the same!*

In that moment, the entire Christian indoctrination collapsed in my mind like a house of cards. The benighted, retrograde social views that I had labored so hard to force upon my twentieth-century mind fell down suddenly like a row of dominoes. For me, the collapse of the Christian indoctrination was a sudden, ecstatic setting right of things that had been all wrong—much as many a Christian is bidden to "testify" the conversion to Christianity to have been. Looking back, I saw that in the intervening three years, I had grown not in righteousness but in rigidness, not in purity but in priggishness, not in holiness but in assholiness! While closing off any number of positive avenues of expression, Christianity had provided approved avenues of expression for many of my worst temperamental weaknesses. I was myself again after a miserable illness—a self-induced mental illness—like waking up from an unusually long, convoluted bad dream. There was no time to follow through on the theme of the closing door, since I had to go to class. For the rest of that week, I kept my own counsel and went through the motions of seminary life. The following Monday I quit the seminary and openly renounced the Christian religion.

In the afternoon of the day when I found my way out of the semantic labyrinth, I read *The Trial* for the first time since undergraduate days. The part that had been the source of my healing insight, Kafka had written first in 1914 as a fragment entitled "Before the Law." The rest of the novel, the only one Kafka completed, was built around it.

In *The Trial,* an unsuspecting man is awakened one morning by two apparently official men in insignialess uniform, and is told he is under arrest. The man, identified only as "Josef K.," makes many resourceful attempts to find out the nature of the charge against him, who the legal authorities involved in it are, and how he may defend himself. Although his experiences are full of portentous symbolism, he can get no substantive answers. He learns more about the system he is up against from an artist whom he visits than from the lawyer he tries to hire to defend him. Since no one has laid a hand on him, and his freedom to come and go has not yet been restricted, it even seems as though the whole thing might be a bluff. But in the end, without K. ever having had his trial or been confronted by any accuser, two other robotlike apparent officials take him out beneath a streetlight and execute him with dagger stabs.

In the chapter penultimate to his death, K. is in a great cathedral, and sits alone as a cleric stands in one of the minor, side pulpits and preaches. Then a conversation ensues between K. and the cleric, who evidently has some knowledge of and involvement in K's case.

> "Don't kid yourself," said the cleric.
>
> "How am I kidding myself?" asked K.
>
> "You kid yourself about the court," said the cleric. "In the preamble to the law, this is set forth about that deception: Before the law is situated a doorkeeper. A man from the country comes up to this doorkeeper and asks to be admitted to the law. But the doorkeeper says he cannot grant him admission now. The man thinks it over and then asks if it would be possible, then, for him to enter later. 'It is possible,' said the doorkeeper, 'but not now.'

"Since the door to the law stood open as always, and the doorkeeper stood to one side, the man leaned over, to see through the door into the interior. When the doorkeeper saw that, he laughed and said, 'If it attracts you so, then go ahead and try to go in despite my prohibition. But keep in mind: I am mighty. And I am only the lowest doorkeeper. In one chamber after another are situated nothing but doorkeepers, one mightier than the other. The mere sight of the third one is more than I can stand.'

"The man from the country had not expected such difficulties, since the law ought to be accessible to everyone always, he thought, but now as he looked more closely at the doorkeeper in his fur coat, with his big pointed nose, the long, thin, black Tartar beard, he made up his mind that he had better, after all, wait until he received leave to enter. The doorkeeper gave him a stool, and let him sit down catercorner to the door. There he sat, days and years. He sought repeatedly to be let pass, and wearied the doorkeeper with his pleading. The doorkeeper would often give him a little hearing and question him about his home town and many other things, the sort of indifferent questions important men ask, and would always conclude by telling him he would not yet be able to admit him. The man, who had equipped himself with many things for his trip, expended them all, that they might have value for bribing the doorkeeper. The latter, to be sure, accepted them all, but said in so doing, 'I am only accepting so you won't think you have neglected anything.'

"During all those years, the man observed the doorkeeper almost continuously. He forgot about the other doorkeepers, and this first one seemed to him the only obstacle to his entry to the law. He cursed his misfortune aloud in the early years; later, as he grew old, he only muttered to himself. He became childish, and since, in the years of studying the doorman, he had even become familiar with the fleas in his fur collar, he asked the fleas as well to help him change the doorkeeper's mind. Finally the man's eyesight bccame weak, and he could not tell whether it was really getting darker or his eyes were deceiving him. But he perceived clearly enough a shimmer in the darkness emanating inextinguishably out of the doorway to the law. Now he had not much longer to live. Before his death all his experiences from that entire time coalesced in his head, into one question, that he until then had not asked the doorkeeper. He gestured to him, since he could no longer raise his feeble body up. The doorkeeper had to bend down very far, since the size differential between them had shifted, much to the disadvantage of the man. 'What do you still want to know?' asked the doorkeeper. 'You are insatiable.'

"'Everybody seeks the law, of course,' said the man. 'How come in all these years nobody besides me sought to be let in?'

"The doorkeeper could see that it was almost all over for the man, and to penetrate his failing hearing, bellowed at him, 'No one else could gain entry here, because this entrance was appointed only for you. Now I'll go and close it.'"[520]

---

520. *Der Prozess* (Frankfurt: Fischer Bücherei, 1960), pp. 155-56. My translation.

Although literature scholars generally have not looked for New Testament themes in Kafka, who had little overt interest in or experience with Christianity,[521] the Parable of the Unjust Judge, the theme of renouncing worldly possessions to be let into the Kingdom of God at hand, and the juxtaposition of the "law" to a destination so attractive that one pines away one's earthly life over it are all quite clearly suggested in the passage. The notion of two entirely disparate realms with a divine agency managing their interface—just what we have found to be the main New Testament paradigm—is evoked. And the New Testament does, indeed, express it as a doorway from time to time:

> For every one that asketh receiveth; and he that seeketh findeth; and to him that knocketh it shall be opened.[522]
>
> Strive to enter in at the strait gate: for many . . . will seek to enter in, and shall not be able. When once the master of the house is risen up, and hath shut to the door, and ye begin to stand without, and to knock at the door, saying, Lord, Lord, open unto us; and he shall answer and say unto you, I know you not whence ye are. . . .[523]
>
> Verily, verily, I say unto you, He that entereth not by the door into the sheepfold, but climbeth up some other way, the same is a thief and a robber. But he that entereth in by the door is the shepherd of the sheep. To him the porter openeth; and the sheep hear his voice: and he calleth his own sheep by name, and leadeth them out. . . . I am the door of the sheep. . . . I am the door: by me if any man enter in, he shall be saved, and shall go in and out, and find pasture.[524]

---

521. Kafka has been variously interpreted in terms of his milieu, i.e., the authoritarian governmental institutions he dealt with as a lawyer and civil servant (he worked in the Czech equivalent of a workmen's compensation board), his family influences, the fragile state of health that made his life tragically short, existentialism, Jewish mysticism and Freudianism. After he had written the works mentioned herein, he read Kierkegaard; that fact has suggested a liberal, neo-Gnostic Christian interpretation. Besides the chronological discrepancy and the cheapening and falsification of the very real seismic warning of the terrible political events that were to come—that warning being the most significant feature of his work in my opinion—such an interpretation is objectionable in that it insinuates Kafka into a project to which he had no relation, in which he had no part. In his personal life, Kafka succeeded in being a helpful, supportive son, brother, public servant and coworker, and he yearned to be the progenitor of a family, as his health would not permit. He was no apostle of hyperintroverted hypereccentricity.

The expression *Kafkaesque* has come to stand for any absurd and menacing exercise of authority. Kafka's friend and not entirely faithful literary executor, Max Brod, placed this neologism in perspective: "The ugly adjective, "Kafkaesque," has been invented. But that sort of Kafkaesqueness is precisely what Kafka most vigorously abhored and combatted. *Kafkaesqueness is that which Kafka was not.* The natural, unspoiled, great, good, and constructive, he loved. Not the no-exit, disturbed-fantastic, not the strange, that he continually noticed and chronicled in the world as he found it, and sorted out with grim humor, without making it his center. Not toward destruction, but toward unfolding, was that sweet and steely strong soul inclined. Kafka nourished no illusions about the difficulty of that unfolding and upbuilding. . . . The more honest one is, the more necessarily must that be so." *Der Prager Kreis* (Stuttgart: W. Kohlhammer Verlag, 1968), p. 84. My translation.

522. Luke 11:10.

523. Luke 13:24–25. See also Matt. 25:8–12.

524. John 10:1–3, 7, 9.

And when they were come [Paul and his entourage to Antioch], and had gathered the church together, they rehearsed [told, announced] all that God had done with them, and how he had opened the door of faith unto the Gentiles.[525]

Grudge not one against another, brethren, lest ye be condemned: behold, the judge standeth before the door.[526]

And to the angel of the church in Philadelphia write; These things saith he that is holy, he that is true, he that hath the key of David, he that openeth, and no man shutteth; and shutteth, and no man openeth; I know thy works: behold I have set before thee an open door, and no man can shut it. . . .[527]

Behold, I stand at the door, and knock: if any man hear my voice, and open the door, I will come in to him, and will sup with him, and he with me. To him that overcometh [*nikao,* conquers, gets victory] will I grant to sit with me in my throne, even as I also overcame, and am set down with my Father in his throne. He that hath an ear, let him hear. . . .[528]

After marinating my mind in all those embedded references to doors, calculated not to give the believer reassurance or comfort, but to instill desperate suspense as to whether the door will be open or shut, it is small wonder that the Kafka passage was evoked. After I had reread *The Trial,* and compared the various New Testament slamming doors with one another, I understood how badly I had been had by the Bible manipulation, and was bitterly ashamed of myself.

Despite the absence of focussed Christian influence in Kafka's life, the implications that he was influenced very much by the New Testament and that his writings largely represent an outsider's empathic response to the unique psychic misery of Christianity are inescapable.[529] The image of the door is a

---

525. Acts 14:27. See also Col. 4:3.
526. James 5:9.
527. Rev. 3:7-8.
528. Rev. 3:20.
529. It is reasonable to suppose that an inquisitive and literarily inclined German speaker would read the Luther Bible with great interest, since its prose is superb and indeed had been instrumental in standardizing modern High German. It does not come off stilted or overly quaint, as English translations of the Bible invariably do. I suspect that Kafka may have read it at an early age and not remembered it consciously.

While these pages were in preparation, I read some of Kafka's early short stories for the first time, and was flabbergasted to find many of the ideas I have presented herein expressed in his symbolism.

In 1913, his first published short story, "The Judgment," appeared. A son's relation to his father, who is self-characterized as senile and failing, is described. The father penetratingly analyzes the motives behind some of the son's actions, none of them intrinsically very terrible, and the son is mortified. The father then ups and sentences his son to death by drowning. There immediately arises in the son an irresistable impulse to carry out the sentence, and the story ends as he runs right out and drowns himself in the river. My impression that the biblical God-image emanates from generations of senile authority figures is echoed in it.

The next year, Kafka wrote "In the Penal Colony," of particular interest since it foreshadows the Nazi concentration camps—where his surviving sisters died. In that short story, an explorer visits a penal colony in a tropical locale, operated by the military of a distant, powerful nation. It seems that a generation earlier, the penal colony had enjoyed a golden age, under a great, revered

fitting place to bring our expedition into the subterranean psychic landscape of Christianity to its culmination, since the largest of its issues culminate in that image.

Besides presenting one of the most concise images of the Bible's largest trend of contradiction, the one that oscillates around the question of whether the

---

commandant, since deceased, who invented an exquisite, high-tech machine for putting people to death. Its operation, everyone has always found marvelously admirable and noble. The machine is divided into three main parts, the uppermost called the "drawer," below it, the "harrow," and under it, a bed for the condemned to be fastened to, with straps of just the right elasticity. Automatically, a gag made of felt forces itself into the condemned's mouth, so that were he not to relax his jaw to let it in, his neck would be broken. Then, the harrow, made of glass so that the condemned and the spectators can see what takes place, comes down, and by the artful co-ordination of movements of the bed and the longer of the spikes protruding from the harrow, a phrase appropriate to the condemned's crime is engraved in his skin, several times simultaneously and that over and over, the condemned being rotated so that his entire body is covered. Smaller projections from the harrow irrigate the areas of skin so engraved with water, also aiding visibility, and the bloody water collects in a trench dug around the machine. After two hours, since the condemned is by then too weak and his throat too dry for him to cry out, the gag automatically comes out, and the condemned is permitted to lap rice gruel from an electrically heated dispenser. Experience had shown that a subject would invariably lap gruel the third through the sixth hour. When twelve hours have been completed, the condemned is dead from a combination of blood loss and being skinned alive. The machine automatically ejects the body in a crumpled heap, into the trench with the bloody water.

The explorer is to witness such an execution, and is given a guided tour by an officer, who had been a youthful disciple of the old commandant. The condemned (without any semblance of a trial) is a soldier who has committed disrespect toward a noncommissioned officer, and the legend to be engraved is "Honor thy superiors." (The story contains no hint of use of the machine on anyone other than the regime's own military personnel.) The officer complains that since the days of the old commandant, budgetary support for the program has declined. The machine is often out of commission, while spare parts are being procured. As replacements for some of its worn main mechanical parts are unobtainable, it now squeaks loudly while operating. Now, the condemned's muffled noises are drowned out, and the bed and the harrow move at less than the most rhythmically efficient speed. Spectator enthusiasm is way down, and dignitaries seldom witness these executions anymore. One of the straps fastening the condemned's arm snaps, and a less elastic pair of handcuffs has to be substituted, further detracting from the elegant smoothness of the machine's normal operation. In the old days, the parts coming in contact with the condemned's naked body had always been hygienically clean; but now, they are soiled from previous executions and their disgustingness constitutes another unwanted distraction of the condemned's mind from the business at hand. Because the officer is no longer able to get enough cooperation to ensure that the condemned will be brought to him fasting, this particular condemned vomits when the foully encrusted gag pushes into his mouth, further wounding the pride of the officer in his work. The vomit is rinsed away, and the execution proceeds.

The officer looks to the explorer, expecting the program to have met with the latter's enthusiastic approval, and to be inspiring him to lobby in the home country for support to restore the program to its former glorious efficiencies. The officer is taken entirely by surprise when the explorer says he is against the program, and will work to have it discontinued. Indeed, the officer is so stricken and abashed that he directs the soldier assisting him to stop the execution, and the condemned, not yet badly injured, is disengaged from the machine, unnecessarily inflicting a few more cuts on himself trying to get out before the officer and the soldier can release the harrow and move it away. The officer readjusts the machine, strips off all his own clothes, and climbs into the business end of it himself. The harrow comes down much farther than before, and munches the officer speedily to death. This indication that the particular horror portrayed ultimately is done to oneself, that all the actors in it are part of the intrapsychic transpiration going on within one person, also occurs in *The Trial,* where the victim is named K., and the more talkative of the apparent officials who come to place him under arrest, "Franz," indicating that both are aspects of Kafka himself.

Then, the explorer, the soldier who had assisted, and the one who had been condemned go to a teahouse together, and afterwards visit the grave of the old commandant. They talk of the legend that the old commandant will one day be resurrected and come again.

salvation plan be closed or open, and that has manifested itself historically as the Calvinist/Arminian polemic, the door image presents the pervasive theme of drastic discrepancy between the realms, symbolized as separated by the door. An additional observation about that theme of drastic separation of realms, evoked by the image of the door, turned out to be crucial in helping me demolish the structure of obsessive biblical thoughts and compulsive biblical habits I had built up. During my Jungian period, I had learned a great deal about symbols of transformation in primitive myths and religions and contemporary people's dreams. In all of these, a certain degree of balance between the starting point of a transformation and its result is always present. A frog turns into a prince, an inanimate thing turns into an animal or person (or vice versa), base metal turns into gold, two beings merge into a different, energetically more potent being, one imago disappears and the appearance of a different one subsequently in a different place points to the transformation of the former into the latter. Only in the Bible is that rule of balance or conservation violated. God creates the cosmos out of nothing. In the New Testament, God becomes a sort of bottomless pit (like the memory-hole system, in *1984*), where a quantity, "sin," is transformed into nothingness. Jesus absorbs any amount of "sin," and yet its concentration in him remains zero: he is always without "sin." Apparently it is incinerated so thoroughly that there are no products of its transformation. In ordinary, spontaneously arising human mythology, unspoiled by self-conscious sophistication and reflection, such a thing simply never happens.

Although I did not consciously recognize it, that feature of the Bible was instrumental early on, in convincing me that there was some enormously consequential, qualitative difference between it and other mythologies purported to be, and tacitly acknowledged by Jungians and Tillichians to be, its equivalent. That difference from other ancient mythology turns out to be, instead of an indication of divinity to the Bible, the fingerprints of the self-conscious, sophisticated humans who contrived it. New Testament Christianity, I conclude, is no spontaneous symbolic expression of shared human experience, as most religions probably are, but a deliberate, invented counterfeit of such expression. Instead of developing and evolving as the experiences calling it into being accumulated generation by generation, and the responses of people to those experiences gradually changed, this one must have come into the form we know in a few eventful decades, through a process resembling nothing so much as field testing a product in our own time, finding out which cola flavor or fast-food baked-potato topping more people prefer. What got in the Bible must simply be what got saluted when Paul and his boys ran it up the flagpole.

Another feature of the insight symbolized for me by the Kafka passage is the conspicuous lack of resolution of the question of what lies beyond the door. Had the man from the country gone forward, would he have been set upon by the higher-ranking doorkeepers as threatened, or would something totally different from what he had heard about been encountered, or would his attempt to pass through the doorway have been like bumping into a mirror? There can be no answer, but the implication is clear that the man was somehow much harmed by officially promulgated deceptions. What I tacitly realized at that point was that, just as there is only incidental similarity between the kind of God an Einstein, a Kant, or a Jung could profess to believe in and the God of the Bible when one has adequately internalized the information given about him, there is only incidental similarity between the latter realm portrayed in the Bible and the reality beyond the apparent universe of space, time and causality, whereof we receive hints from various advances in human knowledge. The thinkable ultimate reconciliation of the outer dimensions that had seemed to make Christianity defensible now seemed too far-fetched to me, and unnecessary. When it came home to me just how monstrous and, in human terms, perverted the implications of the biblical salvation plan are, why would I want to have them be true anyhow? Like the phlogiston theory, the flat-earth theory, and the divine right of kings, the biblical view is not information but disinformation in which someone else has a vested interest.

Yet, once firmly in place in my mind, even without roots going back to formative years, the mind-control system was stable enough that it took those two strong lines of circumstantial evidence—namely the disorderliness of there being ultimately no harmony at all between the natural and the supernatural, and the explicability of all the strange and unexpected human behavior I had seen arise from Christianity in the terms I have herein developed—to bring it down.[530] At once, I understood and felt an aching appreciation for all those religious revisionists who labored to humanize Christianity over the years, to invert the inversion, and finally arrive at Wesley's kindly falsification of the biblical message. I understood why the more educated of the clergymen from the Civil War on, so lacked desire to mount the defense they might have against

530. Although my deconversion was almost instantaneous, and clearly a positive development when it happened, it did leave behind it a feeling of disorientation that lasted for some days. It was like the first efforts to use a limb that has been bandaged up and immobilized. Since I am not one of those in whom different personality integuments can carry on a consciously perceptible dialogue under normal conditions, the feeling that there was a divine other present, to whom to address prayers and who was always watching with that omniscient, single eye, had been difficult for me to develop. Its disappearance was instantaneous, like a bubble popping, and good riddance! There remained a certain tenseness at thoughts possibly blaspheming the Holy Spirit, which I worked out one afternoon by forcing myself to recite to myself every idea I could think of that might meet the criterion for the unforgivable sin.

About a week after I had quit Westminster Theological Seminary, I dreamed I was on the walkway outside its library, on my way out as three unknown young women were on their way in. (In my incoming class, there had been three young women, then allowed to study for a master's degree, but not a first professional degree. With one of them I had a previous history: she had been involved in one of the displays of reactionary fervor that had recently offended me, and when I asked her about in private, days afterwards, it was clear that she had noticed nothing wrong about it.) The three unknown women approached, and one of them came very close, and clapped a gauze mask over my mouth and nose, which stuck securely with adhesive. It smelled of chloroform, and lacking the presence of mind to hold my breath, I got one whiff. I felt dulled, but was not put out. I held my breath to avoid getting any more, and raised my left hand to try to pull the mask off. I awakened before my hand reached the mask.

There is a non-self-evident aspect of this dream to be pointed out. Anima figures usually appear singly in men's dreams (in contradistinction to the plural animus figures common in women's dreams). I can recall no other dream of mine with a plural, much less triune, anima. That clue put me onto the theme of fragmentation that I have developed herein.

Darwinism and materialism: they had suffered the most from the Bible's true implications because they had taken more of it in than anyone else and were silently glad to see the thing hewn down. How could they have known that new purveyors of the buried horror would arise and debunk their falsification, without understanding that when you debunk a falsification of a falsification, the original falsification is what you have left? I appreciate the unsung heroism of the clergy who went liberal in those days, but criticize them also for having left unknown psychic hazardous waste buried in unmarked dumps. Alongside those conservative pastors and believers, I was busily digging it up, thinking I was uncovering buried treasure, but really contaminating myself with psychological poison through and through!

I submit that it is relatively rare for someone who gets deeply enough immersed in the Bible to break its code and to penetrate the usual misconceptions about it, to come out again. The Evangelical mind-control system is the psychological equivalent of Roach Motel. "They check in, but they don't check out!"

Recent past generations have coped with the Evangelical mind-control system by avoidance. This is reflected in the pervasive tradition handed down in mainline liberal churches of very superficial Bible knowledge, and the almost universal Bible illiteracy of collegians, even those who specialize (often in colleges and universities that started under religious auspices) in literature and history whereto the religious ethos of past times directly pertains. The benign falsification has gone so far, that none of the tolerant, progressive, democratic things that *Christian* connotes to the great majority of Gentiles so labeled is biblically authentic. The new, upstart mind-control practitioners have almost as clean a slate to write on, almost as unsuspecting a crop of prospective clientèle, as their first-century counterparts. Once again, people's minds are "open" to be convinced that one kind of war is the best kind of peace, that freedom is slavery, and that weakness—i.e., inner dividedness (if not ignorance)—strength—the same kind of strength as a fasces. Add to the recipe a period of malaise in those fields of endeavor that ought to be adding most to the application of human intelligence to improving the quality of human life, a readiness of the new practitioners to falsify history so as to appoint themselves the heirs of all good traditions, an underlying end-of-the-world hysteria encouraged by the resemblance of some biblical images to a nuclear holocaust and the approach of the magic-numbered year 2000 A.D., and you may have quite a socially dangerous situation. Even in the best-case scenario, convince people that they are to apply the biblical prescripts blindly to their personal lives, under no circumstances to trust their common sense, and above all, not to listen to those "secular humanist" archenemies, the mental-health professionals, and entirely needless fear, manipulation and private suffering will be spread far and wide.

And now today, we grieve for four young men [Marines murdered in El Salvador] taken from us too soon. And we receive them in death as they were on the last night of their lives—together, and following the radiant light, following it toward heaven, toward home. And if we reach, or when we reach, Heaven's scenes, we truly will find it guarded by United States Marines. —President Ronald Reagan, June 22, 1985

Chapter 5

Conclusion

Mental-Health Implications: A First Impression

To put oneself under Evangelical mind-control, one needs normally functioning processes of cognition and attention. While the *form* taken by the disturbed thoughts, delusions and hallucinations of the person diagnosed as schizophrenic[1] may be religious symbolism, the *content* and the emotive power come from within and are not imposed from outside (i.e., the source is autochthonous, not heterochthonous). Psychotic disorders, apparently, are not to be laid at the door of biblicism.[2]

There are almost no usable quantitative data on the interaction of biblical influence and the lesser psychopathologies, wherein cognition and attention remain unimpaired and whose etiology could well involve such influence. The few behavioral-science researchers who take the question up nearly always make Tillichian concepts, or at least Device 1 notions, their criteria of religiosity. Also, the researchers all stumble over the problem of classifying kinds of religious influence, and they mistakenly classify together church experiences that we

1. See p. 97, footnote 61.
2. The causation of, or at least the bringing out of a constitutional predisposition to, schizophrenia has often been attributed to "double-bind," i.e., absurd and contradictory situations imposed while growing up, particularly a "schizophrenogenic," i.e., dominating but rejecting, mother. Reflecting, we note that the Evangelical mind-control system could not be better suited to creating "double-bind" situations, or causing parents to have a "schizophrenogenic" demeanor. Yet I have never encountered any indication of a connection between hyperreligious upbringing and schizophrenia. I am fairly well convinced that schizophrenia does not come about in the way contemplated by the "double-bind" hypothesis.

understand to be enormously different.[3]

The relation of the biblical, devotional program and the neuroses is pretty much what Freud led us to expect. That program helps the individual to be more neurotic, i.e., to increase the estrangement of the conscious attitude from the whole personality. Symptoms are shared instead of idiosyncratic: they become "normal," there is social support for them, and spurious intellectual interpretations of them are furnished. Where optimum psychological integration could be pursued, the Christian way of coping is a poor *Ersatz.* Where pursuit of such integration is not feasible, and the person is sufficiently other-directed not to put the implications of the "beliefs" too coherently together, the Christian way of coping may be the best choice from poor alternatives.

Among the conservative Christians, the problems one can observe being induced or, if already present, aggravated by the devotional program are *fear* and *depression.* The fear condition is the more characteristic: it is unlike anything the secular mental-health professional is trained to look for. It was entirely new to me. When persons in Christian fear do come in contact with mental-health professionals, they are usually misdiagnosed as phobic, mostly as agoraphobic. But unlike those who come by irrational fears in other ways, the fearful Christians (the most typical case is a female with an asthenic physique, partly due to accompanying eating and sleep disorders) are consciously aware of and

---

3. E.g., Coval B. MacDonald and Jeffrey B. Luckett, "Religious Affiliation and Psychiatric Diagnosis," *Journal for the Scientific Study of Religion,* 22 (1983):15-37. The researchers looked for correlation of diagnosis with kind of denominational affiliation in 7,050 persons who had been patients at a midwestern psychiatric clinic in the late seventies. The researchers felt there would be some virtue of tolerance in keeping the "liberal-conservative" issue from entering into their classification of denominations. Of their seven categories, the pertinent ones are "Mainline Protestant" and "Nonmainline Protestant." In the former category, these researchers placed the historically older and more populous denominations, making a category predominantly of groups with modernist theology and liberal views, but diluted with some that are strongly Bible-oriented, such as Southern Baptists, Machen-denomination Presbyterians, etc. The "Nonmainline" included primarily conservative churches, but including all those that ameliorate the devotional program with Pentecostal/charismatic exaltation of personal feelings, and further diluted with some smaller denominations that did "go liberal" when most of the "Mainline" ones did, such as Church of the Brethren, Mennonites, and assorted black churches. Had the denominational classification been better conceived so as to classify psychologically similar religious backgrounds together, the trends found would probably have been more pronounced, and some weaker ones in the same vein not found, found. The "Mainline Protestant" were the only group found to manifest phobias, marital maladjustment and acute schizophrenic episodes. What neuroses this group exhibited, the researchers felt were characterized by emotional isolation rather than repression. The researchers characterized these as "psychologically immobilized," "walking on eggshells," "in dread." The "Nonmainline" led in depression, anxiety neurosis, explosive personality, obsessive-compulsive disorder, and other miscellaneous neuroses. The researchers felt that the "Nonmainline" tended more to have progressed from mere emotional isolation to downright repression, than "Mainline"; i.e., to have progressed to hysterical dissociation when attempt at an obsessive-compulsive adaptation would begin to fail. Interestingly, the patients were 43% "no religious preference," in contrast to the 8%-15% typically found by pollsters in the general population. None of these researchers' findings were in discord with any expectation of mine.

could if correctly questioned discuss what they are afraid of. What they are afraid of is, of course, the no-exit concentration camp, and they are constantly wearing themselves down by the stress of anticipating it. That they stay away from anything that might remotely risk sending them there by accidental death and avoid situations that require action, lest they cause more demerits to be totted up in God's record book, reflects faulty epistemology, not illogic. Such persons often give "testimonies" to the effect that increased religious activity has "delivered" them from even greater mental distress. They do not identify the devotional program, often starting in childhood, as the source of the problem as well as the source of a palliative for it. A comparison with addictive behavior suggests itself.

The other mental disorder constant in conservative Christianity is depression. The Bible-believer is constantly in need of exhortation and "encouragement" from others, and, by self-discipline, he builds up momentum and overcomes inertia, to stave off what would otherwise become complete inactivity. In congregations of the few conservative denominations with a long tradition, one is always struck by the depressed and depressing demeanor of the people, the worship, and, especially, the music. In successful and growing mini-Reformationist churches, one encounters a well-planned and well-acted show of cheerfulness, which I now understand to be partly a compensation for the cheerlessness that would really be appropriate for the teaching, and partly, still more Device 1. Without going into detail as to what psychodynamic concepts might apply, it agrees with our expectations that, under a discipline that so distorts normal investment of psychic energy, purposely misrouting that energy, people would feel drained and, to convince themselves, would prattle incessantly about how filled they supposedly feel.

By far the most interesting set of empirical data pertinent to the biblical indoctrination and mental health deals with depression in the Old Order Amish, of Lancaster County, Pennsylvania. In that sect, outside influence is shut out by requiring the members to keep to themselves, affecting the dress, and with minor exceptions, to restrict themselves to the technology of the mid-nineteenth century. The popular impression has it that this Amish existence is idyllic, untroubled, serene, like *Little House on the Prairie.* Standard fare in courses in abnormal psychology includes studies allegedly demonstrating superior mental health in other, outwardly similar groups that avoid the stress of modern life. In its time, the idea was that these groups' favorable experience tacitly encouraged the sixties' counterculture aspiration to simpler, alternative life styles.[4] But the outsiders' notion that the religious ideas affecting the Old Order Amish are the same benevolent, reassuring stuff as in a modernist, mainline church assumes too much. If one thoughtfully puts oneself into the Old Order Amish point of view, one finds that they see the whole secular culture around them as Satanic and temptation-fraught; every outsider, benighted and hell-bound. The Old

4. Joseph W. Eaton and Robert J. Weil, "The Mental Health of the Hutterites," *Scientific American,* December, 1953, pp. 31-37.

Order Amish bucolic world always threatens to snap open a trap door beneath the feet, and send the backslider down the tubes into the no-exit concentration camp if the guard of rigidity be let down. The sect really presents, like the biblical indoctrination itself, a superbly effective set of psychological social controls, continuing to work mechanically after the needs and circumstances that called it into existence have long since gone away, and hardly anyone recalls what they were. The study in question reviewed mental-health facility admissions from the sect: in sharp contrast to the general population, where the major cause of admission is schizophrenia, among the Old Order Amish, depression eclipsed all other causes of admission, and diagnoses inconsistent with depression occurred only as rare, isolated exceptions.[5] The religious content

5. Janice A. Egeland and Abram M. Hostetter, "Amish Study, I: Affective Disorders Among the Amish, 1976-1980," *American Journal of Psychiatry,* 140, no. 1 (January, 1983), pp. 56-61. Studies II and III and related material follow in the same journal issue, through p. 76. (These were summarized in *Science,* May 2, 1986, pp. 575-76.) In this series, the question of cultural factors and kind of mental disorder diagnosed is explored only in the connection that the distinctive demeanor of the Amish particularly conduces to misdiagnosing their manic-depressive or "bipolar" disorder as schizophrenia.

There was no follow-through at all, on the bellowing clue that conservative, New Testament religiosity may be an etiological factor behind depression. When the principal researcher in these studies published Amish data again, it was to show that what few suicides occur among the Old Order Amish cluster within a few family pedigrees, so that any given suicide tends significantly to be someone consanguine with one or more other suicides. Janice A. Egeland and James N. Sussex, "Suicide and Family Loading for Affective Disorders," *Journal of the American Medical Association,* 254, no. 7 (August, 1985), pp. 915-18. That study is touted as a preliminary, suggestive indication that tendency to suicide is hereditary. No mention of the earlier studies' pertinent contents is made in it! Since the group studied is the most closed and immobile of groups one might study, affording maximum opportunity for family customs and foibles to go on unchanged, I can see no substantive justification for the researchers' stated opinion that rates the hereditary factor more important than the environmental one. The logical error is curiously out of place in such a journal! In an interview publicizing the study, on National Public Radio's "All Things Considered," August 16, 1985, Dr. Egeland showed no inkling of any possibility that the religious indoctrination might be other than benign and supportive. Is she too personally involved with the Amish people who cooperate with her, to be able to hear behind their Device 1 sayings? Is she ducking an implication that would make her the unwilling one to point out the coercive, totalitarian, socially pathological character of the Old Order Amish way of life, like Freud when he ducked the implications of his infantile-seduction hypothesis?

Some tendencies for which Old Order Amish are well known, become understandable in the light of our concepts. There is a strong taboo against independent Bible study; the Bible is to be studied only with the guidance of others, lest the biblical discrepancies in the tradition—once a progressive departure from the dominant Lutheranism—be focally studied. Contacts of community members with other conservative religious enthusiasts, particularly those steeped in and talking about the Bible, prove to be much more troublesome and disruptive of discipline, than contacts with secular, educated people. The overriding fear of the hereafter may underlie the unusual and exaggerated health-consciousness of these Amish. Despite their rejection of modern technology (allowing battery lights on buggies and bottled gas to run kitchen stoves and refrigerators have been big concessions), the Amish avail themselves fully of modern medical care, drastically disrupting the economics of their agrarian way of life: they are even more preoccupied than ordinary, secularized unbelievers in delaying the end of earthly life as long as possible! MacDonald and Luckett, *op. cit.,* whose study included some other Amish people probably from less devout groups than Old Order, found alcoholism rather than depression to be that category's salient mental-health problem.

of the Amish patients' flights of ideas and delusions of grandeur in the manic phase often resulted in an early misdiagnosis of schizophrenia. But these patients' confusion traces back to more mundane causes, such as exhaustion, loss of sleep, and their absurd indoctrination coupled with isolation from other educational experiences: it lacks any true, "schizy" quality.

How, then, do negative mental-health results of the biblical indoctrination concern outsiders? We do not claim that because the biblical indoctrination does demonstrable harm, secular mental-health professionals necessarily do good. For us, every existing secular competitor of religion turns out to have entirely too many orthodox proprietors of some doctrine, protecting their enterprises. Each such enterprise, in turn, has at its core, an oversimple, deprecating but uncannily appealing concept of human nature, rendering the enterprise subtly misleading and harmful, even though it be good for some specific, immediate purposes. Our ultimate message is not reliance on secular substitutes, but, rather, self-reliance. All slickly packaged, comprehensive plans for better, more effective living are to be viewed askance. Yet, we can allow that a therapist with his intuition and basic human qualities in the foreground can be a desirable helper for someone who has been put through the wringer by conservative churches. Just being human and reality-oriented is enough in that case. What with all those conservative Christian primary and secondary schools, there will be hundreds of thousands of bright, articulate, high-achieving young people looking for a way out of the semantic labyrinth. That can be an opportunity for many a therapist to render valuable service. But the therapists will have to know in detail, as they now do not, how that labyrinth works.

Three Unproductive Questions

Every time I encounter journalists interviewing conservative Christian leaders, the same three questions get asked, with hardly any variation. "Don't you see that there are many kinds of truth, that truth is not black and white, but comes in many shades of gray?" "Do Jews who reject Jesus go to Heaven or don't they?" "Aren't there any number of ways to interpret the Bible, so that you know you are wrong about your interpretation being any better than anyone else's?" An interview like that leaves outsiders to conservative Christianity with no more insight than they had before. The conservative church person in the audience gets to reassure himself, entirely truthfully and honestly, that no sore point as to his own religious life has been raised, that that know-it-all interviewer has no inkling what his churchy auditor's precious faith′ is about. The transaction speaks volumes about the usual secular educated person's misinformation about conservative Christianity, and the fatal misattribution of the social problems it presents, to the activity of this or that conspicuous Evangelical media personality, or the effect of this or that ultraright political cause.

1. The authoritarian personality ploy. Journalists and most others who have been to college have the expectation that conservative Evangelicals will be

people with clear, pat, oversimple ideas about everything, who cannot tolerate ambiguity, and who structure their views simply and rigidly to accommodate their intellectual and emotional limitations. We have depicted the conservative Evangelical as just the opposite. He tolerates too much ambiguity, lets artificially induced confusion reign when he ought to throw it off, and makes himself dependent on some pastor's rendition of arcane pseudo-issues, to deal with practical matters wherefor one's average, independent common sense would otherwise be sufficient.

Where do the collegians get such an idea? In practically every college course in social psychology or sociology, one learns about the *authoritarian personality theory,*[6] which has it that conservative political attitudes result from personality inadequacy, whose symptoms include defensive overcompensation against antisocial impulses, projective scapegoating against out-group persons, rigid, overly conventional attitudes, and intolerance of ambiguity. The theory came out of the unique misery of the McCarthy era, and implies that persons who are not politically ultraliberal and lack the attitude we have called "radical nonjudgmentalness" are mentally sick. The theory reflects a time when mental-health professionals were still overconfident enough to pronounce ominous diagnoses on all those who did not share their politics. Superficially, it is a very appealing idea: it simply happens not to be true and not to be borne out by the large body of empirical data that has been accumulated in its behalf.

Desires for clarity and consistency have their place. Indeed, the behavioral sciences have brought themselves to their present low ebb by condemning those who tried to maintain decent intellectual standards in them as "authoritarian." If the Evangelical apologist is skillful (and has read his Francis Schaeffer), he can make it seem as if logic, rationality and self-discipline were exclusively Christian virtues that "secular humanists" are all necessarily against. I reiterate a point made earlier: It is good to have high tolerance for ambiguity, but low tolerance for absurdity.

2. The anti-Semitism ploy. Where the first question ultimately carries the innuendo "Aren't you an Evangelical because you're inadequate?" the second might be cynically paraphrased "Aren't you Evangelicals really just a bunch of closet Jew-haters?" No, they are not a bunch of Jew-haters any more, and the leaders these days generally deserve much credit for instilling pro-Jewish and pro-Israel attitudes in their flocks—well beyond what the biblical language will support. The second question also attempts, very inadequately, to get at the obvious guile in a plan having the devout group go to eternal bliss, and all others, to eternal torment. The Evangelical can fairly and honestly reply that unconverted Jews simply do not go to Heaven just as most so-called Christians (i.e., who do not follow his particular doctrinal variations) do not, and that the Evangelical is simply trying to rescue whomever he can. The Evangelical can, entirely consistent with the biblical language, deem it his business to evangelize as kindly and meekly as possible, and always to try to prolong the lives of the

---

6. T. W. Adorno, et. al., *The Authoritarian Personality* (New York: Harper, 1950).

unsaved, never looking prematurely to foreclose the hope of conversion. Such views are unobjectionable in a pluralistic society.

One can, however, easily sharpen the question, so that no Bible-authentic retort is possible, by making it into what I call the "Anne Frank question." One poses to the Evangelical the hypothetical case of Anne Frank, who never responded to the Gospel, never accepted Christ as her personal savior, and never had what could rightly be termed evidences of salvation in her life. Rather, she went down expressing her belief in mankind. She was a "secular humanist" to the bone. The inescapable biblical conclusion is that the next thing Anne Frank will know, after the temporal Nazi death camp, will be the proceedings of judgment day, when she will inevitably be remanded to God's eternal death' camp, where there will never be any let-up, where her torment will go on forever. Oh, what a glorious picture of God's lovingkindness and mercy! Doesn't the prospect of being a sheep in such a God's pasture just warm your heart? (The allusion to the Nazi death camps is entirely fair: the impetus for them was entirely biblical, even though the detail of human usurpation of the godly prerogative kept them from being entirely Bible-authentic. No prototype for the Nazi death camps is to be found in German secular literature or cultural tradition!)

3. The one-size-fits-all ploy. The third question is always asked in a tone conveying "Everybody knows that the Bible is inherently ambiguous and incomprehensible, so anyone can use it just as well as you, to support any conceivable position." The collegian, whose ideas about the matter are conditioned directly or indirectly by the liberal church, can be excused for that misconception. But since the matter is becoming more rather than less material in our national life, anyone who tries to sort it out had better realize that the Bible is very specific about some crucial public-policy issues, and is so absurd and destructive in that specificity that all those who use the Bible to influence others and still sound somewhat reasonable are, perforce, untrue to the Bible in sundry ways. The knowledgeable antiapologist can defeat such wielders of influence by holding them to the precise letter of the Bible they claim to follow in all things.

Religion in Politics

The twisting of the Bible by the politicized, conservative Evangelical to align church people thoughtlessly for or against this or that candidate or position on an issue is a byproduct of the mini-Reformation. To be sure, liberals have twisted the Bible to help their causes in their time. The religious-right variety of Bible twisting could not have significant effect without the local conservative churches gradually and tirelessly bringing their flocks under mind-control. The motives of those who make that happen are not, for the most part, particularly political. The politicized television preachers get a free ride from all those local churches: even in those Pentecostal churches whose theology and clergy are most heavily represented on television, paying participants recruited by television seldom exceed 3 percent. The sincere Bible-believer, despite efforts to politicize him, develops a fatalistic view of worldly affairs. Weariness of those affairs, the desire to put a favorable construction on ceasing to concern oneself with them, is an important factor inducing modern people to become Bible-believers. From the viewpoint of the Bible, extreme concern with such matters is a symptom of unbelief! The tide of the mini-Reformation is ultimately against the religious right as presently constituted.

In encountering the religious right, it is crucial to remember that the failings of our society to which it reacts are real, and its activity usually points to a legitimate issue needing analytic rather than polemic attention. Often, when old-left antagonists of the religious right seek recognition and solicit funds by sounding the alarm about the supposed danger of a religious-right takeover, the strategy is partly to draw attention away from the diminished vitality of old-left positions. The malaise of the old-left intellectuals, their failure to provide much usable counsel in matters of value any more, gives the religious practitioners an opportunity to insert their inferior *Ersatz*.

What few neoconservative or genuinely postideological commentators there are (I hope I am one of the latter) are hesitant to alienate the religious right, whose votes are needed to counterbalance votes cast for liberals simply in the hope of getting more short-term individual benefit from government than is paid for in taxes. But the misreading of history, sociology, and human nature that inevitably result, if the commentator holds himself obliged to affirm the incompetent premises that our country's democratic ideals have a biblical basis or intention underlying them and that the Bible has something constructive yet to contribute to democratic traditions, seriously impedes the progress of such intellectuals. The *niveau* of the dialogue on public policy issues—the life's blood of our democracy—suffers disastrously as a result.

What of those twin Evangelical Big Lies that commentators at every hand so thoughtlessly ratify these days: the notions that our democracy has essentially religious or "Judeo-Christian" historical foundations and that the Bible is capable of further informing our democratic tradition? Some familiar points that form part of the irreducible minimum of U.S. history need to be kept ready for antiapologetic use.

What of the much-publicized Christianity of the Revolution's founding fathers? Mainly, they were Anglicans who sat weekly under the preaching of Tory clergy, nearly all of whom fled to England when it became clear that independence would be declared. The minority of non-Anglican proponents of the American Revolution were Presbyterians, Congregationalists, Baptists, Roman Catholics, and Jews—from a generation not noted for religious fervor. The education of a privileged-class male stressed Latin and Attic Greek, to enable him to read the masterpieces of Greco-Roman antiquity in the original. The Bible was mainly reserved for the indoctrination of peons, women, and slaves, and biblical languages were strictly a specialty of their trainers, the clergy. Prominent among the founding fathers were individuals, including Jefferson, Franklin, and Paine, with religious views more unorthodox than would be tolerated in persons in public life today. Many of the founding fathers, including Washington, Hancock, Revere, and Franklin, were Freemasons, devoting considerable amounts of their spare time to a religious rigmarole inconsistent with the individual Freemason's nominal Protestantism or Judaism. Religious groups that were still in a fervent phase during the Revolutionary period—such as the Amish, Hutterites, Mennonites, Methodists, Moravians, Quakers, and Shakers—remained Tory and sat the Revolutionary War out, largely on pacifistic grounds. Only one signer of the Declaration of Independence was a clergyman.[7] In hindsight, we can see that anyone who consulted the Bible honestly for guidance in those days could have found only exhortation to obey and within oneself to be loyal to constituted authorities generally, and in particular, pointed biblical prohibition against antitaxation protest.[8] During the Articles of Confederation period, Patrick Henry spearheaded a campaign to get a Virginia state tax to subsidize the Episcopalian successor to the absconded Anglican church. The campaign failed, more on account of lack of interest than any concerted opposition.

When the new, old-time-religion churches grew up in the nineteenth century, their contribution was primarily in the area of community organization and social service, in a time before the rise of secular specialists in these areas. I contend that those churches followed the civic trends, and neither led them nor made any ethical or moral contribution not otherwise in the air. As with the pacifist undercutting of the Revolutionary War effort, the biblical defense of slavery by the religious enthusiasts of the day is all too conveniently forgotten by historians oriented to mainline religion.[9] The Wesleyans learned not to look

---

7. John Witherspoon (1723-1794) had railed against humanist culture, particularly the theater, from his pulpit in Scotland. His involvement in Colonial politics required him to alter—like Jerry Falwell long after him—his earlier biblically authentic position that believers had no call to leadership in secular politics.

8. Matt. 17:24-27; Mark 12:13-17; Luke 20:19-26, 23:1-4; Rom. 13:6-7.

9. Mainline religious professionals have long taken the position that their kind of religion deserves the credit for any and all positive developments in the surrounding culture *ipso facto* but none of the blame for negative ones, which they attribute to rejection of their influence. Heads, mainline religion wins; tails, it does not lose. A rendition of that thesis much lauded in conservative policy-making circles in Washington, D.C., including those within the Reagan White House, is Richard John Neuhaus' *The Naked Public Square* (Grand Rapids, Mich.: Wm. B. Erdmans, 1984). Neuhaus takes an equally dim view of the new religious right and the anti-American leftist ideologues who have dominated the mainline Protestant denominations and the National Council of Churches since the sixties.

"The literature of the religious new right is replete with horror stories about liberal Protestantism's support for communist and other subversive activities. Such literature greatly overrates the degree of ideological consistency or seriousness among the functionaries of mainline religion. High up on Riverside Drive they write memoranda about God's call for a new economic order to replace capitalist oppressions and at the end of the day they cross the bridge to New Jersey on their way to places like Ridgewood, Pennsauken, and Basking Ridge, attaché cases loaded with other people's memoranda to be read that night, and minds uneasy about the mortgage and the bill from the orthodontist. It is more Prufrock than Lenin" (p. 237).

Neuhaus sees clearly that the major manifestations of religion in politics in his time are at the odious extremes of the political spectrum. Yet, undaunted, he declares that the moderate, "Judeo-Christian" tradition is responsible for whatever is good in our culture, and that whatever is wrong in our time is due to the decline of that influence, its absence (because mainline religionists misunderstand their religion to be a private matter) from the public square leaving that square naked. For specifics as to that influence, Neuhaus offers only a few paragraphs of tortured

at the Bible too closely, so that they could espouse a humane, nonabsurd salvation plan, and the abolitionists learned to pass over the Bible even more lightly, to evade its unequivocal support of the institution of slavery. We have forgotten that history. It did no harm for people to think of the Bible as a book of benevolent mystery so long as nobody got into it seriously, so long as everyone followed the tradition of superficiality in encountering the Bible to which all that earlier negative experience had given rise. Besides the negative mental-health implications of the new conservative churches' dismantling of that tradition, the archaic social views inherent in the Bible make those churches ultimately subversive to our democratic institutions.[10]

---

commentary (pp. 167-76) on the Bible passages about the believer's relation to secular civil authorities. Repeatedly, he indicates that the biblical notion that history moves in a progression toward a culmination, as opposed to cyclical or random notions of human history, has somehow furnished the prototype for American civic responsibility; however, he conveniently neglects to mention the particular revolting culmination of world history the Bible presents.

To presume and benevolently to allow that some lowest common denominator of the older Christian bodies and Judaism is also the historic root of our civic values does not make it so. Pressed from one side by the greater social and economic power that conservative Christianity has developed and from the other by the leftist radicals within their own ranks, well-meaning moderates like Neuhaus will no longer be able to maintain their illusions. I now see that when all those pastors followed Carl Rogers in deeming it worthwhile to spend their time and receive compensation for a kind of counseling where the pastoral counselor only repeats back to the counselee the latter's own contribution to the counseling, and the counselor takes special care not to utter any opinions or value judgments, *a pantomime of the relation of their kind of church to the surrounding society was taking place.* To focus on the intellectual idea of hyperrelativism or radical nonjudgmentalness involved in that pantomime is to miss its point, much as epistemological or scientific criticism of the Bible's supposed didactic content misses the point. Those pastors' underlying, nagging intimation that the mainline church, having put away from it the operative parts of its biblical origins, could do no more than recapitulate the culture where it was found, was no source of light but only a reflector of light emitted by secular humanists, was being acted out.

The best advice for those who have deep investments in mainline religion is to look very practically at being useful in social service and community organization, in competing with secular providers of those services as churches in an earlier day did not need to do. If mainline churches lose what historical continuity and momentum they have left, in providing those services, they can never get it back. Also, when atypical pastors in the mainline denominations find they can make some headway by imitating the conservative churches, it becomes important for it to be understood why that works, and for leaders to take a strong stand against mainline churches becoming competitors—probably not particularly successful competitors—in the conservative churches' destructive activities.

Although Neuhaus never says so in so many words, the hope of his readers is that the conservative churches will introduce people to Christianity, and that these will, in turn, "mature" to appreciate its "true" ineffable meaning, to be found only in the mainline houses of worship. Not a shred of sociological data supports such an expectation. I suspect that the Reagan advisors received Neuhaus' book so gladly because that rationalization assuaged whatever qualms they had about courting the new religious right. That situation had its parallel in the Carter White House, where presidential advisors embraced Christopher Lasch's *The Culture of Narcissism* (New York: W. W. Norton, 1978) because it allowed them to blame policy failures on the "me-generation" rather than on themselves. What needs to be emphasized is that rhetoric about the supposed inherent beneficence of the prevalent American religions, so called "Judeo-Christianity" in general and the Bible in particular, plays into the hands of the new conservative Christian hucksters. Moderate Republicans and mainline Christians and Jews end up underwriting a public-relations effort that ultimately inures to the benefit of destructive conservative churches.

10. Until the eighties, publicly visible religious leaders (except for civil-rights leaders) were either relatively neutral or else were clearly perceived as representing some disreputable extreme. Now

What of the supposed biblical basis for our morality and our legal institutions? We can illustrate how tenuous that basis really is by applying it thought-

---

we can understand the biblical origins of Billy Graham's unexpectedly sanguine statements about repression in communist countries after his visits to them. We ought to have appreciated better his efforts to be an agent of conciliation with the Soviet bloc, instead of encouraging the usual fundamentalist mind-set to see that relationship in terms of God's American people pitted against Satan's communists, leading up to the inevitable and desirable finale of Armageddon. Such is the perspective of all the current crop of politicized Evangelical media personalities.

The rise of Jerry Falwell as a politicized Evangelical with some very extreme views, who yet receives respectful treatment from the media and the political leadership, is an unprecedented development. Some implications of that development missed by political commentators need to be highlighted. Falwell's constituency is wholly political; it is not religiously homogeneous. A plurality of Moral Majority membership is Roman Catholic, and the deep rifts between the Pentecostal/charismatic sector and the rest of the conservative Evangelicals, and between conservative Evangelicals and politically conservative persons in the various special-doctrine, Christ-centered religions, are not healed, only tentatively smoothed over for the sake of shared short-range political goals. It needs to be emphasized that such a coalition is perfectly legitimate in our political system, and the point is well taken that it is hypocritical to say that clergy civil-rights leaders have been within their rights, but Falwell somehow is not within his. He works within the system, and his willingness to compromise is so facile that it calls his supposed strong principles into question. I detect in him no serious expectation of disenfranchising his antagonists. His use of lurid, homophobic, pornographic propaganda to raise money is the only consistent indecency for which I can fault him.

Recently he reached his zenith, appearing on the cover of *Time* (Sept. 2, 1985). But he squandered the media blitz by engaging in public relations for status quo apartheid in the Republic of South Africa. The thinly veiled old-time segregationist message must have been seen as a betrayal by many a younger Evangelical, who senses that it would be far harder to be an Evangelical if that made one go against the obvious moral verity of our civil-rights revolution. In the meantime, political analysts have generally come to view endorsement by Falwell more as a liability than an asset to most candidates for public office. (See Dudley Clendinen, "Virginia Polls and Politicians Indicate Falwell Is Slipping in His Home State," *New York Times,* Nov. 24, 1985, p. 26.)

Contemporaneously, Falwell's most powerful competitor, Marion G. "Pat" Robertson, began vigorously promoting himself as a candidate for president of the United States. Falwell promptly indicated his support of George Bush. (Robertson is a recent convert to the Republican Party, and many party faithful resent his interference.) Falwell started a new organization, Liberty Federation, apparently in an effort to evade the fallout from the Moral Majority's deteriorating public image. Vice-president Bush addressed the inaugural meeting of Liberty Federation in January 1986, probably with an eye toward containing Robertson and minimizing the danger of Robertson's getting in a position to make a Jesse Jackson style pitch at the 1988 Republican convention. Ironically, Falwell is the major beneficiary of his competitor's presidential aspirations, since the Republicans, who would otherwise have been distancing themselves from Falwell, need him to help them offset Robertson.

Although Robertson is receiving enormous publicity as this book goes to press (he, too, got his *Time* cover, Feb. 17, 1986), the commentators particularly fail to identify what is important about him. Despite his Southern Baptist background and ordination, Robertson is exclusively identified with the Pentecostal/charismatic sector, and his claims of being an immediate recipient of telepathic prophecies from God and of being able to divert hurricanes, knit broken bones, and cure cancer with his prayers are offensive and blasphemous to Bible-believers outside that sector. The unabashed superstitiousness of his approach enables him, for the wrong reasons, to have a substantial black following. Robertson's following, although tightly knit and generous with contributions, is a far smaller constituency than Falwell's theologically mixed one. Even among Pentecostals, the norm is a fine, double-oriented sensitivity that keeps the hysterical displays and superstition that distinguish their form of religion from getting out of hand. I predict that Robertson's violation of that norm will make even Pentecostals uneasy about supporting him, and that he will have far less less political support when the polls and canvasses are taken than political commentators now fear.

fully to any issue. Let us take the Evangelicals' most appealing moral issue and the one most broadly supported by the different elements within the Evangelical

---

Because of the narrowness of Robertson's support base—his organizations' income diminished while his predisential aspirations were being publicized—and the foreseeable preparedness of Republicans to minimize his damage to their cause, I do not see him as a real danger. Yet, it would be better if the news media were better at catching his more interesting and damaging utterances. After carefully monitoring the 700 Club for more than a year (a VCR saves me from having to sit through the whole thing), I conclude that beneath the genial fa £ade, he is radically antidemocratic and that the presidency of the United States as we know it is a euphemism for the kind of head of government he aspires to be. A general trend, which he has toned down drastically since going public as an aspiring head of government, is his fascination with the idea of economic and political collapse. Consistently, Robertson used to exhibit gleeful anticipation of a banking-system collapse caused by third-world public-debt default, the national debt, farm foreclosures, etc. and political collapse caused by the fractiousness of Congress, the executive and the courts—just the conditions that normally accompany the failure of a democracy and its replacement with despotism. His attitude toward Congress (his father was a longtime Democratic senator from Virginia) has been so consistently negative that one realizes that the very idea of time being wasted to air views that disagree with his own is what Robertson really condemns.

When Robertson is not trying to clothe himself in President Reagan's popularity, he shows his loathing for what he regards as Reagan's weakness in failing to override the other branches of government. Congress and the courts apparently faded into the background in Robertson's fantasies of his "presidency." While he carefully avoids criticizing religious groups likely to launch counterpropaganda, it is clear that "cults" and the Jehovah's Witnesses have no right to exist, so far as he is concerned. He states that only spirit-filled Christians and Orthodox Jews should be allowed to hold public office in the United States. (He is very pro-Israel, envisioning Israel playing a key rôle in the destruction of the Soviet Union.) No holds are barred in using the AIDS epidemic as a lead-in for stirring up scapegoat hatred against homosexuals; Robertson advocates what amount to Nuremberg laws against homosexuals.

Robertson has made horrendous statements about what legal institutions he wants, and these are all the more startling coming from a Yale Law School graduate. When the prosecution of members of an eccentric, fundamentalist church for denying their children necessary medical care on religious grounds was discussed, Robertson stated that there should be legally empowered church tribunals to determine whether or not otherwise illegal behavior was prompted by a true message from God, and to shield the accused from prosecution if so. A few weeks later, he stated that there should be special Christian police, empowered to control crime solely on the basis of telepathic messages from God, without regard for familiar Constitutitional protections and without any requirement for the usual kinds of evidence. Purely supernatural evidence has not been part of our law since "spectral evidence" was admitted at the Salem witch trials! Legal institutions under Robertson would be as different from the ones we know as the Third Reich was from the Federal Republic. It may also be significant that Robertson says that considerations of efficiency ought to outweigh individual rights or privacy considerations in the governmental use of computer data about individuals, and that his own headquarters operates along the lines of a high-security military compound.

Worst of all is Robertson's position on genocide, which he set out clearly on two separate occasions, in response to audience questions about the accounts in the Old Testament of the extermination of such peoples as the Midianites and Amorites. Robertson said that from time to time God does order his people to exterminate an inveterately sinful and ungodly people completely, to "kill them all." While this may seem cruel to spiritually uninformed humans, it is really loving and kind, because it stops the victims from producing more generations of candidates for Hell and the number who must eventually go there is reduced. In other words, God has his people carry out genocide as a means of population control for Hell! Now Robertson sets great store by his Mayflower ancestry as a qualification for his supposed calling; I suspect that these detestable utterances have in view the American extermination of the Indians—in which some ancestor of his must have participated—rather than the Nazi extermination of Jews. Interestingly, this rationale would not hold for the number-one category on Robertson's persecution list, the homosexuals. But since Robertson holds himself up as someone who is to receive and carry out telepathic marching orders from God, it is a very ominous hint as to his true proclivities.

Robertson's obvious posturing that an order from him is tantamount to a commandment from God, regardless of what the Bible may teach, and his constant jockeying to put in place the

subculture: the abortion issue.

The apparent biblical basis for opposing abortion is "Whoso sheddeth man's blood, by man shall his blood be shed."[11] Assuming this verse justifies limiting the Sixth Commandment to contemplate murdering humans and not blanket prohibition against killing living things generally as in Hinduism, assuming the verse does not mean what it literally implies, i.e., penalizing sublethal, perhaps trivial, wounding or surgery, and further assuming that the proscribed act retains some consequence even if the death penalty, which may have been rescinded or ceded to the secular state, be not carried out, then the Bible may indeed be telling us that taking the life of a human who has not even been born once is forbidden. Christian parents-to-be may not abort their ensuing child. What about the unborn child of other believers? Jesus provided intrachurch mechanisms for the settlement of disputes between believers. What about the unborn child of unbelievers? Believers are not to judge them. Are believers to agitate to change the secular state's laws, to try to force all to live by believers' laws? Thereto, the Bible is silent, addressing itself only to obedience to law in an authoritarian setting. Does the aborting of fetuses contravene any broader godly purpose stated in the Bible? God uses the killing of firstborn as a curse in the Old Testament, and Herod imitates it, killing the children among whom he thinks the dreaded messiah will be found, in the New. If it is nonelect children who are being killed, then as long as the believers do not unlawfully perpetrate it themselves, it is not their concern. If it is elect children who are being killed, then it would seem that the same rules apply as when the known, twice-born are being persecuted and martyred. The martyrdom simply spares them the fragmentation and travail of earthly life, and they go straight to be with Jesus. In neither case is there a biblical mandate to rescue anyone from what the believer is to regard as the trivial inconsequence of earthly death. "And fear not them which kill the body. . . ."

Take any practical issue, carefully work out the Scriptures touching it, and a similarly absurd analysis will mechanically crank itself out. The believer will object that such an analysis is against the spirit of Christianity, legalistic, pharisaic. And so it is, depending upon whose Christianity one uses for a criterion. After the preceding avalanche of Scripture, demonstrating monstrous implication after monstrous implication in the Bible, the burden shifts to the

premises for the conclusion that, in order to get rid of the fatal inefficiency of the democratic system and to keep governmental edict aligned with the will of God, the thing to do is to vest all governmental power in himself, are too obvious a ploy to take in more than an extraordinarily vulnerable and unintelligent minority of the people. Among Evangelicals, I have received the impression that those who adhere to him do so for the faith-healing hype and the false sense of fellowship, not for the didactic content—which often reaches a respectably high level. The relatively high *niveau* of the show creates a misleading impression of Robertson's paying following. This is confirmed by what happens to the 700 Club at fund-raising time: the didactic content disappears and the show is then composed of a purely propagandistic film piece, faith-healing testimonials, and uninterpretable tallies and scoreboards supposedly reflecting the progress of the fund-raising, resembling nothing so much as a game show. In January 1986, it was done that way for two weeks, featuring the slogan, "The future is ours."

11. Gen. 9:6.

believer to show how it is that some ineffable, benign Spirit nevertheless shines through. That nonlegalistic rendition will still have to be specific enough for each believer not to be left to do merely as he or she pleases. If it all boils down to complete permissiveness, then how is it that the whole justification for the scheme is to provide vitally necessary restraint for humans with totally depraved natures? And what was Paul talking about when he condemned the libertines?

The Big Loophole

Our biblically rigorous analysis of the abortion issue really ends up restating biblical views about other occasions for the loss of human life, and recapitulating those views' shortcomings. But there is more. There is a way that wholesale permissive abortion can be reconciled with every requirement imposed by the Bible!

Much earlier, we covered the rigid biblical rules, requiring absolute obedience to the secular state and elevating all exercizes of temporal authority to the status of God's will being done.[12] The believer is to obey incumbents of authority wholeheartedly and unthinkingly, except where dissemination of the Gospel is interfered with, and then if he has trouble with the authorities, it just means God is conferring the blessing of martyrdom on him. Accordingly, if one can get the state to order a thing not falling within the special, Gospel-dissemination area, then what is ordered becomes God's will *ipso facto* and it ceases to present a "sin" problem for any individual. After all, "sin" largely consists of man usurping God's prerogatives. If the state orders a thing, it is God's action, and there is no human encroachment.

A minor official of Moral Majority was widely publicized for advocating capital punishment for all homosexuals. His view was not quite representative of that organization, and he lost his position in the ensuing flap. But Bible authenticity was not one of the areas wherein one could fault that view. The Old Testament did specify the death penalty for male homosexuality and for bestiality; whatever the right New Testament doctrine of those penalties may be, they must be stood on a footing even with the Old Testament death penalty for murdering a human (or a higher one, since cities of refuge were provided for the Old Testament murderer, but not for the Old Testament sexual deviate). As to the state taking human life, the New Testament adds only that the public official so doing "does not bear the sword in vain," and in the case of the nonmartyr victim of that sword, the mere fact that he is so victimized biblically establishes him as a wrongdoer being dealt with in God's stead.

Thus, all biblical objections to abortion could be gotten around by legally providing for court orders mandating abortions to be issued routinely whenever parties with appropriate standing apply for them. After all, if all people are sinners and come from their mothers' wombs speaking lies anyhow, why not make available official declaration of that spiritual condition, and thereby bring

12. See pp. 61-65.

destruction of the unborn within the biblically defined purview of God's will and act? It makes as much sense as any other rigorously biblical, public-policy position!

Scapegoating

All the while when Evangelicals are hearing what a great guide the Bible is for modern political life, but not consciously making the connection that its ultimate implication is substitution of authoritarian structures for our constitutional ones, they also take in a more immediately destructive kind of indoctrination, that they do not see leads to alienation from and unconcern for others unlike themselves. While conservative Christians have very commendably distanced themselves from racism and anti-Semitism as forms of scapegoating in recent years, they have replaced these with homophobia. In my contacts with conservative Christians, I found bristling, visceral expression of hatred toward homosexuals the unvarying norm. In my opinion, if conservative Christians had their way, a pogrom against homosexuals would commence immediately. In the recent period when Acquired Immune Deficiency Syndrome has been much in the news, the immediate reaction of every conservative Christian spokesperson I have observed has been gloating over God's supposed wrathful judgment on the homosexuals. The afterthought, that the Christian spokespeople ought to evince some compassion and ought not set themselves up for their own setbacks to be thrown up to them as God's wrathful judgments, never occurs to them until the initial, demagogic benefit has been reaped from the "fag-bashing."[13]

Combatting racism, anti-Semitism and other kinds of outgroup hostility has been such a massive civic project in our society in recent decades that the matter may seem too obvious to discuss. Every schoolchild knows that the gratification one gets from attacking another's ethnicity, class origins, gender, disability etc., is illicit, shameful, cheap. Teaching oneself not to do that, as one teaches oneself not to pick one's nose or break wind in public, has become an ingrained norm. The conservative Evangelicals do not see how approving one kind of making oneself feel a little better by disparaging another's involuntary condition defeats the larger society's enlightened project of declaring the entire scapegoating mental approach wrong, and an occasion for bad conscience. Today the conservative Christians bash the homosexuals: tomorrow, to satisfy their appetite, they will have to find more outgroups to bash.

I could almost write another book, about how integral the scapegoating mental approach is to the Bible. Christian love′ explicitly includes expelling from one's conscious mind not only one's negative thoughts and emotions—with the result that one is blind to its mote in one's own eye and thinks it is a beam in

---

13. "Fag-bashing" is so endemic in the Bible that I have to accuse those who think they are able to base a case for tolerance of homosexuals on the Bible of sheer intellectual incompetence. The applicable New Testament passages are Rom. 1:26-27; I Cor. 5:11; 6:9; 11:14; Phil. 3:2; Jude 7; and Rev. 22:15. See also Deut. 22:5.

another's—but also natural affection and the kind of compassion or empathy that, in our provisional, "relatedness" psychology, are of the essence of decent individual conscience and conduct. Like those Roman soldiers who were among the first Gentile converts, the Christian soldier is exhorted to be a good soldier by displacing the grisliness of his work from his mind and doing what he is ordered "heartily, as to the Lord, and not unto men. . . ," because hierarchical authority makes everything all right. It is okay to destroy those the state has declared its enemies, born and unborn, so long as one thinks pure, scriptural thoughts while doing it. That is how the Bible-believer tacitly understands the verse, ". . . love covereth all sins."[14] I submit that such was the mental approach of American slavers' self-righteously engaging in a kind of barbarism for which the rest of that society had become too far advanced. I submit that the present day Afrikaaner, working the inhuman machinery of apartheid (and who typically has had a very severe, Scripture-saturated Christian-school upbringing) does so in such a frame of mind.

The Jewish people occupy a special place in the conservative Christian's maundering, scapegoating inner mental activity. The present remission of Christian animosity toward the Jews will prove, I fear, to be a temporary phase in the longer process of stripping away folkloric ideas about Christianity and replacing them with Bible-authentic ones. The more familiar, folkloric forms taken by anti-Semitism in recent centuries differ greatly from the attitudes toward Judaism implied in the New Testament. On the surface, and as a doctrinal matter, the Jews get a better deal in the Bible than in historic Christianity. They are on precisely the same footing as anyone else, i.e. a limited quota from their nation are to be saved, but many more are to be damned. Christ dies for the sins of God's elect. The atmosphere building up to his crucifixion is intense and claustrophobic: his followers deserting him, the Jewish mob and the properly constituted Roman magistrate, Pilate, condemning him, are caught up and play their rôles more unfreely than other Bible protagonists do. Biblically speaking, to say that the Jews are the ones to whom Christ's death is to be imputed is to say that they are *still* God's elect. The mini-Reformationist Bible-believer will not say that.

But underlying this doctrinally pure equality of Jews and all others, we sense that there is still a difference. The Jewish nation had been the youthful God's beloved first bride, and he had loved her very much indeed, before being betrayed too often and then exercising his prerogative to break his own rules and divorce her, and taking an exotic, new polyglot bride. The true Bible-believer cannot but be impressed by all that history seemingly behind the individual Jew of his acquaintance. The Christian as insecure second wife, never entirely sure that some residual, passionate attachment to the first wife ought not to make her jealous, never quite at ease around that former wife, is an apt analogy. Especially so when God the husband is so adamant against those who have left their first love.[15]

---

14. Prov. 10:12.
15. Rev. 2:4.

To all that has been written about anti-Semitism, we have something original and rather painful to add. We have speculated that after Christianity became Gentilized and Paulinized, it became ineffective at attracting Jewish converts because a sense of personal, historic identification with the Bible characters psychologically defeats the characteristically Christian, allegorical way of relating to them. The Gentile gets snared in the semantic labyrinth, is made inwardly deeply miserable by it, but the deeper in he gets, the less he understands what is happening to him. Deep down, he knows this thing is historically Jewish, even that being a believer somehow makes him an honorary Jew, inwardly. But he sees his Jewish neighbor wanting no part of this psychic misery that has come on the Christians from the Jews. Seeing the Jew happily unaffected by what eats the Christian, the Christian imagines the Jew knows something the Christian does not. Actually, the Jewish neighbor is as much in the dark about the matter as the Christian, having no real connection with the much earlier Jewish masterminds behind the Evangelical mind-control system. What I am saying is that genuine Christian anti-Semitism, before it gets overlaid with historical complications, consists of Christian envy of the relatively free Jewish mind. And my message for other Jewish intellectuals is simply that taking Evangelical mind-control off their backs—our ancestors having put it on them—is the only decent posture for us in the future, and the only one really calculated to keep us or our posterity from irrational outbursts of prejudice in the long run. Having many Christians become more biblical in their approach is not good news for Jews, since the fine print in the Bible is against the Jews, the product of ancient history that ought not be relevant any more. Having good relations with particular Christian leaders is no longer a useful strategy. Liberal Christian leaders have no real clout any more, and the conservative ones, nearly all friendly to Jews and contemporary Israel for the time being, come and go unpredictably.

The End of the World

The shortness of our treatment of eschatology should not cause us to underestimate the topic's crucial importance in understanding contemporary conservative Christianity. It is no coincidence that during the Reformation, when the first thousand years since Jesus' first coming had long since come and gone, and the completion of the second thousand was about as far in the future, there was practically no interest in eschatology. It hardly occurred to Erasmus, Luther, Calvin or Knox, to take an interest in the events that would accompany the end of the world. Sustained interest in the topic has manifested itself only in the last century or so.

The operative New Testament passage about the end of this world reads:

> The Lord is not slack concerning his promise, as some men count slackness; but is longsuffering to us-ward, not willing that any should perish, but that all should

> come to repentance. But the day of the Lord will come as a thief in the night; in the which the heavens shall pass away with a great noise, and the elements shall melt with fervent heat, the earth also and the works that are therein shall be burned up. *Seeing* then *that* all these things shall be dissolved, what manner *of persons* ought ye to be in *all* holy conversation and godliness, Looking for and hasting unto the coming of the day of God, wherein the heavens being on fire shall be dissolved, and the elements shall melt with fervent heat? Nevertheless we, according to his promise, look for new heavens and a new earth, wherein dwelleth righteousness. Wherefore, beloved, seeing that ye look for such things, be diligent that ye may be found of him in peace, without spot, and blameless. And account *that* the longsuffering of our Lord *is* salvation; even as our beloved brother Paul also according to the wisdom given unto him hath written unto you. . . .[16]

How quaint, that the passage should end with kudos for Paulinism. We have encountered before how a drastic end of all that the four Jungian functions can relate to—the so-called hope of the Christian—and the drastic separation of different mental compartments—combine and augment one another. The Christian who is really serious about Bible-authenticity will cultivate unconcern for the natural world, emotional disinvestment in it.

Three consequences of the Christian view, requiring the believer to regard the destruction of the natural world as immanent, concern us. The most obvious of these is the similarity of the calamity the Christian is to anticipate so happily to a nuclear war. I believe that the subtle sense of futility about the future that forty years of atomic age and the cold war have brought us account for the mini-Reformation more than any other influence. That situation corresponds to the civic futility in ruined Israel, prompting people to seek to shift everything important to them to a different plane, away from earthly calamity. I only thank God that She made the other side in the potential nuclear conflict doctrinaire atheists, who cannot see in the end of the world an opportunity for themselves to be transported to bliss and to see their hated antagonists transported off to eternal torment. A tragic end to the cold war would be a certainty, if both nations had influential persons capable of reaching such a conclusion. The second consequence is complete lack of interest in conservation, in preserving the natural environment for distant future generations at the expense of short-range objectives. One notes a complete lack of interest in conservation among politicized Evangelicals: James Watt, as Secretary of the Interior, was next to perfect in his Bible-authenticity. (Accordingly, since the biblical end of the "world" takes place entirely on planet earth, a biblicist would have no use for space exploration.) The third consequence touches the Jewish people. With some biblical justification, the end-time scenarios cranked out by the conservative Evangelicals typically include a sensationally gory end for contemporary Israel. It is on this topic that every one of the major television evangelists shows himself up as less benign in his feelings toward the Jews and Israel than he otherwise lets on.

---

16. 2 Pet. 3:9-15. Cf., Isa. 13:11-16; 24:3-6; 65:17; 66:22-24; and, contradicting these, Eccles. 1:4.

What, Then, Is Christianity?

Having challenged the standard theories of religion as being an ongoing cultural expression, an attempt to explain the origins of human existence, an attempt to take control over life's uncertainties—at least as these theories apply to Christianity—there remains an obligation to make a summary statement as to what Christianity is. Bertrand Russell, in his widely read criticisms of Christianity, thought it resembled nothing so much as Stoicism. There is, indeed, a resemblance; both Stoicism and Christianity arose in situations where civic virtues that had once been productive became futile. Noting also that the contemporary resurgence of conservative Christianity comes in a time when people are tired of rapid social and technological change and when the events that can end the existence of all those who are living and their posterity are at once real and immediate, yet unimaginable and perhaps beyond human efforts to control them, we can identify a deep sense of futility about real events as the possible key factor. Having experienced it before, in my Jungian phase, I call giving up on reality and withdrawal into fantasy and fiction by a different name: *decadence*. For me, Christianity is simply a cleaner form of decadence than recreational drugs, perverse sex, or rock and roll. Christianity has shown me that I, too, could be decadent. But, serious person that I am, I chose the way wherein one can be decadent—and still not have much fun at it.

Postscript

I had nearly finished another long chapter, on the mental-health implications of the Evangelical mind-control system, and was going to follow it with another, on the larger political and social implications. The mental-health chapter was turning out to depend too heavily on Camping's call-in program, and on other, too incomplete impressionistic information. A letter arrived from the publisher, pointing out that the book was already too long. Wasn't it enough to solve in one book a problem that has been hanging around unsolved, consequentially affecting history, for nineteen centuries? Were I to write prematurely on the mental-health implications and this work were well received, might people not develop some misguided scruple against contradicting what I wrote, as happened with Freud? Can the thoughtful reader not deduce anyhow more or less what I would write about such topics as biblicism and family relations, biblicism and sexuality, and the similarity of the biblical program to our century's totalitarian ideologies, which, like it, are mind-games of the second kind? It was time to make an end and say no more without the benefit of feedback and additional information.

On the subject of feedback, I would welcome communication from people concerned with the things we have covered. Please write to me in care of the publisher. I have in mind the founding of a membership organization, which will gather and disseminate information.[1] A likely activity for it would be to furnish

1. Two organizations with a somewhat related intent exist. People for the American Way was founded by Norman Lear; it functions mainly as a lobby, countering initiatives from religious-right lobbies, particularly the Moral Majority. I support it and contribute to it with some reservations. Its actions evince the same sort of old-left orientation as Americans for Democratic Action or the National Education Association. To the extent that People for the American Way purports to be somehow active in protecting freedom of expression for all viewpoints generally, as opposed to advocating its own rather narrow and ideological viewpoint, its solicitations and advertisements are misleading. But its efforts against the Evangelical enthusiasts among Reagan-administration appointees have been useful. Except for Surgeon General C. Everett Koop, every conspicuous Reagan-administration Evangelical enthusiast has left office under a cloud; others have been blocked at the nomination stage. The organization's masthead includes many leaders of the liberal, mainline denominations.

In the Spring of 1985, an organization called Fundamentalists Anonymous appeared, based in New York City. (See *Newsweek,* Aug. 5, 1985, p. 63.) It purports to reach out to individuals who leave fundamentalist churches, and are confused, bitter, and isolated thereafter. On slight acquaintance, one finds out that it is more interested in repopulating liberal, mainline churches

copies of this book to conservative pastors. I request persons interested in receiving a solicitation when and if one is made to respond on a standard-sized postcard.

---

with former fundamentalists than with understanding the fundamentalist experience. It observes a curious scruple against attempting to reach individuals who have not clearly broken with their fundamentalist affiliation, reminiscent of the unwritten rule against "sheep stealing" in the pastoring trade. I contacted it, and when its principals learned the nature of my book, they broke their promises to send me a press kit and set up a meeting. I think it fair to infer that this organization has something to hide.

Both organizations demonstrate the oblique and ineffective attack on the conservative church resurgence, to which a liberal theological orientation limits one. The stones will have to be thrown, not by those who are without sin but by those who do not live in glass houses.

Postscript to the Paperback Edition

There has been too little time since this work's first publication for many additional psychological insights about people renouncing militant conservative Christianity to have emerged.[1] There has been enough time for new friends who were once believers to share their experiences with me. Joe Edward Barnhart, Barbara Bellis Egelkamp, Austin Miles, Charles "Skipp" Porteous, and Gerard Thomas Straub have meant especially much to me. But so far, too few former conservative church insiders have found their way to me to make systematic study possible.

One mental-health matter that does seem ripe for further comment now is the rather long period of readjustment often needed by those who "come out." It may be useful to speak of that period when the fictitious ideas and values of the devotee have collapsed, but have not yet been adequately replaced with other, more salutary views, as a *refractory period.* The former believers I know best have reported that they sought new intellectual stimulation to counteract the biblical pseudophilosophy in which their minds had been immersed, that it took a lot of quiet time for the devotional bad habits ingrained in them to be extinguished, and that intellectual and emotional self-reliance was the next major life issue they needed to address. It may be that only people with the potential to become strongly independent and self-reliant do come out at present.[2] The

---

1. My short encapsulation of this book, "The Psychology of the Bible-Believer," was published in *Free Inquiry* (7, no. 2, Spring 1987, pp. 22-27).

Wendell W. Watters, a psychiatry professor at McMaster University, began theorizing about the detrimental effects of Christian doctrine on mental health long before I did. "Christianity and Mental Health" (*Humanist,* 47, no. 6, Nov./Dec. 1987, p. 5ff.) is a preliminary rendition of his views. I hope that his nearly completed book on the subject will soon appear.

2. Fundamentalists Anonymous' experiment with support groups for former conservative church participants—notwithstanding their grossly exaggerated promotional and fund-raising claims—has not been a success. The "Anonymous" format is inappropriate where there is no compulsive habit or problem needing management. Fighting off an urge to return is not the problem. Once the conservative church illusion is punctured, the person who has labored under it experiences no compulsion to go back. Also, the peculiar mix of the ambiguous religious overtones carried over from Alcoholics Anonymous and the staunch National Council of Churches loyalties of the national leaders of Fundamentalists Anonymous can be rather unsettling to a person who has recently been on a completely different kind of God-trip. Fundamentalists Anonymous definitely pursues a hidden agenda disparaging to nontheists. All this makes for a confused and confusing approach to counseling.

The yet-to-come successful outreach to people shaking off the influence of a conservative church will need to take a much more didactic approach than Fundamentalists Anonymous has done, one that maintains a careful balance, allowing neither intolerance nor deference toward individual religious idiosyncrasies. Those who become skeptics and those who opt for some less noxious form of religion will have to cultivate an ethic of civility toward one another—just as the several religious denominations present when the United States was founded had to do. But germane new vocabulary and concepts—not necessarily mine—are needed to come to terms with the experience of having been under evangelical mind-control. These cannot be developed if discussions of substance are avoided and certain selected theological sacred cows are allowed to roam at will.

objective of bringing about release of more ordinary captives of the conservative churches is yet to be attempted. And we are almost entirely unprepared for the thorny question of how the liberated can manage their continuing loyalties to those who remain captive.[3]

The dormancy in the 1986-1988 period of the topic of mental health and conservative Christianity has been more than made up for by watershed developments in religion and politics. I was fortunate to be able to play a pivotal rôle in the period's premier religion-in-politics story. My videotape monitoring of Pat Robertson figured significantly in the demolition of his 1988 presidential candidacy and enabled me to have some marvelous adventures along the way.[4]

I read Gerard Thomas Straub's *Salvation for Sale* in page proofs some months before its first publication.[5] As producer of the "700 Club" and creator of the Christian soap opera "Another Life," Straub was one of Robertson's most trusted lieutenants from 1978 to 1980. In March 1987, I first met Gerry Straub. He had come to Philadelphia to be on "People Are Talking," a local television talk-show, and I was in the studio audience. He had just been to see Paul Kurtz (the publisher of both Gerry's and my books) in Buffalo, New York, where, in rapid succession, Gerry learned about the Robertson material I had collected and had a public confrontation with Robertson, who had been in town for a convention of the National Association of Evangelicals. Gerry and I began an intellectual dialogue, a working cooperation, and a friendship of downright historic significance.

In *Salvation for Sale,* Gerry had primarily chronicled his own "refractory period" journey and had included enough illustration of Robertson's intolerance, impulsiveness, and capacity for self-delusion, as well as of the downright medieval atmosphere he cultivated at his Christian Broadcasting Network (CBN), to lead one to infer that a Robertson presidency would be a catastrophe. Gerry and I pooled our information. He had not realized that Robertson was capable of statements so wantonly radical as the ones I had gathered. I had not followed how Robertson, during the seventies and early eighties, had been obsessed with an eschatological scenario placing the Battle of Armageddon in or about 1982, and the Second Coming (which CBN was preparing to televise) before 1990. It became clear to us both that Robertson's presidential aspirations had followed in the wake of the failure of his cataclysmic prophecies to come true. Gerry

---

3. A higher rate of marriage dissolution was found among Fundamentalist Protestants than among mainline Protestants or Catholics in extensive survey data collected by the National Opinion Research Center from 1972 to 1980 (Kenneth S. Chi and Sharon K. Houseknecht, "Protestant Fundamentalism and Marital Success: A Comparative Approach," *Sociology and Social Research,* 69, no. 3, April 1985, pp. 351-375). In my opinion, the alienation ensuing when one spouse ceases to talk *to* the other and begins instead to talk *at* the other in biblical clichés is the central experience these findings reflect. So much for conservative church as the preserver of "family values"!

When I showed the study to Gerard Straub, he was reminded of the extraordinarily large number of marriage break-ups he had witnessed inside Pat Robertson's Christian Broadcasting Network. Statistics were unnecessary to ascertain that there had been an epidemic of marriage dissolution in the "secret kingdom" during the time when Straub worked there.

4. See p. 396-399, footnote 10.

5. (Buffalo, N.Y.: Prometheus Books, 1986). Updated Edition, 1988.

discovered an audiotape of the New Year's Day 1980 CBN-staff prayer meeting where Robertson, sounding like Ayatollah Khomeini, Jim Jones, and Dr. Strangelove all rolled into one, spun out his Armageddon-in-'82 scenario. Selected excerpts from the transcripts of that tape and my own tape collection were incorporated into a new chapter added to *Salvation for Sale* for the updated paperback edition, published in early January 1988.

Throughout the rest of 1987 and until Super Tuesday 1988, when Robertson's presidential campaign got blown out of the water, Gerry and I worked to get the word out. Gerry gave more than 150 radio interviews and made 19 television appearances. We both talked with many journalists and furnished them with great quantities of written material and tape.[6] "NBC Nightly News with Tom Brokaw"[7] and CBS' "West 57th Street" broadcast strategically scheduled pieces in which Gerry was interviewed, and rebroadcast my home videotape of some of Robertson's more radical utterances.[8]

Robertson would, in any event, have ceased to make political progress as soon as his "packing" of straw polls and caucuses with relatively small numbers

---

6. Information we provided was used particularly well in articles by Wayne King in the *New York Times,* Michael Kranish in the *Boston Globe,* and T. R. Reid and Susan Kelleher in the *Washington Post.*

By far the most discussed item from my tape monitoring was an excerpt from the January 11, 1985, "700 Club," in which Robertson said that only ultrareligious Christians and Jews ought to be allowed to hold government posts. (Some of his other comments render his sincerity in including Jews in the charmed circle highly dubious.) When first asked about the matter, Robertson, with a great flourish of sham indignation, denied ever having said any such thing. No other Robertson utterance received such wide coverage or embarrassed him more often in interviews. *Time* revisited the matter repeatedly and, in an editorial written by Walter Shapiro and reported by Laurence J. Barrett ("The Teflon Twins of 1988," January 11, 1988, p. 30), declared it the Robertson equivalent of Jesse Jackson's "Hymietown" gaffe.

7. December 21, 1987. This piece, produced by Stephanie Meagher, set the tone for much of the subsequent news coverage of Robertson. It also prompted Robertson to charge NBC News with "religious bigotry" for failing in what he regarded as a duty of journalists not to report extremist statements couched in religious terms. Robertson made a second charge of religious bigotry, against Brokaw, for characterizing Robertson as a "television evangelist."

8. The copyright law implications of rebroadcasting copyrighted videotape excerpts from the "700 Club" played an interesting part in my adventures. Before I began my tape monitoring, People for the American Way (PFAW) had conducted a similar monitoring and made available in 1986 a fifteen-minute reel of Robertson utterances. Its highlights were Robertson praying Hurricane Gloria away and a pre-1982 offer of teaching tapes about the imminent end of the world. (Most of the reel consisted of Robertson reciting stock ultraconservative political doctrine, which I did not find inherently outrageous.) Robertson threatened to sue PFAW for infringement of copyright. During the 1988 presidential campaign, PFAW provided no tape footage other than what had been on its 1986 reel. PFAW has been very fair about giving me credit for what my tape monitoring accomplished. Apparently, my providing tape for rebroadcast obviated a legal problem for PFAW.

The first television program to brave the copyright hazard and rebroadcast some of my tape—the January 11, 1985 excerpt—was WWOR's "People are Talking," hosted by Richard Bey. (See Edmund D. Cohen, "Rebroadcasting the True Pat Robertson," *Free Inquiry,* 8, no. 1, Winter 1987-88, p. 20.) Bey had been the host of a show by the same name in Philadelphia, where Gerry Straub and I first met. I have received no allegations of copyright infringement from the Robertson camp.

of militants, and his lack of genuine popular support in primaries, became obvious. Even so, Gerry and I find it disconcerting to realize that without our efforts Robertson would have largely succeeded in finessing his past, posing as someone he never was, and suppressing what was most interesting about him. In my estimation, Robertson is now discredited to too great an extent for him to return as an influential participant in national decisions.[9] Having presented his presidential prospects to his hard-core followers as a prophesied miracle, while at the same time wooing the trust and support of the general public by pretending to have renounced the peculiar views so admired by those followers, Robertson will have to contend with no small disillusionment problem. Unless he can successfully launch another prophetic gimmick even more grandiose than the first two, I expect Robertson to fade from view. As time goes on, he will resemble the late Herbert W. Armstrong more and more. When someone does come along who can overcome the fragmentation and disagreement on issues that now substantially neutralize the Religious Right as a force in national politics—and it will take a few years for that to occur—he will not particularly resemble Robertson or any other current Religious Right leader.

The Robertson-era adventure most memorable for me began when Gerry sent a copy of *Salvation for Sale* to Frank Zappa in May 1987. The two got acquainted, and plans were soon formed to produce and market a home videocassette with Gerry, Frank, Waleed Ali,[10] and me talking about Robertson. We all met in the studio beneath Frank's house in Los Angeles, and for a day and

---

9. The one other person who was of major help in puncturing the false image Robertson sought to project was former Congressman Paul N. "Pete" McCloskey, Jr. He and Robertson had served together as Marine junior officers in the Korean War. In 1986, McCloskey wrote a letter to Congressman Andrew Jacobs, Jr., accusing Robertson of having used the political influence of his late father, Senator A. Willis Robertson, to evade dangerous duty in Korea. The letter became public, and Robertson, apparently expecting to prevail by dint of financial might, sued for defamation. The evidence developed in pretrial discovery ran heavily in favor of McCloskey, as did prospects of winning at trial. On the eve of the date set for trial—ironically, Super Tuesday 1988—Robertson dropped the suit, accepting as conditions a ban on initiating the same claim again and the obligation to pay McCloskey's court costs (subsequently set at $28,000). Much of Robertson's conduct in the case fit the classical pattern of the bad-faith litigant.

Although McCloskey could have got off with a perfunctory apology, he stood his ground and took Robertson on at great personal sacrifice—and with personal valor that I deeply admire.

10. Waleed Ali and his brothers founded MPI Home Video, a pioneer distributor of home entertainment videocassettes. As Palestinian-Americans, the Alis detested Robertson's touting the Israelis as divinely mandated to keep the occupied territories and his portrayal of Palestinians as nonpersons—like the Philistines, Canaanites, Midianites, etc., in the Old Testament. MPI's videocassette "Oliver North: Memo to History" was probably the first attempt ever at a public affairs home video. Although it got better critical notices than the imitating competitors that rapidly appeared, the public demonstrated its good sense regarding Lt. Col. North, and bought few North videocassettes. Our Robertson discussion would have been the second in MPI's public affairs series, had the failure of the first project not made its sales prospects appear bleak.

Later in 1987, I got another dry run at television. Videotape interviews of Paul Kurtz and me were shot for "Moyers: God and Politics—On Earth As It Is In Heaven," PBS' documentary on the Reconstructionist movement. For the version that was finally broadcast, the criticisms of the Reconstructionists by other fundamentalists were felt to be so sufficient that we skeptics were edited out of it.

a night, shot videotape.

Although the project was never completed, it found its fruition in songs that were part of Frank's next concert tour. At a Frank Zappa concert in Philadelphia in February 1988, I heard him perform them. His song "When the Lie's So Big" included the lyrics:

> . . . With a big ol' lie
> And a Flag and a Pie
> And a Mom and a Bible
> Most folks are just liable
> To buy any line
> any Place, any time.
> When the lie's so big,
> As in Robertson's case,
> (That sinister face
> Behind all the Jesus hurrah)
> Could result in the end
> To a worrisome trend
> In which every American
> Not BORN AGAIN
> Could be punished in cruel and unusual ways
> By this treacherous cretin
> Who tells everyone
> That he's Jesus' best friend.

It had taken me a lot of explaining to get some of those earthbound political journalists to envision the mad, super-Christian dystopia implicit in Robertson's words. Perhaps an excess of sanity had made it hard for them to put together. But here, for once, was someone who picked up on it instantly. Frank filled the air with it. He even worked my name into a song containing a collage of public figures' names. Another song, "Jesus Thinks You're a Jerk," had the lines:

> There's an ugly little weasel 'bout three-foot nine
> Face puffed up from cryin' 'n' lyin'
> 'Cause her sweet little hubby's
> Suckin' prong part time
> In the name of The Lord. . . .
> Robertson says that he's the one
> Oh he sure is if Armageddon
> Is your idea of family fun
> An' he's got some planned for you
> Now, tell me that ain't true.
> Now what if Jimbo's slightly gay,
> Will Pat let Jimbo get away?
> Everything we've heard him say
> Indicates that Jim must pay,
> (And it just might hurt a bit)
> But keep that money rollin' in,

'Cause Pat and Jimbo,
Can't get enough of it. . . .
Well they took those Jeezo-bucks and ran
To the bank to the bank to the bank
And every night we can hear them thank
Their buddy up above
For sending down his love
While you all smell the glove. . . .
Imagine if you will
A multi-millionaire TV evangelist
Saved from Korean combat duty
By his father, a U.S. Senator.
Studied law, but is not qualified to practice it.
Father of a "love child"
Who in adulthood hosts the remnants
Of papa's religious propaganda program.
Claims not to be a "Faith Healer"
But has, in the past,
Dealt sternly with everything from
Hemorrhoids to hurricanes.
Involved with funding
For a secret war in Central America,
Claiming Ronald Reagan and Oliver
    North as close friends.[11]
Involved in suspicious tax-avoidance schemes,
Under investigation for sixteen months
    by the I.R.S.
Claims to be a MAN OF GOD;
. . . Hoping we will all follow him
Into the Twilight Zone. . . .

---

11. Frank Zappa got his information about Robertson's connection with the Iran/Contra scandal from me. In my videotape monitoring, I had picked up several statements by Robertson describing contacts between North and himself and recounting some of Robertson's activities in support of the Contras. I had relayed summaries of these to the Independent Counsel and to the Iran/Contra Committee. (There had also been a fascinating news account of a Robertson/North meeting in a Washington, D.C., hotel room in November 1986. Although Robertson described that meeting as a nonclassified briefing given as a courtesy to a presidential aspirant, the timing pointed more to a purpose of getting cover stories straight on the eve of a criminal probe.)

During the days when North was being questioned by the Iran/Contra Committee, Robertson told the press of his chance meeting with North in the Page Airways Terminal at Washington National Airport in September 1985, when North said he was on his way to Tehran to negotiate for the release of hostages. (This was long before the McFarlane mission, with the cake in the shape of a key and that singular master stroke of sensitive cross-cultural diplomacy to the Mullahs, the Bible autographed by President Reagan.) When Senator Sam Nunn asked North about Robertson's account, North denied it.

That colloquy prompted me to recall that I had recorded a long one-on-one interview of President Reagan by Robertson, with mention of something along those lines. It had been on September 19, 1985, and in it Robertson had said that the existence of such a mission had been leaked to him. Robertson asked Reagan to comment on the mission and Reagan adroitly deflected the question. This proved that Robertson had indeed been aware of something

Far too few people attempted to follow Robertson over the fringe into the Twilight Zone to drag the rest of the country across. Instead, the cycle that had started with the secular conservative leaders' recruiting of Jerry Falwell and the creation of the Moral Majority movement in the mid-seventies came full circle on Super Tuesday 1988. The secular economic and foreign policy conservatives and the Religious Right conservatives had progressed to the realization that they are different constituencies with different agendas: The pollsters had begun to distinguish them as "enterprisers" and "moralizers," respectively. The internecine battles within many state Republican parties sparked by the sudden, aggressive influx of the Robertson supporters would hurt Republican prospects more than those supporters' added numbers would help them. The Religious Right was left with few consensus political issues, none of which were capable of energizing more than small subgroups to activism.

Being "born again" was now out of fashion. A window in history had closed. One of the great historic waves of Christian revival was coming to an end. Or so it seemed to some commentators who also saw the Religious Right narrowly in terms of its political activists and television evangelists. The unholy trinity of Pentecostal televangelists terminally wounded in holy wars, the eclipse of the influence of Jerry Falwell, and the discrediting of Robertson coming in such rapid succession—apparently with no viable replacements waiting in the wings—all made it look as if the whole problem would go away.[12]

But never forget that television evangelism and Religious Right political activism were never more than relatively minor extracurricular activities for the captives of the conservative churches. Administering the devotional program and maintaining evangelical mind-control day in and day out remain their principal endeavors. When new activities meant to embellish that endeavor turn out to detract from it instead, they are dropped. The new mini-Reformationist leader learns from his mistakes. In the long run, the problem of psychological pressure-

---

pertinent at the time he claimed. I immediately wrote to Nunn, suggesting that witnesses claiming their illegal withholding of information from Congress to have been justified in order to prevent leaks be asked why so conspicuous a gusher spewing from Robertson was never investigated. Nunn used my information and adopted the line of questioning I suggested in his examinations of Admiral Poindexter and Attorney General Meese: They each claimed they had never heard of the matter.

Lest too strong an impression of a Robertson-North conspiracy be conveyed, it should be emphasized that none of the titillating information Robertson claimed to have received from North (or from an unnamed "National Security Council source") ever turned out to be correct. Despite North's own heavy involvement in Pentecostalism, I have the impression that he neither took Robertson seriously nor truly confided in him. Instead, North used Robertson as a sounding board for disinformation.

12. In April 1988, I was a guest on the "Morton Downey Jr. Show" with Jerry Falwell. I commented that I thought that the era of huge national television ministries was ending, and that the current state of the television medium (I had in mind the rise of local cable channels and the availability of affordable television production equipment) would redirect the focus to regional ministries emanating from local churches. Falwell agreed that such might well be the case. But we two agreed to disagree as to whether or not strengthening the local Bible-believing church is a good thing.

cooker churches, with their potential to trap sensitive people in lives of silent desperation and to persuade formidable throngs of people to desire a political environment less free and less tolerant than the one we have known, will not go away. The same problem will be back in ever more virulent and ever better camouflaged guises. The conservative church movement may experience a lull, and for a while find few new recruits, but such setbacks will prove temporary. Recent events have given no accurate indication of the immense raw social power potential that is latent in the conservative church movement. Never think that we will be spared some sort of dangerous brush with that power in years to come.

Philadelphia, Pennsylvania
June 1988

Index of Scriptures

Page numbers are in bold face.

Index of Selected Names, Subjects and Titles

About This Book

Could it be that a subconscious impression of the torments of Hell awaiting the unchosen—in the Calvinist sense of election—led the Germans to build the concentration camps? Were they unknowingly imitating the destruction of the Jewish firstborn early in the time of Jesus, even as Herod had been imitating God's last plague on Egypt? Does the imago of a wrathful and avenging God in the Bible furnish the model for man's inhumanity to man, far outweighing the injunction to "love one another"? Does the present resurgence of fundamentalist Christianity in the United States, with its radical-right political cutting edge, prefigure a dark age of prejudice and persecution—like the thousand-year dark age brought on Greco-Roman civilization by the original rise of New Testament religion?

When Edmund D. Cohen sensed the pyschologically powerful effects of the New Testament among the new, conservative Evangelicals, he became engrossed in their experience. Reworking and expanding on familiar ideas of Jung, Freud, Feuerbach, and others, Dr. Cohen found he could uncover the disguised psychological ploys around which the New Testament is built, and analyze them.

The unsurpassed psychological acumen of the New Testament authors is explained here for modern readers. It will unsettle both liberal and conservative proponents of Christianity, inform those concerned with the mental-health problems fundamentalism causes its unsuspecting participants, and warn of its potential adverse social effects.

Edmund D. Cohen is the author of *C. G. Jung and the Scientific Attitude.* He received his Ph.D. in psychology from Case-Western Reserve University in 1968, taught in college, and was a postdoctoral trainee at the C. G. Jung Institute in Zürich, Switzerland. Later, he earned a J.D. from the National Law Center of the George Washington University, and was a respected general-practice attorney and hearing officer in the Virginia suburbs of Washington, D.C. He is currently a full-time author and lecturer.